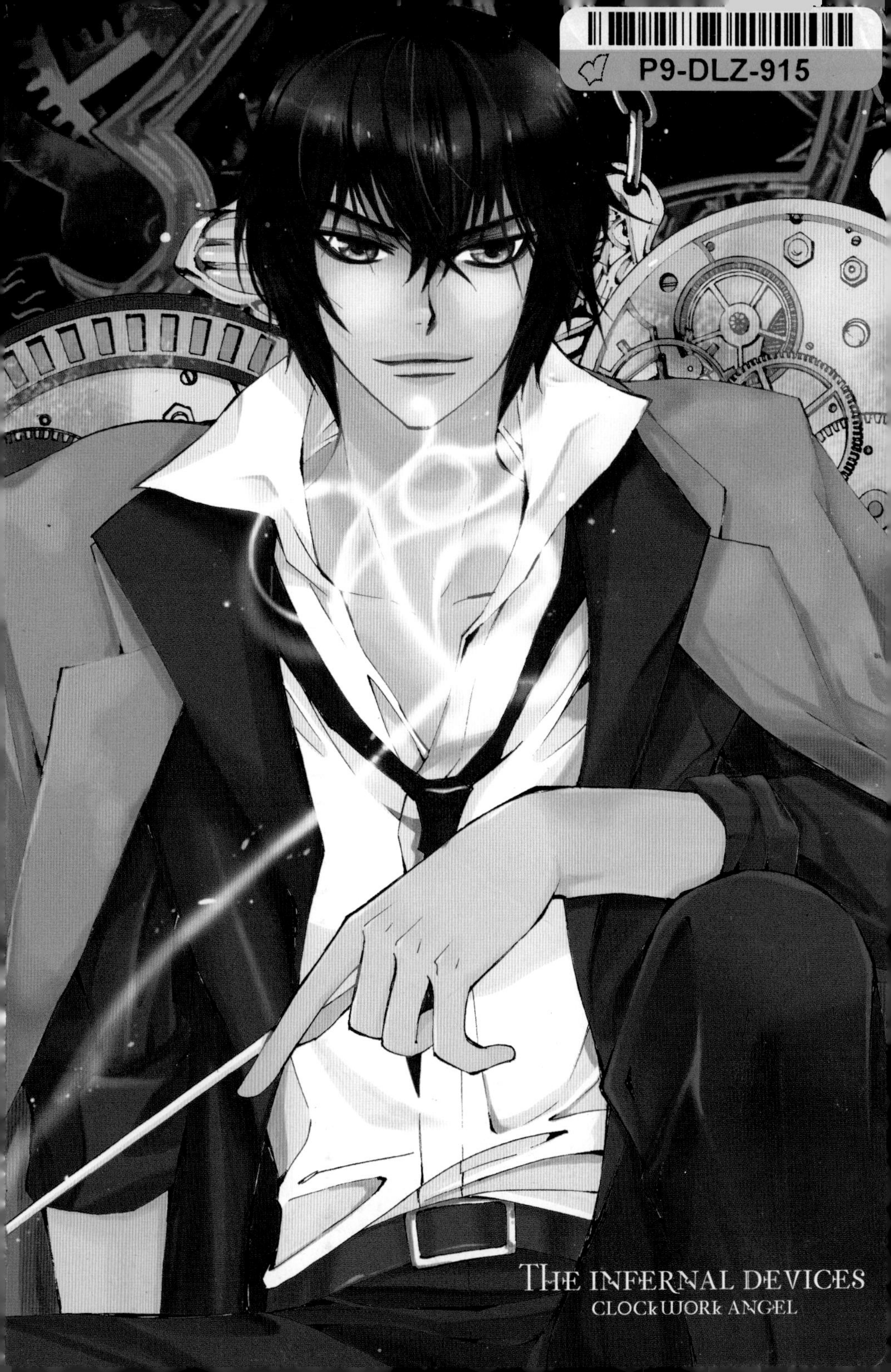
THE INFERNAL DEVICES
CLOCKWORK ANGEL

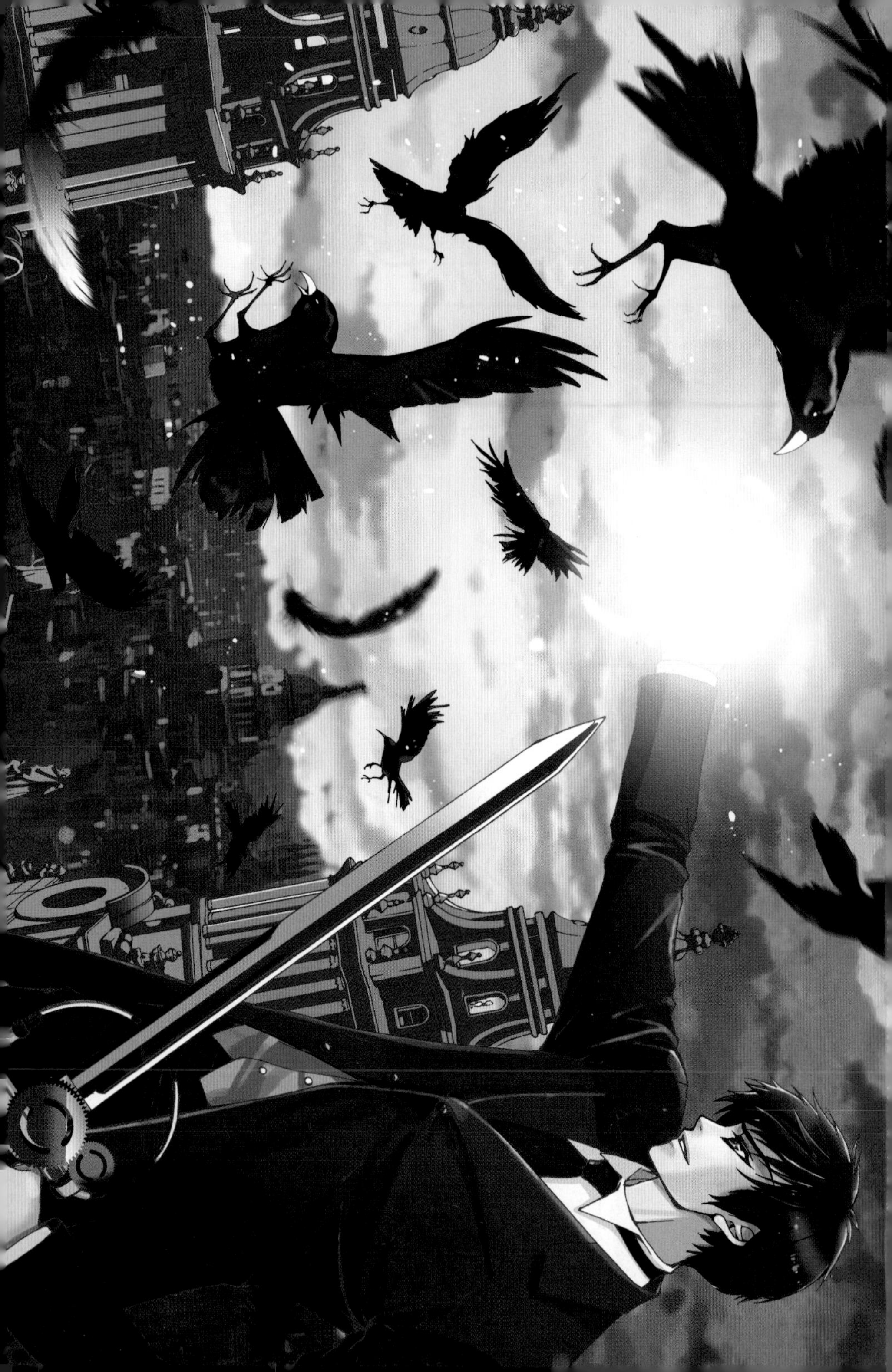

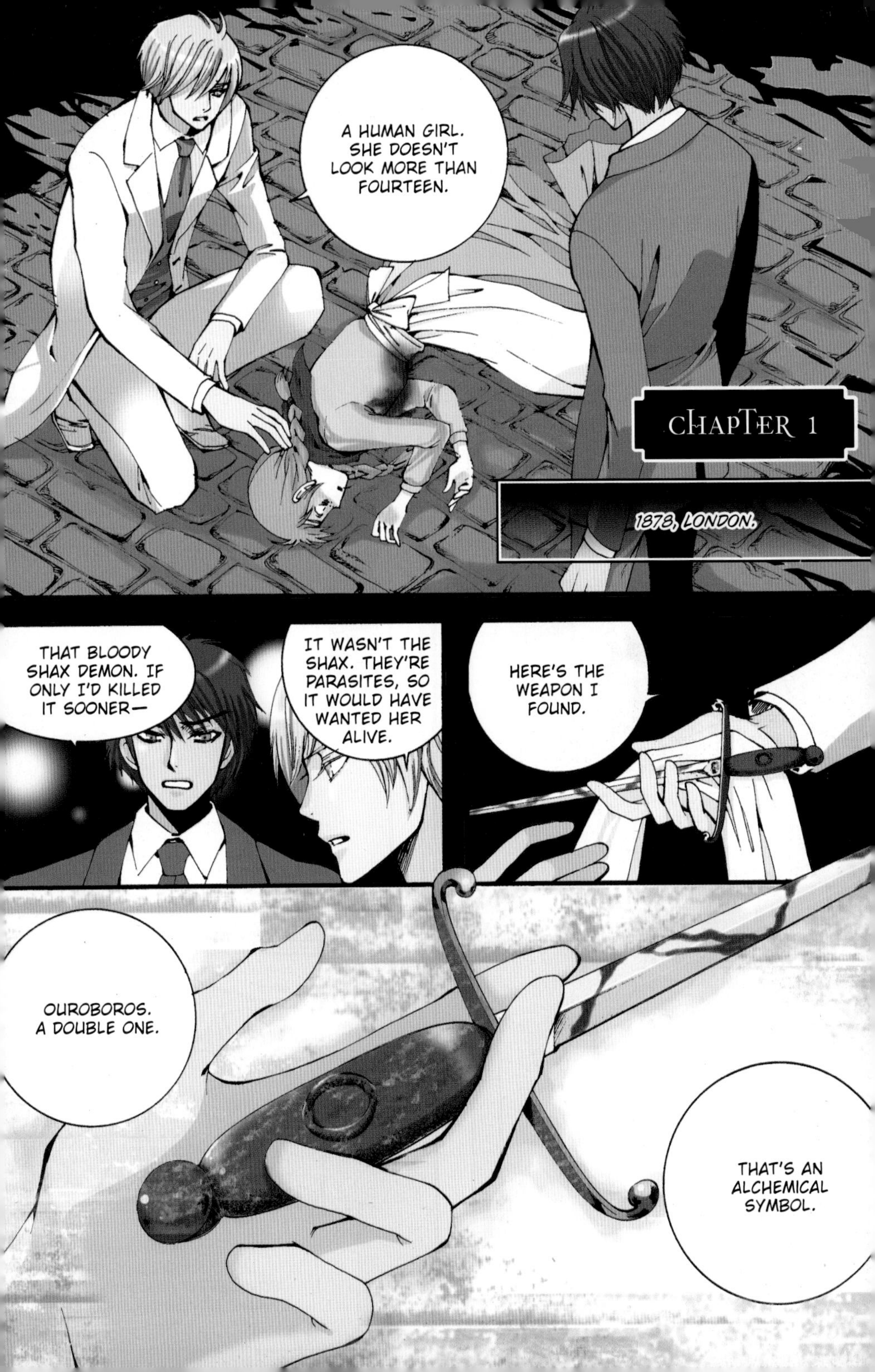
A HUMAN GIRL. SHE DOESN'T LOOK MORE THAN FOURTEEN.
CHAPTER 1
1878, LONDON.
THAT BLOODY SHAX DEMON. IF ONLY I'D KILLED IT SOONER—
IT WASN'T THE SHAX. THEY'RE PARASITES, SO IT WOULD HAVE WANTED HER ALIVE.
HERE'S THE WEAPON I FOUND.
OUROBOROS. A DOUBLE ONE.
THAT'S AN ALCHEMICAL SYMBOL.

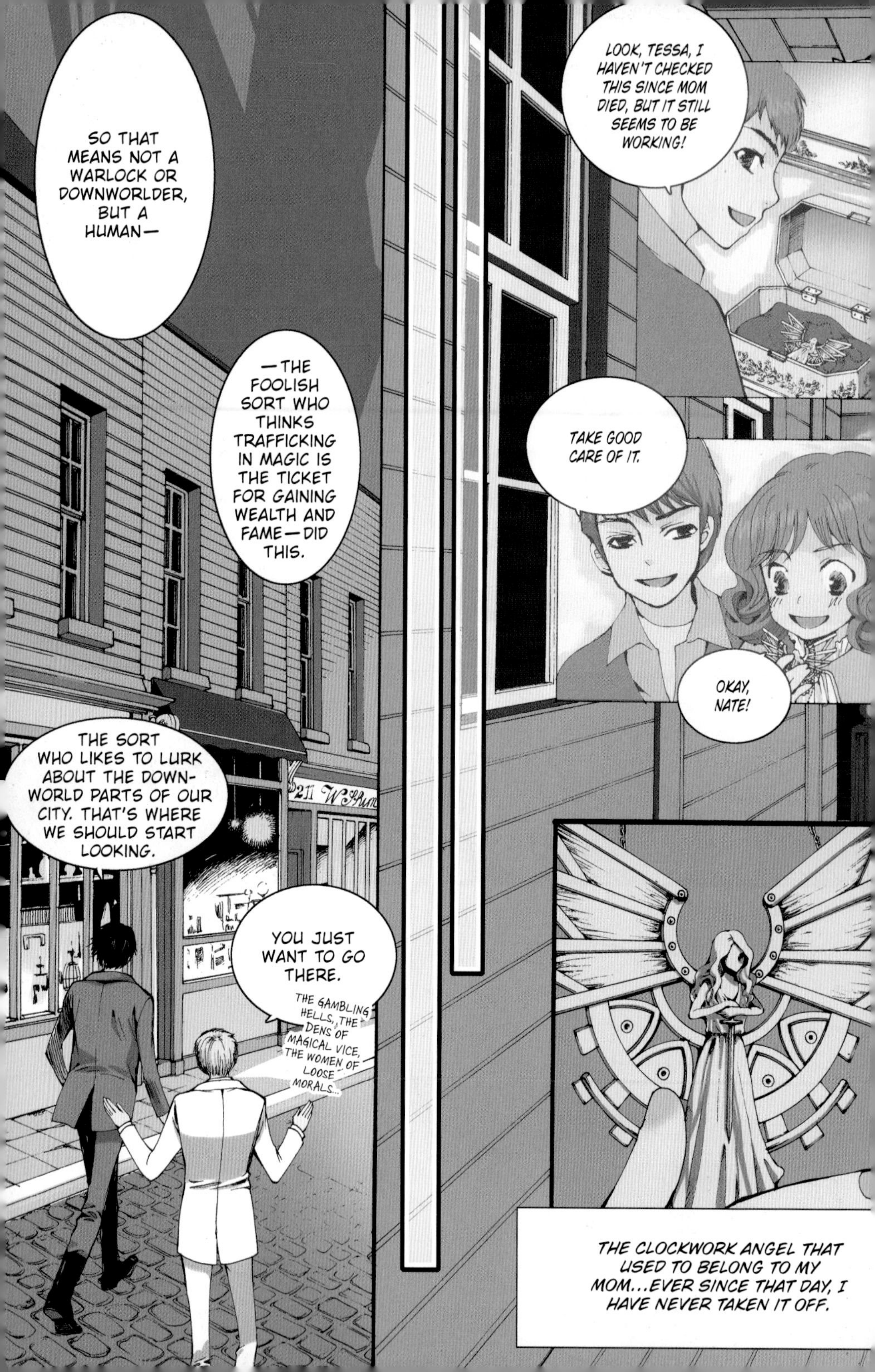
SO THAT MEANS NOT A WARLOCK OR DOWNWORLDER, BUT A HUMAN—
—THE FOOLISH SORT WHO THINKS TRAFFICKING IN MAGIC IS THE TICKET FOR GAINING WEALTH AND FAME—DID THIS.
THE SORT WHO LIKES TO LURK ABOUT THE DOWN-WORLD PARTS OF OUR CITY. THAT'S WHERE WE SHOULD START LOOKING.
YOU JUST WANT TO GO THERE.
THE GAMBLING HELLS, THE DENS OF MAGICAL VICE, THE WOMEN OF LOOSE MORALS...
LOOK, TESSA, I HAVEN'T CHECKED THIS SINCE MOM DIED, BUT IT STILL SEEMS TO BE WORKING!
TAKE GOOD CARE OF IT.
OKAY, NATE!
THE CLOCKWORK ANGEL THAT USED TO BELONG TO MY MOM...EVER SINCE THAT DAY, I HAVE NEVER TAKEN IT OFF.

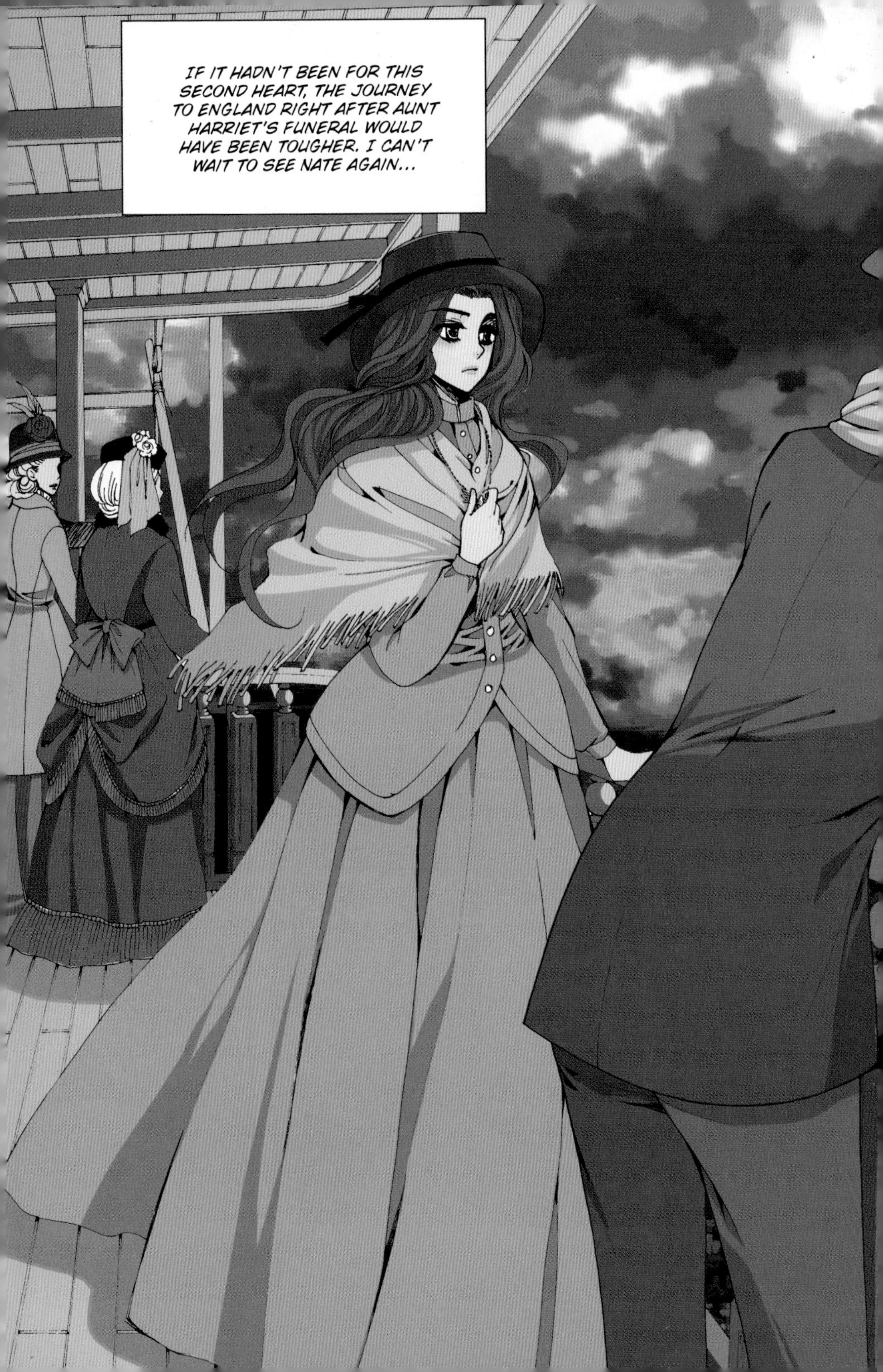
IF IT HADN'T BEEN FOR THIS SECOND HEART, THE JOURNEY TO ENGLAND RIGHT AFTER AUNT HARRIET'S FUNERAL WOULD HAVE BEEN TOUGHER. I CAN'T WAIT TO SEE NATE AGAIN...

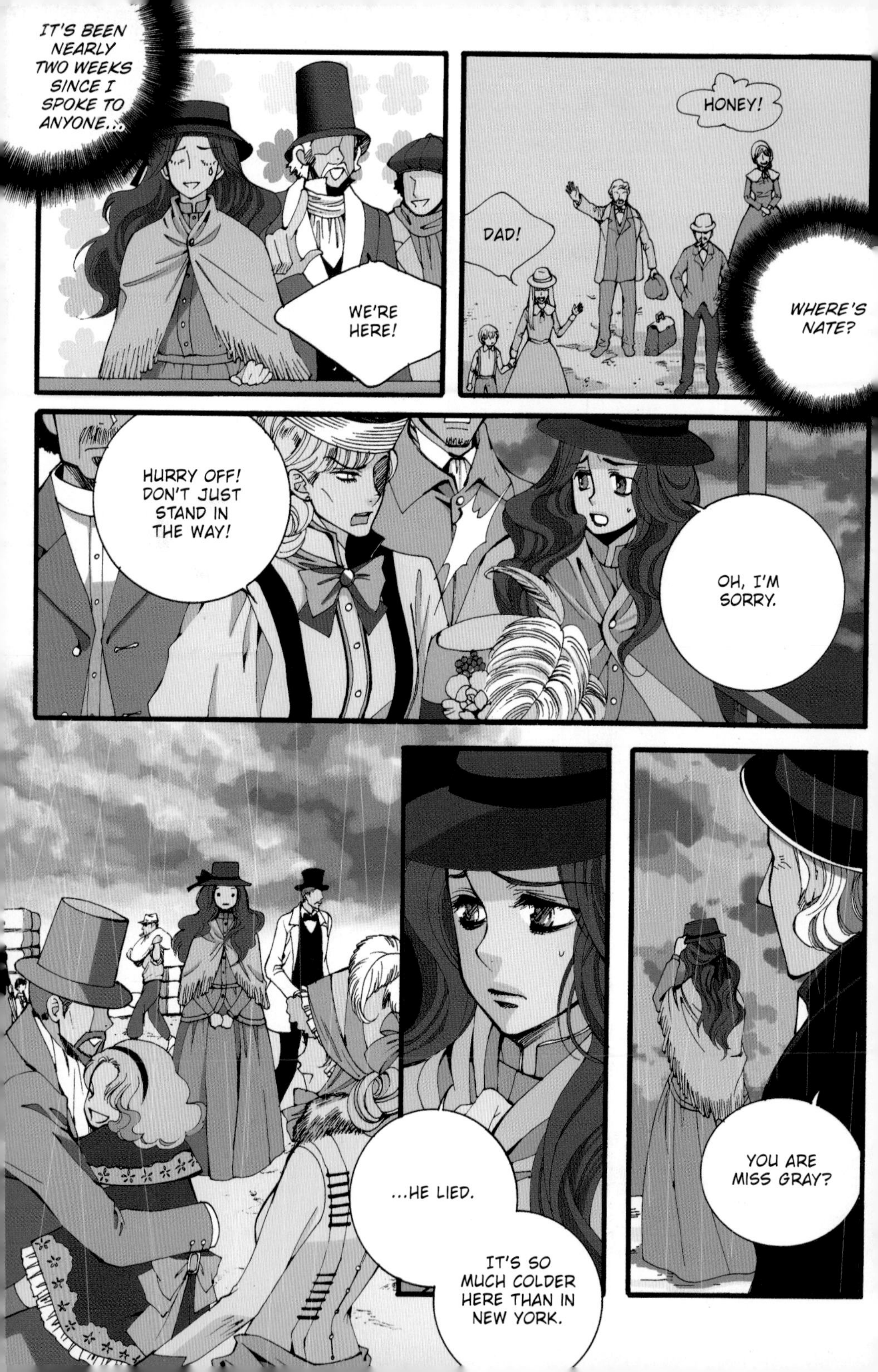
IT'S BEEN NEARLY TWO WEEKS SINCE I SPOKE TO ANYONE...
WE'RE HERE!
HONEY!
DAD!
WHERE'S NATE?
HURRY OFF! DON'T JUST STAND IN THE WAY!
OH, I'M SORRY.
...HE LIED.
IT'S SO MUCH COLDER HERE THAN IN NEW YORK.
YOU ARE MISS GRAY?

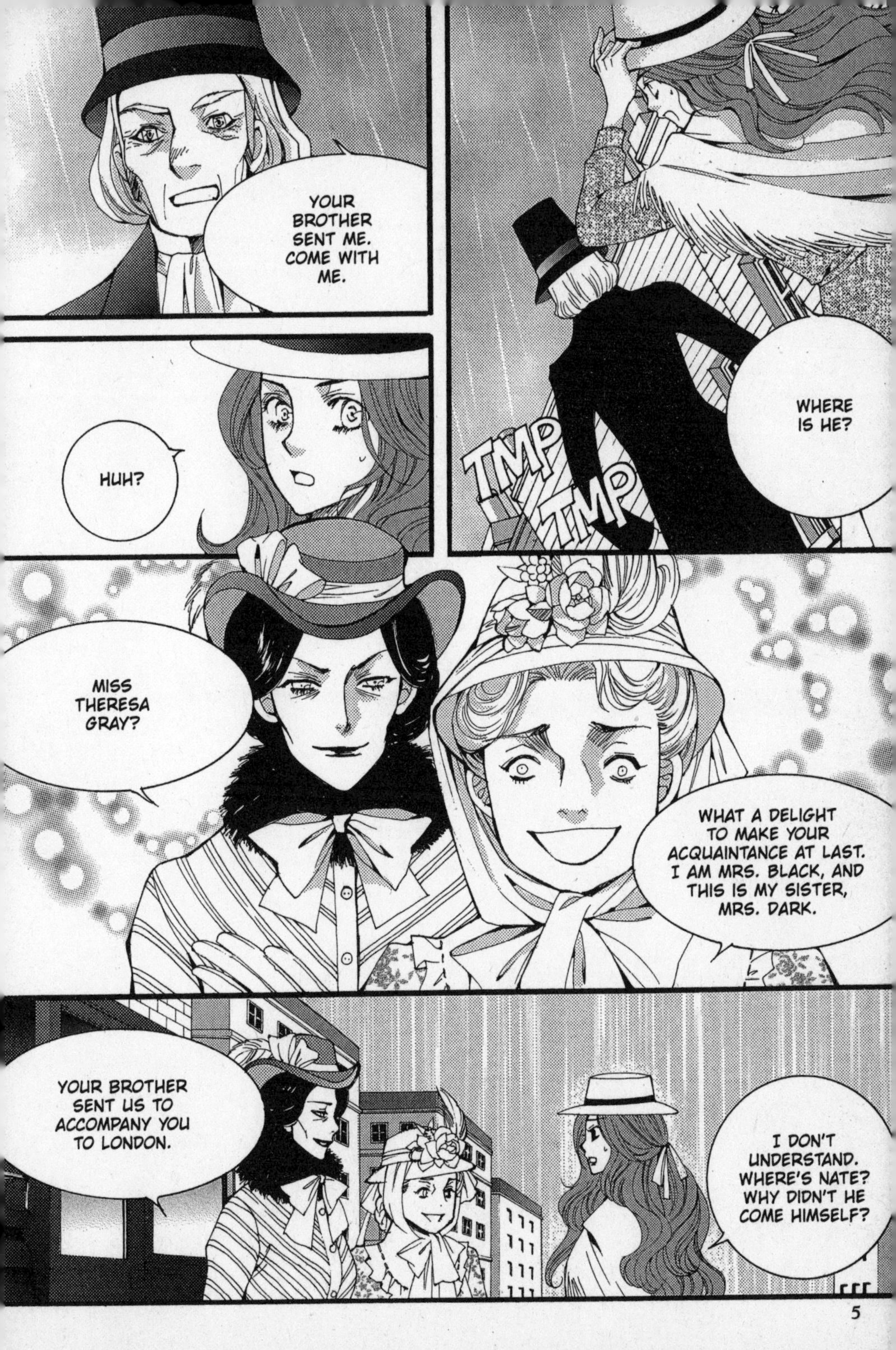
YOUR BROTHER SENT ME. COME WITH ME.
WHERE IS HE?
TMP TMP
HUH?
MISS THERESA GRAY?
WHAT A DELIGHT TO MAKE YOUR ACQUAINTANCE AT LAST. I AM MRS. BLACK, AND THIS IS MY SISTER, MRS. DARK.
YOUR BROTHER SENT US TO ACCOMPANY YOU TO LONDON.
I DON'T UNDERSTAND. WHERE'S NATE? WHY DIDN'T HE COME HIMSELF?

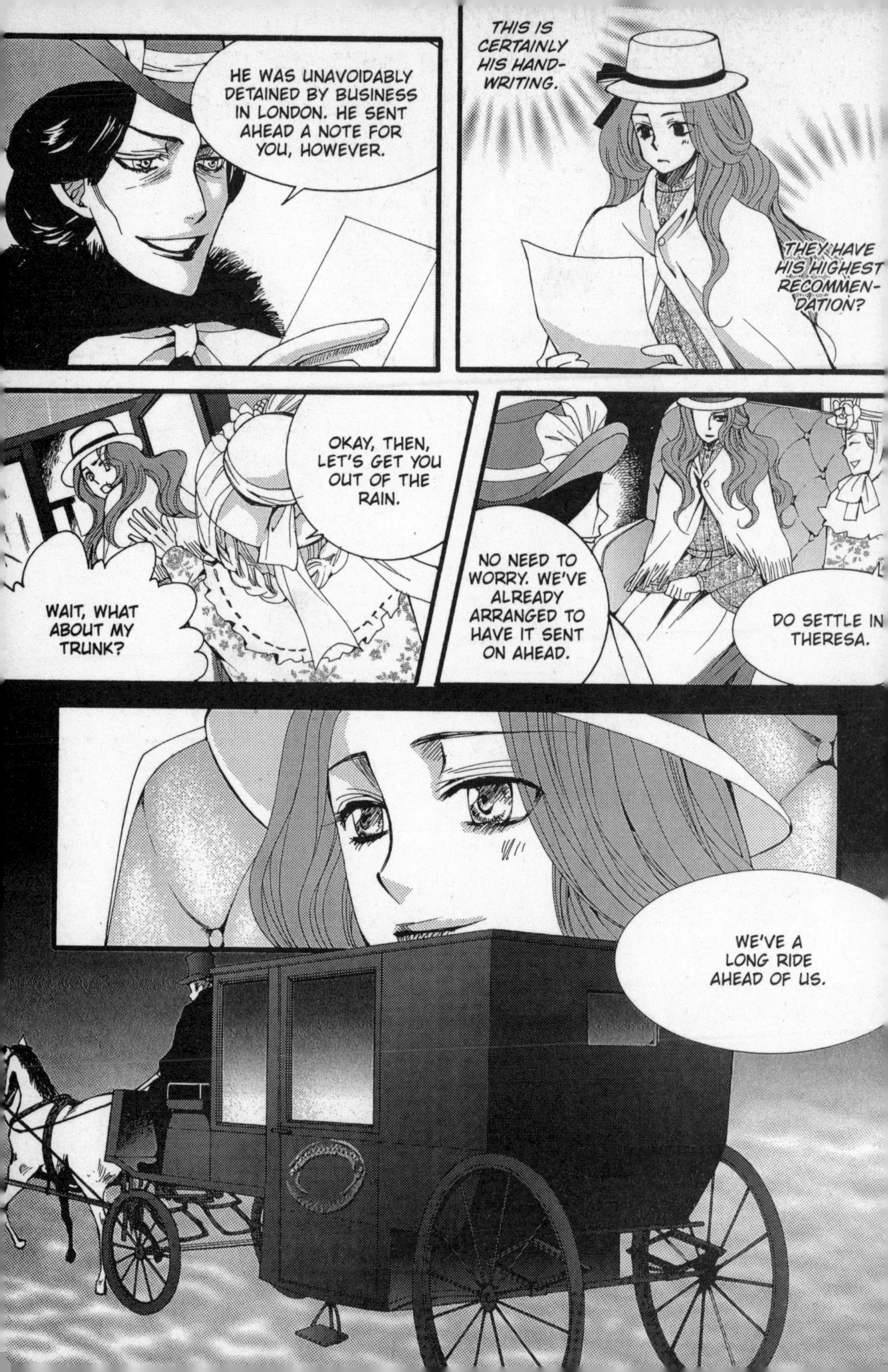
HE WAS UNAVOIDABLY DETAINED BY BUSINESS IN LONDON. HE SENT AHEAD A NOTE FOR YOU, HOWEVER.
THIS IS CERTAINLY HIS HAND-WRITING.
THEY HAVE HIS HIGHEST RECOMMEN-DATION?
OKAY, THEN, LET'S GET YOU OUT OF THE RAIN.
WAIT, WHAT ABOUT MY TRUNK?
NO NEED TO WORRY. WE'VE ALREADY ARRANGED TO HAVE IT SENT ON AHEAD.
DO SETTLE IN THERESA.
WE'VE A LONG RIDE AHEAD OF US.

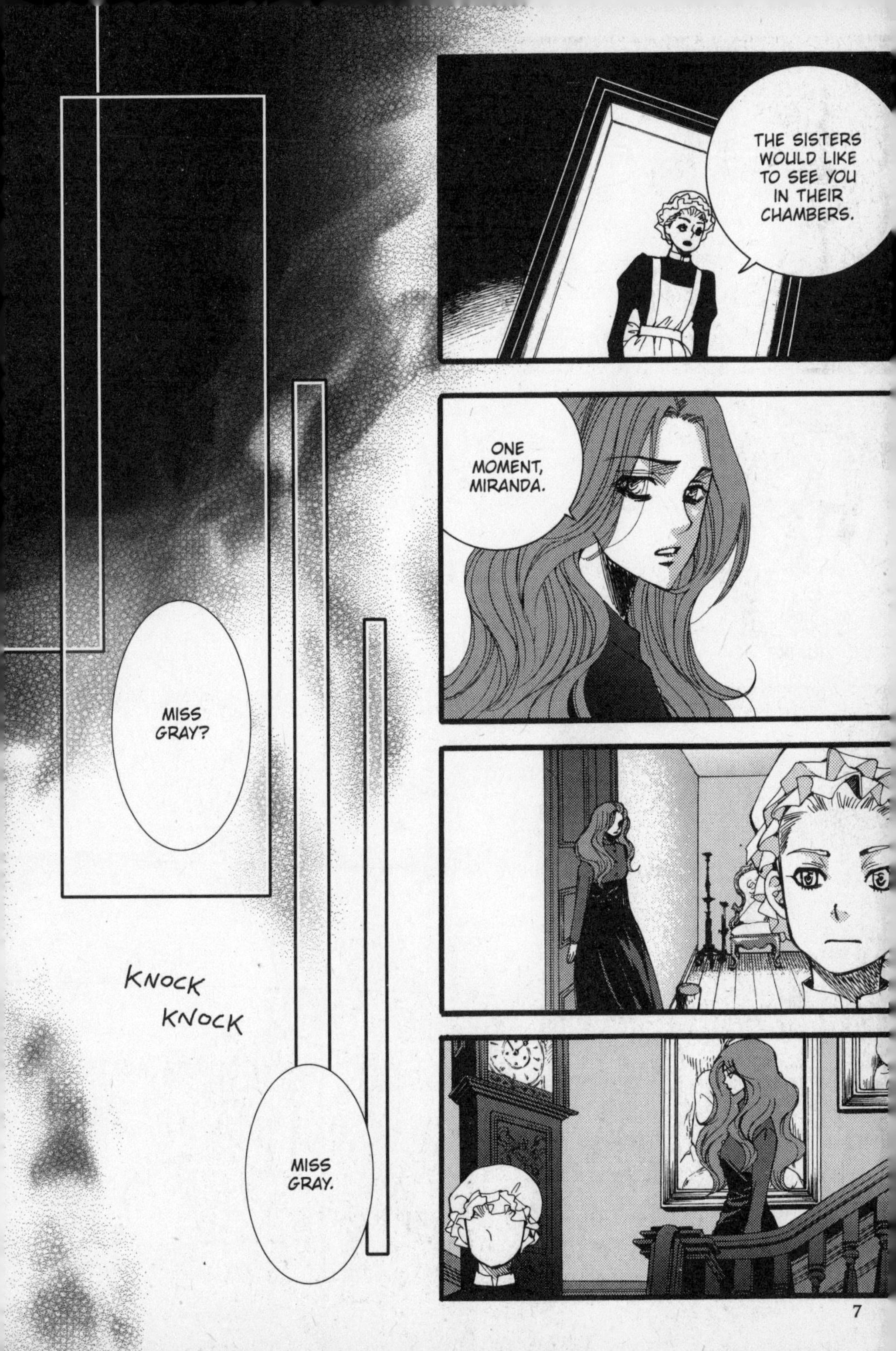
MISS GRAY?
KNOCK KNOCK
MISS GRAY.
THE SISTERS WOULD LIKE TO SEE YOU IN THEIR CHAMBERS.
ONE MOMENT, MIRANDA.

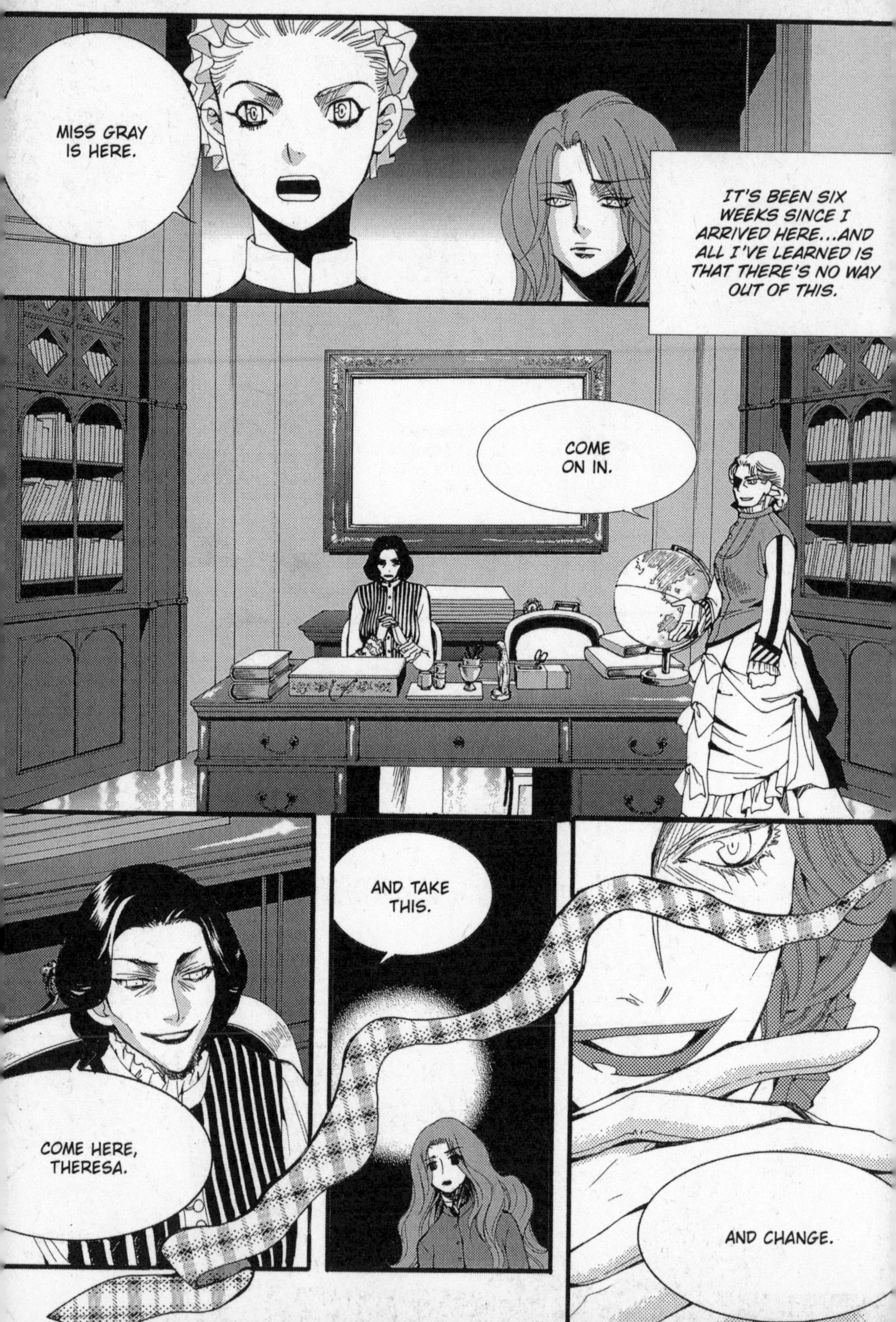
MISS GRAY IS HERE.
IT'S BEEN SIX WEEKS SINCE I ARRIVED HERE...AND ALL I'VE LEARNED IS THAT THERE'S NO WAY OUT OF THIS.
COME ON IN.
COME HERE, THERESA.
AND TAKE THIS.
AND CHANGE.

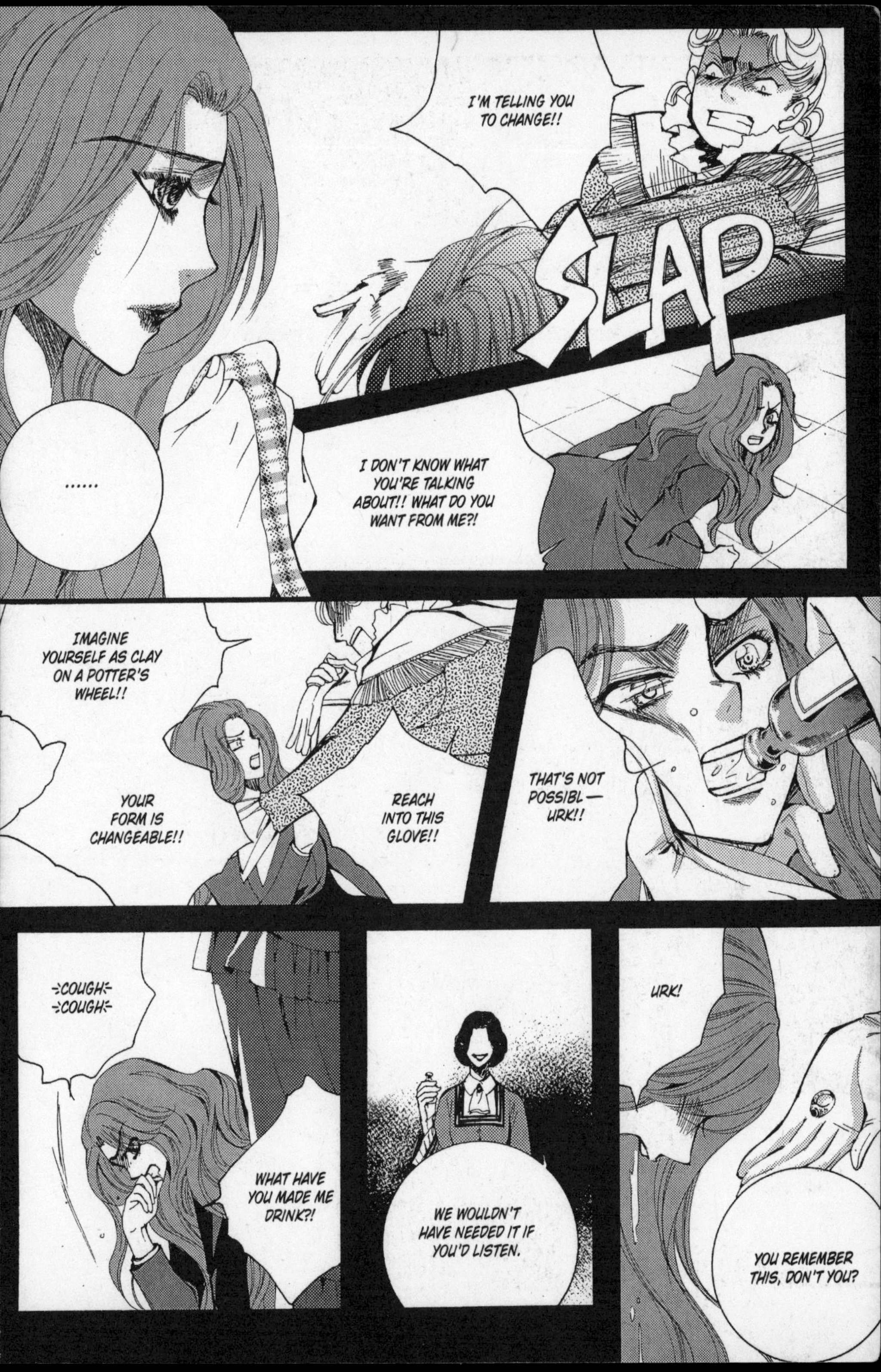
I'M TELLING YOU TO CHANGE!!
SLAP
......
I DON'T KNOW WHAT YOU'RE TALKING ABOUT!! WHAT DO YOU WANT FROM ME?!
IMAGINE YOURSELF AS CLAY ON A POTTER'S WHEEL!!
YOUR FORM IS CHANGEABLE!!
REACH INTO THIS GLOVE!!
THAT'S NOT POSSIBL— URK!!
COUGH COUGH
WHAT HAVE YOU MADE ME DRINK?!
WE WOULDN'T HAVE NEEDED IT IF YOU'D LISTEN.
URK!
YOU REMEMBER THIS, DON'T YOU?

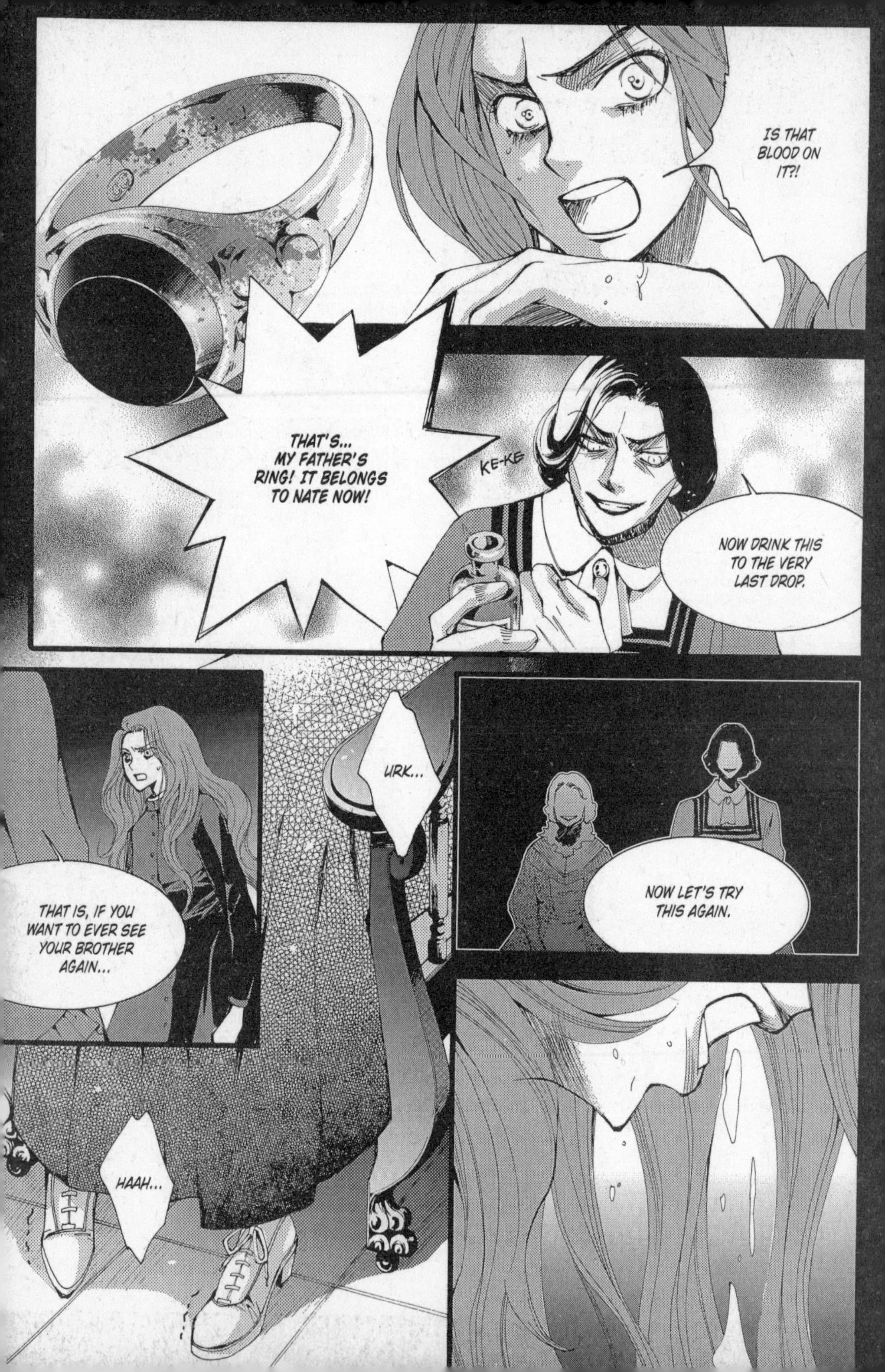
IS THAT BLOOD ON IT?!
THAT'S... MY FATHER'S RING! IT BELONGS TO NATE NOW!
KE-KE
NOW DRINK THIS TO THE VERY LAST DROP.
THAT IS, IF YOU WANT TO EVER SEE YOUR BROTHER AGAIN...
URK...
HAAH...
NOW LET'S TRY THIS AGAIN.

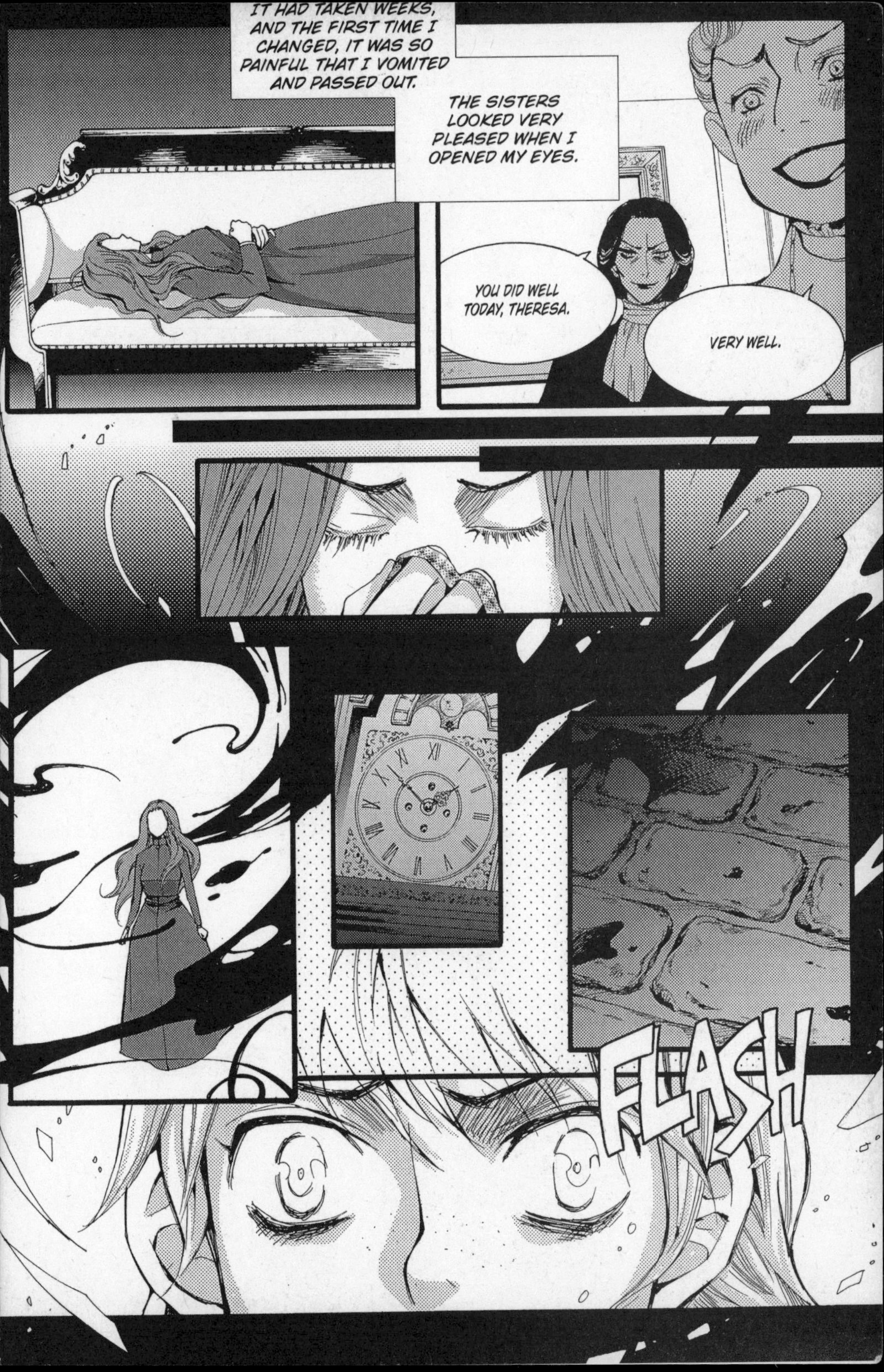
IT HAD TAKEN WEEKS, AND THE FIRST TIME I CHANGED, IT WAS SO PAINFUL THAT I VOMITED AND PASSED OUT.
THE SISTERS LOOKED VERY PLEASED WHEN I OPENED MY EYES.
YOU DID WELL TODAY, THERESA.
VERY WELL.
FLASH

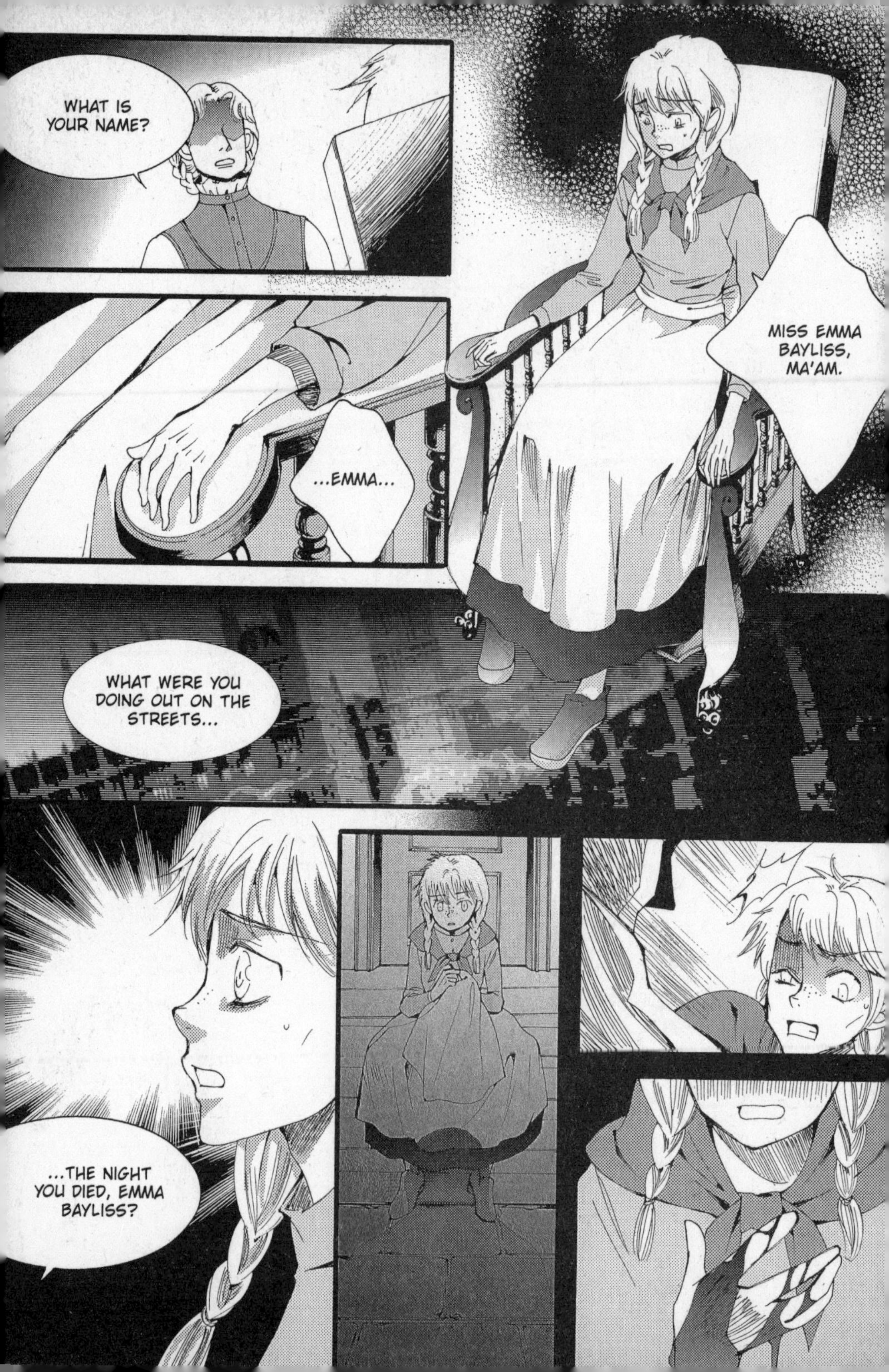
WHAT IS YOUR NAME?
MISS EMMA BAYLISS, MA'AM.
...EMMA...
WHAT WERE YOU DOING OUT ON THE STREETS...
...THE NIGHT YOU DIED, EMMA BAYLISS?

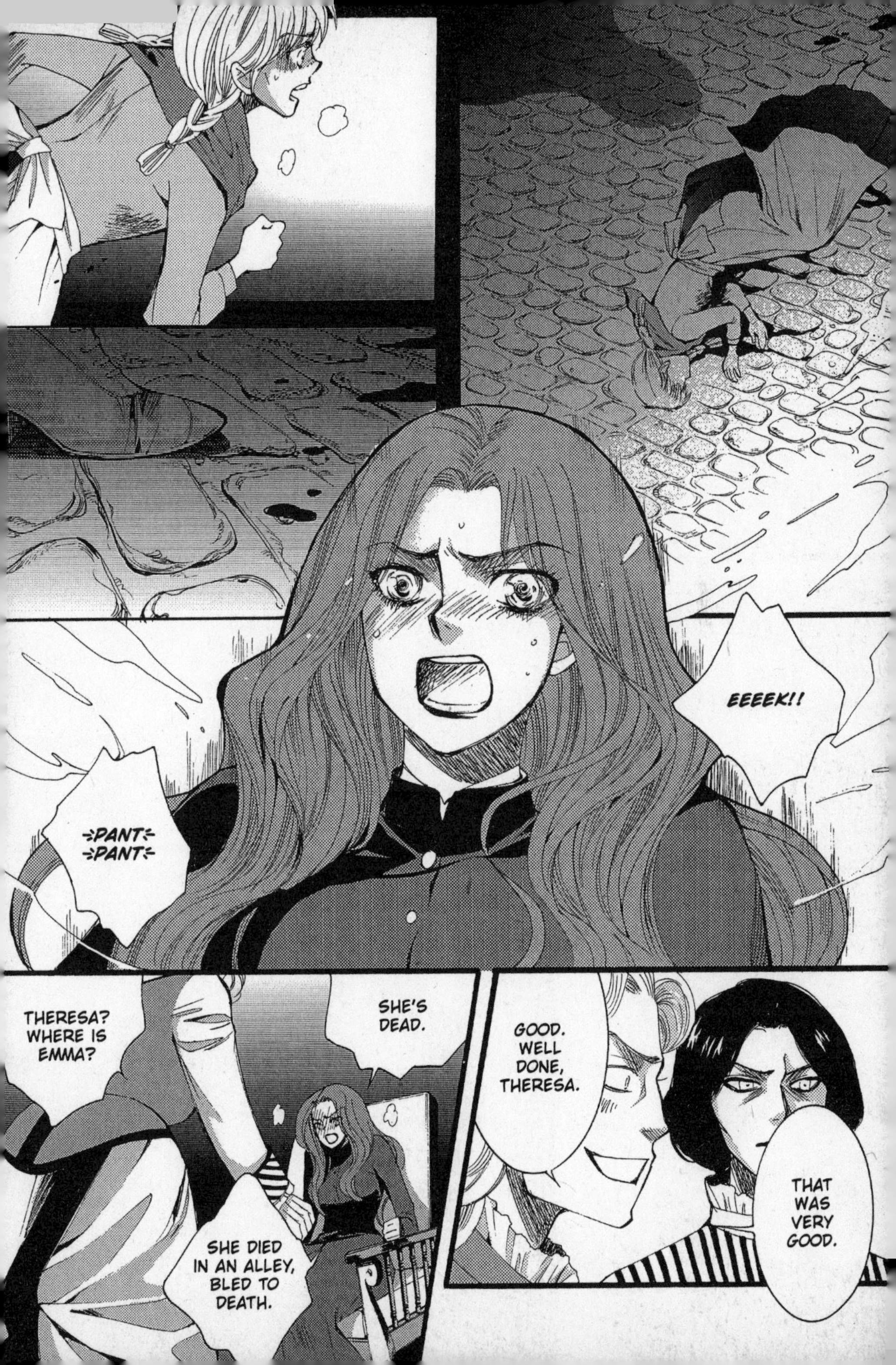

EEEEK!!
PANT PANT
THERESA? WHERE IS EMMA?
SHE'S DEAD.
SHE DIED IN AN ALLEY, BLED TO DEATH.
GOOD. WELL DONE, THERESA.
THAT WAS VERY GOOD.

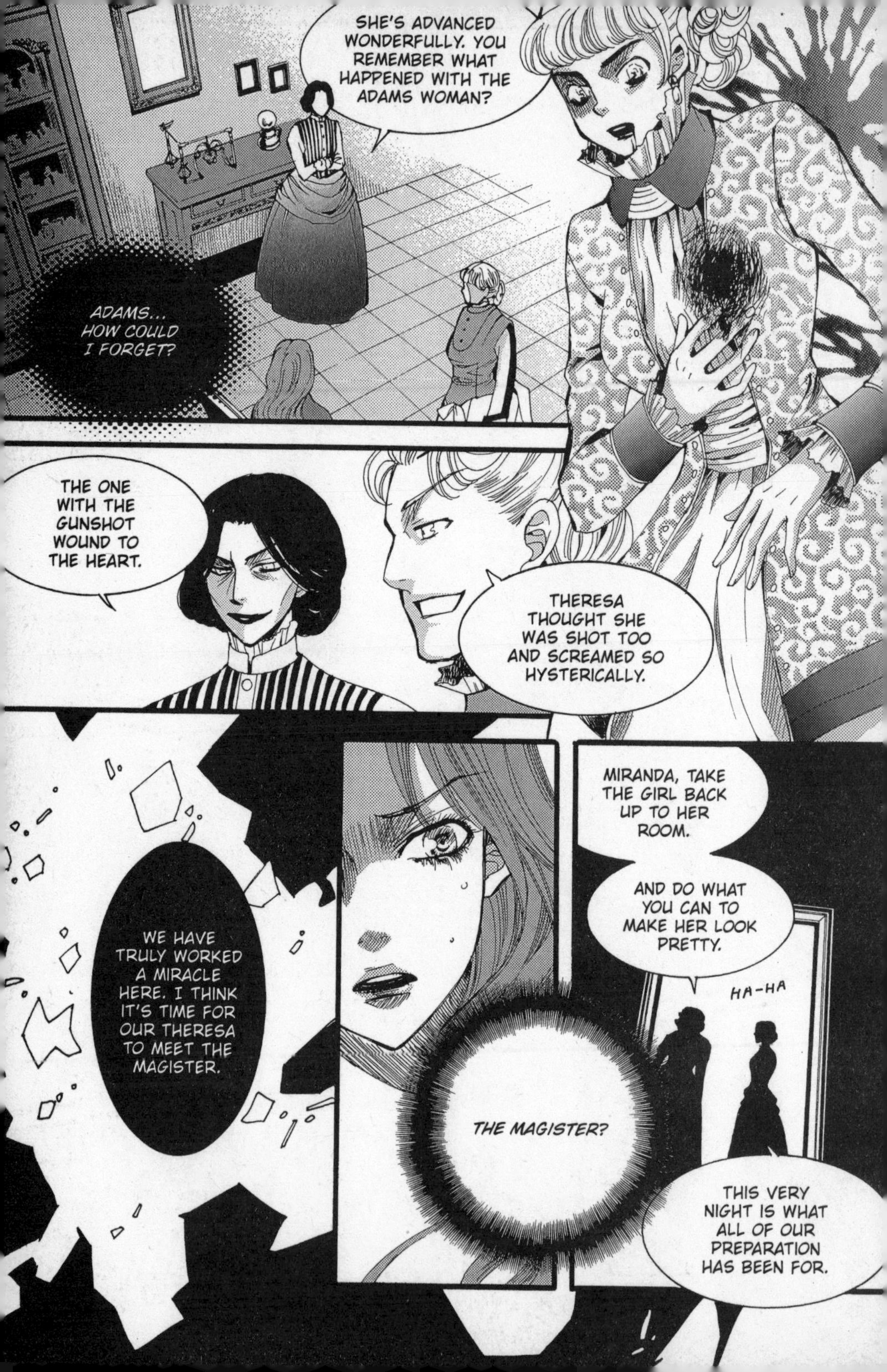
SHE'S ADVANCED WONDERFULLY. YOU REMEMBER WHAT HAPPENED WITH THE ADAMS WOMAN?
ADAMS... HOW COULD I FORGET?
THE ONE WITH THE GUNSHOT WOUND TO THE HEART.
THERESA THOUGHT SHE WAS SHOT TOO AND SCREAMED SO HYSTERICALLY.
WE HAVE TRULY WORKED A MIRACLE HERE. I THINK IT'S TIME FOR OUR THERESA TO MEET THE MAGISTER.
THE MAGISTER?
MIRANDA, TAKE THE GIRL BACK UP TO HER ROOM.
AND DO WHAT YOU CAN TO MAKE HER LOOK PRETTY.
HA-HA
THIS VERY NIGHT IS WHAT ALL OF OUR PREPARATION HAS BEEN FOR.

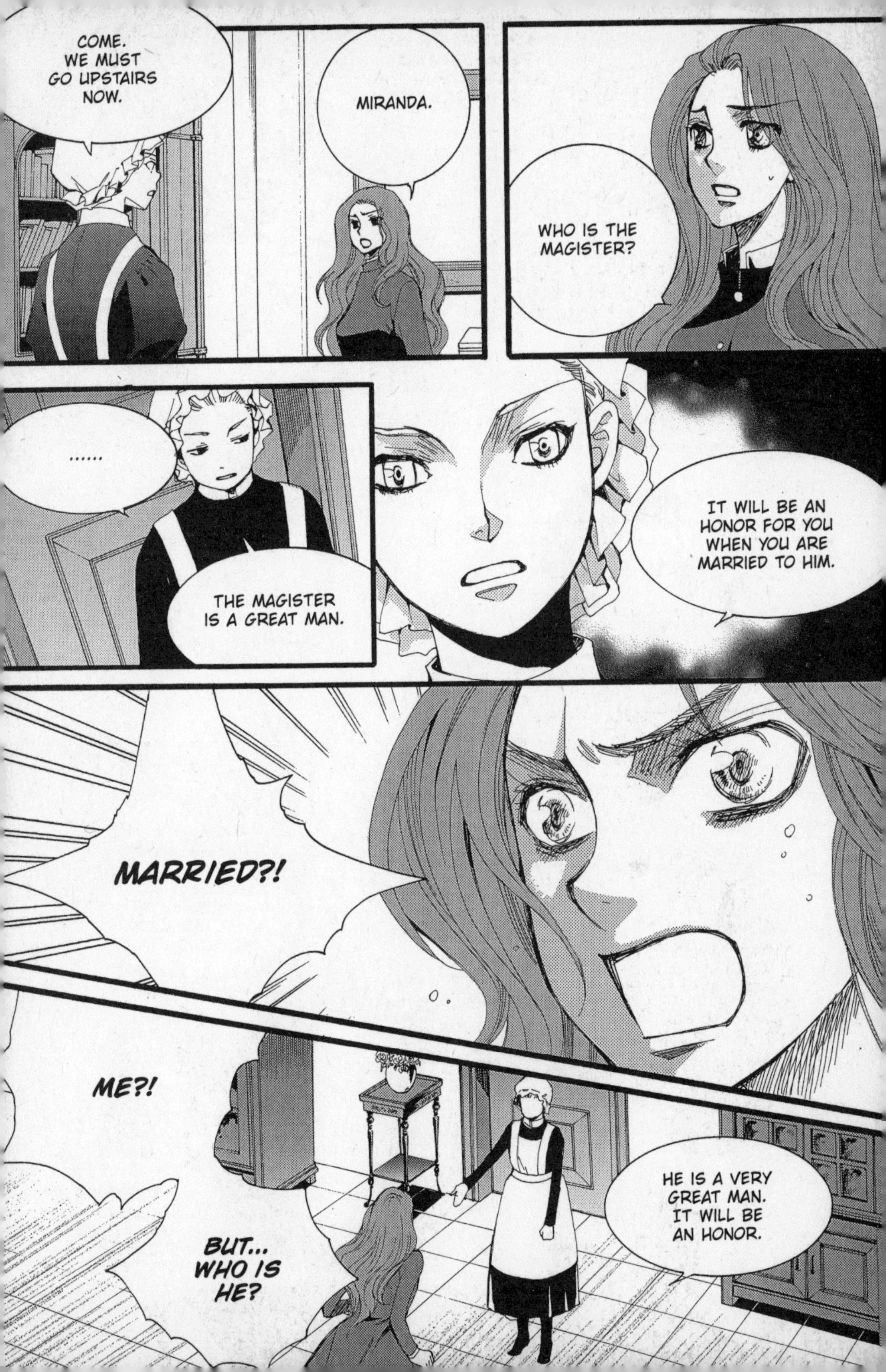
COME. WE MUST GO UPSTAIRS NOW.
MIRANDA.
WHO IS THE MAGISTER?
......
THE MAGISTER IS A GREAT MAN.
IT WILL BE AN HONOR FOR YOU WHEN YOU ARE MARRIED TO HIM.
MARRIED?!
ME?!
BUT... WHO IS HE?
HE IS A VERY GREAT MAN. IT WILL BE AN HONOR.

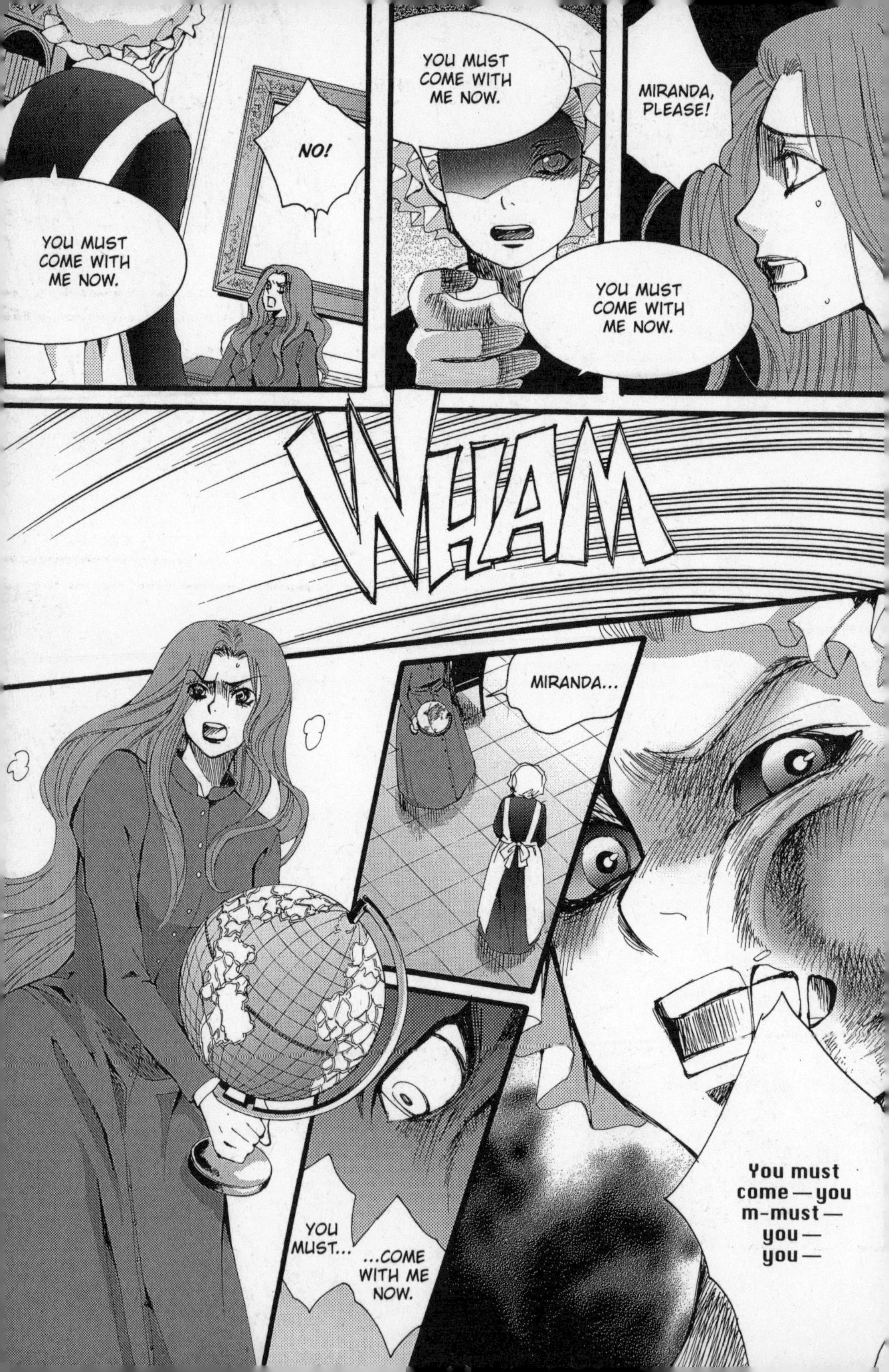
NO!
YOU MUST COME WITH ME NOW.
YOU MUST COME WITH ME NOW.
YOU MUST COME WITH ME NOW.
MIRANDA, PLEASE!
WHAM
MIRANDA...
YOU MUST...
...COME WITH ME NOW.
You must come—you m-must—you—you—

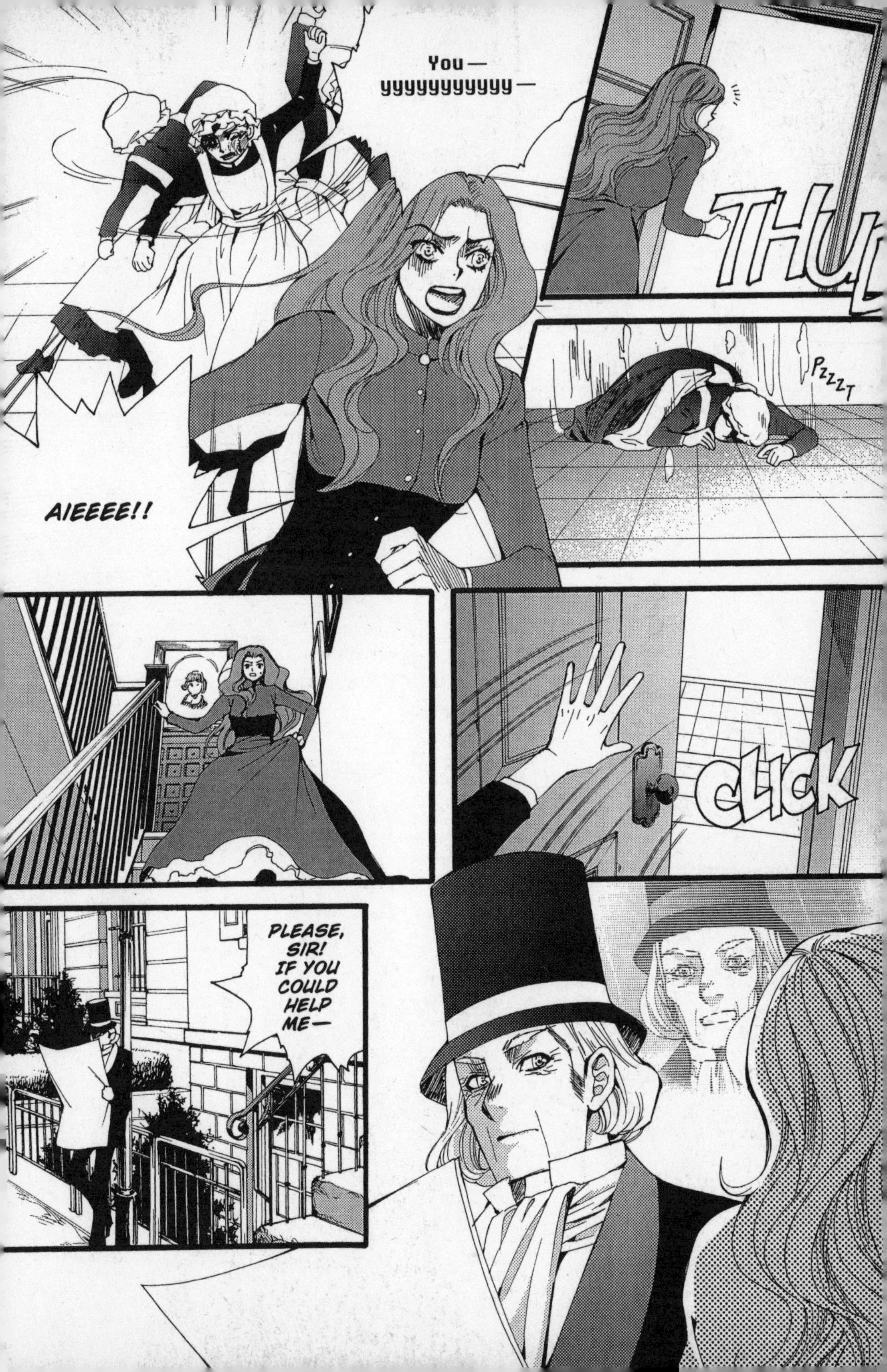
You—
yyyyyyyyyy—
AIEEEE!!
THUD
PZZZT
CLICK
PLEASE, SIR! IF YOU COULD HELP ME—

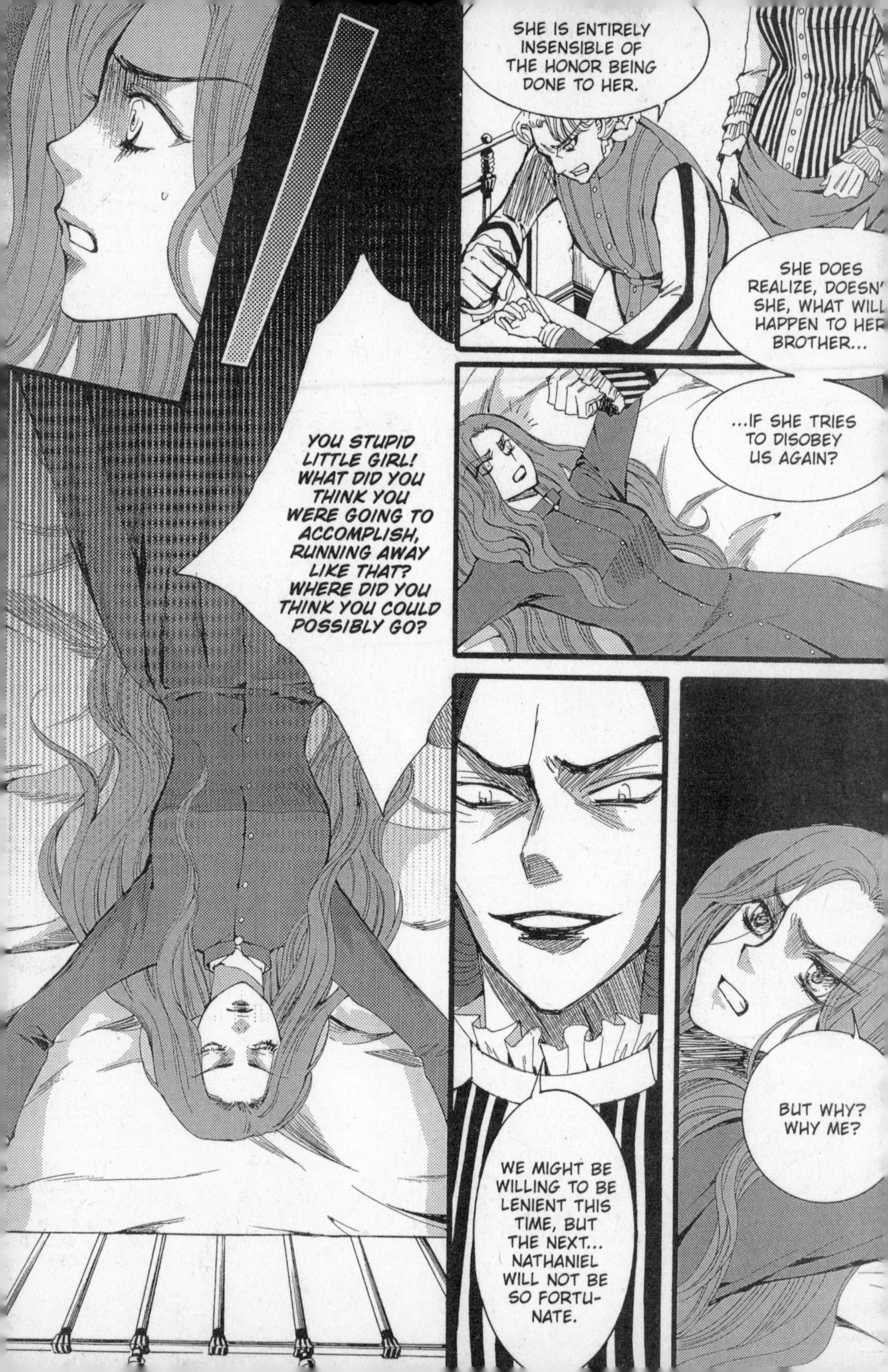
YOU STUPID LITTLE GIRL! WHAT DID YOU THINK YOU WERE GOING TO ACCOMPLISH, RUNNING AWAY LIKE THAT? WHERE DID YOU THINK YOU COULD POSSIBLY GO?
SHE IS ENTIRELY INSENSIBLE OF THE HONOR BEING DONE TO HER.
SHE DOES REALIZE, DOESN'T SHE, WHAT WILL HAPPEN TO HER BROTHER...
...IF SHE TRIES TO DISOBEY US AGAIN?
WE MIGHT BE WILLING TO BE LENIENT THIS TIME, BUT THE NEXT... NATHANIEL WILL NOT BE SO FORTU-NATE.
BUT WHY? WHY ME?

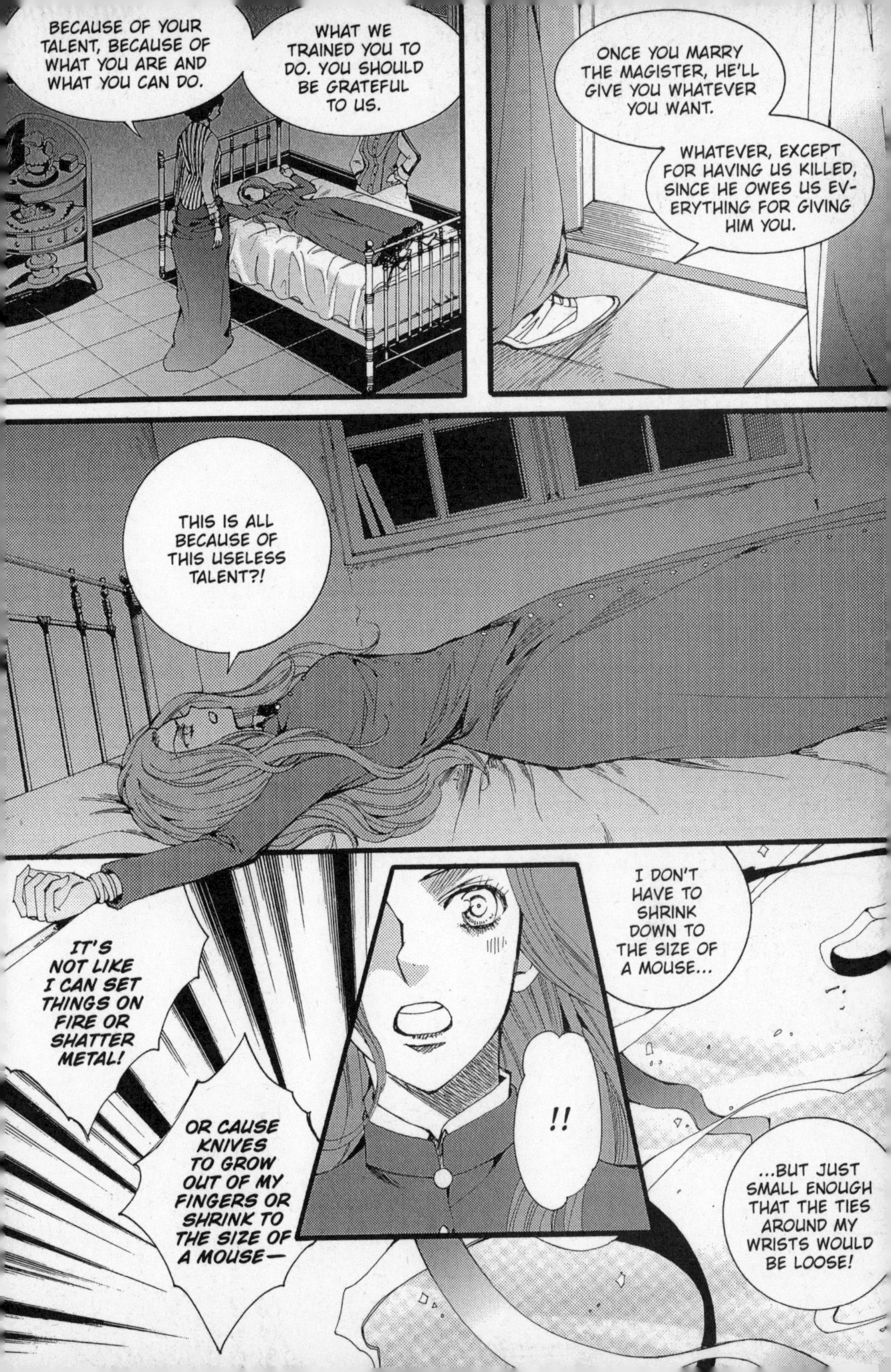
BECAUSE OF YOUR TALENT, BECAUSE OF WHAT YOU ARE AND WHAT YOU CAN DO.
WHAT WE TRAINED YOU TO DO. YOU SHOULD BE GRATEFUL TO US.
ONCE YOU MARRY THE MAGISTER, HE'LL GIVE YOU WHATEVER YOU WANT.
WHATEVER, EXCEPT FOR HAVING US KILLED, SINCE HE OWES US EV-ERYTHING FOR GIVING HIM YOU.
THIS IS ALL BECAUSE OF THIS USELESS TALENT?!
IT'S NOT LIKE I CAN SET THINGS ON FIRE OR SHATTER METAL!
OR CAUSE KNIVES TO GROW OUT OF MY FINGERS OR SHRINK TO THE SIZE OF A MOUSE—
!!
I DON'T HAVE TO SHRINK DOWN TO THE SIZE OF A MOUSE...
...BUT JUST SMALL ENOUGH THAT THE TIES AROUND MY WRISTS WOULD BE LOOSE!

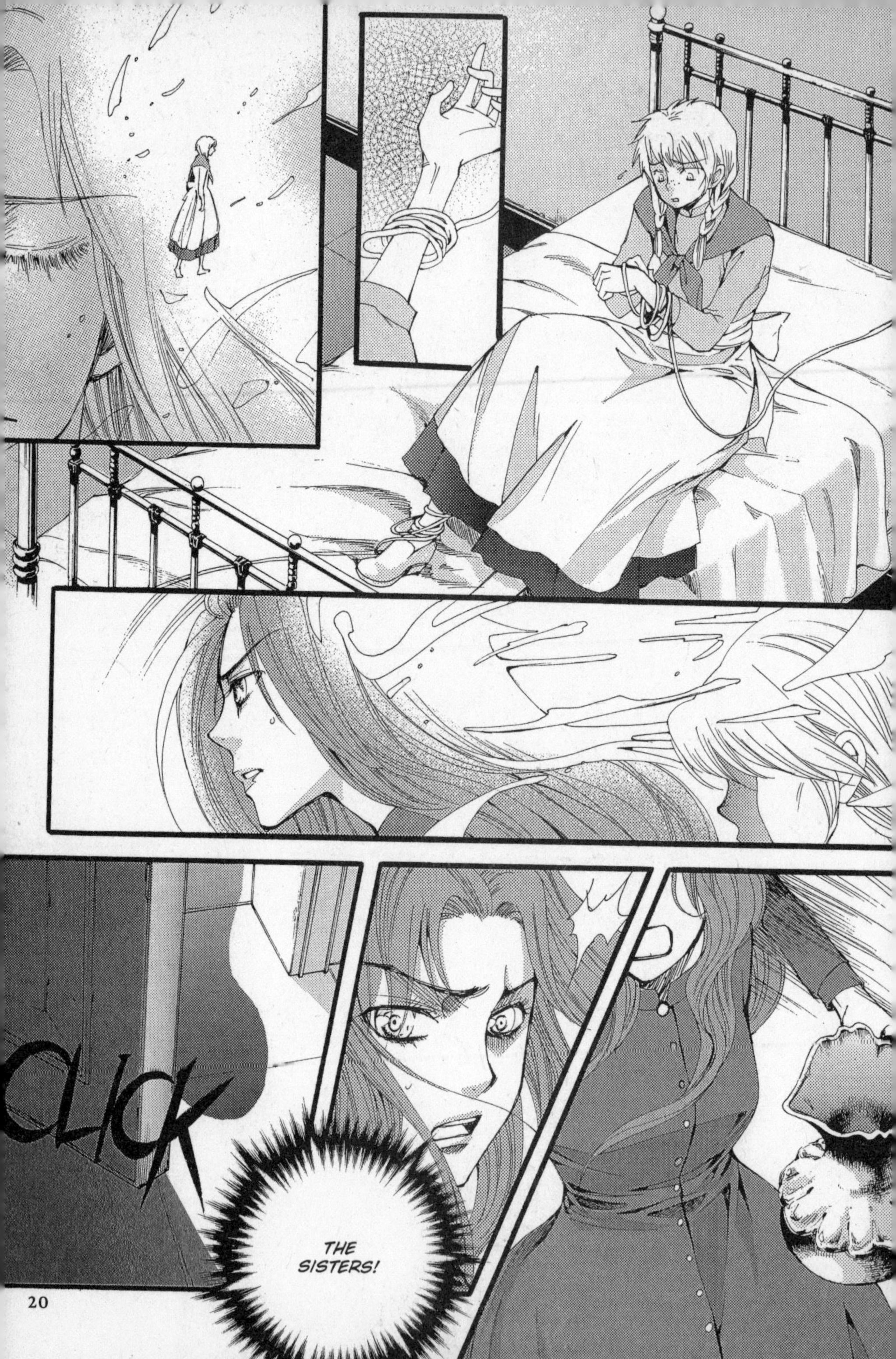
CLICK
THE SISTERS!

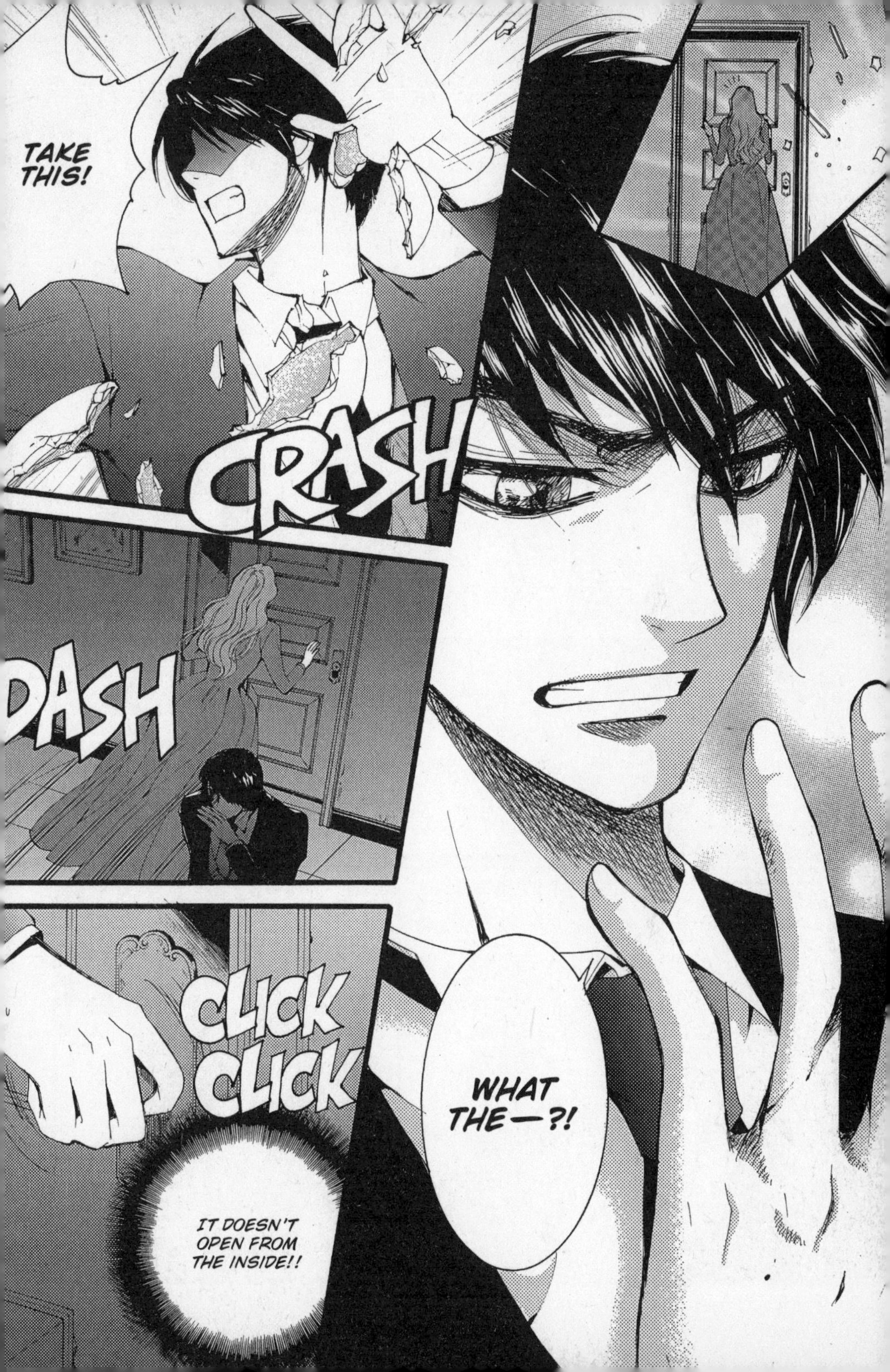
TAKE THIS!
CRASH
DASH
CLICK CLICK
IT DOESN'T OPEN FROM THE INSIDE!!
WHAT THE—?!

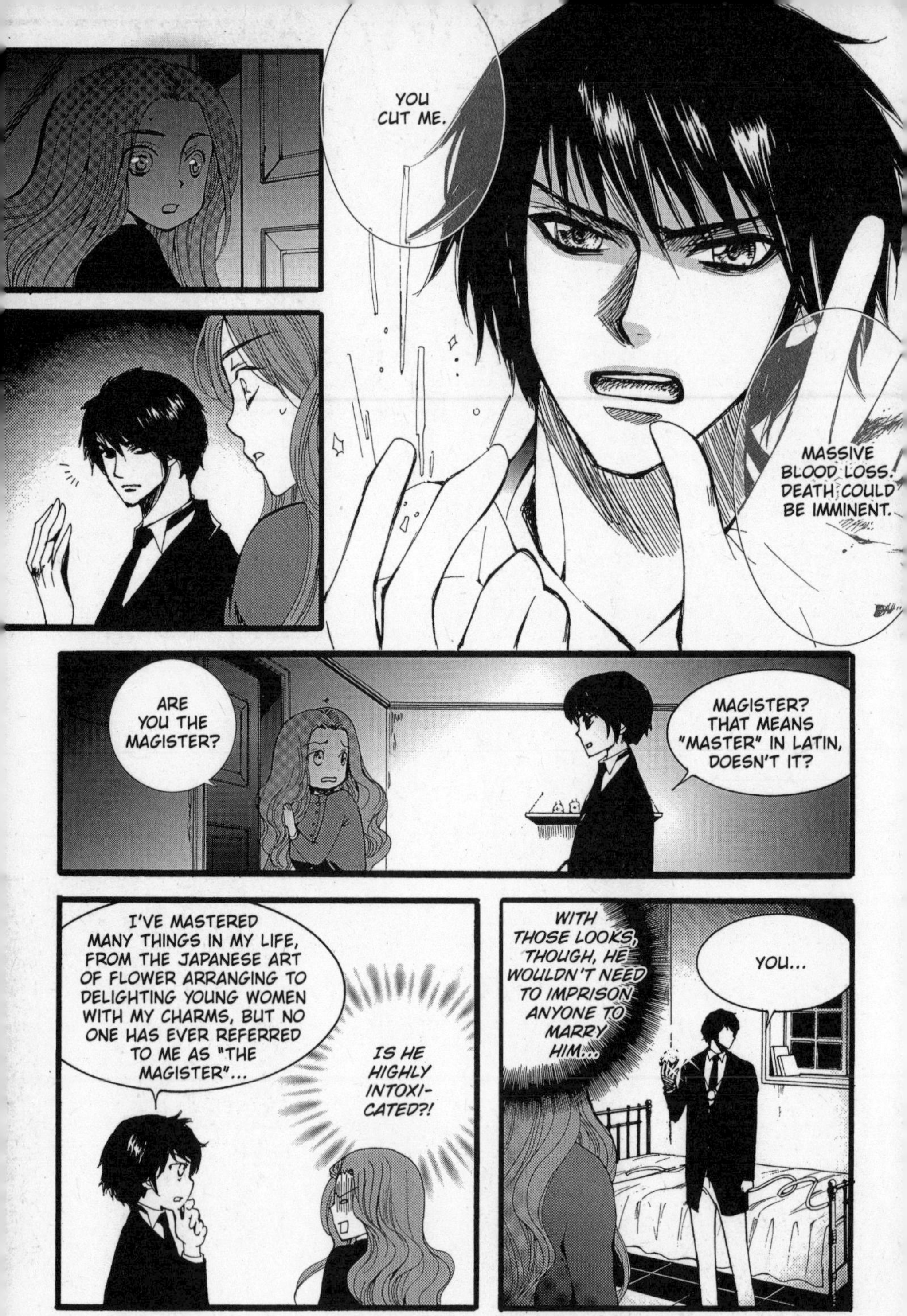
YOU CUT ME.
MASSIVE BLOOD LOSS. DEATH COULD BE IMMINENT.
ARE YOU THE MAGISTER?
MAGISTER? THAT MEANS "MASTER" IN LATIN, DOESN'T IT?
I'VE MASTERED MANY THINGS IN MY LIFE, FROM THE JAPANESE ART OF FLOWER ARRANGING TO DELIGHTING YOUNG WOMEN WITH MY CHARMS, BUT NO ONE HAS EVER REFERRED TO ME AS "THE MAGISTER"...
IS HE HIGHLY INTOXI-CATED?!
WITH THOSE LOOKS, THOUGH, HE WOULDN'T NEED TO IMPRISON ANYONE TO MARRY HIM...
YOU...

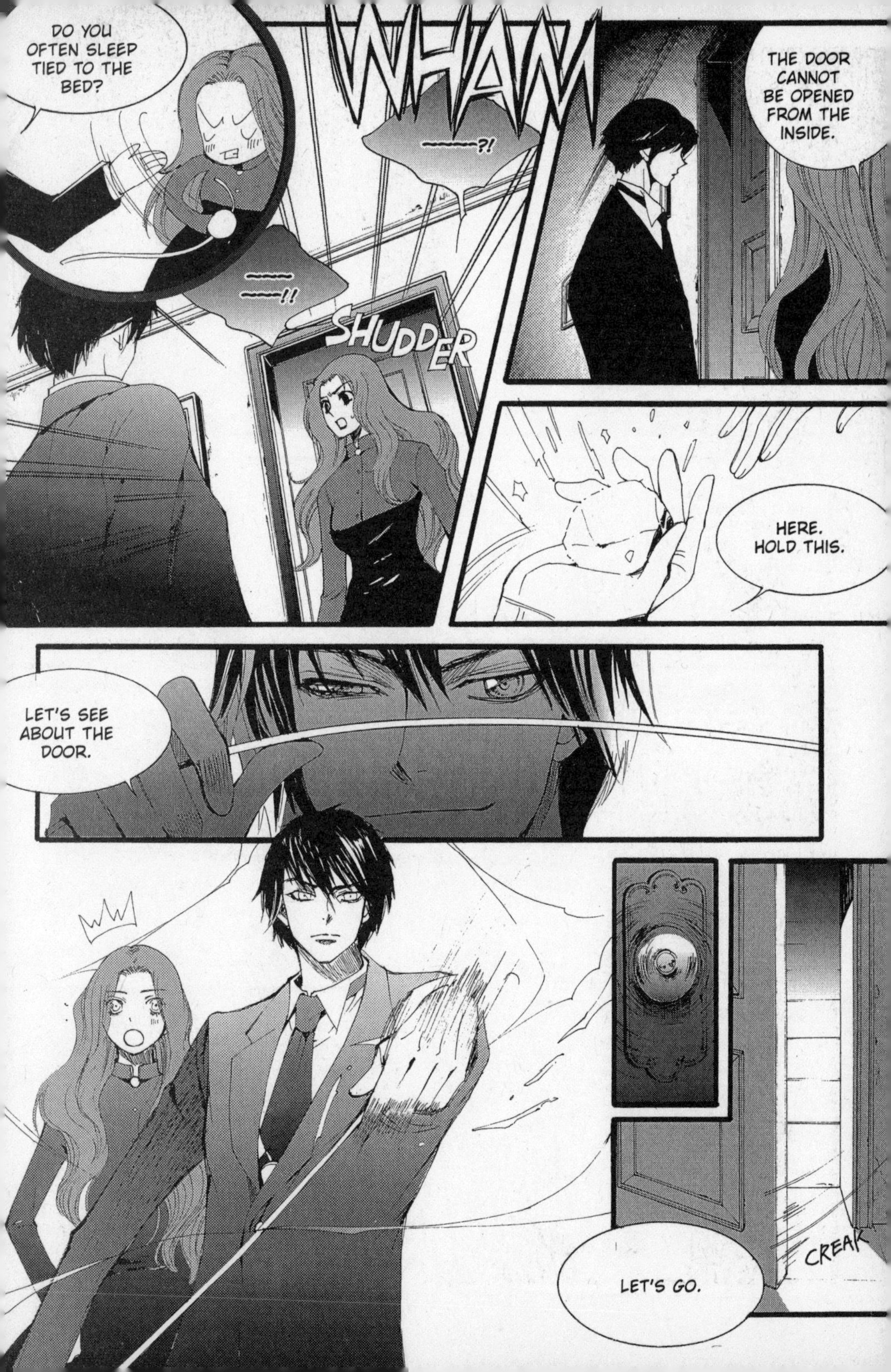
DO YOU OFTEN SLEEP TIED TO THE BED?
WHAM
——?!
——
——!!
SHUDDER
THE DOOR CANNOT BE OPENED FROM THE INSIDE.
HERE. HOLD THIS.
LET'S SEE ABOUT THE DOOR.
LET'S GO.
CREAK

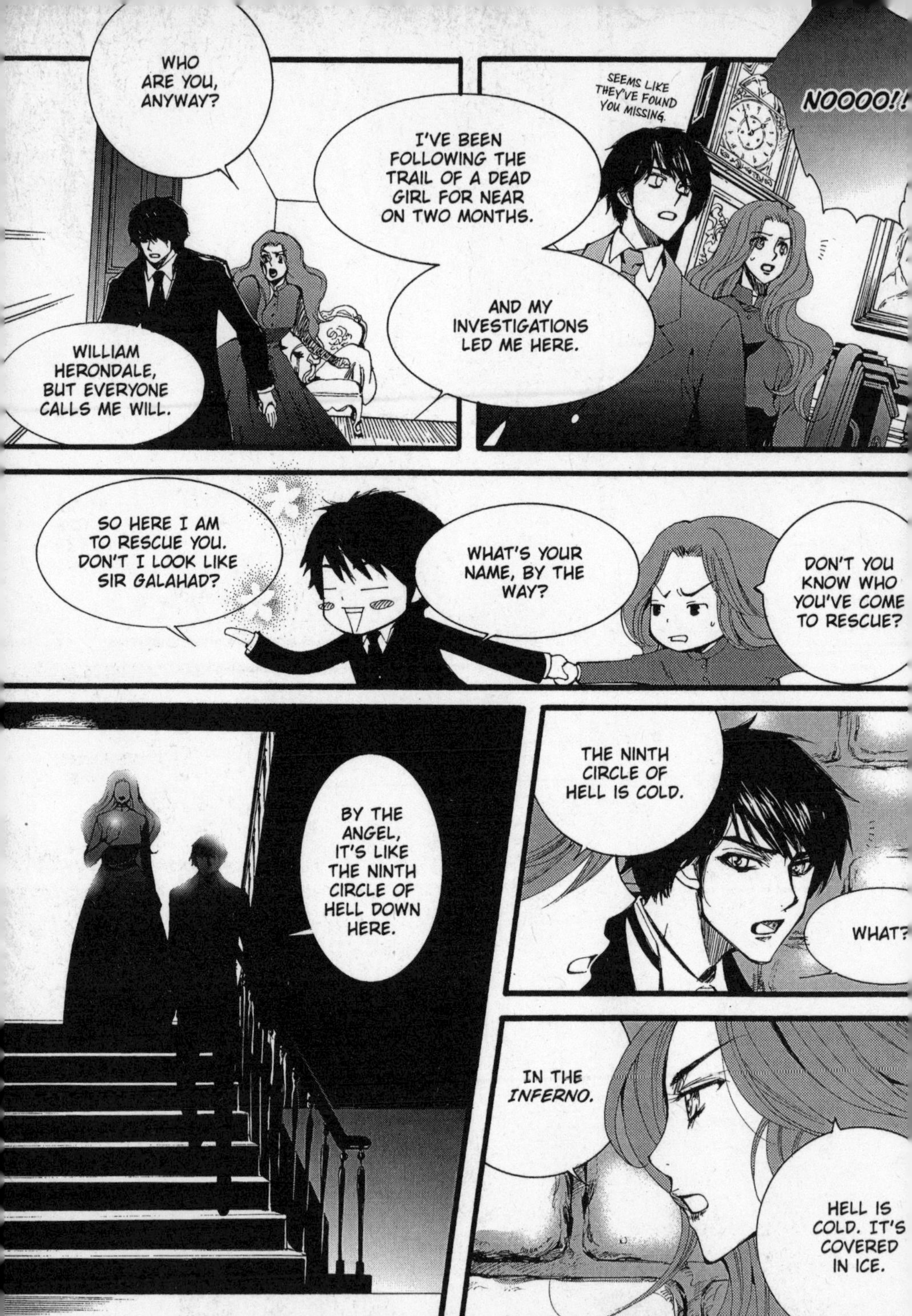
WHO ARE YOU, ANYWAY?
WILLIAM HERONDALE, BUT EVERYONE CALLS ME WILL.
I'VE BEEN FOLLOWING THE TRAIL OF A DEAD GIRL FOR NEAR ON TWO MONTHS.
AND MY INVESTIGATIONS LED ME HERE.
SEEMS LIKE THEY'VE FOUND YOU MISSING.
NOOOO!!
SO HERE I AM TO RESCUE YOU. DON'T I LOOK LIKE SIR GALAHAD?
WHAT'S YOUR NAME, BY THE WAY?
DON'T YOU KNOW WHO YOU'VE COME TO RESCUE?
BY THE ANGEL, IT'S LIKE THE NINTH CIRCLE OF HELL DOWN HERE.
THE NINTH CIRCLE OF HELL IS COLD.
WHAT?
IN THE *INFERNO*.
HELL IS COLD. IT'S COVERED IN ICE.

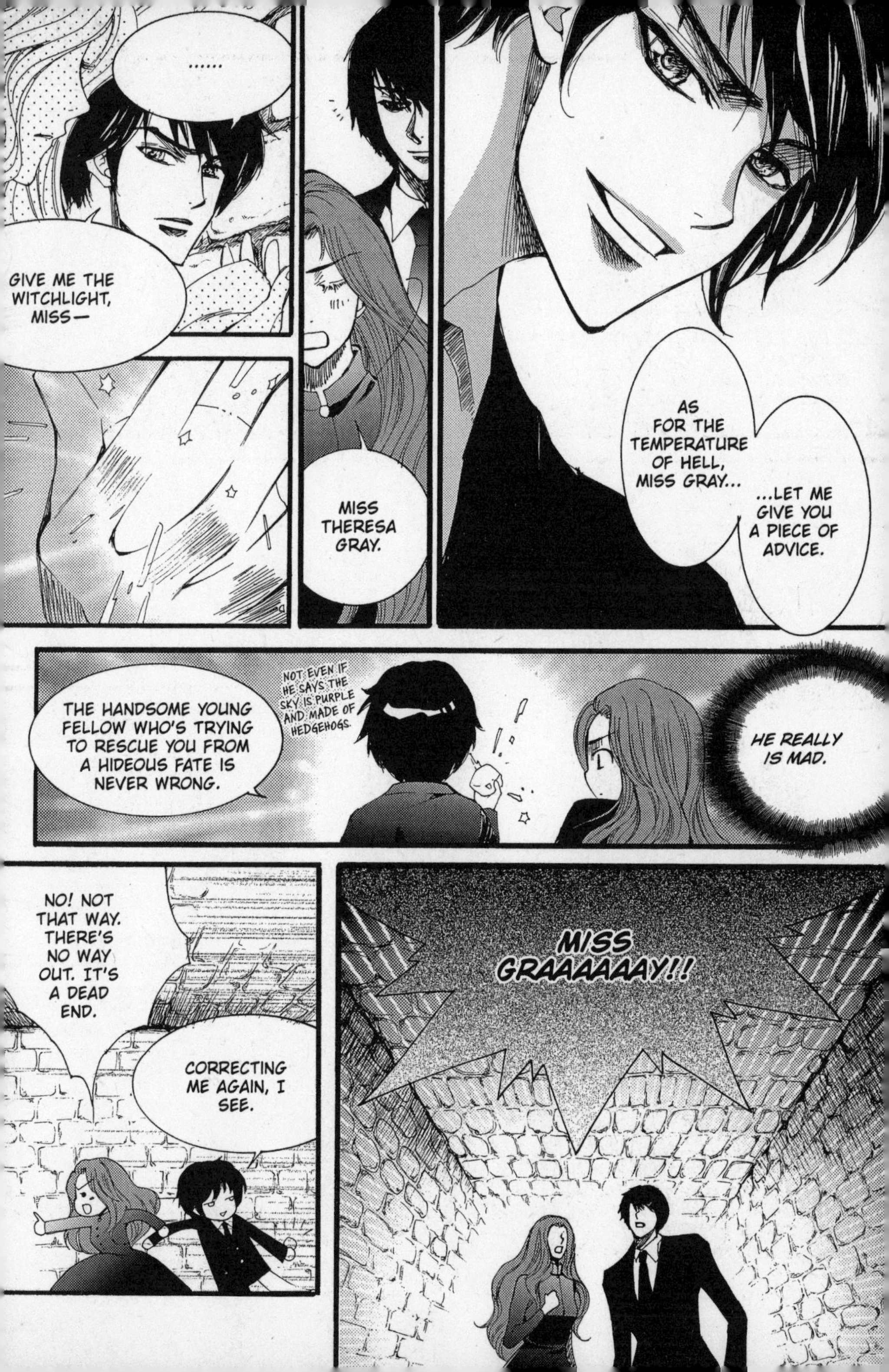

......
GIVE ME THE WITCHLIGHT, MISS—
MISS THERESA GRAY.
AS FOR THE TEMPERATURE OF HELL, MISS GRAY...
...LET ME GIVE YOU A PIECE OF ADVICE.
THE HANDSOME YOUNG FELLOW WHO'S TRYING TO RESCUE YOU FROM A HIDEOUS FATE IS NEVER WRONG.
NOT EVEN IF HE SAYS THE SKY IS PURPLE AND MADE OF HEDGEHOGS.
HE REALLY IS MAD.
NO! NOT THAT WAY. THERE'S NO WAY OUT. IT'S A DEAD END.
CORRECTING ME AGAIN, I SEE.
MISS GRAAAAAAY!!

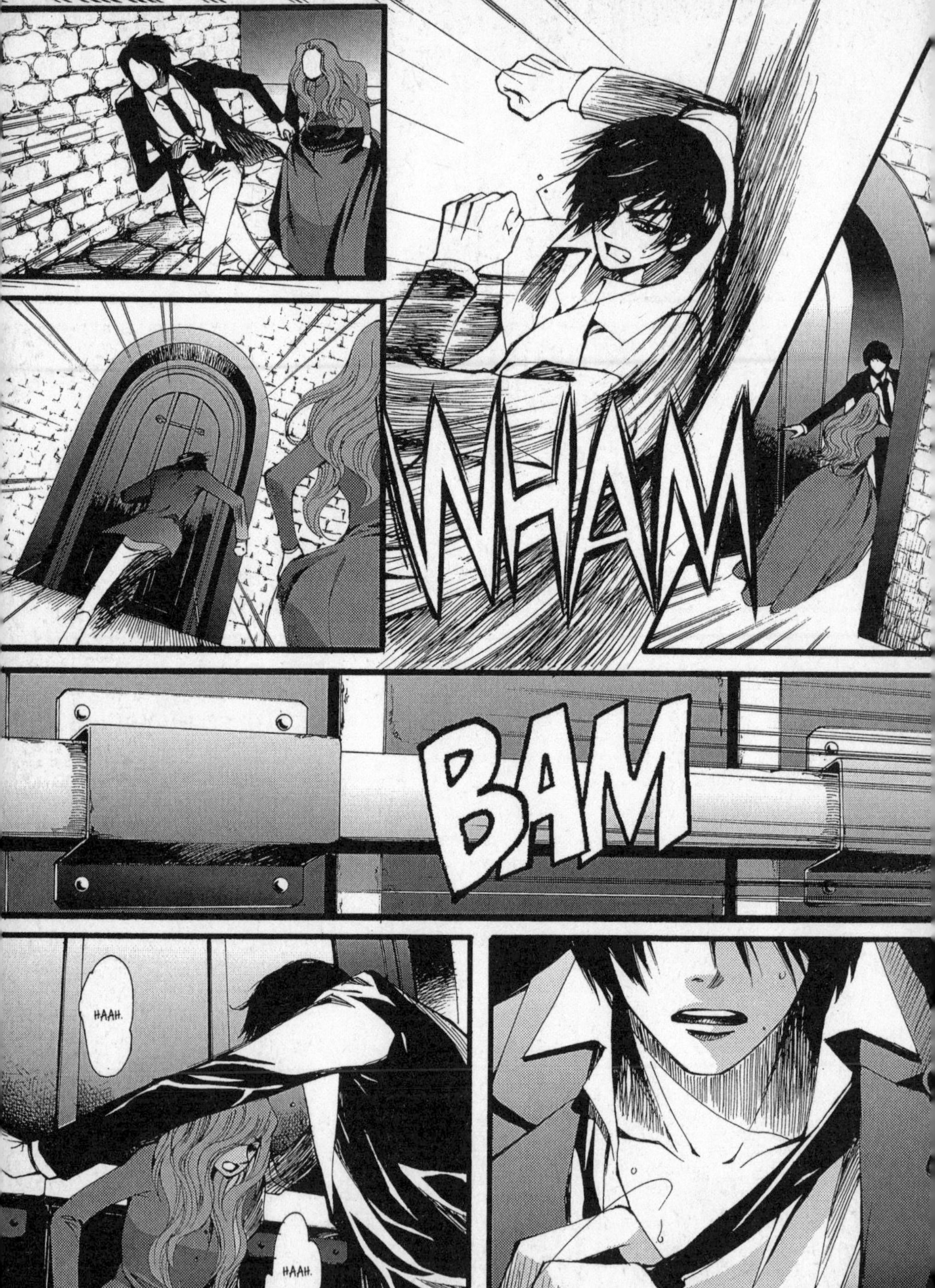
WHAM
BAM
HAAH.
HAAH.

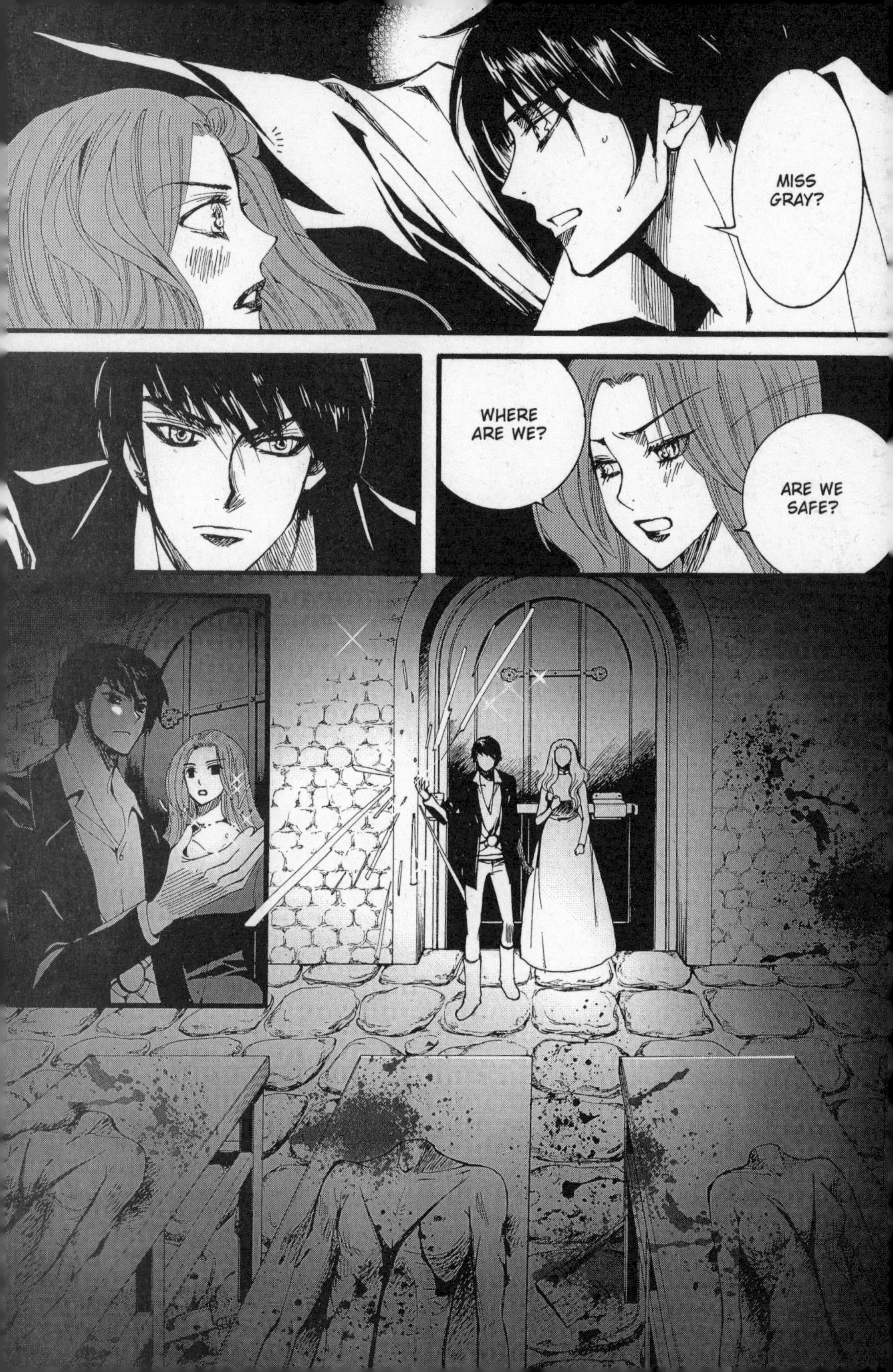
MISS GRAY?
WHERE ARE WE?
ARE WE SAFE?

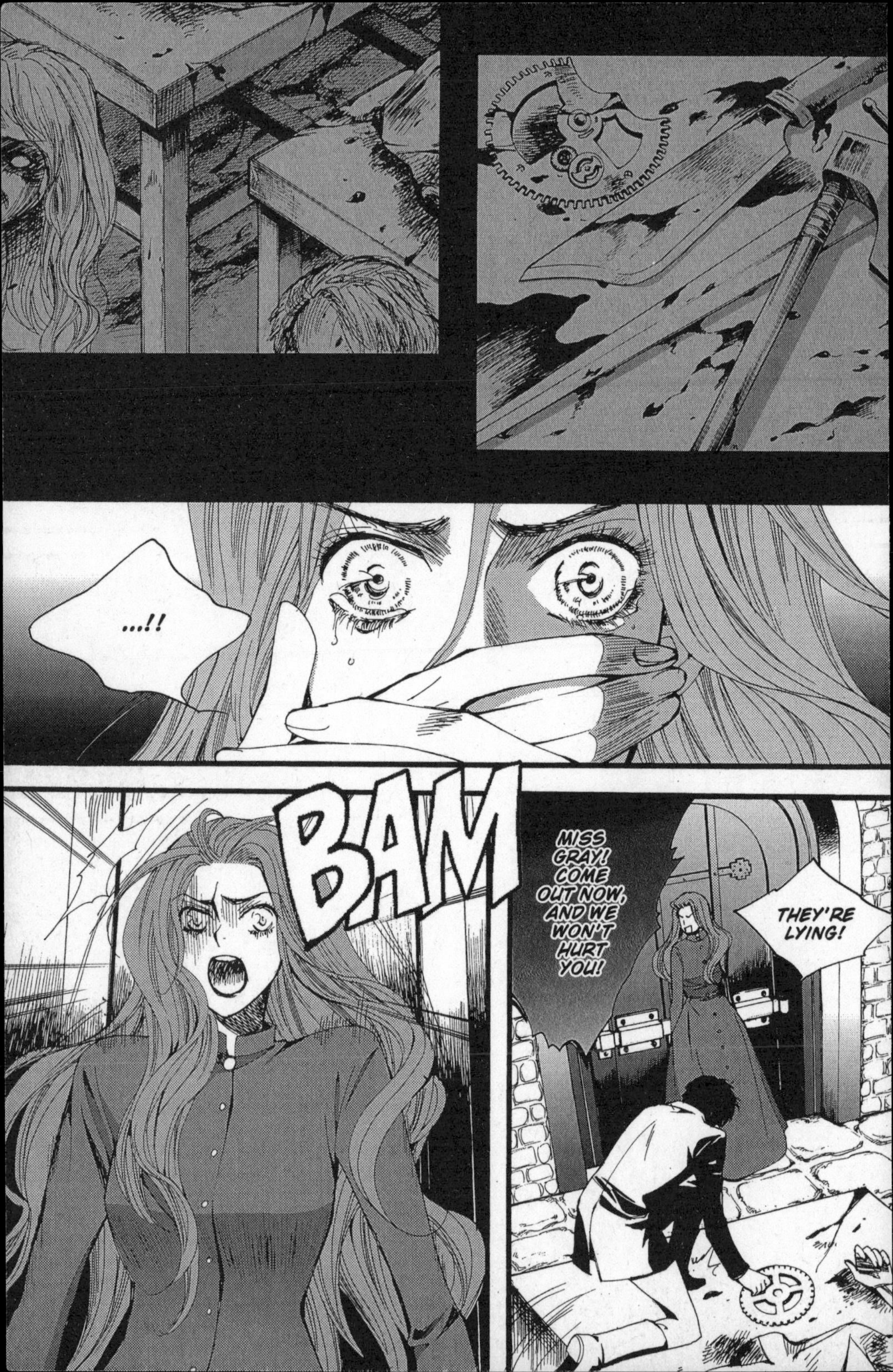
...!!
BAM
MISS GRAY! COME OUT NOW, AND WE WON'T HURT YOU!
THEY'RE LYING!

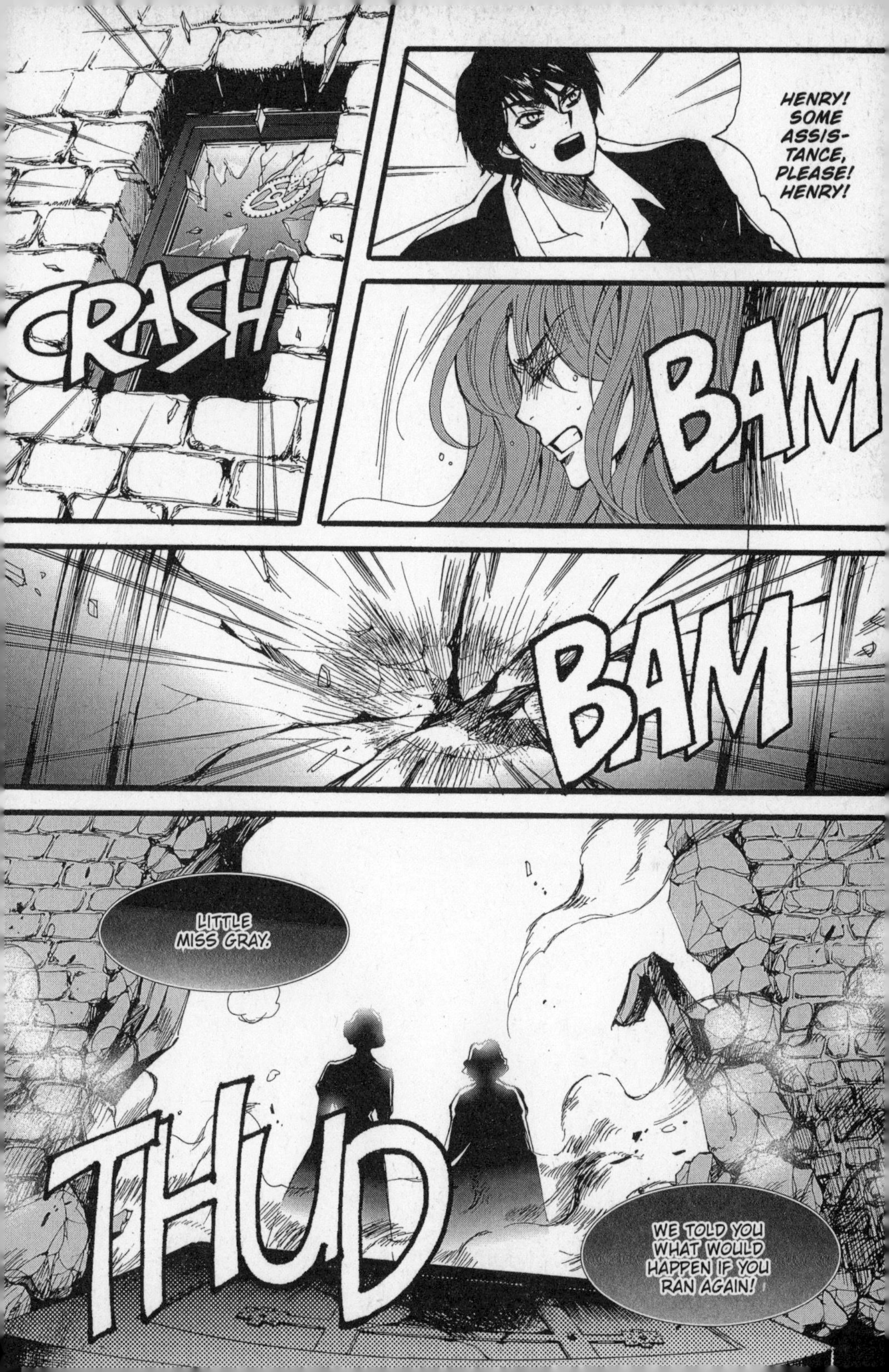
CRASH
HENRY! SOME ASSIS-TANCE, PLEASE! HENRY!
BAM
BAM
LITTLE MISS GRAY.
THUD
WE TOLD YOU WHAT WOULD HAPPEN IF YOU RAN AGAIN!

THE INFERNAL DEVICES
CLOCKWORK ANGEL

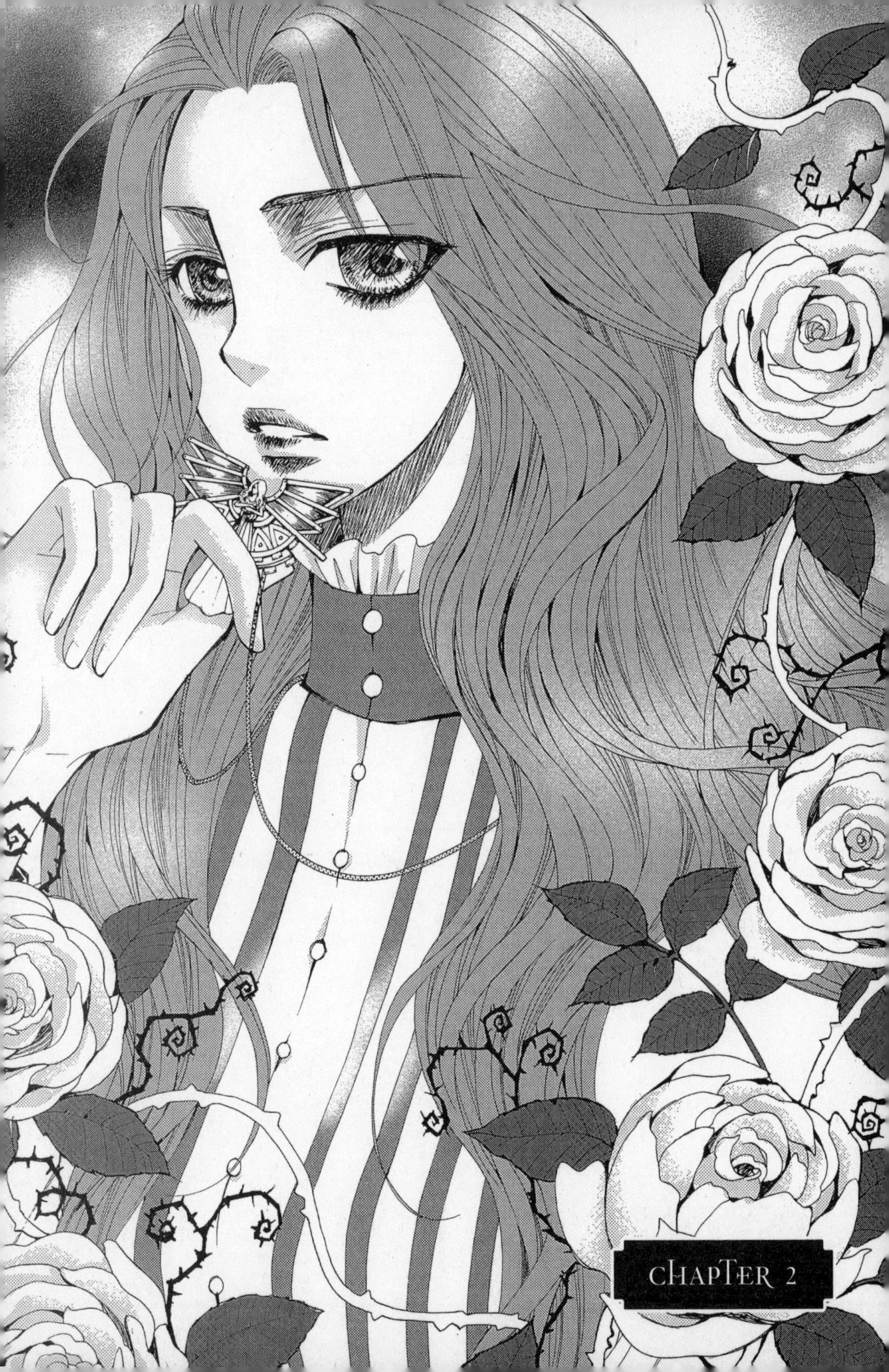
CHAPTER 2

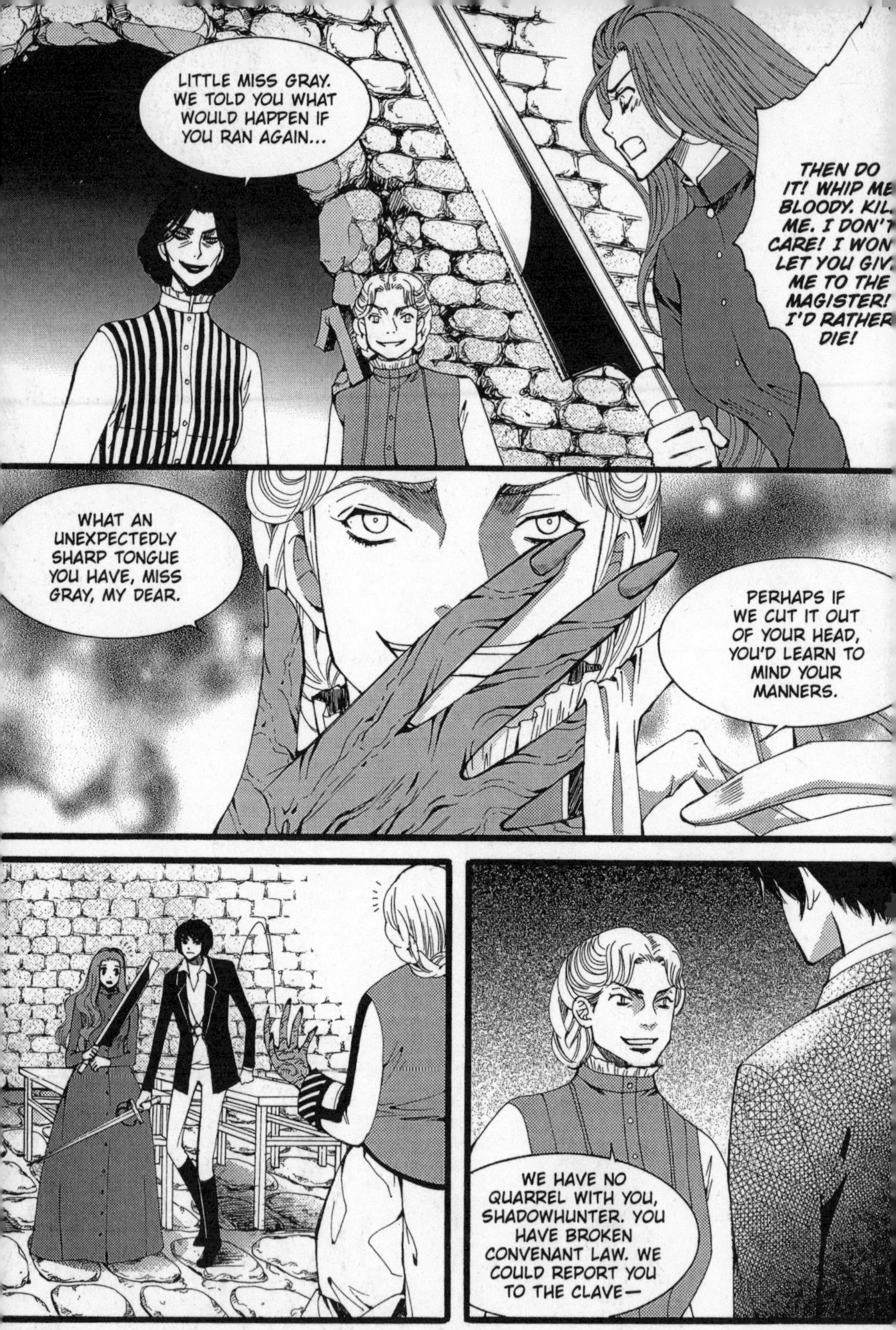
LITTLE MISS GRAY. WE TOLD YOU WHAT WOULD HAPPEN IF YOU RAN AGAIN...
THEN DO IT! WHIP ME BLOODY. KIL ME. I DON'T CARE! I WON LET YOU GIV ME TO THE MAGISTER! I'D RATHER DIE!
WHAT AN UNEXPECTEDLY SHARP TONGUE YOU HAVE, MISS GRAY, MY DEAR.
PERHAPS IF WE CUT IT OUT OF YOUR HEAD, YOU'D LEARN TO MIND YOUR MANNERS.
WE HAVE NO QUARREL WITH YOU, SHADOWHUNTER. YOU HAVE BROKEN COVENANT LAW. WE COULD REPORT YOU TO THE CLAVE—

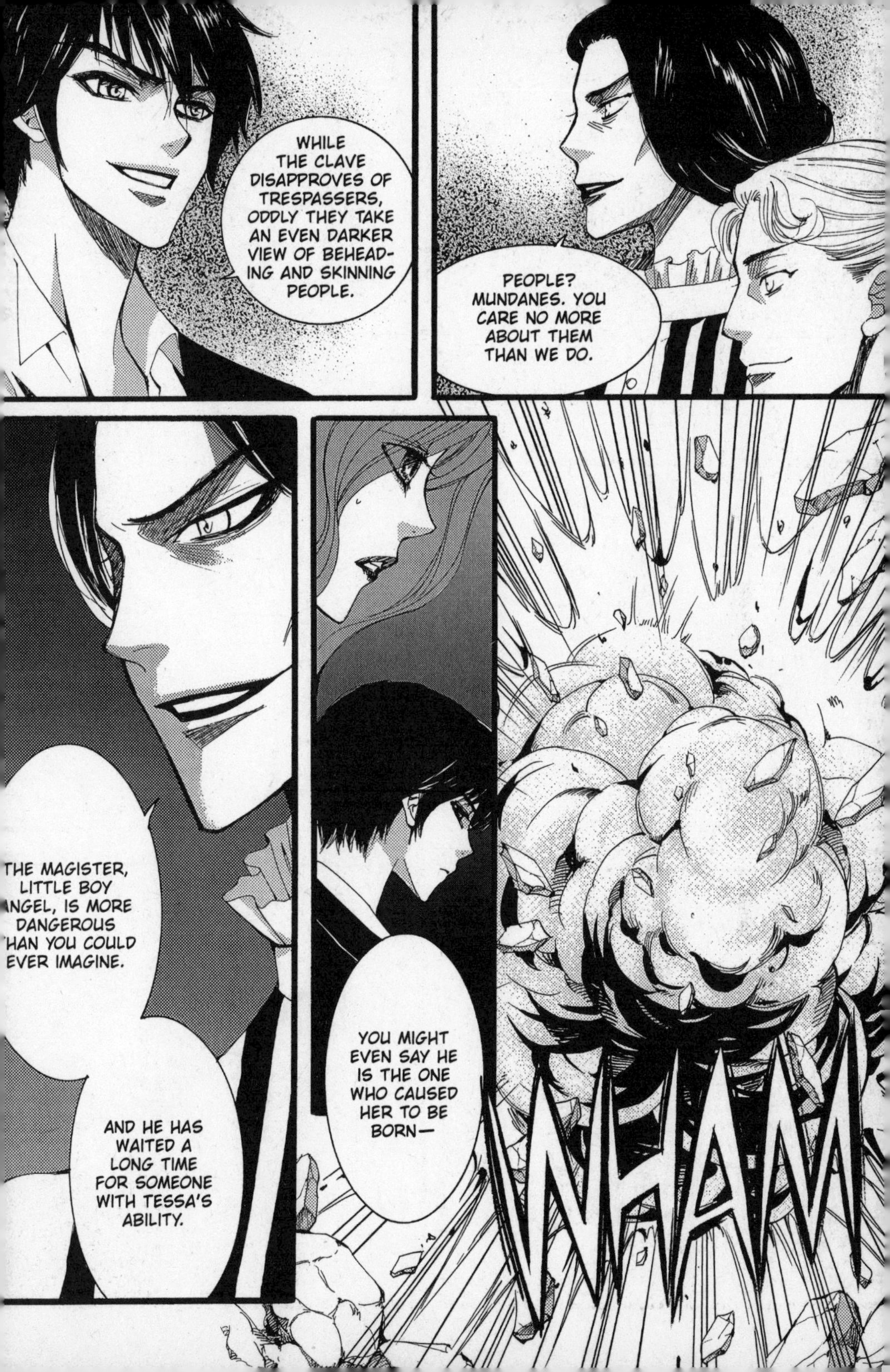
WHILE THE CLAVE DISAPPROVES OF TRESPASSERS, ODDLY THEY TAKE AN EVEN DARKER VIEW OF BEHEAD-ING AND SKINNING PEOPLE.
PEOPLE? MUNDANES. YOU CARE NO MORE ABOUT THEM THAN WE DO.
THE MAGISTER, LITTLE BOY ANGEL, IS MORE DANGEROUS THAN YOU COULD EVER IMAGINE.
AND HE HAS WAITED A LONG TIME FOR SOMEONE WITH TESSA'S ABILITY.
YOU MIGHT EVEN SAY HE IS THE ONE WHO CAUSED HER TO BE BORN—
WHAM

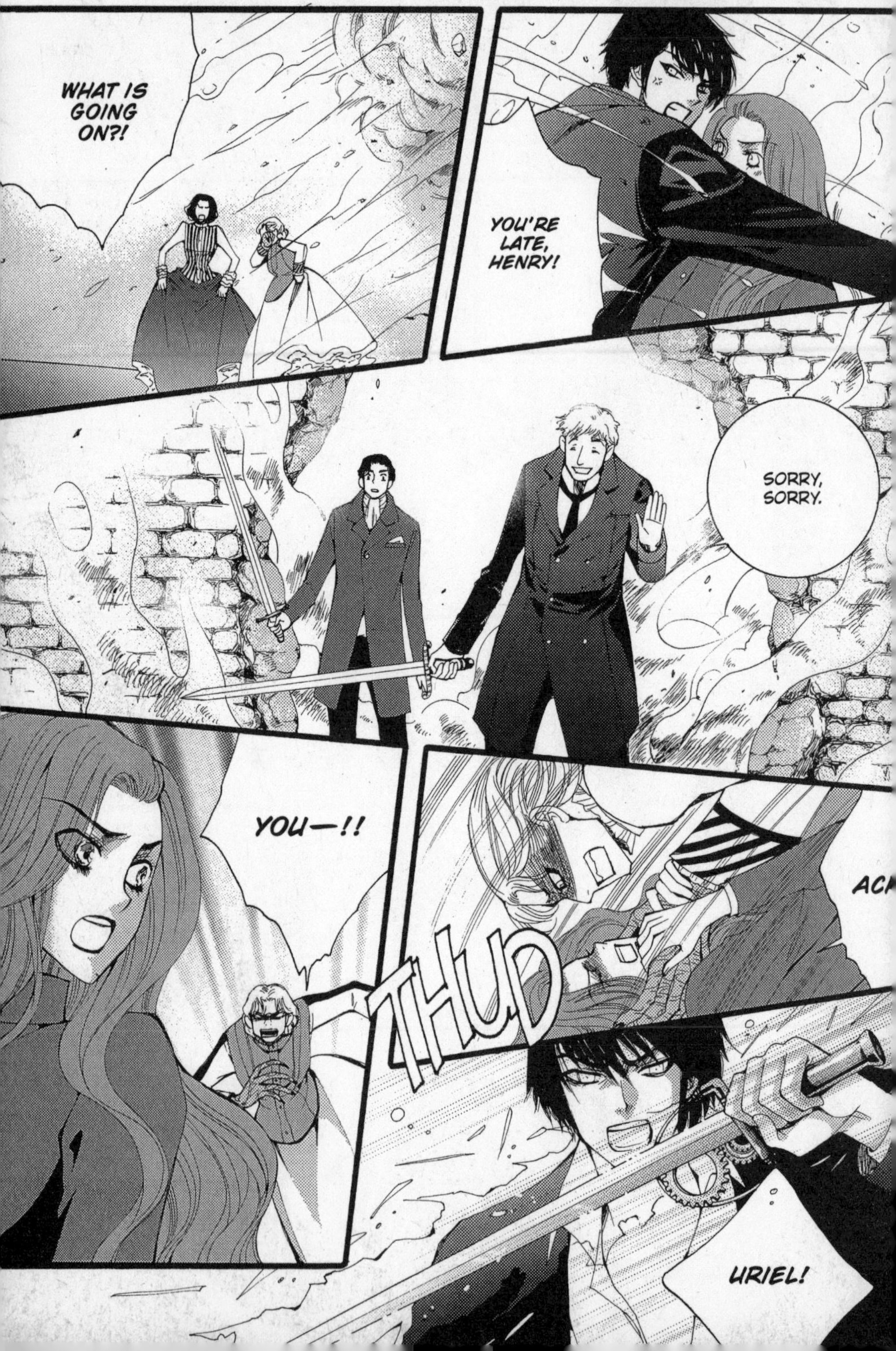
WHAT IS GOING ON?!
YOU'RE LATE, HENRY!
SORRY, SORRY.
YOU—!!
THUD
AC
URIEL!

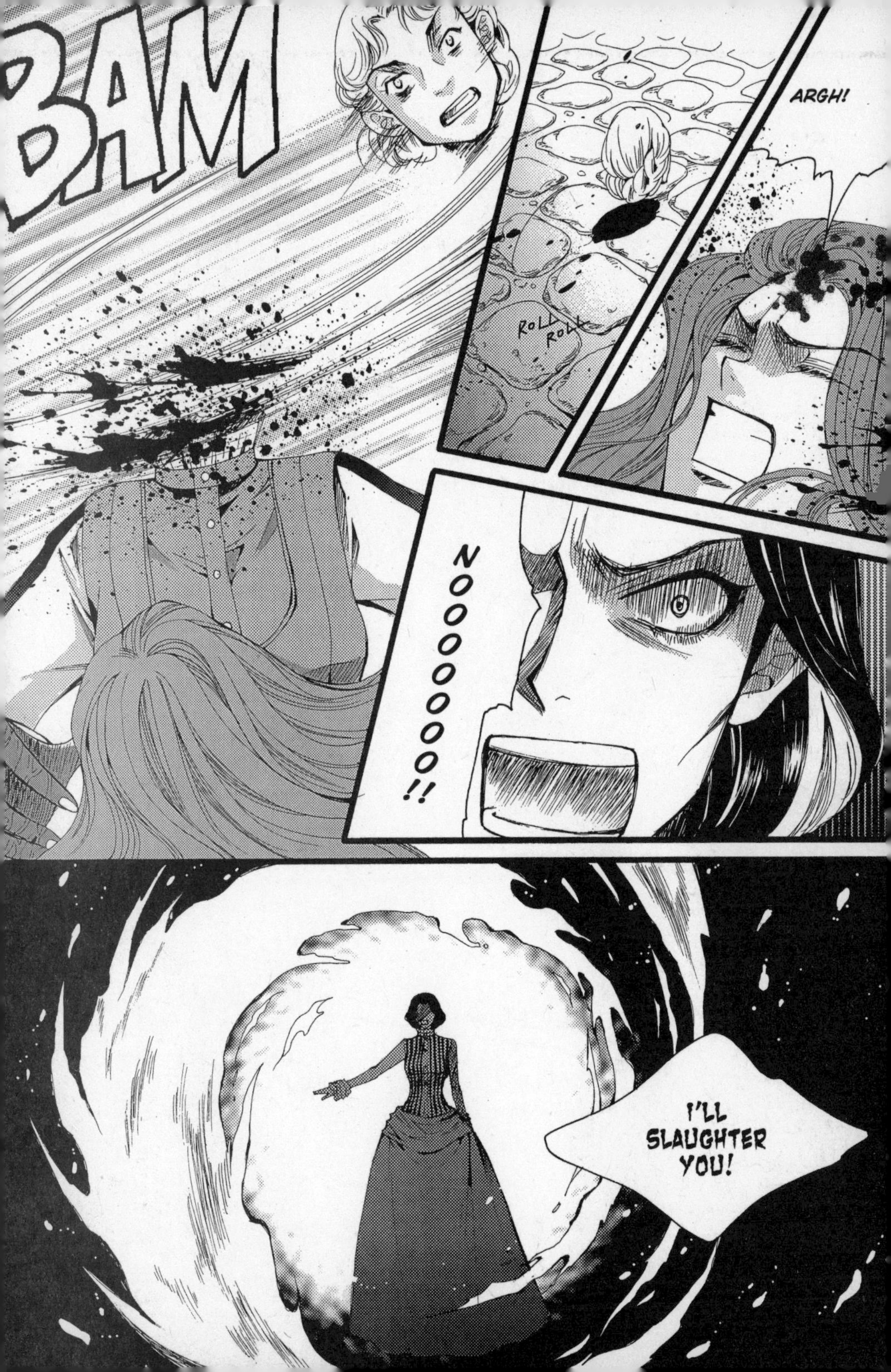
BAM
ROLL ROLL
ARGH!
NOOOOOOOOO!!
I'LL SLAUGHTER YOU!

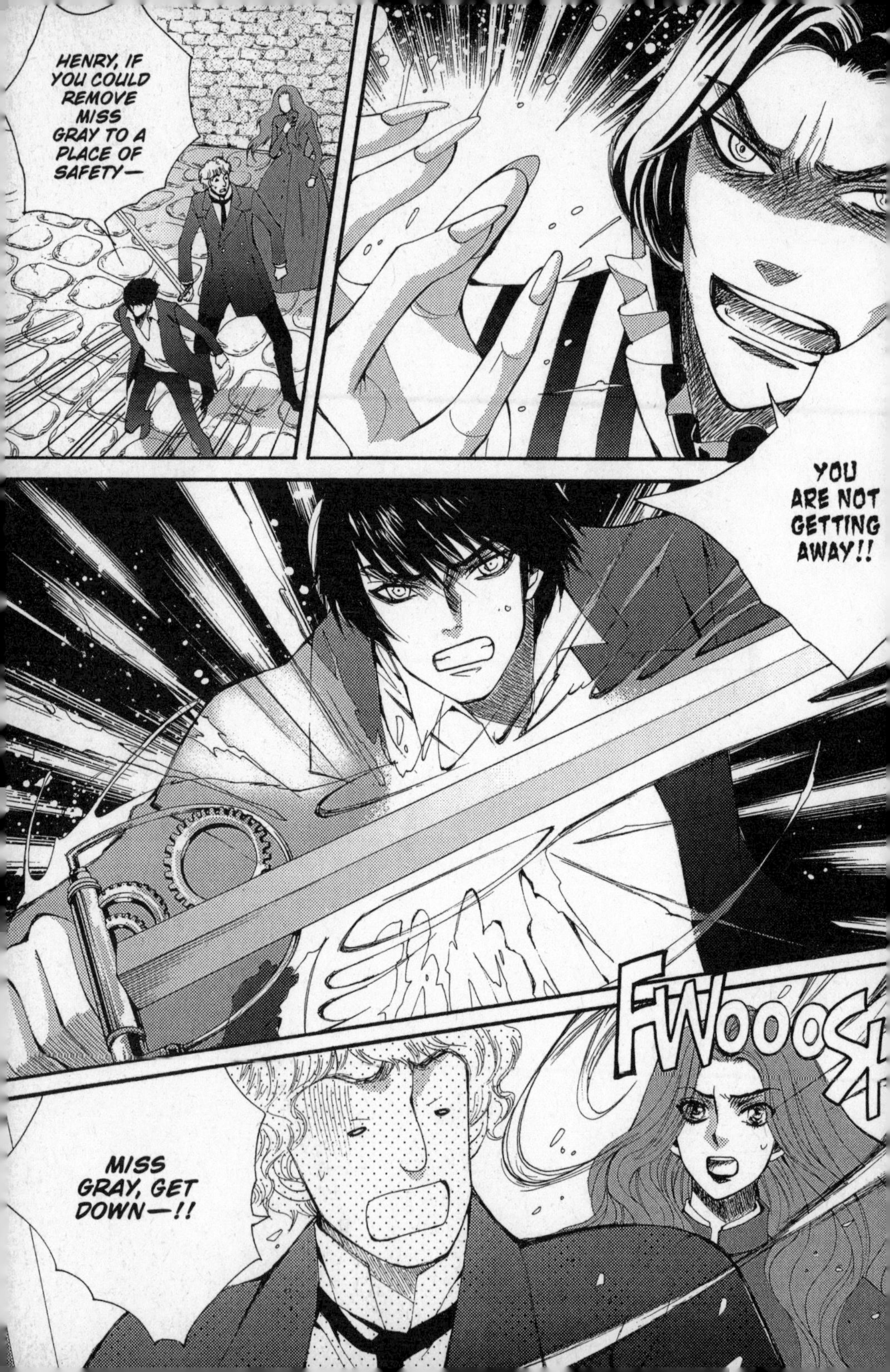
HENRY, IF YOU COULD REMOVE MISS GRAY TO A PLACE OF SAFETY—
YOU ARE NOT GETTING AWAY!!
FWOOOSH
MISS GRAY, GET DOWN—!!

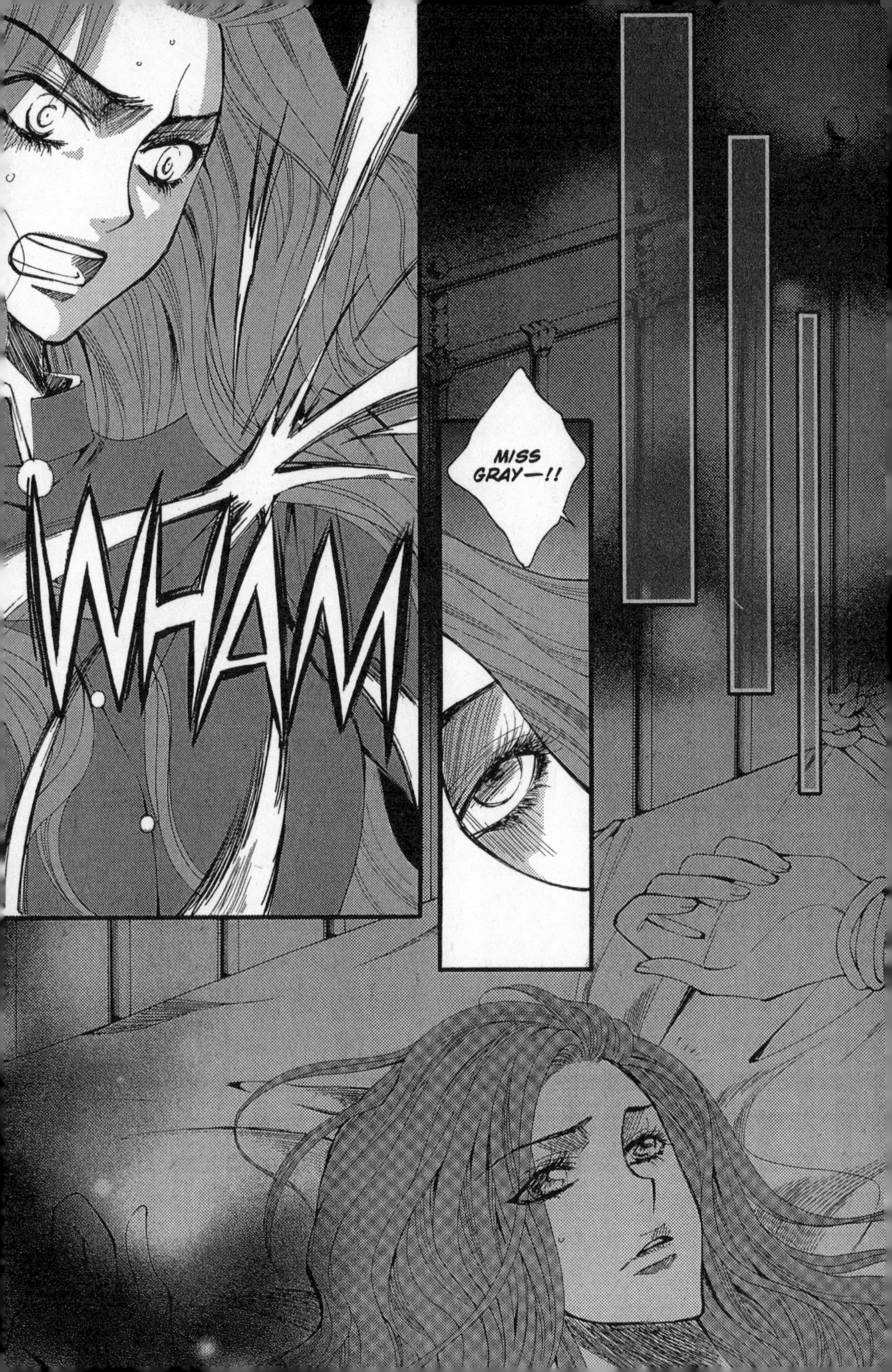
WHAM
MISS GRAY—!!

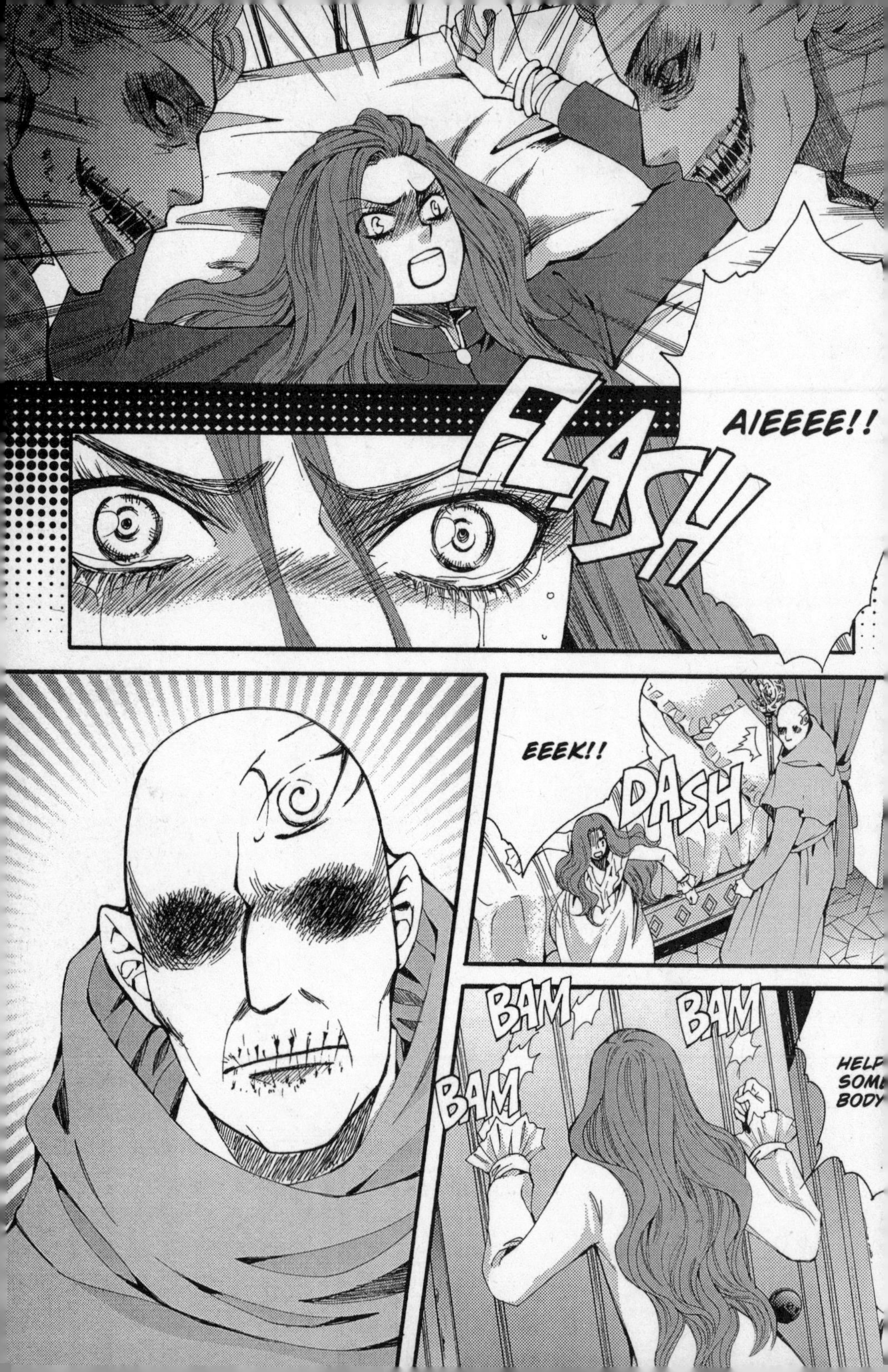
FLASH
AIEEEEE!!
EEEK!!
DASH
BAM
BAM
BAM
HELP SOME BODY

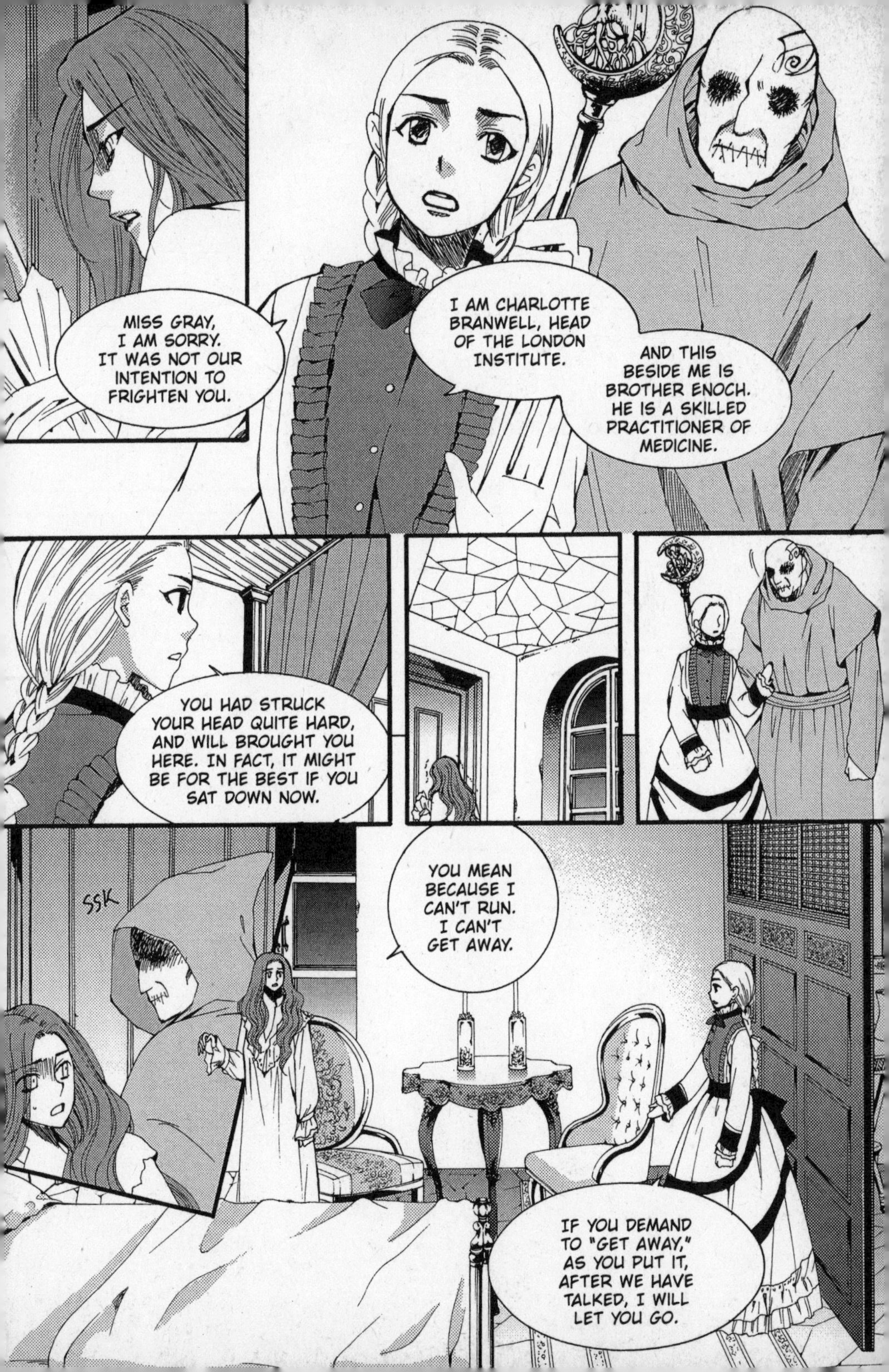
MISS GRAY, I AM SORRY. IT WAS NOT OUR INTENTION TO FRIGHTEN YOU.
I AM CHARLOTTE BRANWELL, HEAD OF THE LONDON INSTITUTE.
AND THIS BESIDE ME IS BROTHER ENOCH. HE IS A SKILLED PRACTITIONER OF MEDICINE.
YOU HAD STRUCK YOUR HEAD QUITE HARD, AND WILL BROUGHT YOU HERE. IN FACT, IT MIGHT BE FOR THE BEST IF YOU SAT DOWN NOW.
SSK
YOU MEAN BECAUSE I CAN'T RUN. I CAN'T GET AWAY.
IF YOU DEMAND TO "GET AWAY," AS YOU PUT IT, AFTER WE HAVE TALKED, I WILL LET YOU GO.

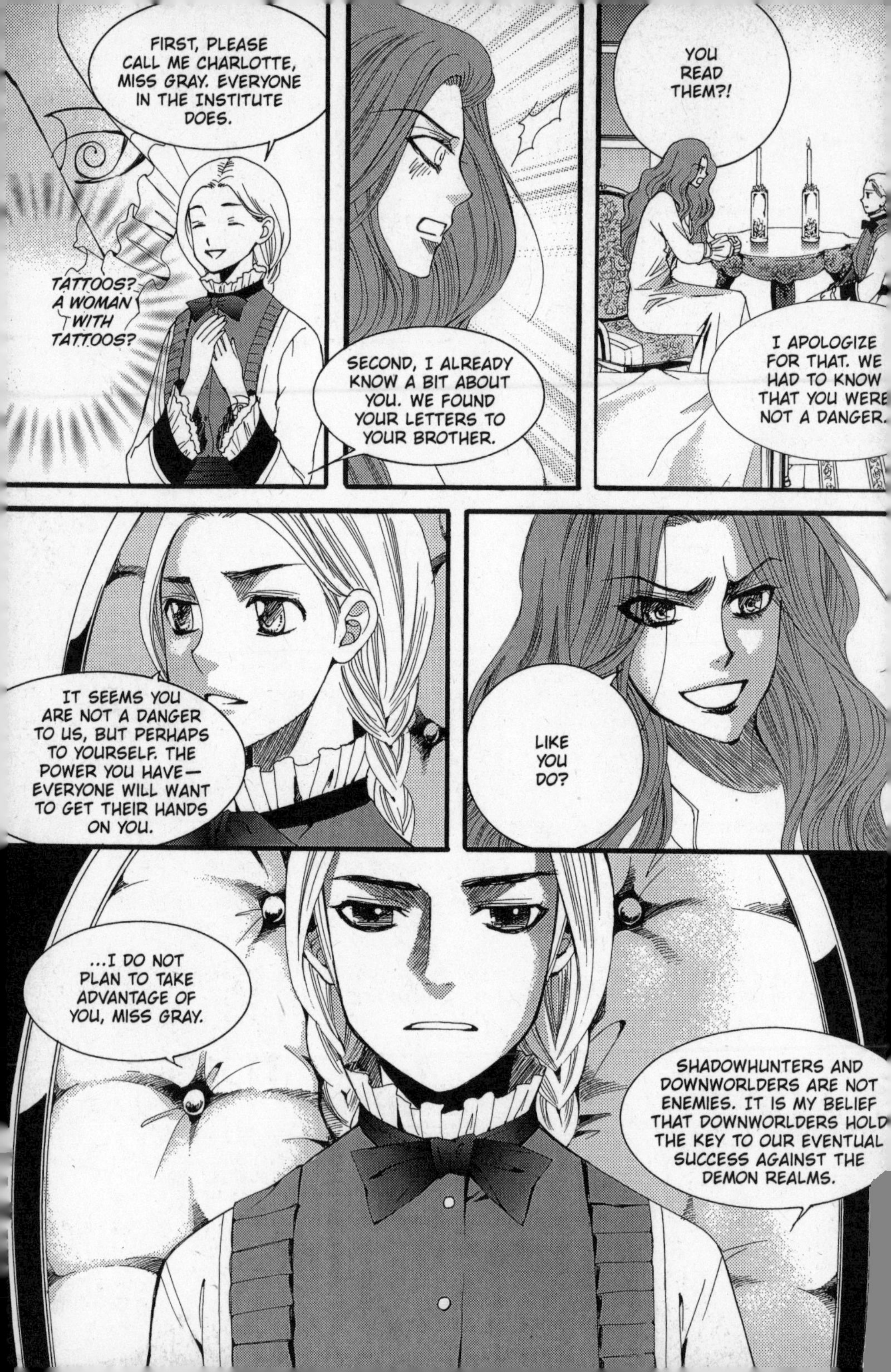
FIRST, PLEASE CALL ME CHARLOTTE, MISS GRAY. EVERYONE IN THE INSTITUTE DOES.
TATTOOS? A WOMAN WITH TATTOOS?
SECOND, I ALREADY KNOW A BIT ABOUT YOU. WE FOUND YOUR LETTERS TO YOUR BROTHER.
YOU READ THEM?!
I APOLOGIZE FOR THAT. WE HAD TO KNOW THAT YOU WERE NOT A DANGER.
IT SEEMS YOU ARE NOT A DANGER TO US, BUT PERHAPS TO YOURSELF. THE POWER YOU HAVE—EVERYONE WILL WANT TO GET THEIR HANDS ON YOU.
LIKE YOU DO?
...I DO NOT PLAN TO TAKE ADVANTAGE OF YOU, MISS GRAY.
SHADOWHUNTERS AND DOWNWORLDERS ARE NOT ENEMIES. IT IS MY BELIEF THAT DOWNWORLDERS HOLD THE KEY TO OUR EVENTUAL SUCCESS AGAINST THE DEMON REALMS.

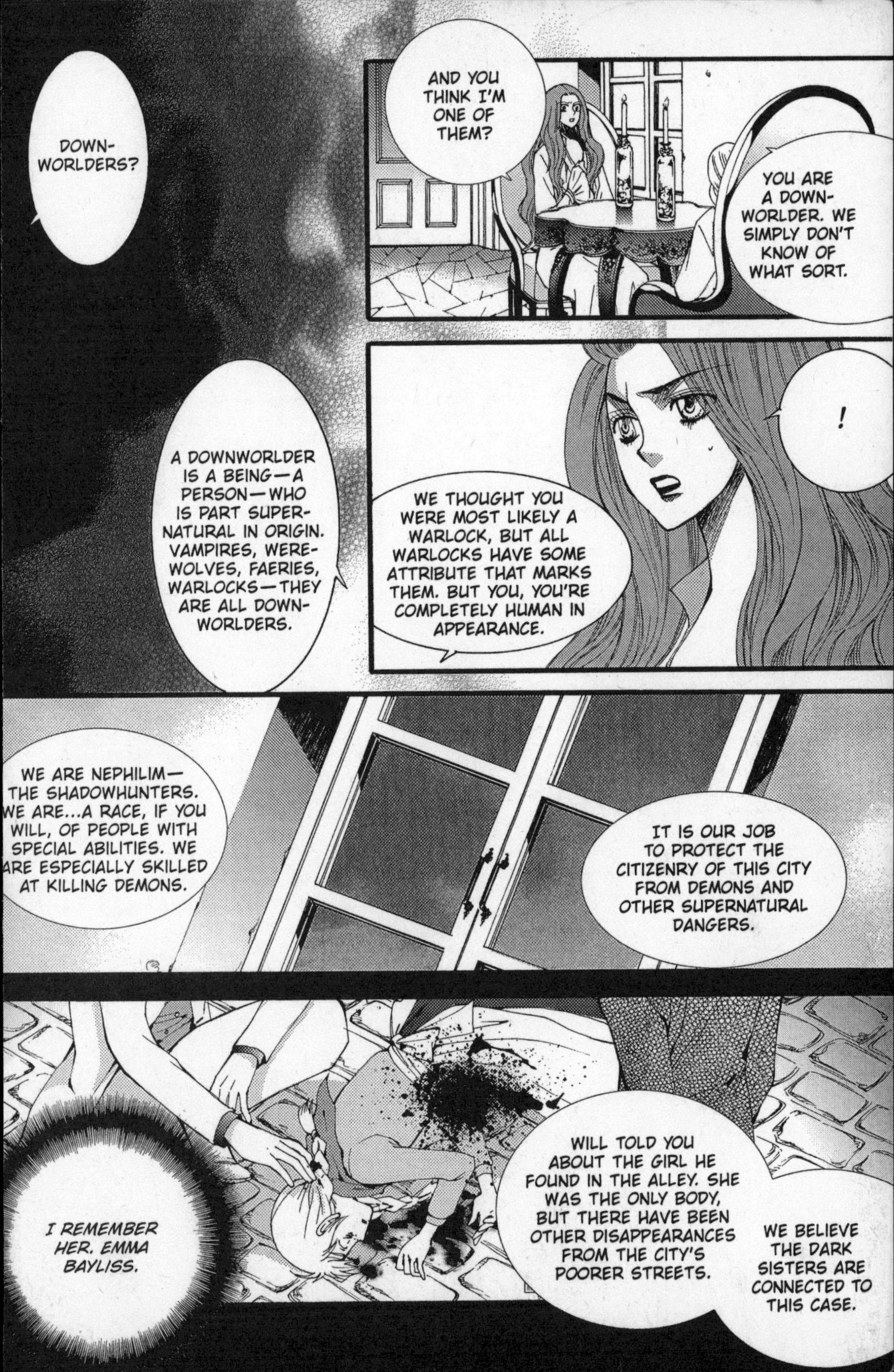
DOWN-WORLDERS?
AND YOU THINK I'M ONE OF THEM?
YOU ARE A DOWN-WORLDER. WE SIMPLY DON'T KNOW OF WHAT SORT.
A DOWNWORLDER IS A BEING—A PERSON—WHO IS PART SUPER-NATURAL IN ORIGIN. VAMPIRES, WERE-WOLVES, FAERIES, WARLOCKS—THEY ARE ALL DOWN-WORLDERS.
!
WE THOUGHT YOU WERE MOST LIKELY A WARLOCK, BUT ALL WARLOCKS HAVE SOME ATTRIBUTE THAT MARKS THEM. BUT YOU, YOU'RE COMPLETELY HUMAN IN APPEARANCE.
WE ARE NEPHILIM—THE SHADOWHUNTERS. WE ARE...A RACE, IF YOU WILL, OF PEOPLE WITH SPECIAL ABILITIES. WE ARE ESPECIALLY SKILLED AT KILLING DEMONS.
IT IS OUR JOB TO PROTECT THE CITIZENRY OF THIS CITY FROM DEMONS AND OTHER SUPERNATURAL DANGERS.
I REMEMBER HER. EMMA BAYLISS.
WILL TOLD YOU ABOUT THE GIRL HE FOUND IN THE ALLEY. SHE WAS THE ONLY BODY, BUT THERE HAVE BEEN OTHER DISAPPEARANCES FROM THE CITY'S POORER STREETS.
WE BELIEVE THE DARK SISTERS ARE CONNECTED TO THIS CASE.

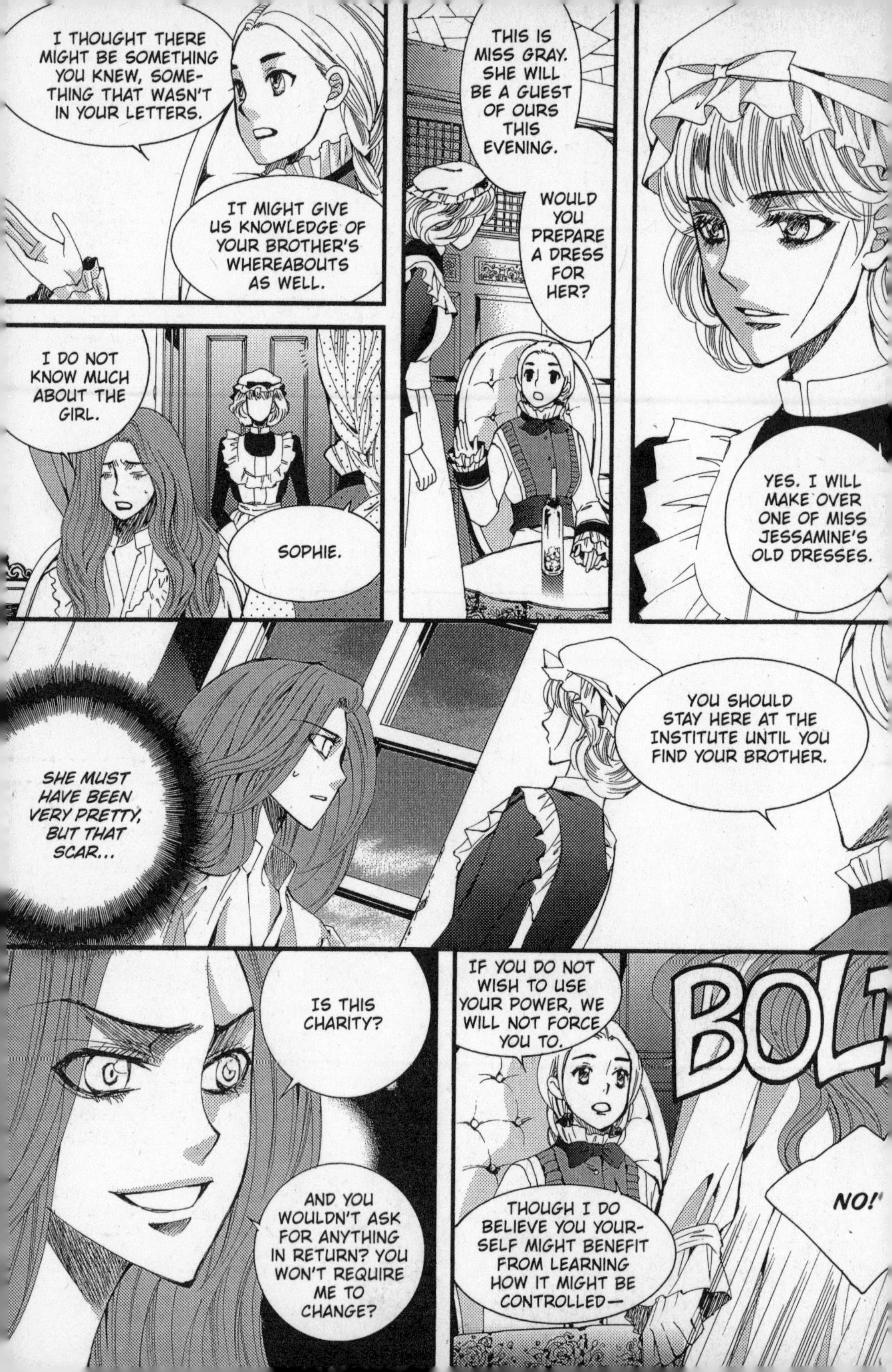
I THOUGHT THERE MIGHT BE SOMETHING YOU KNEW, SOMETHING THAT WASN'T IN YOUR LETTERS.
IT MIGHT GIVE US KNOWLEDGE OF YOUR BROTHER'S WHEREABOUTS AS WELL.
THIS IS MISS GRAY. SHE WILL BE A GUEST OF OURS THIS EVENING.
WOULD YOU PREPARE A DRESS FOR HER?
I DO NOT KNOW MUCH ABOUT THE GIRL.
SOPHIE.
YES. I WILL MAKE OVER ONE OF MISS JESSAMINE'S OLD DRESSES.
SHE MUST HAVE BEEN VERY PRETTY, BUT THAT SCAR...
YOU SHOULD STAY HERE AT THE INSTITUTE UNTIL YOU FIND YOUR BROTHER.
IS THIS CHARITY?
AND YOU WOULDN'T ASK FOR ANYTHING IN RETURN? YOU WON'T REQUIRE ME TO CHANGE?
IF YOU DO NOT WISH TO USE YOUR POWER, WE WILL NOT FORCE YOU TO.
THOUGH I DO BELIEVE YOU YOURSELF MIGHT BENEFIT FROM LEARNING HOW IT MIGHT BE CONTROLLED—
BOL
NO!

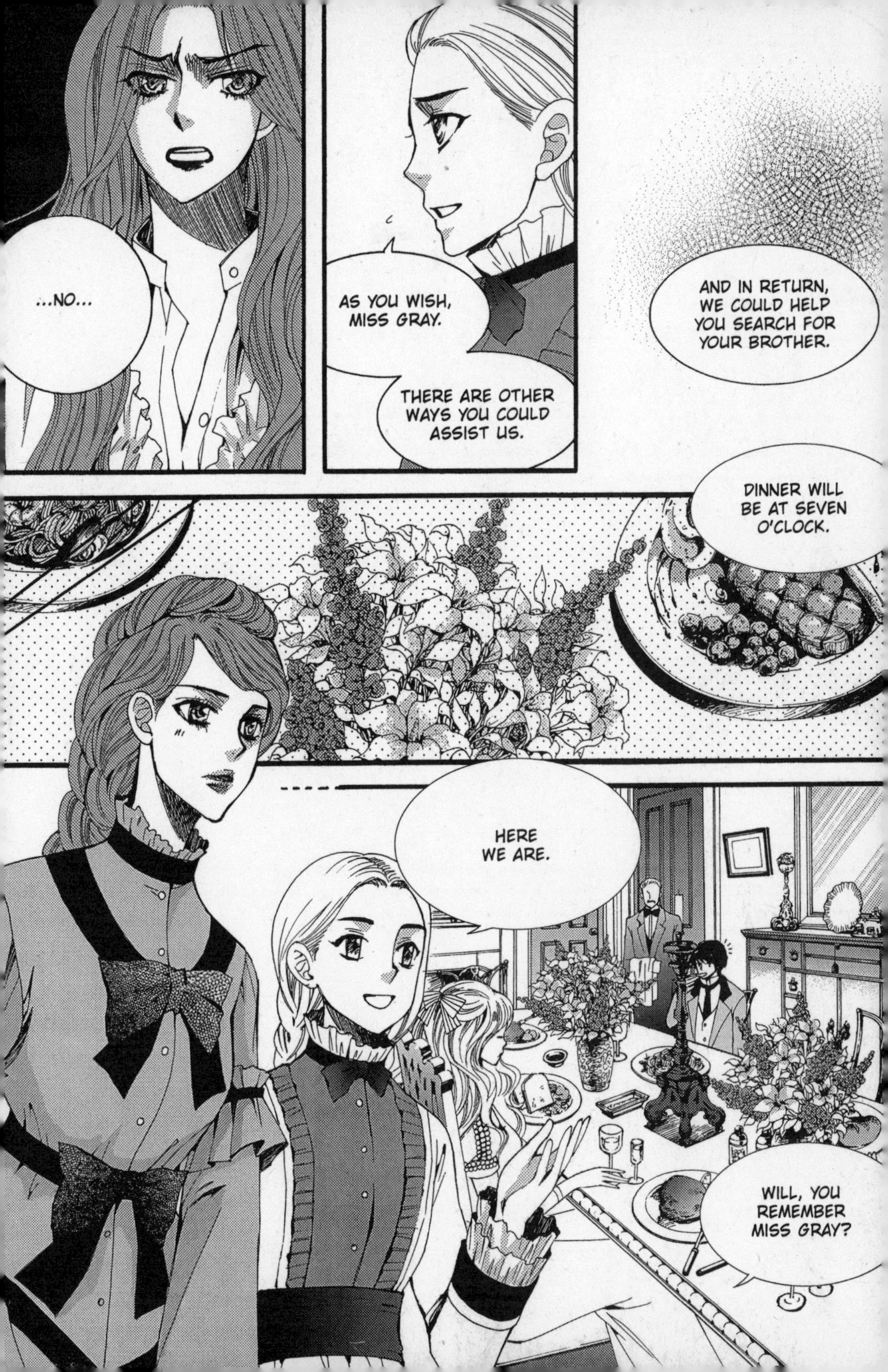
...NO...
AS YOU WISH, MISS GRAY.
THERE ARE OTHER WAYS YOU COULD ASSIST US.
AND IN RETURN, WE COULD HELP YOU SEARCH FOR YOUR BROTHER.
DINNER WILL BE AT SEVEN O'CLOCK.
HERE WE ARE.
WILL, YOU REMEMBER MISS GRAY?

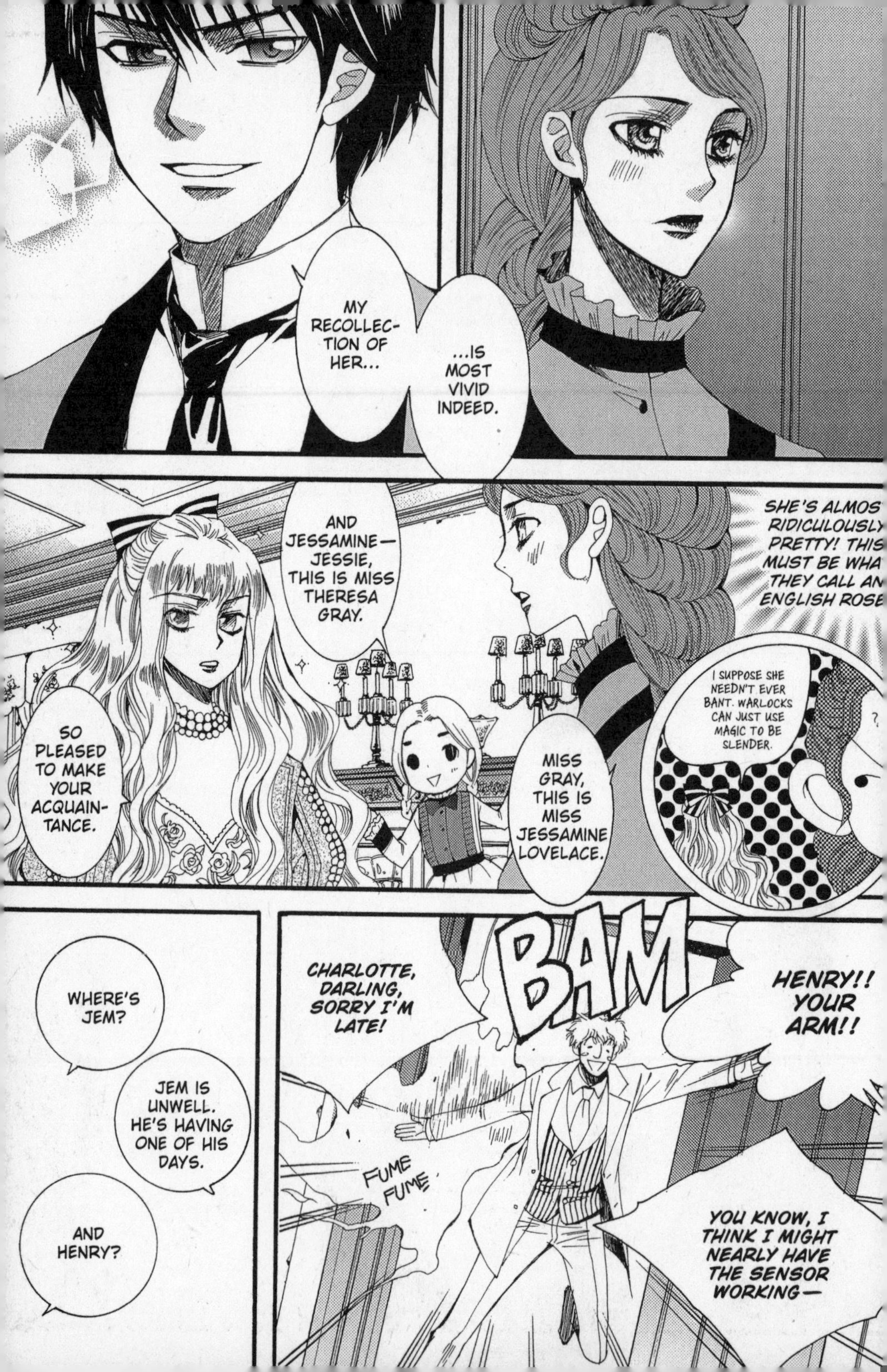
MY RECOLLECTION OF HER...
...IS MOST VIVID INDEED.
AND JESSAMINE—JESSIE, THIS IS MISS THERESA GRAY.
SO PLEASED TO MAKE YOUR ACQUAINTANCE.
MISS GRAY, THIS IS MISS JESSAMINE LOVELACE.
SHE'S ALMOS RIDICULOUSL PRETTY! THIS MUST BE WHA THEY CALL AN ENGLISH ROSE
I SUPPOSE SHE NEEDN'T EVER BANT. WARLOCKS CAN JUST USE MAGIC TO BE SLENDER.
?
WHERE'S JEM?
JEM IS UNWELL. HE'S HAVING ONE OF HIS DAYS.
AND HENRY?
CHARLOTTE, DARLING, SORRY I'M LATE!
BAM
HENRY!! YOUR ARM!!
FUME FUME
YOU KNOW, I THINK I MIGHT NEARLY HAVE THE SENSOR WORKING—

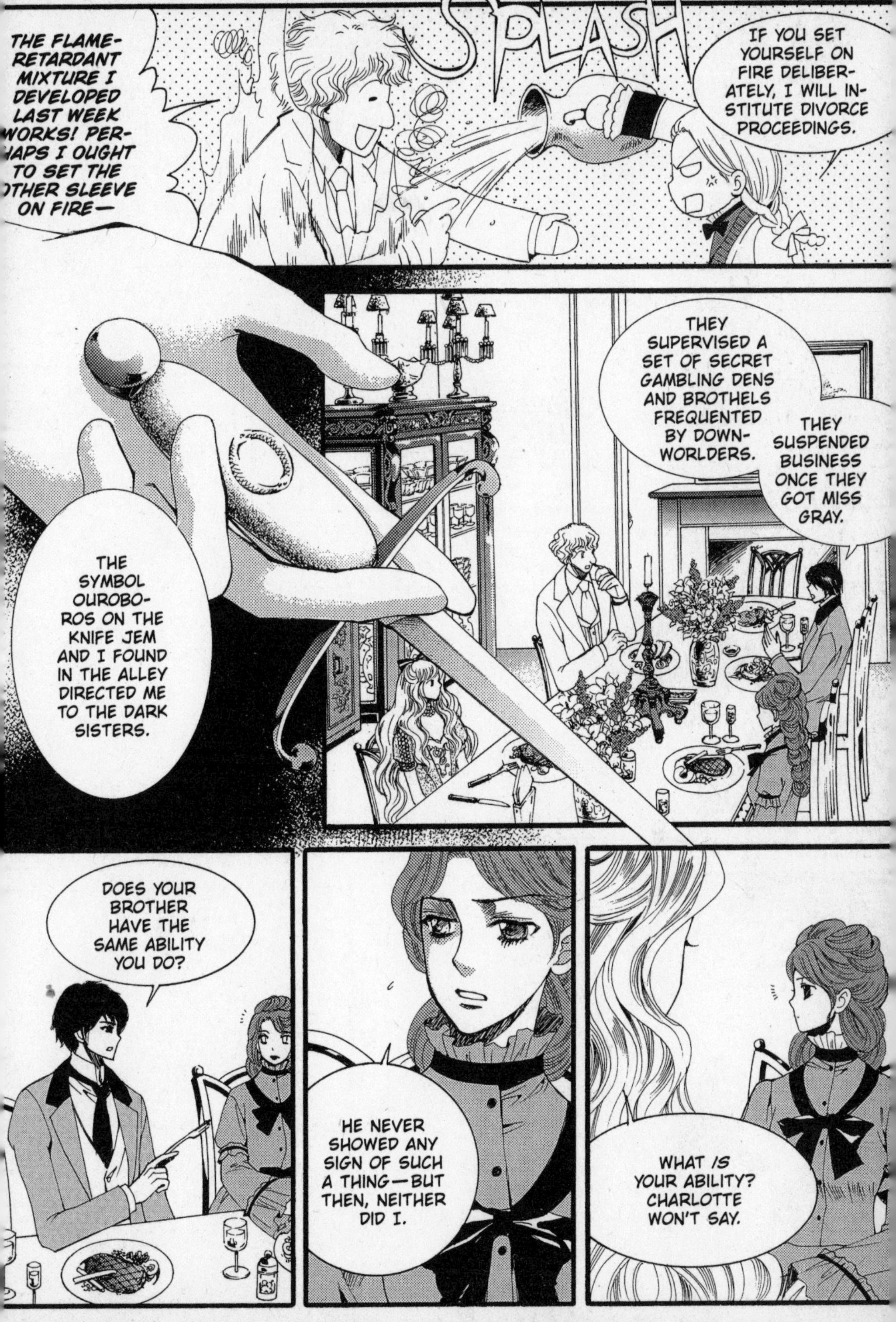

THE FLAME-RETARDANT MIXTURE I DEVELOPED LAST WEEK WORKS! PERHAPS I OUGHT TO SET THE OTHER SLEEVE ON FIRE—
SPLASH
IF YOU SET YOURSELF ON FIRE DELIBERATELY, I WILL INSTITUTE DIVORCE PROCEEDINGS.
THE SYMBOL OUROBOROS ON THE KNIFE JEM AND I FOUND IN THE ALLEY DIRECTED ME TO THE DARK SISTERS.
THEY SUPERVISED A SET OF SECRET GAMBLING DENS AND BROTHELS FREQUENTED BY DOWNWORLDERS.
THEY SUSPENDED BUSINESS ONCE THEY GOT MISS GRAY.
DOES YOUR BROTHER HAVE THE SAME ABILITY YOU DO?
HE NEVER SHOWED ANY SIGN OF SUCH A THING—BUT THEN, NEITHER DID I.
WHAT *IS* YOUR ABILITY? CHARLOTTE WON'T SAY.

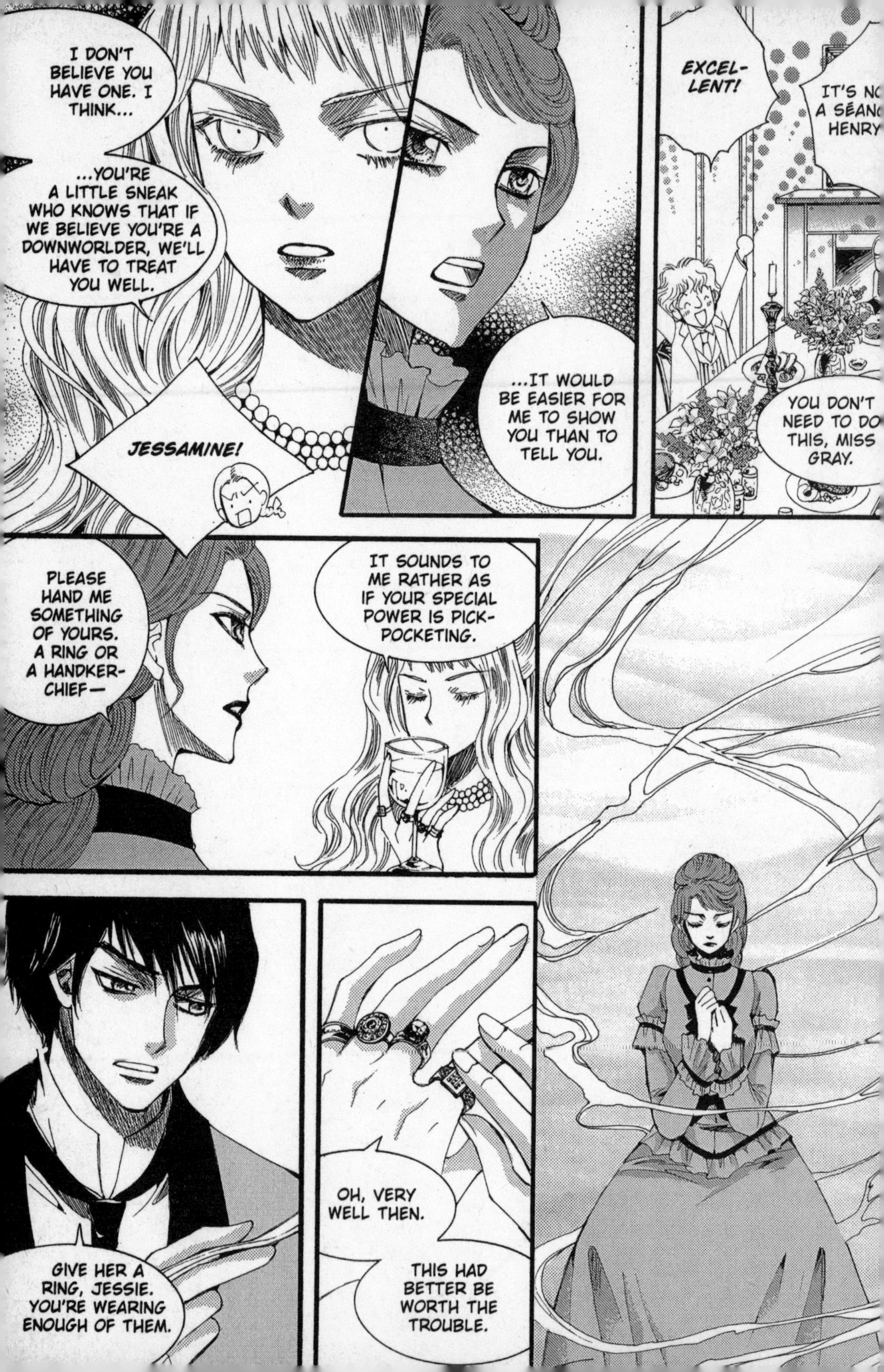
I DON'T BELIEVE YOU HAVE ONE. I THINK...
...YOU'RE A LITTLE SNEAK WHO KNOWS THAT IF WE BELIEVE YOU'RE A DOWNWORLDER, WE'LL HAVE TO TREAT YOU WELL.
JESSAMINE!
...IT WOULD BE EASIER FOR ME TO SHOW YOU THAN TO TELL YOU.
EXCEL-LENT!
IT'S NO A SÉANC HENRY
YOU DON'T NEED TO DO THIS, MISS GRAY.
PLEASE HAND ME SOMETHING OF YOURS. A RING OR A HANDKER-CHIEF—
IT SOUNDS TO ME RATHER AS IF YOUR SPECIAL POWER IS PICK-POCKETING.
GIVE HER A RING, JESSIE. YOU'RE WEARING ENOUGH OF THEM.
OH, VERY WELL THEN.
THIS HAD BETTER BE WORTH THE TROUBLE.

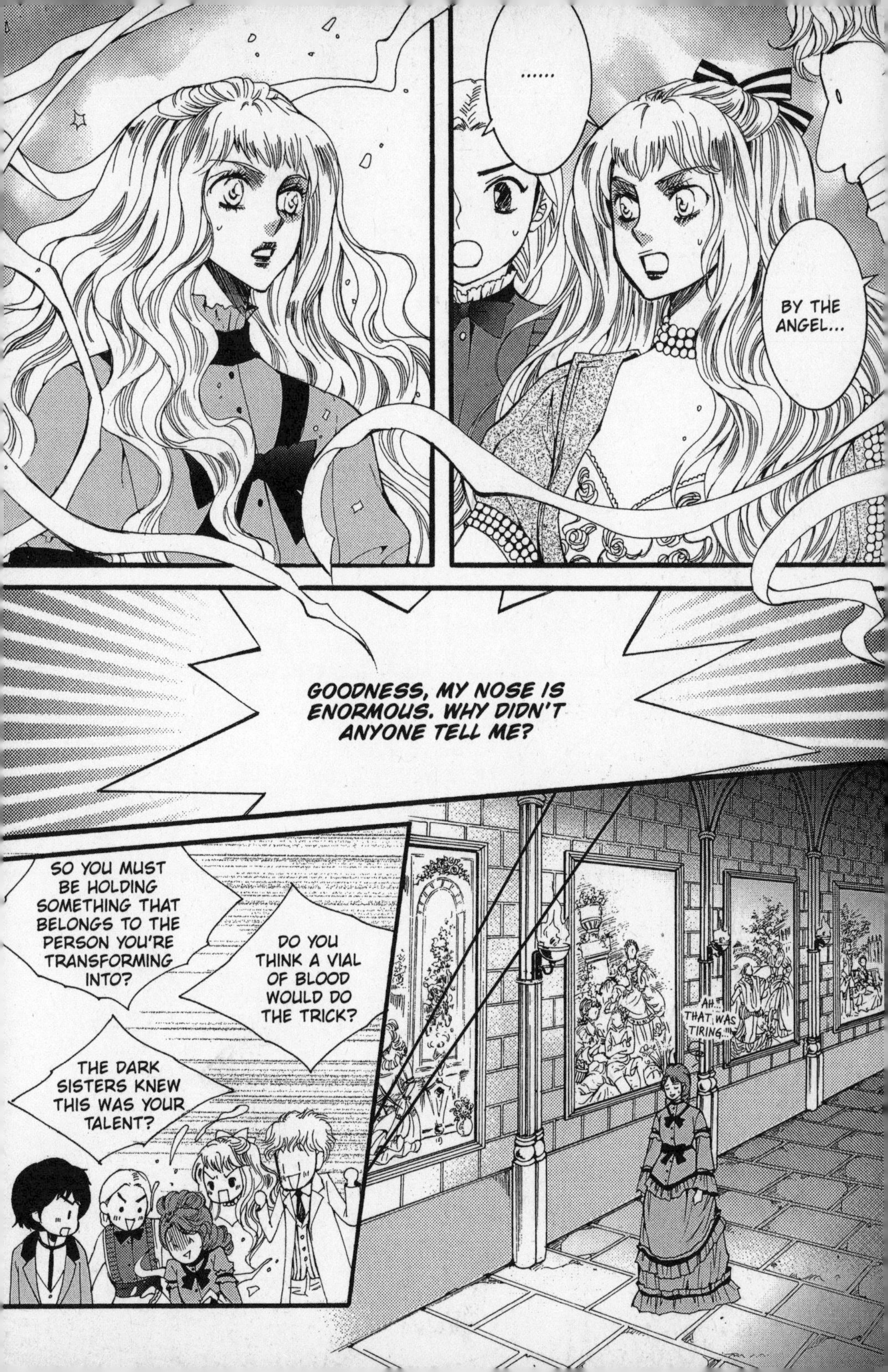
......
BY THE ANGEL...
GOODNESS, MY NOSE IS ENORMOUS. WHY DIDN'T ANYONE TELL ME?
SO YOU MUST BE HOLDING SOMETHING THAT BELONGS TO THE PERSON YOU'RE TRANSFORMING INTO?
DO YOU THINK A VIAL OF BLOOD WOULD DO THE TRICK?
THE DARK SISTERS KNEW THIS WAS YOUR TALENT?
AH... THAT WAS TIRING...

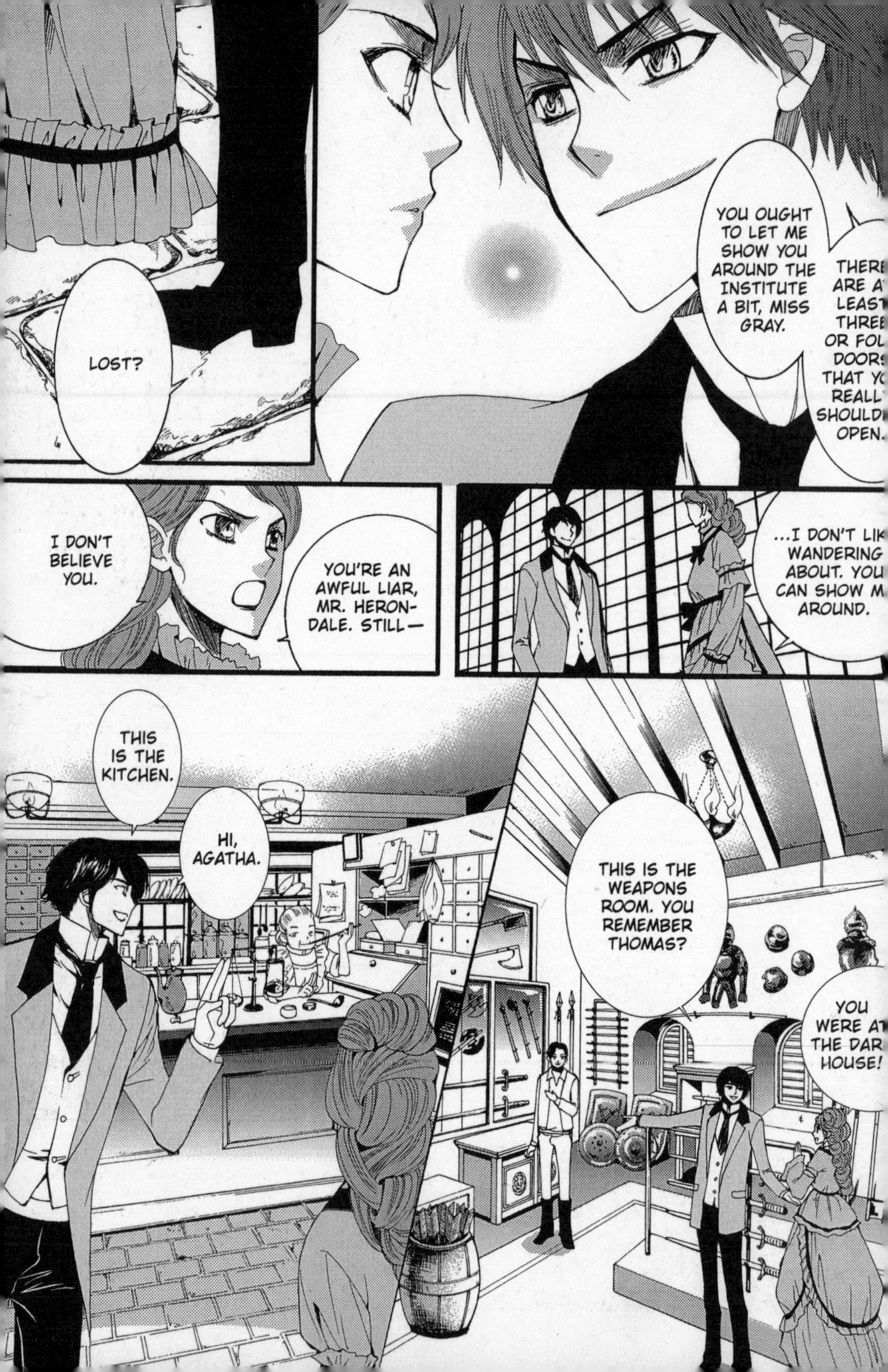
LOST?
YOU OUGHT TO LET ME SHOW YOU AROUND THE INSTITUTE A BIT, MISS GRAY.
THERE ARE A LEAST THREE OR FOL DOORS THAT YO REALL SHOULD OPEN.
I DON'T BELIEVE YOU.
YOU'RE AN AWFUL LIAR, MR. HERON-DALE. STILL—
...I DON'T LIK WANDERING ABOUT. YOU CAN SHOW M AROUND.
THIS IS THE KITCHEN.
HI, AGATHA.
THIS IS THE WEAPONS ROOM. YOU REMEMBER THOMAS?
YOU WERE AT THE DAR HOUSE!

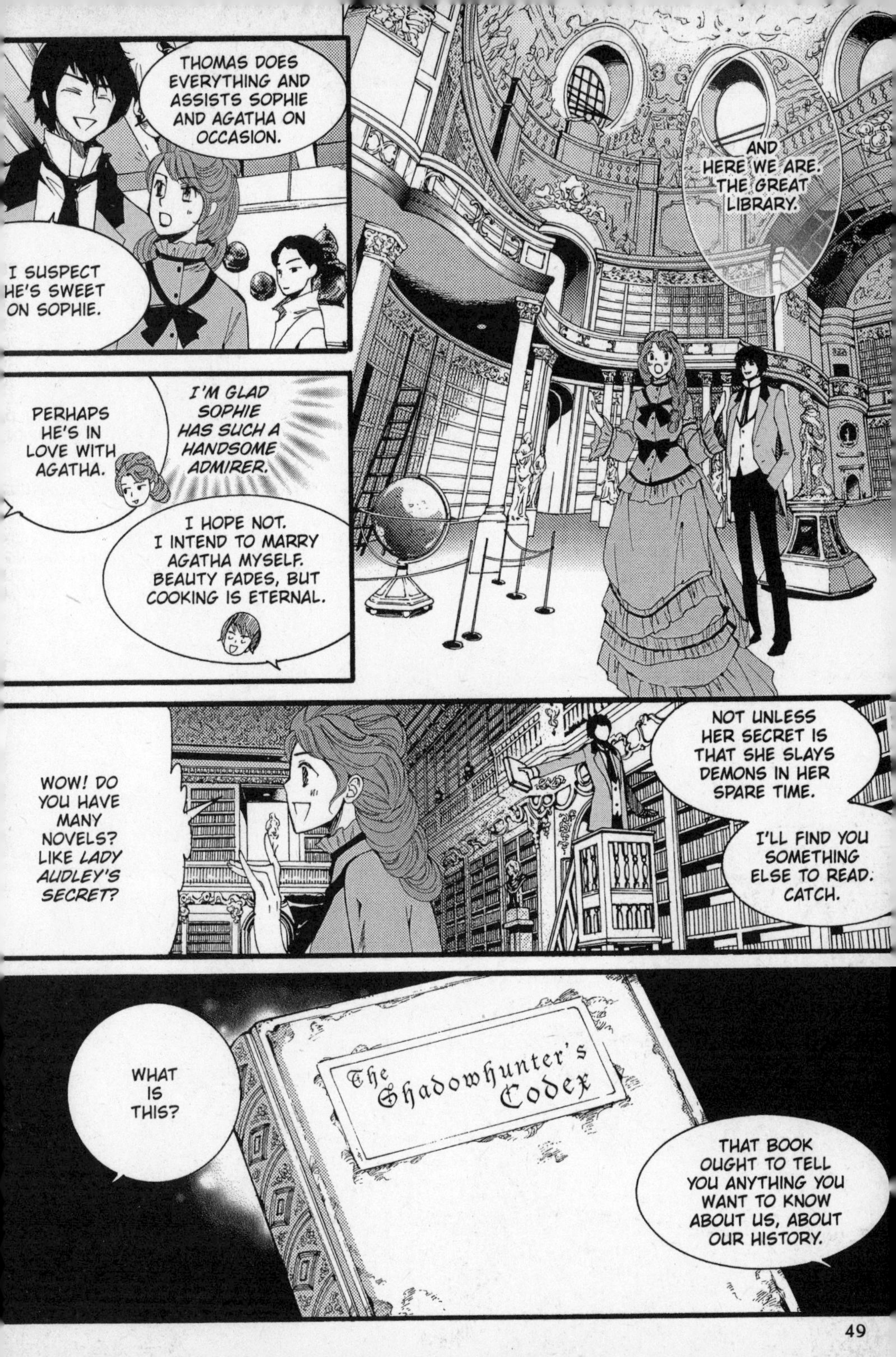
THOMAS DOES EVERYTHING AND ASSISTS SOPHIE AND AGATHA ON OCCASION.
I SUSPECT HE'S SWEET ON SOPHIE.
PERHAPS HE'S IN LOVE WITH AGATHA.
I'M GLAD SOPHIE HAS SUCH A HANDSOME ADMIRER.
I HOPE NOT. I INTEND TO MARRY AGATHA MYSELF. BEAUTY FADES, BUT COOKING IS ETERNAL.
AND HERE WE ARE. THE GREAT LIBRARY.
WOW! DO YOU HAVE MANY NOVELS? LIKE *LADY AUDLEY'S SECRET?*
NOT UNLESS HER SECRET IS THAT SHE SLAYS DEMONS IN HER SPARE TIME.
I'LL FIND YOU SOMETHING ELSE TO READ. CATCH.
WHAT IS THIS?
The Shadowhunter's Codex
THAT BOOK OUGHT TO TELL YOU ANYTHING YOU WANT TO KNOW ABOUT US, ABOUT OUR HISTORY.

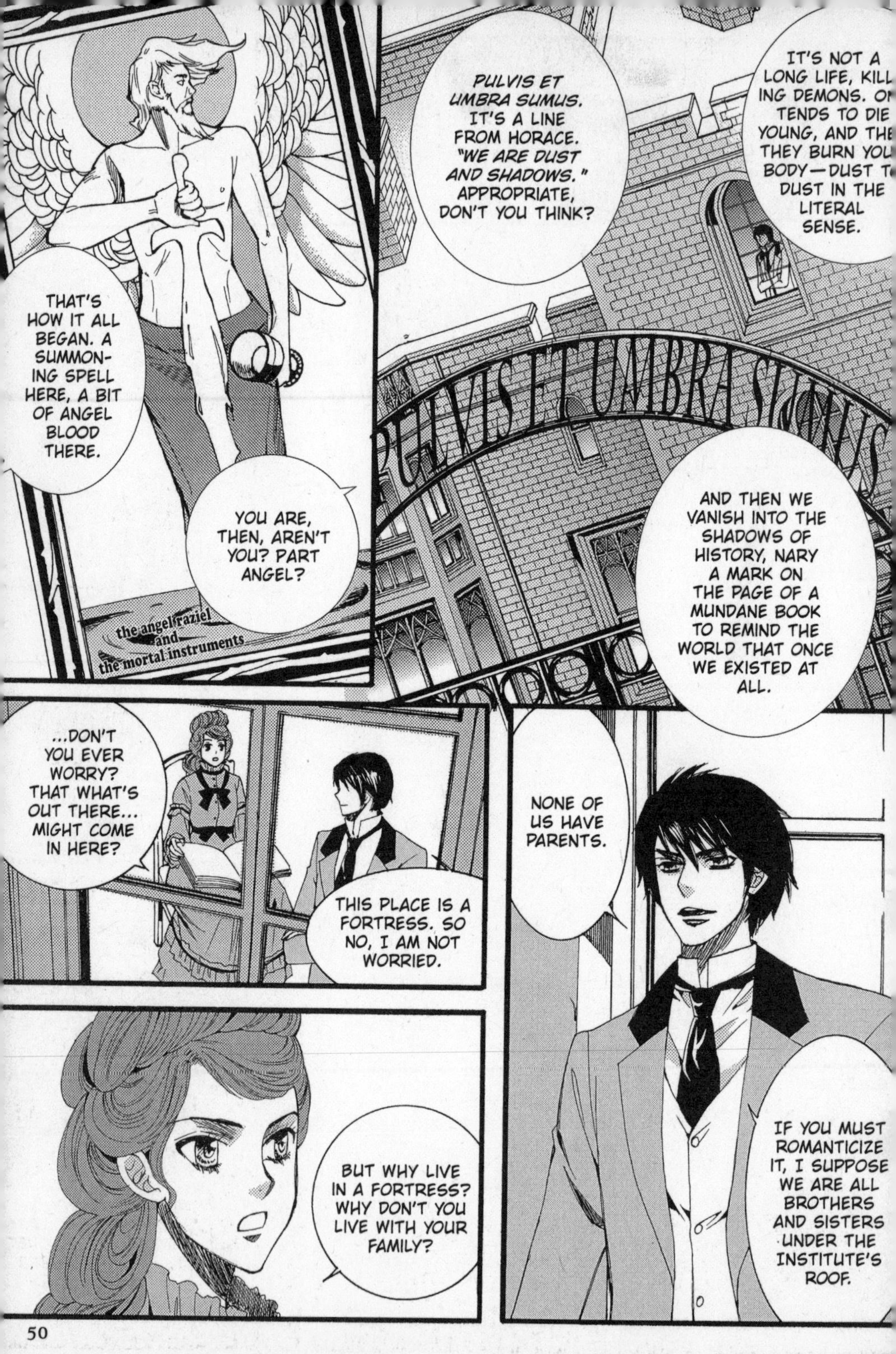
THAT'S HOW IT ALL BEGAN. A SUMMONING SPELL HERE, A BIT OF ANGEL BLOOD THERE.
YOU ARE, THEN, AREN'T YOU? PART ANGEL?
the angel raziel and the mortal instruments
PULVIS ET UMBRA SUMUS. IT'S A LINE FROM HORACE. "WE ARE DUST AND SHADOWS." APPROPRIATE, DON'T YOU THINK?
IT'S NOT A LONG LIFE, KILL ING DEMONS. O TENDS TO DIE YOUNG, AND THE THEY BURN YOU BODY—DUST T DUST IN THE LITERAL SENSE.
PULVIS ET UMBRA SUMUS
AND THEN WE VANISH INTO THE SHADOWS OF HISTORY, NARY A MARK ON THE PAGE OF A MUNDANE BOOK TO REMIND THE WORLD THAT ONCE WE EXISTED AT ALL.
...DON'T YOU EVER WORRY? THAT WHAT'S OUT THERE... MIGHT COME IN HERE?
THIS PLACE IS A FORTRESS. SO NO, I AM NOT WORRIED.
BUT WHY LIVE IN A FORTRESS? WHY DON'T YOU LIVE WITH YOUR FAMILY?
NONE OF US HAVE PARENTS.
IF YOU MUST ROMANTICIZE IT, I SUPPOSE WE ARE ALL BROTHERS AND SISTERS UNDER THE INSTITUTE'S ROOF.

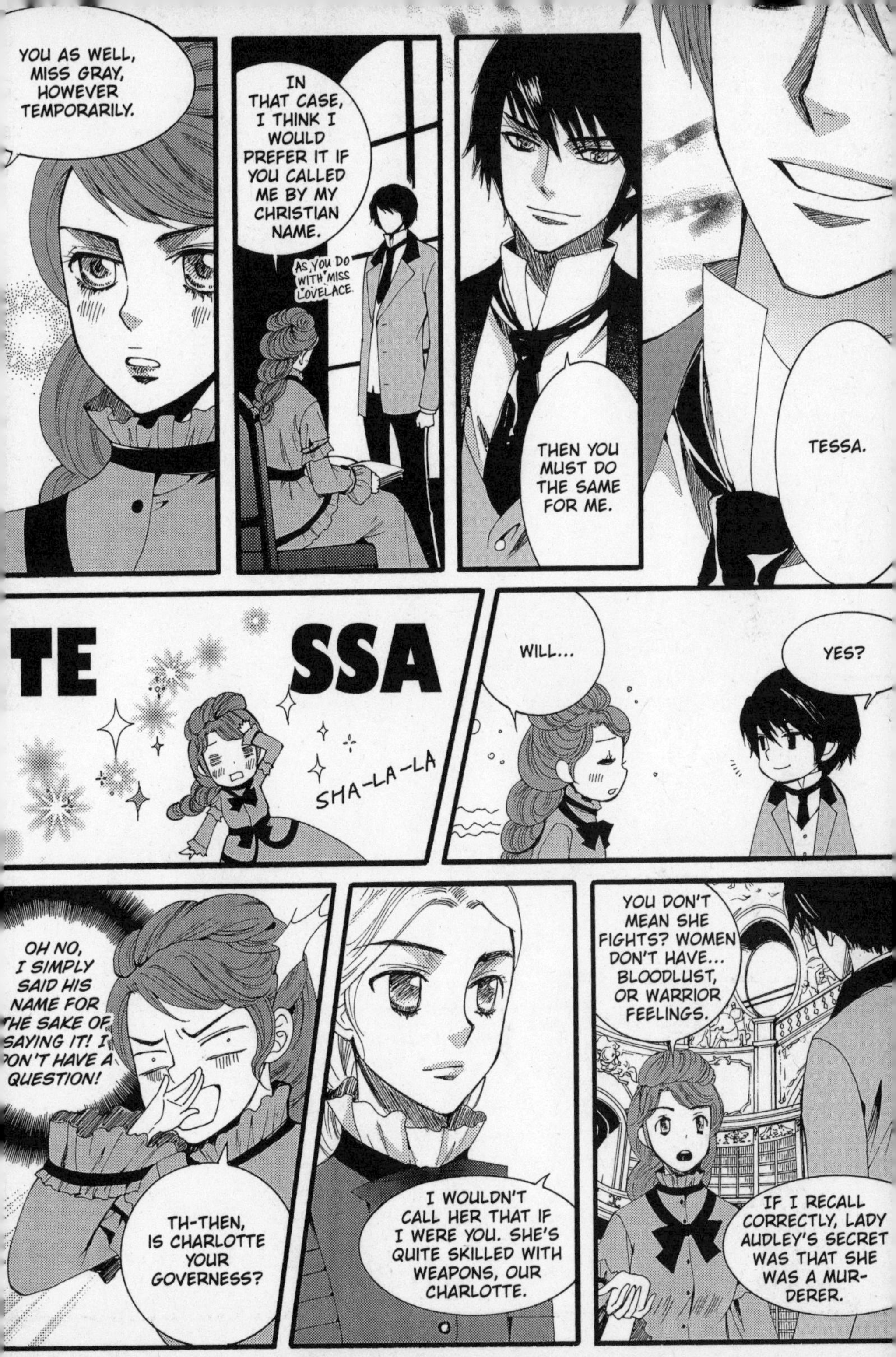
YOU AS WELL, MISS GRAY, HOWEVER TEMPORARILY.
IN THAT CASE, I THINK I WOULD PREFER IT IF YOU CALLED ME BY MY CHRISTIAN NAME.
AS YOU DO WITH MISS LOVELACE.
THEN YOU MUST DO THE SAME FOR ME.
TESSA.
TE SSA
SHA-LA-LA
WILL...
YES?
OH NO, I SIMPLY SAID HIS NAME FOR THE SAKE OF SAYING IT! I DON'T HAVE A QUESTION!
TH-THEN, IS CHARLOTTE YOUR GOVERNESS?
I WOULDN'T CALL HER THAT IF I WERE YOU. SHE'S QUITE SKILLED WITH WEAPONS, OUR CHARLOTTE.
YOU DON'T MEAN SHE FIGHTS? WOMEN DON'T HAVE... BLOODLUST, OR WARRIOR FEELINGS.
IF I RECALL CORRECTLY, LADY AUDLEY'S SECRET WAS THAT SHE WAS A MURDERER.

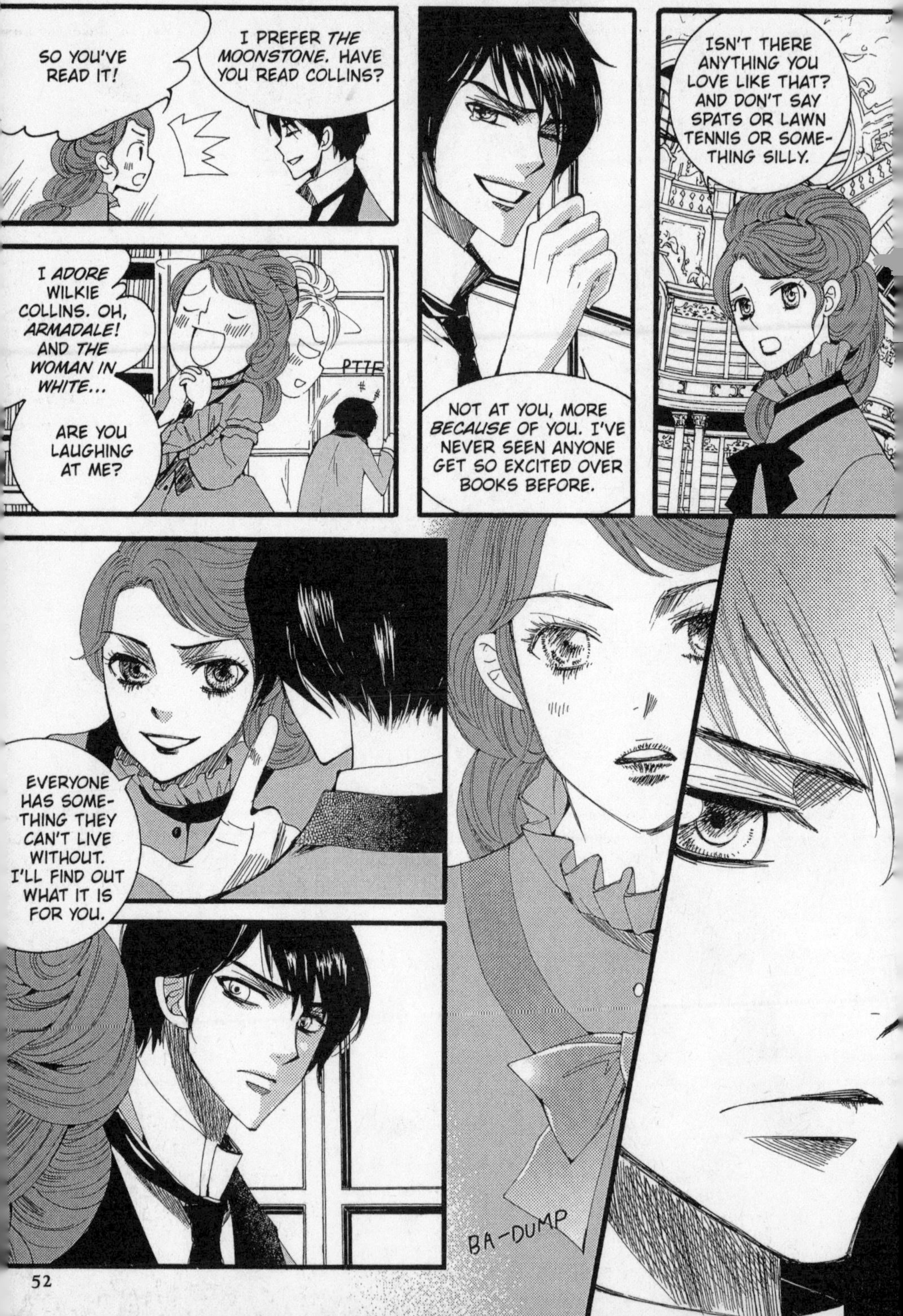

SO YOU'VE READ IT!
I PREFER *THE MOONSTONE*. HAVE YOU READ COLLINS?
I *ADORE* WILKIE COLLINS. OH, *ARMADALE*! AND *THE WOMAN IN WHITE*...
PTTF
ARE YOU LAUGHING AT ME?
NOT AT YOU, MORE *BECAUSE* OF YOU. I'VE NEVER SEEN ANYONE GET SO EXCITED OVER BOOKS BEFORE.
ISN'T THERE ANYTHING YOU LOVE LIKE THAT? AND DON'T SAY SPATS OR LAWN TENNIS OR SOMETHING SILLY.
EVERYONE HAS SOMETHING THEY CAN'T LIVE WITHOUT. I'LL FIND OUT WHAT IT IS FOR YOU.
BA-DUMP

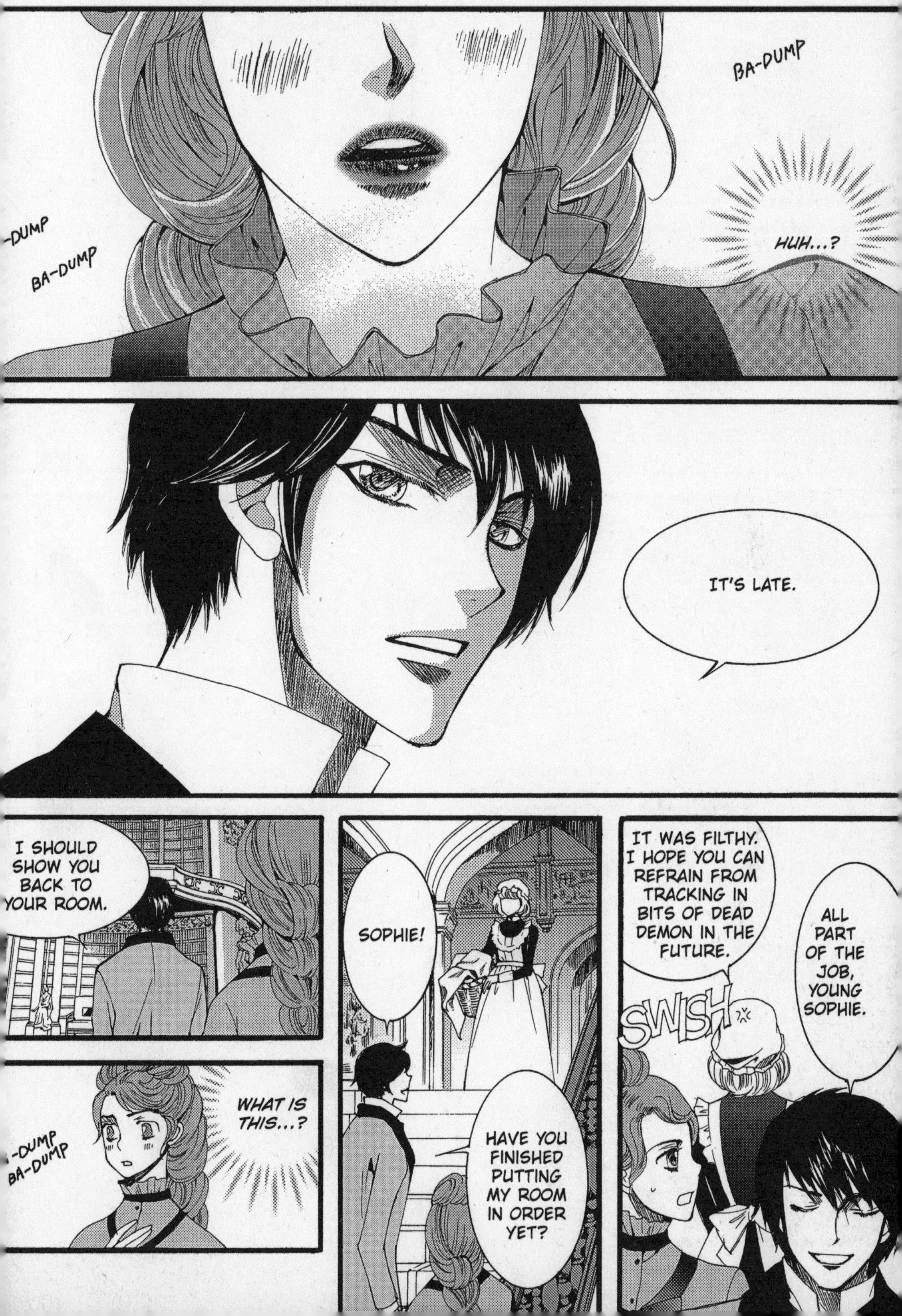
BA-DUMP
-DUMP
BA-DUMP
HUH...?
IT'S LATE.
I SHOULD SHOW YOU BACK TO YOUR ROOM.
WHAT IS THIS...?
-DUMP
BA-DUMP
SOPHIE!
HAVE YOU FINISHED PUTTING MY ROOM IN ORDER YET?
IT WAS FILTHY. I HOPE YOU CAN REFRAIN FROM TRACKING IN BITS OF DEAD DEMON IN THE FUTURE.
SWISH
ALL PART OF THE JOB, YOUNG SOPHIE.

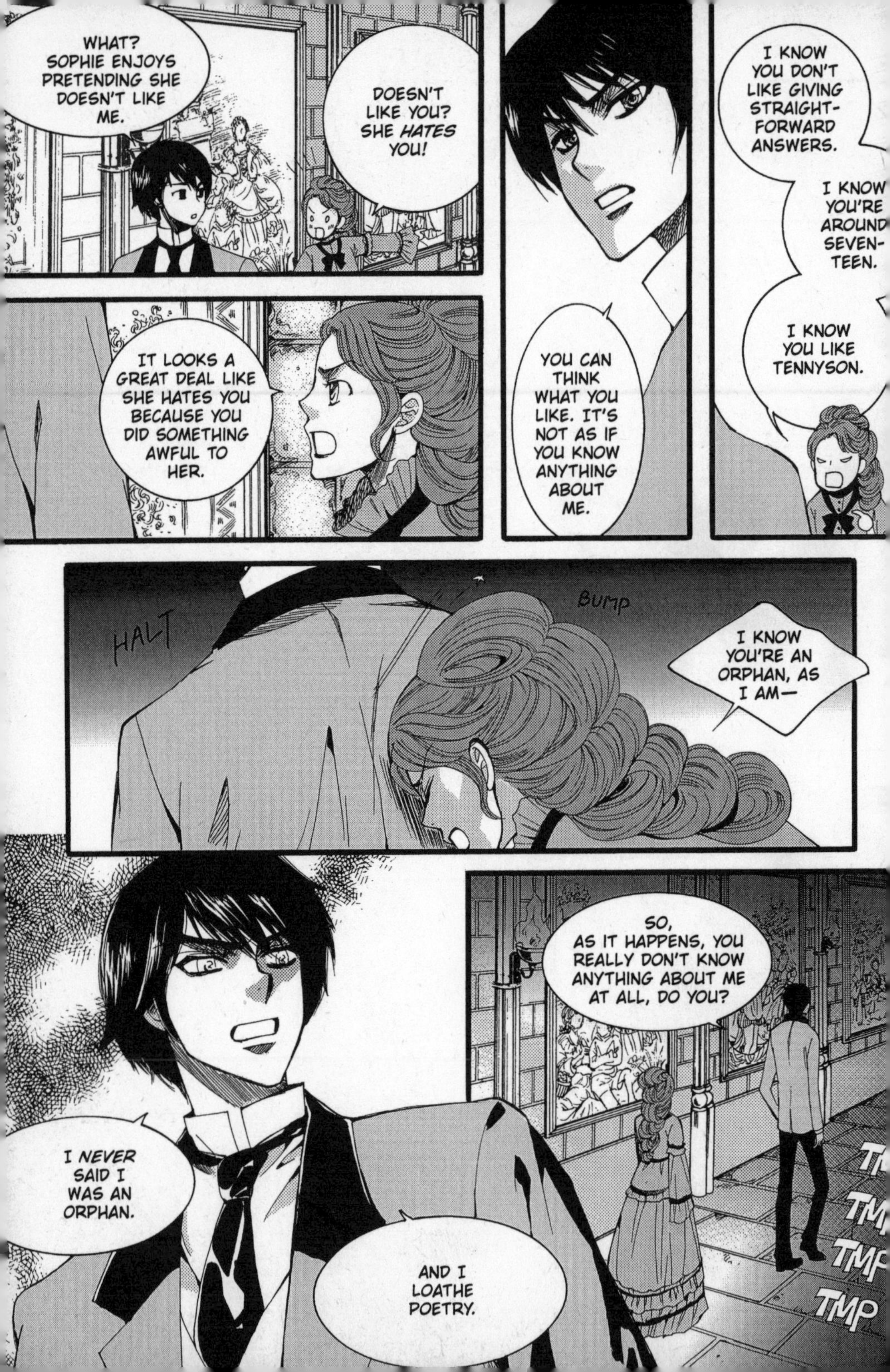
WHAT? SOPHIE ENJOYS PRETENDING SHE DOESN'T LIKE ME.
DOESN'T LIKE YOU? SHE *HATES* YOU!
IT LOOKS A GREAT DEAL LIKE SHE HATES YOU BECAUSE YOU DID SOMETHING AWFUL TO HER.
YOU CAN THINK WHAT YOU LIKE. IT'S NOT AS IF YOU KNOW ANYTHING ABOUT ME.
I KNOW YOU DON'T LIKE GIVING STRAIGHT-FORWARD ANSWERS.
I KNOW YOU'RE AROUND SEVEN-TEEN.
I KNOW YOU LIKE TENNYSON.
HALT
BUMP
I KNOW YOU'RE AN ORPHAN, AS I AM—
I *NEVER* SAID I WAS AN ORPHAN.
AND I LOATHE POETRY.
SO, AS IT HAPPENS, YOU REALLY DON'T KNOW ANYTHING ABOUT ME AT ALL, DO YOU?
TMP
TMP
TMP
TMP

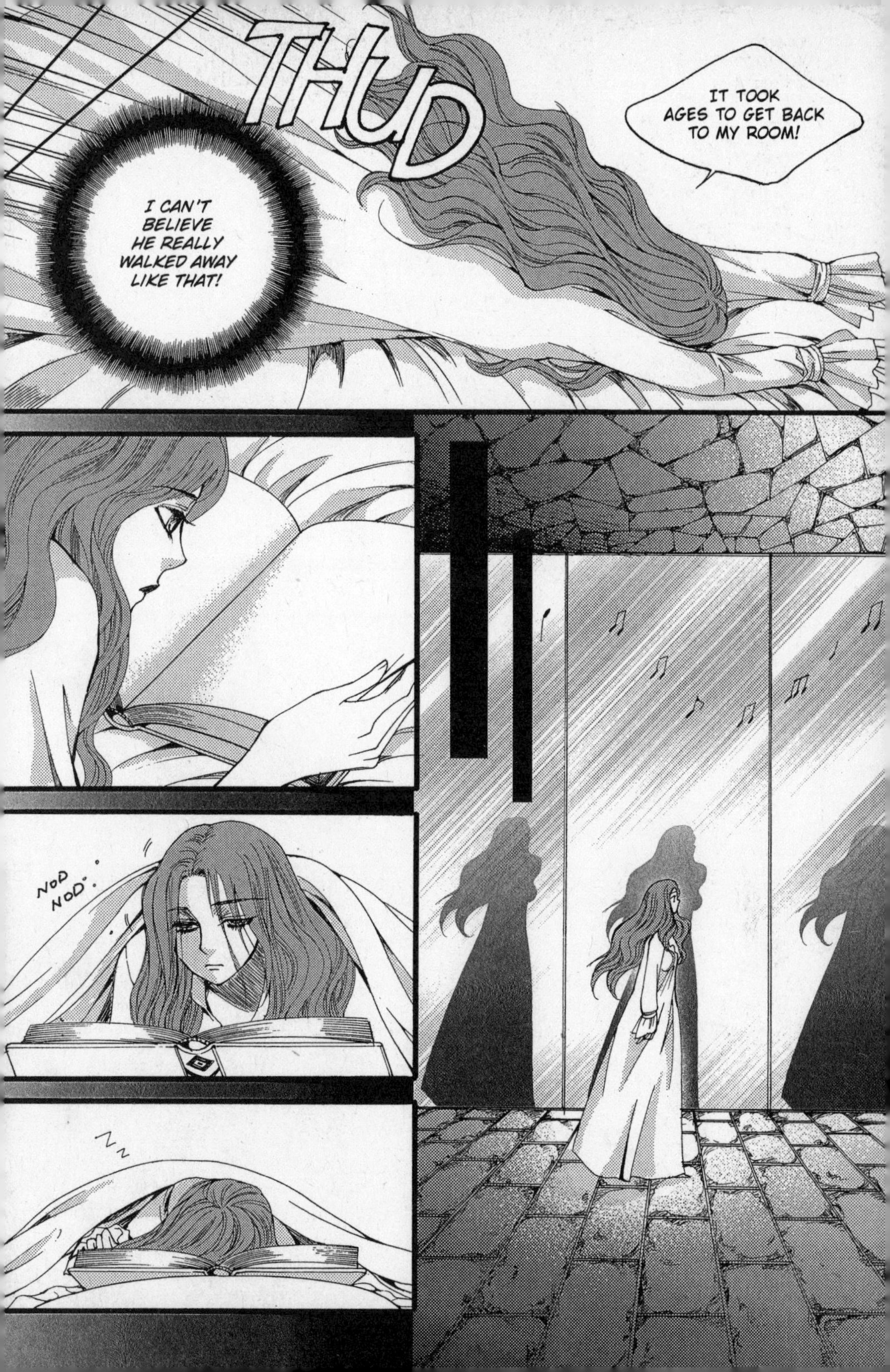
THUD
IT TOOK AGES TO GET BACK TO MY ROOM!
I CAN'T BELIEVE HE REALLY WALKED AWAY LIKE THAT!
NOD NOD
Z z

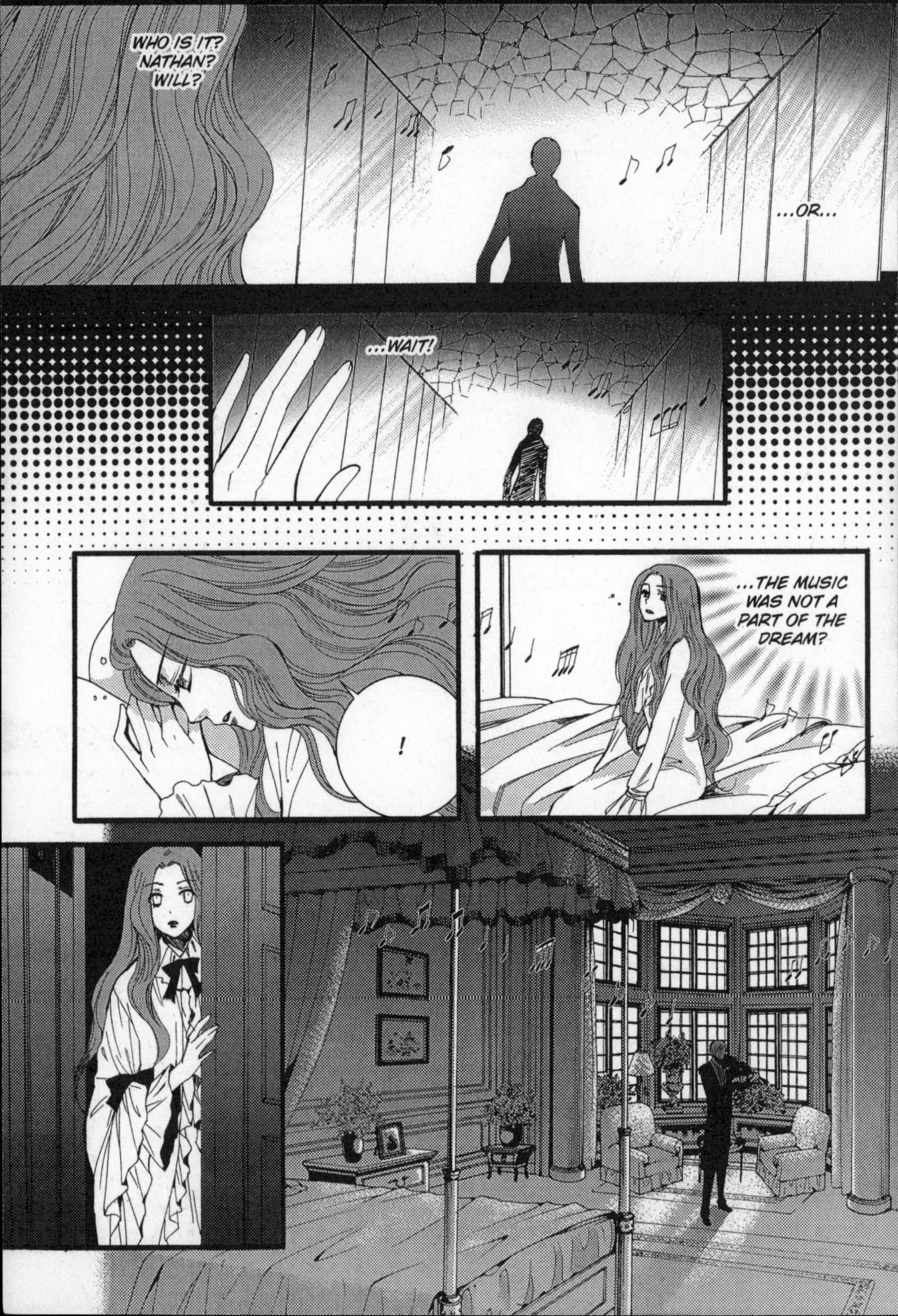

WHO IS IT? NATHAN? WILL?
...OR...
...WAIT!
!
...THE MUSIC WAS NOT A PART OF THE DREAM?

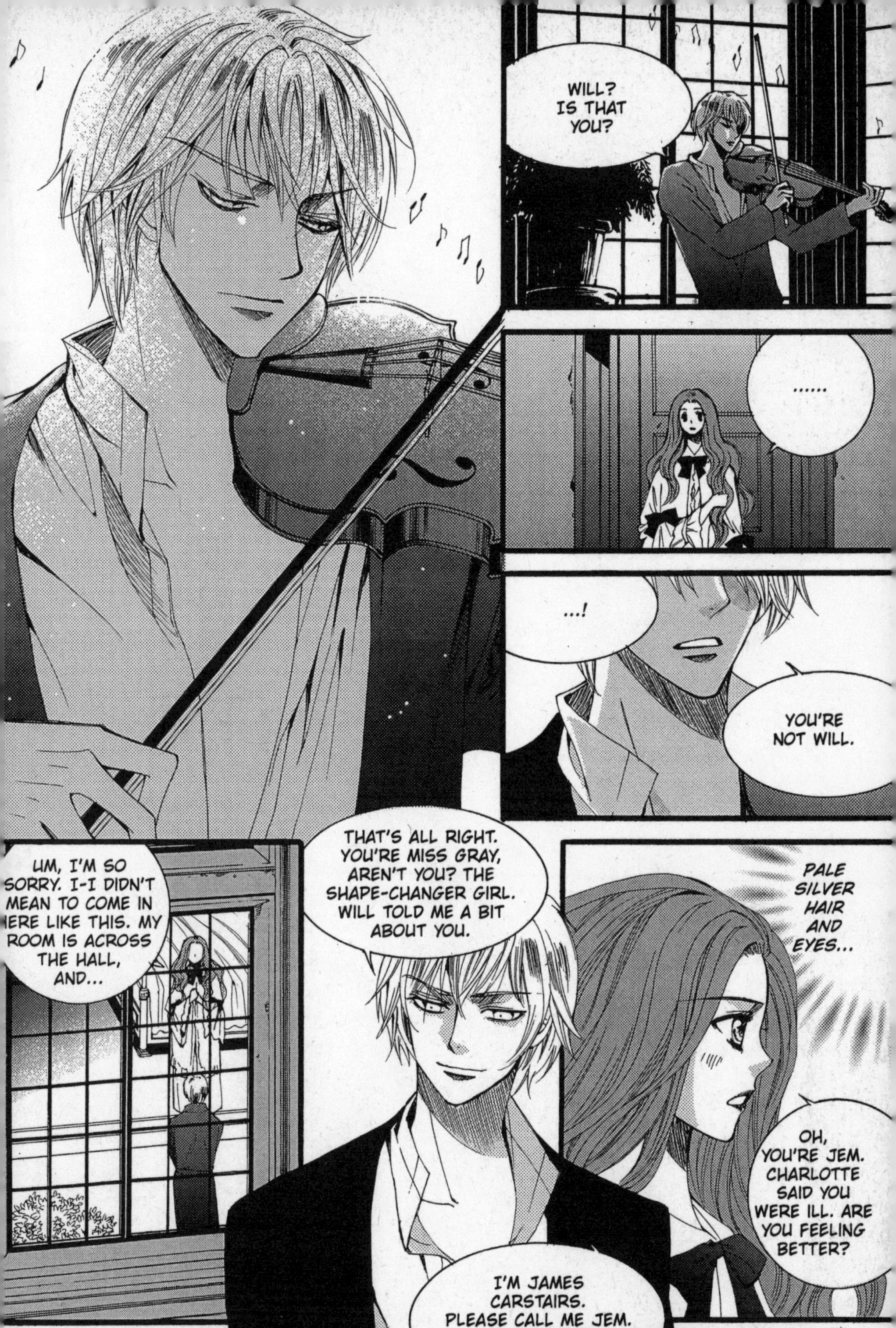
WILL? IS THAT YOU?
......
...!
YOU'RE NOT WILL.
UM, I'M SO SORRY. I-I DIDN'T MEAN TO COME IN HERE LIKE THIS. MY ROOM IS ACROSS THE HALL, AND...
THAT'S ALL RIGHT. YOU'RE MISS GRAY, AREN'T YOU? THE SHAPE-CHANGER GIRL. WILL TOLD ME A BIT ABOUT YOU.
PALE SILVER HAIR AND EYES...
OH, YOU'RE JEM. CHARLOTTE SAID YOU WERE ILL. ARE YOU FEELING BETTER?
I'M JAMES CARSTAIRS. PLEASE CALL ME JEM. EVERYONE DOES.

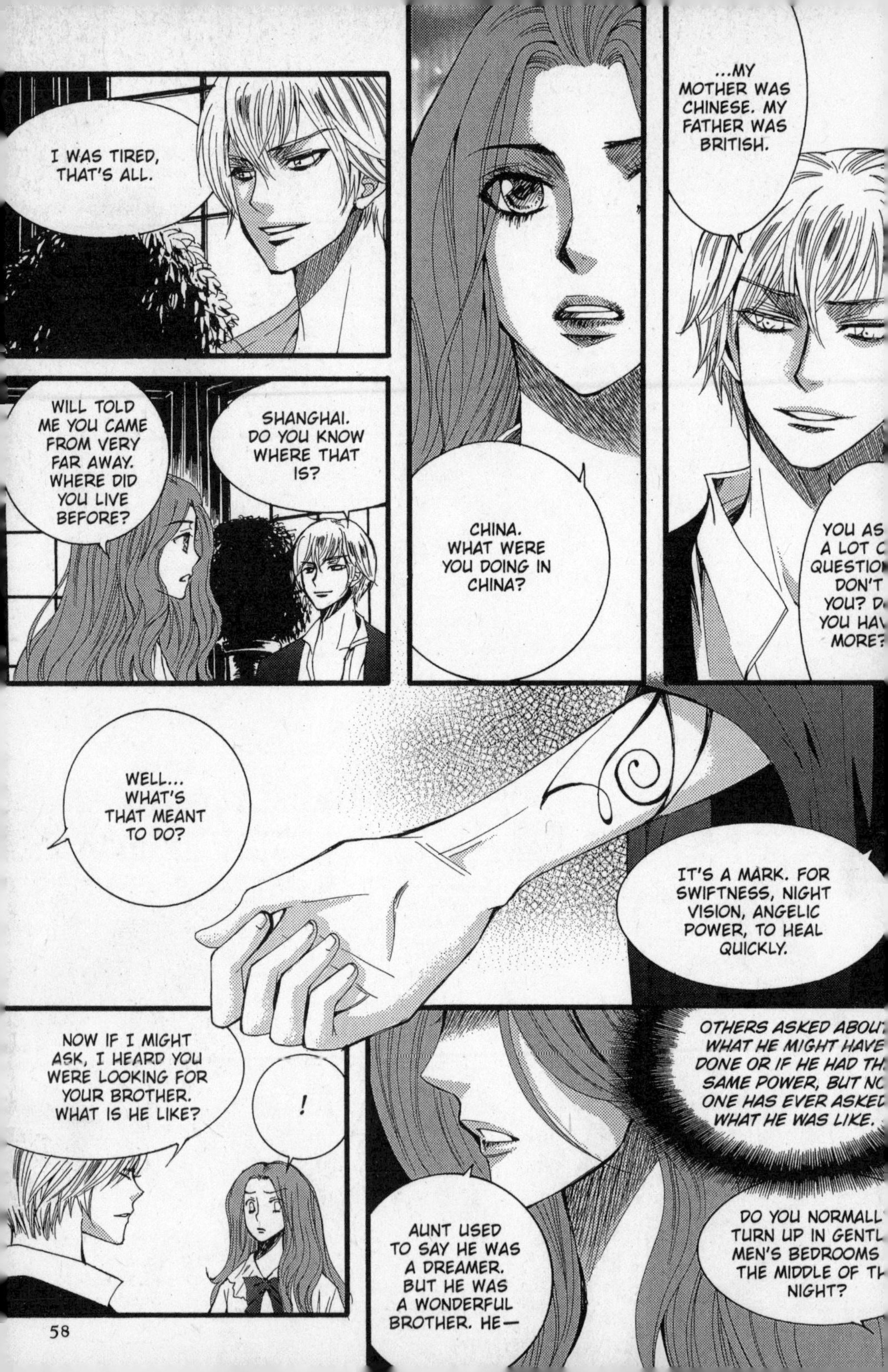
I WAS TIRED, THAT'S ALL.
WILL TOLD ME YOU CAME FROM VERY FAR AWAY. WHERE DID YOU LIVE BEFORE?
SHANGHAI. DO YOU KNOW WHERE THAT IS?
CHINA. WHAT WERE YOU DOING IN CHINA?
...MY MOTHER WAS CHINESE. MY FATHER WAS BRITISH.
YOU AS A LOT C QUESTIO DON'T YOU? D YOU HAV MORE?
WELL... WHAT'S THAT MEANT TO DO?
IT'S A MARK. FOR SWIFTNESS, NIGHT VISION, ANGELIC POWER, TO HEAL QUICKLY.
NOW IF I MIGHT ASK, I HEARD YOU WERE LOOKING FOR YOUR BROTHER. WHAT IS HE LIKE?
!
OTHERS ASKED ABOU WHAT HE MIGHT HAVE DONE OR IF HE HAD TH SAME POWER, BUT NO ONE HAS EVER ASKED WHAT HE WAS LIKE.
AUNT USED TO SAY HE WAS A DREAMER. BUT HE WAS A WONDERFUL BROTHER. HE—
DO YOU NORMALL TURN UP IN GENTL MEN'S BEDROOMS THE MIDDLE OF T NIGHT?

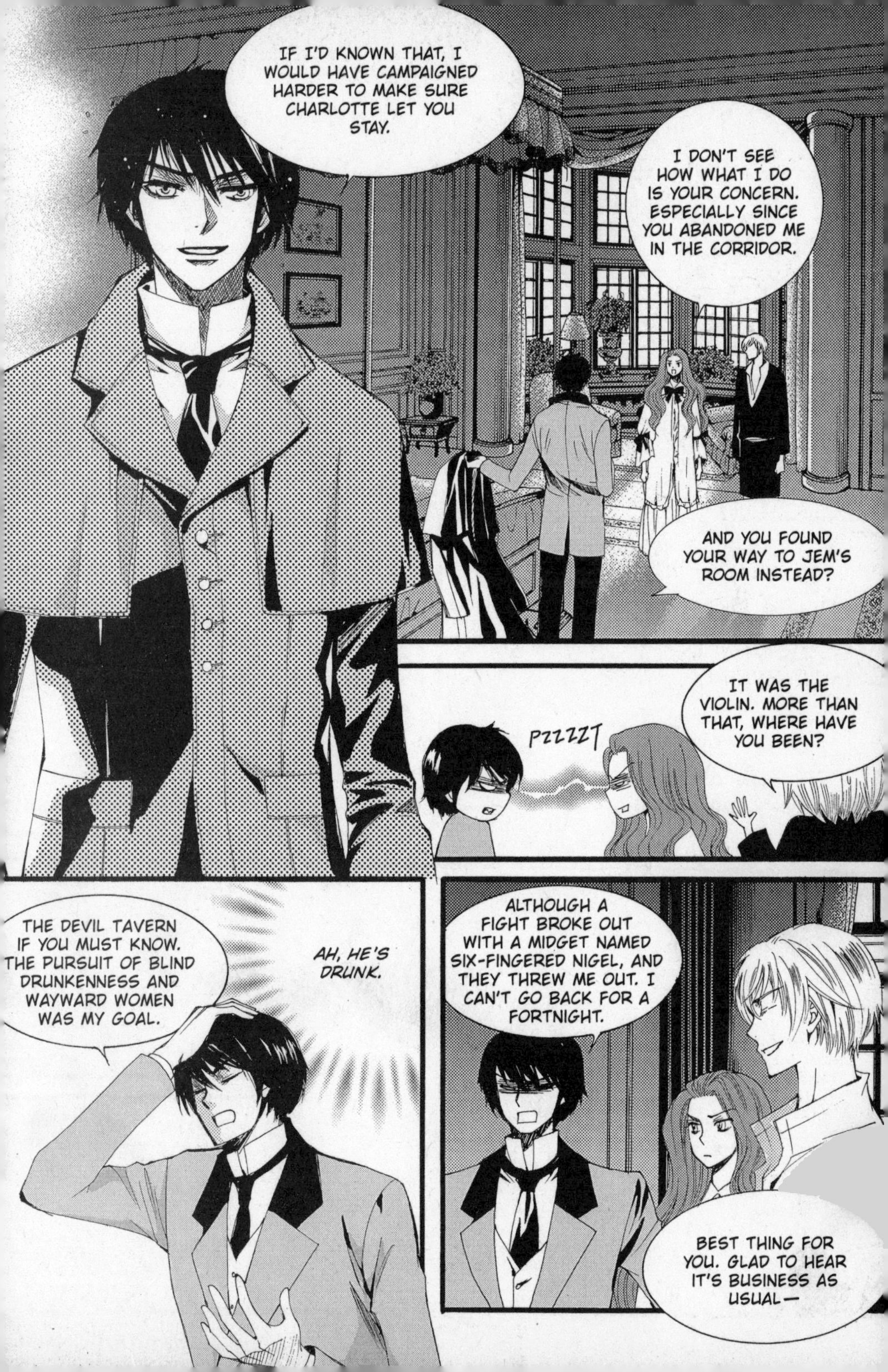
IF I'D KNOWN THAT, I WOULD HAVE CAMPAIGNED HARDER TO MAKE SURE CHARLOTTE LET YOU STAY.
I DON'T SEE HOW WHAT I DO IS YOUR CONCERN. ESPECIALLY SINCE YOU ABANDONED ME IN THE CORRIDOR.
AND YOU FOUND YOUR WAY TO JEM'S ROOM INSTEAD?
PZZZZT
IT WAS THE VIOLIN. MORE THAN THAT, WHERE HAVE YOU BEEN?
THE DEVIL TAVERN IF YOU MUST KNOW. THE PURSUIT OF BLIND DRUNKENNESS AND WAYWARD WOMEN WAS MY GOAL.
AH, HE'S DRUNK.
ALTHOUGH A FIGHT BROKE OUT WITH A MIDGET NAMED SIX-FINGERED NIGEL, AND THEY THREW ME OUT. I CAN'T GO BACK FOR A FORTNIGHT.
BEST THING FOR YOU. GLAD TO HEAR IT'S BUSINESS AS USUAL—

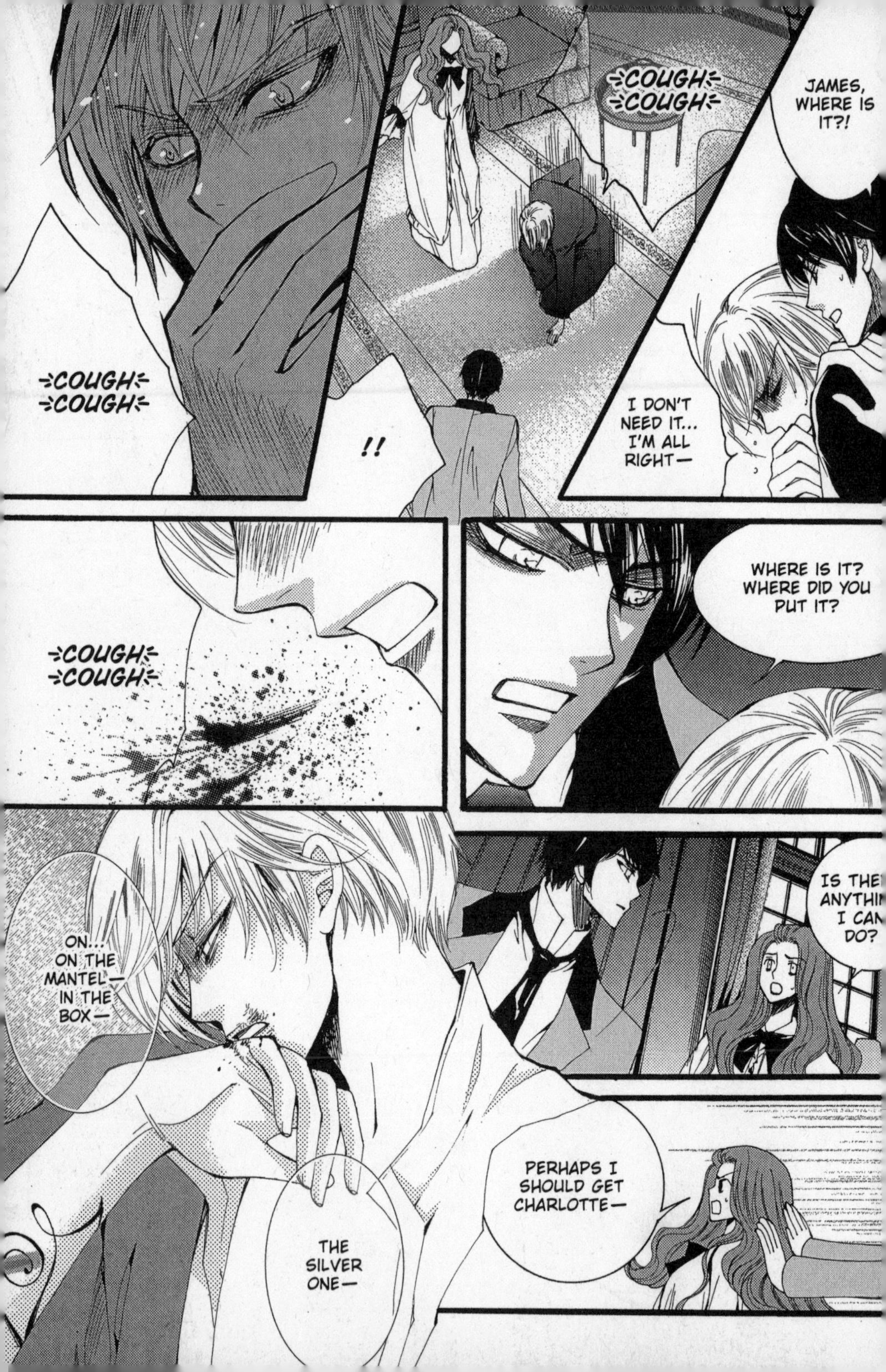
COUGH COUGH
COUGH COUGH
!!
JAMES, WHERE IS IT?!
I DON'T NEED IT... I'M ALL RIGHT—
COUGH COUGH
WHERE IS IT? WHERE DID YOU PUT IT?
ON... ON THE MANTEL— IN THE BOX—
THE SILVER ONE—
IS THE ANYTHI I CAN DO?
PERHAPS I SHOULD GET CHARLOTTE—

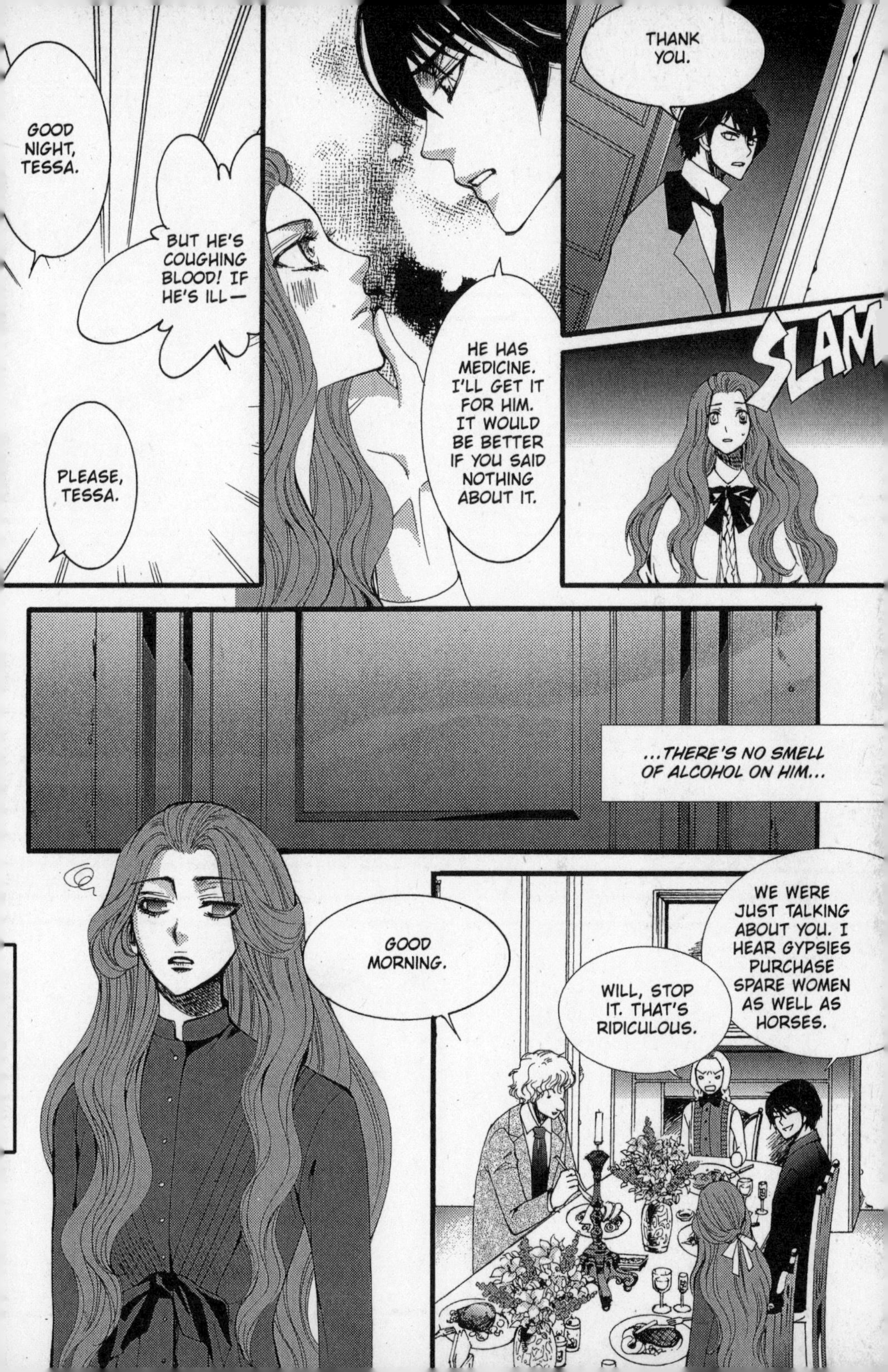
GOOD NIGHT, TESSA.
BUT HE'S COUGHING BLOOD! IF HE'S ILL—
PLEASE, TESSA.
HE HAS MEDICINE. I'LL GET IT FOR HIM. IT WOULD BE BETTER IF YOU SAID NOTHING ABOUT IT.
THANK YOU.
SLAM
...THERE'S NO SMELL OF ALCOHOL ON HIM...
GOOD MORNING.
WE WERE JUST TALKING ABOUT YOU. I HEAR GYPSIES PURCHASE SPARE WOMEN AS WELL AS HORSES.
WILL, STOP IT. THAT'S RIDICULOUS.

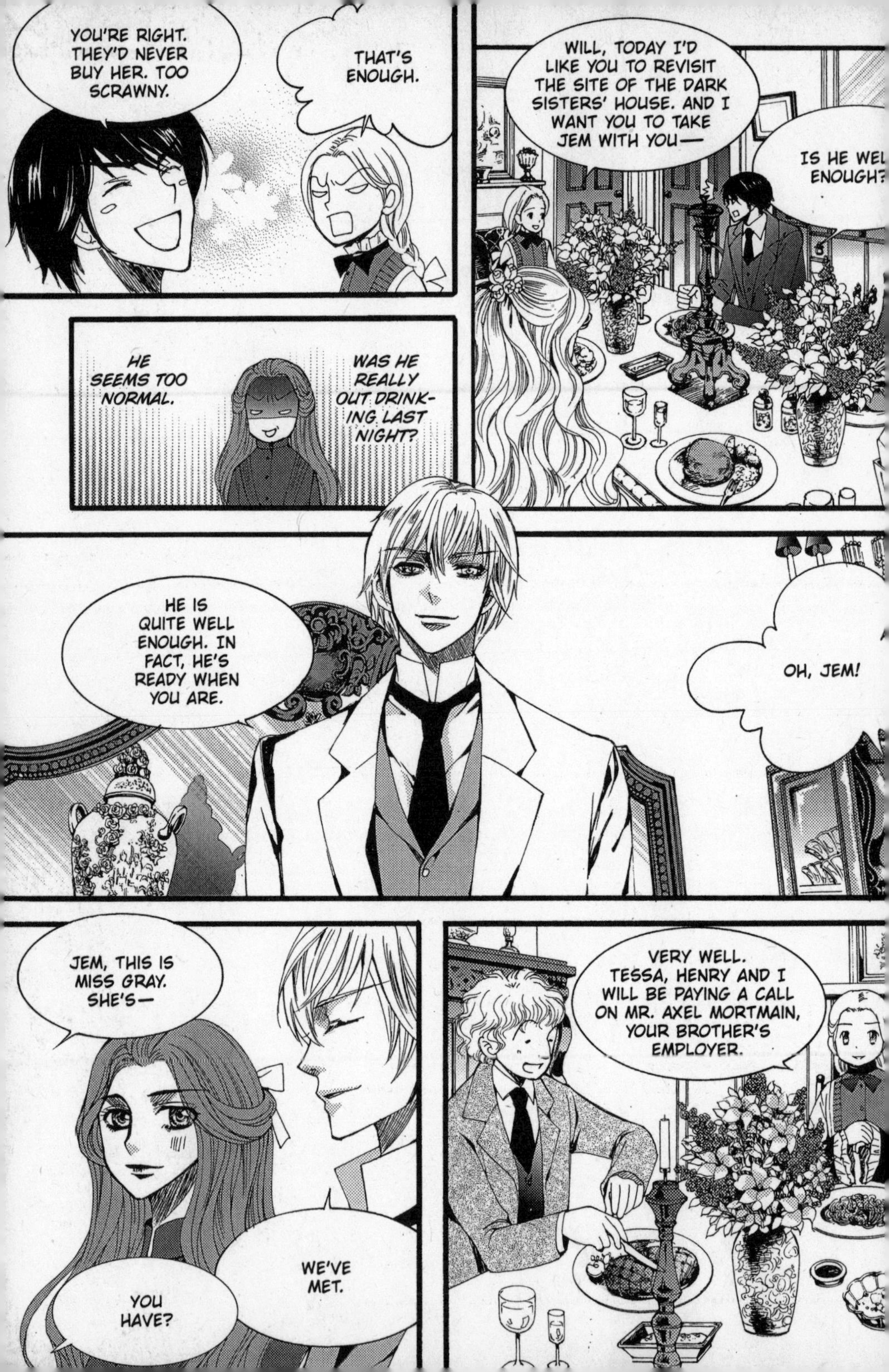
YOU'RE RIGHT. THEY'D NEVER BUY HER. TOO SCRAWNY.
THAT'S ENOUGH.
WILL, TODAY I'D LIKE YOU TO REVISIT THE SITE OF THE DARK SISTERS' HOUSE. AND I WANT YOU TO TAKE JEM WITH YOU—
IS HE WEL ENOUGH?
HE SEEMS TOO NORMAL.
WAS HE REALLY OUT DRINKING LAST NIGHT?
HE IS QUITE WELL ENOUGH. IN FACT, HE'S READY WHEN YOU ARE.
OH, JEM!
JEM, THIS IS MISS GRAY. SHE'S—
WE'VE MET.
YOU HAVE?
VERY WELL. TESSA, HENRY AND I WILL BE PAYING A CALL ON MR. AXEL MORTMAIN, YOUR BROTHER'S EMPLOYER.

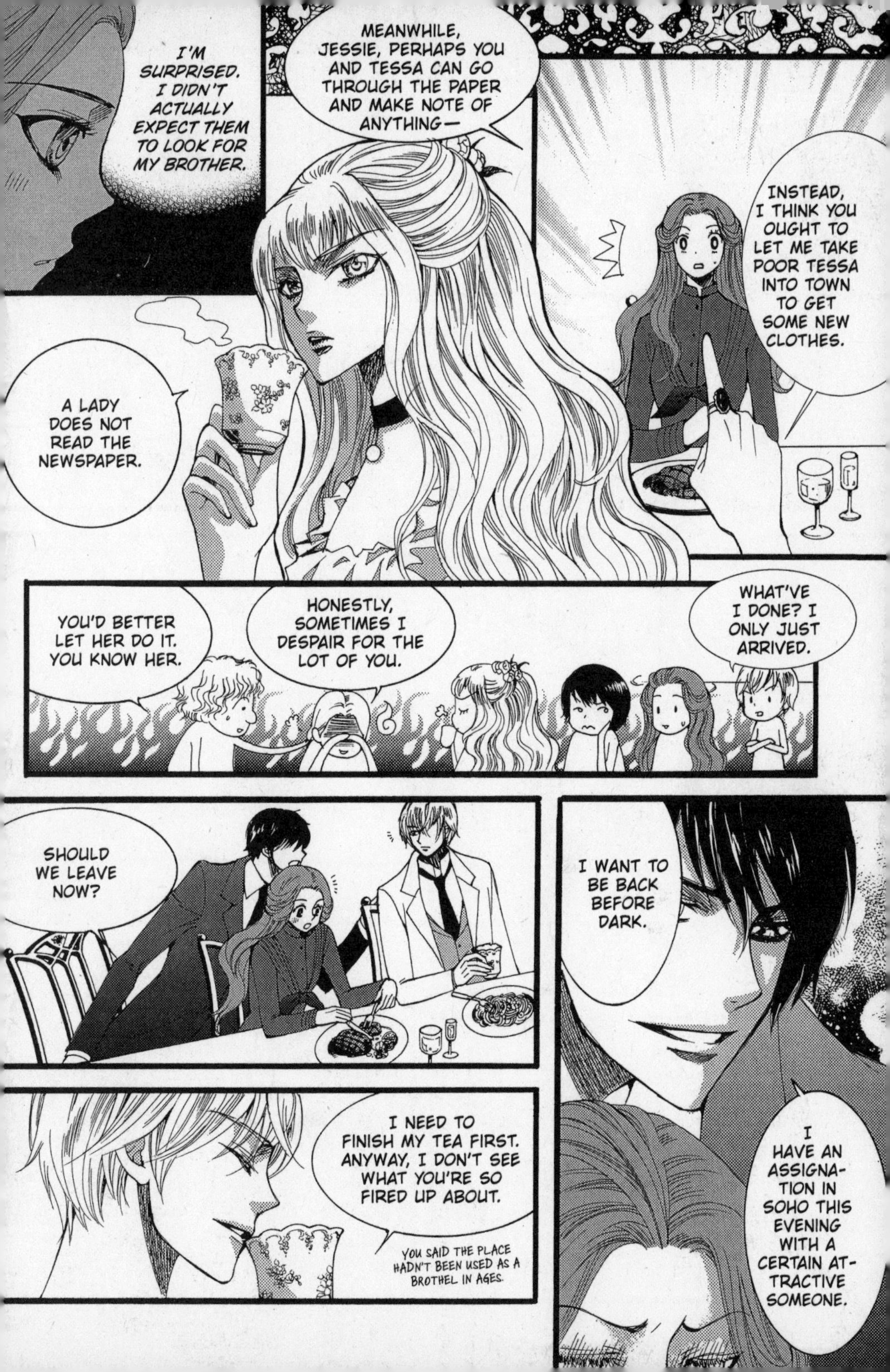
I'M SURPRISED. I DIDN'T ACTUALLY EXPECT THEM TO LOOK FOR MY BROTHER.
MEANWHILE, JESSIE, PERHAPS YOU AND TESSA CAN GO THROUGH THE PAPER AND MAKE NOTE OF ANYTHING—
A LADY DOES NOT READ THE NEWSPAPER.
INSTEAD, I THINK YOU OUGHT TO LET ME TAKE POOR TESSA INTO TOWN TO GET SOME NEW CLOTHES.
YOU'D BETTER LET HER DO IT. YOU KNOW HER.
HONESTLY, SOMETIMES I DESPAIR FOR THE LOT OF YOU.
WHAT'VE I DONE? I ONLY JUST ARRIVED.
SHOULD WE LEAVE NOW?
I NEED TO FINISH MY TEA FIRST. ANYWAY, I DON'T SEE WHAT YOU'RE SO FIRED UP ABOUT.
YOU SAID THE PLACE HADN'T BEEN USED AS A BROTHEL IN AGES.
I WANT TO BE BACK BEFORE DARK.
I HAVE AN ASSIGNATION IN SOHO THIS EVENING WITH A CERTAIN ATTRACTIVE SOMEONE.

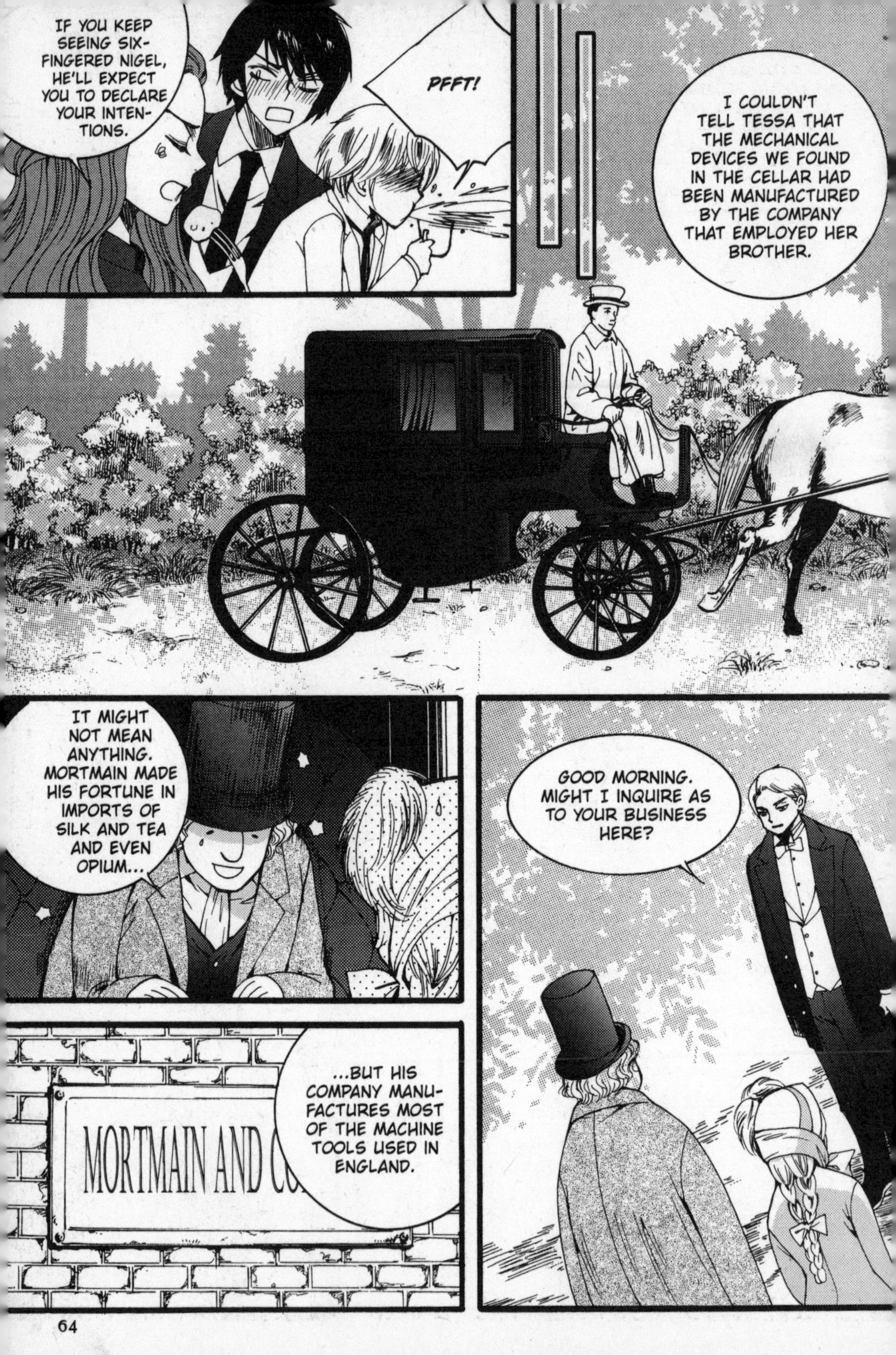

IF YOU KEEP SEEING SIX-FINGERED NIGEL, HE'LL EXPECT YOU TO DECLARE YOUR INTEN-TIONS.
PFFT!
I COULDN'T TELL TESSA THAT THE MECHANICAL DEVICES WE FOUND IN THE CELLAR HAD BEEN MANUFACTURED BY THE COMPANY THAT EMPLOYED HER BROTHER.
IT MIGHT NOT MEAN ANYTHING. MORTMAIN MADE HIS FORTUNE IN IMPORTS OF SILK AND TEA AND EVEN OPIUM...
MORTMAIN AND CO
...BUT HIS COMPANY MANU-FACTURES MOST OF THE MACHINE TOOLS USED IN ENGLAND.
GOOD MORNING. MIGHT I INQUIRE AS TO YOUR BUSINESS HERE?

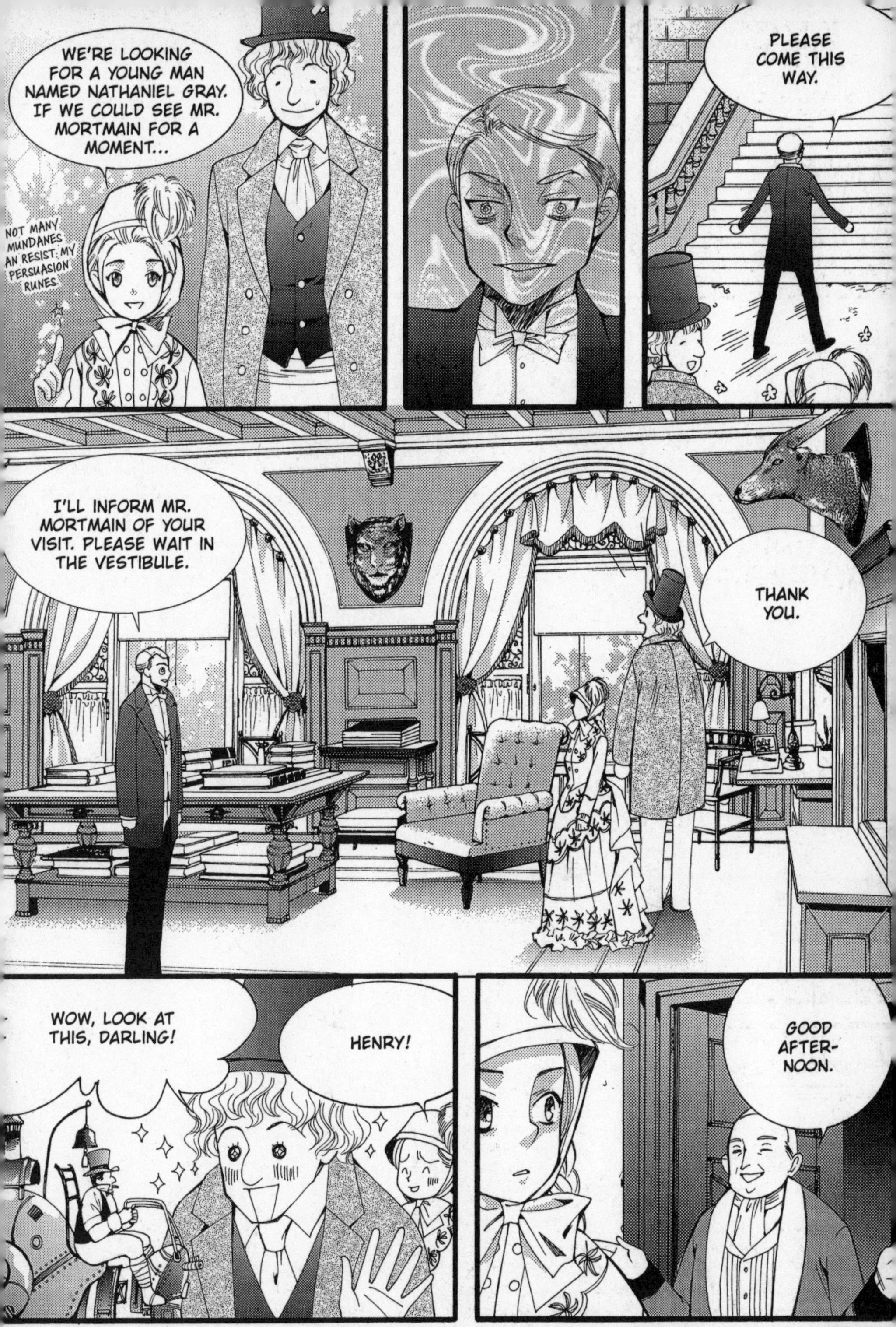
WE'RE LOOKING FOR A YOUNG MAN NAMED NATHANIEL GRAY. IF WE COULD SEE MR. MORTMAIN FOR A MOMENT...
NOT MANY MUNDANES CAN RESIST MY PERSUASION RUNES.
PLEASE COME THIS WAY.
I'LL INFORM MR. MORTMAIN OF YOUR VISIT. PLEASE WAIT IN THE VESTIBULE.
THANK YOU.
WOW, LOOK AT THIS, DARLING!
HENRY!
GOOD AFTER-NOON.

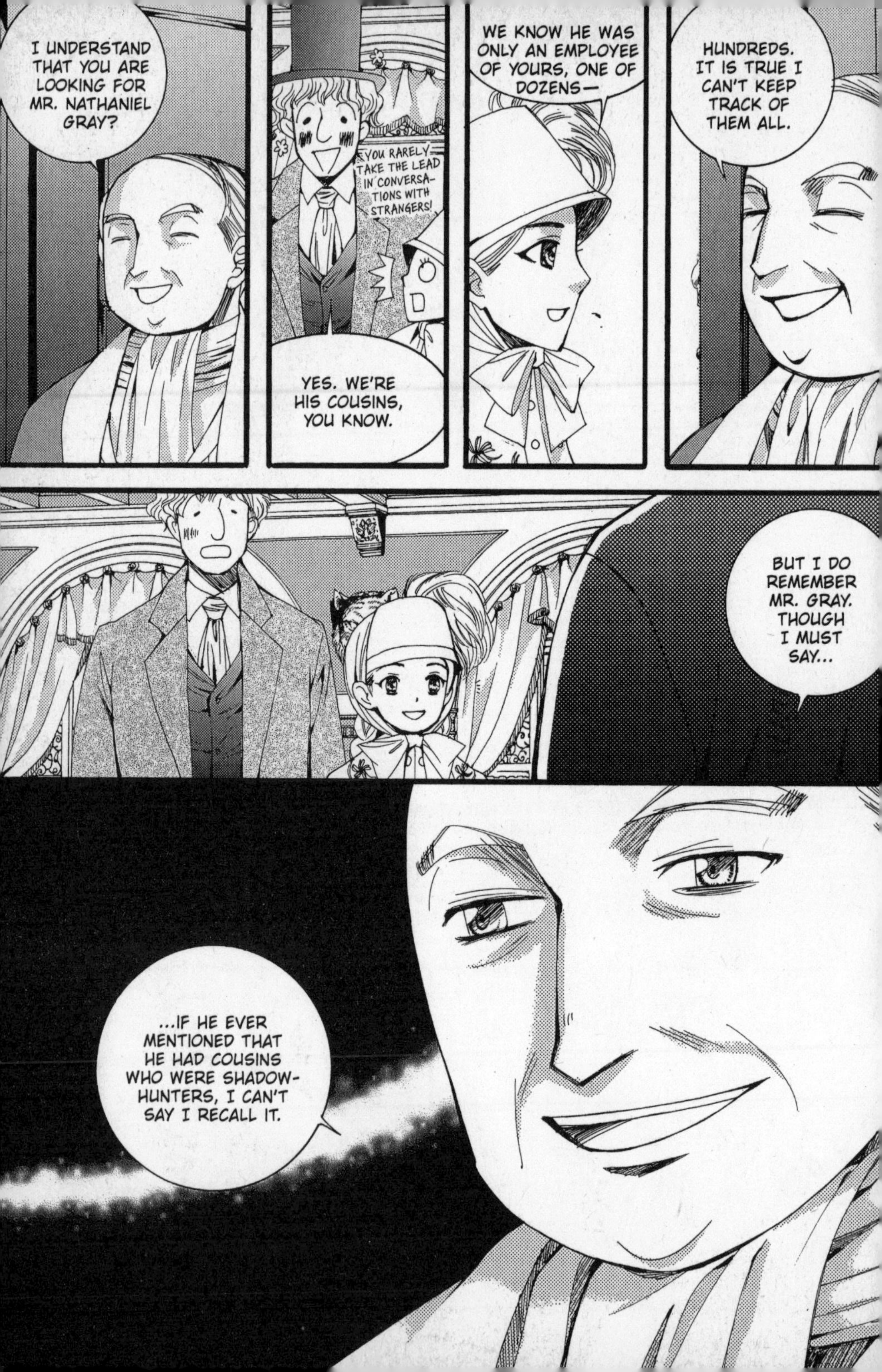
I UNDERSTAND THAT YOU ARE LOOKING FOR MR. NATHANIEL GRAY?
YOU RARELY TAKE THE LEAD IN CONVERSATIONS WITH STRANGERS!
YES. WE'RE HIS COUSINS, YOU KNOW.
WE KNOW HE WAS ONLY AN EMPLOYEE OF YOURS, ONE OF DOZENS—
HUNDREDS. IT IS TRUE I CAN'T KEEP TRACK OF THEM ALL.
BUT I DO REMEMBER MR. GRAY. THOUGH I MUST SAY...
...IF HE EVER MENTIONED THAT HE HAD COUSINS WHO WERE SHADOW-HUNTERS, I CAN'T SAY I RECALL IT.

CHAPTER 3

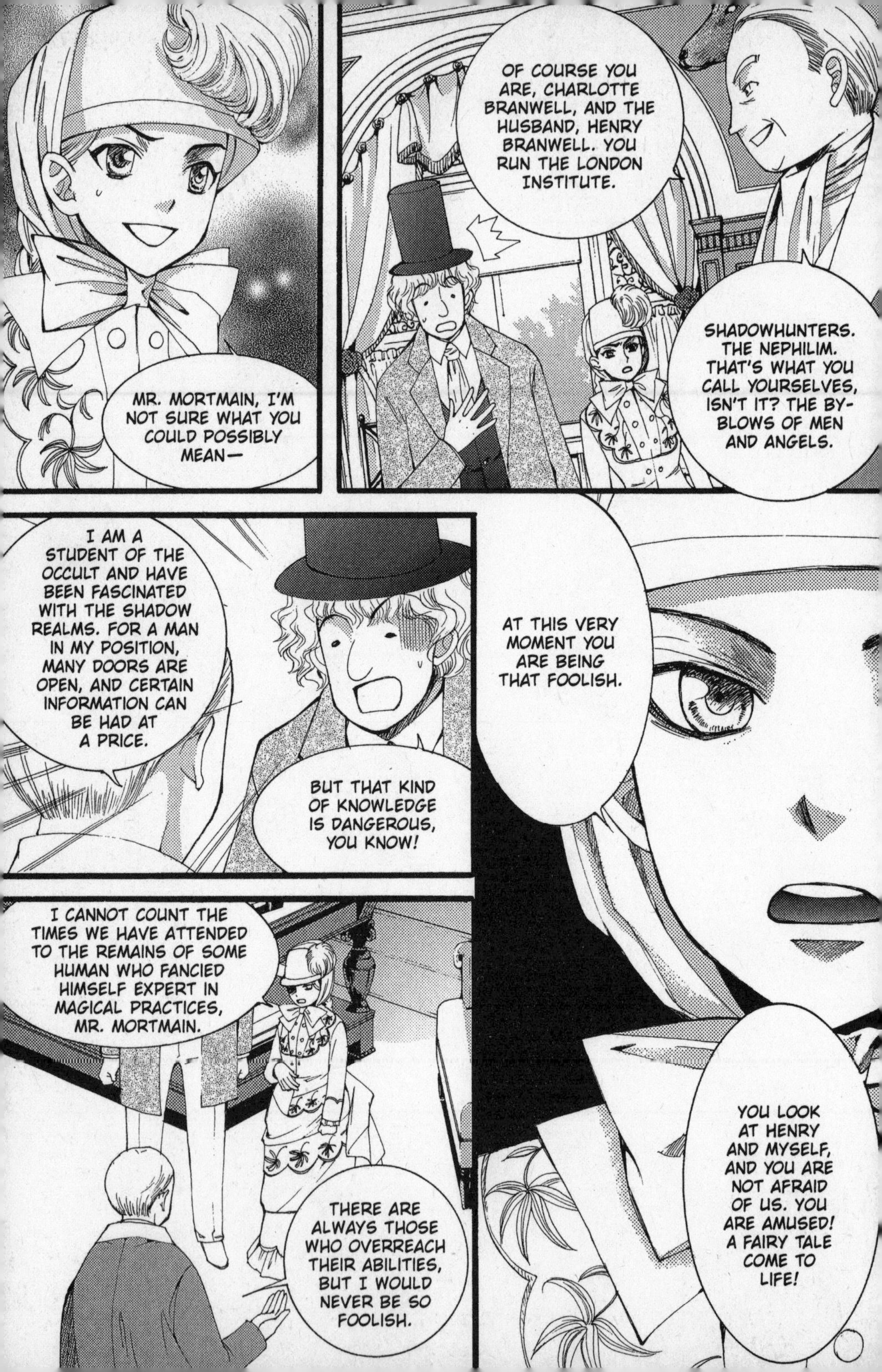
MR. MORTMAIN, I'M NOT SURE WHAT YOU COULD POSSIBLY MEAN—
OF COURSE YOU ARE, CHARLOTTE BRANWELL, AND THE HUSBAND, HENRY BRANWELL. YOU RUN THE LONDON INSTITUTE.
SHADOWHUNTERS. THE NEPHILIM. THAT'S WHAT YOU CALL YOURSELVES, ISN'T IT? THE BY-BLOWS OF MEN AND ANGELS.
I AM A STUDENT OF THE OCCULT AND HAVE BEEN FASCINATED WITH THE SHADOW REALMS. FOR A MAN IN MY POSITION, MANY DOORS ARE OPEN, AND CERTAIN INFORMATION CAN BE HAD AT A PRICE.
BUT THAT KIND OF KNOWLEDGE IS DANGEROUS, YOU KNOW!
I CANNOT COUNT THE TIMES WE HAVE ATTENDED TO THE REMAINS OF SOME HUMAN WHO FANCIED HIMSELF EXPERT IN MAGICAL PRACTICES, MR. MORTMAIN.
THERE ARE ALWAYS THOSE WHO OVERREACH THEIR ABILITIES, BUT I WOULD NEVER BE SO FOOLISH.
AT THIS VERY MOMENT YOU ARE BEING THAT FOOLISH.
YOU LOOK AT HENRY AND MYSELF, AND YOU ARE NOT AFRAID OF US. YOU ARE AMUSED! A FAIRY TALE COME TO LIFE!

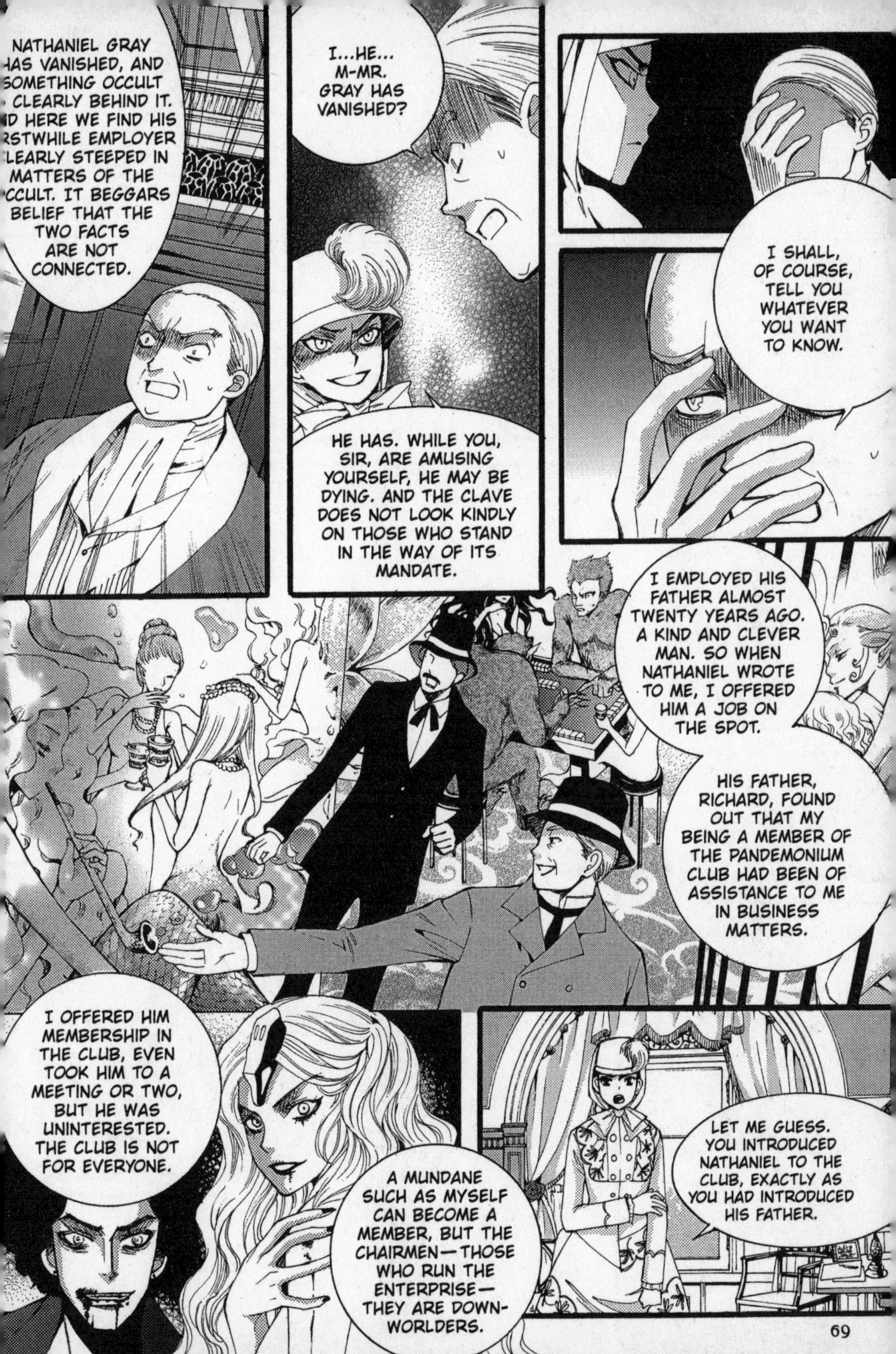
NATHANIEL GRAY HAS VANISHED, AND SOMETHING OCCULT CLEARLY BEHIND IT. D HERE WE FIND HIS RSTWHILE EMPLOYER LEARLY STEEPED IN MATTERS OF THE CCULT. IT BEGGARS BELIEF THAT THE TWO FACTS ARE NOT CONNECTED.
I...HE... M-MR. GRAY HAS VANISHED?
HE HAS. WHILE YOU, SIR, ARE AMUSING YOURSELF, HE MAY BE DYING. AND THE CLAVE DOES NOT LOOK KINDLY ON THOSE WHO STAND IN THE WAY OF ITS MANDATE.
I SHALL, OF COURSE, TELL YOU WHATEVER YOU WANT TO KNOW.
I EMPLOYED HIS FATHER ALMOST TWENTY YEARS AGO. A KIND AND CLEVER MAN. SO WHEN NATHANIEL WROTE TO ME, I OFFERED HIM A JOB ON THE SPOT.
HIS FATHER, RICHARD, FOUND OUT THAT MY BEING A MEMBER OF THE PANDEMONIUM CLUB HAD BEEN OF ASSISTANCE TO ME IN BUSINESS MATTERS.
I OFFERED HIM MEMBERSHIP IN THE CLUB, EVEN TOOK HIM TO A MEETING OR TWO, BUT HE WAS UNINTERESTED. THE CLUB IS NOT FOR EVERYONE.
A MUNDANE SUCH AS MYSELF CAN BECOME A MEMBER, BUT THE CHAIRMEN—THOSE WHO RUN THE ENTERPRISE—THEY ARE DOWN-WORLDERS.
LET ME GUESS. YOU INTRODUCED NATHANIEL TO THE CLUB, EXACTLY AS YOU HAD INTRODUCED HIS FATHER.

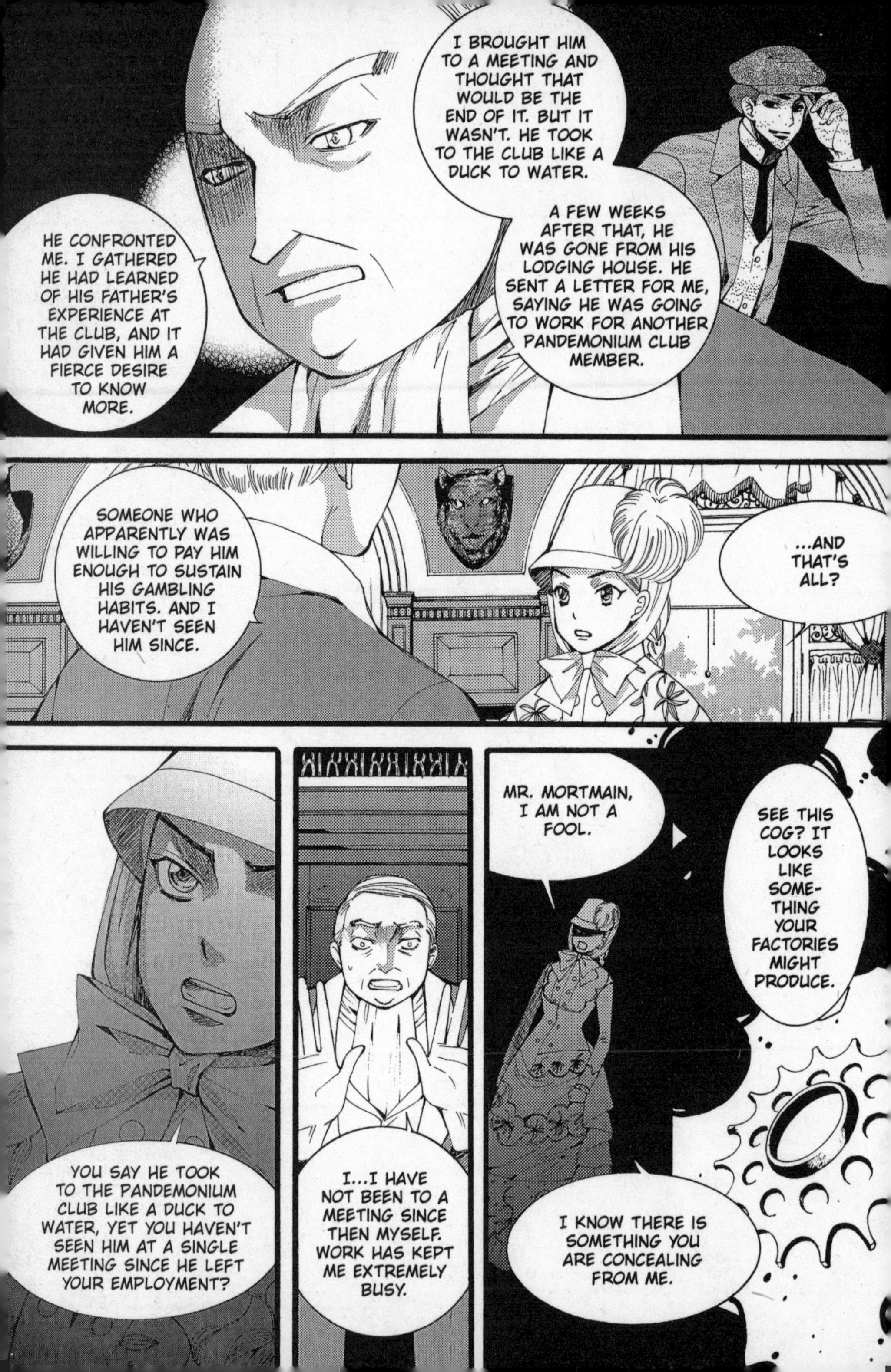
HE CONFRONTED ME. I GATHERED HE HAD LEARNED OF HIS FATHER'S EXPERIENCE AT THE CLUB, AND IT HAD GIVEN HIM A FIERCE DESIRE TO KNOW MORE.
I BROUGHT HIM TO A MEETING AND THOUGHT THAT WOULD BE THE END OF IT. BUT IT WASN'T. HE TOOK TO THE CLUB LIKE A DUCK TO WATER.
A FEW WEEKS AFTER THAT, HE WAS GONE FROM HIS LODGING HOUSE. HE SENT A LETTER FOR ME, SAYING HE WAS GOING TO WORK FOR ANOTHER PANDEMONIUM CLUB MEMBER.
SOMEONE WHO APPARENTLY WAS WILLING TO PAY HIM ENOUGH TO SUSTAIN HIS GAMBLING HABITS. AND I HAVEN'T SEEN HIM SINCE.
...AND THAT'S ALL?
YOU SAY HE TOOK TO THE PANDEMONIUM CLUB LIKE A DUCK TO WATER, YET YOU HAVEN'T SEEN HIM AT A SINGLE MEETING SINCE HE LEFT YOUR EMPLOYMENT?
I...I HAVE NOT BEEN TO A MEETING SINCE THEN MYSELF. WORK HAS KEPT ME EXTREMELY BUSY.
MR. MORTMAIN, I AM NOT A FOOL.
I KNOW THERE IS SOMETHING YOU ARE CONCEALING FROM ME.
SEE THIS COG? IT LOOKS LIKE SOME-THING YOUR FACTORIES MIGHT PRODUCE.

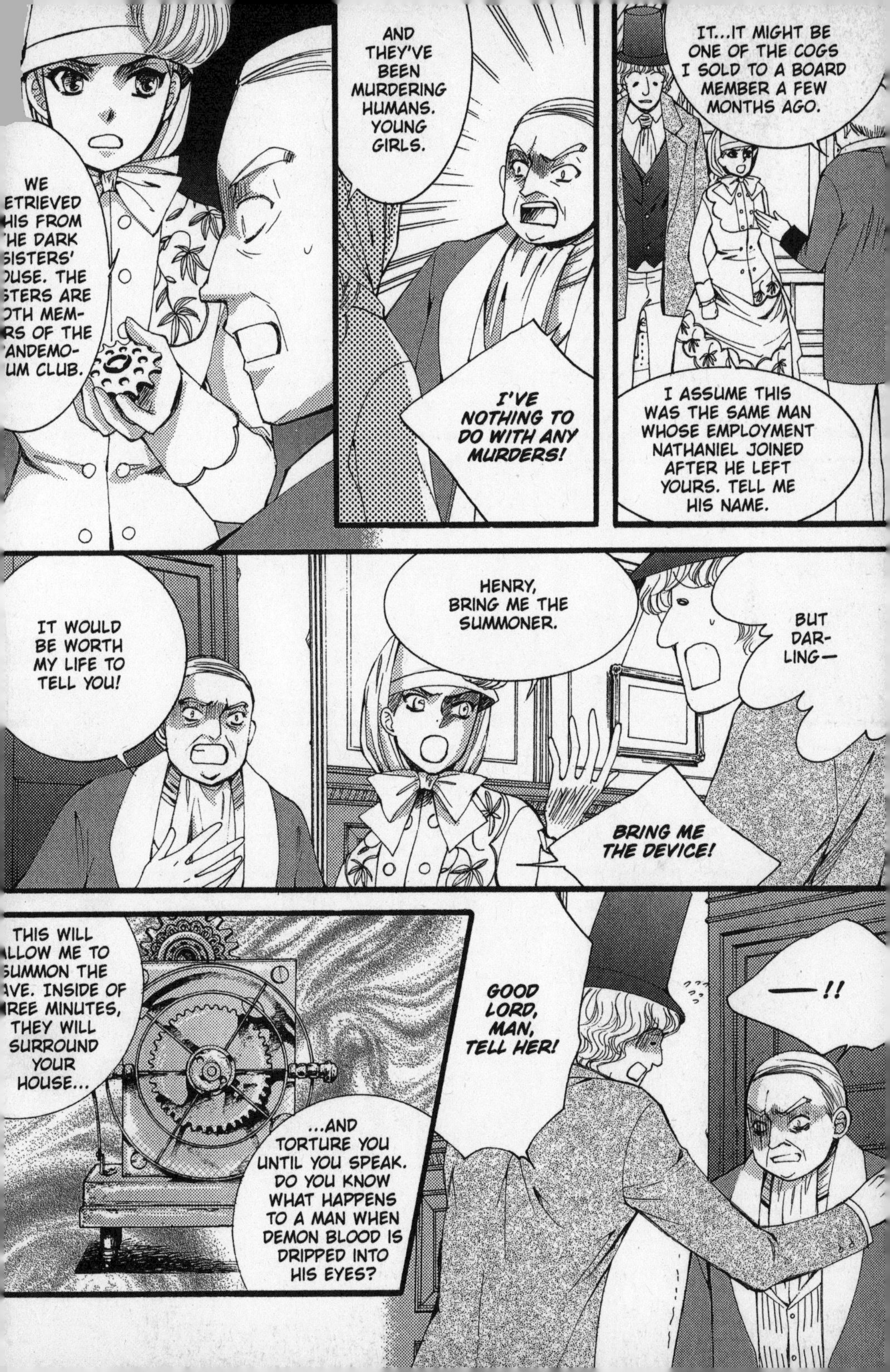
WE ETRIEVED HIS FROM HE DARK SISTERS' OUSE. THE STERS ARE OTH MEM-RS OF THE ANDEMO-UM CLUB.
AND THEY'VE BEEN MURDERING HUMANS. YOUNG GIRLS.
I'VE NOTHING TO DO WITH ANY MURDERS!
IT...IT MIGHT BE ONE OF THE COGS I SOLD TO A BOARD MEMBER A FEW MONTHS AGO.
I ASSUME THIS WAS THE SAME MAN WHOSE EMPLOYMENT NATHANIEL JOINED AFTER HE LEFT YOURS. TELL ME HIS NAME.
IT WOULD BE WORTH MY LIFE TO TELL YOU!
HENRY, BRING ME THE SUMMONER.
BUT DAR-LING—
BRING ME THE DEVICE!
THIS WILL LLOW ME TO UMMON THE AVE. INSIDE OF REE MINUTES, THEY WILL SURROUND YOUR HOUSE...
...AND TORTURE YOU UNTIL YOU SPEAK. DO YOU KNOW WHAT HAPPENS TO A MAN WHEN DEMON BLOOD IS DRIPPED INTO HIS EYES?
GOOD LORD, MAN, TELL HER!
—!!

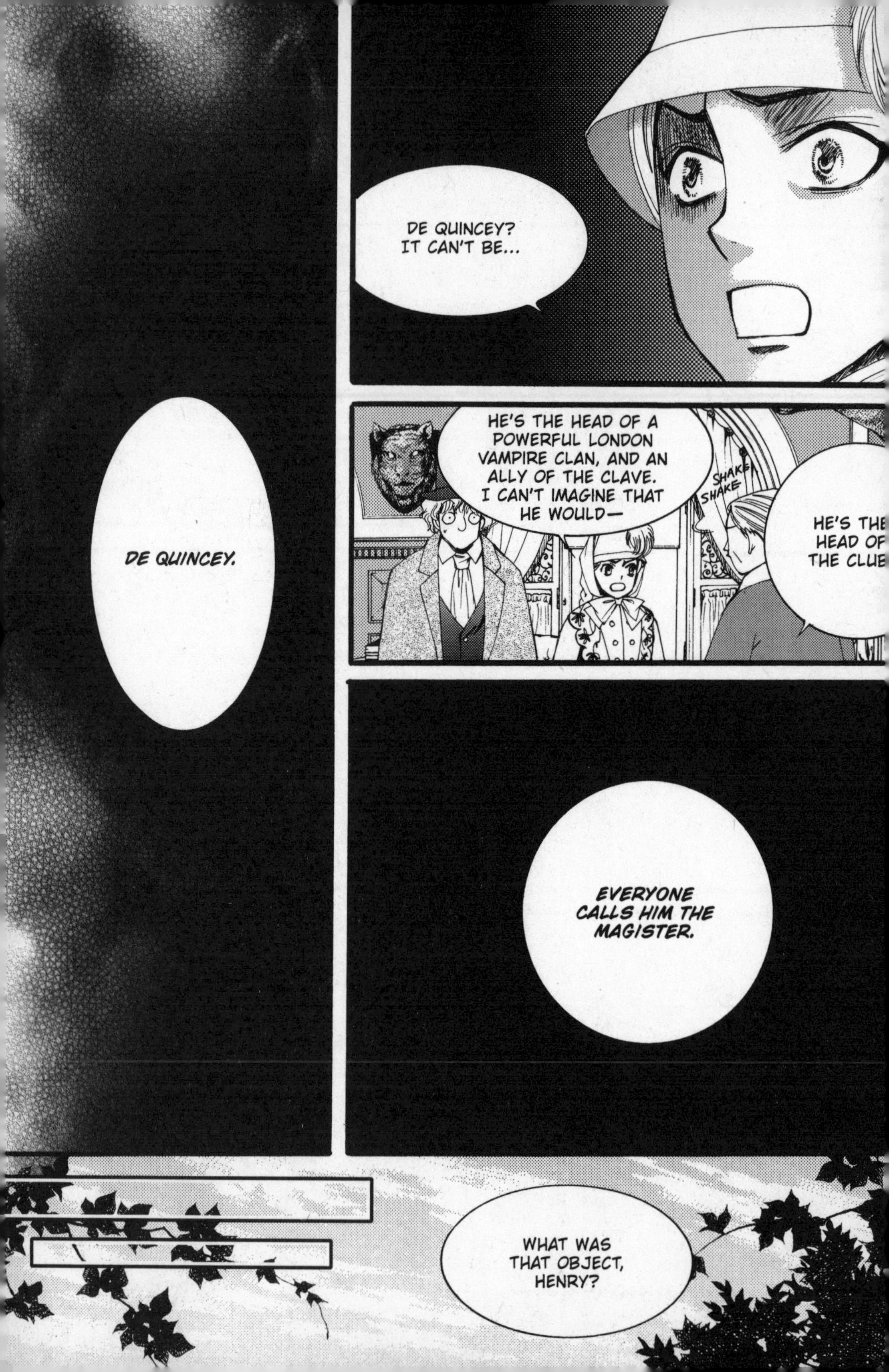
DE QUINCEY.
DE QUINCEY? IT CAN'T BE...
HE'S THE HEAD OF A POWERFUL LONDON VAMPIRE CLAN, AND AN ALLY OF THE CLAVE. I CAN'T IMAGINE THAT HE WOULD—
SHAKE SHAKE
HE'S THE HEAD OF THE CLUB
EVERYONE CALLS HIM THE MAGISTER.
WHAT WAS THAT OBJECT, HENRY?

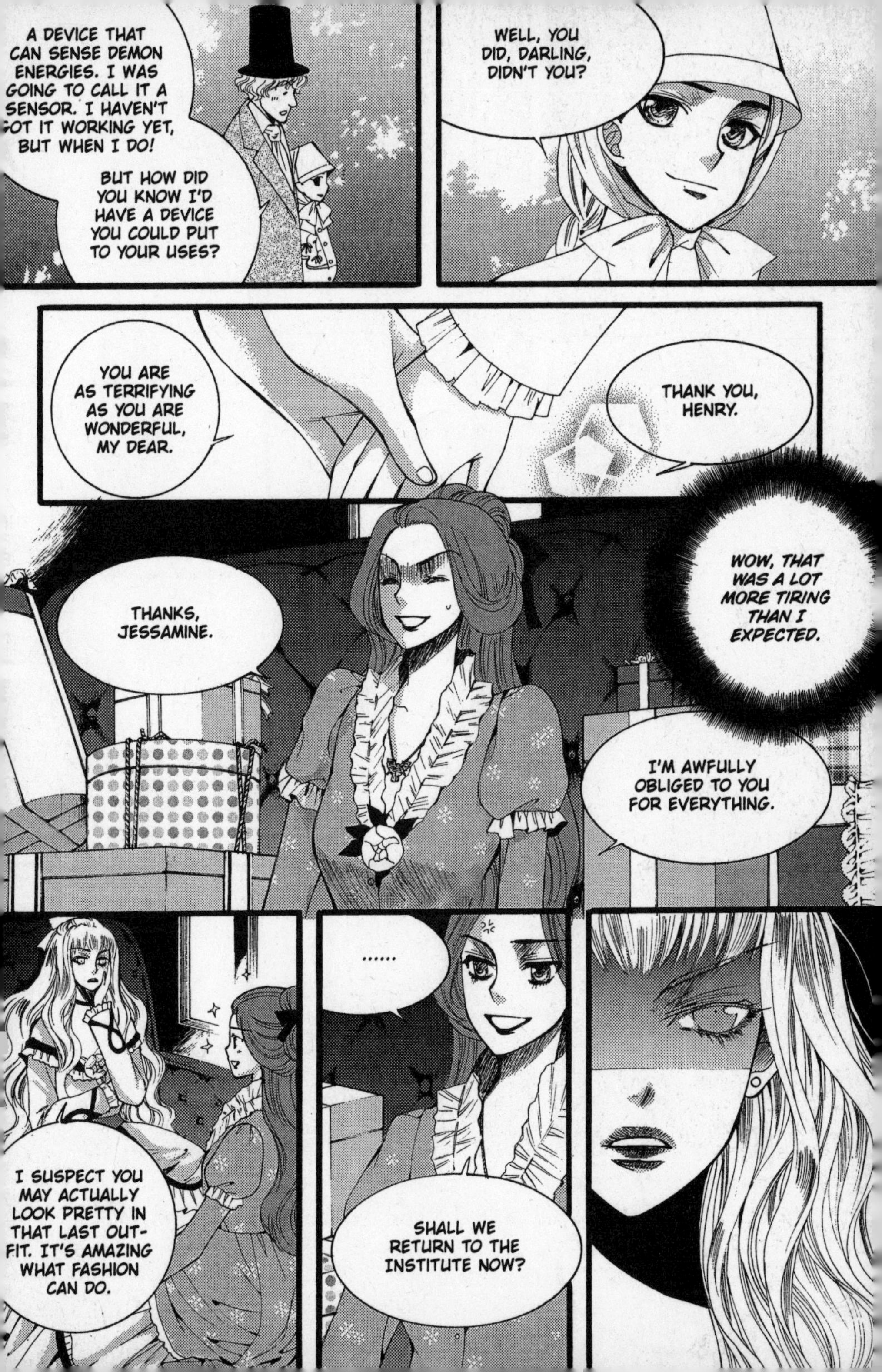
A DEVICE THAT CAN SENSE DEMON ENERGIES. I WAS GOING TO CALL IT A SENSOR. I HAVEN'T GOT IT WORKING YET, BUT WHEN I DO!
BUT HOW DID YOU KNOW I'D HAVE A DEVICE YOU COULD PUT TO YOUR USES?
WELL, YOU DID, DARLING, DIDN'T YOU?
YOU ARE AS TERRIFYING AS YOU ARE WONDERFUL, MY DEAR.
THANK YOU, HENRY.
THANKS, JESSAMINE.
WOW, THAT WAS A LOT MORE TIRING THAN I EXPECTED.
I'M AWFULLY OBLIGED TO YOU FOR EVERYTHING.
I SUSPECT YOU MAY ACTUALLY LOOK PRETTY IN THAT LAST OUT-FIT. IT'S AMAZING WHAT FASHION CAN DO.
......
SHALL WE RETURN TO THE INSTITUTE NOW?

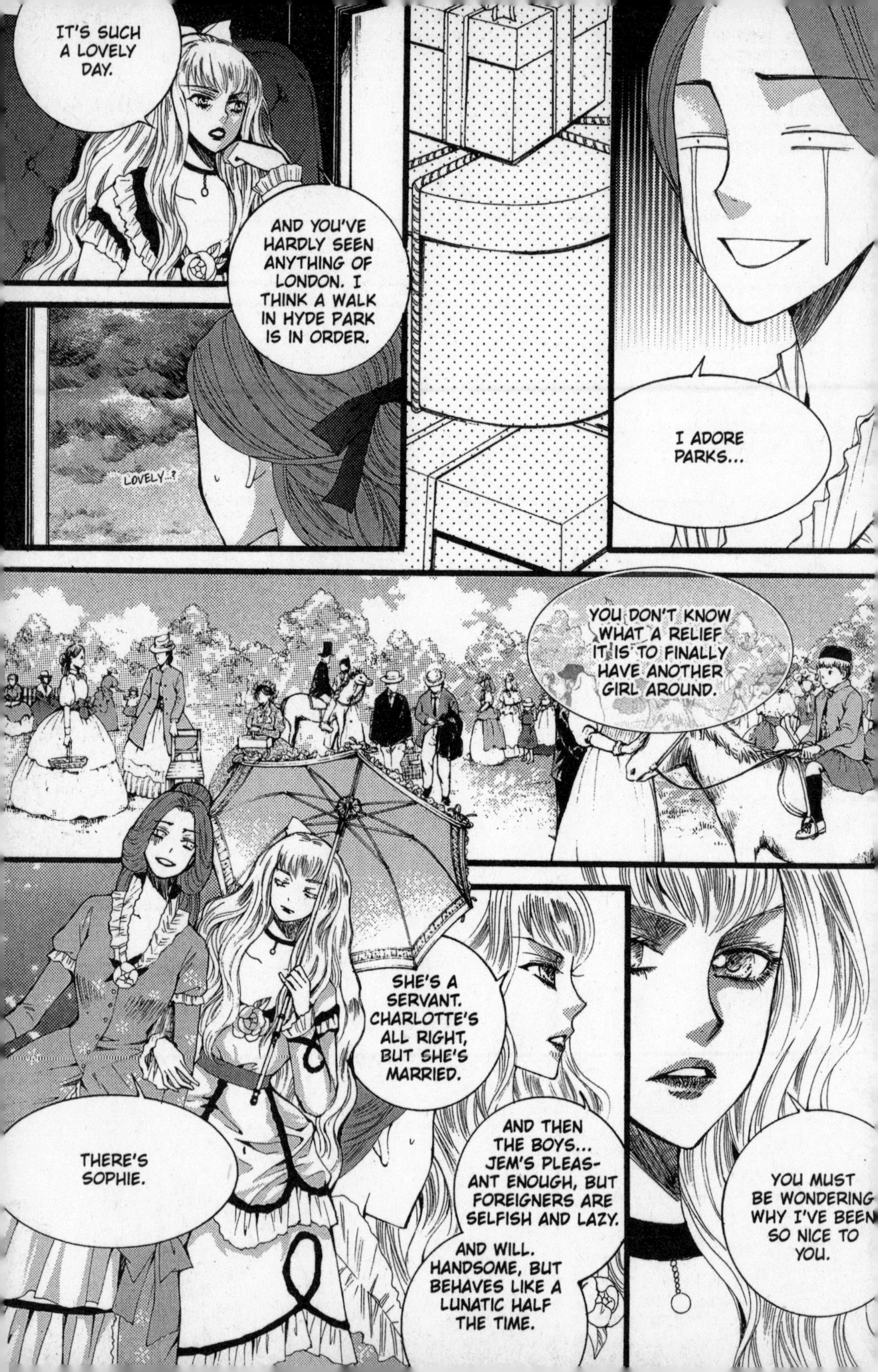
IT'S SUCH A LOVELY DAY.
AND YOU'VE HARDLY SEEN ANYTHING OF LONDON. I THINK A WALK IN HYDE PARK IS IN ORDER.
LOVELY...?
I ADORE PARKS...
YOU DON'T KNOW WHAT A RELIEF IT IS TO FINALLY HAVE ANOTHER GIRL AROUND.
THERE'S SOPHIE.
SHE'S A SERVANT. CHARLOTTE'S ALL RIGHT, BUT SHE'S MARRIED.
AND THEN THE BOYS... JEM'S PLEAS-ANT ENOUGH, BUT FOREIGNERS ARE SELFISH AND LAZY.
AND WILL. HANDSOME, BUT BEHAVES LIKE A LUNATIC HALF THE TIME.
YOU MUST BE WONDERING WHY I'VE BEEN SO NICE TO YOU.

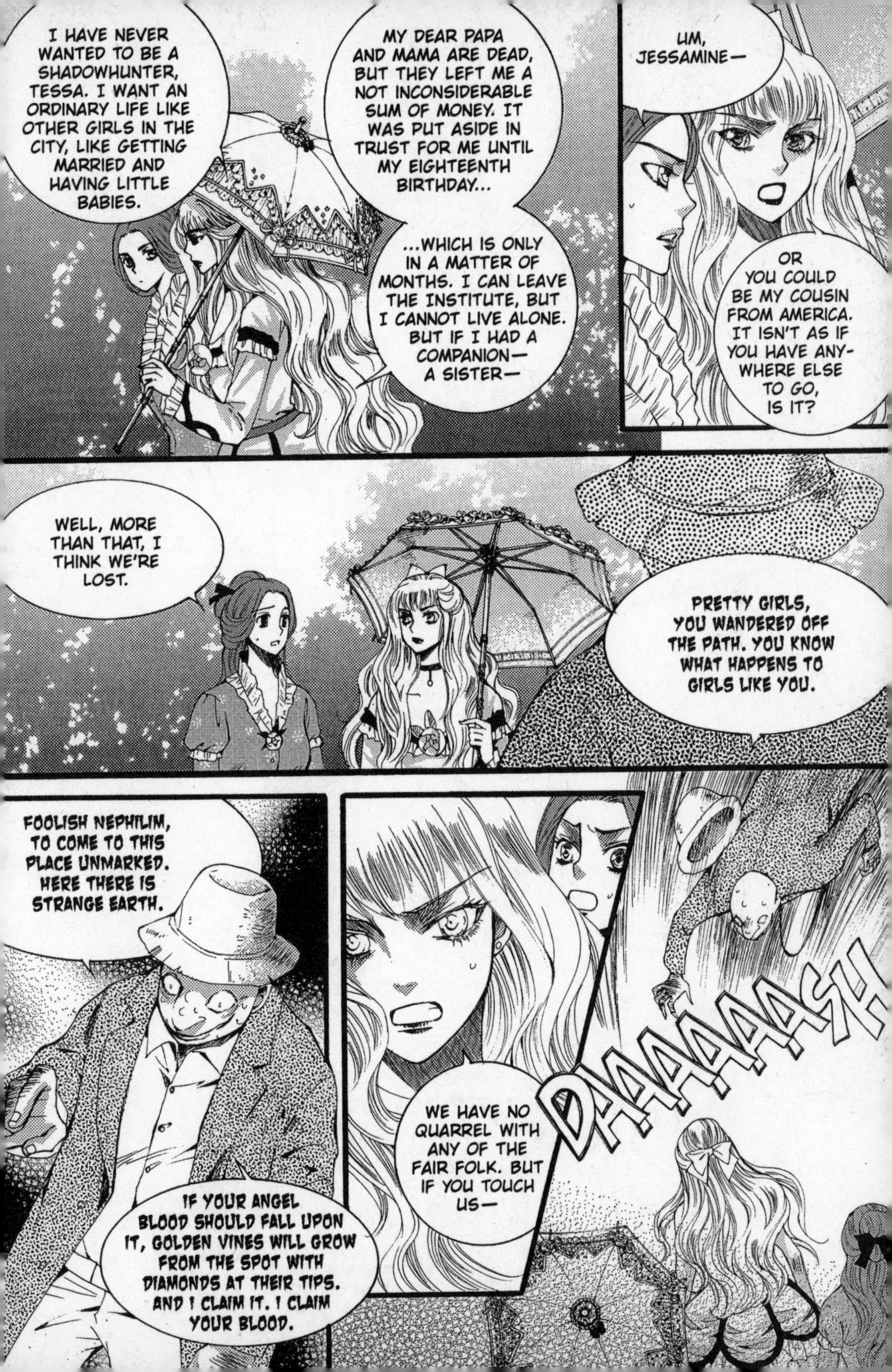
I HAVE NEVER WANTED TO BE A SHADOWHUNTER, TESSA. I WANT AN ORDINARY LIFE LIKE OTHER GIRLS IN THE CITY, LIKE GETTING MARRIED AND HAVING LITTLE BABIES.
MY DEAR PAPA AND MAMA ARE DEAD, BUT THEY LEFT ME A NOT INCONSIDERABLE SUM OF MONEY. IT WAS PUT ASIDE IN TRUST FOR ME UNTIL MY EIGHTEENTH BIRTHDAY...
...WHICH IS ONLY IN A MATTER OF MONTHS. I CAN LEAVE THE INSTITUTE, BUT I CANNOT LIVE ALONE. BUT IF I HAD A COMPANION— A SISTER—
UM, JESSAMINE—
OR YOU COULD BE MY COUSIN FROM AMERICA. IT ISN'T AS IF YOU HAVE ANY-WHERE ELSE TO GO, IS IT?
WELL, MORE THAN THAT, I THINK WE'RE LOST.
PRETTY GIRLS, YOU WANDERED OFF THE PATH. YOU KNOW WHAT HAPPENS TO GIRLS LIKE YOU.
FOOLISH NEPHILIM, TO COME TO THIS PLACE UNMARKED. HERE THERE IS STRANGE EARTH.
IF YOUR ANGEL BLOOD SHOULD FALL UPON IT, GOLDEN VINES WILL GROW FROM THE SPOT WITH DIAMONDS AT THEIR TIPS. AND I CLAIM IT. I CLAIM YOUR BLOOD.
WE HAVE NO QUARREL WITH ANY OF THE FAIR FOLK. BUT IF YOU TOUCH US—
DAAAAASH!

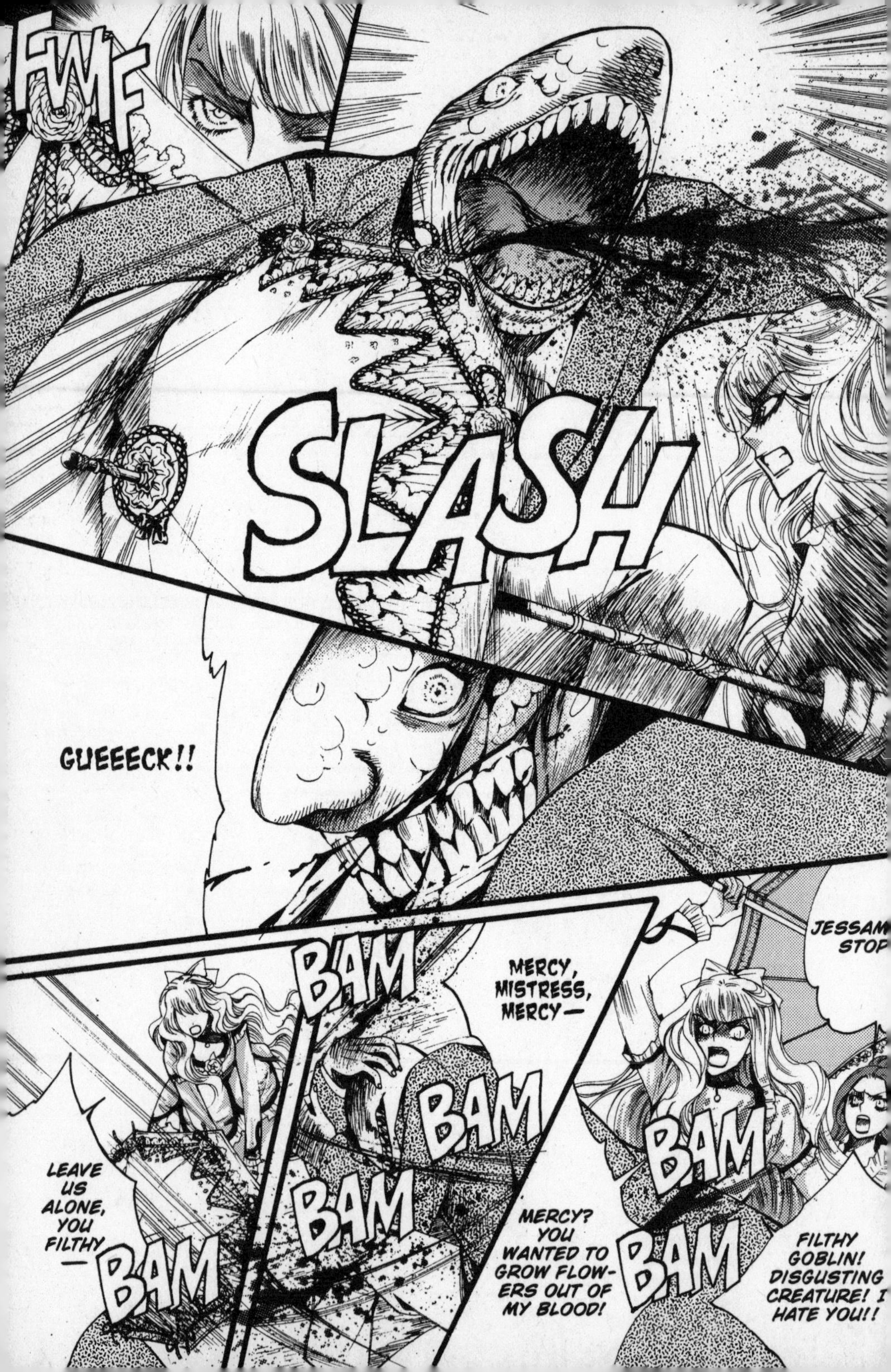
FWF
SLASH
GUEEEECK!!
LEAVE US ALONE, YOU FILTHY—
BAM
BAM
MERCY, MISTRESS, MERCY—
BAM
BAM
MERCY? YOU WANTED TO GROW FLOW-ERS OUT OF MY BLOOD!
JESSAM STOP
BAM
BAM
FILTHY GOBLIN! DISGUSTING CREATURE! I HATE YOU!!

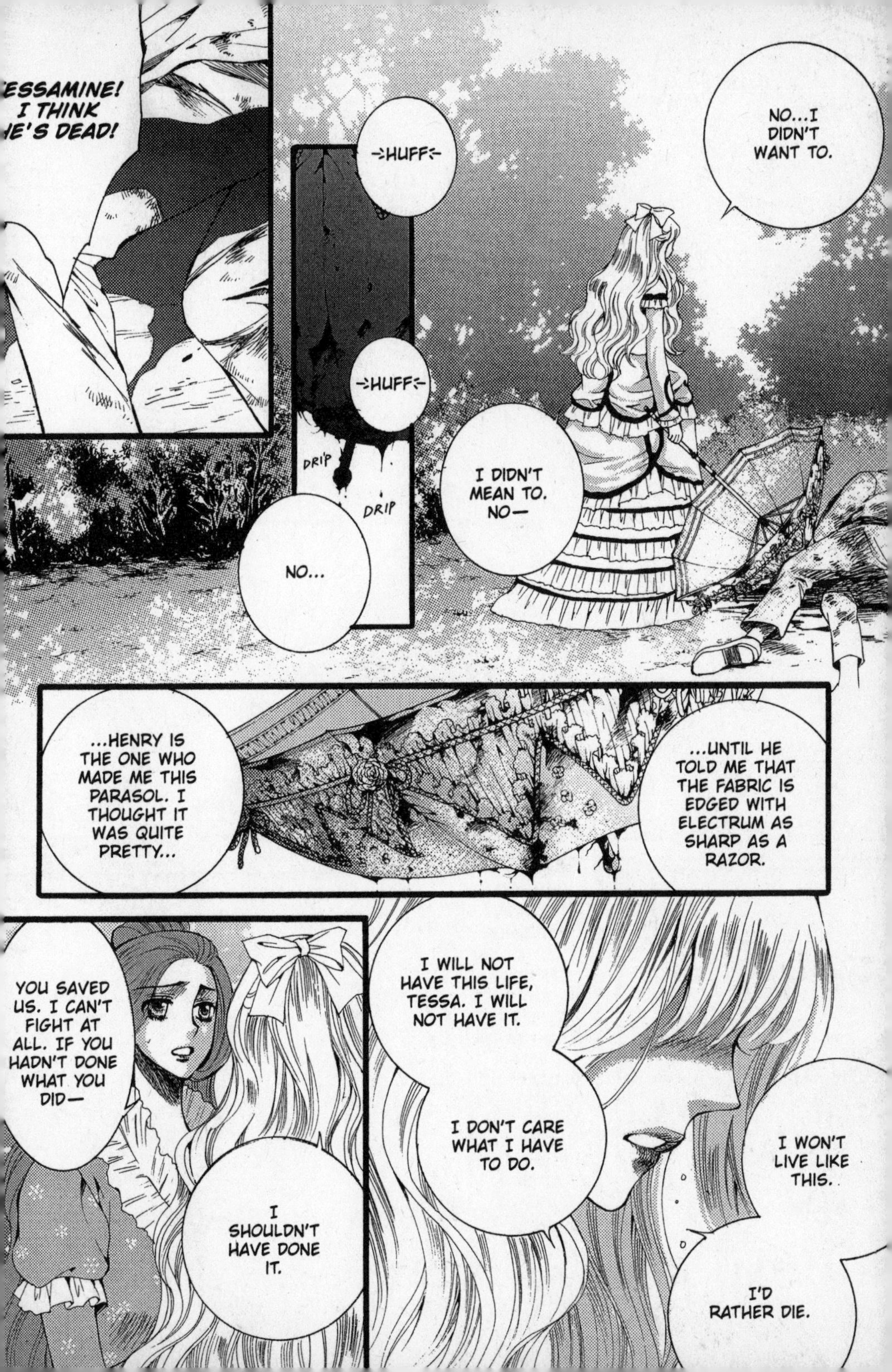
ESSAMINE! I THINK E'S DEAD!
HUFF
HUFF
DRIP
DRIP
NO...
I DIDN'T MEAN TO. NO—
NO...I DIDN'T WANT TO.
...HENRY IS THE ONE WHO MADE ME THIS PARASOL. I THOUGHT IT WAS QUITE PRETTY...
...UNTIL HE TOLD ME THAT THE FABRIC IS EDGED WITH ELECTRUM AS SHARP AS A RAZOR.
YOU SAVED US. I CAN'T FIGHT AT ALL. IF YOU HADN'T DONE WHAT YOU DID—
I SHOULDN'T HAVE DONE IT.
I WILL NOT HAVE THIS LIFE, TESSA. I WILL NOT HAVE IT.
I DON'T CARE WHAT I HAVE TO DO.
I WON'T LIVE LIKE THIS.
I'D RATHER DIE.

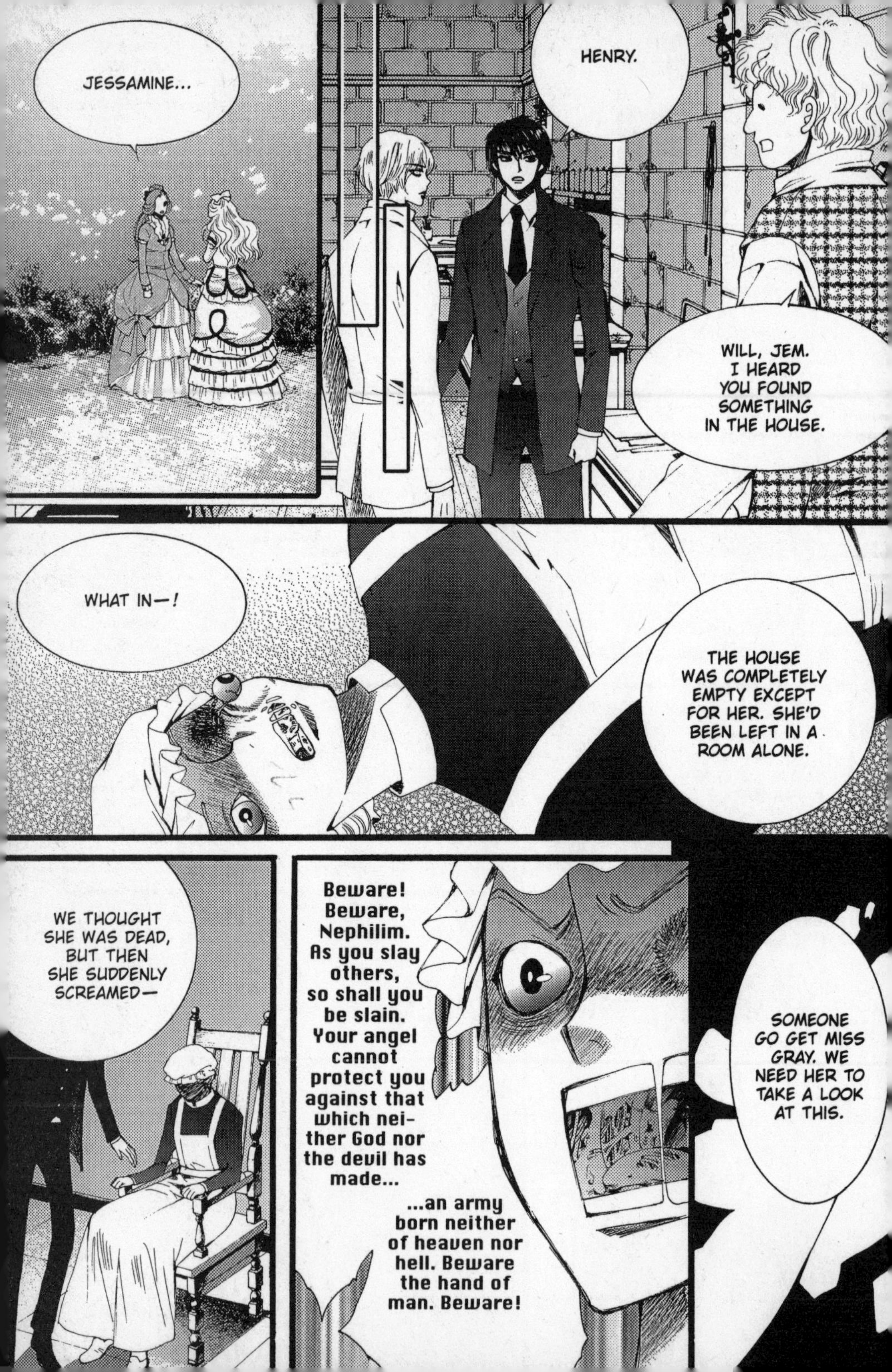
JESSAMINE...
HENRY.
WILL, JEM. I HEARD YOU FOUND SOMETHING IN THE HOUSE.
WHAT IN—!
THE HOUSE WAS COMPLETELY EMPTY EXCEPT FOR HER. SHE'D BEEN LEFT IN A ROOM ALONE.
WE THOUGHT SHE WAS DEAD, BUT THEN SHE SUDDENLY SCREAMED—
Beware! Beware, Nephilim. As you slay others, so shall you be slain. Your angel cannot protect you against that which neither God nor the devil has made...
...an army born neither of heaven nor hell. Beware the hand of man. Beware!
SOMEONE GO GET MISS GRAY. WE NEED HER TO TAKE A LOOK AT THIS.

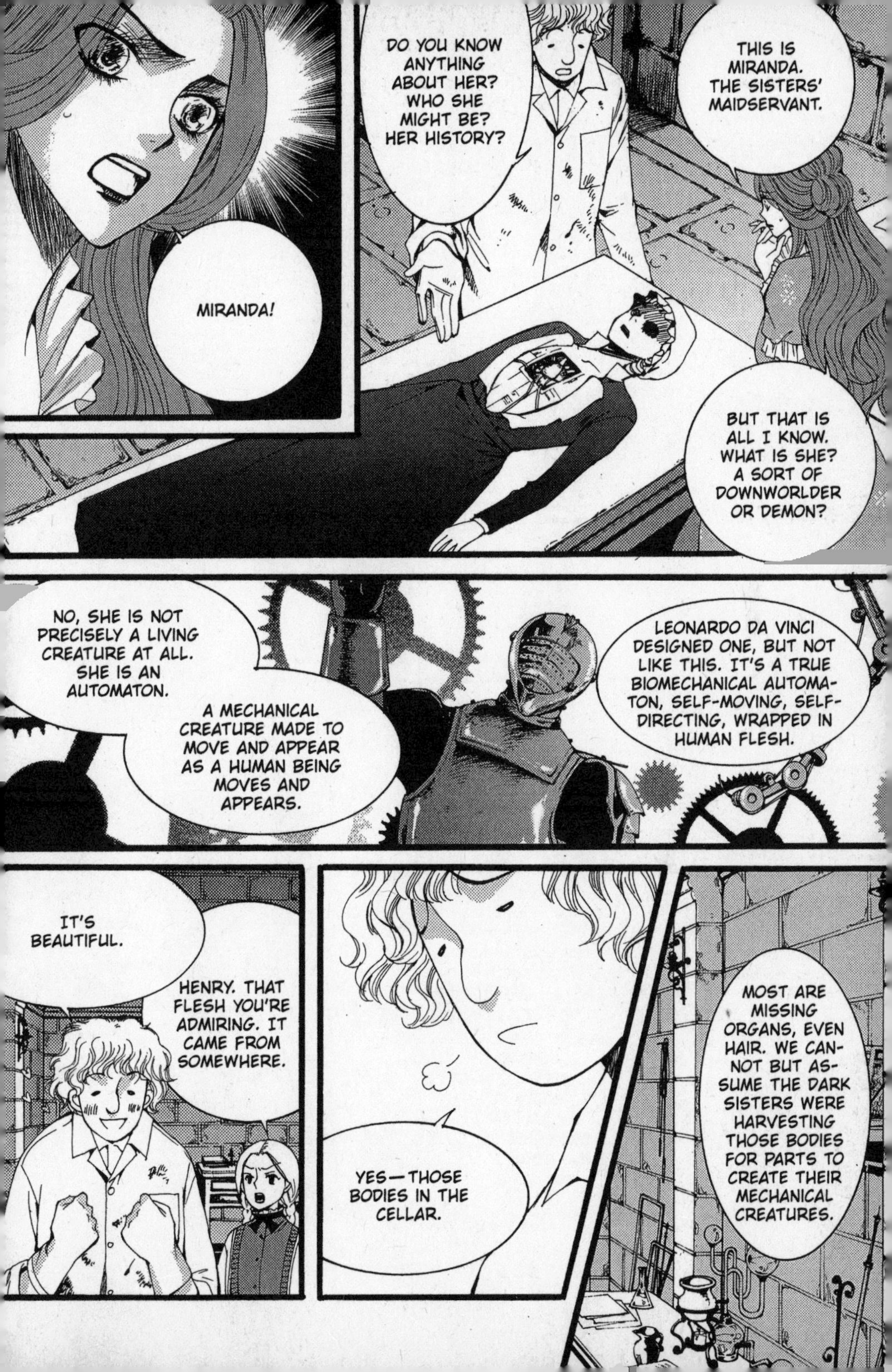
MIRANDA!
DO YOU KNOW ANYTHING ABOUT HER? WHO SHE MIGHT BE? HER HISTORY?
THIS IS MIRANDA. THE SISTERS' MAIDSERVANT.
BUT THAT IS ALL I KNOW. WHAT IS SHE? A SORT OF DOWNWORLDER OR DEMON?
NO, SHE IS NOT PRECISELY A LIVING CREATURE AT ALL. SHE IS AN AUTOMATON.
A MECHANICAL CREATURE MADE TO MOVE AND APPEAR AS A HUMAN BEING MOVES AND APPEARS.
LEONARDO DA VINCI DESIGNED ONE, BUT NOT LIKE THIS. IT'S A TRUE BIOMECHANICAL AUTOMATON, SELF-MOVING, SELF-DIRECTING, WRAPPED IN HUMAN FLESH.
IT'S BEAUTIFUL.
HENRY. THAT FLESH YOU'RE ADMIRING. IT CAME FROM SOMEWHERE.
YES—THOSE BODIES IN THE CELLAR.
MOST ARE MISSING ORGANS, EVEN HAIR. WE CANNOT BUT ASSUME THE DARK SISTERS WERE HARVESTING THOSE BODIES FOR PARTS TO CREATE THEIR MECHANICAL CREATURES.

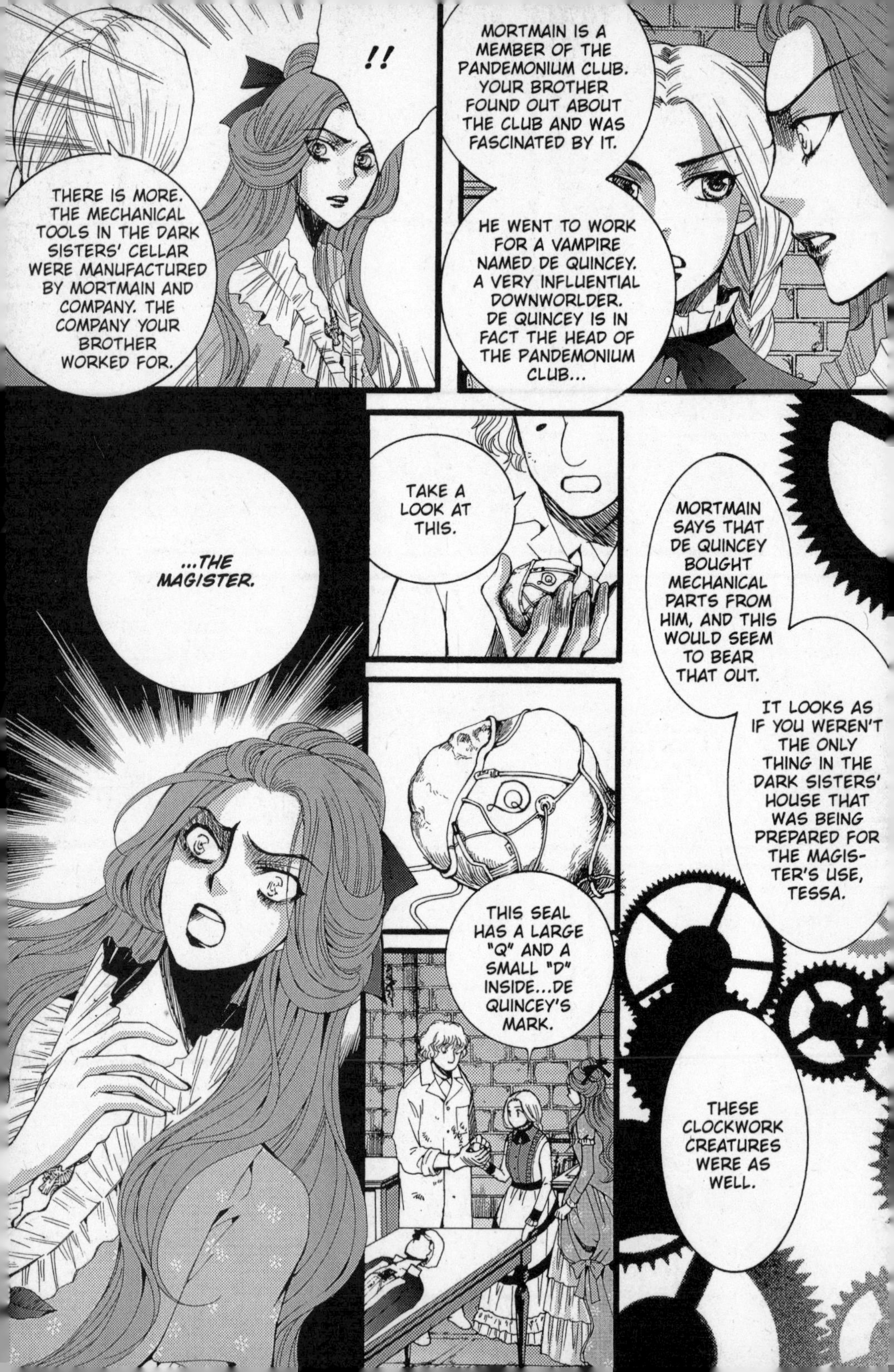
!!
THERE IS MORE. THE MECHANICAL TOOLS IN THE DARK SISTERS' CELLAR WERE MANUFACTURED BY MORTMAIN AND COMPANY. THE COMPANY YOUR BROTHER WORKED FOR.
MORTMAIN IS A MEMBER OF THE PANDEMONIUM CLUB. YOUR BROTHER FOUND OUT ABOUT THE CLUB AND WAS FASCINATED BY IT.
HE WENT TO WORK FOR A VAMPIRE NAMED DE QUINCEY. A VERY INFLUENTIAL DOWNWORLDER. DE QUINCEY IS IN FACT THE HEAD OF THE PANDEMONIUM CLUB...
...THE MAGISTER.
TAKE A LOOK AT THIS.
THIS SEAL HAS A LARGE "Q" AND A SMALL "D" INSIDE...DE QUINCEY'S MARK.
MORTMAIN SAYS THAT DE QUINCEY BOUGHT MECHANICAL PARTS FROM HIM, AND THIS WOULD SEEM TO BEAR THAT OUT.
IT LOOKS AS IF YOU WEREN'T THE ONLY THING IN THE DARK SISTERS' HOUSE THAT WAS BEING PREPARED FOR THE MAGISTER'S USE, TESSA.
THESE CLOCKWORK CREATURES WERE AS WELL.

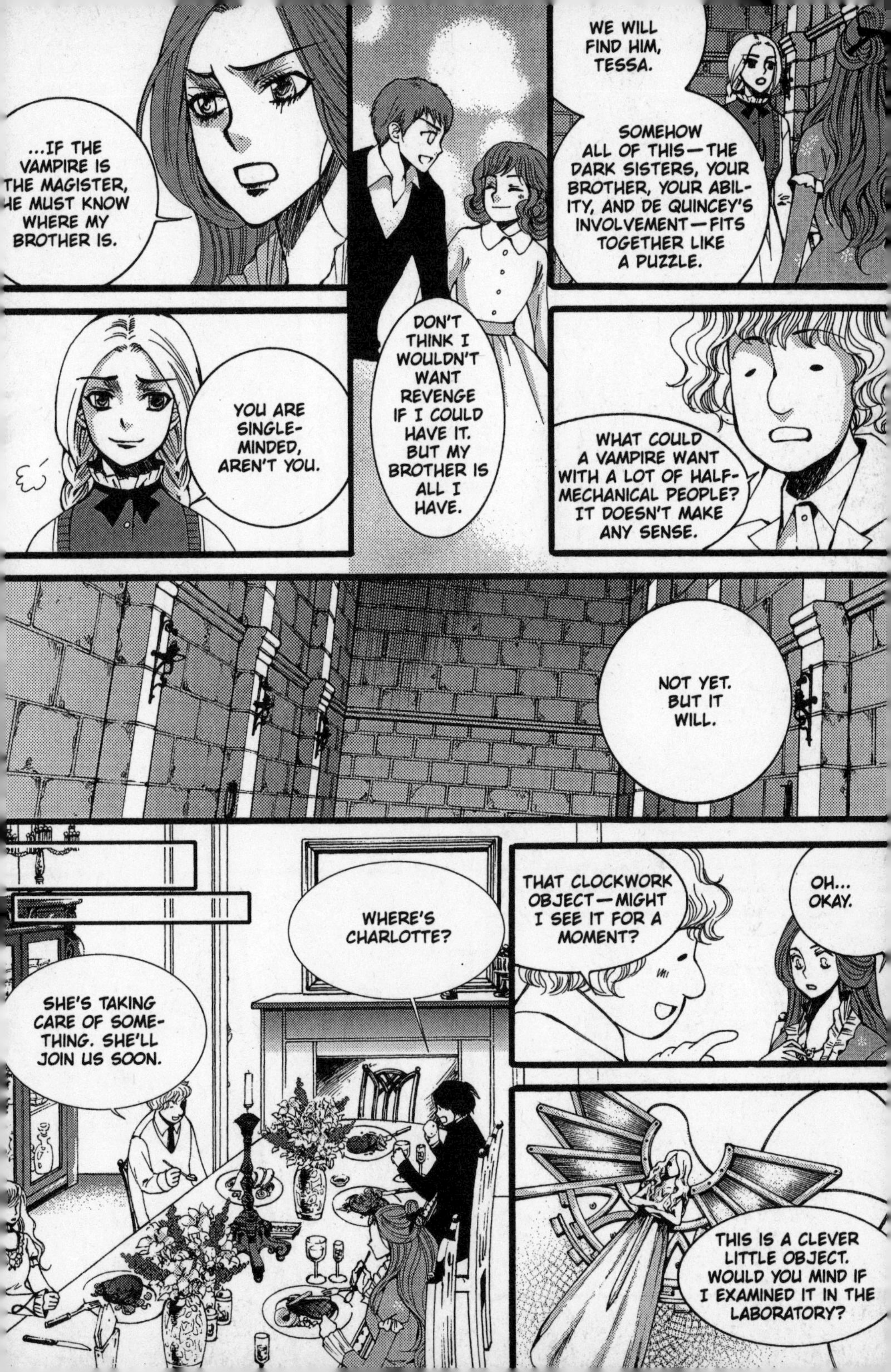
...IF THE VAMPIRE IS THE MAGISTER, HE MUST KNOW WHERE MY BROTHER IS.
WE WILL FIND HIM, TESSA.
SOMEHOW ALL OF THIS—THE DARK SISTERS, YOUR BROTHER, YOUR ABILITY, AND DE QUINCEY'S INVOLVEMENT—FITS TOGETHER LIKE A PUZZLE.
YOU ARE SINGLE-MINDED, AREN'T YOU.
DON'T THINK I WOULDN'T WANT REVENGE IF I COULD HAVE IT. BUT MY BROTHER IS ALL I HAVE.
WHAT COULD A VAMPIRE WANT WITH A LOT OF HALF-MECHANICAL PEOPLE? IT DOESN'T MAKE ANY SENSE.
NOT YET. BUT IT WILL.
WHERE'S CHARLOTTE?
SHE'S TAKING CARE OF SOMETHING. SHE'LL JOIN US SOON.
THAT CLOCKWORK OBJECT—MIGHT I SEE IT FOR A MOMENT?
OH... OKAY.
THIS IS A CLEVER LITTLE OBJECT. WOULD YOU MIND IF I EXAMINED IT IN THE LABORATORY?

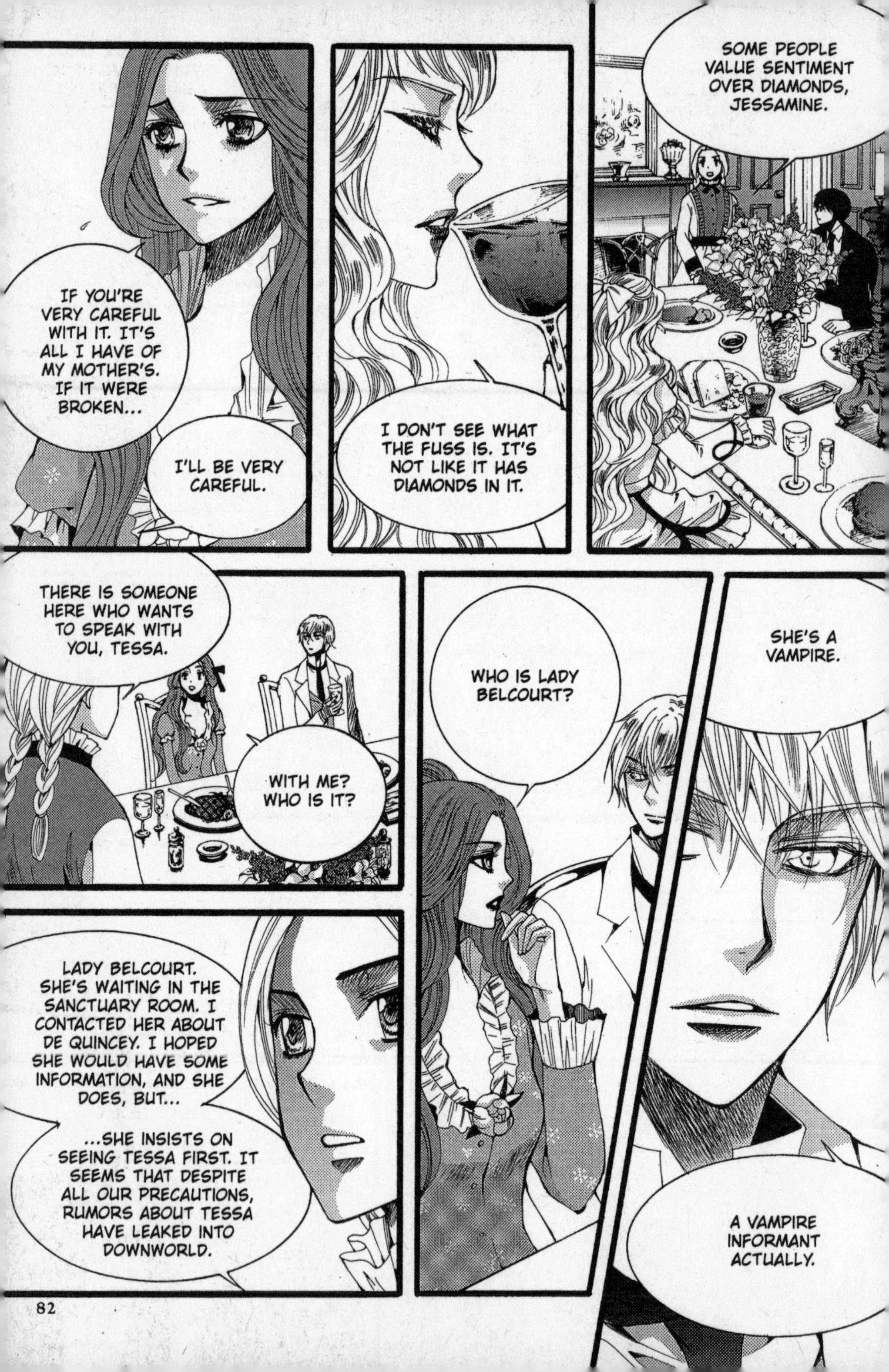
IF YOU'RE VERY CAREFUL WITH IT. IT'S ALL I HAVE OF MY MOTHER'S. IF IT WERE BROKEN...
I'LL BE VERY CAREFUL.
I DON'T SEE WHAT THE FUSS IS. IT'S NOT LIKE IT HAS DIAMONDS IN IT.
SOME PEOPLE VALUE SENTIMENT OVER DIAMONDS, JESSAMINE.
THERE IS SOMEONE HERE WHO WANTS TO SPEAK WITH YOU, TESSA.
WITH ME? WHO IS IT?
LADY BELCOURT. SHE'S WAITING IN THE SANCTUARY ROOM. I CONTACTED HER ABOUT DE QUINCEY. I HOPED SHE WOULD HAVE SOME INFORMATION, AND SHE DOES, BUT...
...SHE INSISTS ON SEEING TESSA FIRST. IT SEEMS THAT DESPITE ALL OUR PRECAUTIONS, RUMORS ABOUT TESSA HAVE LEAKED INTO DOWNWORLD.
WHO IS LADY BELCOURT?
SHE'S A VAMPIRE.
A VAMPIRE INFORMANT ACTUALLY.

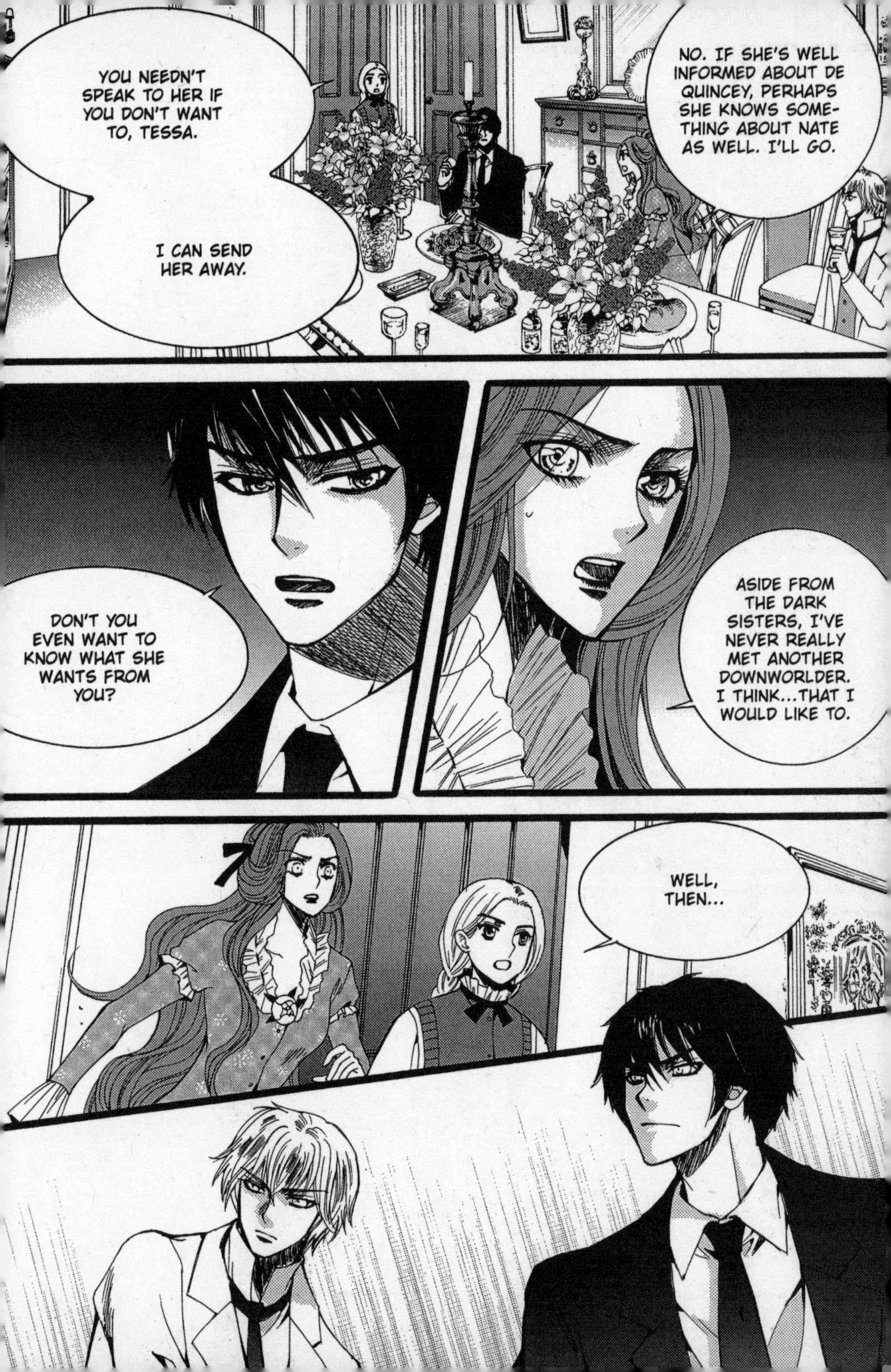

YOU NEEDN'T SPEAK TO HER IF YOU DON'T WANT TO, TESSA.
I CAN SEND HER AWAY.
NO. IF SHE'S WELL INFORMED ABOUT DE QUINCEY, PERHAPS SHE KNOWS SOMETHING ABOUT NATE AS WELL. I'LL GO.
DON'T YOU EVEN WANT TO KNOW WHAT SHE WANTS FROM YOU?
ASIDE FROM THE DARK SISTERS, I'VE NEVER REALLY MET ANOTHER DOWNWORLDER. I THINK...THAT I WOULD LIKE TO.
WELL, THEN...

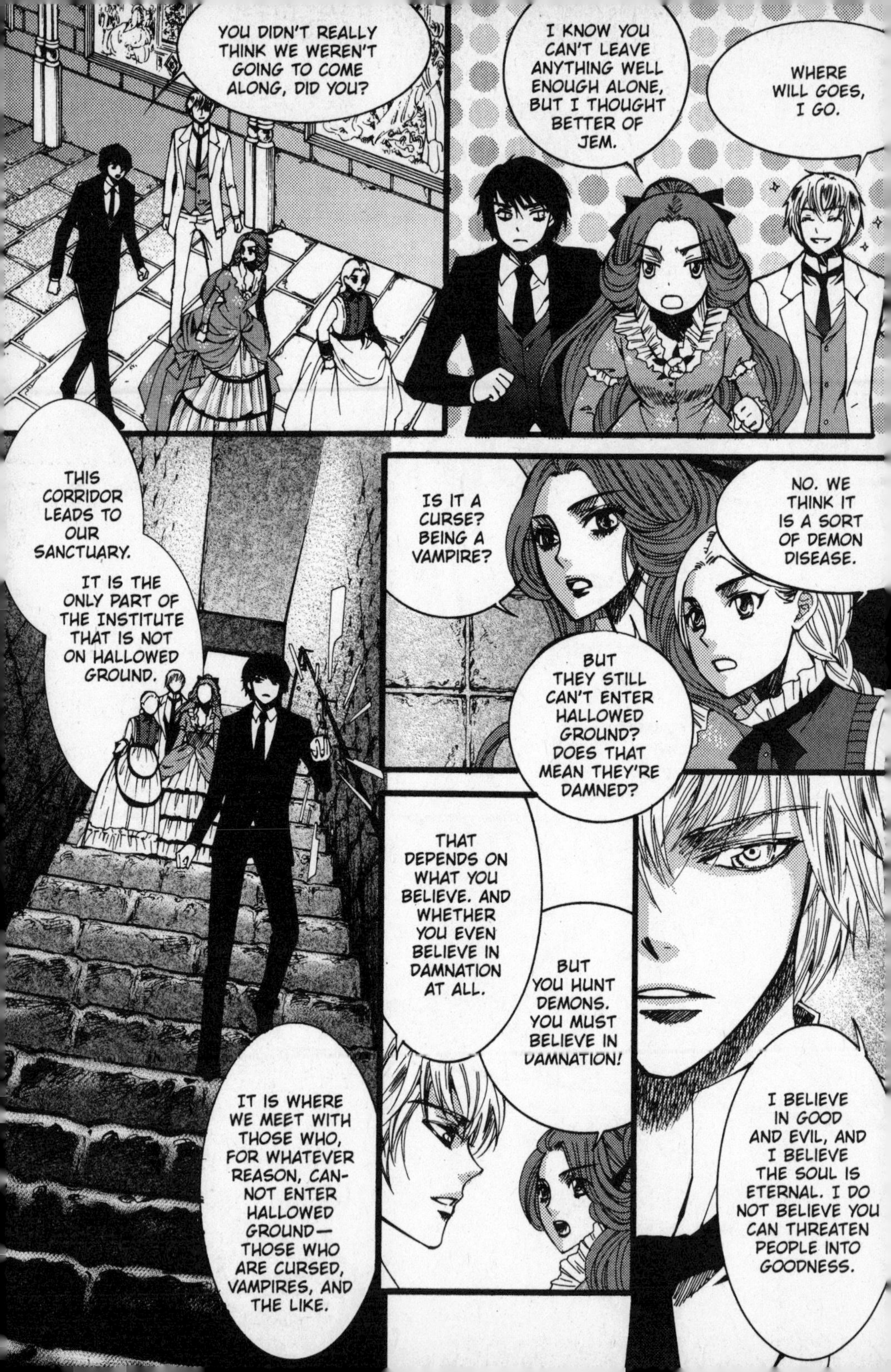

YOU DIDN'T REALLY THINK WE WEREN'T GOING TO COME ALONG, DID YOU?
I KNOW YOU CAN'T LEAVE ANYTHING WELL ENOUGH ALONE, BUT I THOUGHT BETTER OF JEM.
WHERE WILL GOES, I GO.
THIS CORRIDOR LEADS TO OUR SANCTUARY.
IT IS THE ONLY PART OF THE INSTITUTE THAT IS NOT ON HALLOWED GROUND.
IT IS WHERE WE MEET WITH THOSE WHO, FOR WHATEVER REASON, CAN-NOT ENTER HALLOWED GROUND— THOSE WHO ARE CURSED, VAMPIRES, AND THE LIKE.
IS IT A CURSE? BEING A VAMPIRE?
NO. WE THINK IT IS A SORT OF DEMON DISEASE.
BUT THEY STILL CAN'T ENTER HALLOWED GROUND? DOES THAT MEAN THEY'RE DAMNED?
THAT DEPENDS ON WHAT YOU BELIEVE. AND WHETHER YOU EVEN BELIEVE IN DAMNATION AT ALL.
BUT YOU HUNT DEMONS. YOU MUST BELIEVE IN DAMNATION!
I BELIEVE IN GOOD AND EVIL, AND I BELIEVE THE SOUL IS ETERNAL. I DO NOT BELIEVE YOU CAN THREATEN PEOPLE INTO GOODNESS.

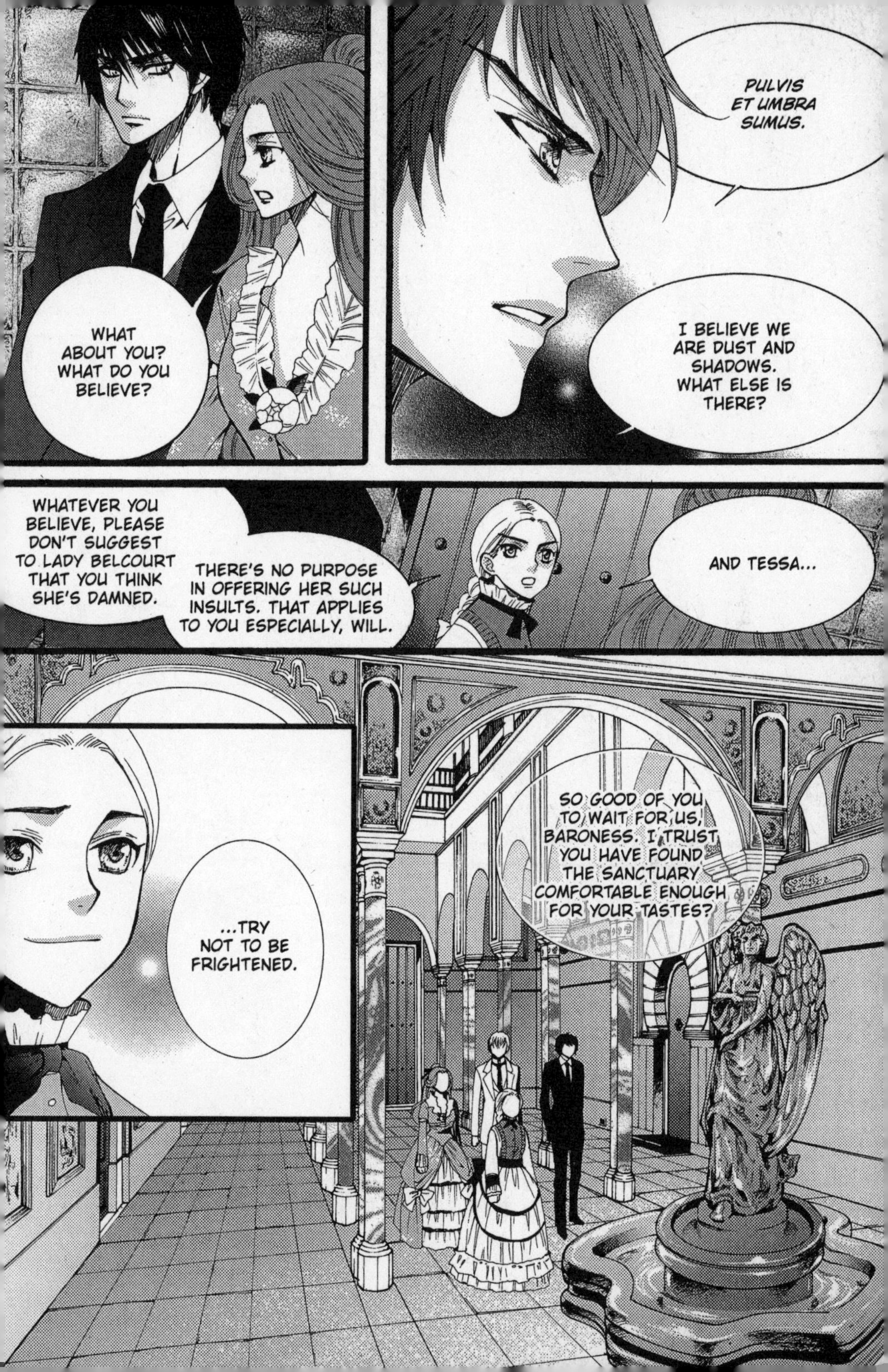
WHAT ABOUT YOU? WHAT DO YOU BELIEVE?
PULVIS ET UMBRA SUMUS.
I BELIEVE WE ARE DUST AND SHADOWS. WHAT ELSE IS THERE?
WHATEVER YOU BELIEVE, PLEASE DON'T SUGGEST TO LADY BELCOURT THAT YOU THINK SHE'S DAMNED.
THERE'S NO PURPOSE IN OFFERING HER SUCH INSULTS. THAT APPLIES TO YOU ESPECIALLY, WILL.
AND TESSA...
...TRY NOT TO BE FRIGHTENED.
SO GOOD OF YOU TO WAIT FOR US, BARONESS. I TRUST YOU HAVE FOUND THE SANCTUARY COMFORTABLE ENOUGH FOR YOUR TASTES?

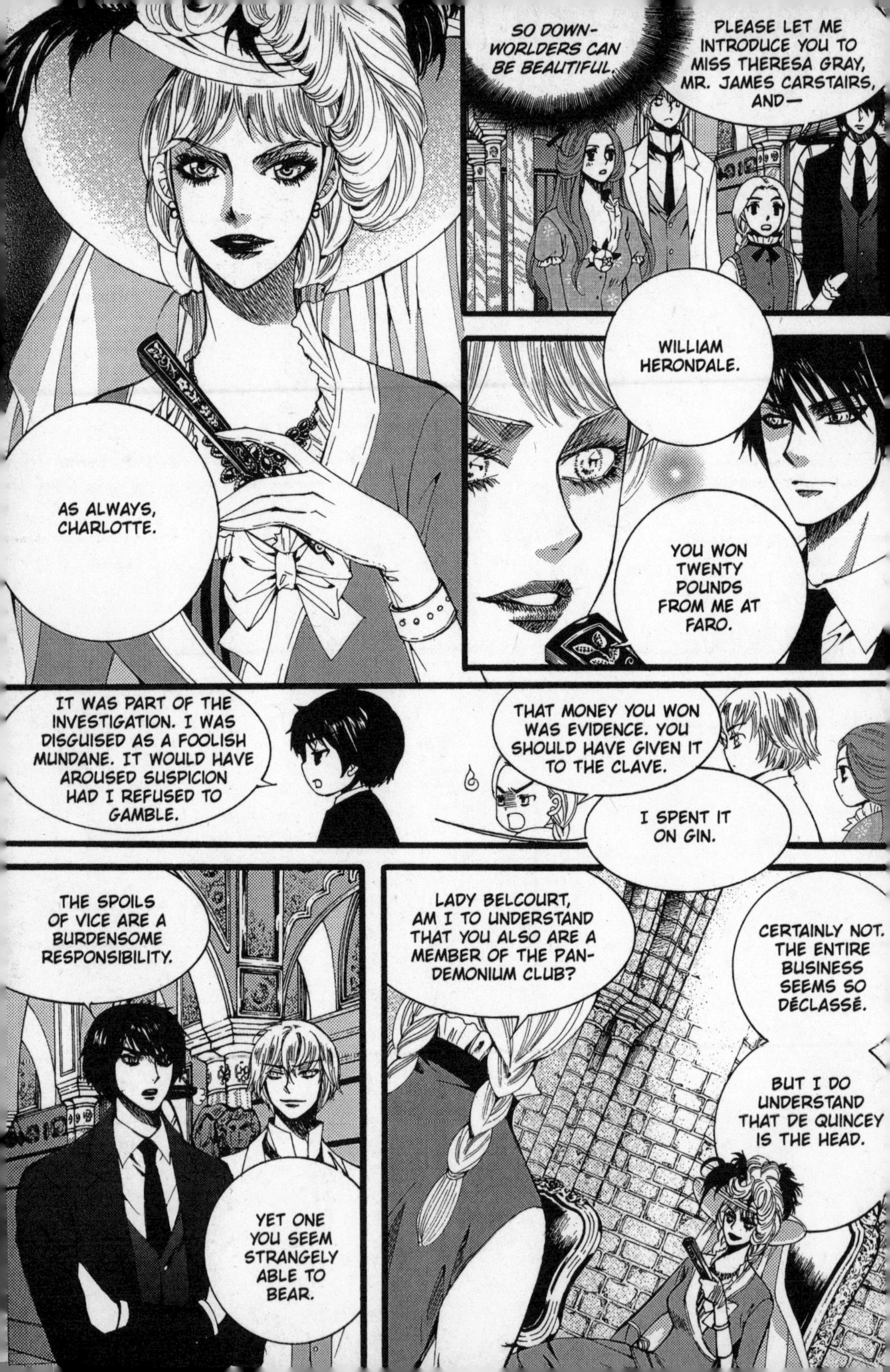
AS ALWAYS, CHARLOTTE.
SO DOWN-WORLDERS CAN BE BEAUTIFUL.
PLEASE LET ME INTRODUCE YOU TO MISS THERESA GRAY, MR. JAMES CARSTAIRS, AND—
WILLIAM HERONDALE.
YOU WON TWENTY POUNDS FROM ME AT FARO.
IT WAS PART OF THE INVESTIGATION. I WAS DISGUISED AS A FOOLISH MUNDANE. IT WOULD HAVE AROUSED SUSPICION HAD I REFUSED TO GAMBLE.
THAT MONEY YOU WON WAS EVIDENCE. YOU SHOULD HAVE GIVEN IT TO THE CLAVE.
I SPENT IT ON GIN.
THE SPOILS OF VICE ARE A BURDENSOME RESPONSIBILITY.
YET ONE YOU SEEM STRANGELY ABLE TO BEAR.
LADY BELCOURT, AM I TO UNDERSTAND THAT YOU ALSO ARE A MEMBER OF THE PAN-DEMONIUM CLUB?
CERTAINLY NOT. THE ENTIRE BUSINESS SEEMS SO DÉCLASSÉ.
BUT I DO UNDERSTAND THAT DE QUINCEY IS THE HEAD.

THE FIRST THING YOU MUST UNDERSTAND ABOUT DE QUINCEY IS THAT HE IS THE MOST DANGEROUS VAMPIRE IN LONDON. THE SECOND THING IS THAT DE QUINCEY IS OLD.

HE LIVED MOST OF HIS LIFE BEFORE THE ACCORDS, AND HE LOATHES THEM AND LOATHES LIVING BENEATH THE YOKE OF THE LAW. AND MOST OF ALL, HE HATES THE NEPHILIM.

HOW COULD ANYONE DESPISE US WHEN WE ARE SO CHARMING?

I AM SURE YOU KNOW THAT YOU ARE NOT LOVED BY MOST DOWN-WORLDERS.

HMMM. I CAN SEE THE FAMILY RESEMBLANCE.

TO NATHANIEL, TO YOUR BROTHER.

YOU'VE SEEN MY BROTHER?

I SAW HIM A FEW TIMES AT VARIOUS PANDEMONIUM CLUB OCCASIONS.

CHARLOTTE, DID YOU KNOW HE HOLDS PARTIES AT HIS TOWN HOUSE?

I'VE HEARD IT MENTIONED.

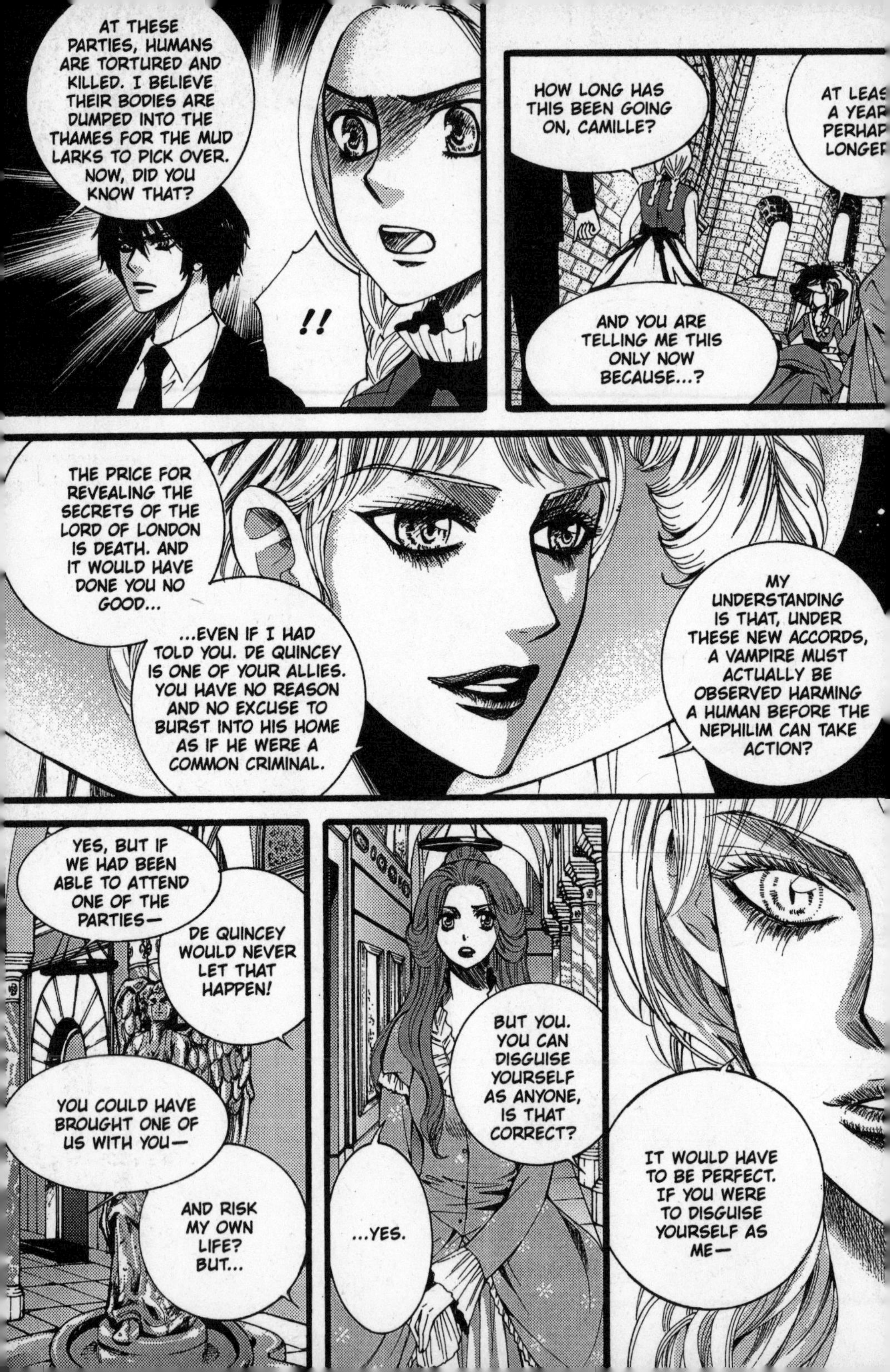
AT THESE PARTIES, HUMANS ARE TORTURED AND KILLED. I BELIEVE THEIR BODIES ARE DUMPED INTO THE THAMES FOR THE MUD LARKS TO PICK OVER. NOW, DID YOU KNOW THAT?
!!
HOW LONG HAS THIS BEEN GOING ON, CAMILLE?
AT LEAS A YEAR PERHAP LONGER
AND YOU ARE TELLING ME THIS ONLY NOW BECAUSE...?
THE PRICE FOR REVEALING THE SECRETS OF THE LORD OF LONDON IS DEATH. AND IT WOULD HAVE DONE YOU NO GOOD...
...EVEN IF I HAD TOLD YOU. DE QUINCEY IS ONE OF YOUR ALLIES. YOU HAVE NO REASON AND NO EXCUSE TO BURST INTO HIS HOME AS IF HE WERE A COMMON CRIMINAL.
MY UNDERSTANDING IS THAT, UNDER THESE NEW ACCORDS, A VAMPIRE MUST ACTUALLY BE OBSERVED HARMING A HUMAN BEFORE THE NEPHILIM CAN TAKE ACTION?
YES, BUT IF WE HAD BEEN ABLE TO ATTEND ONE OF THE PARTIES—
DE QUINCEY WOULD NEVER LET THAT HAPPEN!
YOU COULD HAVE BROUGHT ONE OF US WITH YOU—
AND RISK MY OWN LIFE? BUT...
BUT YOU. YOU CAN DISGUISE YOURSELF AS ANYONE, IS THAT CORRECT?
...YES.
IT WOULD HAVE TO BE PERFECT. IF YOU WERE TO DISGUISE YOURSELF AS ME—

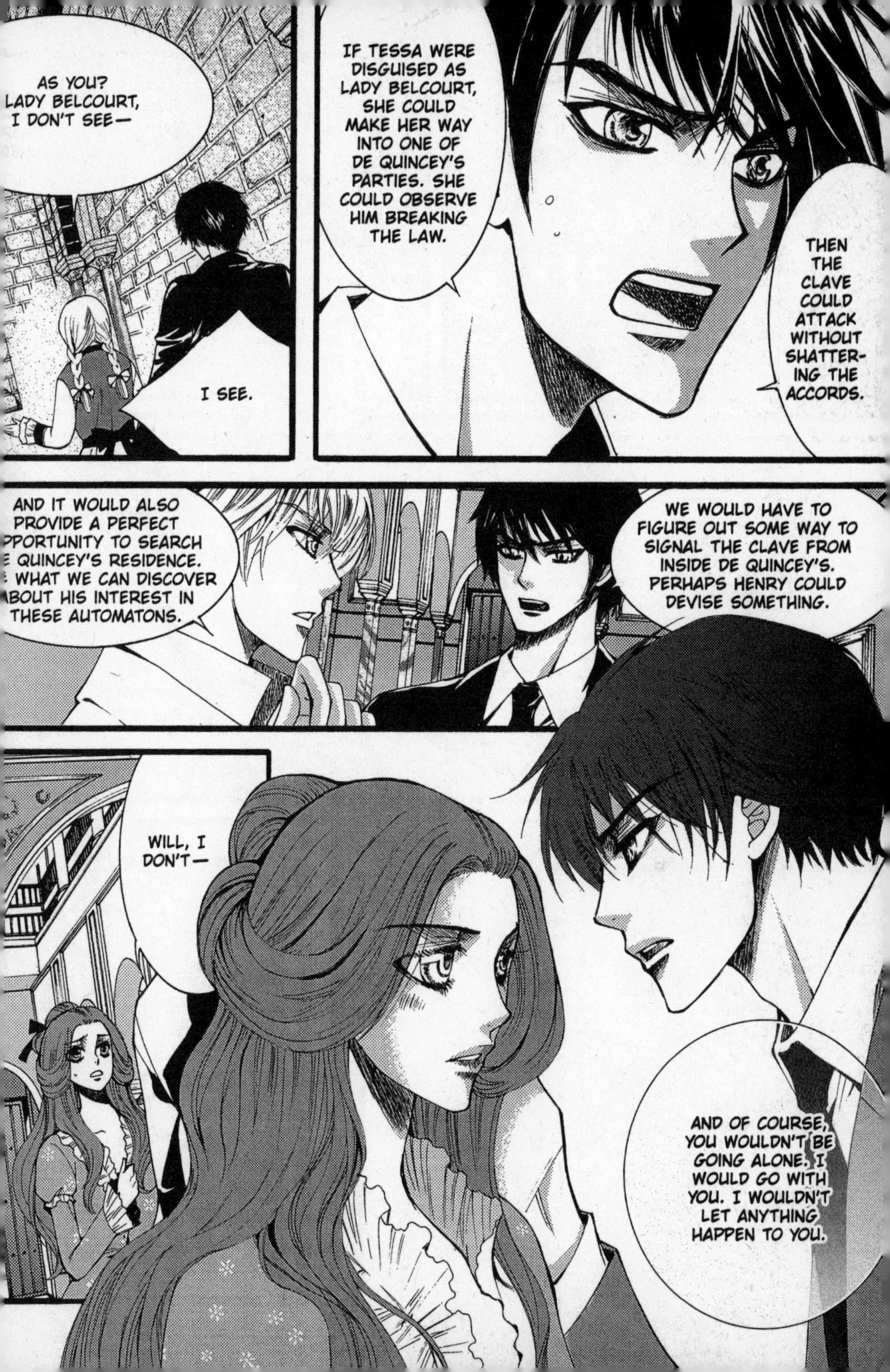
AS YOU? LADY BELCOURT, I DON'T SEE—
I SEE.
IF TESSA WERE DISGUISED AS LADY BELCOURT, SHE COULD MAKE HER WAY INTO ONE OF DE QUINCEY'S PARTIES. SHE COULD OBSERVE HIM BREAKING THE LAW.
THEN THE CLAVE COULD ATTACK WITHOUT SHATTERING THE ACCORDS.
AND IT WOULD ALSO PROVIDE A PERFECT PPORTUNITY TO SEARCH E QUINCEY'S RESIDENCE. E WHAT WE CAN DISCOVER ABOUT HIS INTEREST IN THESE AUTOMATONS.
WE WOULD HAVE TO FIGURE OUT SOME WAY TO SIGNAL THE CLAVE FROM INSIDE DE QUINCEY'S. PERHAPS HENRY COULD DEVISE SOMETHING.
WILL, I DON'T—
AND OF COURSE, YOU WOULDN'T BE GOING ALONE. I WOULD GO WITH YOU. I WOULDN'T LET ANYTHING HAPPEN TO YOU.

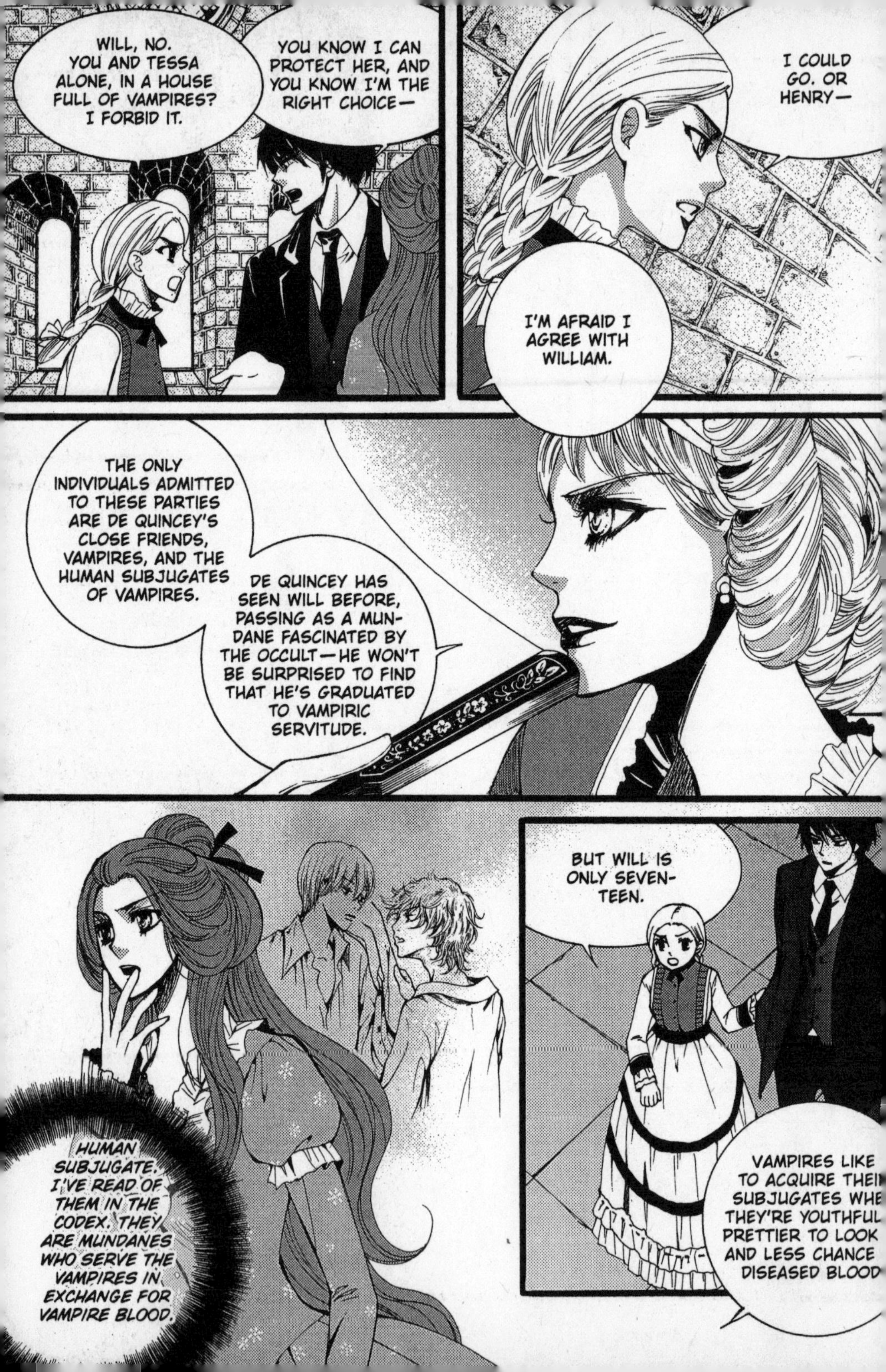
WILL, NO. YOU AND TESSA ALONE, IN A HOUSE FULL OF VAMPIRES? I FORBID IT.
YOU KNOW I CAN PROTECT HER, AND YOU KNOW I'M THE RIGHT CHOICE—
I COULD GO. OR HENRY—
I'M AFRAID I AGREE WITH WILLIAM.
THE ONLY INDIVIDUALS ADMITTED TO THESE PARTIES ARE DE QUINCEY'S CLOSE FRIENDS, VAMPIRES, AND THE HUMAN SUBJUGATES OF VAMPIRES.
DE QUINCEY HAS SEEN WILL BEFORE, PASSING AS A MUNDANE FASCINATED BY THE OCCULT—HE WON'T BE SURPRISED TO FIND THAT HE'S GRADUATED TO VAMPIRIC SERVITUDE.
HUMAN SUBJUGATE. I'VE READ OF THEM IN THE CODEX. THEY ARE MUNDANES WHO SERVE THE VAMPIRES IN EXCHANGE FOR VAMPIRE BLOOD.
BUT WILL IS ONLY SEVENTEEN.
VAMPIRES LIKE TO ACQUIRE THEI SUBJUGATES WHE THEY'RE YOUTHFUL PRETTIER TO LOOK AND LESS CHANCE DISEASED BLOOD

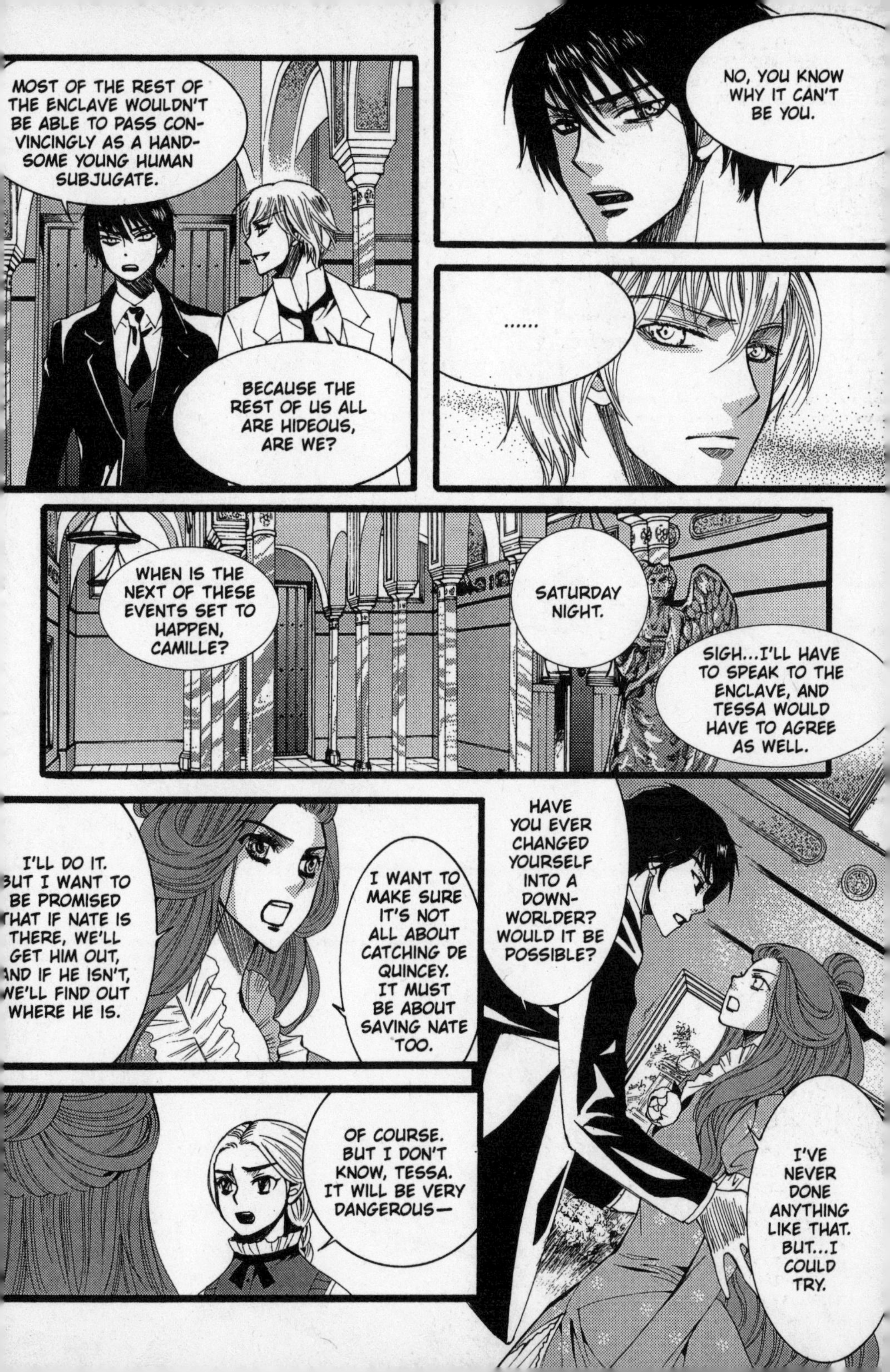
MOST OF THE REST OF THE ENCLAVE WOULDN'T BE ABLE TO PASS CON-VINCINGLY AS A HAND-SOME YOUNG HUMAN SUBJUGATE.
BECAUSE THE REST OF US ALL ARE HIDEOUS, ARE WE?
NO, YOU KNOW WHY IT CAN'T BE YOU.
......
WHEN IS THE NEXT OF THESE EVENTS SET TO HAPPEN, CAMILLE?
SATURDAY NIGHT.
SIGH...I'LL HAVE TO SPEAK TO THE ENCLAVE, AND TESSA WOULD HAVE TO AGREE AS WELL.
I'LL DO IT. BUT I WANT TO BE PROMISED THAT IF NATE IS THERE, WE'LL GET HIM OUT, AND IF HE ISN'T, WE'LL FIND OUT WHERE HE IS.
I WANT TO MAKE SURE IT'S NOT ALL ABOUT CATCHING DE QUINCEY. IT MUST BE ABOUT SAVING NATE TOO.
OF COURSE. BUT I DON'T KNOW, TESSA. IT WILL BE VERY DANGEROUS—
HAVE YOU EVER CHANGED YOURSELF INTO A DOWN-WORLDER? WOULD IT BE POSSIBLE?
I'VE NEVER DONE ANYTHING LIKE THAT. BUT...I COULD TRY.

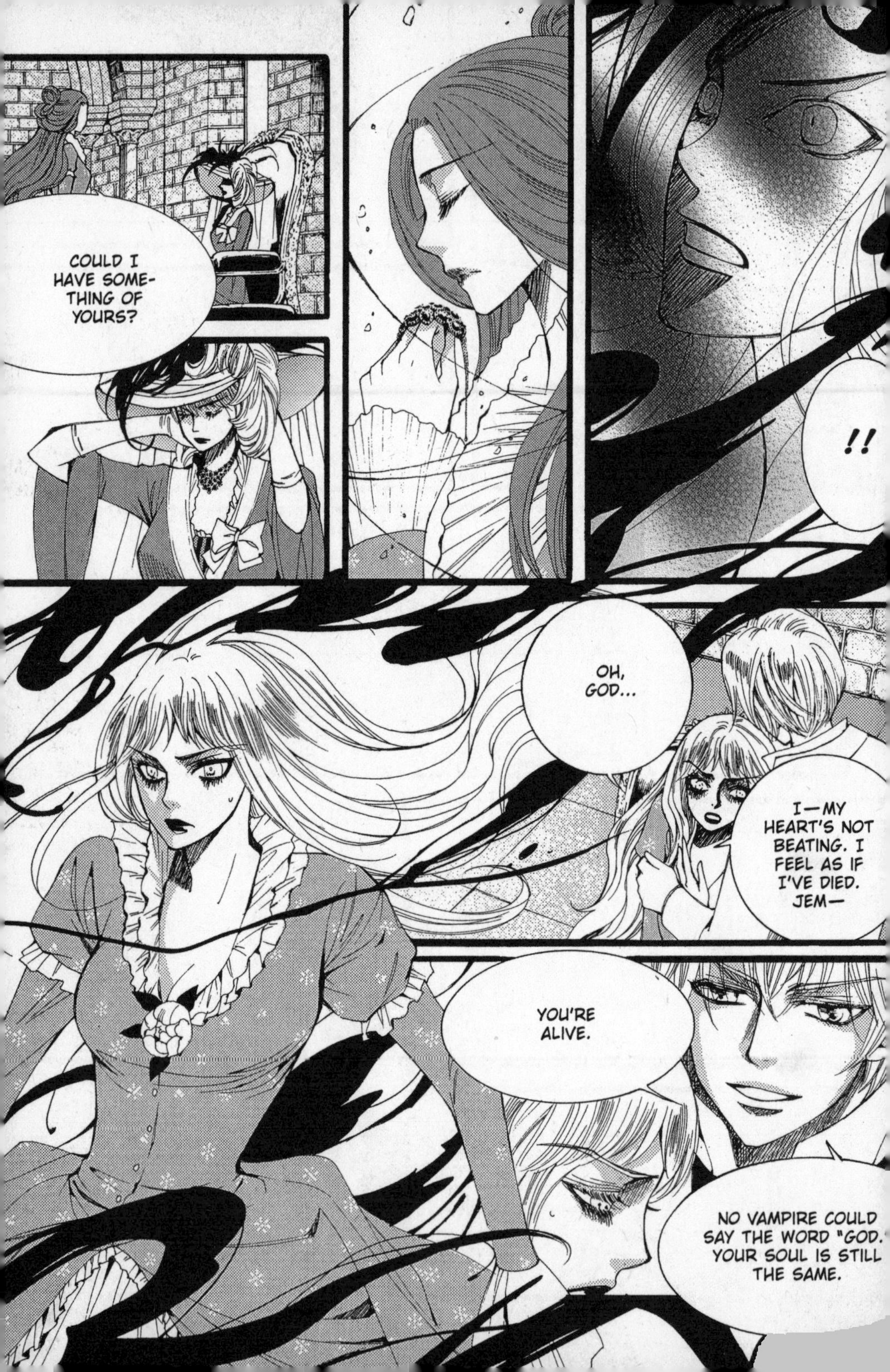
COULD I HAVE SOME-THING OF YOURS?
!!
OH, GOD...
I—MY HEART'S NOT BEATING. I FEEL AS IF I'VE DIED. JEM—
YOU'RE ALIVE.
NO VAMPIRE COULD SAY THE WORD "GOD. YOUR SOUL IS STILL THE SAME.

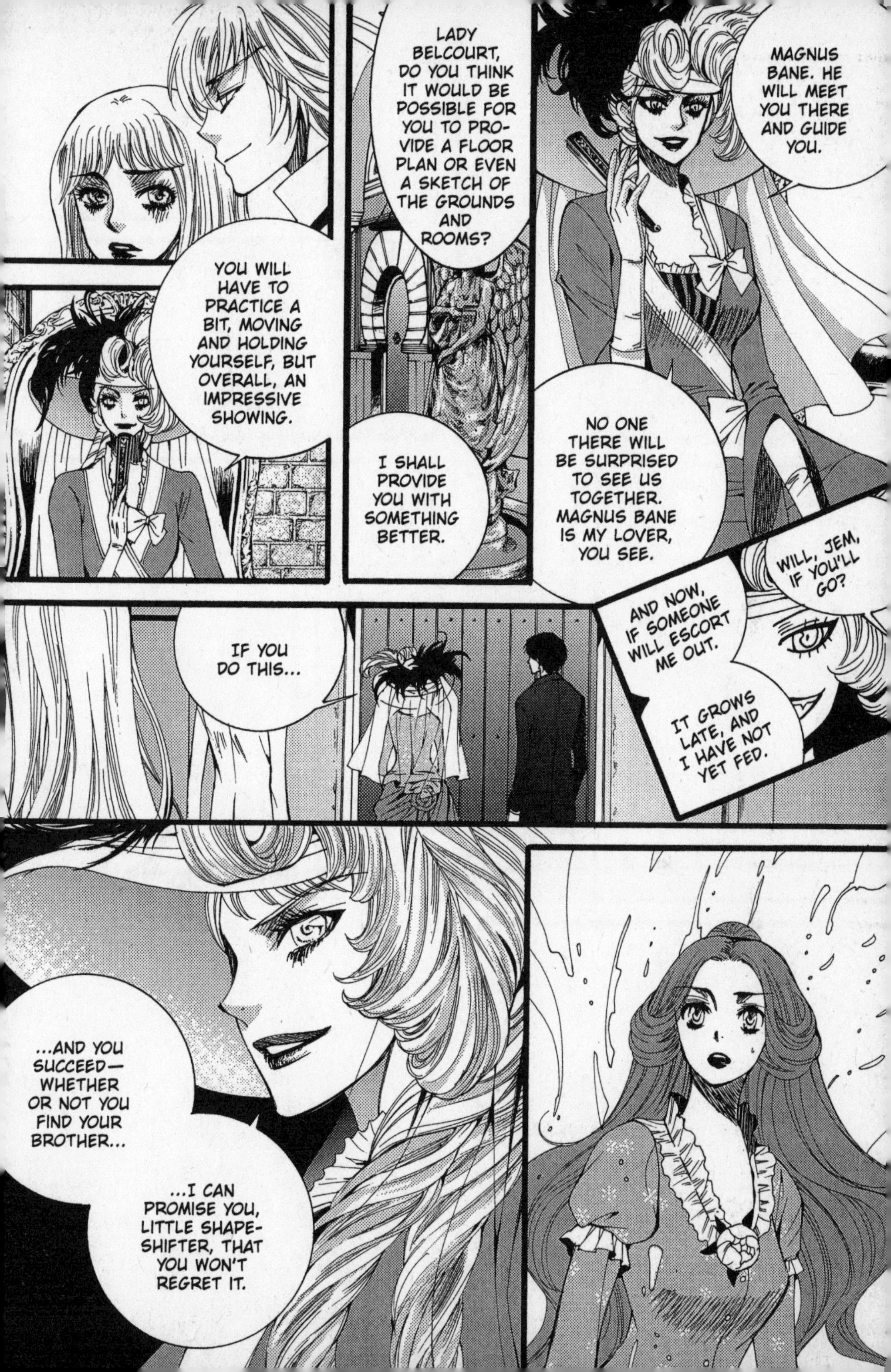
LADY BELCOURT, DO YOU THINK IT WOULD BE POSSIBLE FOR YOU TO PROVIDE A FLOOR PLAN OR EVEN A SKETCH OF THE GROUNDS AND ROOMS?
MAGNUS BANE. HE WILL MEET YOU THERE AND GUIDE YOU.
YOU WILL HAVE TO PRACTICE A BIT, MOVING AND HOLDING YOURSELF, BUT OVERALL, AN IMPRESSIVE SHOWING.
I SHALL PROVIDE YOU WITH SOMETHING BETTER.
NO ONE THERE WILL BE SURPRISED TO SEE US TOGETHER. MAGNUS BANE IS MY LOVER, YOU SEE.
IF YOU DO THIS...
AND NOW, IF SOMEONE WILL ESCORT ME OUT.
WILL, JEM, IF YOU'LL GO?
IT GROWS LATE, AND I HAVE NOT YET FED.
...AND YOU SUCCEED—WHETHER OR NOT YOU FIND YOUR BROTHER...
...I CAN PROMISE YOU, LITTLE SHAPE-SHIFTER, THAT YOU WON'T REGRET IT.

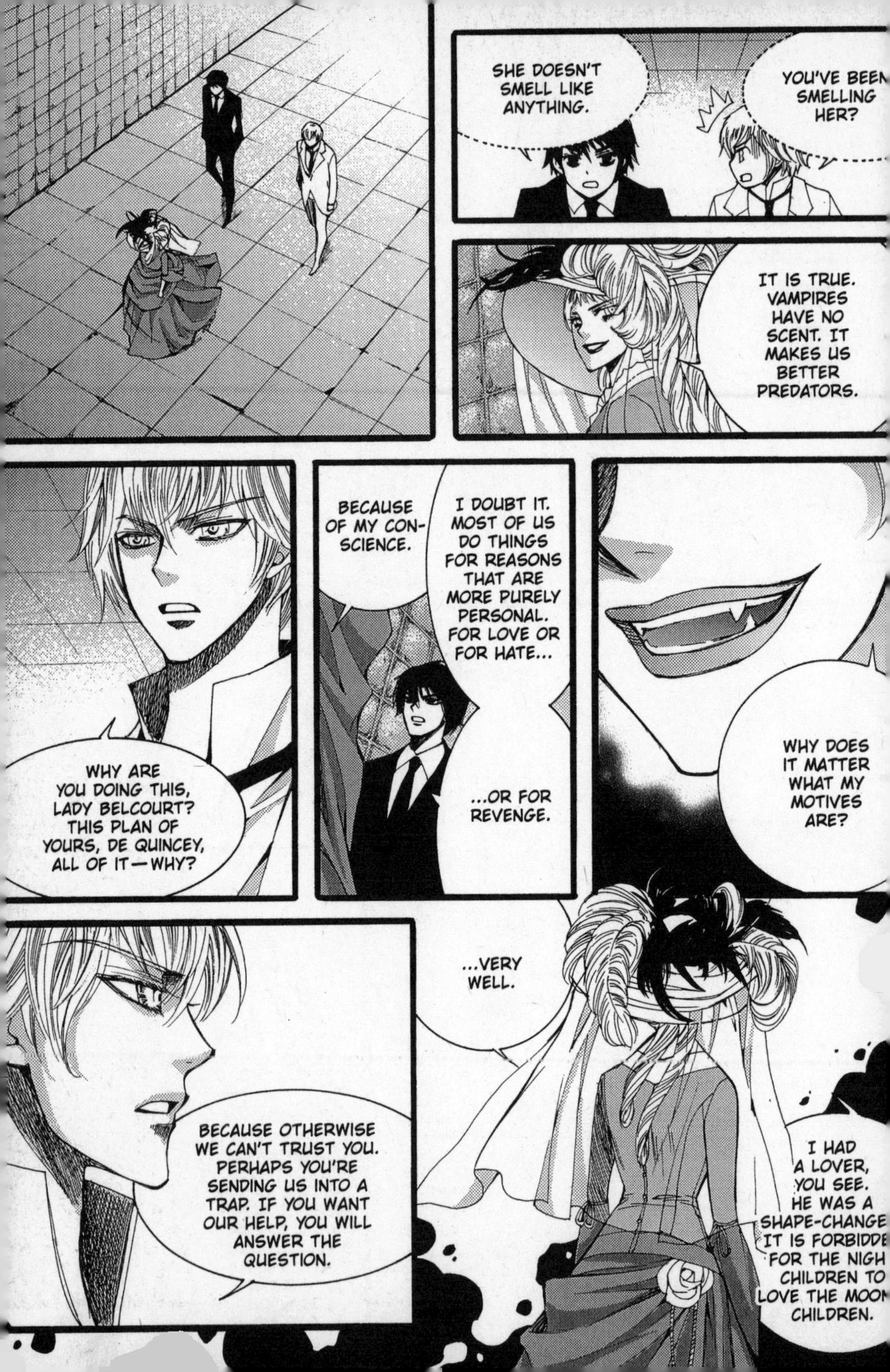

SHE DOESN'T SMELL LIKE ANYTHING.
YOU'VE BEEN SMELLING HER?
IT IS TRUE. VAMPIRES HAVE NO SCENT. IT MAKES US BETTER PREDATORS.
WHY ARE YOU DOING THIS, LADY BELCOURT? THIS PLAN OF YOURS, DE QUINCEY, ALL OF IT—WHY?
BECAUSE OF MY CON-SCIENCE.
I DOUBT IT. MOST OF US DO THINGS FOR REASONS THAT ARE MORE PURELY PERSONAL. FOR LOVE OR FOR HATE...
...OR FOR REVENGE.
WHY DOES IT MATTER WHAT MY MOTIVES ARE?
BECAUSE OTHERWISE WE CAN'T TRUST YOU. PERHAPS YOU'RE SENDING US INTO A TRAP. IF YOU WANT OUR HELP, YOU WILL ANSWER THE QUESTION.
...VERY WELL.
I HAD A LOVER, YOU SEE. HE WAS A SHAPE-CHANGE IT IS FORBIDDE FOR THE NIGH CHILDREN TO LOVE THE MOON CHILDREN.

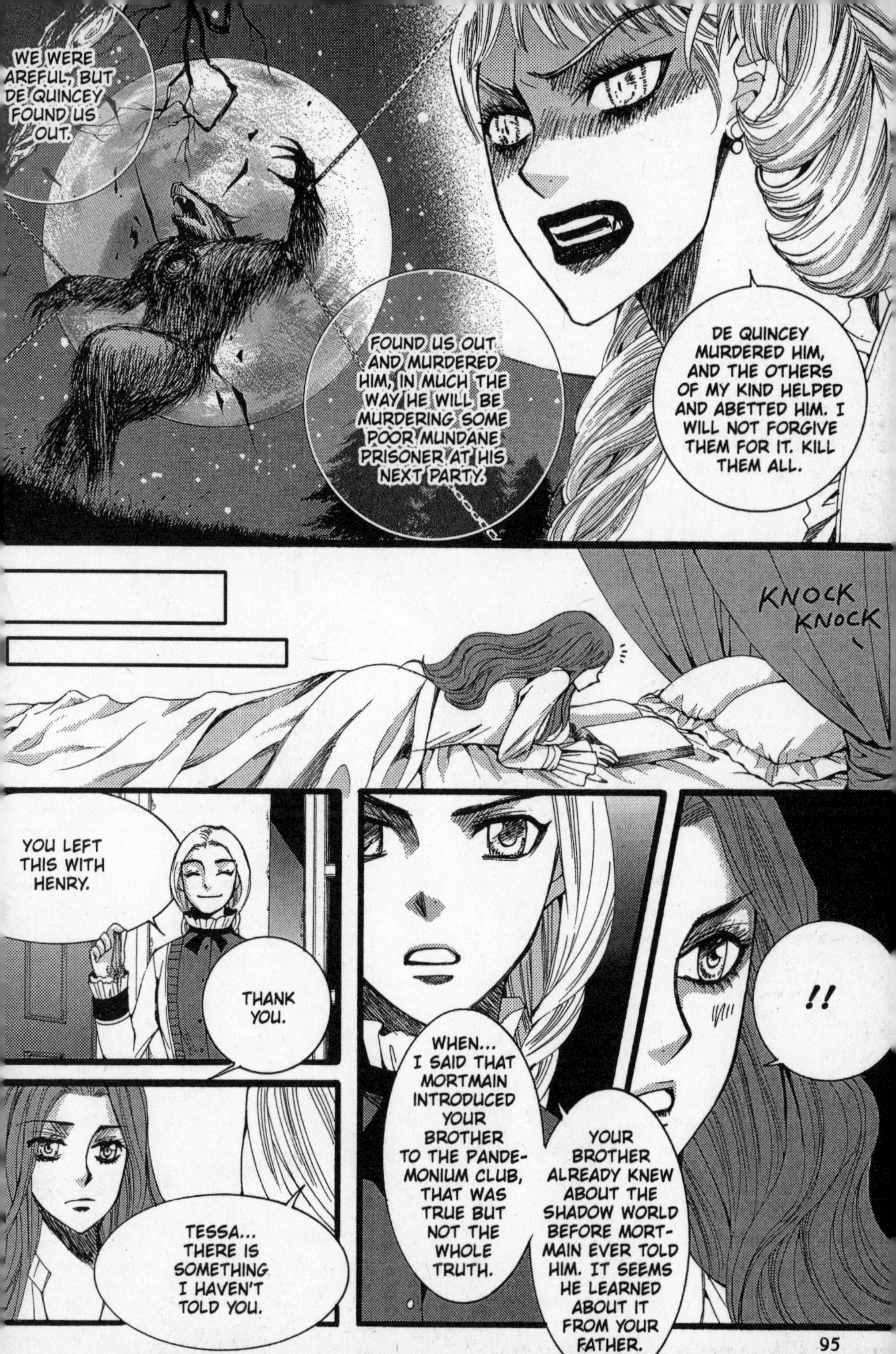
WE WERE AREFUL, BUT DE QUINCEY FOUND US OUT.
FOUND US OUT AND MURDERED HIM, IN MUCH THE WAY HE WILL BE MURDERING SOME POOR MUNDANE PRISONER AT HIS NEXT PARTY.
DE QUINCEY MURDERED HIM, AND THE OTHERS OF MY KIND HELPED AND ABETTED HIM. I WILL NOT FORGIVE THEM FOR IT. KILL THEM ALL.
KNOCK KNOCK
YOU LEFT THIS WITH HENRY.
THANK YOU.
TESSA... THERE IS SOMETHING I HAVEN'T TOLD YOU.
WHEN... I SAID THAT MORTMAIN INTRODUCED YOUR BROTHER TO THE PANDE-MONIUM CLUB, THAT WAS TRUE BUT NOT THE WHOLE TRUTH.
YOUR BROTHER ALREADY KNEW ABOUT THE SHADOW WORLD BEFORE MORT-MAIN EVER TOLD HIM. IT SEEMS HE LEARNED ABOUT IT FROM YOUR FATHER.
!!

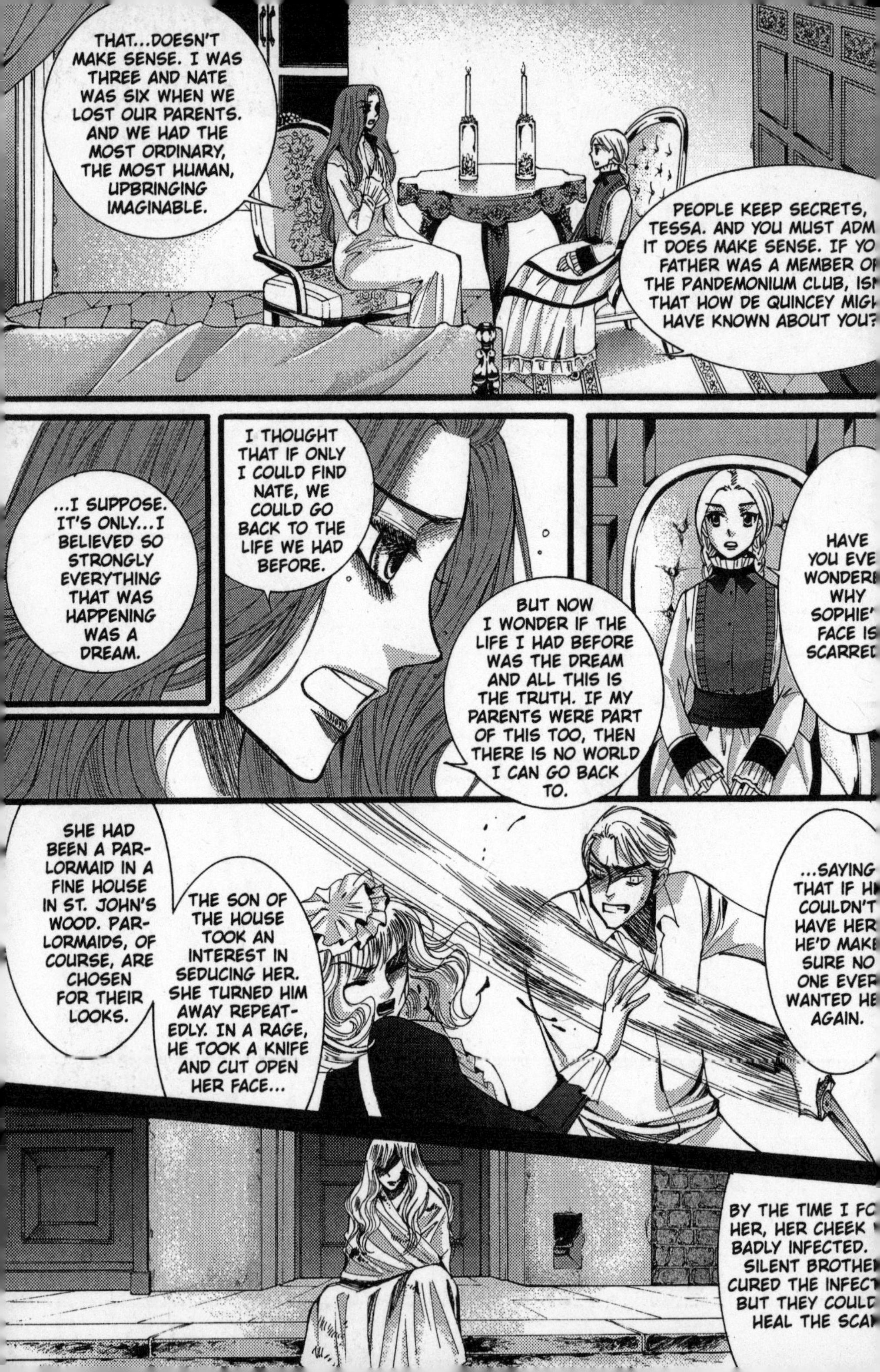

THAT...DOESN'T MAKE SENSE. I WAS THREE AND NATE WAS SIX WHEN WE LOST OUR PARENTS. AND WE HAD THE MOST ORDINARY, THE MOST HUMAN, UPBRINGING IMAGINABLE.
PEOPLE KEEP SECRETS, TESSA. AND YOU MUST ADM IT DOES MAKE SENSE. IF YO FATHER WAS A MEMBER OF THE PANDEMONIUM CLUB, ISN THAT HOW DE QUINCEY MIGH HAVE KNOWN ABOUT YOU?
...I SUPPOSE. IT'S ONLY...I BELIEVED SO STRONGLY EVERYTHING THAT WAS HAPPENING WAS A DREAM.
I THOUGHT THAT IF ONLY I COULD FIND NATE, WE COULD GO BACK TO THE LIFE WE HAD BEFORE.
BUT NOW I WONDER IF THE LIFE I HAD BEFORE WAS THE DREAM AND ALL THIS IS THE TRUTH. IF MY PARENTS WERE PART OF THIS TOO, THEN THERE IS NO WORLD I CAN GO BACK TO.
HAVE YOU EVE WONDERI WHY SOPHIE' FACE IS SCARRED
SHE HAD BEEN A PARLORMAID IN A FINE HOUSE IN ST. JOHN'S WOOD. PARLORMAIDS, OF COURSE, ARE CHOSEN FOR THEIR LOOKS.
THE SON OF THE HOUSE TOOK AN INTEREST IN SEDUCING HER. SHE TURNED HIM AWAY REPEATEDLY. IN A RAGE, HE TOOK A KNIFE AND CUT OPEN HER FACE...
...SAYING THAT IF HI COULDN'T HAVE HER HE'D MAKE SURE NO ONE EVER WANTED HE AGAIN.
BY THE TIME I FO HER, HER CHEEK BADLY INFECTED. SILENT BROTHE CURED THE INFECT BUT THEY COULD HEAL THE SCA

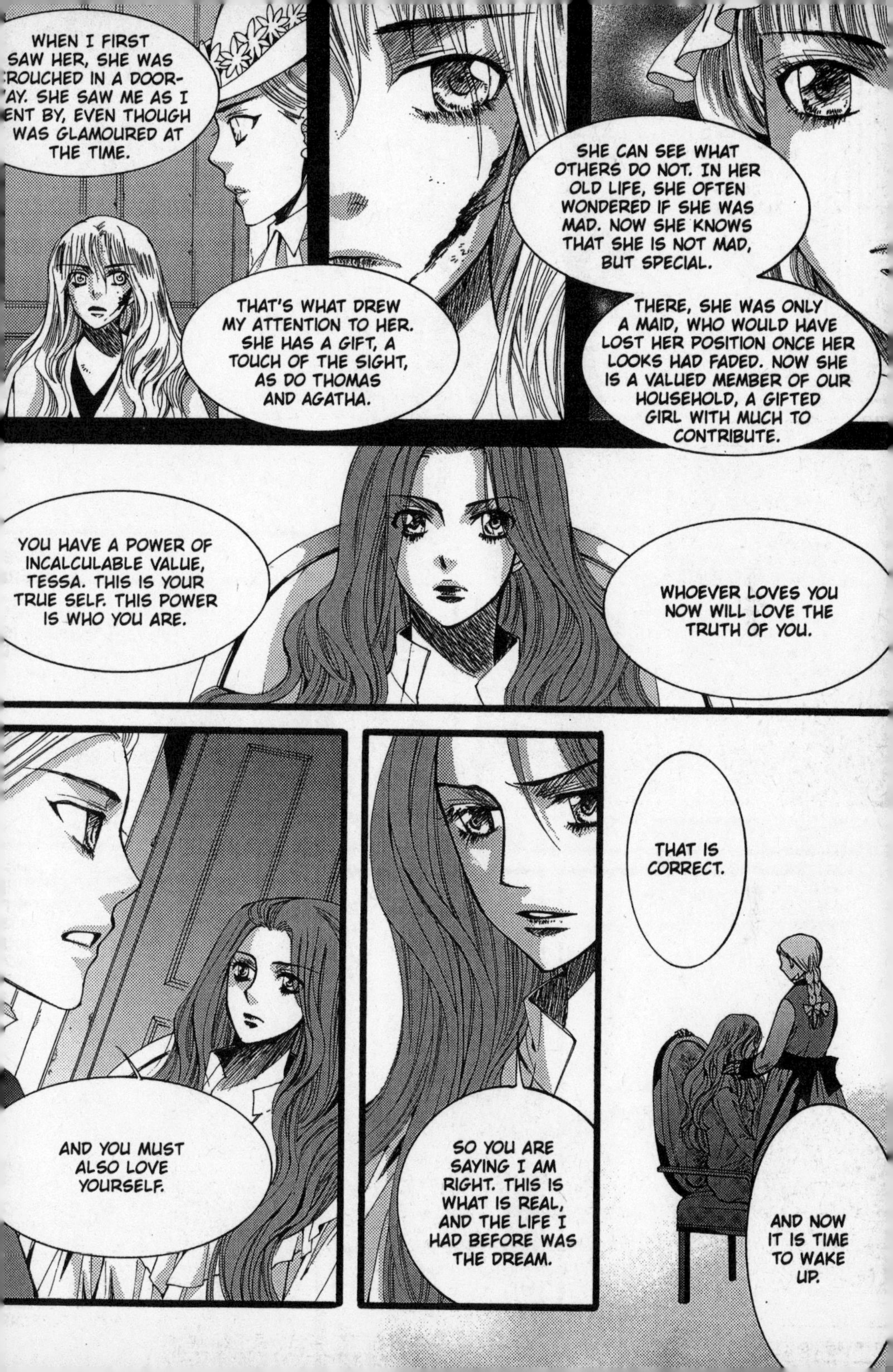

WHEN I FIRST SAW HER, SHE WAS ROUCHED IN A DOOR-AY. SHE SAW ME AS I ENT BY, EVEN THOUGH WAS GLAMOURED AT THE TIME.
THAT'S WHAT DREW MY ATTENTION TO HER. SHE HAS A GIFT, A TOUCH OF THE SIGHT, AS DO THOMAS AND AGATHA.
SHE CAN SEE WHAT OTHERS DO NOT. IN HER OLD LIFE, SHE OFTEN WONDERED IF SHE WAS MAD. NOW SHE KNOWS THAT SHE IS NOT MAD, BUT SPECIAL.
THERE, SHE WAS ONLY A MAID, WHO WOULD HAVE LOST HER POSITION ONCE HER LOOKS HAD FADED. NOW SHE IS A VALUED MEMBER OF OUR HOUSEHOLD, A GIFTED GIRL WITH MUCH TO CONTRIBUTE.
YOU HAVE A POWER OF INCALCULABLE VALUE, TESSA. THIS IS YOUR TRUE SELF. THIS POWER IS WHO YOU ARE.
WHOEVER LOVES YOU NOW WILL LOVE THE TRUTH OF YOU.
AND YOU MUST ALSO LOVE YOURSELF.
SO YOU ARE SAYING I AM RIGHT. THIS IS WHAT IS REAL, AND THE LIFE I HAD BEFORE WAS THE DREAM.
THAT IS CORRECT.
AND NOW IT IS TIME TO WAKE UP.

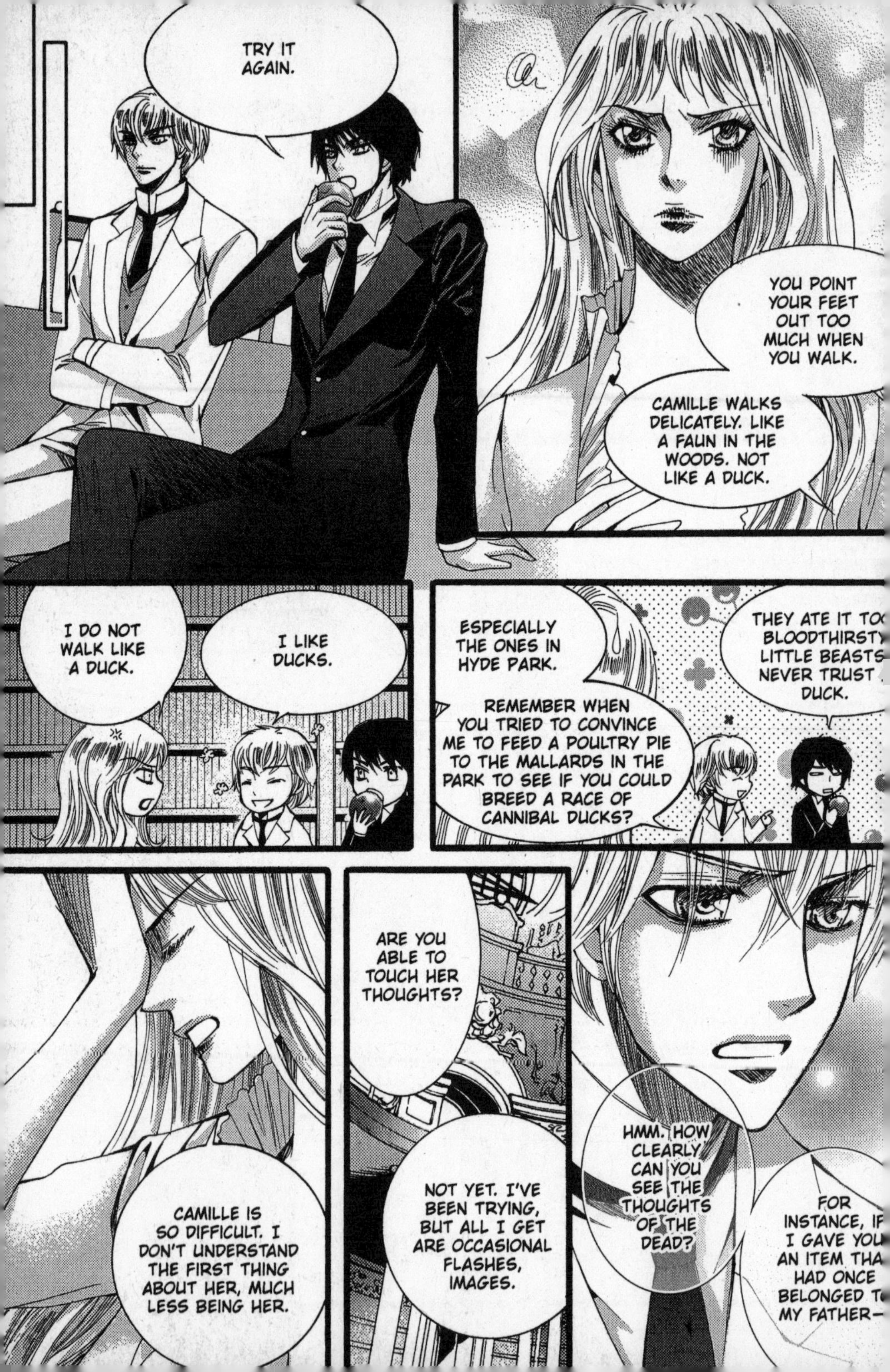
TRY IT AGAIN.
YOU POINT YOUR FEET OUT TOO MUCH WHEN YOU WALK.
CAMILLE WALKS DELICATELY. LIKE A FAUN IN THE WOODS. NOT LIKE A DUCK.
I DO NOT WALK LIKE A DUCK.
I LIKE DUCKS.
ESPECIALLY THE ONES IN HYDE PARK.
REMEMBER WHEN YOU TRIED TO CONVINCE ME TO FEED A POULTRY PIE TO THE MALLARDS IN THE PARK TO SEE IF YOU COULD BREED A RACE OF CANNIBAL DUCKS?
THEY ATE IT TO BLOODTHIRSTY LITTLE BEASTS NEVER TRUST DUCK.
CAMILLE IS SO DIFFICULT. I DON'T UNDERSTAND THE FIRST THING ABOUT HER, MUCH LESS BEING HER.
ARE YOU ABLE TO TOUCH HER THOUGHTS?
NOT YET. I'VE BEEN TRYING, BUT ALL I GET ARE OCCASIONAL FLASHES, IMAGES.
HMM. HOW CLEARLY CAN YOU SEE THE THOUGHTS OF THE DEAD?
FOR INSTANCE, IF I GAVE YOU AN ITEM THA HAD ONCE BELONGED T MY FATHER—

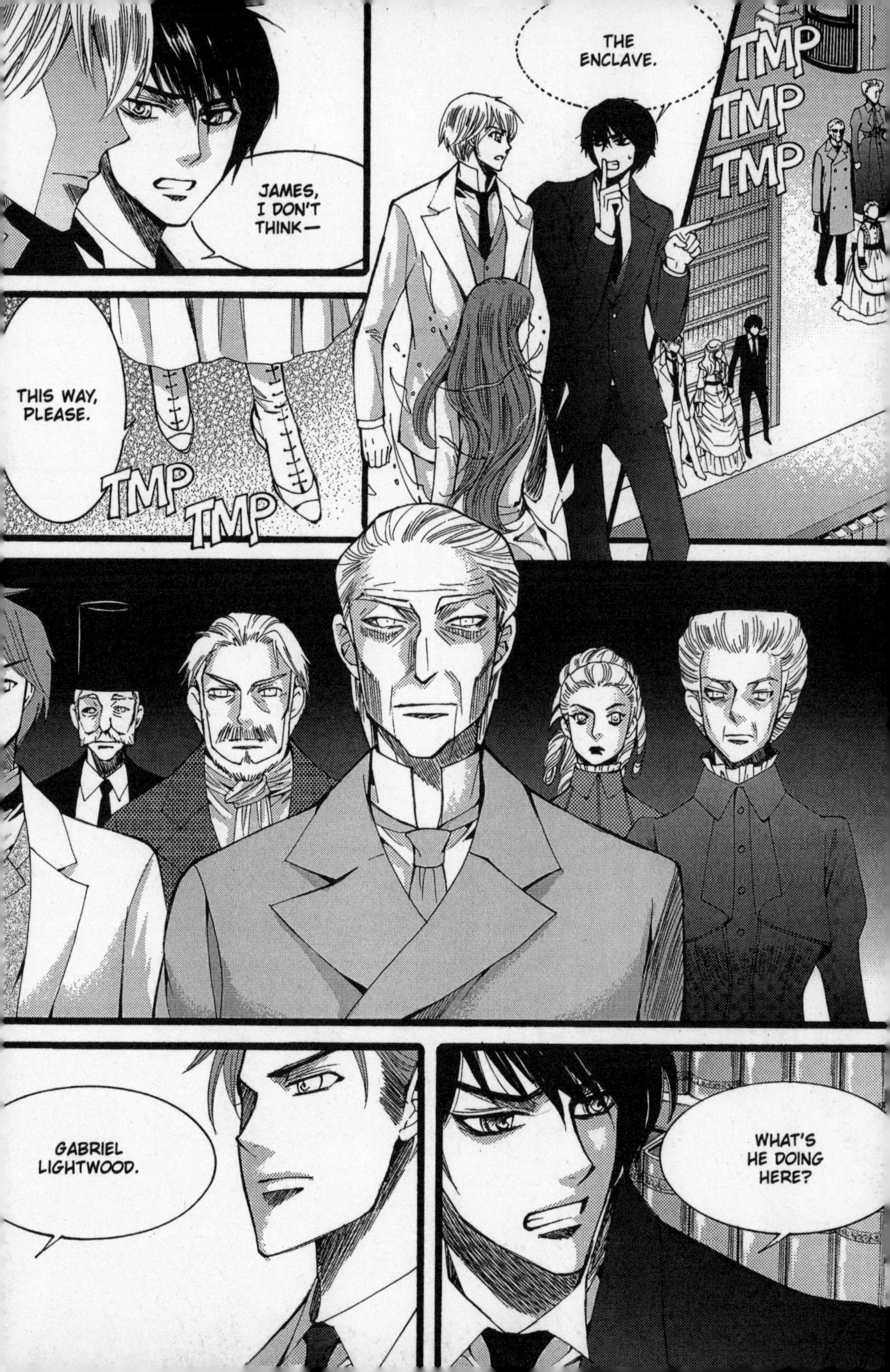
JAMES, I DON'T THINK—
THE ENCLAVE.
TMP TMP TMP
THIS WAY, PLEASE.
TMP TMP
GABRIEL LIGHTWOOD.
WHAT'S HE DOING HERE?

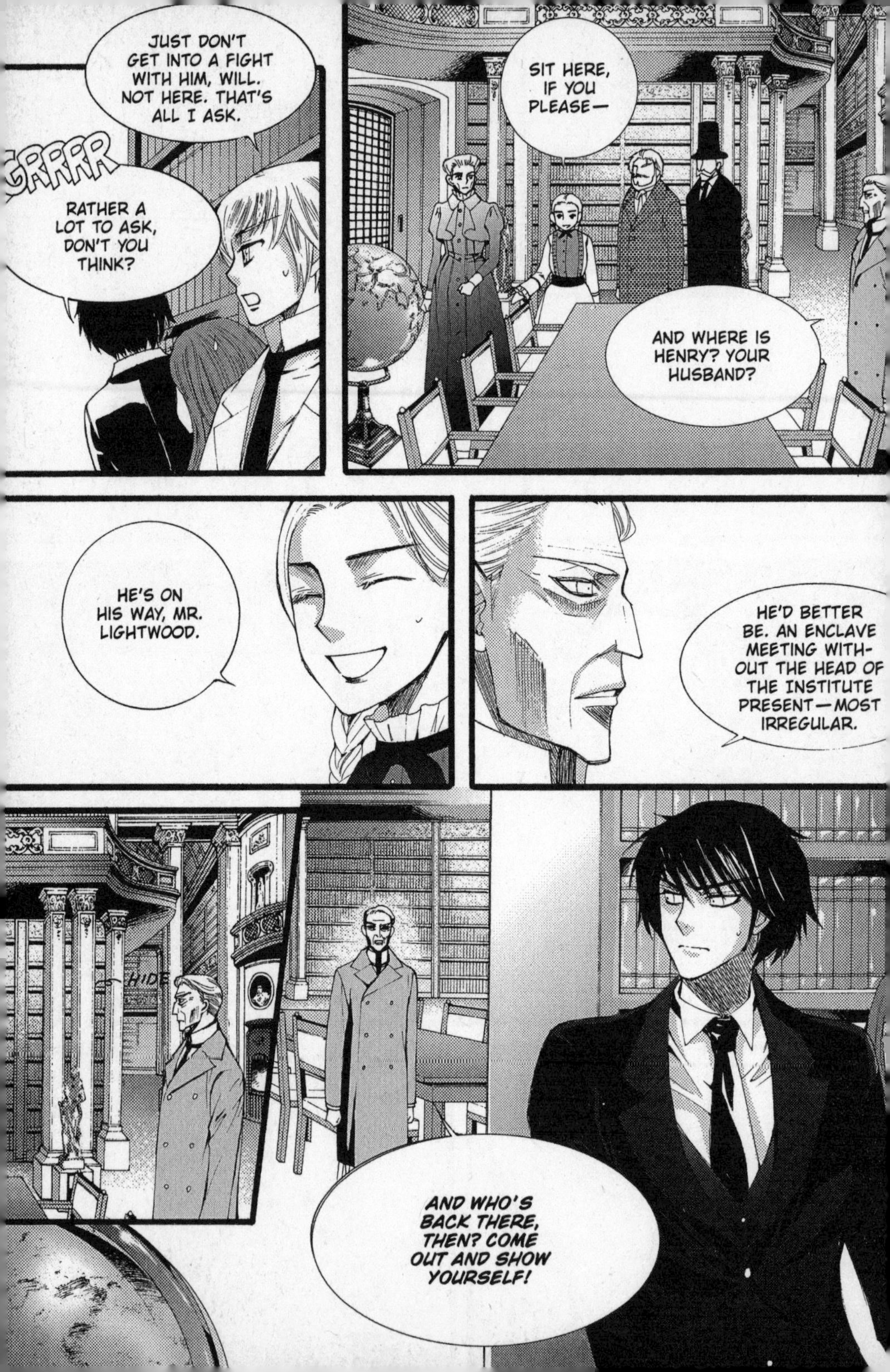
JUST DON'T GET INTO A FIGHT WITH HIM, WILL. NOT HERE. THAT'S ALL I ASK.
GRRRR
RATHER A LOT TO ASK, DON'T YOU THINK?
SIT HERE, IF YOU PLEASE—
AND WHERE IS HENRY? YOUR HUSBAND?
HE'S ON HIS WAY, MR. LIGHTWOOD.
HE'D BETTER BE. AN ENCLAVE MEETING WITH-OUT THE HEAD OF THE INSTITUTE PRESENT—MOST IRREGULAR.
HIDE
AND WHO'S BACK THERE, THEN? COME OUT AND SHOW YOURSELF!

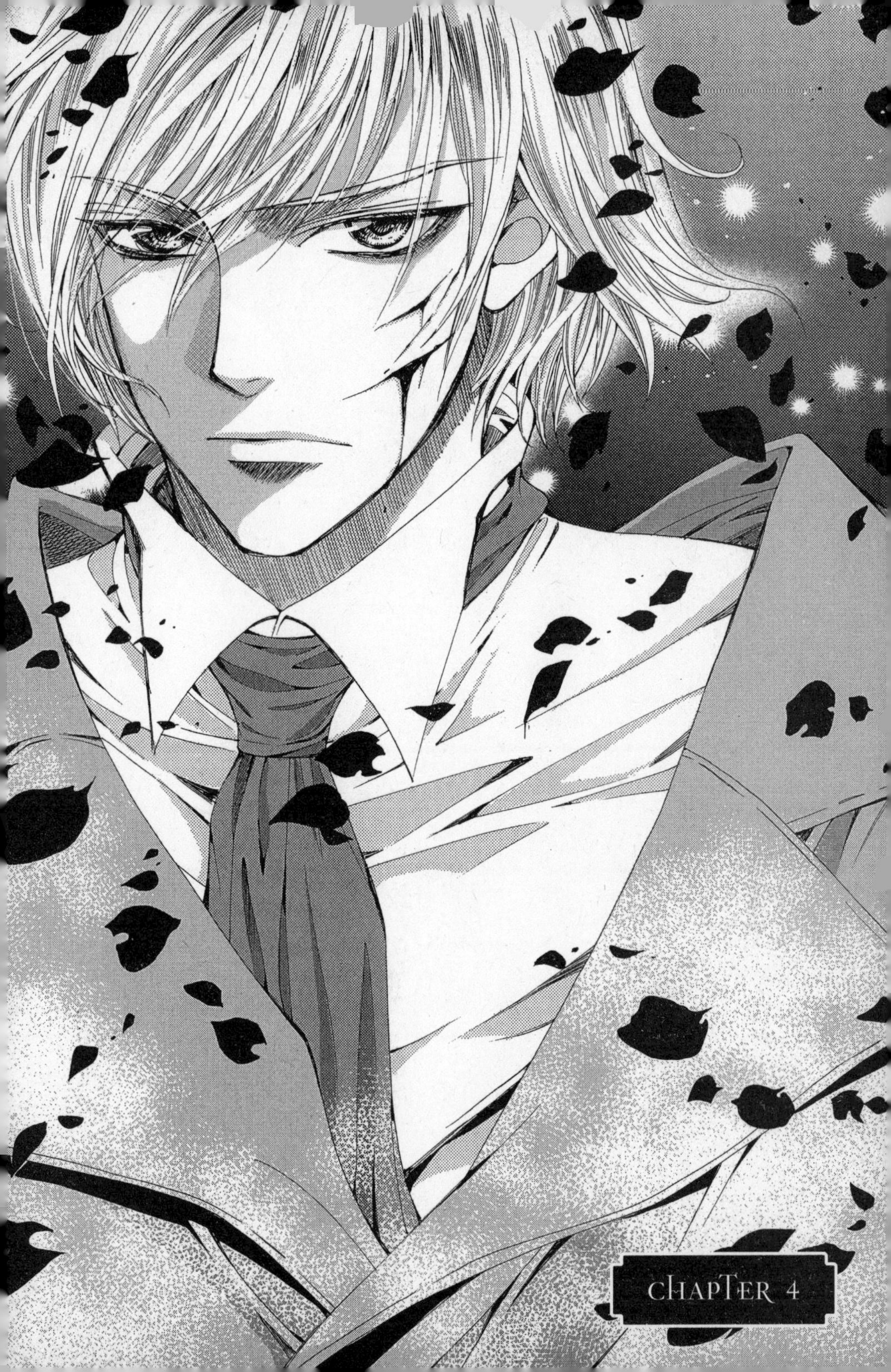
CHAPTER 4

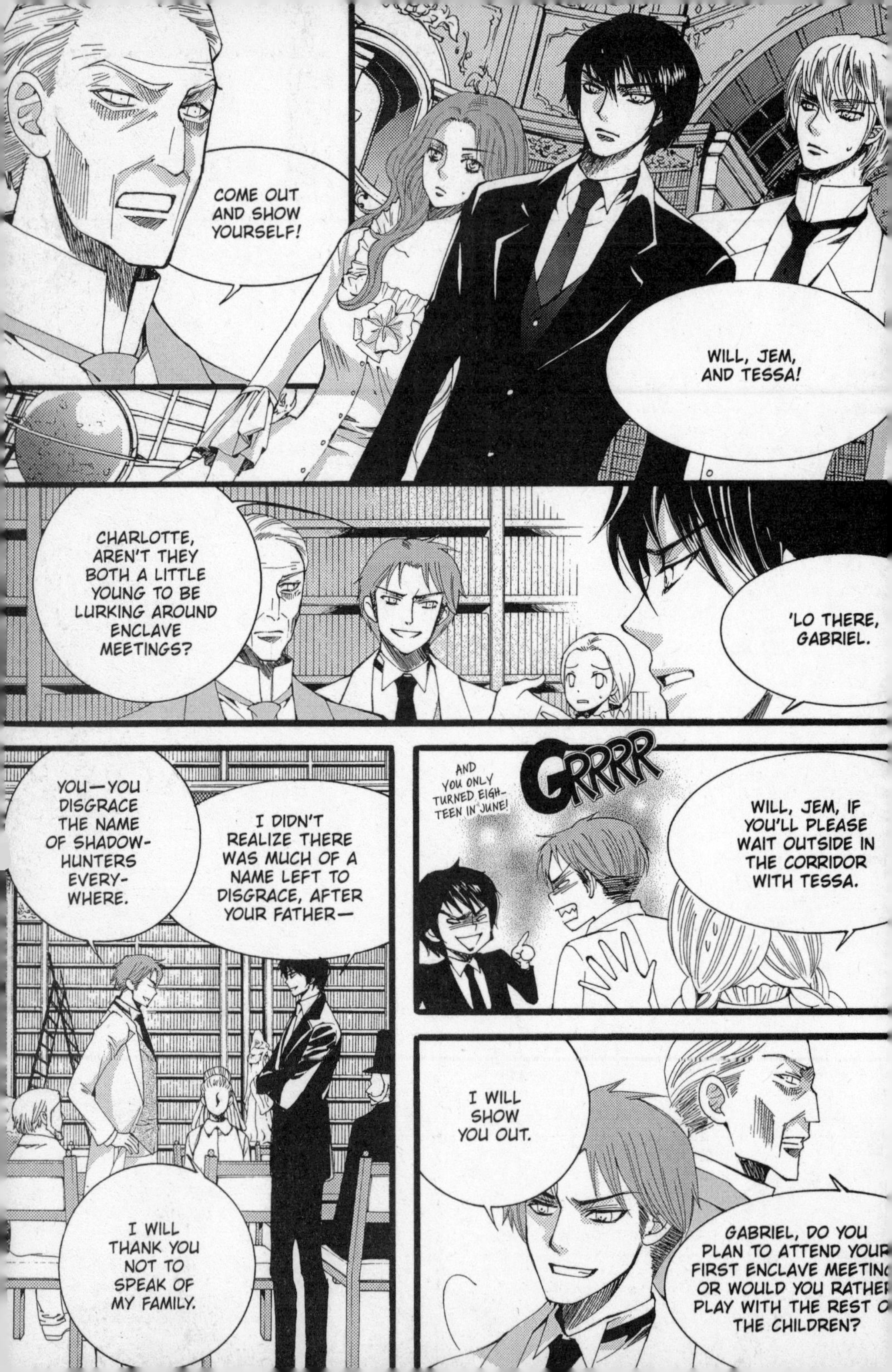
COME OUT AND SHOW YOURSELF!
WILL, JEM, AND TESSA!
CHARLOTTE, AREN'T THEY BOTH A LITTLE YOUNG TO BE LURKING AROUND ENCLAVE MEETINGS?
'LO THERE, GABRIEL.
YOU—YOU DISGRACE THE NAME OF SHADOW-HUNTERS EVERY-WHERE.
I DIDN'T REALIZE THERE WAS MUCH OF A NAME LEFT TO DISGRACE, AFTER YOUR FATHER—
I WILL THANK YOU NOT TO SPEAK OF MY FAMILY.
AND YOU ONLY TURNED EIGH-TEEN IN JUNE!
GRRRR
WILL, JEM, IF YOU'LL PLEASE WAIT OUTSIDE IN THE CORRIDOR WITH TESSA.
I WILL SHOW YOU OUT.
GABRIEL, DO YOU PLAN TO ATTEND YOUR FIRST ENCLAVE MEETIN OR WOULD YOU RATHE PLAY WITH THE REST O THE CHILDREN?

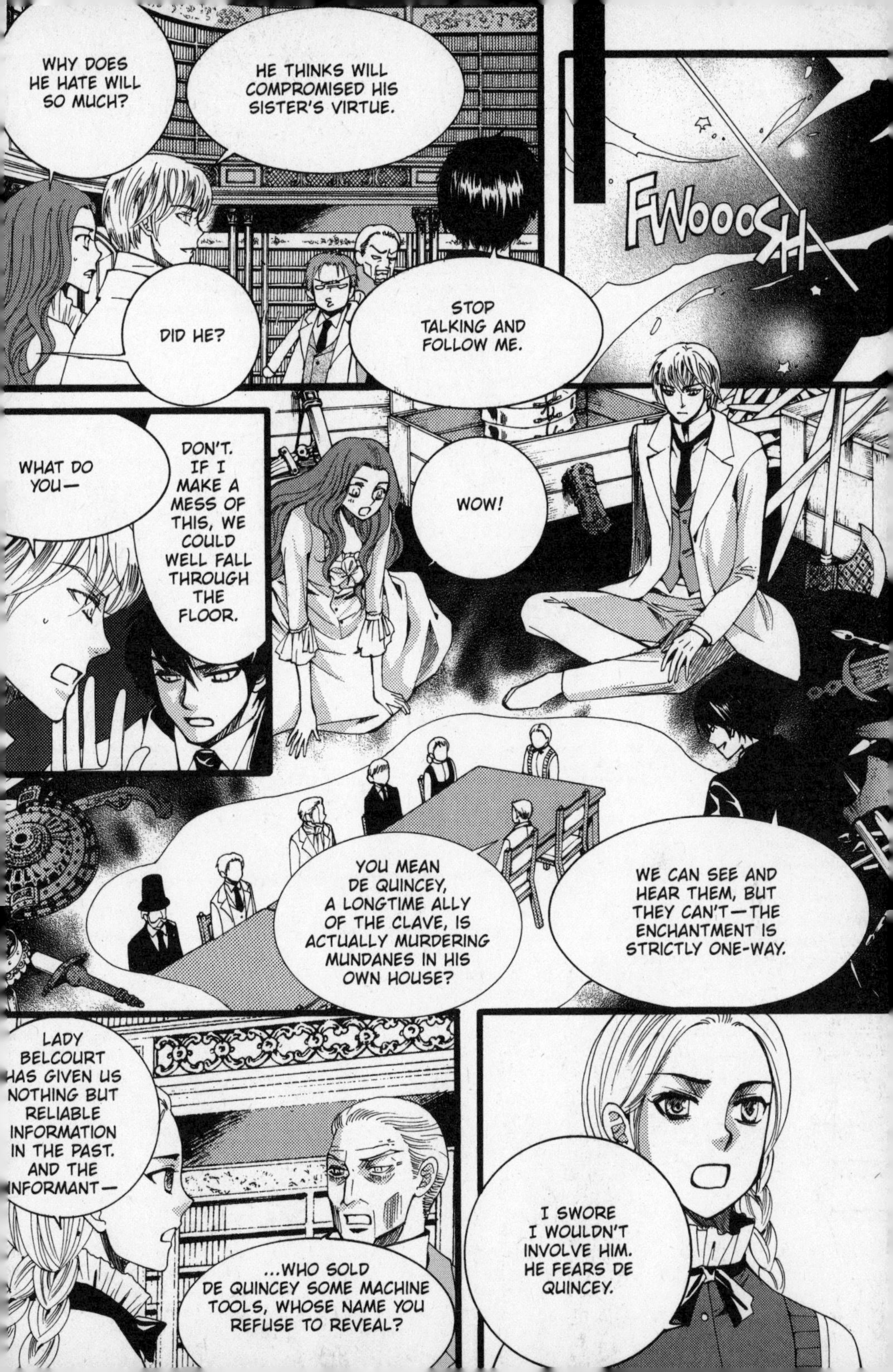
WHY DOES HE HATE WILL SO MUCH?
HE THINKS WILL COMPROMISED HIS SISTER'S VIRTUE.
DID HE?
STOP TALKING AND FOLLOW ME.
FWOOOSH
WHAT DO YOU—
DON'T. IF I MAKE A MESS OF THIS, WE COULD WELL FALL THROUGH THE FLOOR.
WOW!
YOU MEAN DE QUINCEY, A LONGTIME ALLY OF THE CLAVE, IS ACTUALLY MURDERING MUNDANES IN HIS OWN HOUSE?
WE CAN SEE AND HEAR THEM, BUT THEY CAN'T—THE ENCHANTMENT IS STRICTLY ONE-WAY.
LADY BELCOURT HAS GIVEN US NOTHING BUT RELIABLE INFORMATION IN THE PAST. AND THE INFORMANT—
...WHO SOLD DE QUINCEY SOME MACHINE TOOLS, WHOSE NAME YOU REFUSE TO REVEAL?
I SWORE I WOULDN'T INVOLVE HIM. HE FEARS DE QUINCEY.

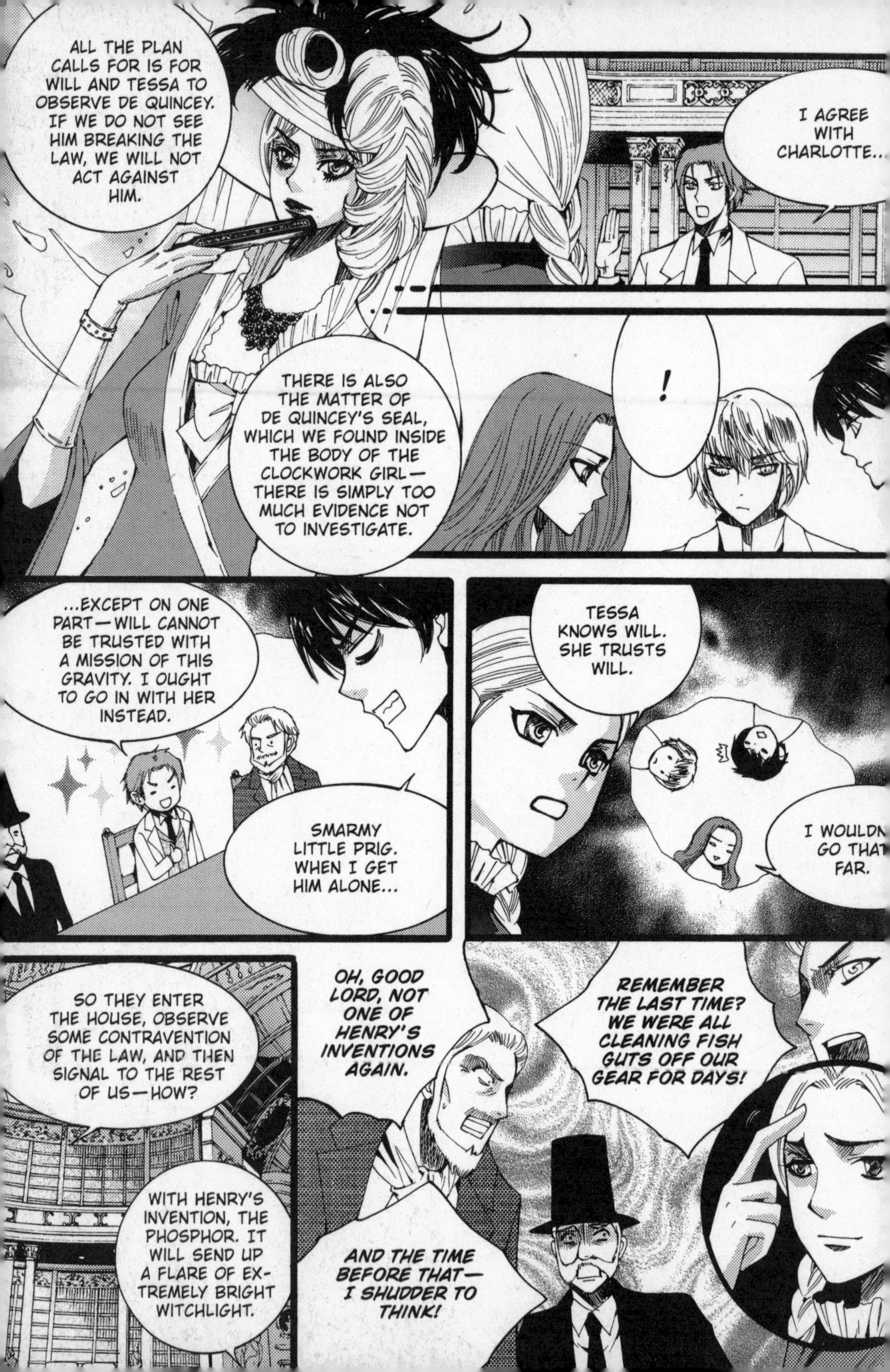
ALL THE PLAN CALLS FOR IS FOR WILL AND TESSA TO OBSERVE DE QUINCEY. IF WE DO NOT SEE HIM BREAKING THE LAW, WE WILL NOT ACT AGAINST HIM.
I AGREE WITH CHARLOTTE...
THERE IS ALSO THE MATTER OF DE QUINCEY'S SEAL, WHICH WE FOUND INSIDE THE BODY OF THE CLOCKWORK GIRL—THERE IS SIMPLY TOO MUCH EVIDENCE NOT TO INVESTIGATE.
!
...EXCEPT ON ONE PART—WILL CANNOT BE TRUSTED WITH A MISSION OF THIS GRAVITY. I OUGHT TO GO IN WITH HER INSTEAD.
SMARMY LITTLE PRIG. WHEN I GET HIM ALONE...
TESSA KNOWS WILL. SHE TRUSTS WILL.
I WOULDN GO THAT FAR.
SO THEY ENTER THE HOUSE, OBSERVE SOME CONTRAVENTION OF THE LAW, AND THEN SIGNAL TO THE REST OF US—HOW?
WITH HENRY'S INVENTION, THE PHOSPHOR. IT WILL SEND UP A FLARE OF EXTREMELY BRIGHT WITCHLIGHT.
OH, GOOD LORD, NOT ONE OF HENRY'S INVENTIONS AGAIN.
REMEMBER THE LAST TIME? WE WERE ALL CLEANING FISH GUTS OFF OUR GEAR FOR DAYS!
AND THE TIME BEFORE THAT—I SHUDDER TO THINK!

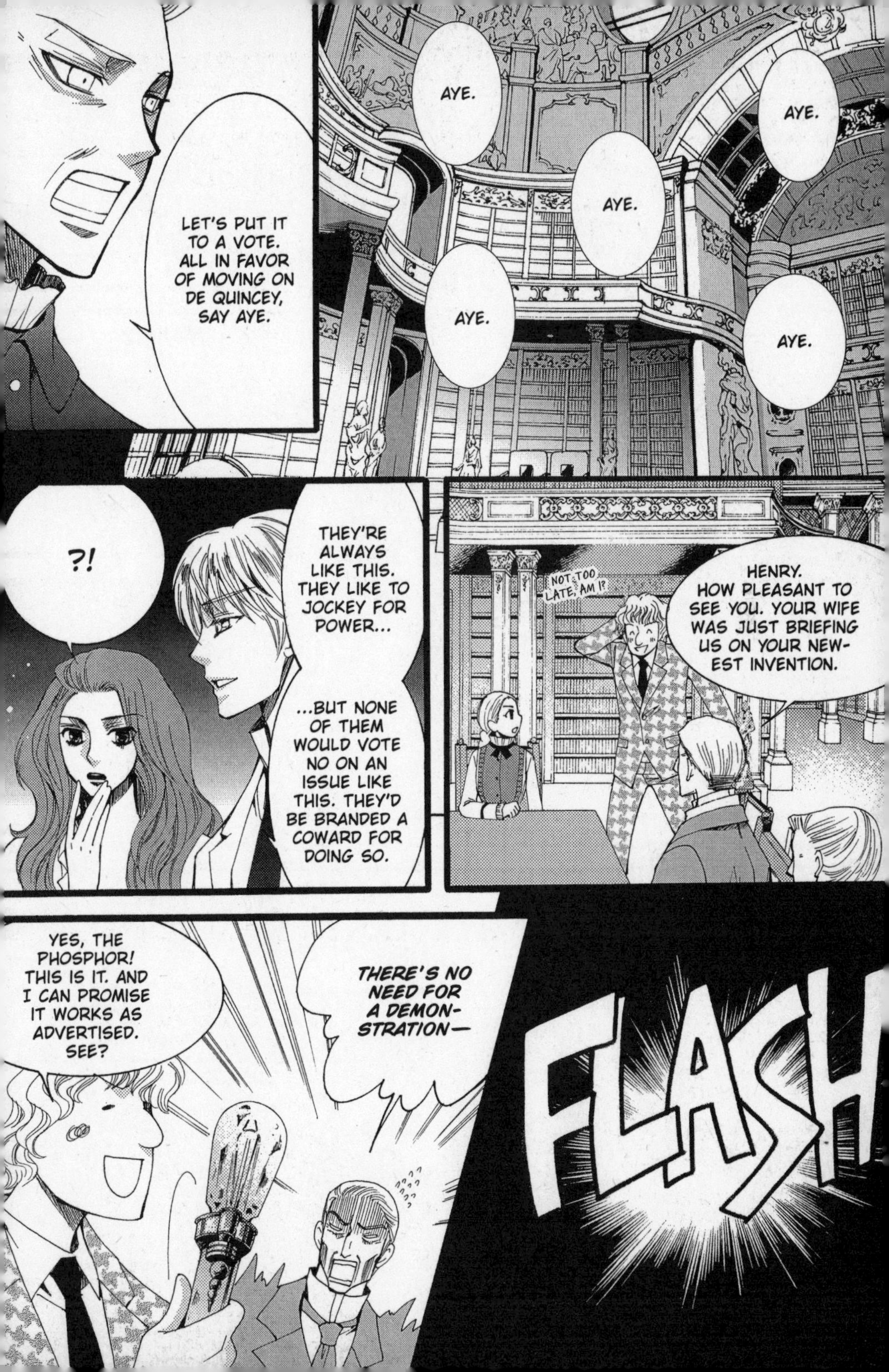
LET'S PUT IT TO A VOTE. ALL IN FAVOR OF MOVING ON DE QUINCEY, SAY AYE.
AYE.
AYE.
AYE.
AYE.
AYE.
?!
THEY'RE ALWAYS LIKE THIS. THEY LIKE TO JOCKEY FOR POWER...
...BUT NONE OF THEM WOULD VOTE NO ON AN ISSUE LIKE THIS. THEY'D BE BRANDED A COWARD FOR DOING SO.
NOT TOO LATE, AM I?
HENRY. HOW PLEASANT TO SEE YOU. YOUR WIFE WAS JUST BRIEFING US ON YOUR NEW-EST INVENTION.
YES, THE PHOSPHOR! THIS IS IT. AND I CAN PROMISE IT WORKS AS ADVERTISED. SEE?
THERE'S NO NEED FOR A DEMON-STRATION—
FLASH

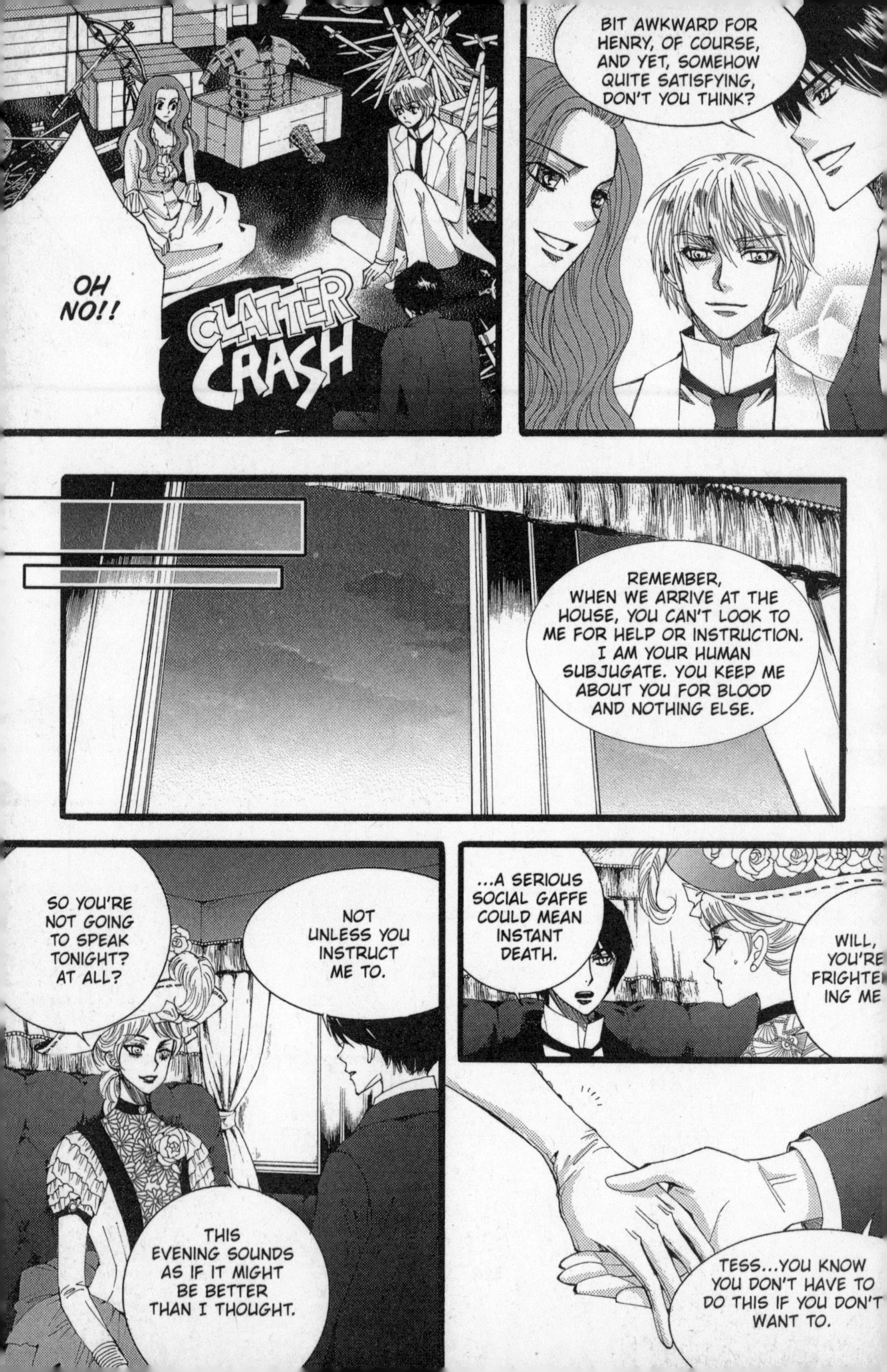

OH NO!!
CLATTER CRASH
BIT AWKWARD FOR HENRY, OF COURSE, AND YET, SOMEHOW QUITE SATISFYING, DON'T YOU THINK?
REMEMBER, WHEN WE ARRIVE AT THE HOUSE, YOU CAN'T LOOK TO ME FOR HELP OR INSTRUCTION. I AM YOUR HUMAN SUBJUGATE. YOU KEEP ME ABOUT YOU FOR BLOOD AND NOTHING ELSE.
SO YOU'RE NOT GOING TO SPEAK TONIGHT? AT ALL?
NOT UNLESS YOU INSTRUCT ME TO.
THIS EVENING SOUNDS AS IF IT MIGHT BE BETTER THAN I THOUGHT.
...A SERIOUS SOCIAL GAFFE COULD MEAN INSTANT DEATH.
WILL, YOU'RE FRIGHTE ING ME
TESS...YOU KNOW YOU DON'T HAVE TO DO THIS IF YOU DON'T WANT TO.

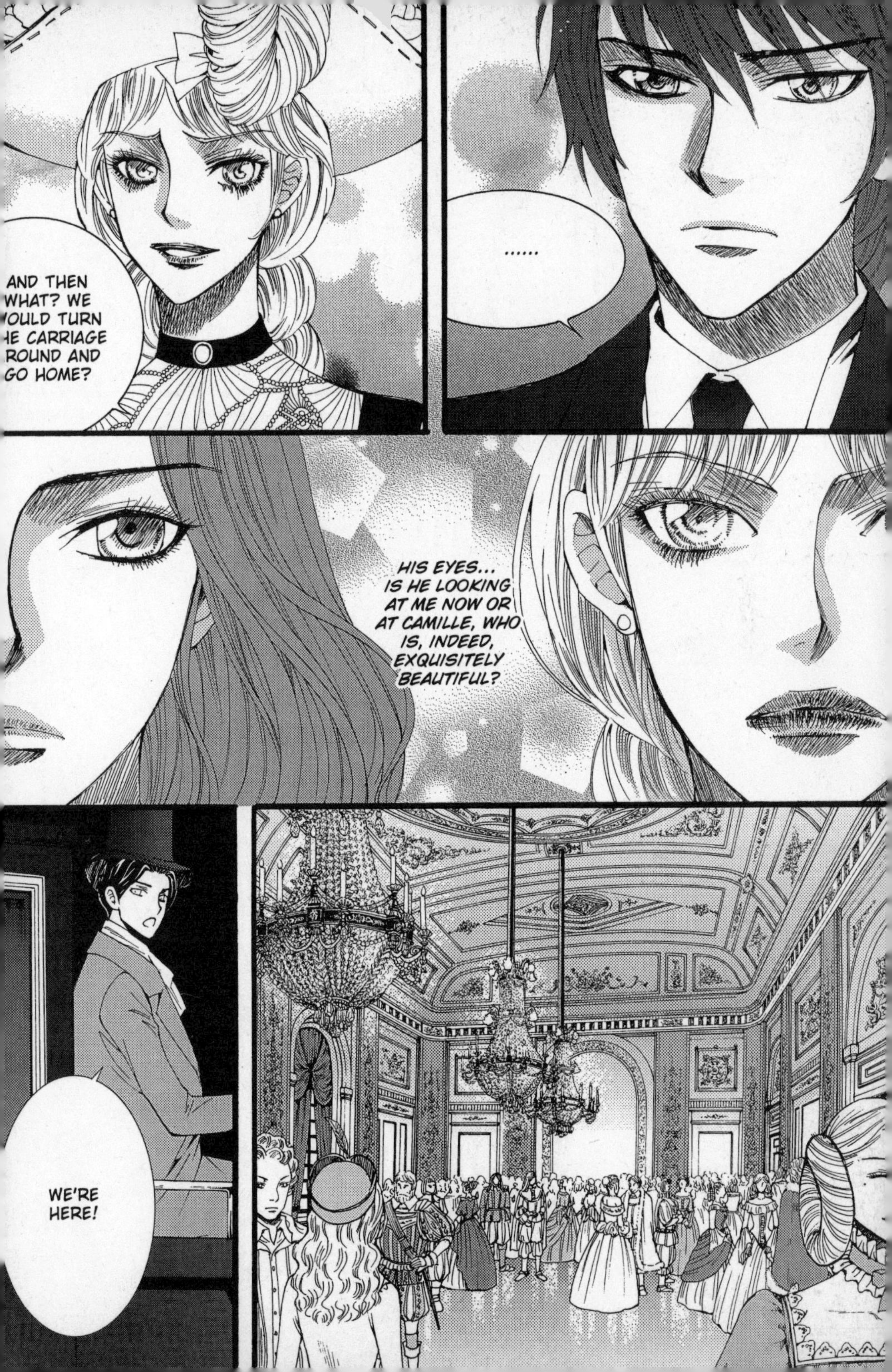

......
AND THEN WHAT? WE WOULD TURN THE CARRIAGE AROUND AND GO HOME?
HIS EYES... IS HE LOOKING AT ME NOW OR AT CAMILLE, WHO IS, INDEED, EXQUISITELY BEAUTIFUL?
WE'RE HERE!

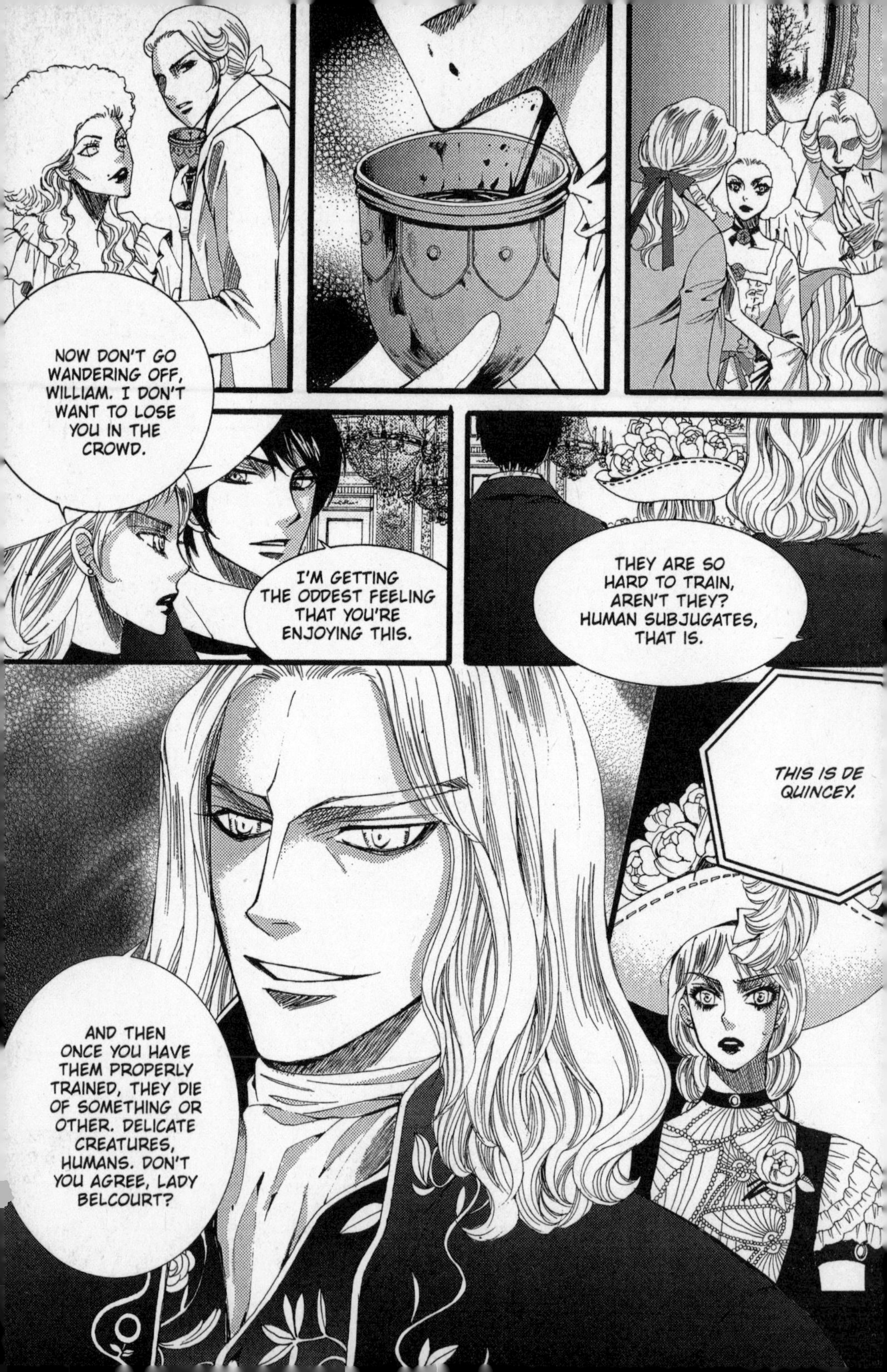
NOW DON'T GO WANDERING OFF, WILLIAM. I DON'T WANT TO LOSE YOU IN THE CROWD.
I'M GETTING THE ODDEST FEELING THAT YOU'RE ENJOYING THIS.
THEY ARE SO HARD TO TRAIN, AREN'T THEY? HUMAN SUBJUGATES, THAT IS.
THIS IS DE QUINCEY.
AND THEN ONCE YOU HAVE THEM PROPERLY TRAINED, THEY DIE OF SOMETHING OR OTHER. DELICATE CREATURES, HUMANS. DON'T YOU AGREE, LADY BELCOURT?

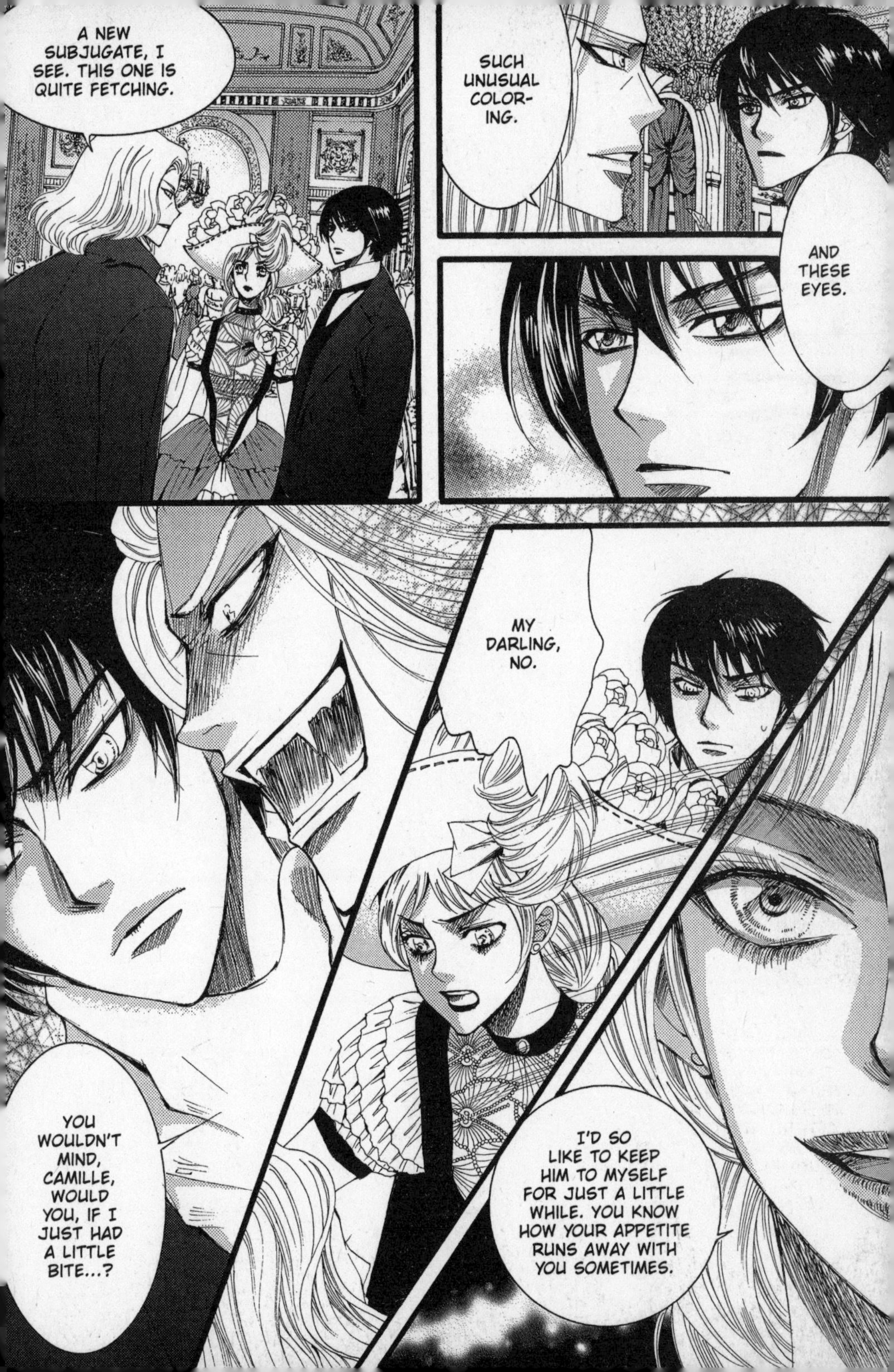
A NEW SUBJUGATE, I SEE. THIS ONE IS QUITE FETCHING.
SUCH UNUSUAL COLOR-ING.
AND THESE EYES.
YOU WOULDN'T MIND, CAMILLE, WOULD YOU, IF I JUST HAD A LITTLE BITE...?
MY DARLING, NO.
I'D SO LIKE TO KEEP HIM TO MYSELF FOR JUST A LITTLE WHILE. YOU KNOW HOW YOUR APPETITE RUNS AWAY WITH YOU SOMETIMES.

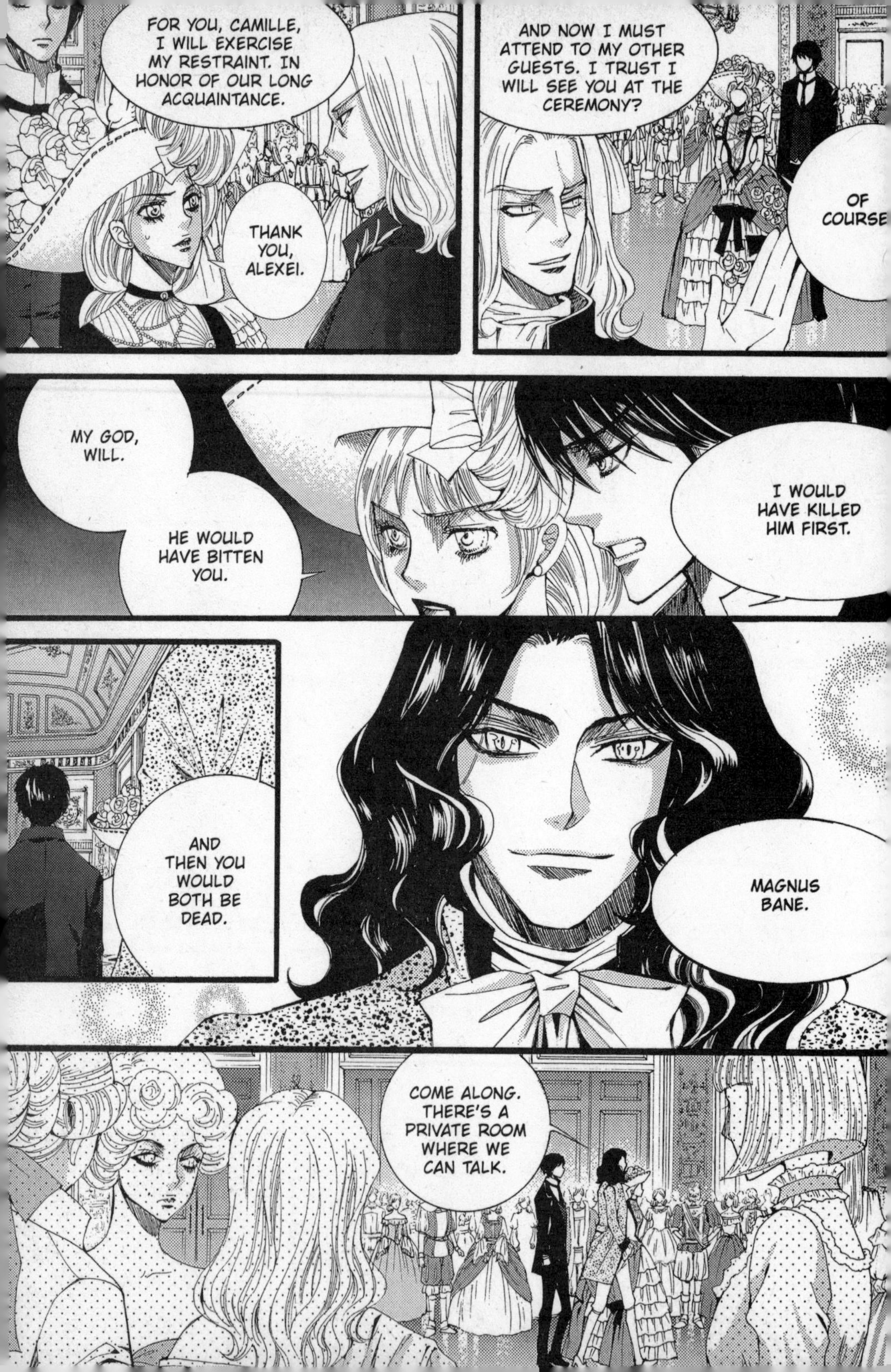

FOR YOU, CAMILLE, I WILL EXERCISE MY RESTRAINT. IN HONOR OF OUR LONG ACQUAINTANCE.
THANK YOU, ALEXEI.
AND NOW I MUST ATTEND TO MY OTHER GUESTS. I TRUST I WILL SEE YOU AT THE CEREMONY?
OF COURSE
MY GOD, WILL.
HE WOULD HAVE BITTEN YOU.
I WOULD HAVE KILLED HIM FIRST.
AND THEN YOU WOULD BOTH BE DEAD.
MAGNUS BANE.
COME ALONG. THERE'S A PRIVATE ROOM WHERE WE CAN TALK.

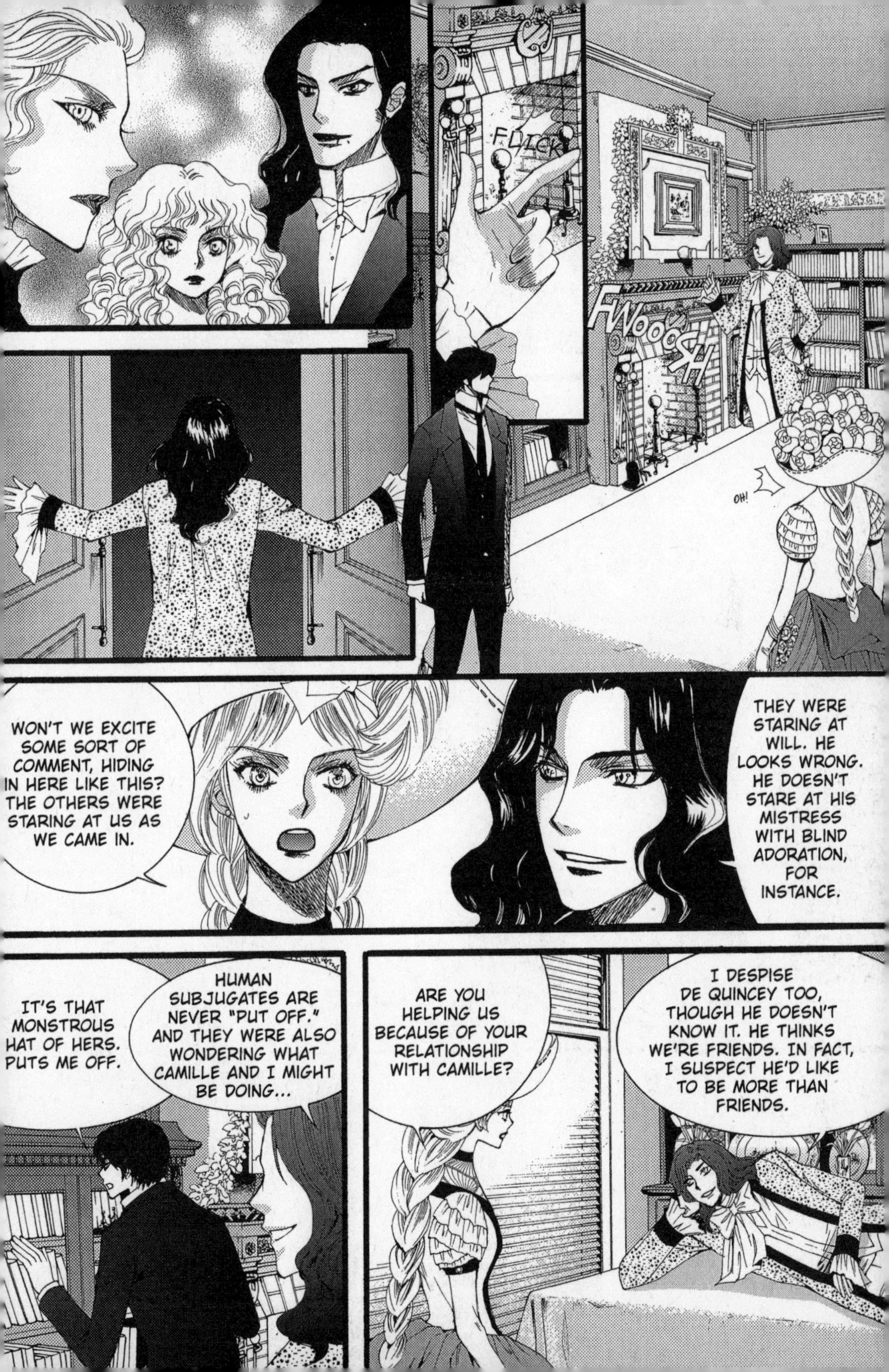
FLICK
FWOOOSH
OH!
WON'T WE EXCITE SOME SORT OF COMMENT, HIDING IN HERE LIKE THIS? THE OTHERS WERE STARING AT US AS WE CAME IN.
THEY WERE STARING AT WILL. HE LOOKS WRONG. HE DOESN'T STARE AT HIS MISTRESS WITH BLIND ADORATION, FOR INSTANCE.
IT'S THAT MONSTROUS HAT OF HERS. PUTS ME OFF.
HUMAN SUBJUGATES ARE NEVER "PUT OFF." AND THEY WERE ALSO WONDERING WHAT CAMILLE AND I MIGHT BE DOING...
ARE YOU HELPING US BECAUSE OF YOUR RELATIONSHIP WITH CAMILLE?
I DESPISE DE QUINCEY TOO, THOUGH HE DOESN'T KNOW IT. HE THINKS WE'RE FRIENDS. IN FACT, I SUSPECT HE'D LIKE TO BE MORE THAN FRIENDS.

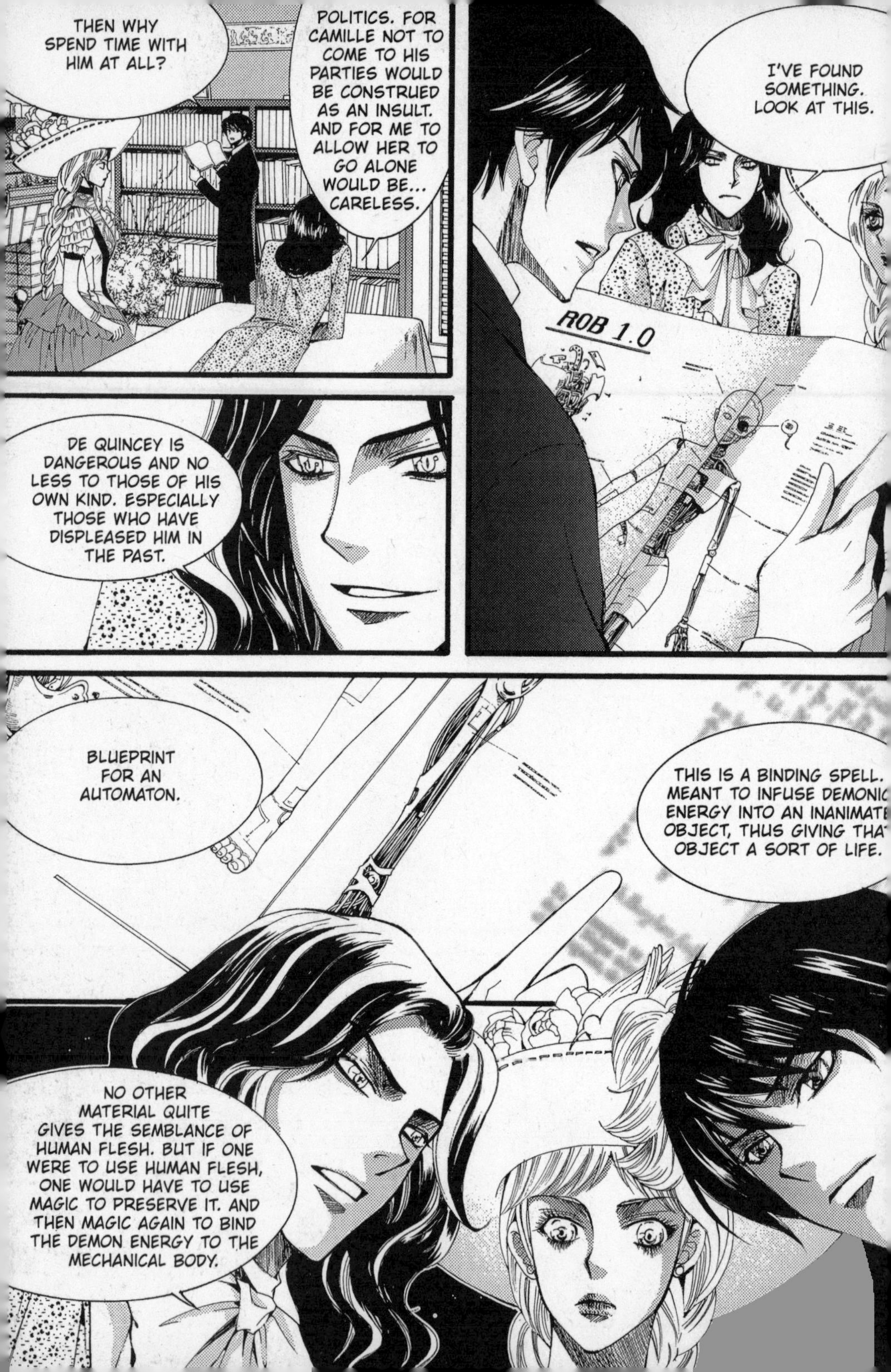
THEN WHY SPEND TIME WITH HIM AT ALL?
POLITICS. FOR CAMILLE NOT TO COME TO HIS PARTIES WOULD BE CONSTRUED AS AN INSULT. AND FOR ME TO ALLOW HER TO GO ALONE WOULD BE... CARELESS.
DE QUINCEY IS DANGEROUS AND NO LESS TO THOSE OF HIS OWN KIND. ESPECIALLY THOSE WHO HAVE DISPLEASED HIM IN THE PAST.
I'VE FOUND SOMETHING. LOOK AT THIS.
ROB 1.0
BLUEPRINT FOR AN AUTOMATON.
THIS IS A BINDING SPELL. MEANT TO INFUSE DEMONIC ENERGY INTO AN INANIMATE OBJECT, THUS GIVING THAT OBJECT A SORT OF LIFE.
NO OTHER MATERIAL QUITE GIVES THE SEMBLANCE OF HUMAN FLESH. BUT IF ONE WERE TO USE HUMAN FLESH, ONE WOULD HAVE TO USE MAGIC TO PRESERVE IT. AND THEN MAGIC AGAIN TO BIND THE DEMON ENERGY TO THE MECHANICAL BODY.

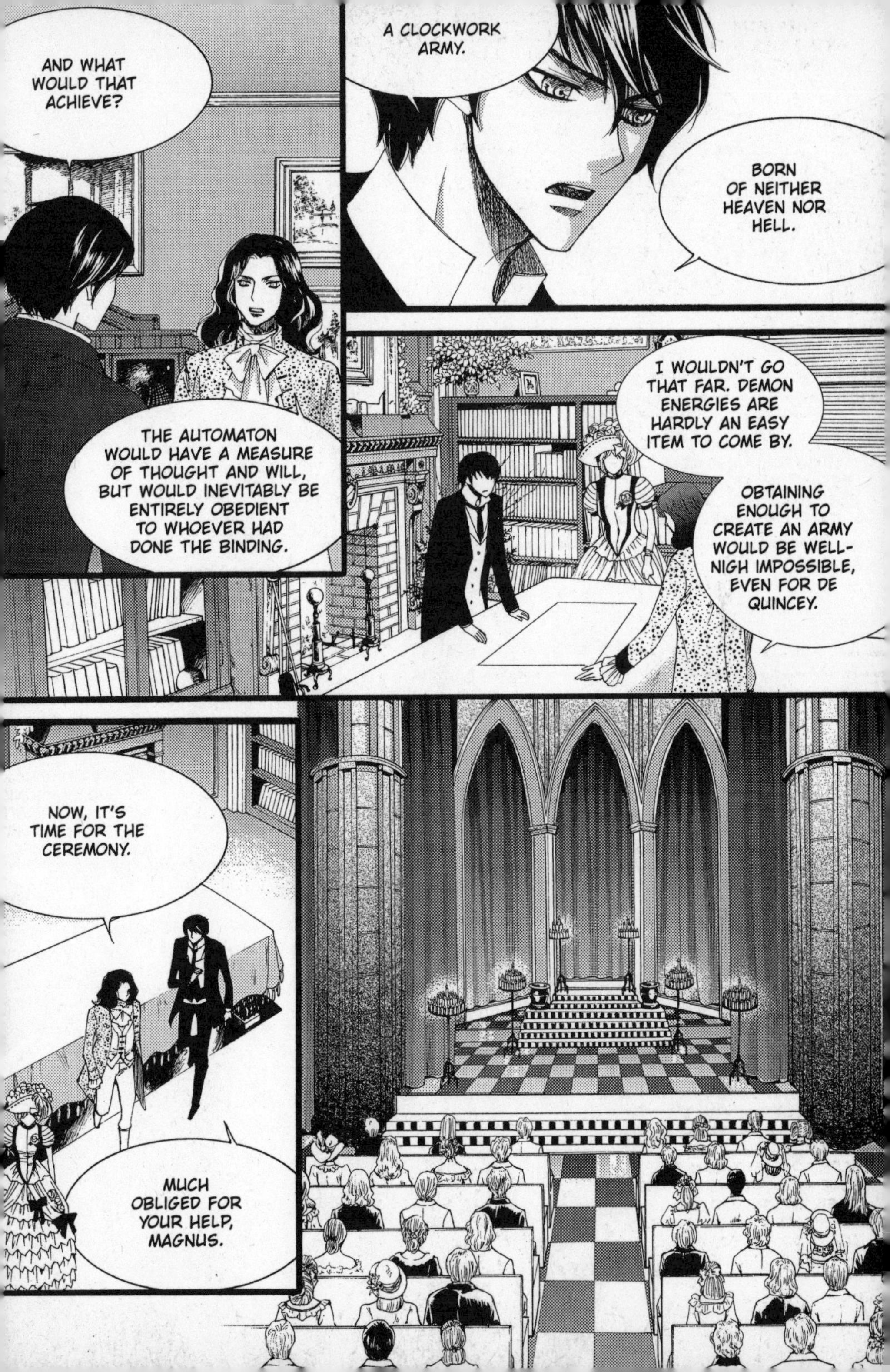
AND WHAT WOULD THAT ACHIEVE?
A CLOCKWORK ARMY.
BORN OF NEITHER HEAVEN NOR HELL.
THE AUTOMATON WOULD HAVE A MEASURE OF THOUGHT AND WILL, BUT WOULD INEVITABLY BE ENTIRELY OBEDIENT TO WHOEVER HAD DONE THE BINDING.
I WOULDN'T GO THAT FAR. DEMON ENERGIES ARE HARDLY AN EASY ITEM TO COME BY.
OBTAINING ENOUGH TO CREATE AN ARMY WOULD BE WELL-NIGH IMPOSSIBLE, EVEN FOR DE QUINCEY.
NOW, IT'S TIME FOR THE CEREMONY.
MUCH OBLIGED FOR YOUR HELP, MAGNUS.

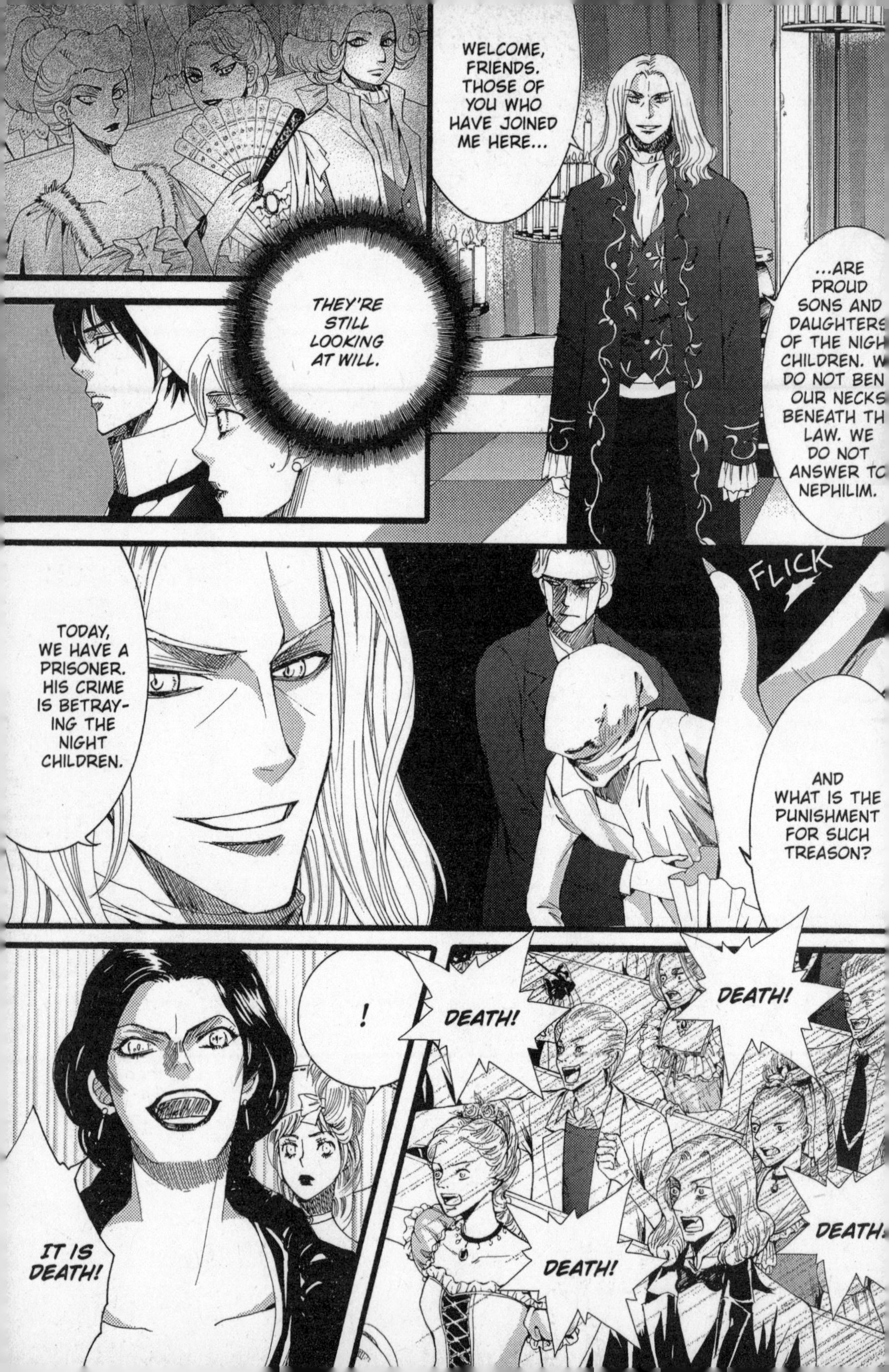
THEY'RE STILL LOOKING AT WILL.
WELCOME, FRIENDS. THOSE OF YOU WHO HAVE JOINED ME HERE...
...ARE PROUD SONS AND DAUGHTERS OF THE NIGH CHILDREN. W DO NOT BEN OUR NECKS BENEATH TH LAW. WE DO NOT ANSWER TO NEPHILIM.
TODAY, WE HAVE A PRISONER. HIS CRIME IS BETRAYING THE NIGHT CHILDREN.
FLICK
AND WHAT IS THE PUNISHMENT FOR SUCH TREASON?
!
IT IS DEATH!
DEATH!
DEATH!
DEATH!
DEATH!
DEATH!

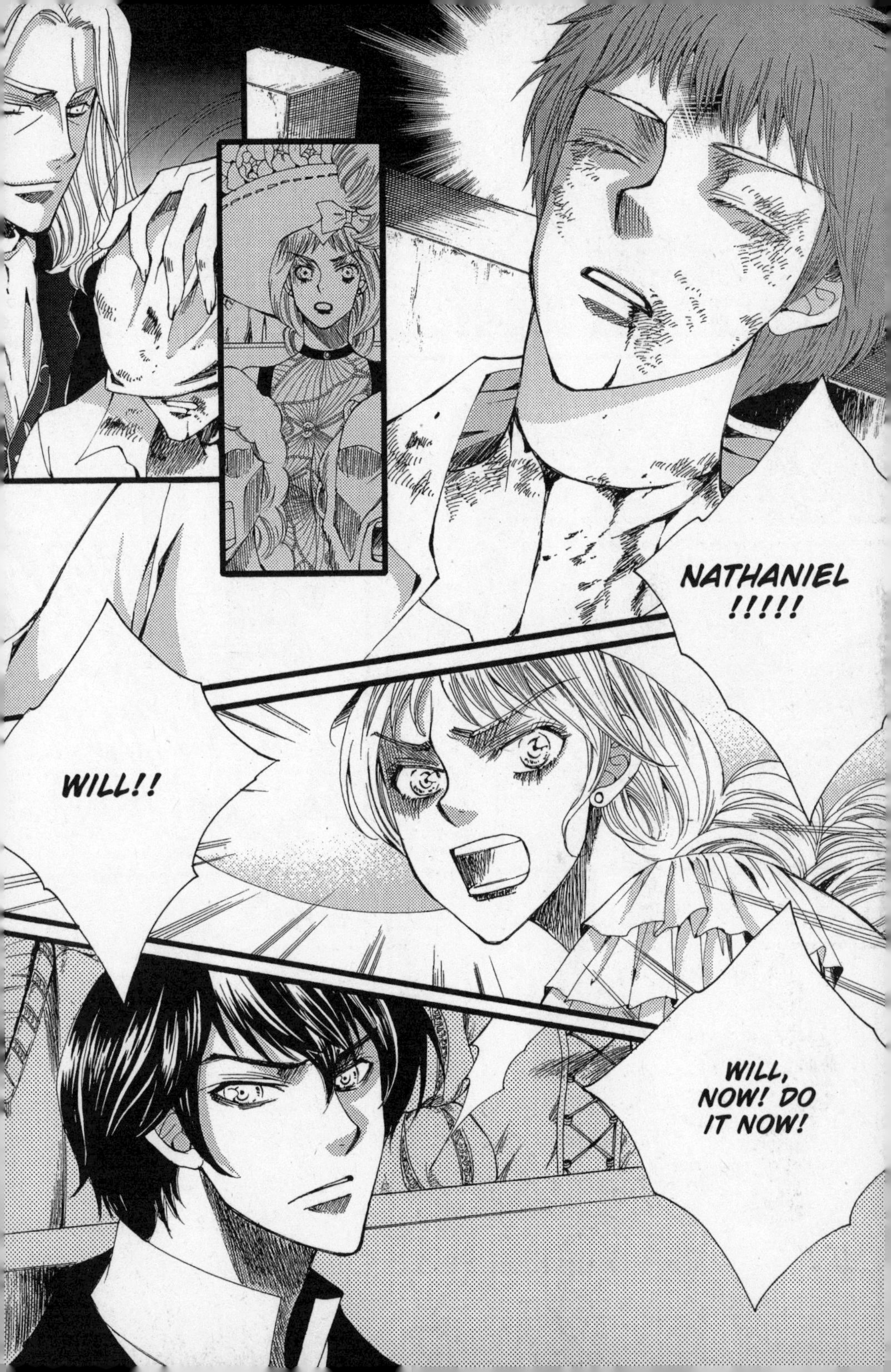
NATHANIEL !!!!!
WILL!!
WILL, NOW! DO IT NOW!

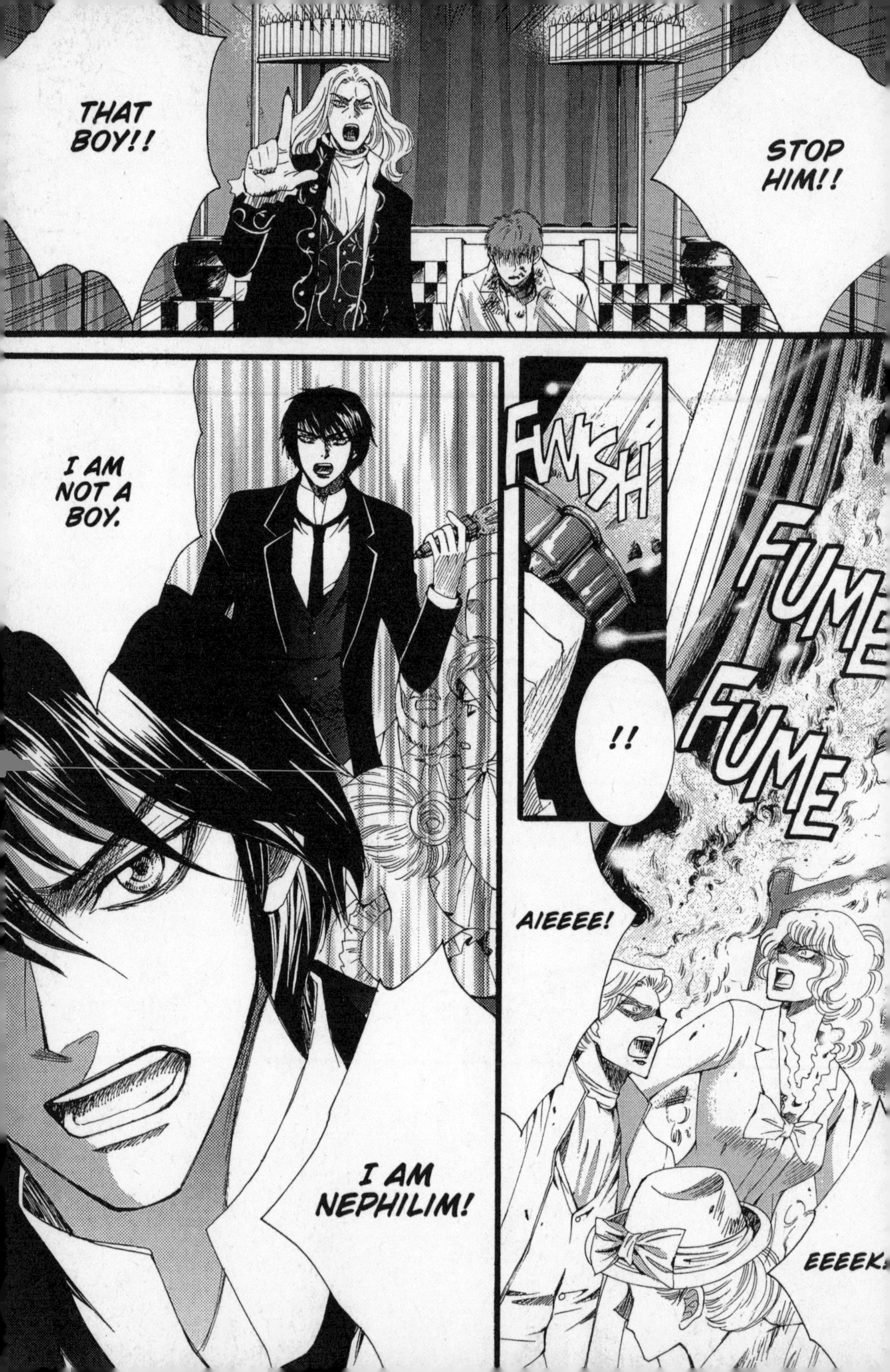
THAT BOY!!
STOP HIM!!
I AM NOT A BOY.
I AM NEPHILIM!
FWISH
!!
FUME FUME
AIEEEE!
EEEEK!

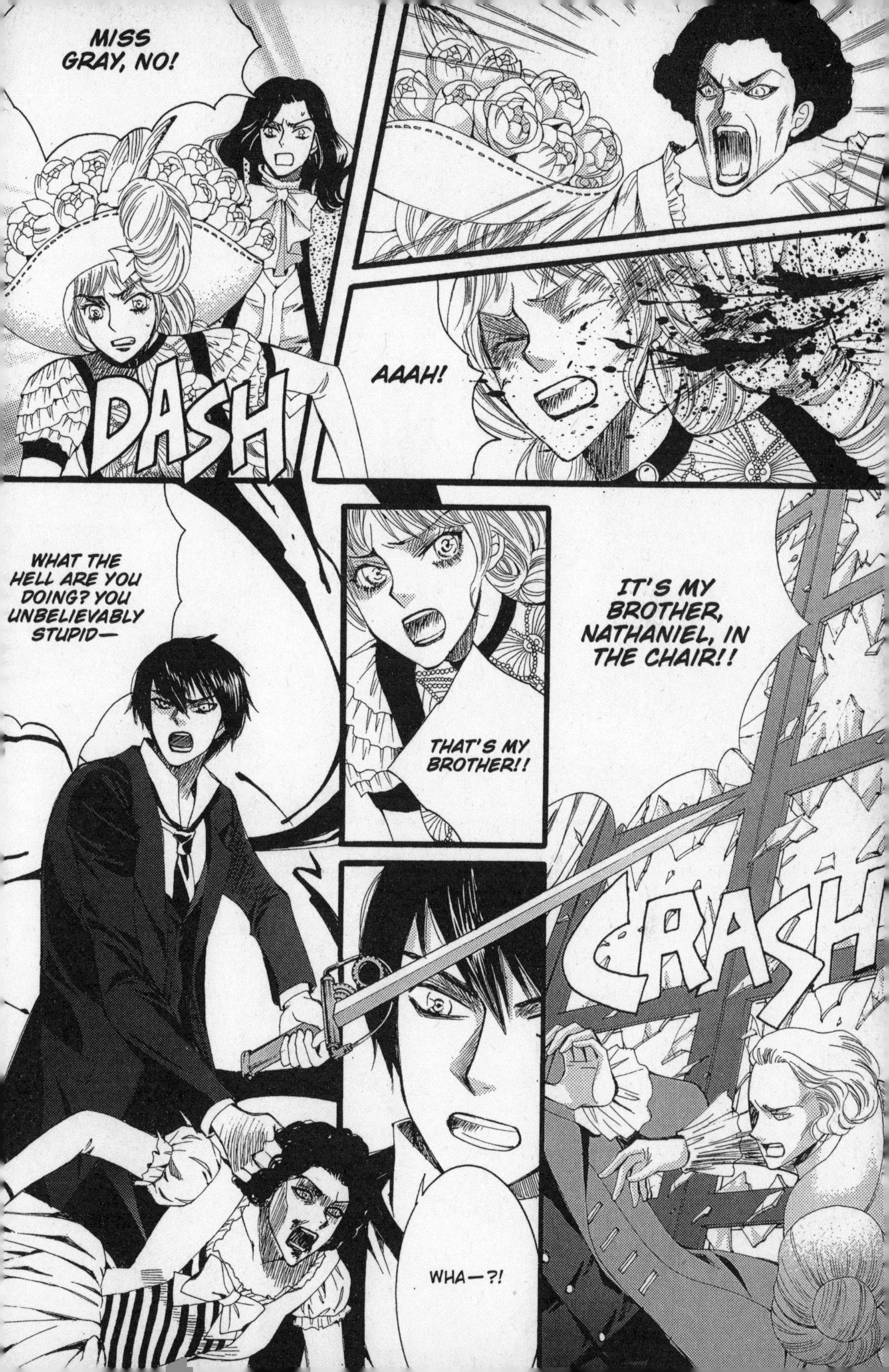
MISS GRAY, NO!
DASH
AAAH!
WHAT THE HELL ARE YOU DOING? YOU UNBELIEVABLY STUPID—
THAT'S MY BROTHER!!
IT'S MY BROTHER, NATHANIEL, IN THE CHAIR!!
CRASH
WHA—?!

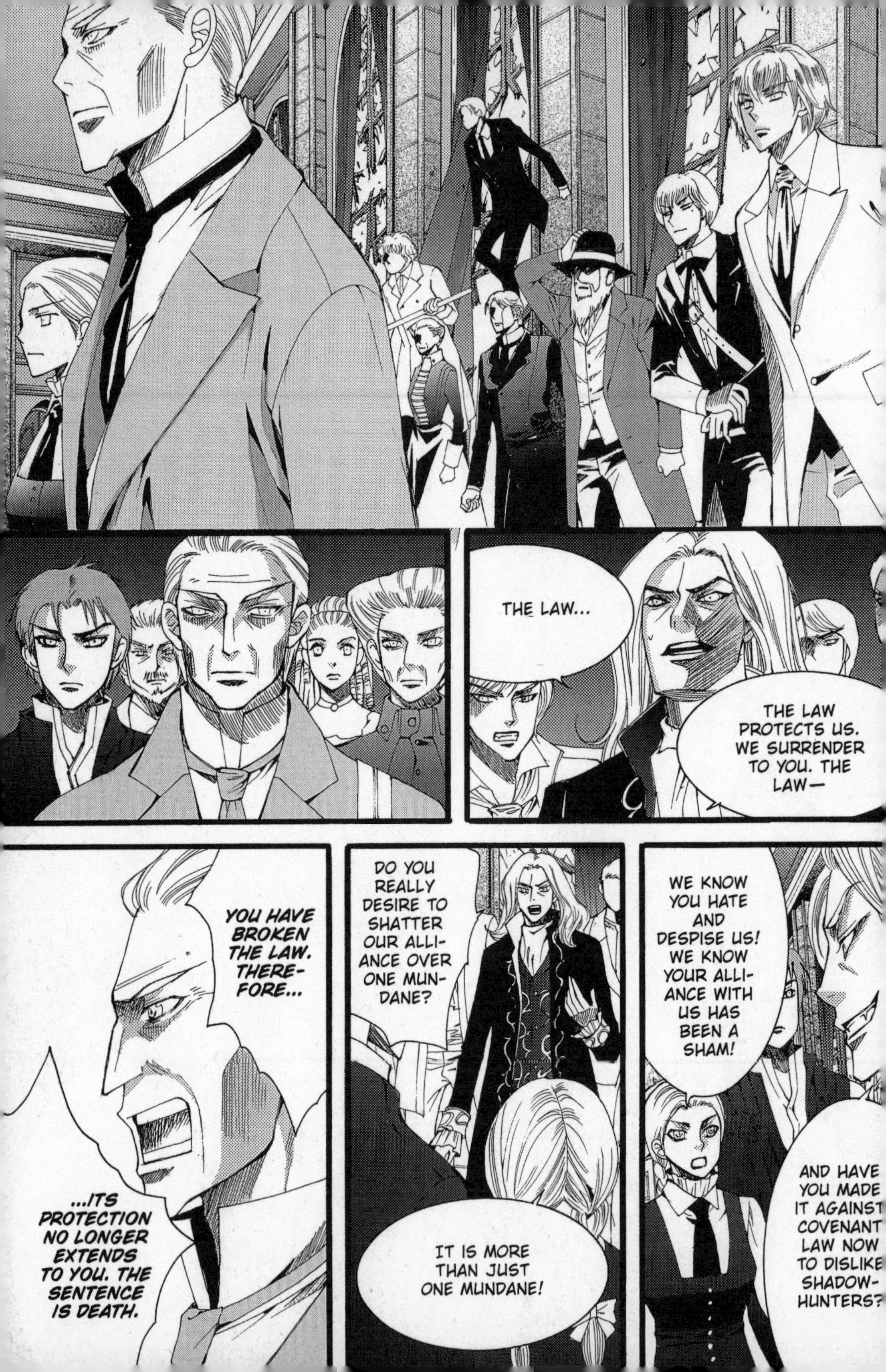
THE LAW...
THE LAW PROTECTS US. WE SURRENDER TO YOU. THE LAW—
YOU HAVE BROKEN THE LAW. THERE-FORE...
...ITS PROTECTION NO LONGER EXTENDS TO YOU. THE SENTENCE IS DEATH.
DO YOU REALLY DESIRE TO SHATTER OUR ALLI-ANCE OVER ONE MUN-DANE?
IT IS MORE THAN JUST ONE MUNDANE!
WE KNOW YOU HATE AND DESPISE US! WE KNOW YOUR ALLI-ANCE WITH US HAS BEEN A SHAM!
AND HAVE YOU MADE IT AGAINST COVENANT LAW NOW TO DISLIKE SHADOW-HUNTERS?

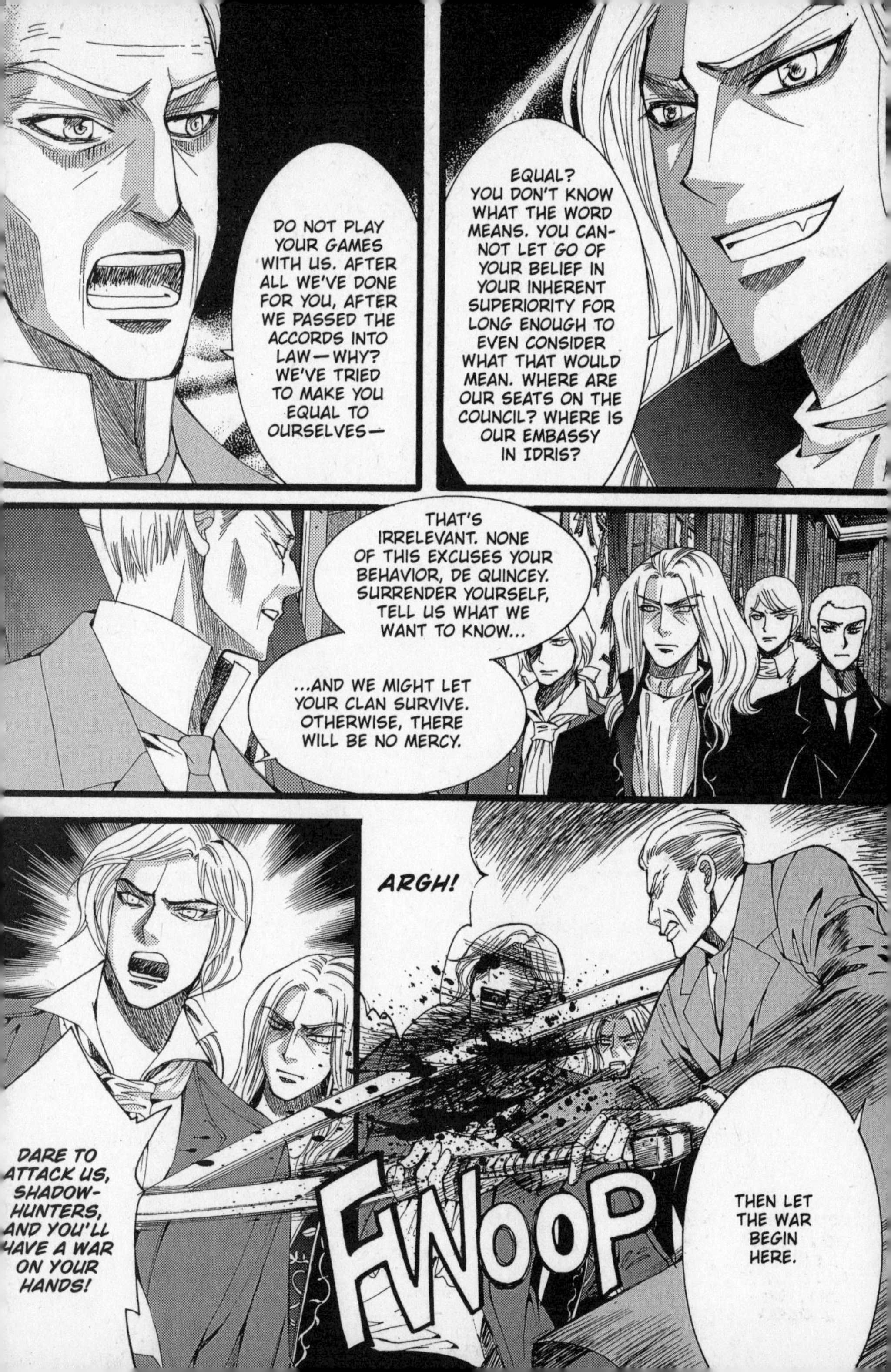
DO NOT PLAY YOUR GAMES WITH US. AFTER ALL WE'VE DONE FOR YOU, AFTER WE PASSED THE ACCORDS INTO LAW—WHY? WE'VE TRIED TO MAKE YOU EQUAL TO OURSELVES—
EQUAL? YOU DON'T KNOW WHAT THE WORD MEANS. YOU CAN-NOT LET GO OF YOUR BELIEF IN YOUR INHERENT SUPERIORITY FOR LONG ENOUGH TO EVEN CONSIDER WHAT THAT WOULD MEAN. WHERE ARE OUR SEATS ON THE COUNCIL? WHERE IS OUR EMBASSY IN IDRIS?
THAT'S IRRELEVANT. NONE OF THIS EXCUSES YOUR BEHAVIOR, DE QUINCEY. SURRENDER YOURSELF, TELL US WHAT WE WANT TO KNOW...
...AND WE MIGHT LET YOUR CLAN SURVIVE. OTHERWISE, THERE WILL BE NO MERCY.
DARE TO ATTACK US, SHADOW-HUNTERS, AND YOU'LL HAVE A WAR ON YOUR HANDS!
ARGH!
FWOOP
THEN LET THE WAR BEGIN HERE.

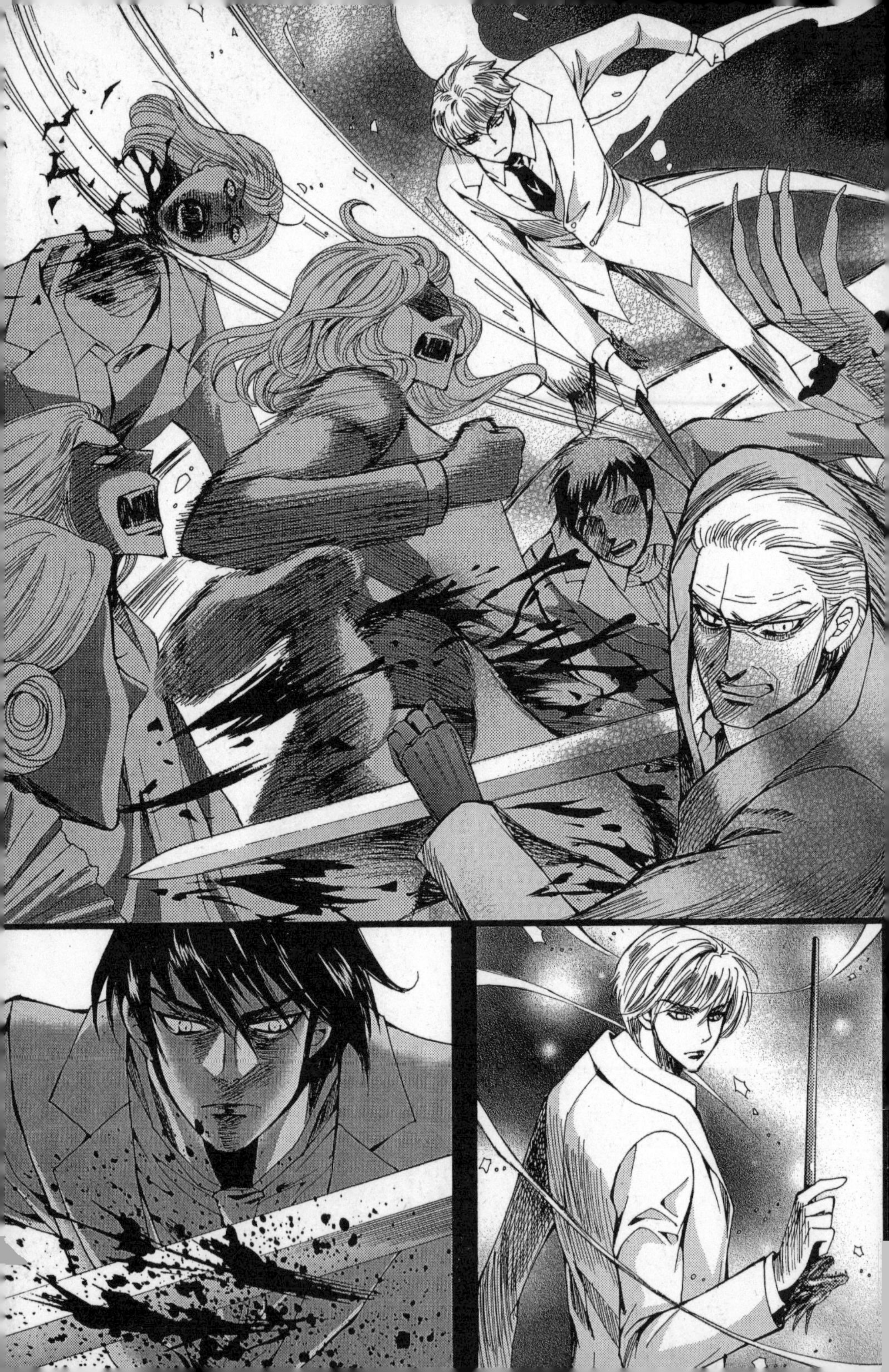

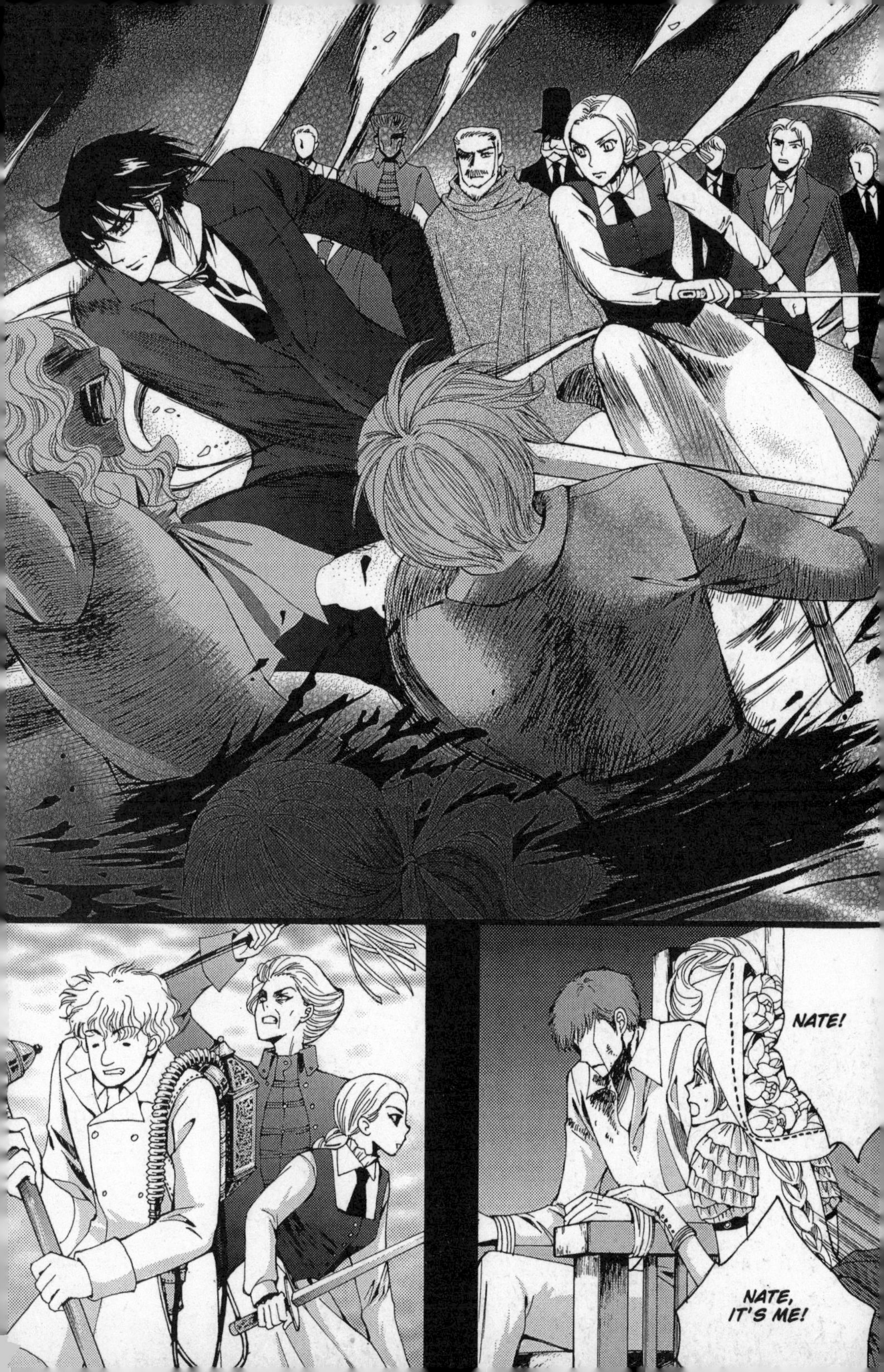
NATE!
NATE, IT'S ME!

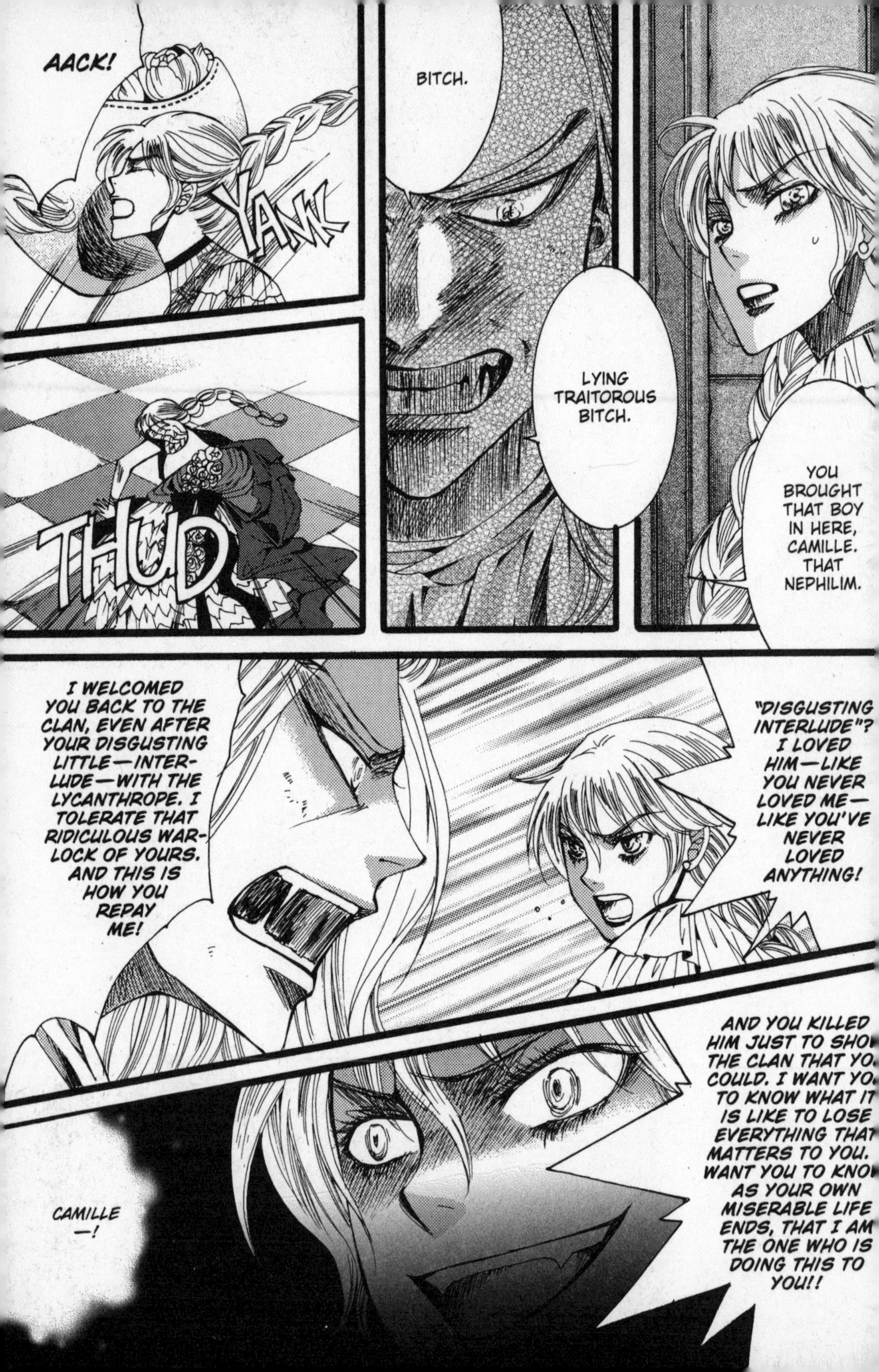
AACK!
YANK
THUD
BITCH.
LYING TRAITOROUS BITCH.
YOU BROUGHT THAT BOY IN HERE, CAMILLE. THAT NEPHILIM.
I WELCOMED YOU BACK TO THE CLAN, EVEN AFTER YOUR DISGUSTING LITTLE—INTER-LUDE—WITH THE LYCANTHROPE. I TOLERATE THAT RIDICULOUS WAR-LOCK OF YOURS. AND THIS IS HOW YOU REPAY ME!
"DISGUSTING INTERLUDE"? I LOVED HIM—LIKE YOU NEVER LOVED ME—LIKE YOU'VE NEVER LOVED ANYTHING!
CAMILLE—!
AND YOU KILLED HIM JUST TO SHO THE CLAN THAT YO COULD. I WANT YO TO KNOW WHAT IT IS LIKE TO LOSE EVERYTHING THAT MATTERS TO YOU. WANT YOU TO KNO AS YOUR OWN MISERABLE LIFE ENDS, THAT I AM THE ONE WHO IS DOING THIS TO YOU!!

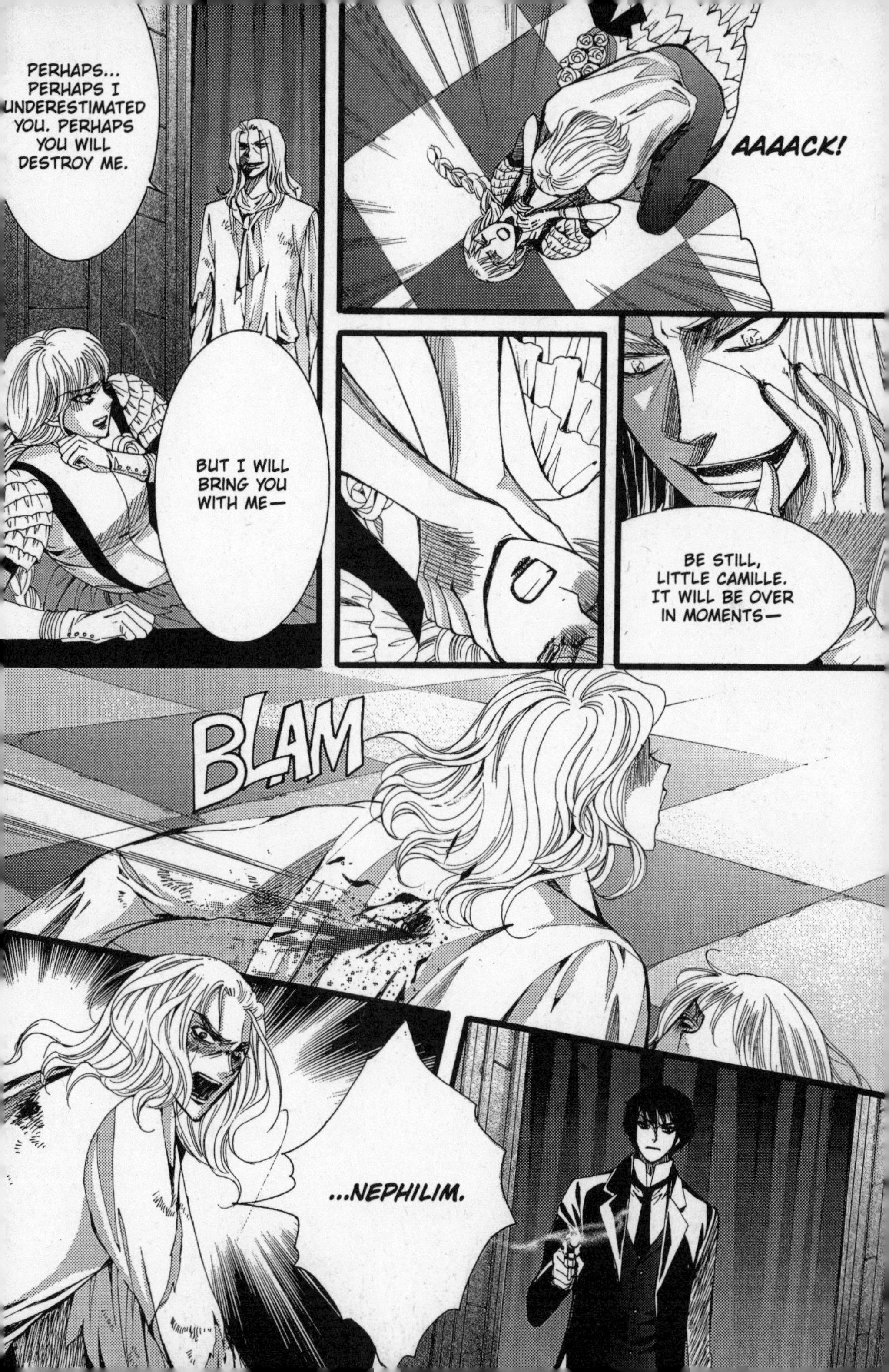
PERHAPS... PERHAPS I UNDERESTIMATED YOU. PERHAPS YOU WILL DESTROY ME.
BUT I WILL BRING YOU WITH ME—
AAAACK!
BE STILL, LITTLE CAMILLE. IT WILL BE OVER IN MOMENTS—
BLAM
...NEPHILIM.

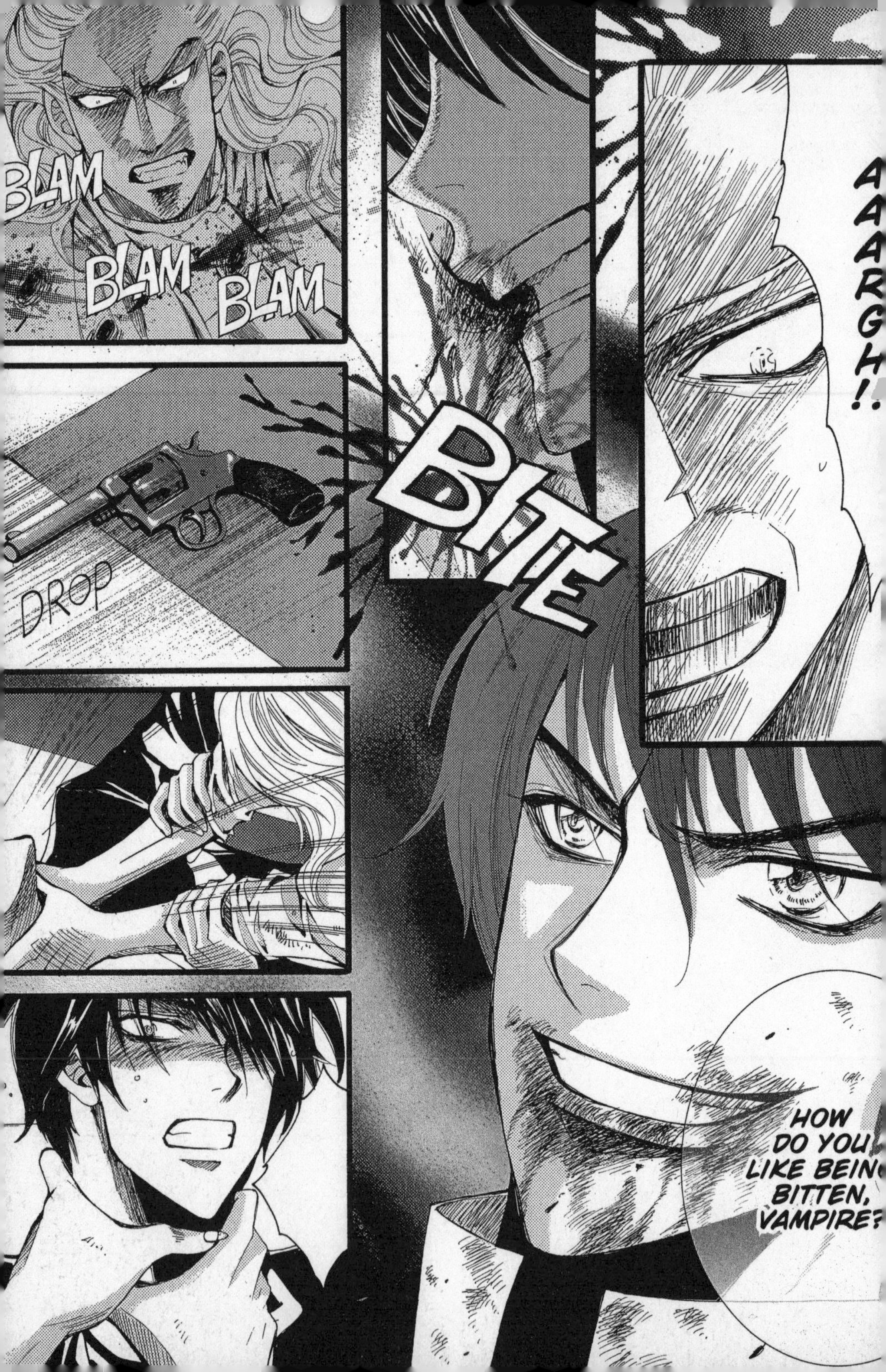
BLAM
BLAM
BLAM
DROP
BITE
AAARGH!!
HOW DO YOU LIKE BEIN BITTEN, VAMPIRE?

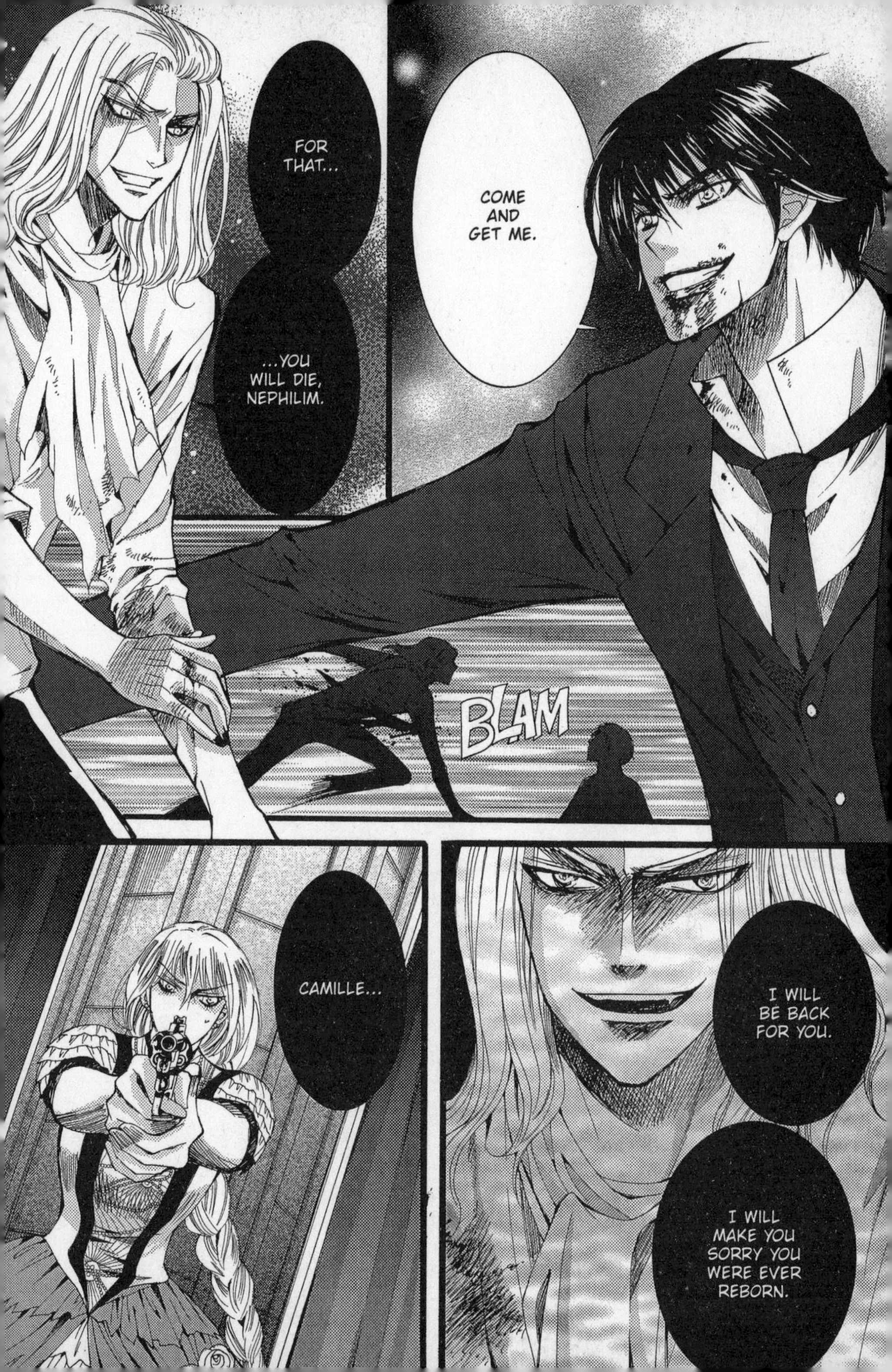
FOR THAT...
...YOU WILL DIE, NEPHILIM.
COME AND GET ME.
BLAM
CAMILLE...
I WILL BE BACK FOR YOU.
I WILL MAKE YOU SORRY YOU WERE EVER REBORN.

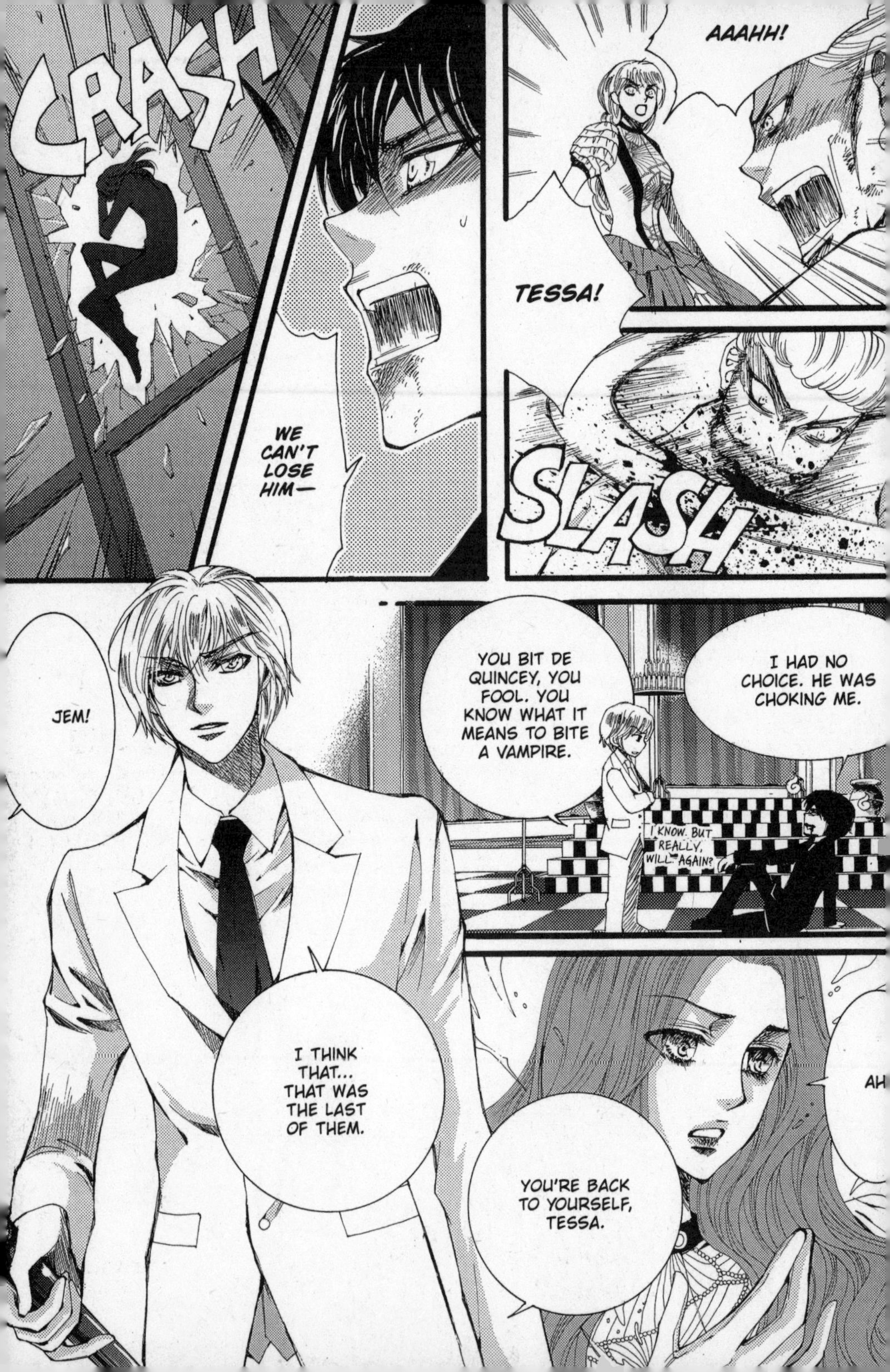
CRASH
WE CAN'T LOSE HIM—
AAAHH!
TESSA!
SLASH
JEM!
I THINK THAT... THAT WAS THE LAST OF THEM.
YOU BIT DE QUINCEY, YOU FOOL. YOU KNOW WHAT IT MEANS TO BITE A VAMPIRE.
I HAD NO CHOICE. HE WAS CHOKING ME.
I KNOW. BUT REALLY, WILL. AGAIN?
YOU'RE BACK TO YOURSELF, TESSA.
AH

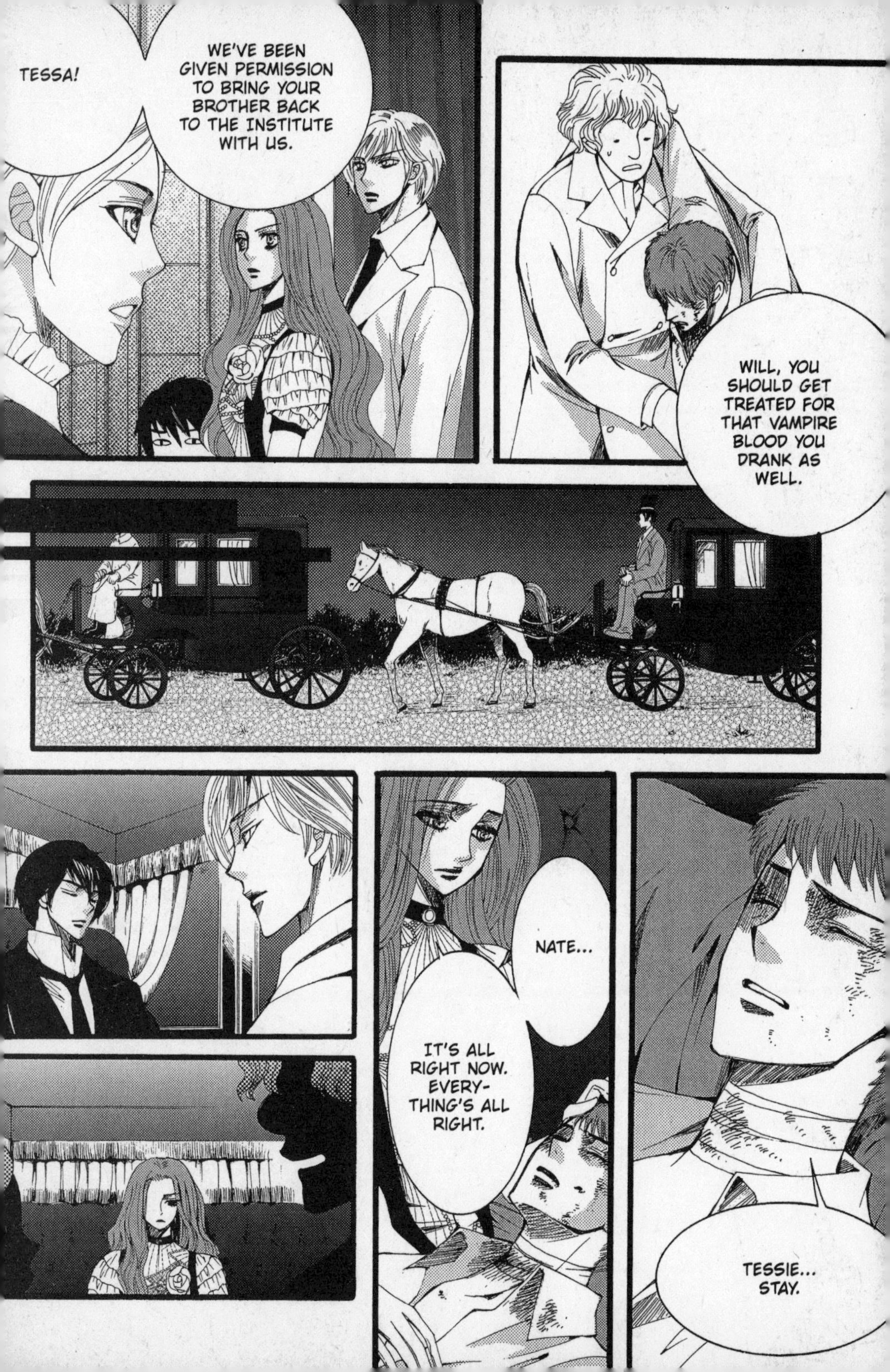
TESSA!
WE'VE BEEN GIVEN PERMISSION TO BRING YOUR BROTHER BACK TO THE INSTITUTE WITH US.
WILL, YOU SHOULD GET TREATED FOR THAT VAMPIRE BLOOD YOU DRANK AS WELL.
NATE...
IT'S ALL RIGHT NOW. EVERY-THING'S ALL RIGHT.
TESSIE... STAY.

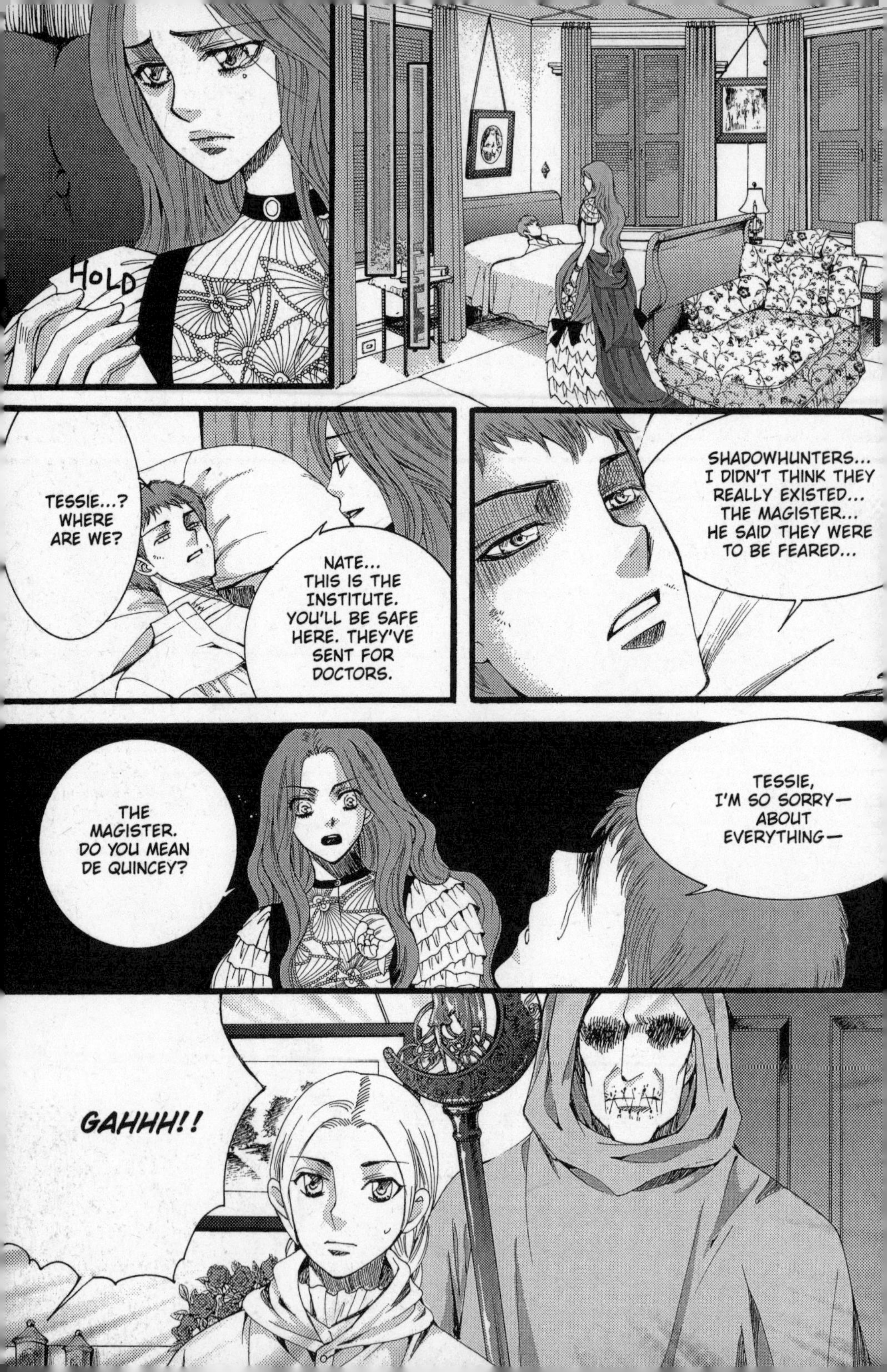
HOLD
TESSIE...? WHERE ARE WE?
NATE... THIS IS THE INSTITUTE. YOU'LL BE SAFE HERE. THEY'VE SENT FOR DOCTORS.
SHADOWHUNTERS... I DIDN'T THINK THEY REALLY EXISTED... THE MAGISTER... HE SAID THEY WERE TO BE FEARED...
THE MAGISTER. DO YOU MEAN DE QUINCEY?
TESSIE, I'M SO SORRY— ABOUT EVERYTHING—
GAHHH!!

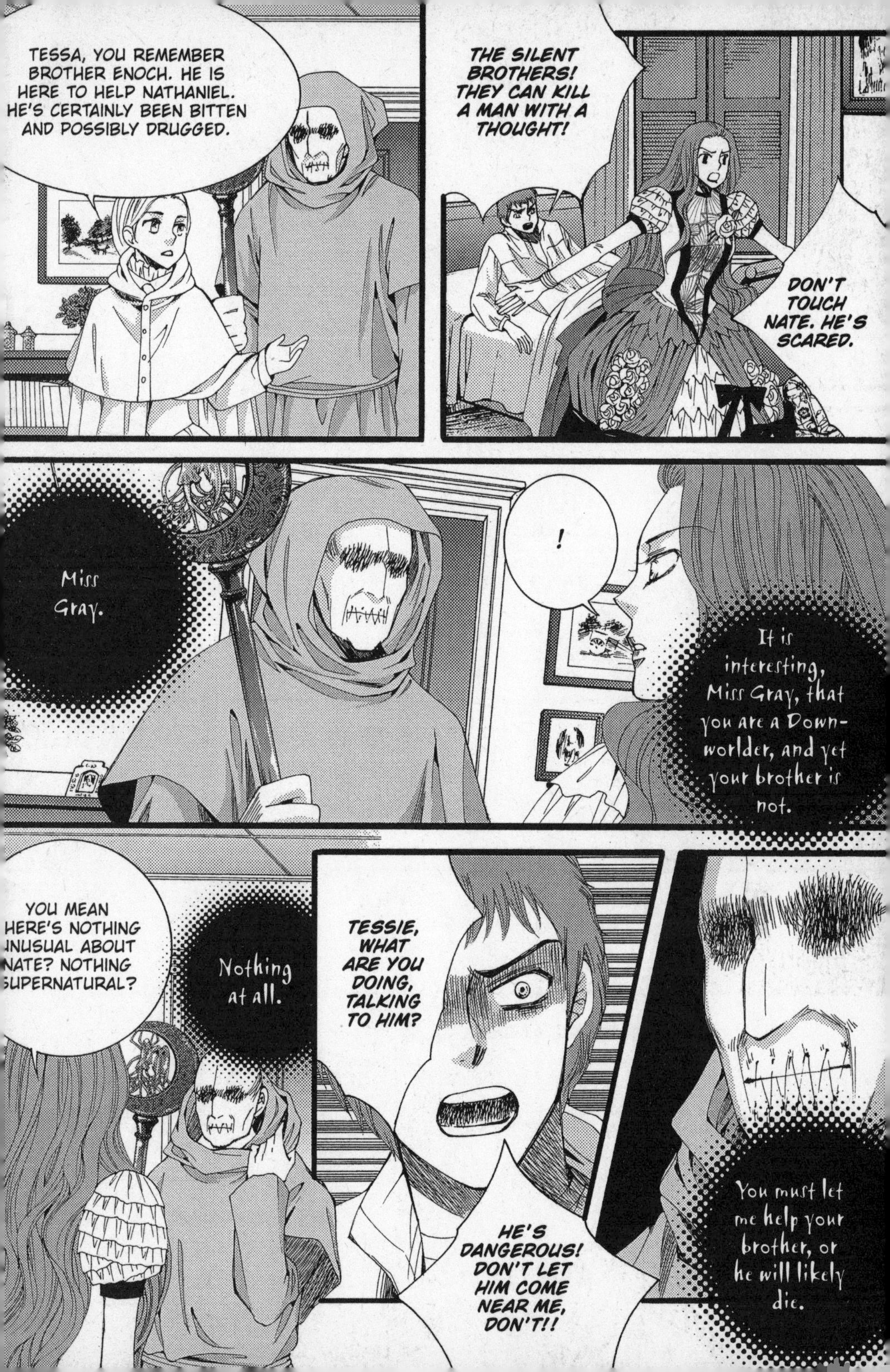
TESSA, YOU REMEMBER BROTHER ENOCH. HE IS HERE TO HELP NATHANIEL. HE'S CERTAINLY BEEN BITTEN AND POSSIBLY DRUGGED.
THE SILENT BROTHERS! THEY CAN KILL A MAN WITH A THOUGHT!
DON'T TOUCH NATE. HE'S SCARED.
Miss Gray.
!
It is interesting, Miss Gray, that you are a Down-worlder, and yet your brother is not.
YOU MEAN HERE'S NOTHING UNUSUAL ABOUT NATE? NOTHING SUPERNATURAL?
Nothing at all.
TESSIE, WHAT ARE YOU DOING, TALKING TO HIM?
HE'S DANGEROUS! DON'T LET HIM COME NEAR ME, DON'T!!
You must let me help your brother, or he will likely die.

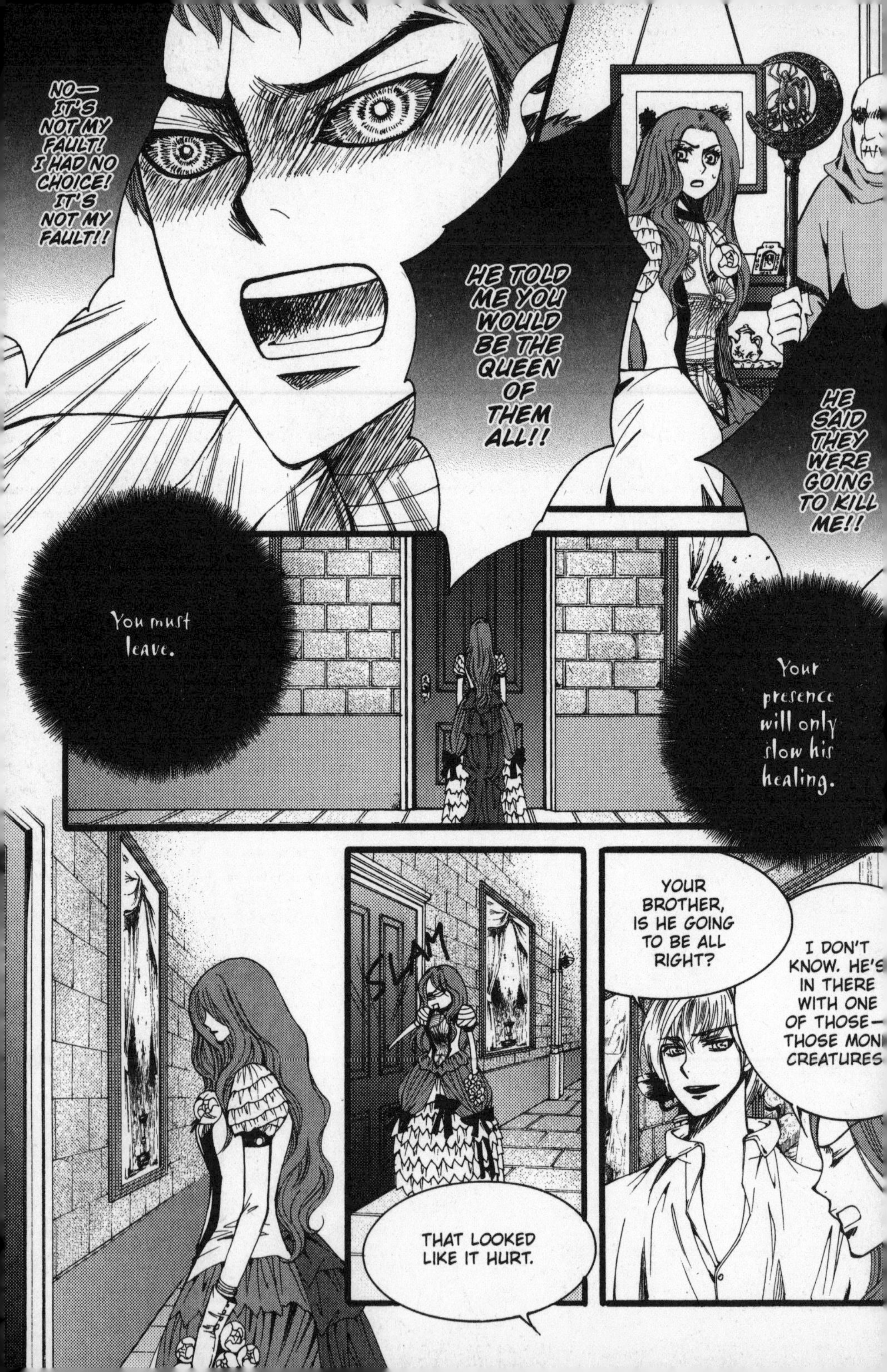
NO— IT'S NOT MY FAULT! I HAD NO CHOICE! IT'S NOT MY FAULT!!
HE TOLD ME YOU WOULD BE THE QUEEN OF THEM ALL!!
HE SAID THEY WERE GOING TO KILL ME!!
You must leave.
Your presence will only slow his healing.
SLAM
THAT LOOKED LIKE IT HURT.
YOUR BROTHER, IS HE GOING TO BE ALL RIGHT?
I DON'T KNOW. HE'S IN THERE WITH ONE OF THOSE— THOSE MON CREATURES

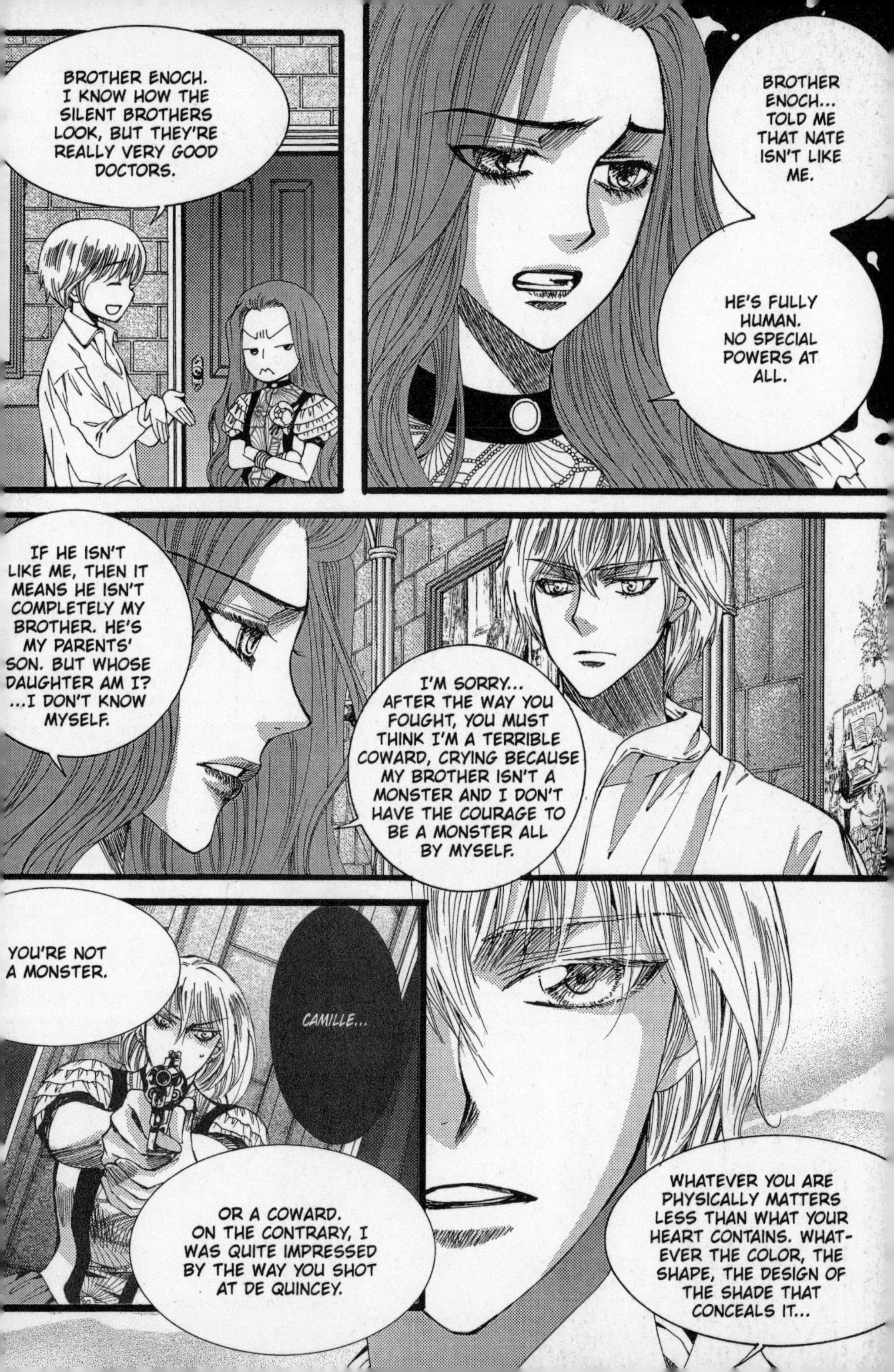
BROTHER ENOCH. I KNOW HOW THE SILENT BROTHERS LOOK, BUT THEY'RE REALLY VERY GOOD DOCTORS.
BROTHER ENOCH... TOLD ME THAT NATE ISN'T LIKE ME.
HE'S FULLY HUMAN. NO SPECIAL POWERS AT ALL.
IF HE ISN'T LIKE ME, THEN IT MEANS HE ISN'T COMPLETELY MY BROTHER. HE'S MY PARENTS' SON. BUT WHOSE DAUGHTER AM I? ...I DON'T KNOW MYSELF.
I'M SORRY... AFTER THE WAY YOU FOUGHT, YOU MUST THINK I'M A TERRIBLE COWARD, CRYING BECAUSE MY BROTHER ISN'T A MONSTER AND I DON'T HAVE THE COURAGE TO BE A MONSTER ALL BY MYSELF.
YOU'RE NOT A MONSTER.
CAMILLE...
OR A COWARD. ON THE CONTRARY, I WAS QUITE IMPRESSED BY THE WAY YOU SHOT AT DE QUINCEY.
WHATEVER YOU ARE PHYSICALLY MATTERS LESS THAN WHAT YOUR HEART CONTAINS. WHAT-EVER THE COLOR, THE SHAPE, THE DESIGN OF THE SHADE THAT CONCEALS IT...

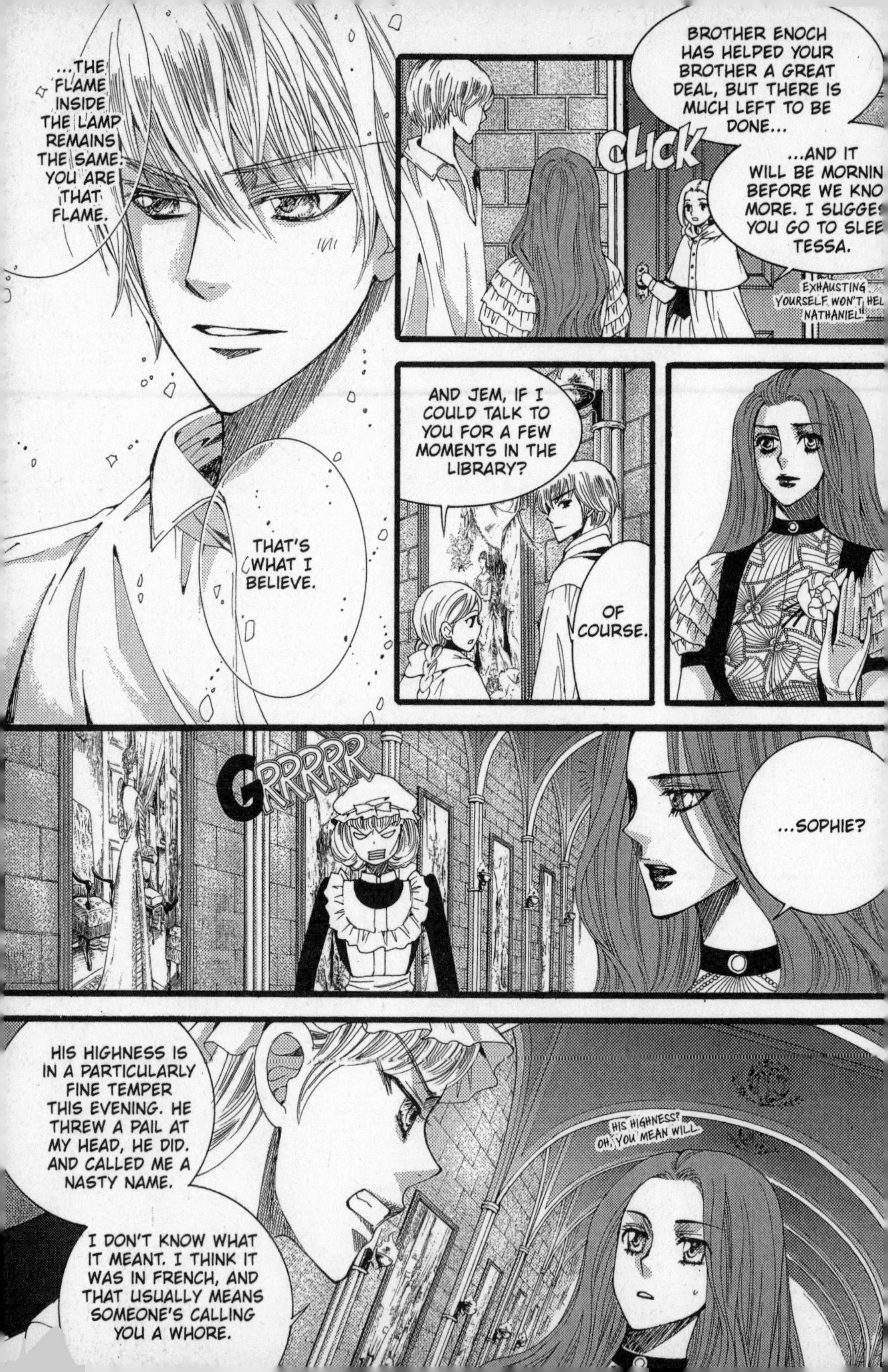
...THE FLAME INSIDE THE LAMP REMAINS THE SAME. YOU ARE THAT FLAME.
THAT'S WHAT I BELIEVE.
BROTHER ENOCH HAS HELPED YOUR BROTHER A GREAT DEAL, BUT THERE IS MUCH LEFT TO BE DONE...
CLICK
...AND IT WILL BE MORNIN BEFORE WE KNO MORE. I SUGGES YOU GO TO SLEE TESSA.
EXHAUSTING YOURSELF WON'T HEL NATHANIEL!
AND JEM, IF I COULD TALK TO YOU FOR A FEW MOMENTS IN THE LIBRARY?
OF COURSE.
GRRRRRR
...SOPHIE?
HIS HIGHNESS IS IN A PARTICULARLY FINE TEMPER THIS EVENING. HE THREW A PAIL AT MY HEAD, HE DID. AND CALLED ME A NASTY NAME.
I DON'T KNOW WHAT IT MEANT. I THINK IT WAS IN FRENCH, AND THAT USUALLY MEANS SOMEONE'S CALLING YOU A WHORE.
HIS HIGHNESS? OH, YOU MEAN WILL.

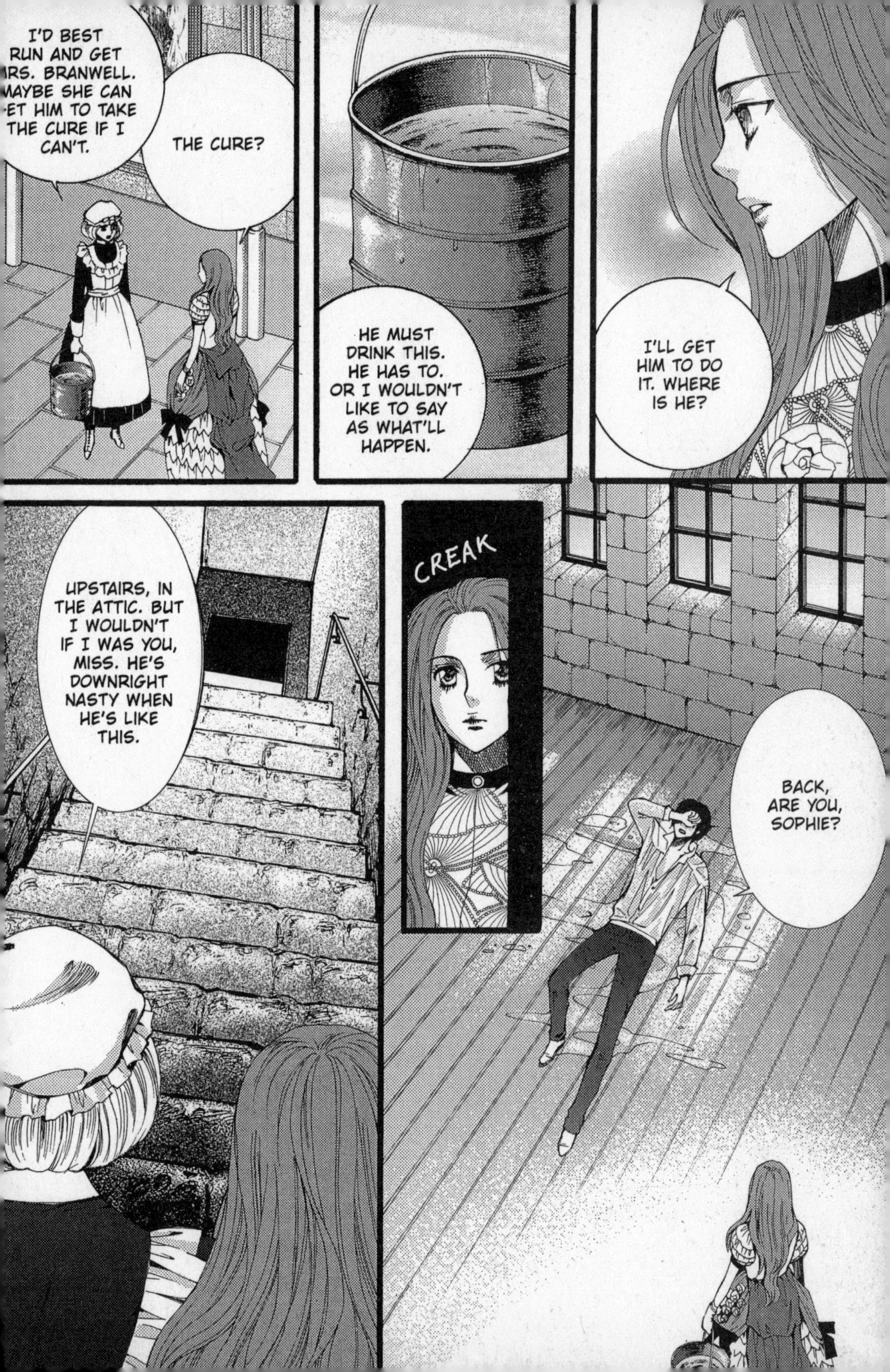
I'D BEST RUN AND GET [M]RS. BRANWELL. MAYBE SHE CAN [G]ET HIM TO TAKE THE CURE IF I CAN'T.
THE CURE?
HE MUST DRINK THIS. HE HAS TO. OR I WOULDN'T LIKE TO SAY AS WHAT'LL HAPPEN.
I'LL GET HIM TO DO IT. WHERE IS HE?
UPSTAIRS, IN THE ATTIC. BUT I WOULDN'T IF I WAS YOU, MISS. HE'S DOWNRIGHT NASTY WHEN HE'S LIKE THIS.
CREAK
BACK, ARE YOU, SOPHIE?

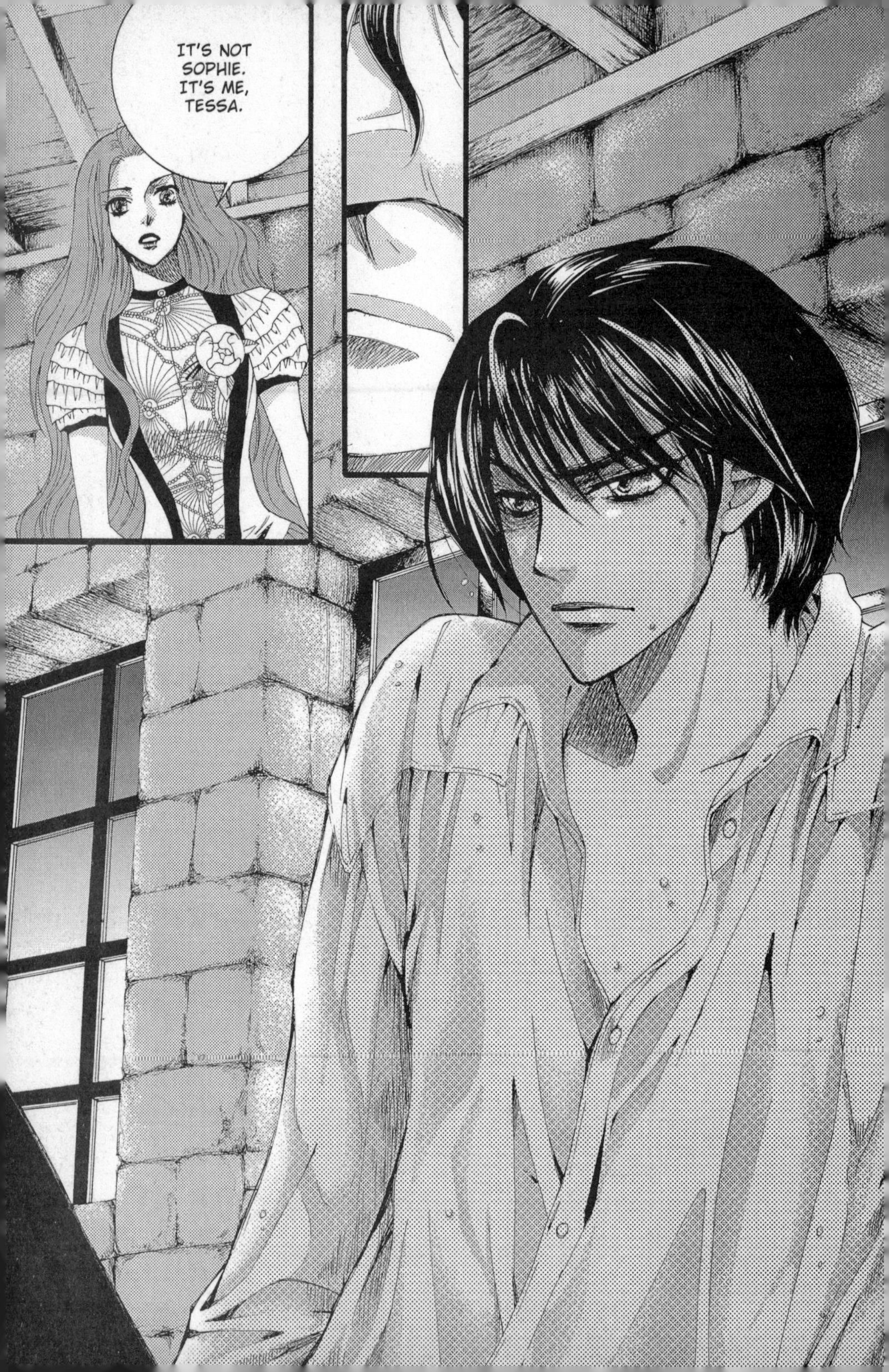
IT'S NOT SOPHIE. IT'S ME, TESSA.

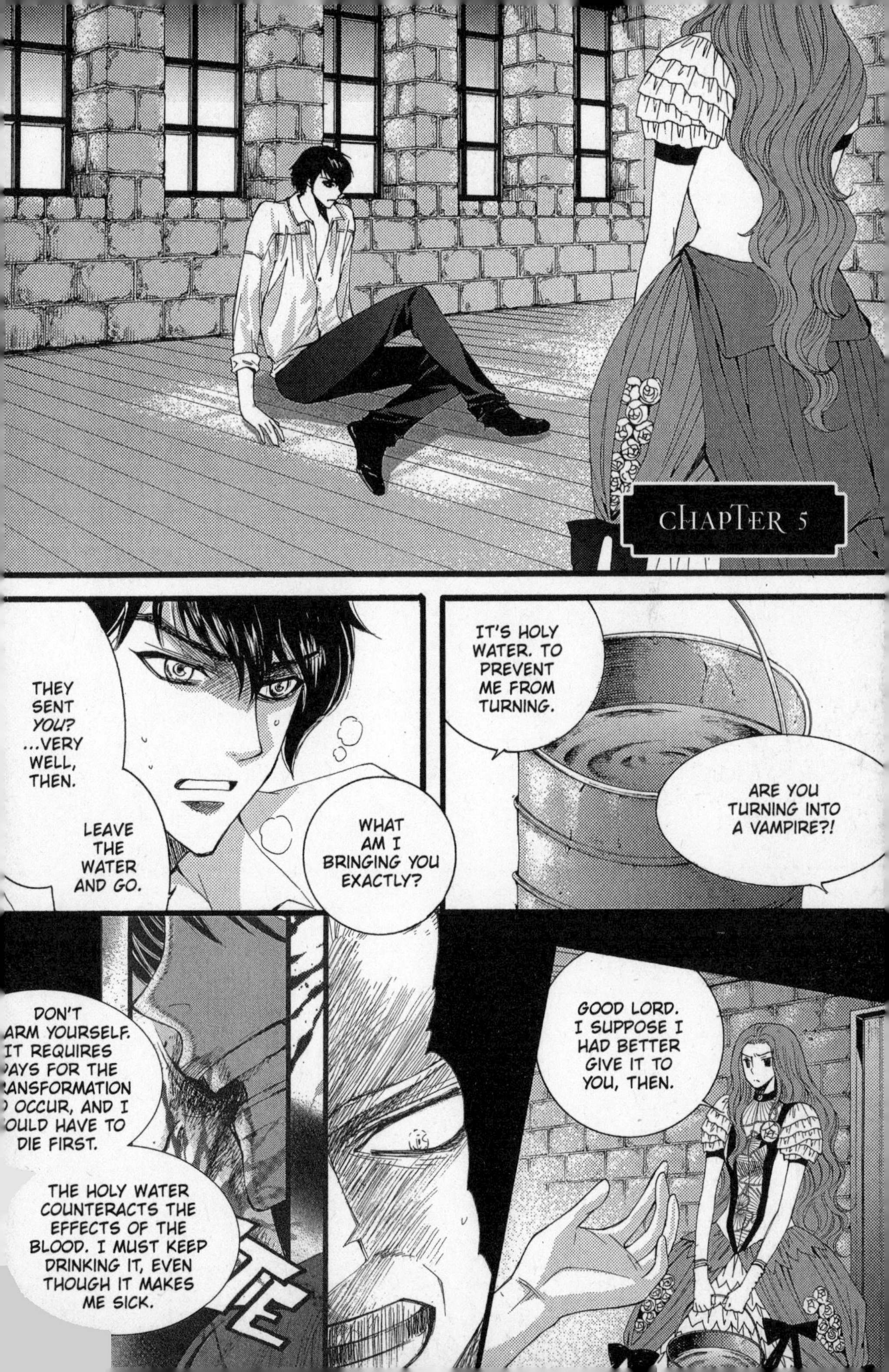
CHAPTER 5
THEY SENT YOU? ...VERY WELL, THEN.
LEAVE THE WATER AND GO.
WHAT AM I BRINGING YOU EXACTLY?
IT'S HOLY WATER. TO PREVENT ME FROM TURNING.
ARE YOU TURNING INTO A VAMPIRE?!
DON'T ARM YOURSELF. IT REQUIRES AYS FOR THE RANSFORMATION O OCCUR, AND I OULD HAVE TO DIE FIRST.
THE HOLY WATER COUNTERACTS THE EFFECTS OF THE BLOOD. I MUST KEEP DRINKING IT, EVEN THOUGH IT MAKES ME SICK.
GOOD LORD. I SUPPOSE I HAD BETTER GIVE IT TO YOU, THEN.

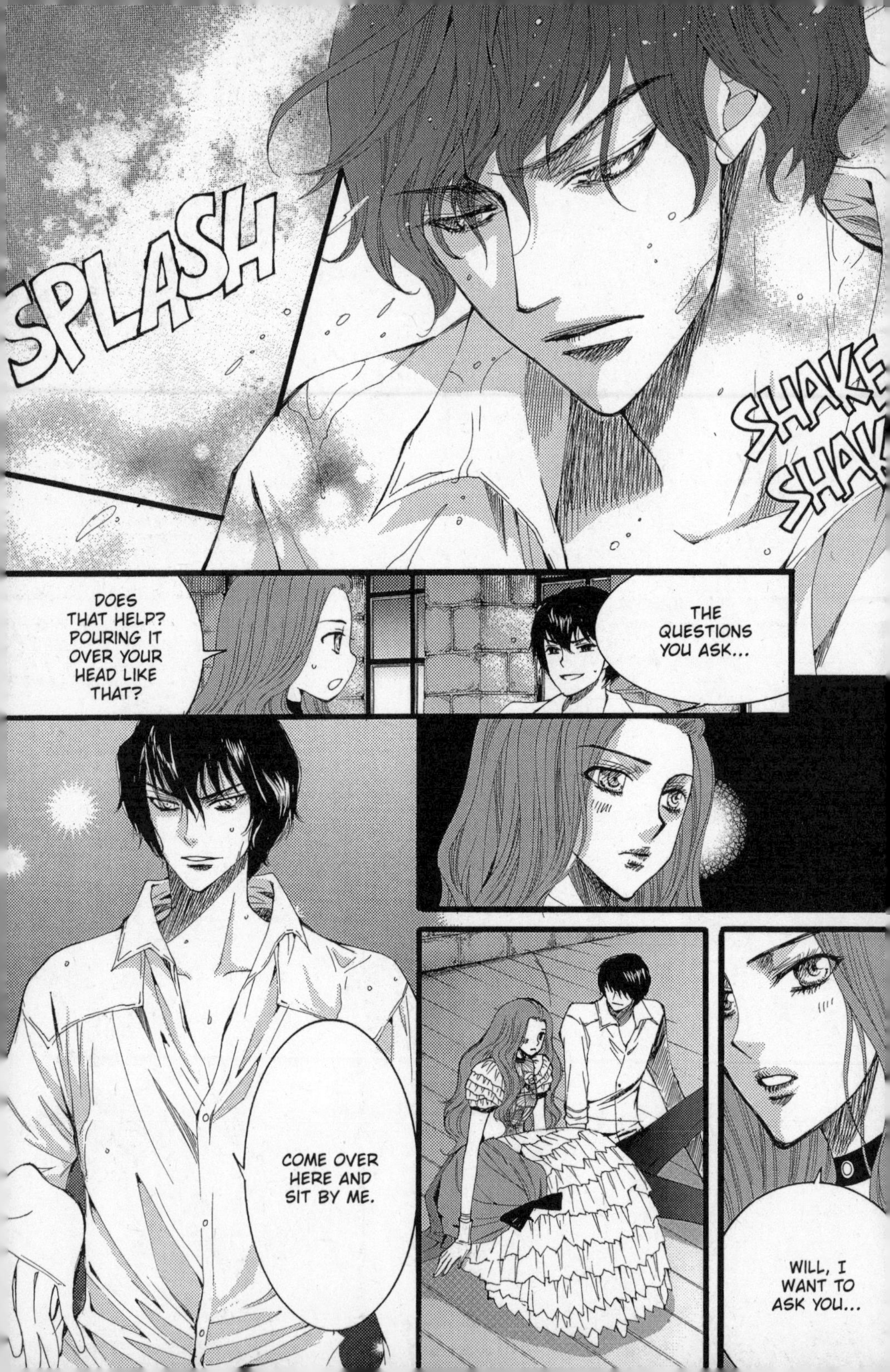
SPLASH
SHAKE SHAK
DOES THAT HELP? POURING IT OVER YOUR HEAD LIKE THAT?
THE QUESTIONS YOU ASK...
COME OVER HERE AND SIT BY ME.
WILL, I WANT TO ASK YOU...

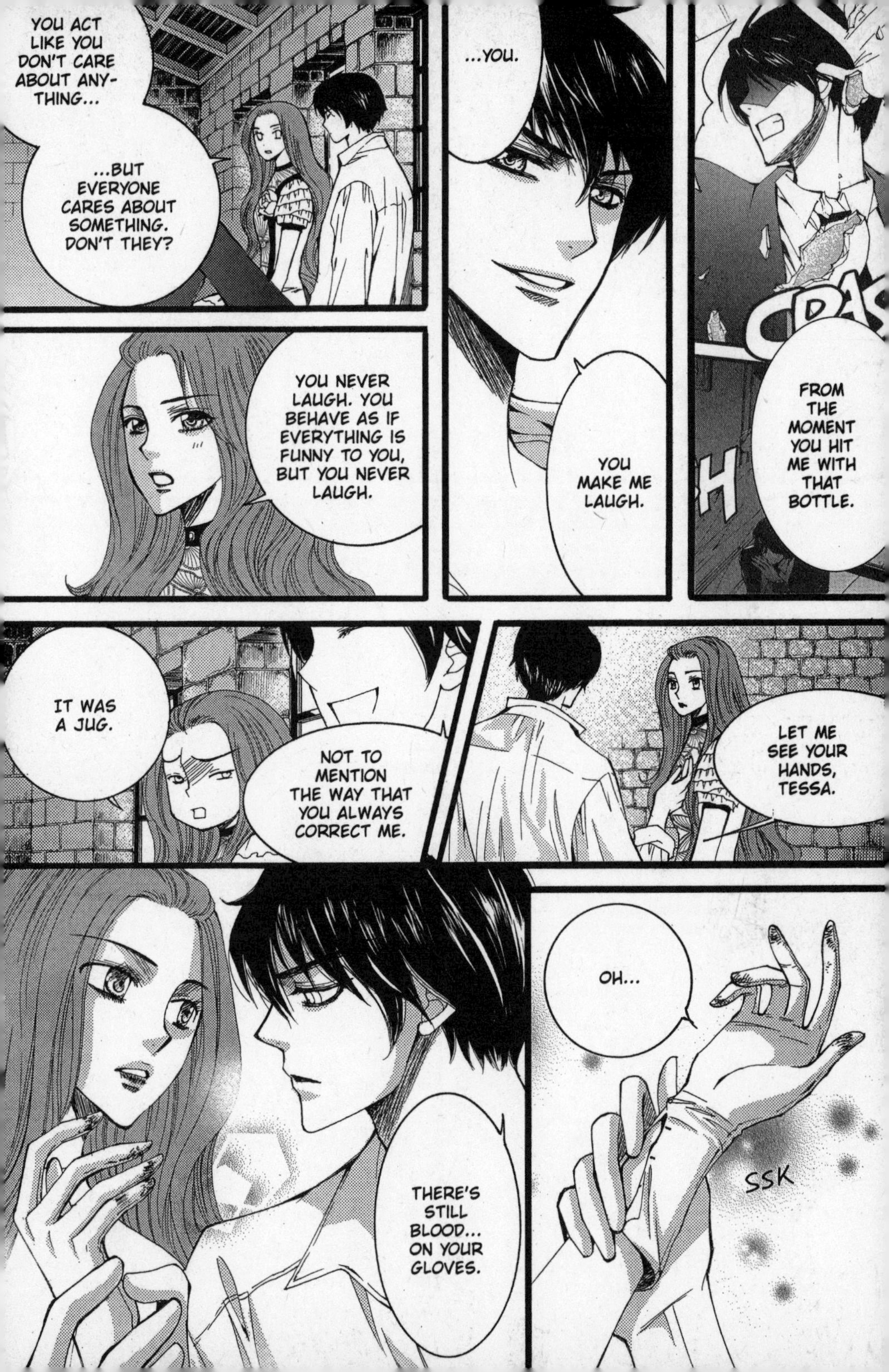
YOU ACT LIKE YOU DON'T CARE ABOUT ANY-THING...
...BUT EVERYONE CARES ABOUT SOMETHING. DON'T THEY?
YOU NEVER LAUGH. YOU BEHAVE AS IF EVERYTHING IS FUNNY TO YOU, BUT YOU NEVER LAUGH.
...YOU.
YOU MAKE ME LAUGH.
CRASH
FROM THE MOMENT YOU HIT ME WITH THAT BOTTLE.
IT WAS A JUG.
NOT TO MENTION THE WAY THAT YOU ALWAYS CORRECT ME.
LET ME SEE YOUR HANDS, TESSA.
THERE'S STILL BLOOD... ON YOUR GLOVES.
OH...
SSK

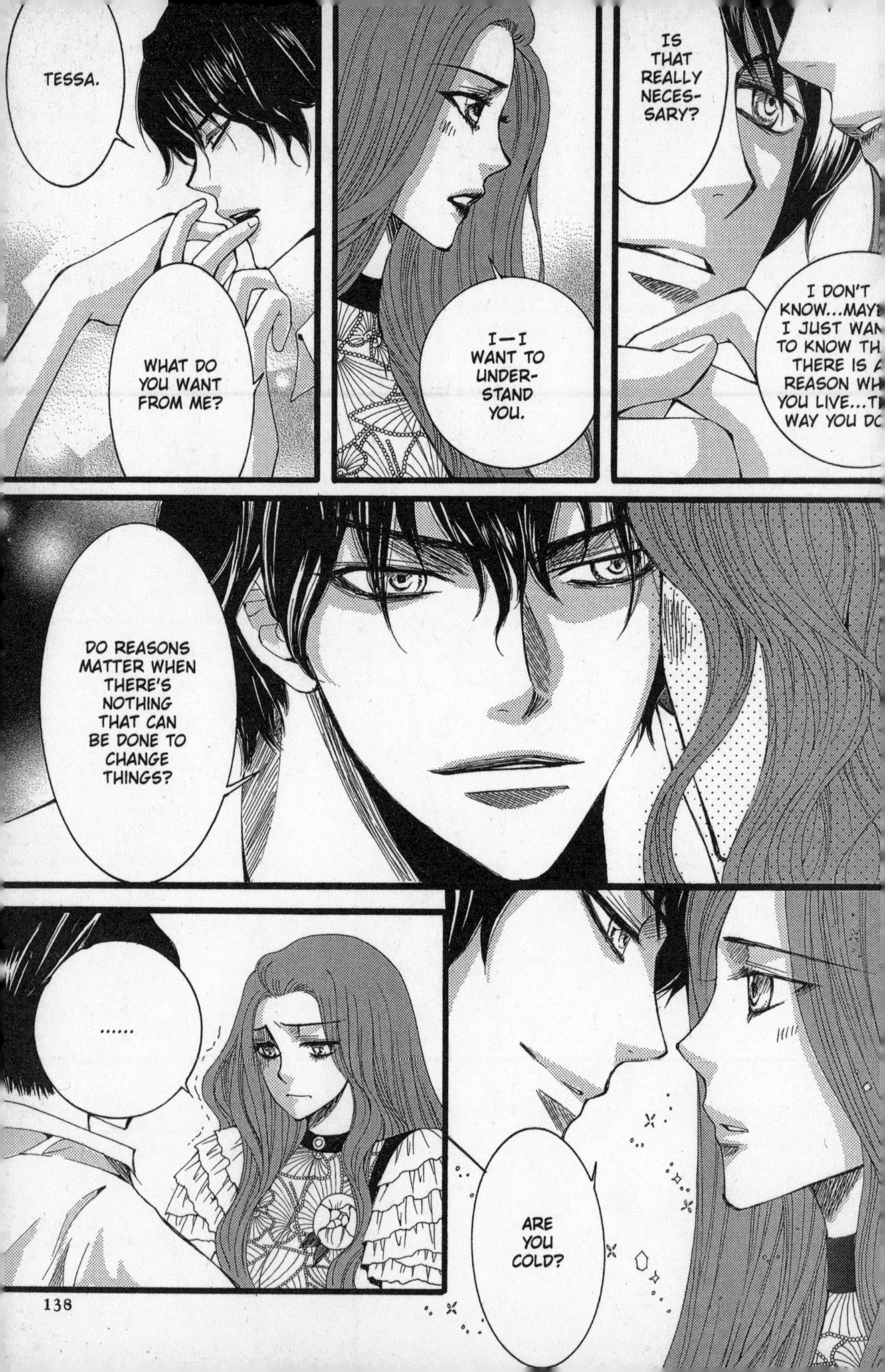

TESSA.
WHAT DO YOU WANT FROM ME?
I—I WANT TO UNDER-STAND YOU.
IS THAT REALLY NECES-SARY?
DO REASONS MATTER WHEN THERE'S NOTHING THAT CAN BE DONE TO CHANGE THINGS?
......
ARE YOU COLD?

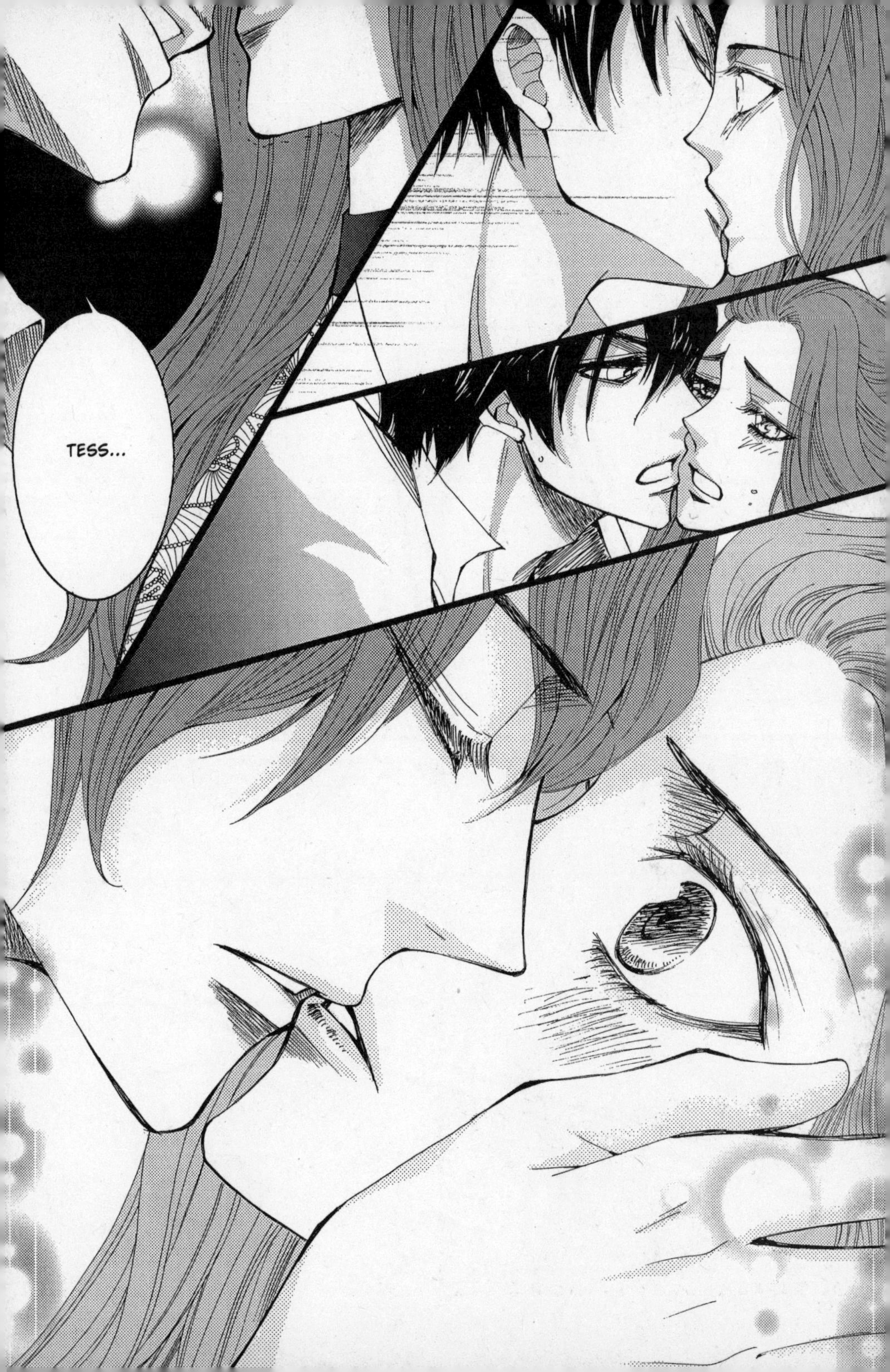
TESS...

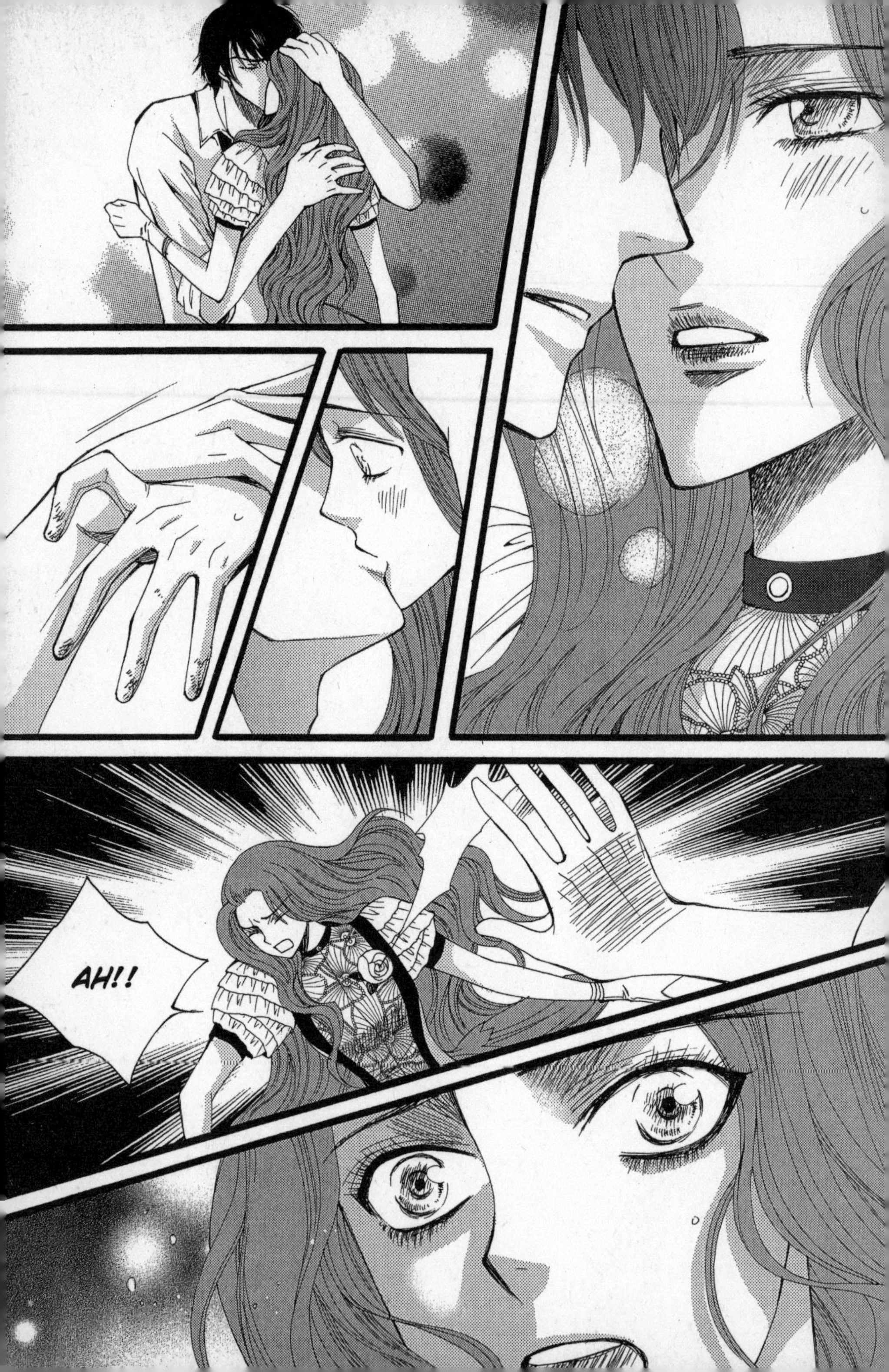
AH!!

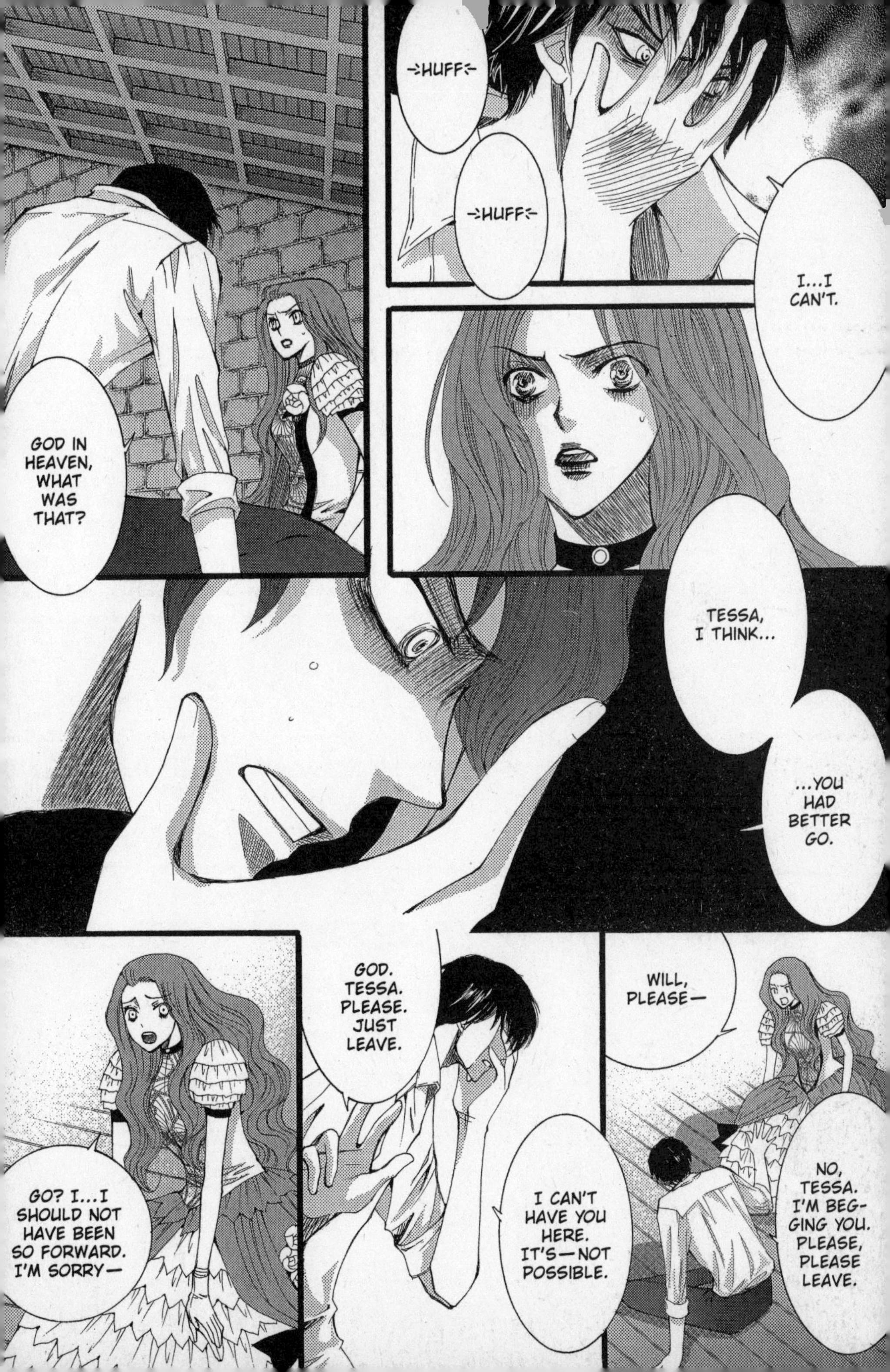
GOD IN HEAVEN, WHAT WAS THAT?
-HUFF-
-HUFF-
I...I CAN'T.
TESSA, I THINK...
...YOU HAD BETTER GO.
GO? I...I SHOULD NOT HAVE BEEN SO FORWARD. I'M SORRY—
GOD. TESSA. PLEASE. JUST LEAVE.
I CAN'T HAVE YOU HERE. IT'S—NOT POSSIBLE.
WILL, PLEASE—
NO, TESSA. I'M BEG-GING YOU. PLEASE, PLEASE LEAVE.

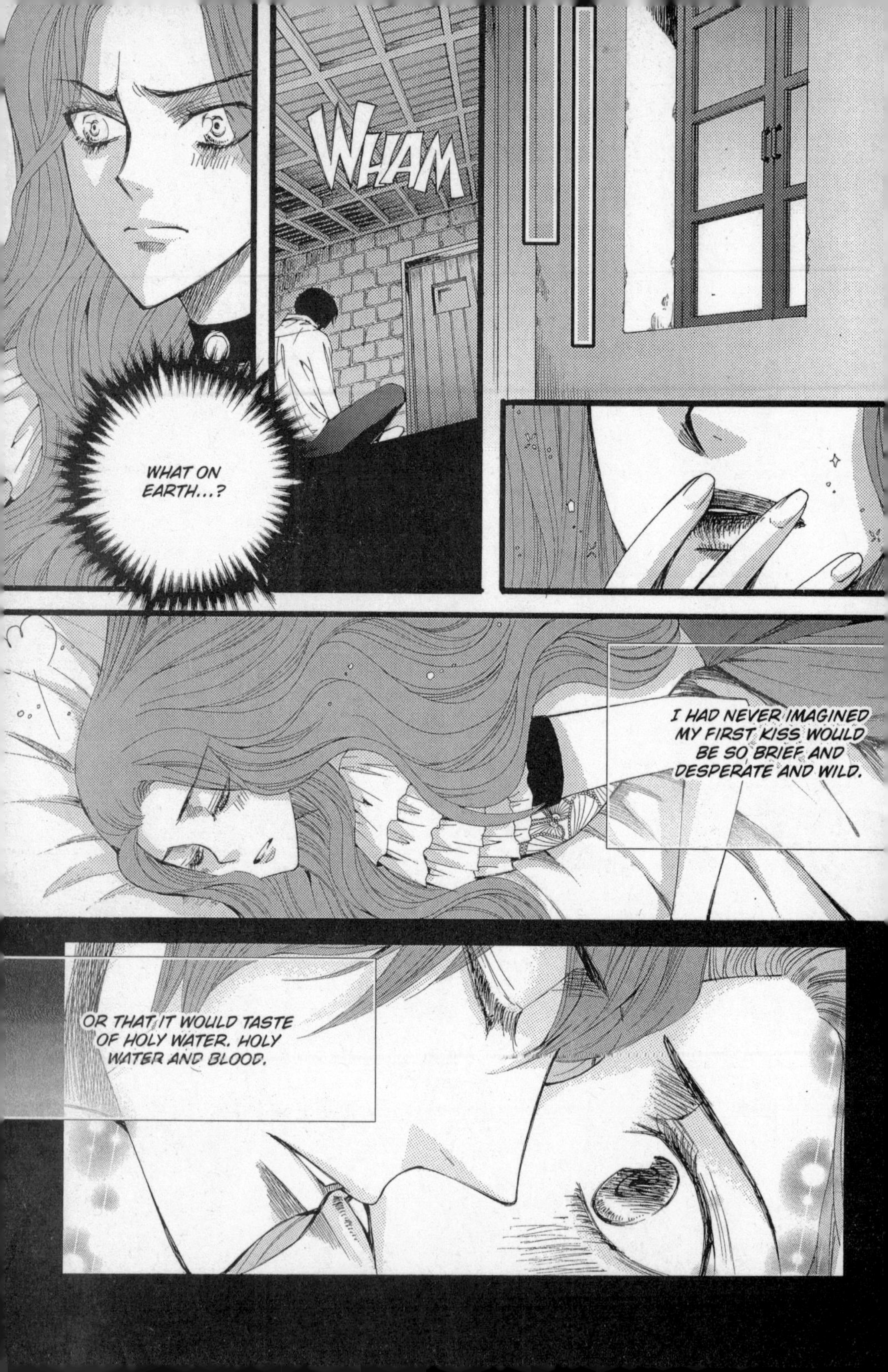
WHAM
WHAT ON EARTH...?
I HAD NEVER IMAGINED MY FIRST KISS WOULD BE SO BRIEF AND DESPERATE AND WILD.
OR THAT IT WOULD TASTE OF HOLY WATER. HOLY WATER AND BLOOD.

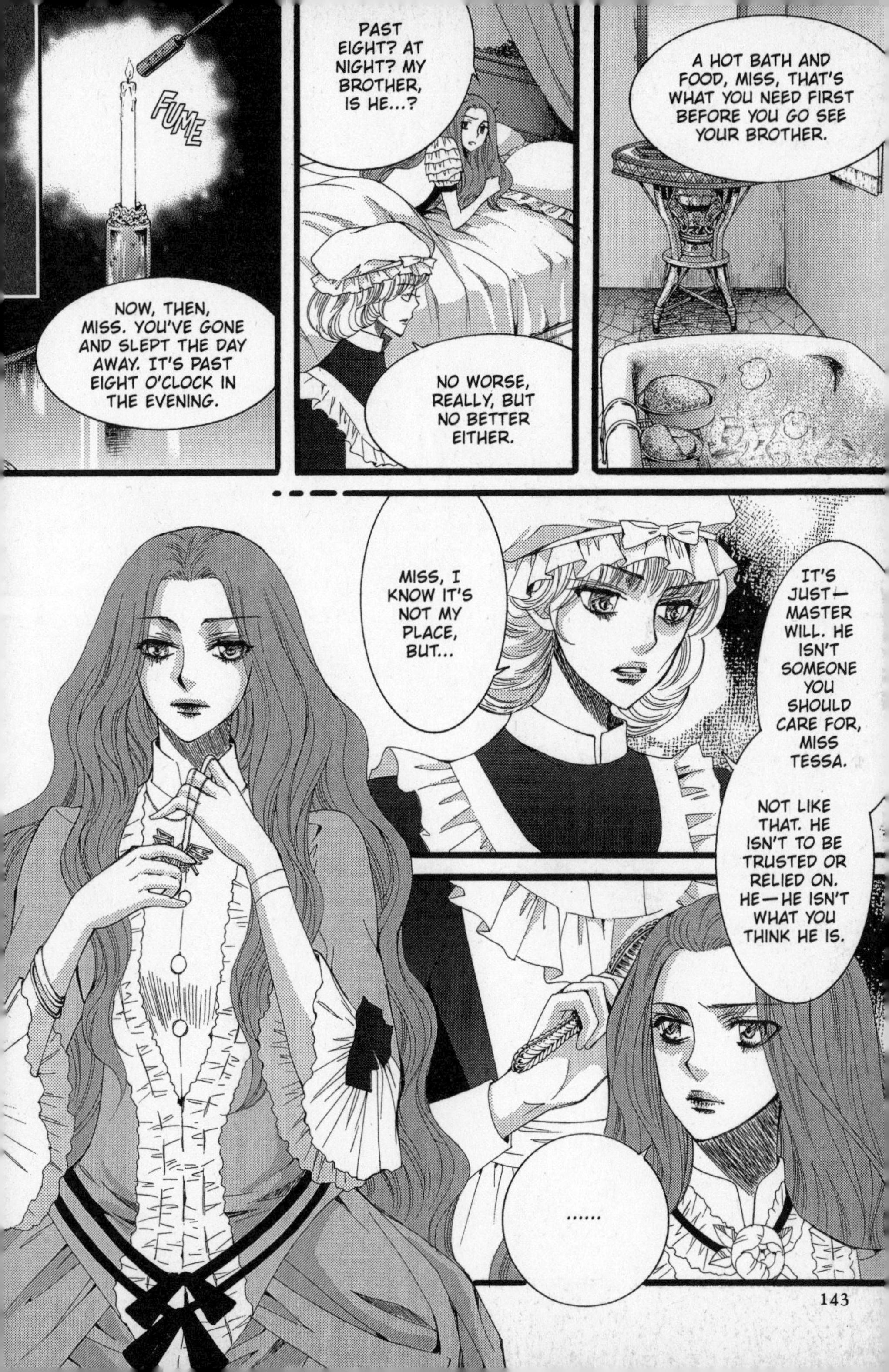

FUME
NOW, THEN, MISS. YOU'VE GONE AND SLEPT THE DAY AWAY. IT'S PAST EIGHT O'CLOCK IN THE EVENING.
PAST EIGHT? AT NIGHT? MY BROTHER, IS HE...?
NO WORSE, REALLY, BUT NO BETTER EITHER.
A HOT BATH AND FOOD, MISS, THAT'S WHAT YOU NEED FIRST BEFORE YOU GO SEE YOUR BROTHER.
MISS, I KNOW IT'S NOT MY PLACE, BUT...
IT'S JUST— MASTER WILL. HE ISN'T SOMEONE YOU SHOULD CARE FOR, MISS TESSA.
NOT LIKE THAT. HE ISN'T TO BE TRUSTED OR RELIED ON. HE—HE ISN'T WHAT YOU THINK HE IS.
......

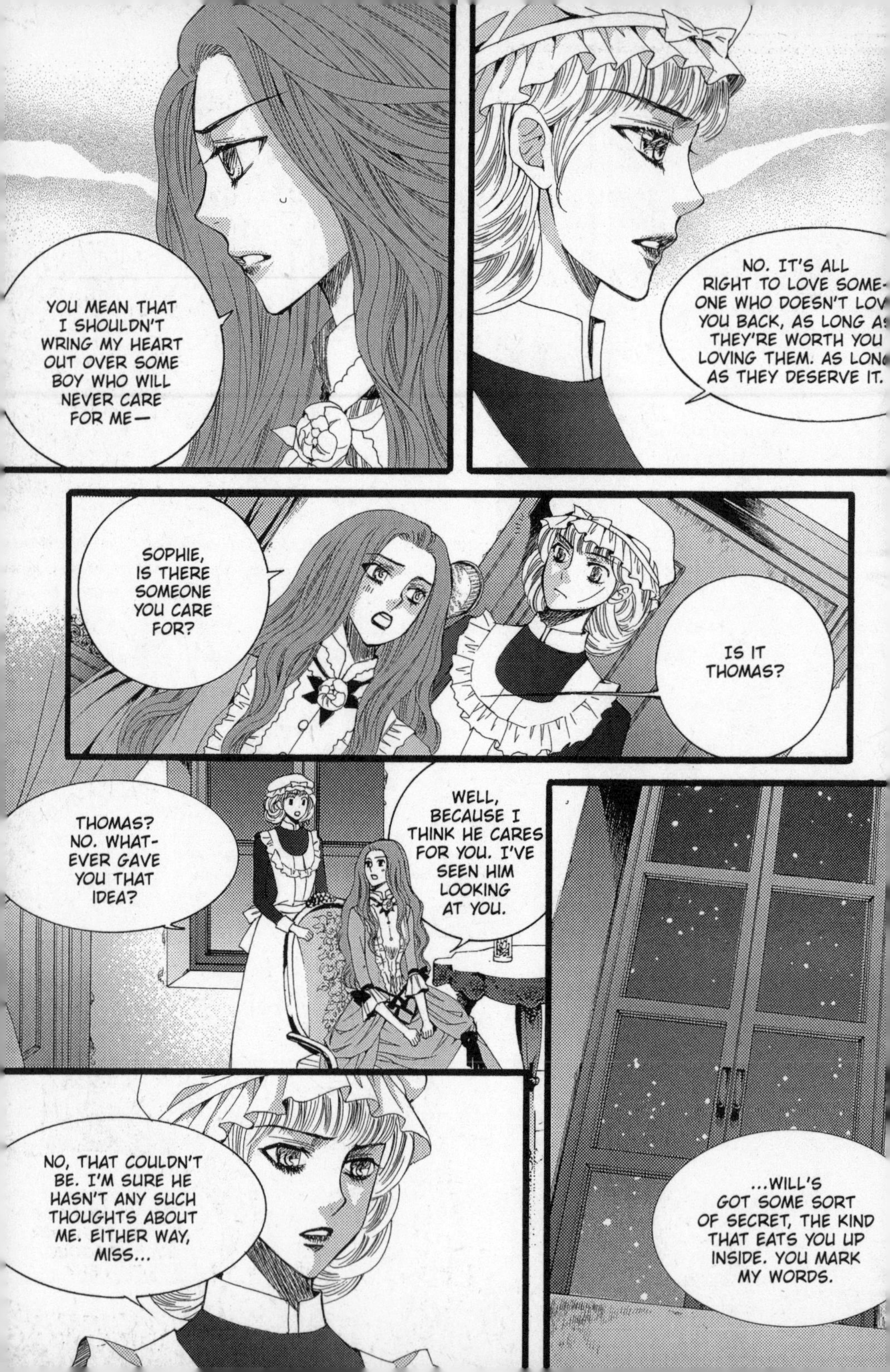

YOU MEAN THAT I SHOULDN'T WRING MY HEART OUT OVER SOME BOY WHO WILL NEVER CARE FOR ME—
NO. IT'S ALL RIGHT TO LOVE SOME-ONE WHO DOESN'T LOV YOU BACK, AS LONG A THEY'RE WORTH YOU LOVING THEM. AS LON AS THEY DESERVE IT.
SOPHIE, IS THERE SOMEONE YOU CARE FOR?
IS IT THOMAS?
THOMAS? NO. WHAT-EVER GAVE YOU THAT IDEA?
WELL, BECAUSE I THINK HE CARES FOR YOU. I'VE SEEN HIM LOOKING AT YOU.
NO, THAT COULDN'T BE. I'M SURE HE HASN'T ANY SUCH THOUGHTS ABOUT ME. EITHER WAY, MISS...
...WILL'S GOT SOME SORT OF SECRET, THE KIND THAT EATS YOU UP INSIDE. YOU MARK MY WORDS.

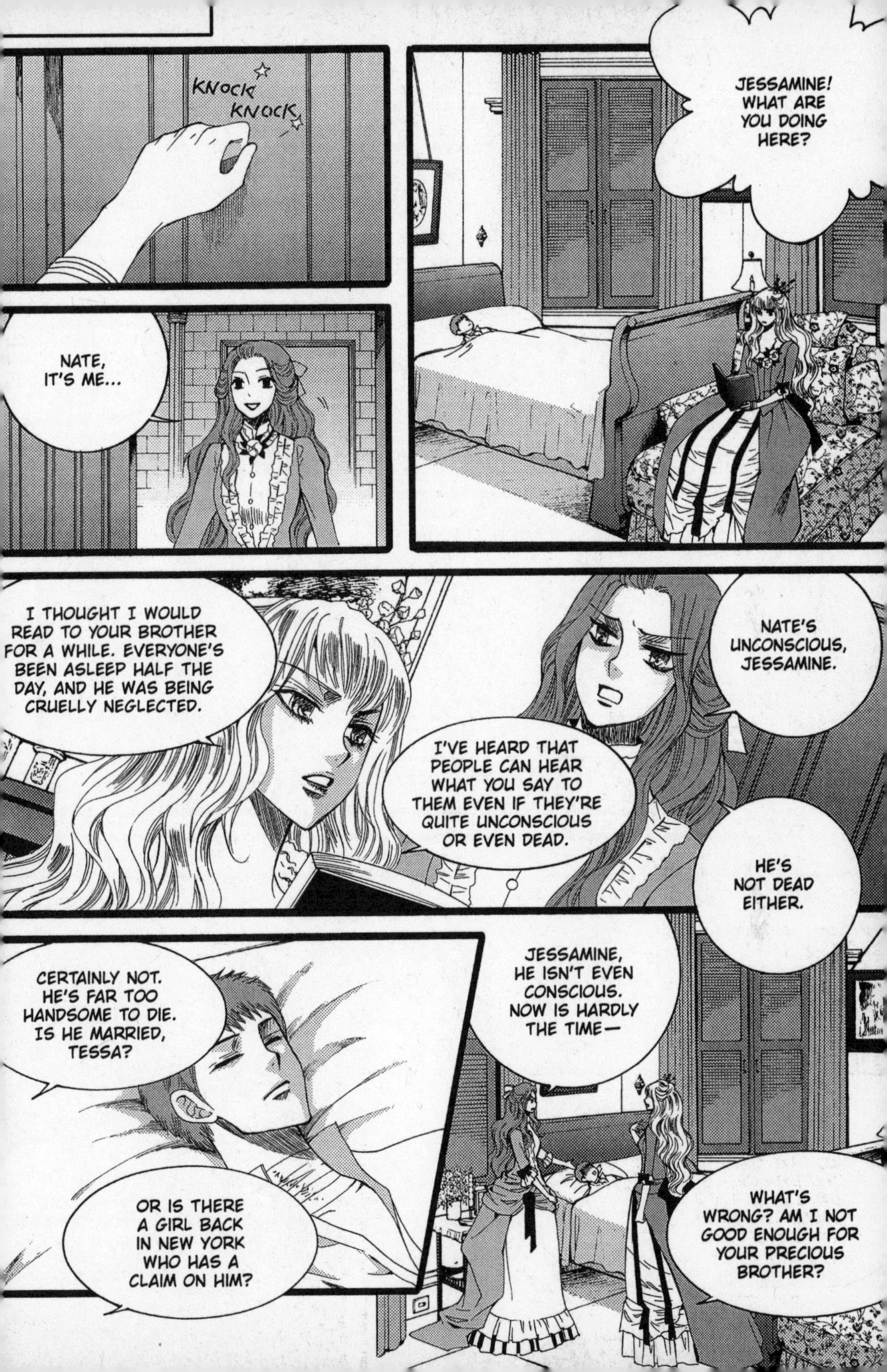
KNOCK KNOCK
NATE, IT'S ME...
JESSAMINE! WHAT ARE YOU DOING HERE?
I THOUGHT I WOULD READ TO YOUR BROTHER FOR A WHILE. EVERYONE'S BEEN ASLEEP HALF THE DAY, AND HE WAS BEING CRUELLY NEGLECTED.
I'VE HEARD THAT PEOPLE CAN HEAR WHAT YOU SAY TO THEM EVEN IF THEY'RE QUITE UNCONSCIOUS OR EVEN DEAD.
NATE'S UNCONSCIOUS, JESSAMINE.
HE'S NOT DEAD EITHER.
CERTAINLY NOT. HE'S FAR TOO HANDSOME TO DIE. IS HE MARRIED, TESSA?
OR IS THERE A GIRL BACK IN NEW YORK WHO HAS A CLAIM ON HIM?
JESSAMINE, HE ISN'T EVEN CONSCIOUS. NOW IS HARDLY THE TIME—
WHAT'S WRONG? AM I NOT GOOD ENOUGH FOR YOUR PRECIOUS BROTHER?

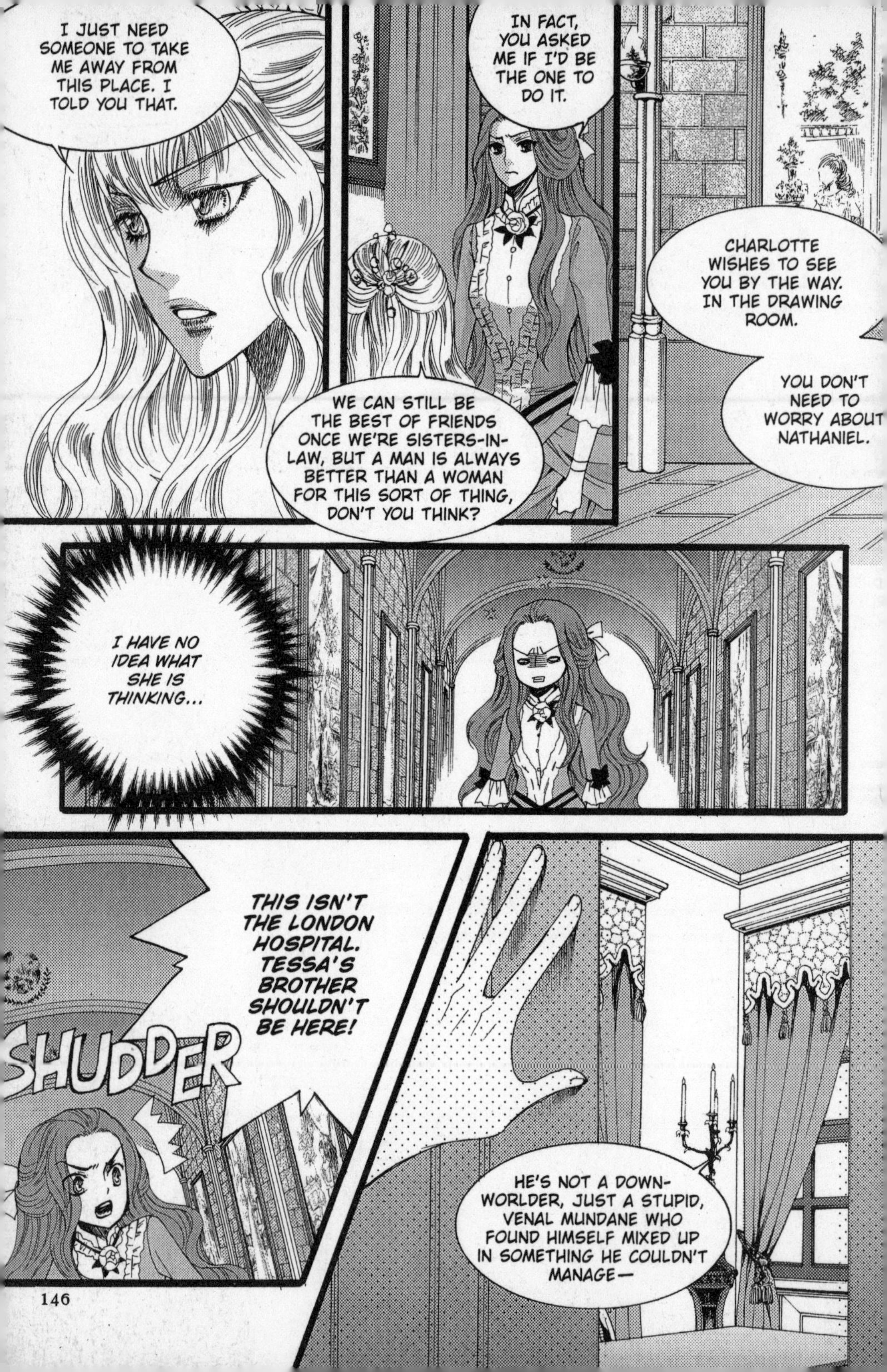
I JUST NEED SOMEONE TO TAKE ME AWAY FROM THIS PLACE. I TOLD YOU THAT.
IN FACT, YOU ASKED ME IF I'D BE THE ONE TO DO IT.
WE CAN STILL BE THE BEST OF FRIENDS ONCE WE'RE SISTERS-IN-LAW, BUT A MAN IS ALWAYS BETTER THAN A WOMAN FOR THIS SORT OF THING, DON'T YOU THINK?
CHARLOTTE WISHES TO SEE YOU BY THE WAY. IN THE DRAWING ROOM.
YOU DON'T NEED TO WORRY ABOUT NATHANIEL.
I HAVE NO IDEA WHAT SHE IS THINKING...
THIS ISN'T THE LONDON HOSPITAL. TESSA'S BROTHER SHOULDN'T BE HERE!
SHUDDER
HE'S NOT A DOWN-WORLDER, JUST A STUPID, VENAL MUNDANE WHO FOUND HIMSELF MIXED UP IN SOMETHING HE COULDN'T MANAGE—

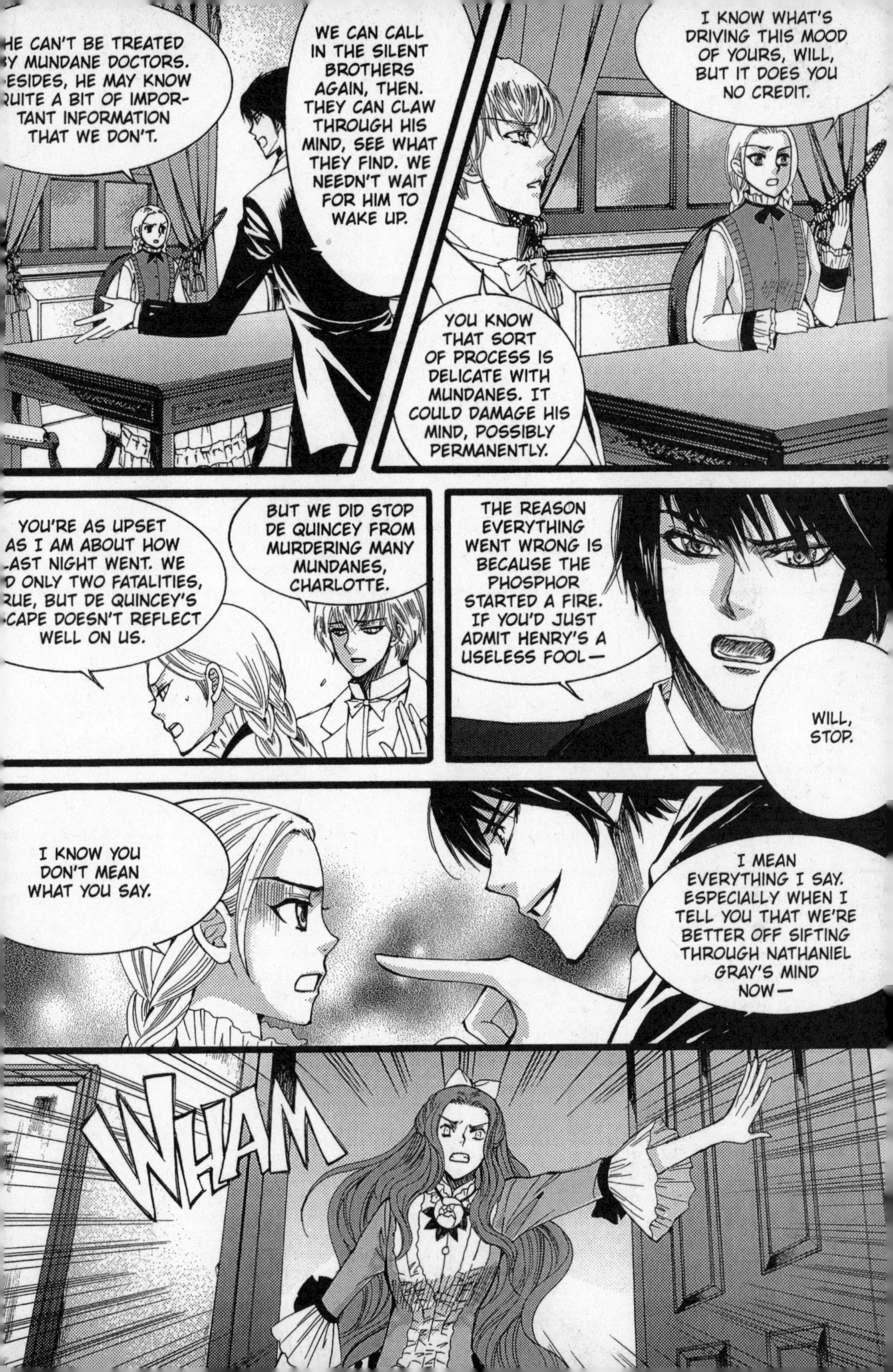
HE CAN'T BE TREATED Y MUNDANE DOCTORS. ESIDES, HE MAY KNOW UITE A BIT OF IMPOR- TANT INFORMATION THAT WE DON'T.
WE CAN CALL IN THE SILENT BROTHERS AGAIN, THEN. THEY CAN CLAW THROUGH HIS MIND, SEE WHAT THEY FIND. WE NEEDN'T WAIT FOR HIM TO WAKE UP.
I KNOW WHAT'S DRIVING THIS MOOD OF YOURS, WILL, BUT IT DOES YOU NO CREDIT.
YOU KNOW THAT SORT OF PROCESS IS DELICATE WITH MUNDANES. IT COULD DAMAGE HIS MIND, POSSIBLY PERMANENTLY.
YOU'RE AS UPSET AS I AM ABOUT HOW LAST NIGHT WENT. WE D ONLY TWO FATALITIES, RUE, BUT DE QUINCEY'S SCAPE DOESN'T REFLECT WELL ON US.
BUT WE DID STOP DE QUINCEY FROM MURDERING MANY MUNDANES, CHARLOTTE.
THE REASON EVERYTHING WENT WRONG IS BECAUSE THE PHOSPHOR STARTED A FIRE. IF YOU'D JUST ADMIT HENRY'S A USELESS FOOL—
WILL, STOP.
I KNOW YOU DON'T MEAN WHAT YOU SAY.
I MEAN EVERYTHING I SAY. ESPECIALLY WHEN I TELL YOU THAT WE'RE BETTER OFF SIFTING THROUGH NATHANIEL GRAY'S MIND NOW—
WHAM

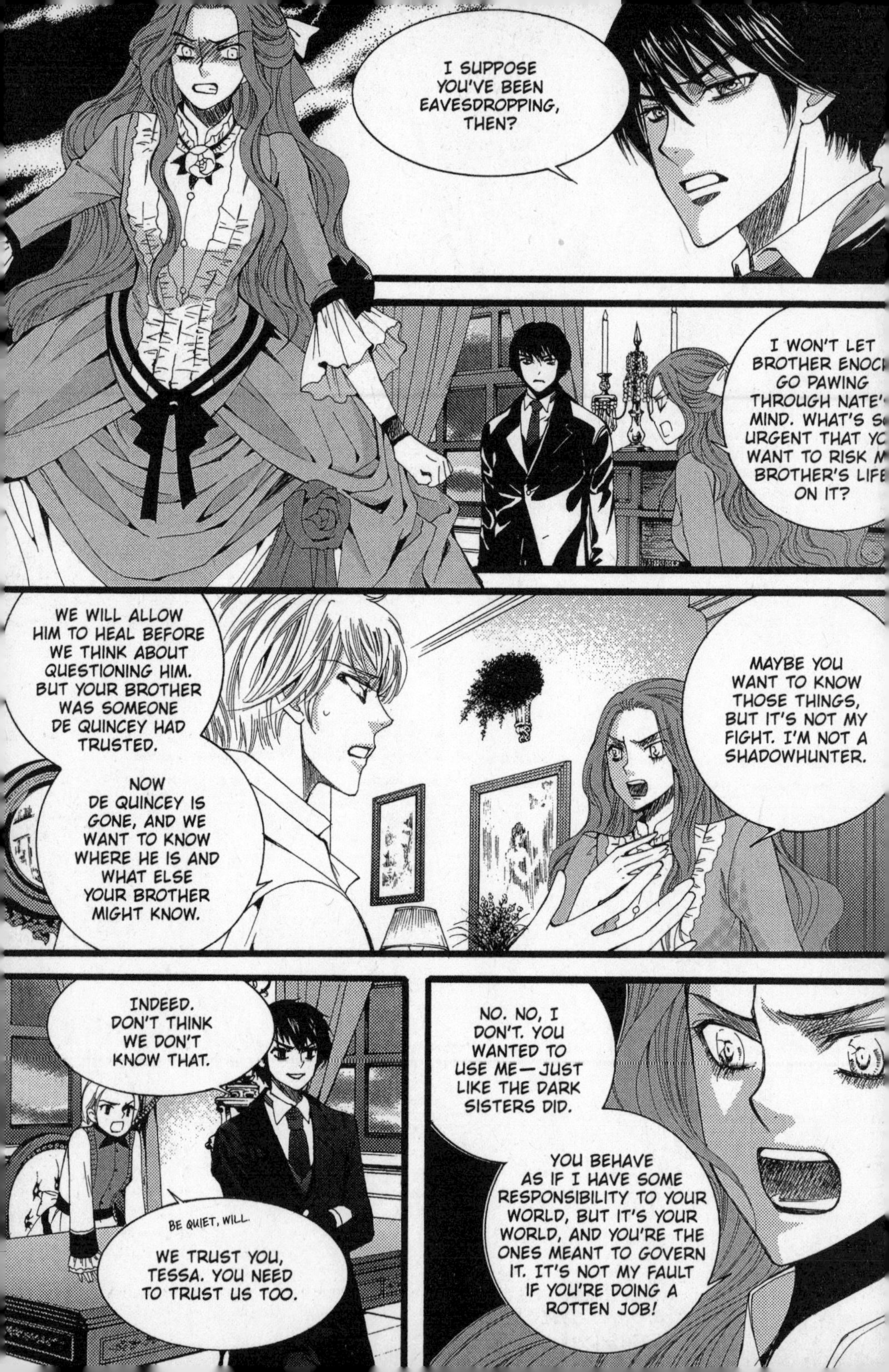
I SUPPOSE YOU'VE BEEN EAVESDROPPING, THEN?
I WON'T LET BROTHER ENOCH GO PAWING THROUGH NATE'S MIND. WHAT'S SO URGENT THAT YOU WANT TO RISK MY BROTHER'S LIFE ON IT?
WE WILL ALLOW HIM TO HEAL BEFORE WE THINK ABOUT QUESTIONING HIM. BUT YOUR BROTHER WAS SOMEONE DE QUINCEY HAD TRUSTED.
NOW DE QUINCEY IS GONE, AND WE WANT TO KNOW WHERE HE IS AND WHAT ELSE YOUR BROTHER MIGHT KNOW.
MAYBE YOU WANT TO KNOW THOSE THINGS, BUT IT'S NOT MY FIGHT. I'M NOT A SHADOWHUNTER.
INDEED. DON'T THINK WE DON'T KNOW THAT.
BE QUIET, WILL.
WE TRUST YOU, TESSA. YOU NEED TO TRUST US TOO.
NO. NO, I DON'T. YOU WANTED TO USE ME—JUST LIKE THE DARK SISTERS DID.
YOU BEHAVE AS IF I HAVE SOME RESPONSIBILITY TO YOUR WORLD, BUT IT'S YOUR WORLD, AND YOU'RE THE ONES MEANT TO GOVERN IT. IT'S NOT MY FAULT IF YOU'RE DOING A ROTTEN JOB!

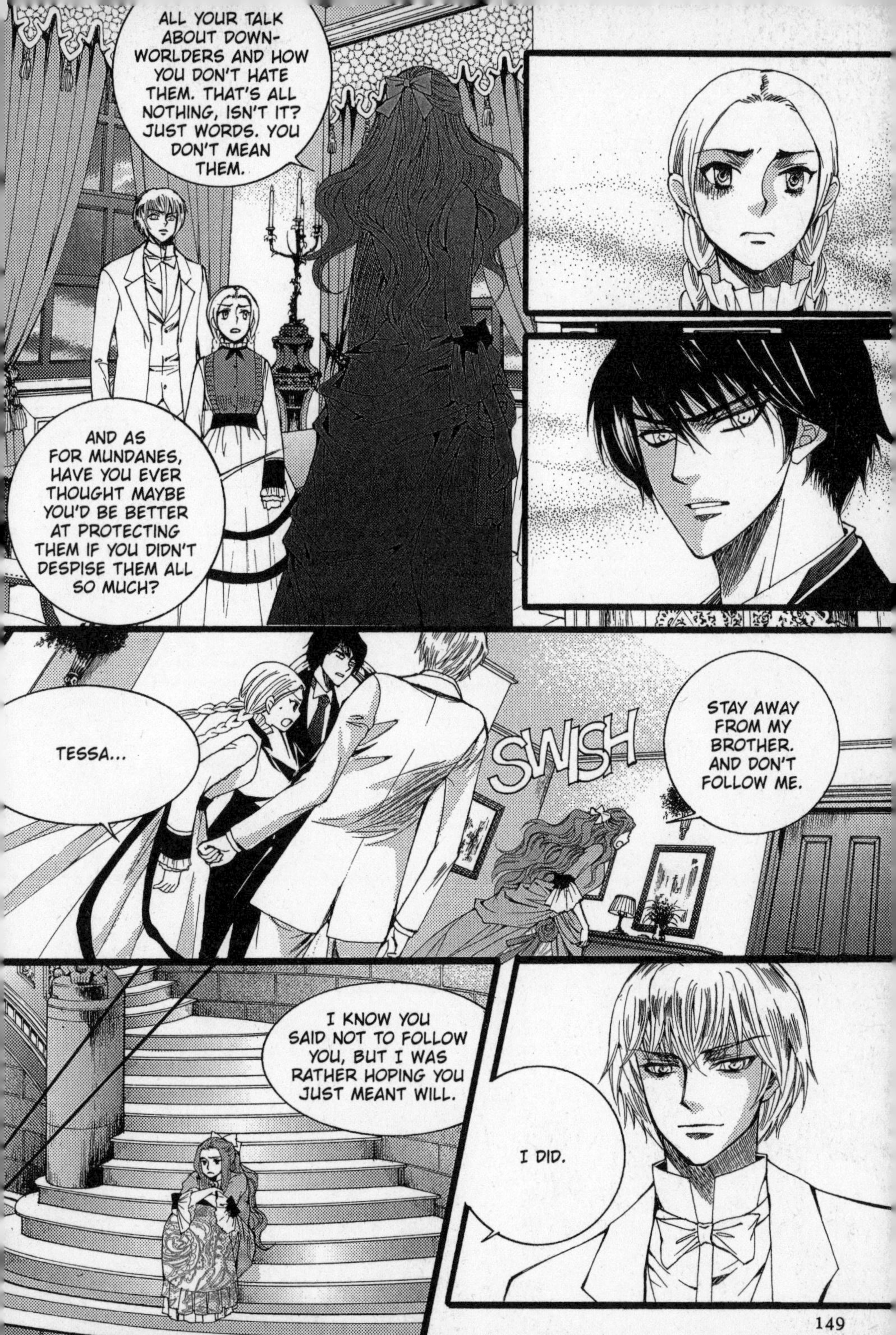
ALL YOUR TALK ABOUT DOWN-WORLDERS AND HOW YOU DON'T HATE THEM. THAT'S ALL NOTHING, ISN'T IT? JUST WORDS. YOU DON'T MEAN THEM.
AND AS FOR MUNDANES, HAVE YOU EVER THOUGHT MAYBE YOU'D BE BETTER AT PROTECTING THEM IF YOU DIDN'T DESPISE THEM ALL SO MUCH?
TESSA...
SWISH
STAY AWAY FROM MY BROTHER. AND DON'T FOLLOW ME.
I KNOW YOU SAID NOT TO FOLLOW YOU, BUT I WAS RATHER HOPING YOU JUST MEANT WILL.
I DID.

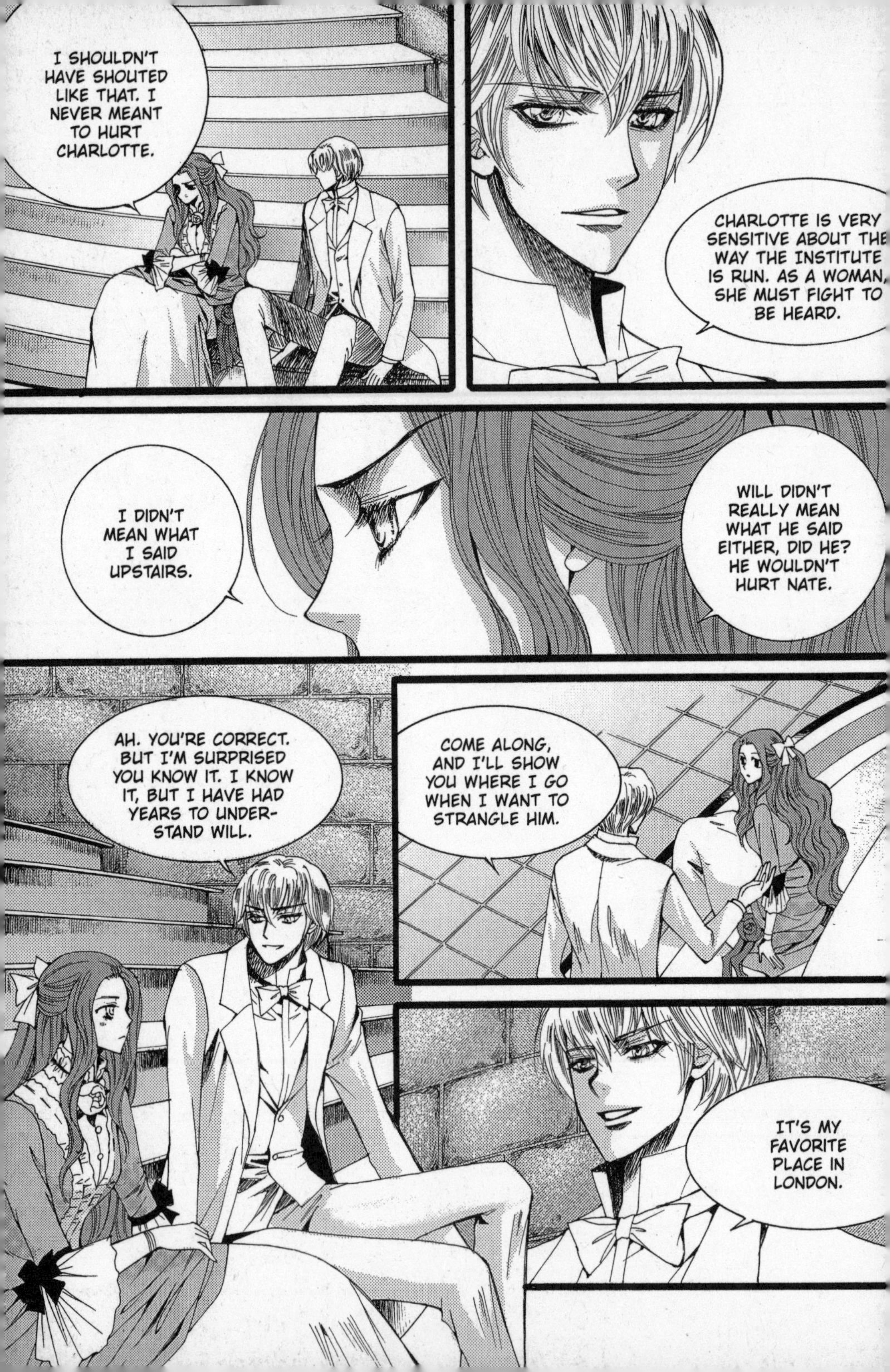
I SHOULDN'T HAVE SHOUTED LIKE THAT. I NEVER MEANT TO HURT CHARLOTTE.
CHARLOTTE IS VERY SENSITIVE ABOUT THE WAY THE INSTITUTE IS RUN. AS A WOMAN, SHE MUST FIGHT TO BE HEARD.
I DIDN'T MEAN WHAT I SAID UPSTAIRS.
WILL DIDN'T REALLY MEAN WHAT HE SAID EITHER, DID HE? HE WOULDN'T HURT NATE.
AH. YOU'RE CORRECT. BUT I'M SURPRISED YOU KNOW IT. I KNOW IT, BUT I HAVE HAD YEARS TO UNDER-STAND WILL.
COME ALONG, AND I'LL SHOW YOU WHERE I GO WHEN I WANT TO STRANGLE HIM.
IT'S MY FAVORITE PLACE IN LONDON.

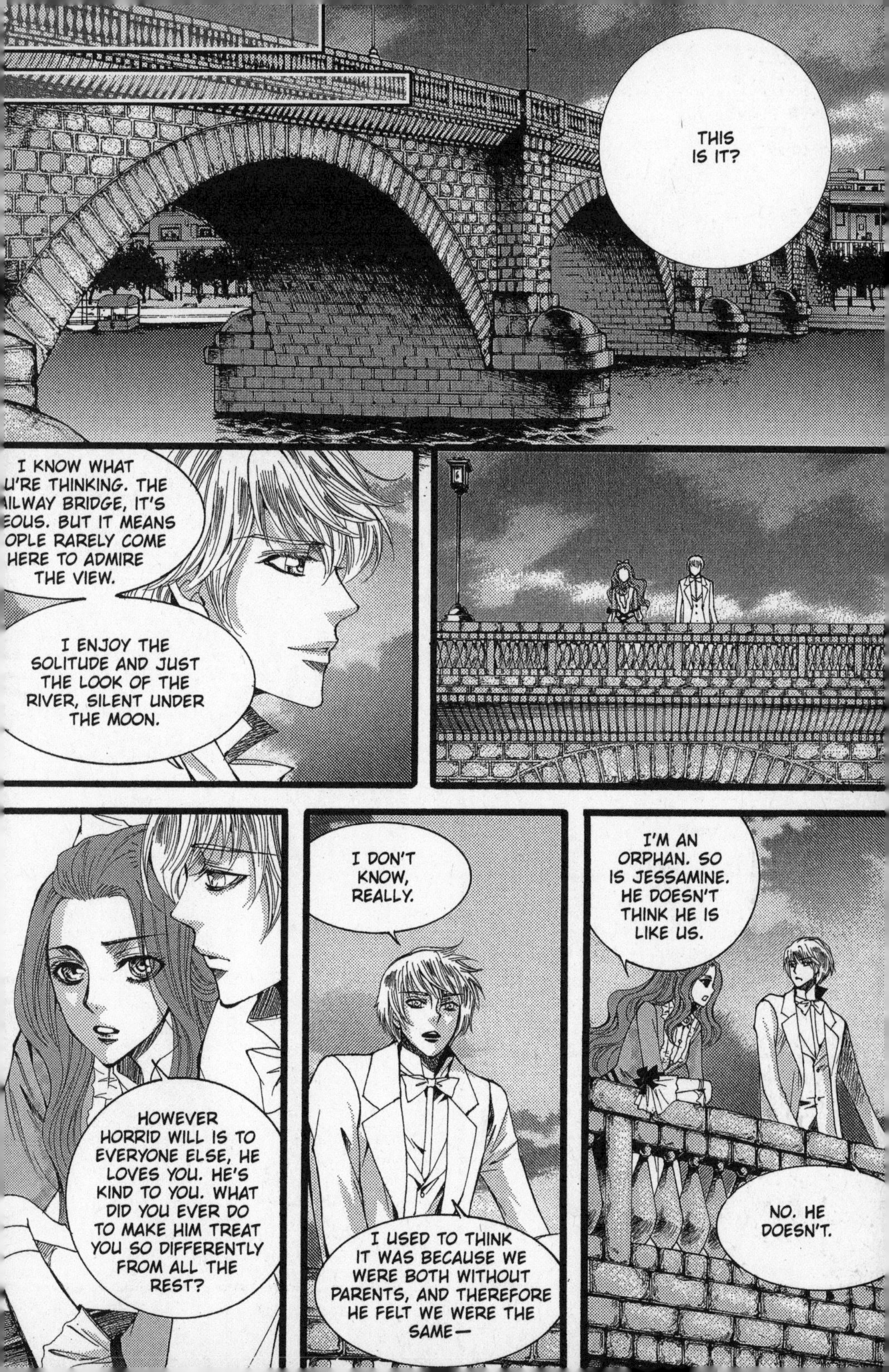
THIS IS IT?
I KNOW WHAT U'RE THINKING. THE AILWAY BRIDGE, IT'S EOUS. BUT IT MEANS OPLE RARELY COME HERE TO ADMIRE THE VIEW.
I ENJOY THE SOLITUDE AND JUST THE LOOK OF THE RIVER, SILENT UNDER THE MOON.
HOWEVER HORRID WILL IS TO EVERYONE ELSE, HE LOVES YOU. HE'S KIND TO YOU. WHAT DID YOU EVER DO TO MAKE HIM TREAT YOU SO DIFFERENTLY FROM ALL THE REST?
I DON'T KNOW, REALLY.
I USED TO THINK IT WAS BECAUSE WE WERE BOTH WITHOUT PARENTS, AND THEREFORE HE FELT WE WERE THE SAME—
I'M AN ORPHAN. SO IS JESSAMINE. HE DOESN'T THINK HE IS LIKE US.
NO. HE DOESN'T.

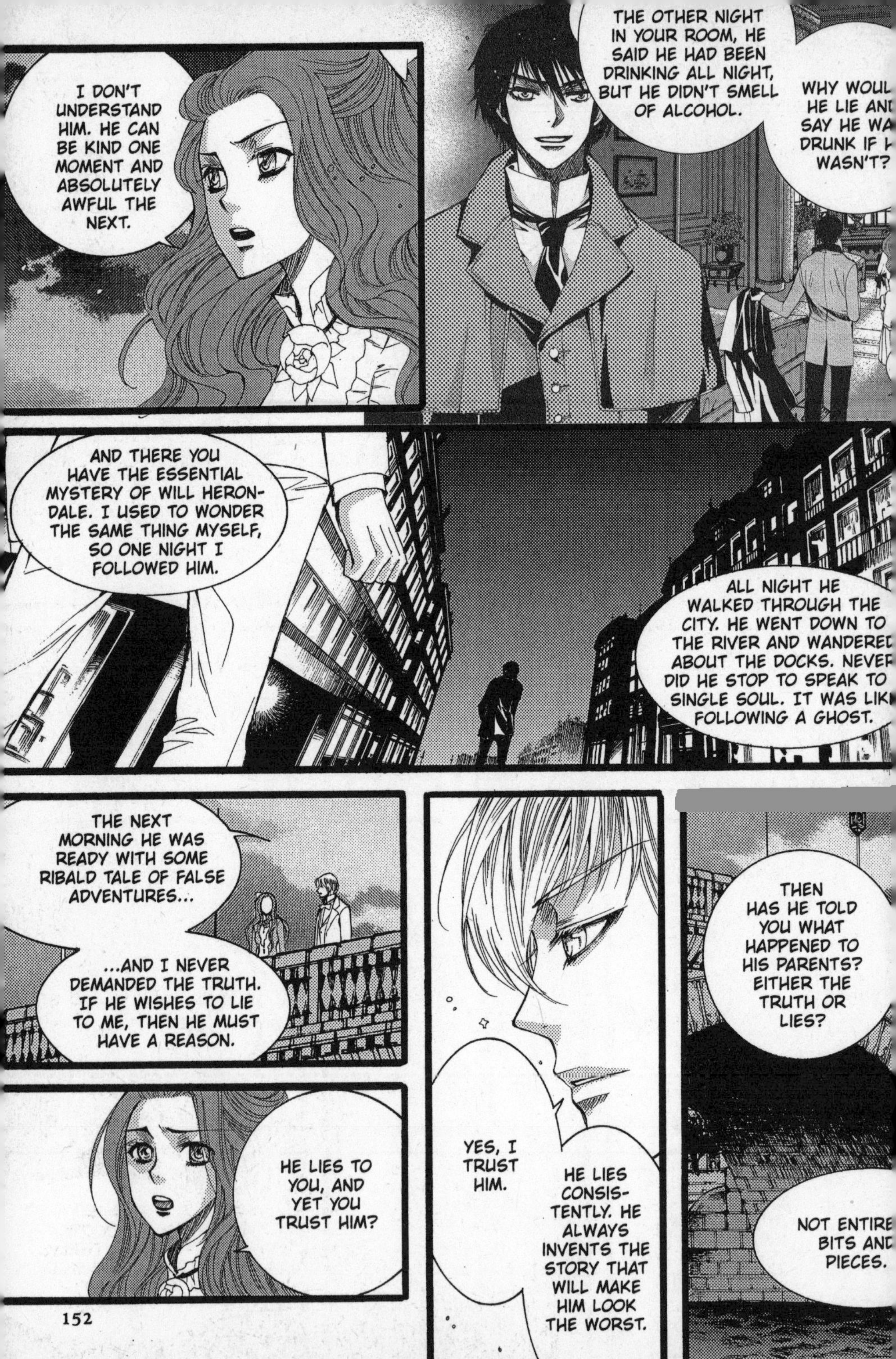
I DON'T UNDERSTAND HIM. HE CAN BE KIND ONE MOMENT AND ABSOLUTELY AWFUL THE NEXT.
THE OTHER NIGHT IN YOUR ROOM, HE SAID HE HAD BEEN DRINKING ALL NIGHT, BUT HE DIDN'T SMELL OF ALCOHOL.
WHY WOUL HE LIE AN SAY HE WA DRUNK IF H WASN'T?
AND THERE YOU HAVE THE ESSENTIAL MYSTERY OF WILL HERON-DALE. I USED TO WONDER THE SAME THING MYSELF, SO ONE NIGHT I FOLLOWED HIM.
ALL NIGHT HE WALKED THROUGH THE CITY. HE WENT DOWN TO THE RIVER AND WANDERED ABOUT THE DOCKS. NEVER DID HE STOP TO SPEAK TO SINGLE SOUL. IT WAS LIK FOLLOWING A GHOST.
THE NEXT MORNING HE WAS READY WITH SOME RIBALD TALE OF FALSE ADVENTURES...
...AND I NEVER DEMANDED THE TRUTH. IF HE WISHES TO LIE TO ME, THEN HE MUST HAVE A REASON.
HE LIES TO YOU, AND YET YOU TRUST HIM?
YES, I TRUST HIM.
HE LIES CONSIS-TENTLY. HE ALWAYS INVENTS THE STORY THAT WILL MAKE HIM LOOK THE WORST.
THEN HAS HE TOLD YOU WHAT HAPPENED TO HIS PARENTS? EITHER THE TRUTH OR LIES?
NOT ENTIRE BITS AND PIECES.

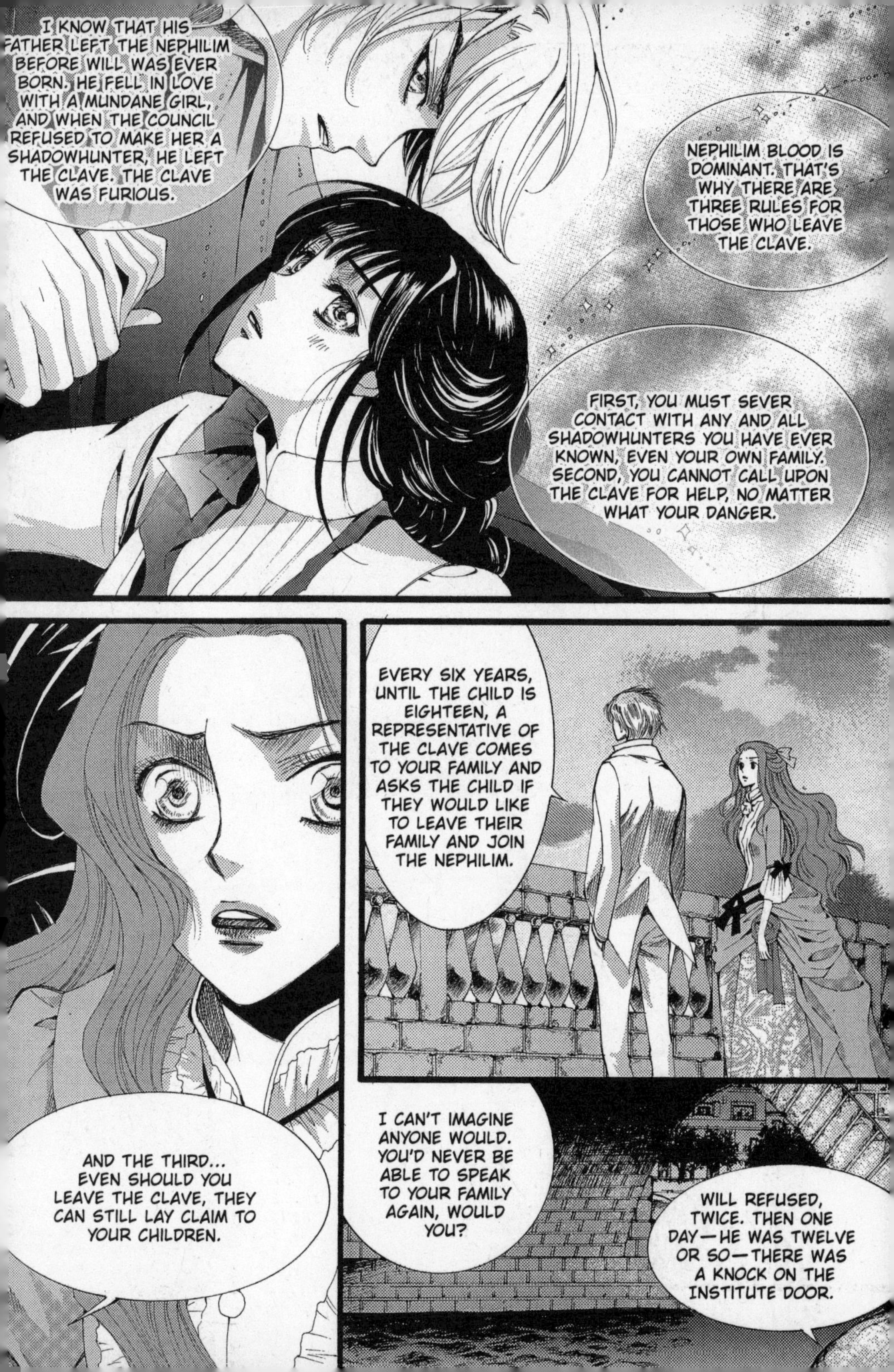
I KNOW THAT HIS FATHER LEFT THE NEPHILIM BEFORE WILL WAS EVER BORN. HE FELL IN LOVE WITH A MUNDANE GIRL, AND WHEN THE COUNCIL REFUSED TO MAKE HER A SHADOWHUNTER, HE LEFT THE CLAVE. THE CLAVE WAS FURIOUS.
NEPHILIM BLOOD IS DOMINANT. THAT'S WHY THERE ARE THREE RULES FOR THOSE WHO LEAVE THE CLAVE.
FIRST, YOU MUST SEVER CONTACT WITH ANY AND ALL SHADOWHUNTERS YOU HAVE EVER KNOWN, EVEN YOUR OWN FAMILY. SECOND, YOU CANNOT CALL UPON THE CLAVE FOR HELP, NO MATTER WHAT YOUR DANGER.
AND THE THIRD... EVEN SHOULD YOU LEAVE THE CLAVE, THEY CAN STILL LAY CLAIM TO YOUR CHILDREN.
EVERY SIX YEARS, UNTIL THE CHILD IS EIGHTEEN, A REPRESENTATIVE OF THE CLAVE COMES TO YOUR FAMILY AND ASKS THE CHILD IF THEY WOULD LIKE TO LEAVE THEIR FAMILY AND JOIN THE NEPHILIM.
I CAN'T IMAGINE ANYONE WOULD. YOU'D NEVER BE ABLE TO SPEAK TO YOUR FAMILY AGAIN, WOULD YOU?
WILL REFUSED, TWICE. THEN ONE DAY—HE WAS TWELVE OR SO—THERE WAS A KNOCK ON THE INSTITUTE DOOR.

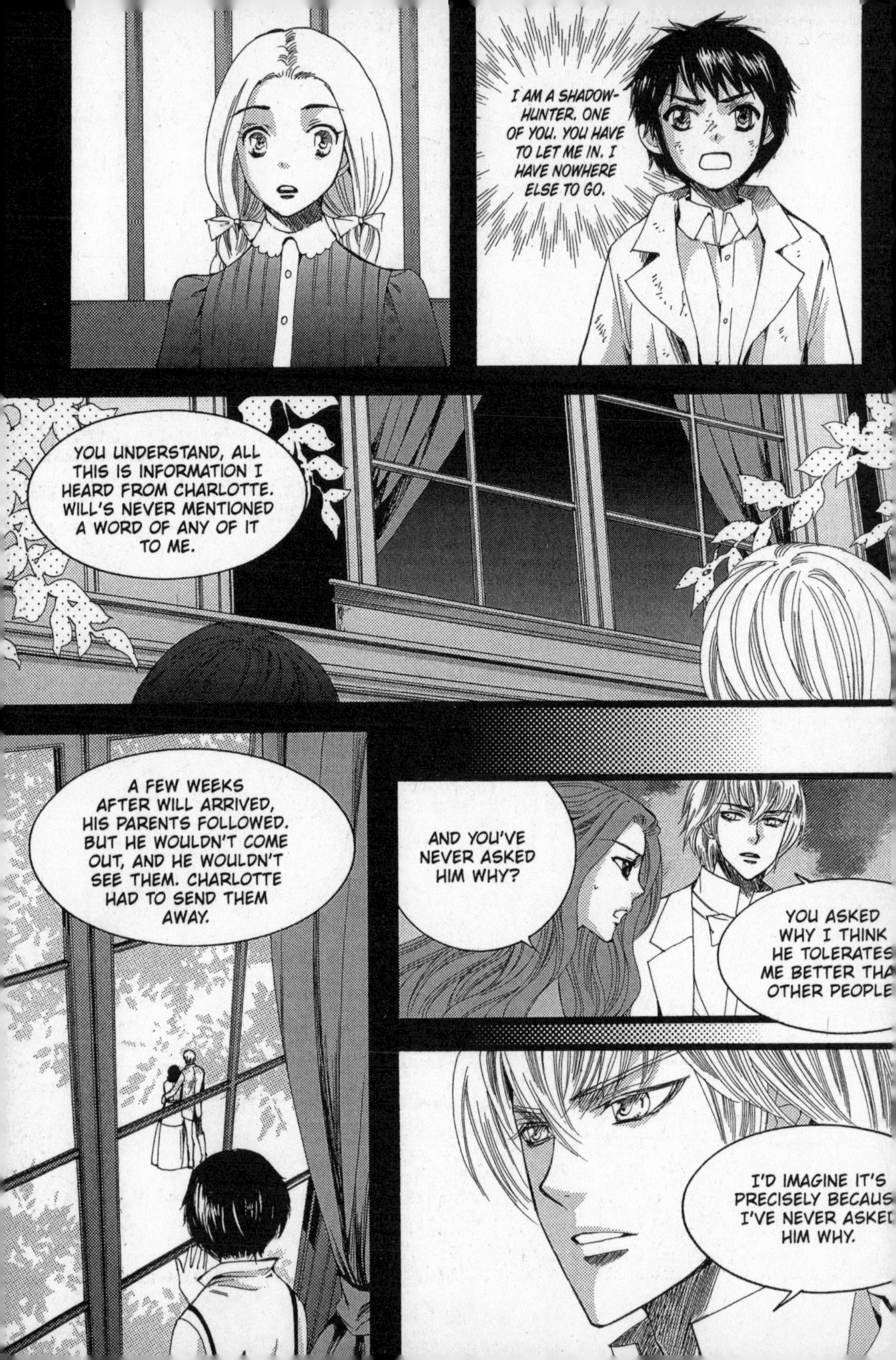
I AM A SHADOW-HUNTER. ONE OF YOU. YOU HAVE TO LET ME IN. I HAVE NOWHERE ELSE TO GO.
YOU UNDERSTAND, ALL THIS IS INFORMATION I HEARD FROM CHARLOTTE. WILL'S NEVER MENTIONED A WORD OF ANY OF IT TO ME.
A FEW WEEKS AFTER WILL ARRIVED, HIS PARENTS FOLLOWED. BUT HE WOULDN'T COME OUT, AND HE WOULDN'T SEE THEM. CHARLOTTE HAD TO SEND THEM AWAY.
AND YOU'VE NEVER ASKED HIM WHY?
YOU ASKED WHY I THINK HE TOLERATES ME BETTER THA OTHER PEOPLE
I'D IMAGINE IT'S PRECISELY BECAUS I'VE NEVER ASKE HIM WHY.

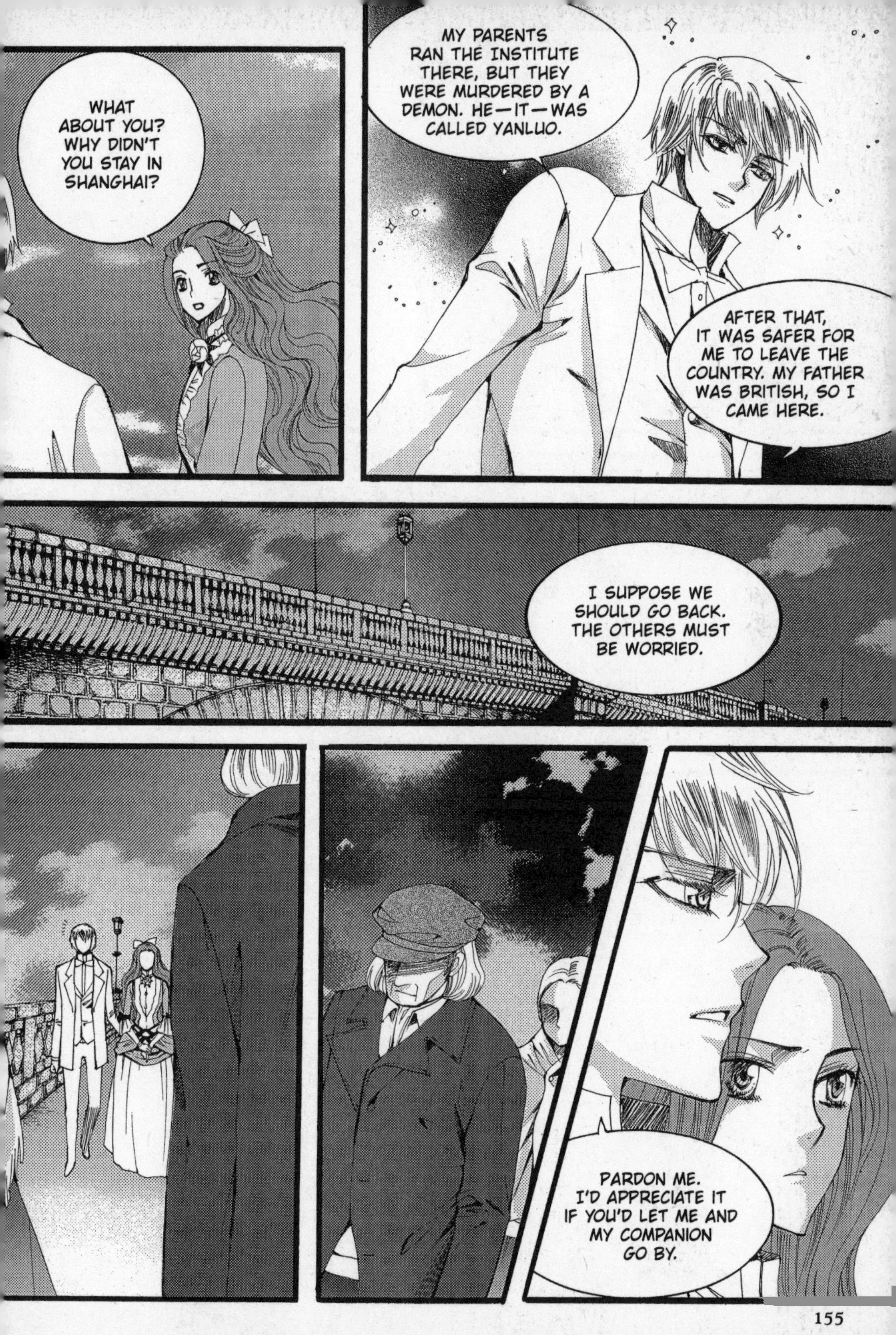
WHAT ABOUT YOU? WHY DIDN'T YOU STAY IN SHANGHAI?
MY PARENTS RAN THE INSTITUTE THERE, BUT THEY WERE MURDERED BY A DEMON. HE—IT—WAS CALLED YANLUO.
AFTER THAT, IT WAS SAFER FOR ME TO LEAVE THE COUNTRY. MY FATHER WAS BRITISH, SO I CAME HERE.
I SUPPOSE WE SHOULD GO BACK. THE OTHERS MUST BE WORRIED.
PARDON ME. I'D APPRECIATE IT IF YOU'D LET ME AND MY COMPANION GO BY.

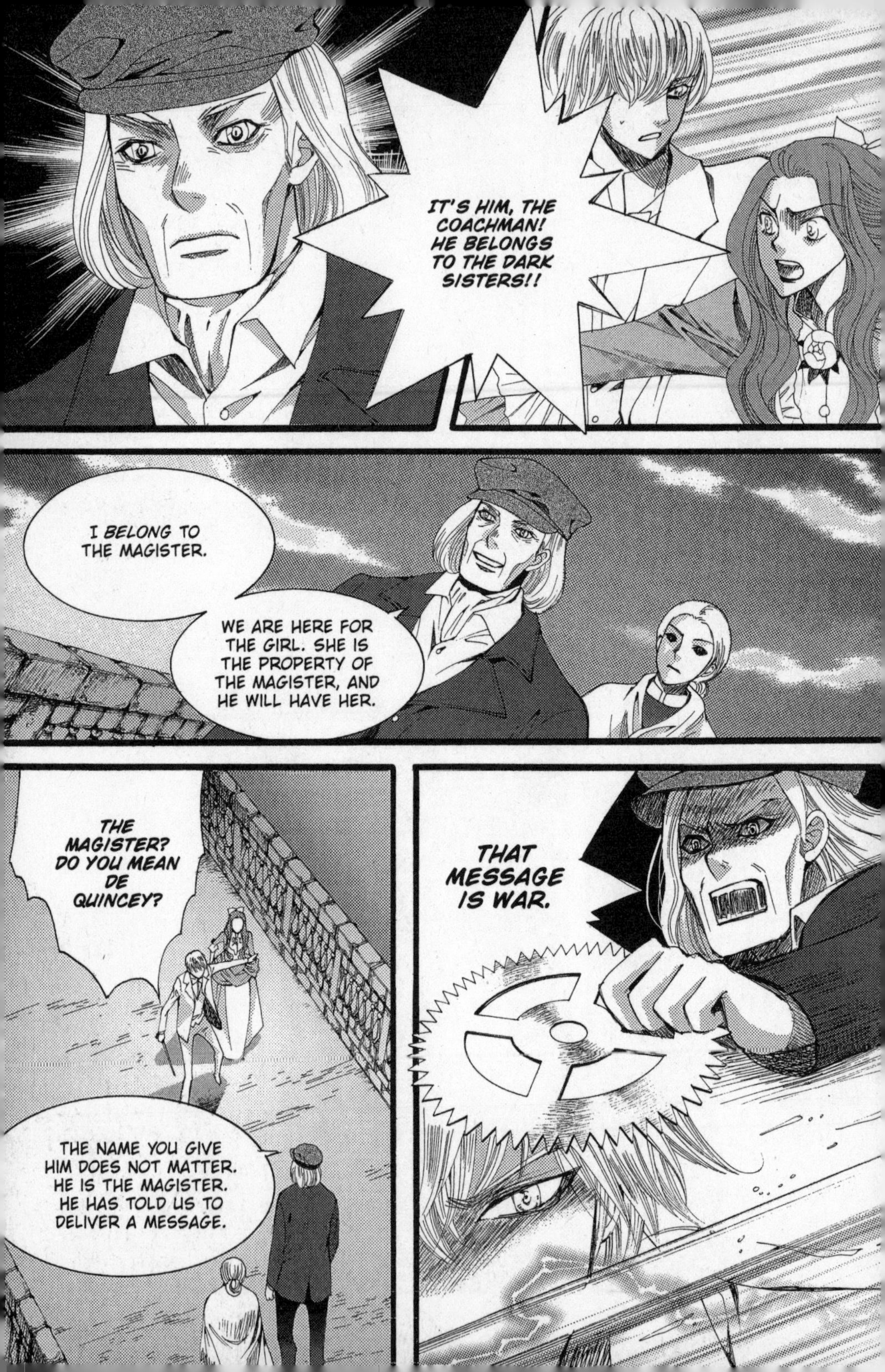
IT'S HIM, THE COACHMAN! HE BELONGS TO THE DARK SISTERS!!
I BELONG TO THE MAGISTER.
WE ARE HERE FOR THE GIRL. SHE IS THE PROPERTY OF THE MAGISTER, AND HE WILL HAVE HER.
THE MAGISTER? DO YOU MEAN DE QUINCEY?
THE NAME YOU GIVE HIM DOES NOT MATTER. HE IS THE MAGISTER. HE HAS TOLD US TO DELIVER A MESSAGE.
THAT MESSAGE IS WAR.

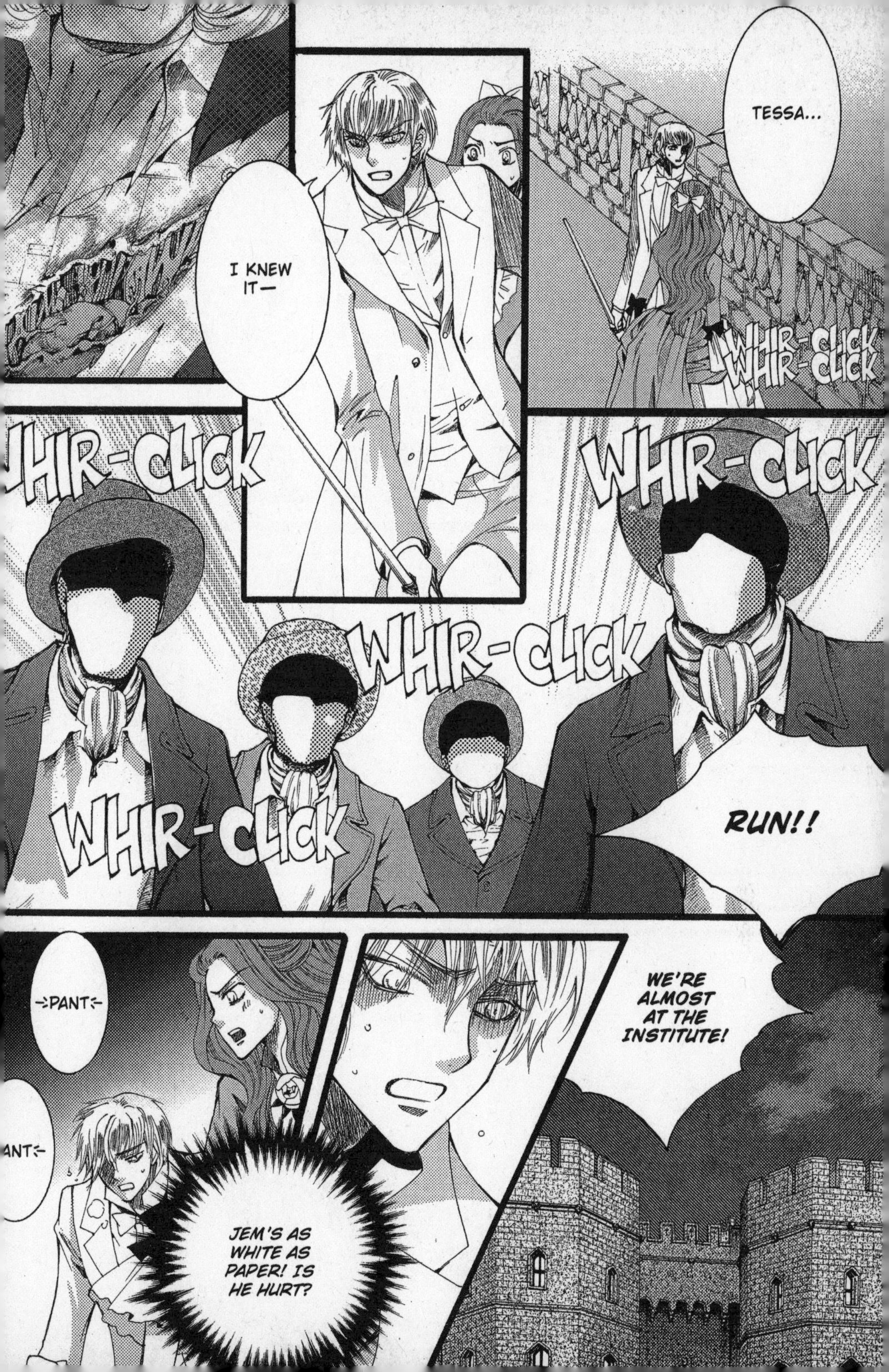
I KNEW IT—
TESSA...
WHIR-CLICK
WHIR-CLICK
HIR-CLICK
WHIR-CLICK
WHIR-CLICK
WHIR-CLICK
RUN!!
-PANT-
ANT-
WE'RE ALMOST AT THE INSTITUTE!
JEM'S AS WHITE AS PAPER! IS HE HURT?

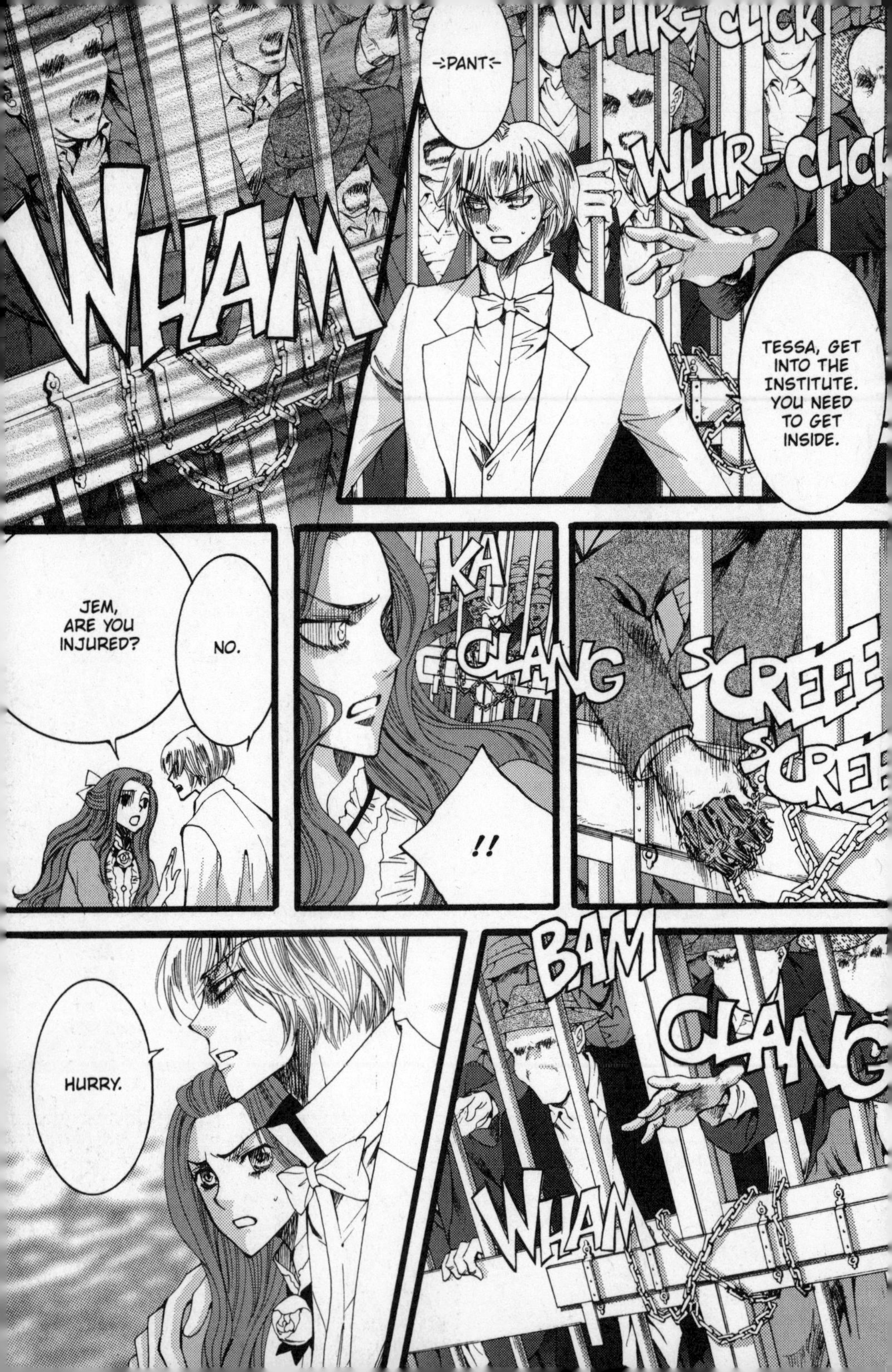
WHAM
PANT
WHIR-CLICK
WHIR-CLICK
TESSA, GET INTO THE INSTITUTE. YOU NEED TO GET INSIDE.
JEM, ARE YOU INJURED?
NO.
KA
CLANG
!!
SCREEE
SCREE
HURRY.
BAM
CLANG
WHAM

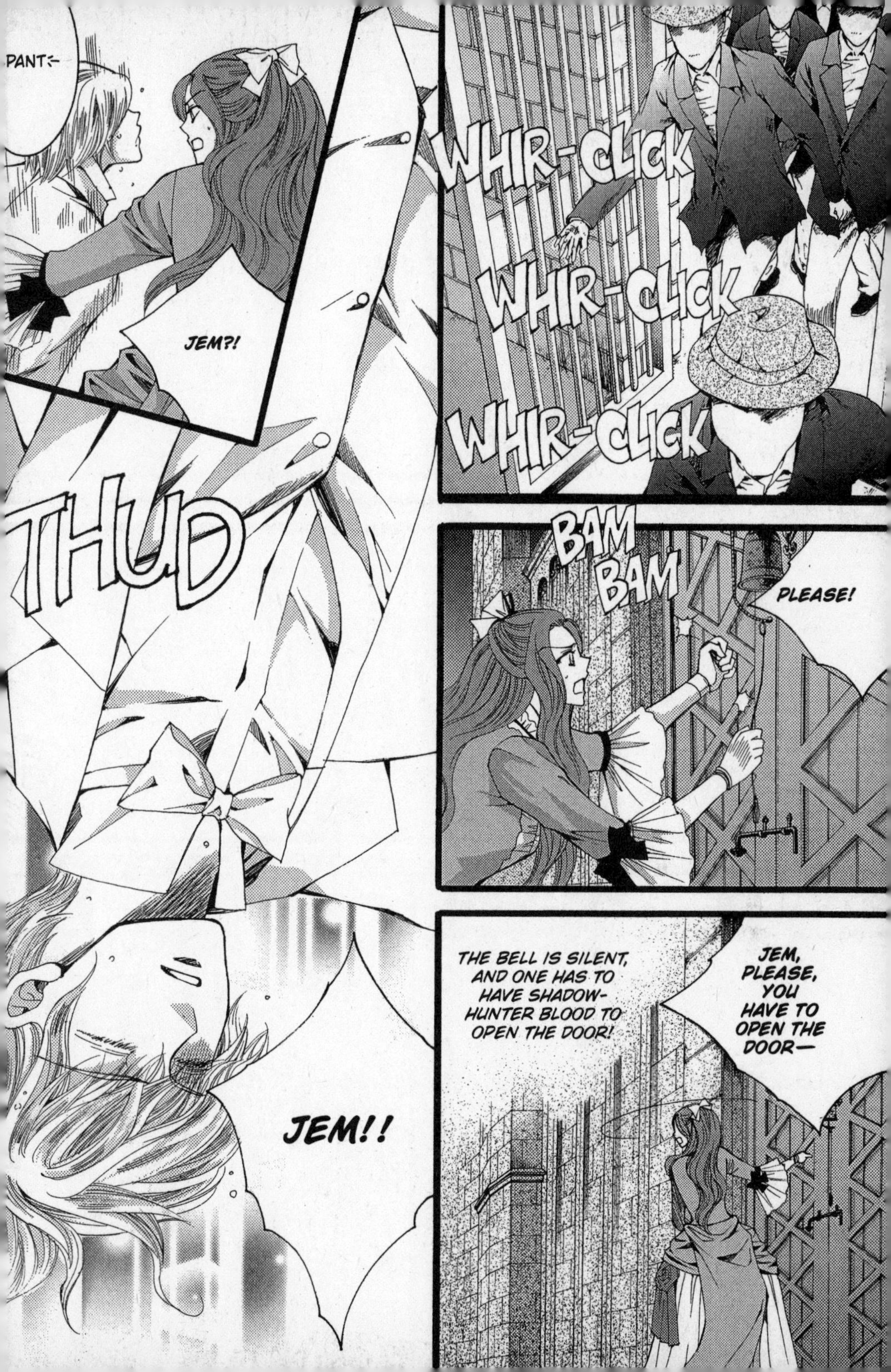
PANT
JEM?!
THUD
JEM!!
WHIR-CLICK
WHIR-CLICK
WHIR-CLICK
BAM
BAM
PLEASE!
THE BELL IS SILENT, AND ONE HAS TO HAVE SHADOW-HUNTER BLOOD TO OPEN THE DOOR!
JEM, PLEASE, YOU HAVE TO OPEN THE DOOR—

GET AWAY FROM HIM!

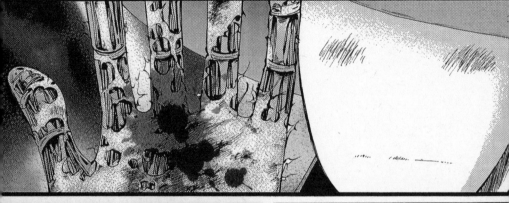

STAY AWAY!!

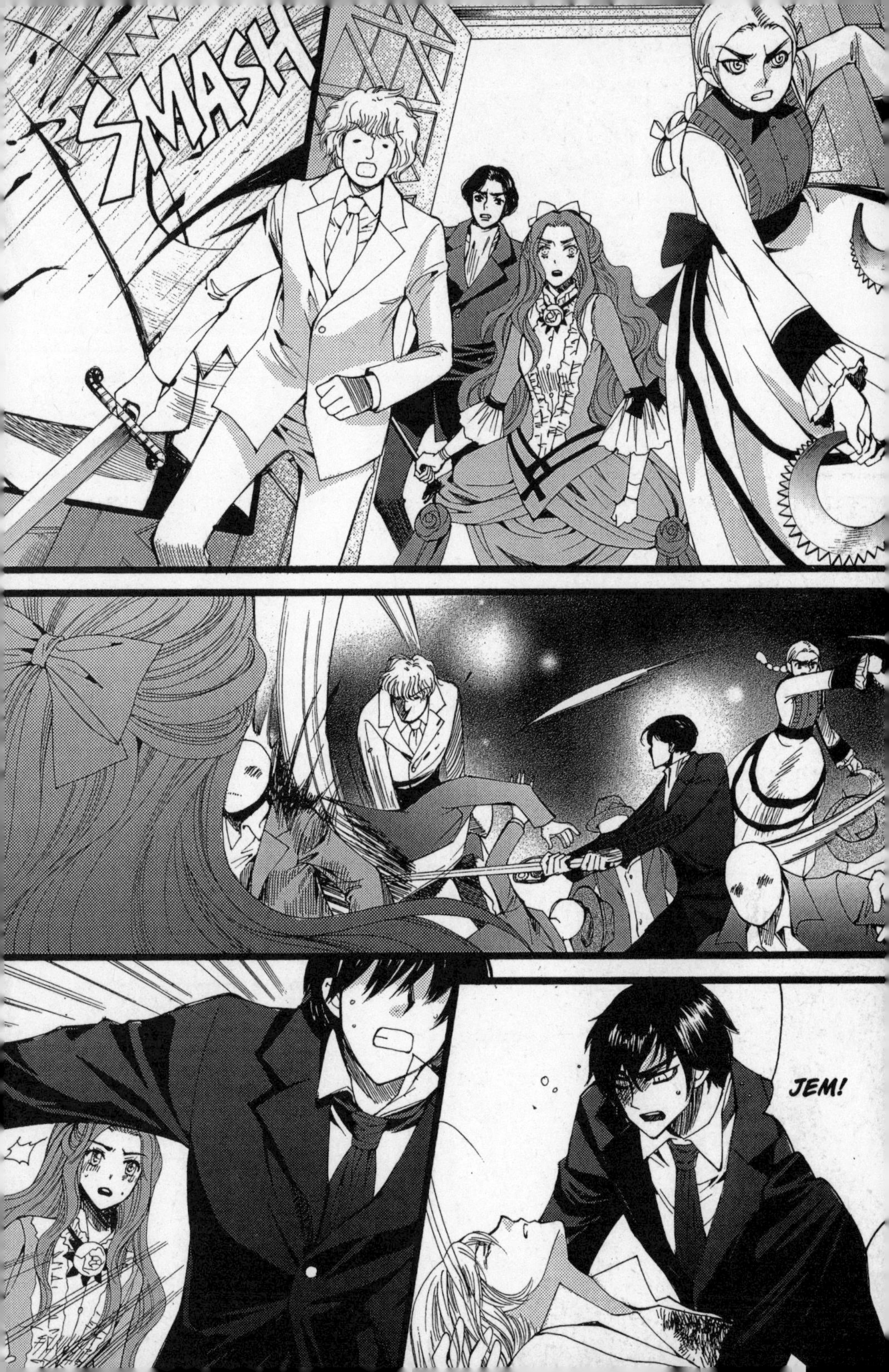
SMASH
JEM!

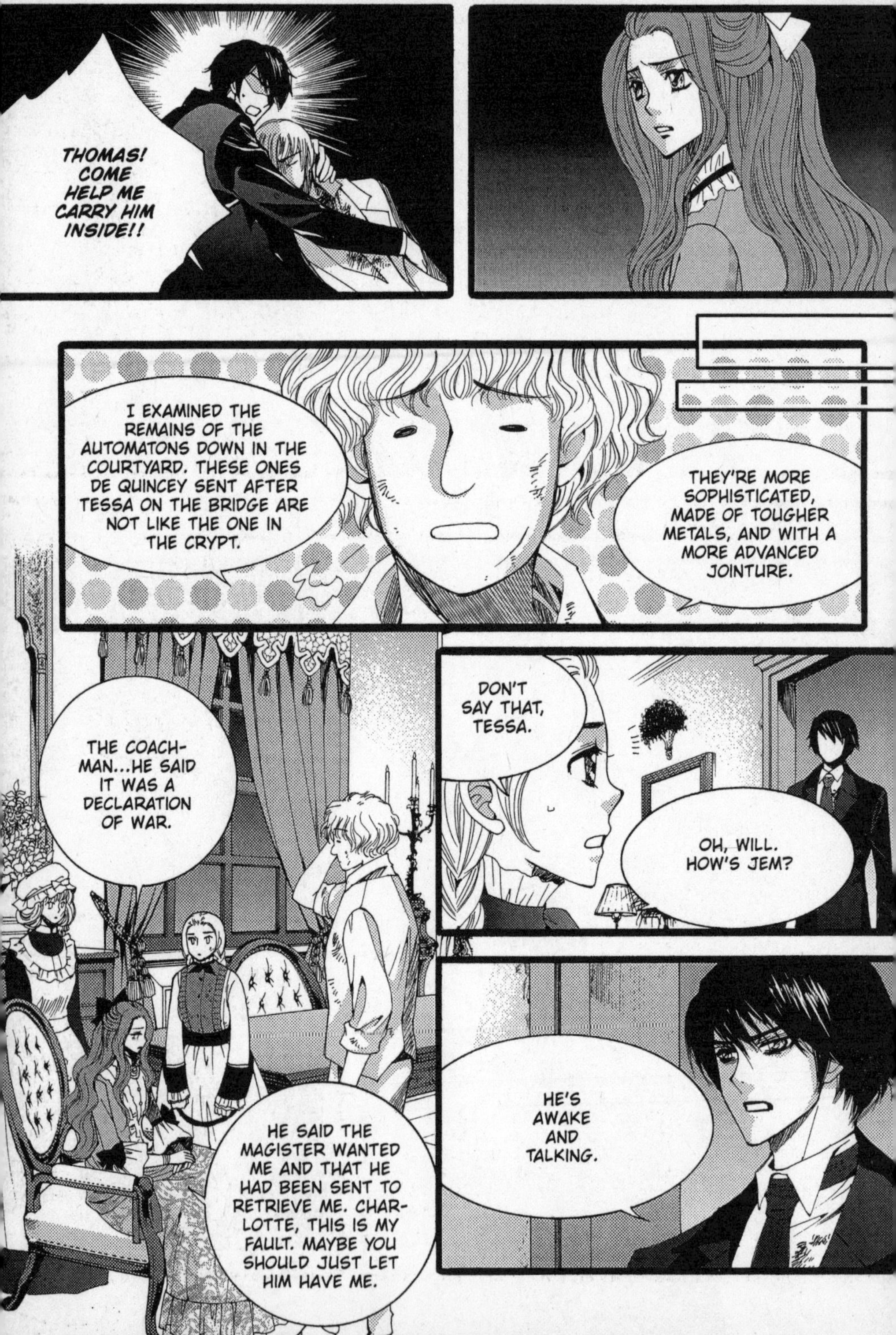
THOMAS! COME HELP ME CARRY HIM INSIDE!!
I EXAMINED THE REMAINS OF THE AUTOMATONS DOWN IN THE COURTYARD. THESE ONES DE QUINCEY SENT AFTER TESSA ON THE BRIDGE ARE NOT LIKE THE ONE IN THE CRYPT.
THEY'RE MORE SOPHISTICATED, MADE OF TOUGHER METALS, AND WITH A MORE ADVANCED JOINTURE.
THE COACH-MAN...HE SAID IT WAS A DECLARATION OF WAR.
HE SAID THE MAGISTER WANTED ME AND THAT HE HAD BEEN SENT TO RETRIEVE ME. CHAR-LOTTE, THIS IS MY FAULT. MAYBE YOU SHOULD JUST LET HIM HAVE ME.
DON'T SAY THAT, TESSA.
OH, WILL. HOW'S JEM?
HE'S AWAKE AND TALKING.

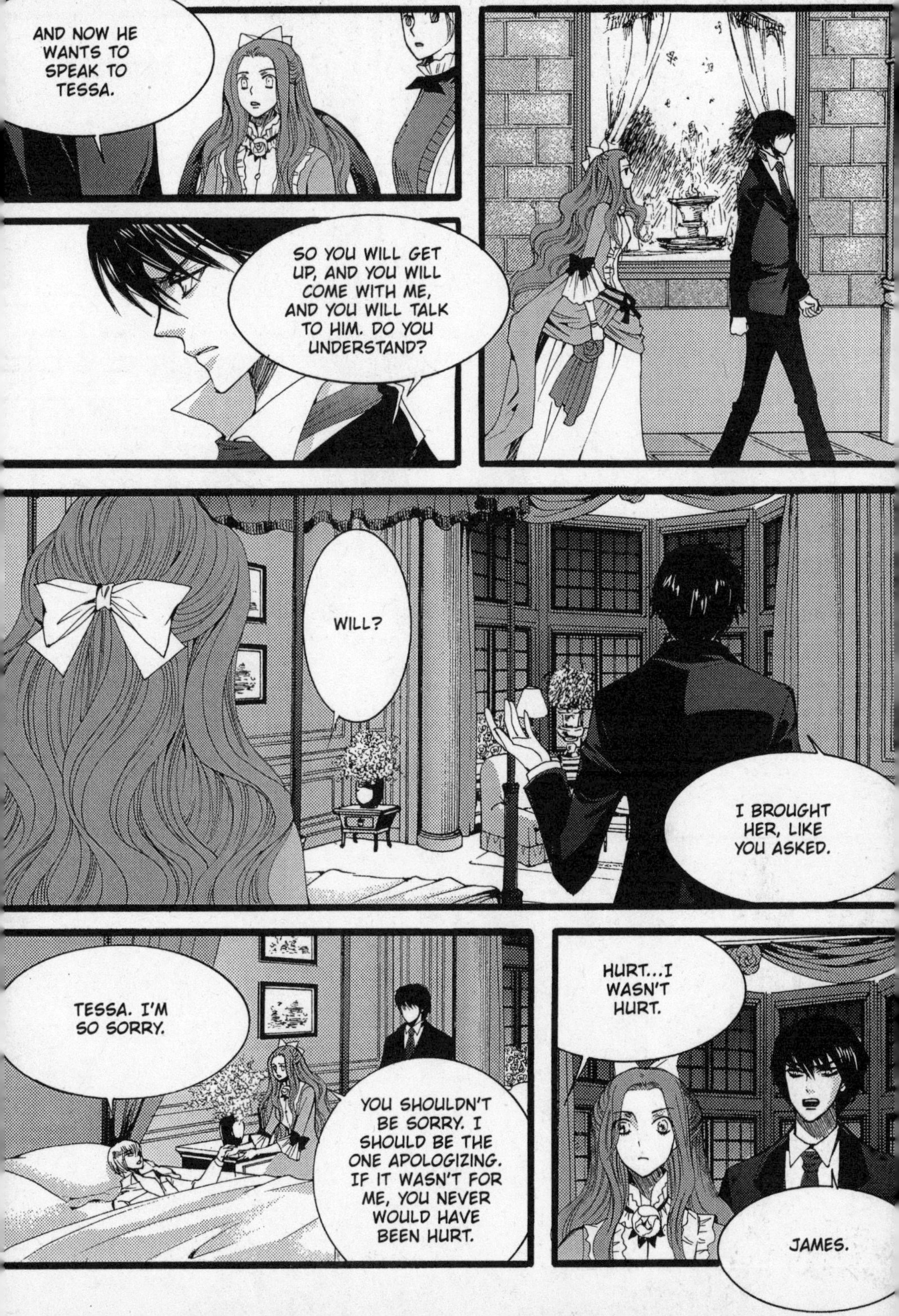
AND NOW HE WANTS TO SPEAK TO TESSA.
SO YOU WILL GET UP, AND YOU WILL COME WITH ME, AND YOU WILL TALK TO HIM. DO YOU UNDERSTAND?
WILL?
I BROUGHT HER, LIKE YOU ASKED.
TESSA. I'M SO SORRY.
YOU SHOULDN'T BE SORRY. I SHOULD BE THE ONE APOLOGIZING. IF IT WASN'T FOR ME, YOU NEVER WOULD HAVE BEEN HURT.
HURT...I WASN'T HURT.
JAMES.

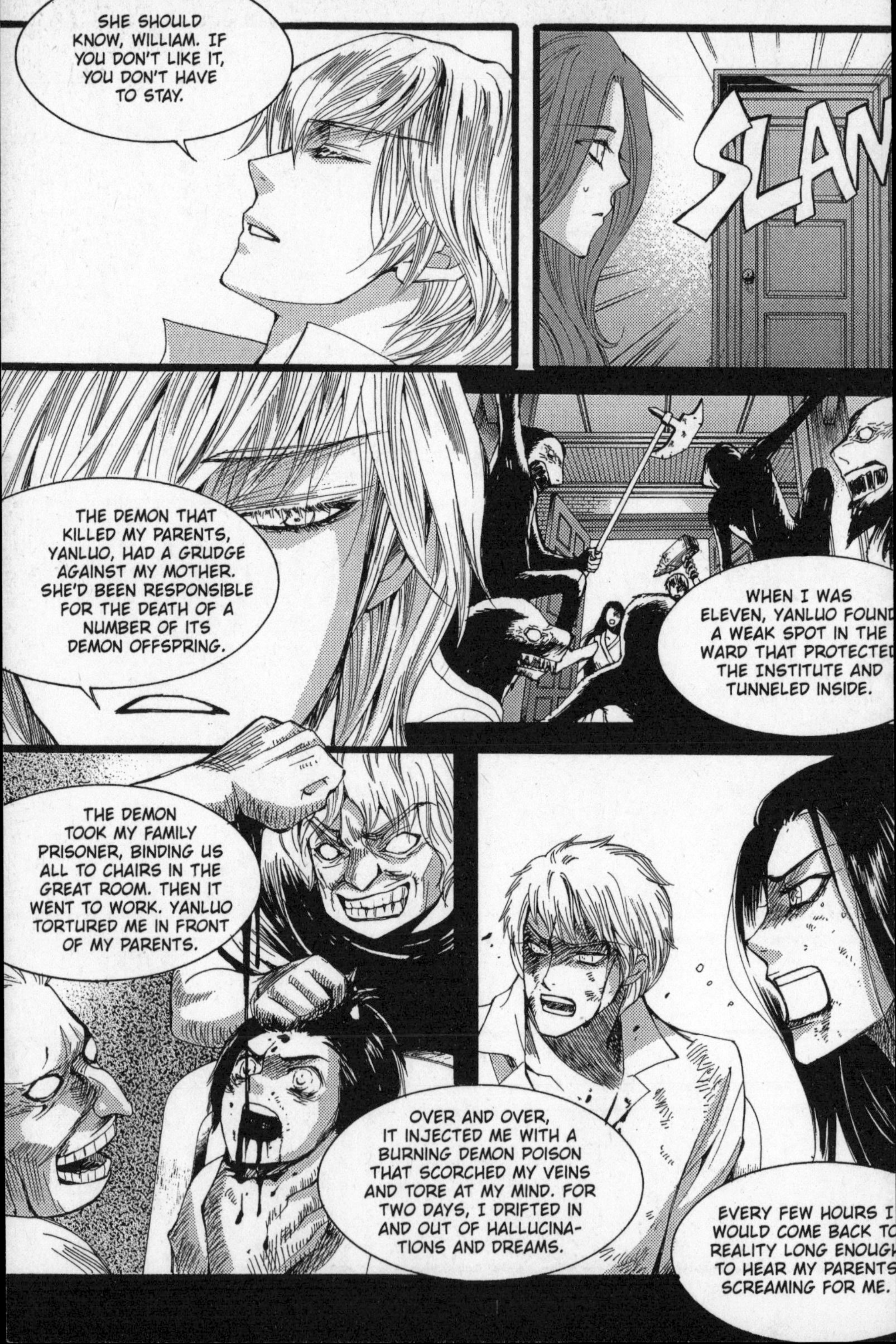
SHE SHOULD KNOW, WILLIAM. IF YOU DON'T LIKE IT, YOU DON'T HAVE TO STAY.
SLAM
THE DEMON THAT KILLED MY PARENTS, YANLUO, HAD A GRUDGE AGAINST MY MOTHER. SHE'D BEEN RESPONSIBLE FOR THE DEATH OF A NUMBER OF ITS DEMON OFFSPRING.
WHEN I WAS ELEVEN, YANLUO FOUND A WEAK SPOT IN THE WARD THAT PROTECTED THE INSTITUTE AND TUNNELED INSIDE.
THE DEMON TOOK MY FAMILY PRISONER, BINDING US ALL TO CHAIRS IN THE GREAT ROOM. THEN IT WENT TO WORK. YANLUO TORTURED ME IN FRONT OF MY PARENTS.
OVER AND OVER, IT INJECTED ME WITH A BURNING DEMON POISON THAT SCORCHED MY VEINS AND TORE AT MY MIND. FOR TWO DAYS, I DRIFTED IN AND OUT OF HALLUCINATIONS AND DREAMS.
EVERY FEW HOURS I WOULD COME BACK TO REALITY LONG ENOUGH TO HEAR MY PARENTS SCREAMING FOR ME.

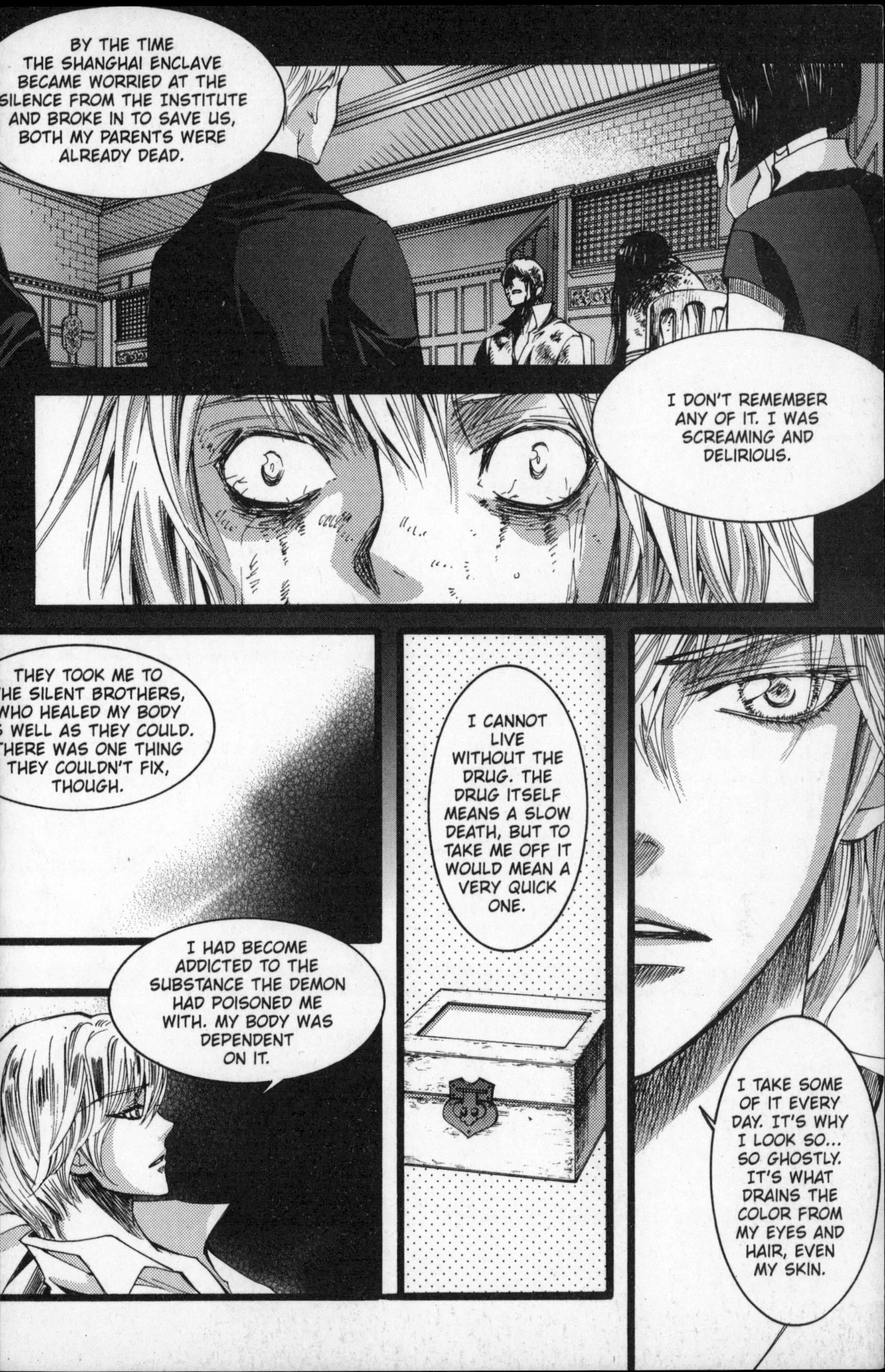
BY THE TIME THE SHANGHAI ENCLAVE BECAME WORRIED AT THE SILENCE FROM THE INSTITUTE AND BROKE IN TO SAVE US, BOTH MY PARENTS WERE ALREADY DEAD.
I DON'T REMEMBER ANY OF IT. I WAS SCREAMING AND DELIRIOUS.
THEY TOOK ME TO HE SILENT BROTHERS, WHO HEALED MY BODY S WELL AS THEY COULD. THERE WAS ONE THING THEY COULDN'T FIX, THOUGH.
I HAD BECOME ADDICTED TO THE SUBSTANCE THE DEMON HAD POISONED ME WITH. MY BODY WAS DEPENDENT ON IT.
I CANNOT LIVE WITHOUT THE DRUG. THE DRUG ITSELF MEANS A SLOW DEATH, BUT TO TAKE ME OFF IT WOULD MEAN A VERY QUICK ONE.
I TAKE SOME OF IT EVERY DAY. IT'S WHY I LOOK SO... SO GHOSTLY. IT'S WHAT DRAINS THE COLOR FROM MY EYES AND HAIR, EVEN MY SKIN.

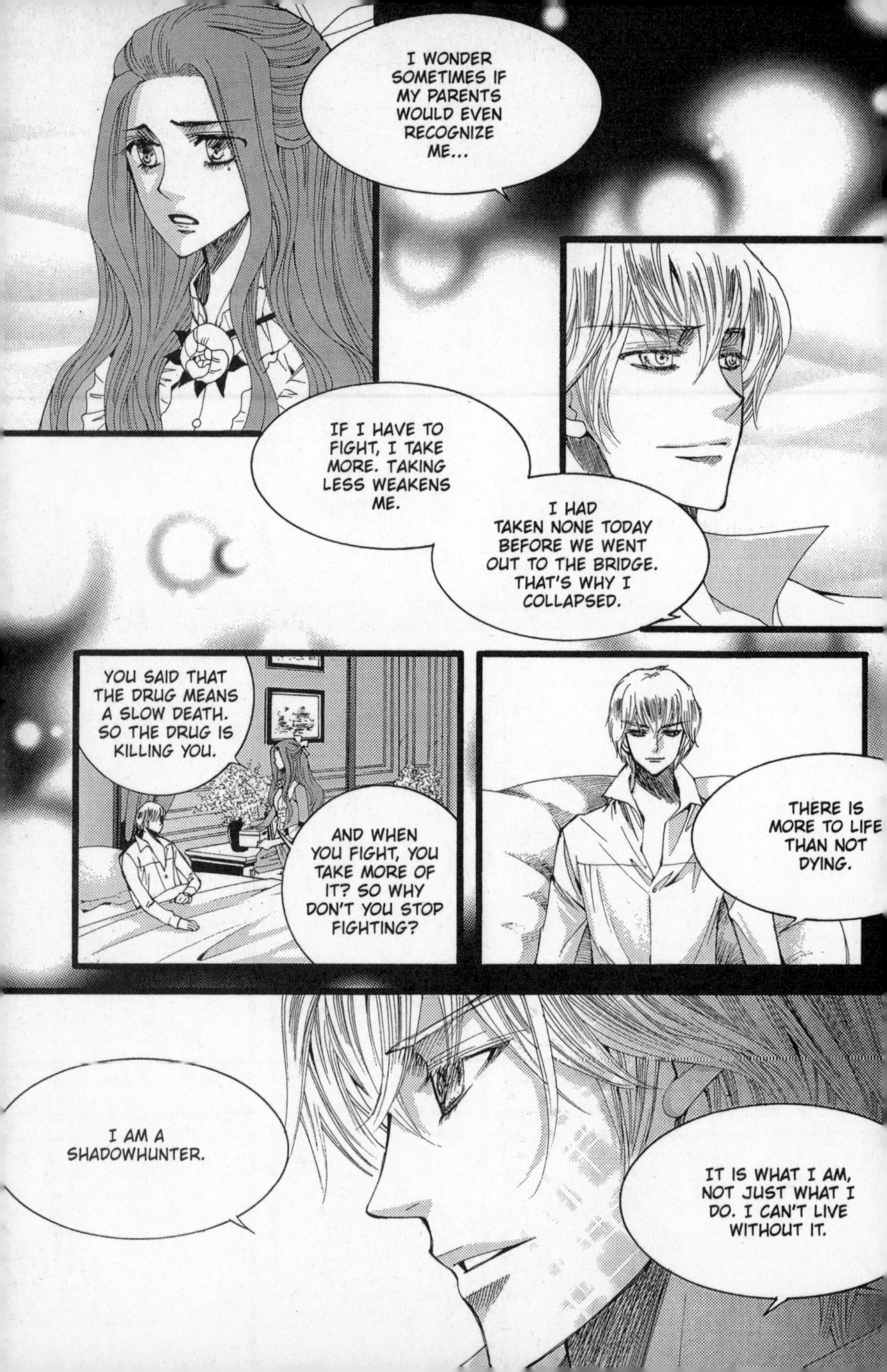
I WONDER SOMETIMES IF MY PARENTS WOULD EVEN RECOGNIZE ME...
IF I HAVE TO FIGHT, I TAKE MORE. TAKING LESS WEAKENS ME.
I HAD TAKEN NONE TODAY BEFORE WE WENT OUT TO THE BRIDGE. THAT'S WHY I COLLAPSED.
YOU SAID THAT THE DRUG MEANS A SLOW DEATH. SO THE DRUG IS KILLING YOU.
AND WHEN YOU FIGHT, YOU TAKE MORE OF IT? SO WHY DON'T YOU STOP FIGHTING?
THERE IS MORE TO LIFE THAN NOT DYING.
I AM A SHADOWHUNTER.
IT IS WHAT I AM, NOT JUST WHAT I DO. I CAN'T LIVE WITHOUT IT.

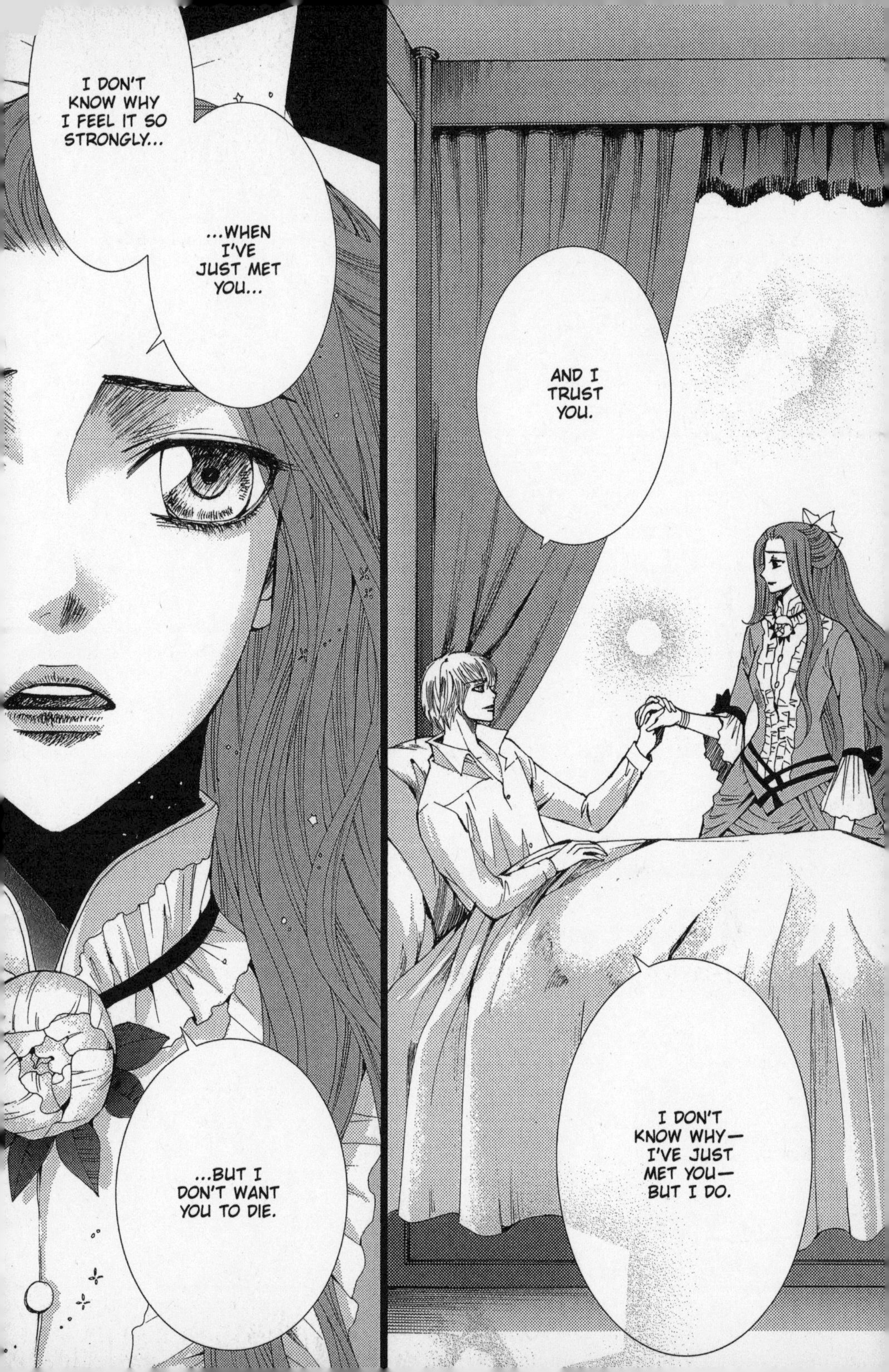
I DON'T KNOW WHY I FEEL IT SO STRONGLY...
...WHEN I'VE JUST MET YOU...
...BUT I DON'T WANT YOU TO DIE.
AND I TRUST YOU.
I DON'T KNOW WHY—I'VE JUST MET YOU—BUT I DO.

THE INFERNAL DEVICES
CLOCKWORK ANGEL

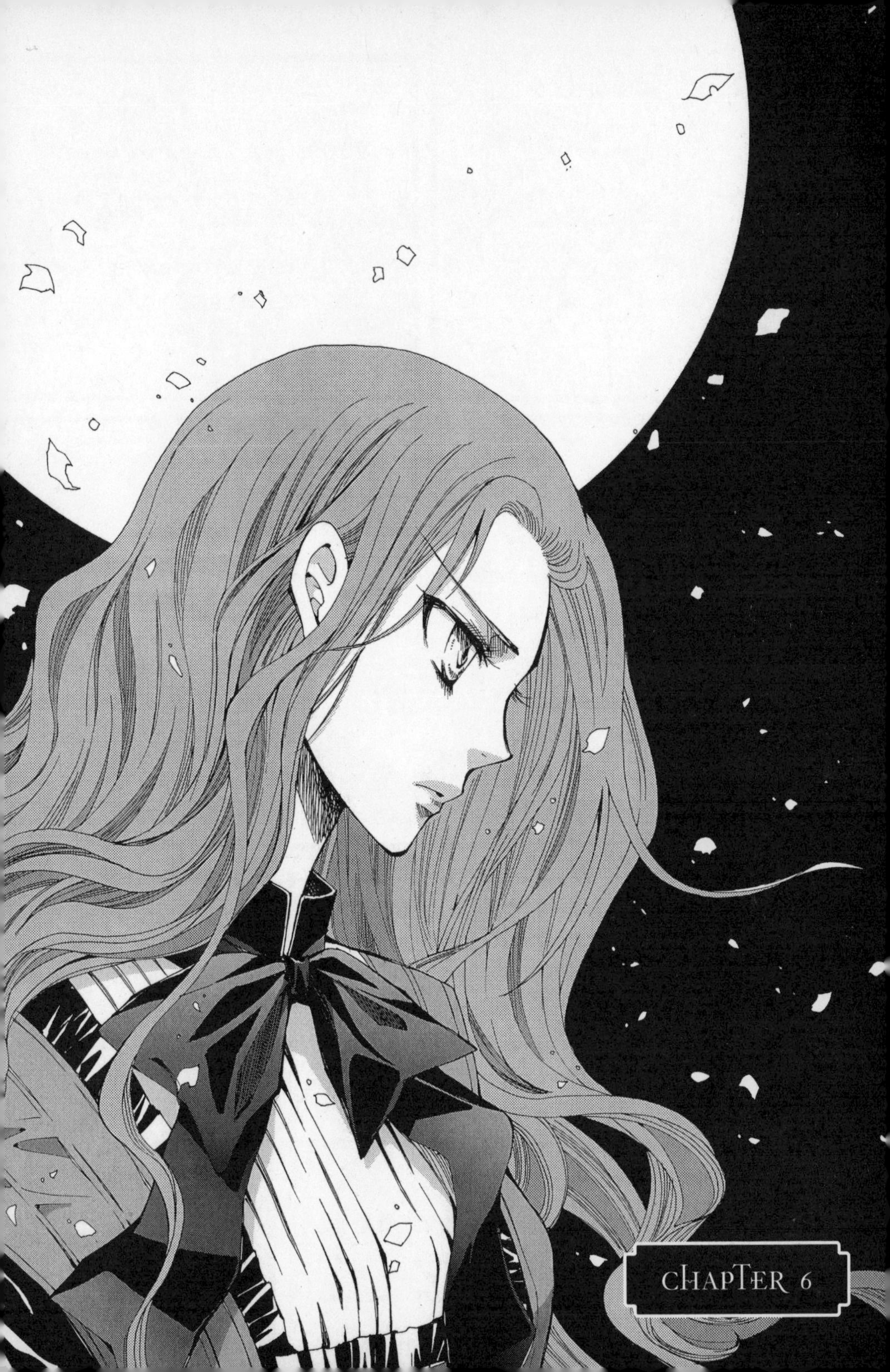
CHAPTER 6

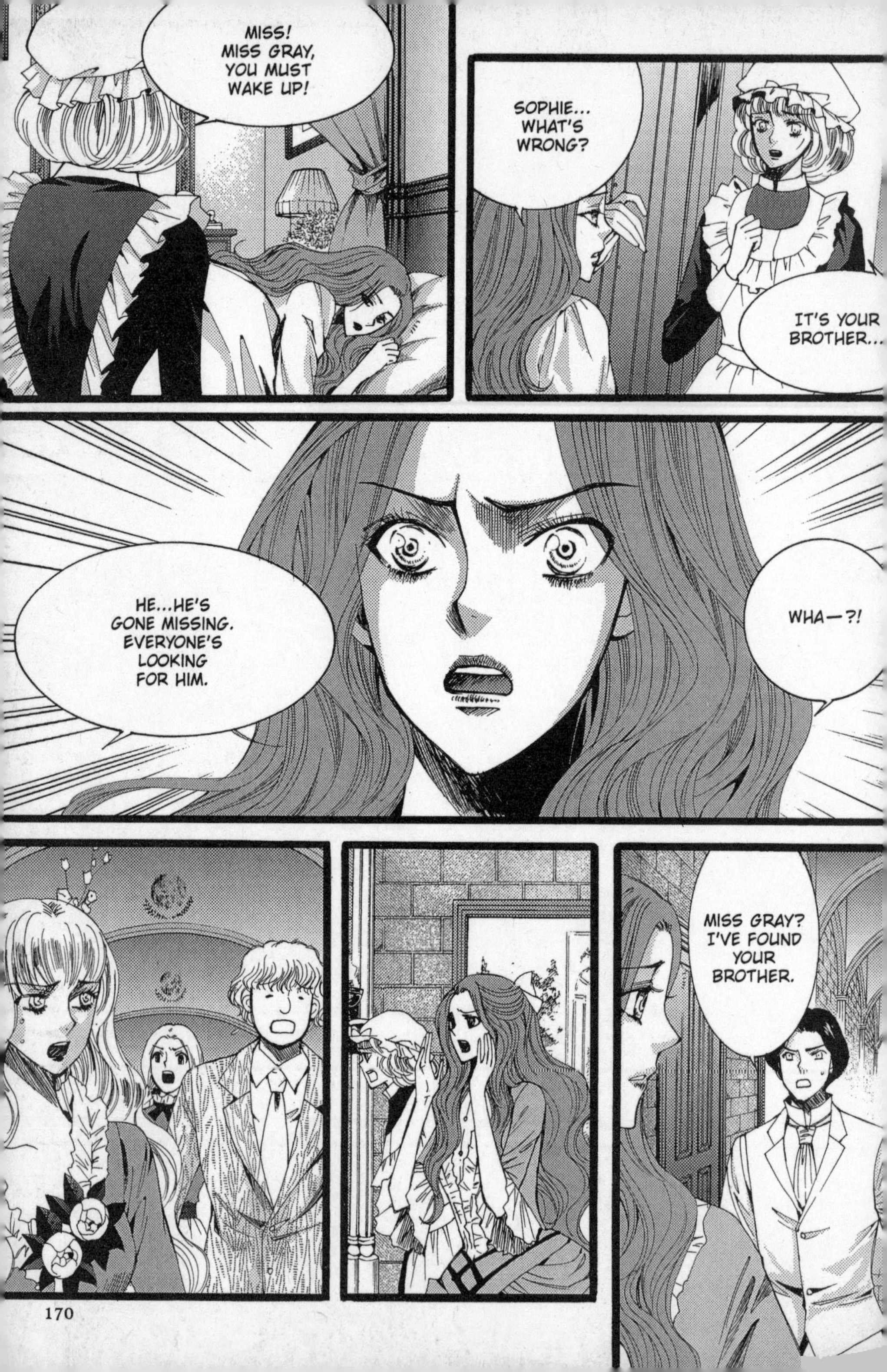
MISS! MISS GRAY, YOU MUST WAKE UP!
SOPHIE... WHAT'S WRONG?
IT'S YOUR BROTHER...
HE...HE'S GONE MISSING. EVERYONE'S LOOKING FOR HIM.
WHA—?!
MISS GRAY? I'VE FOUND YOUR BROTHER.

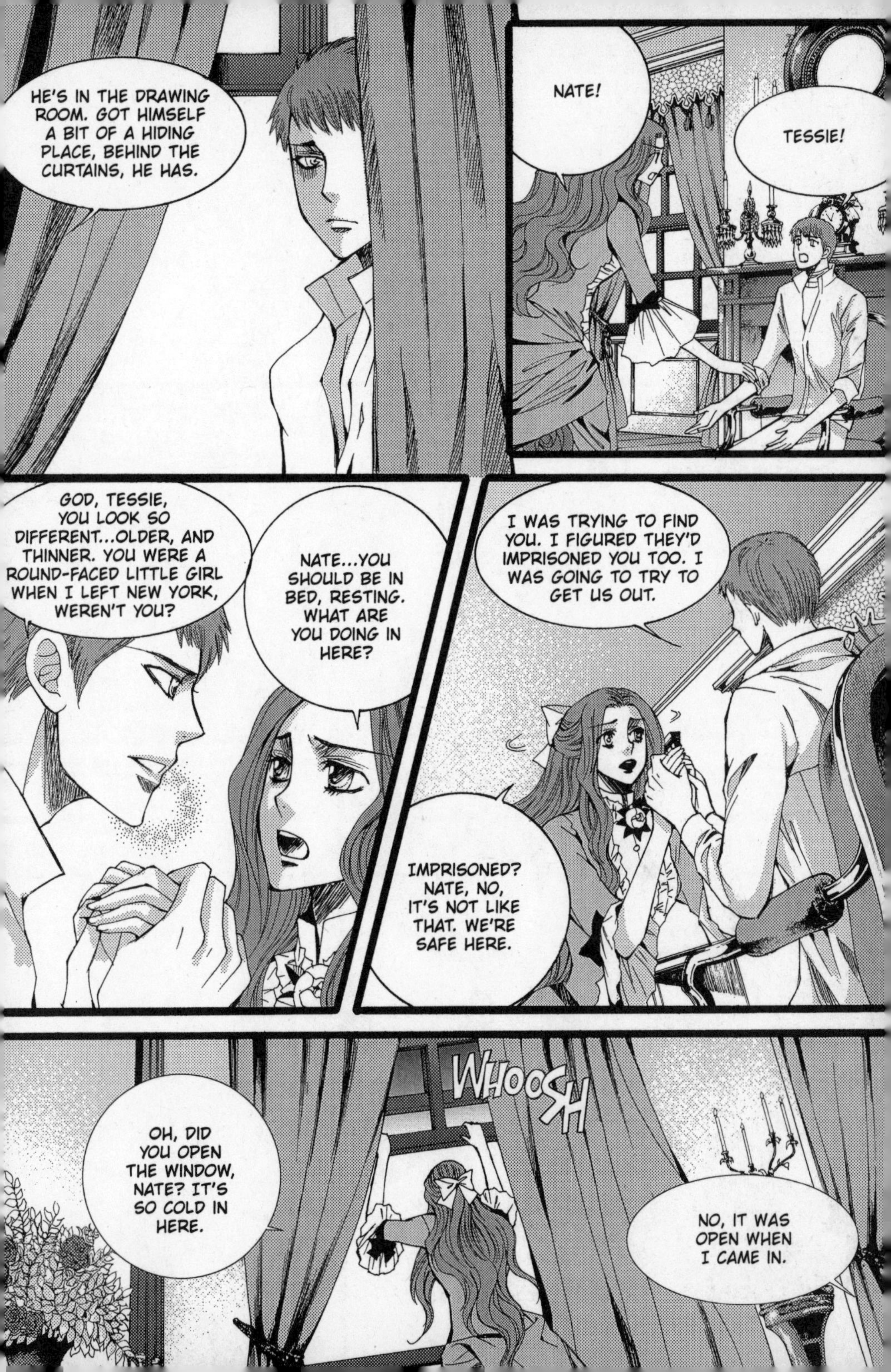
HE'S IN THE DRAWING ROOM. GOT HIMSELF A BIT OF A HIDING PLACE, BEHIND THE CURTAINS, HE HAS.
NATE!
TESSIE!
GOD, TESSIE, YOU LOOK SO DIFFERENT...OLDER, AND THINNER. YOU WERE A ROUND-FACED LITTLE GIRL WHEN I LEFT NEW YORK, WEREN'T YOU?
NATE...YOU SHOULD BE IN BED, RESTING. WHAT ARE YOU DOING IN HERE?
I WAS TRYING TO FIND YOU. I FIGURED THEY'D IMPRISONED YOU TOO. I WAS GOING TO TRY TO GET US OUT.
IMPRISONED? NATE, NO, IT'S NOT LIKE THAT. WE'RE SAFE HERE.
OH, DID YOU OPEN THE WINDOW, NATE? IT'S SO COLD IN HERE.
WHOOSH
NO, IT WAS OPEN WHEN I CAME IN.

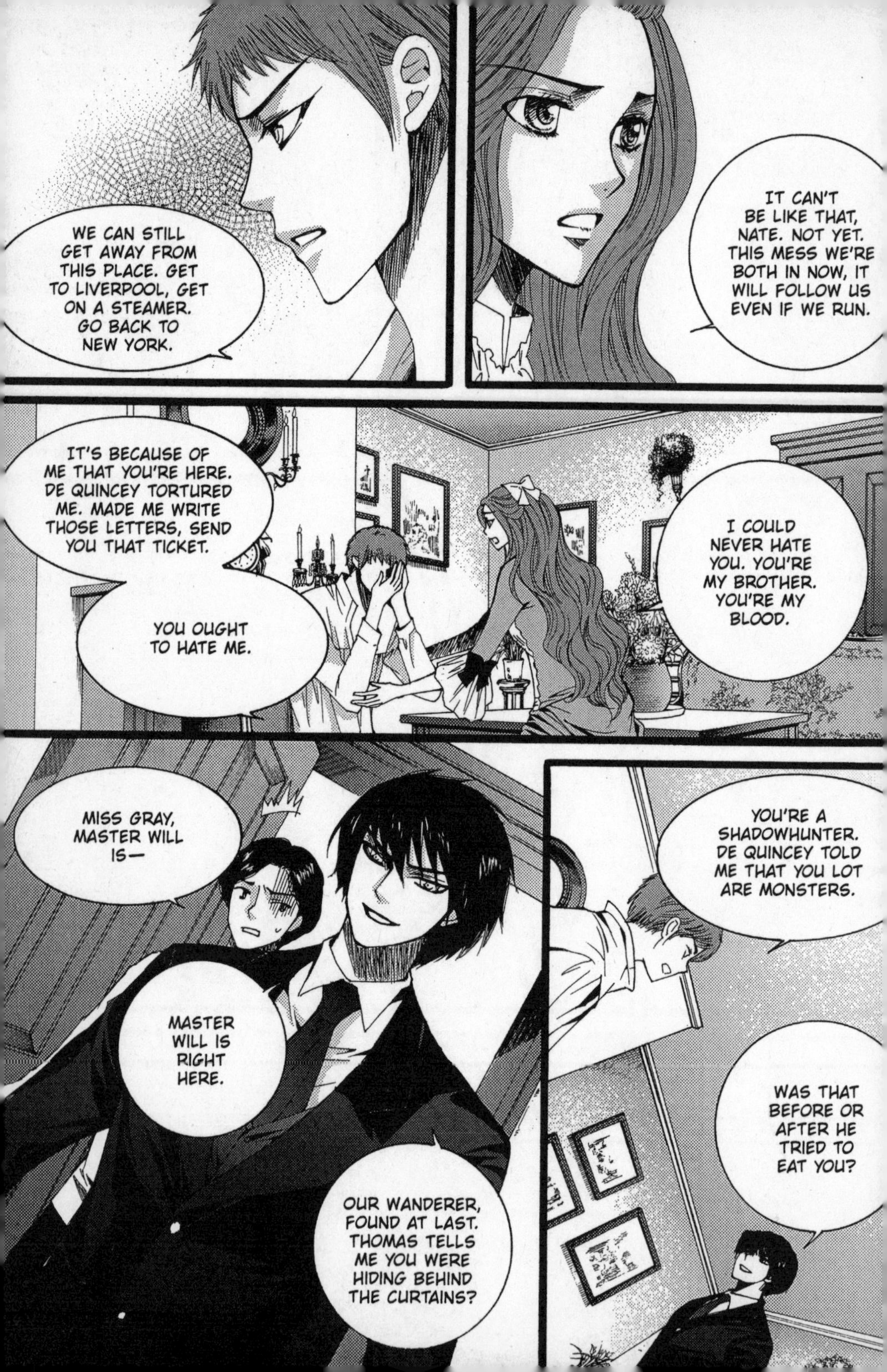
WE CAN STILL GET AWAY FROM THIS PLACE. GET TO LIVERPOOL, GET ON A STEAMER. GO BACK TO NEW YORK.
IT CAN'T BE LIKE THAT, NATE. NOT YET. THIS MESS WE'RE BOTH IN NOW, IT WILL FOLLOW US EVEN IF WE RUN.
IT'S BECAUSE OF ME THAT YOU'RE HERE. DE QUINCEY TORTURED ME. MADE ME WRITE THOSE LETTERS, SEND YOU THAT TICKET.
YOU OUGHT TO HATE ME.
I COULD NEVER HATE YOU. YOU'RE MY BROTHER. YOU'RE MY BLOOD.
MISS GRAY, MASTER WILL IS—
MASTER WILL IS RIGHT HERE.
OUR WANDERER, FOUND AT LAST. THOMAS TELLS ME YOU WERE HIDING BEHIND THE CURTAINS?
YOU'RE A SHADOWHUNTER. DE QUINCEY TOLD ME THAT YOU LOT ARE MONSTERS.
WAS THAT BEFORE OR AFTER HE TRIED TO EAT YOU?

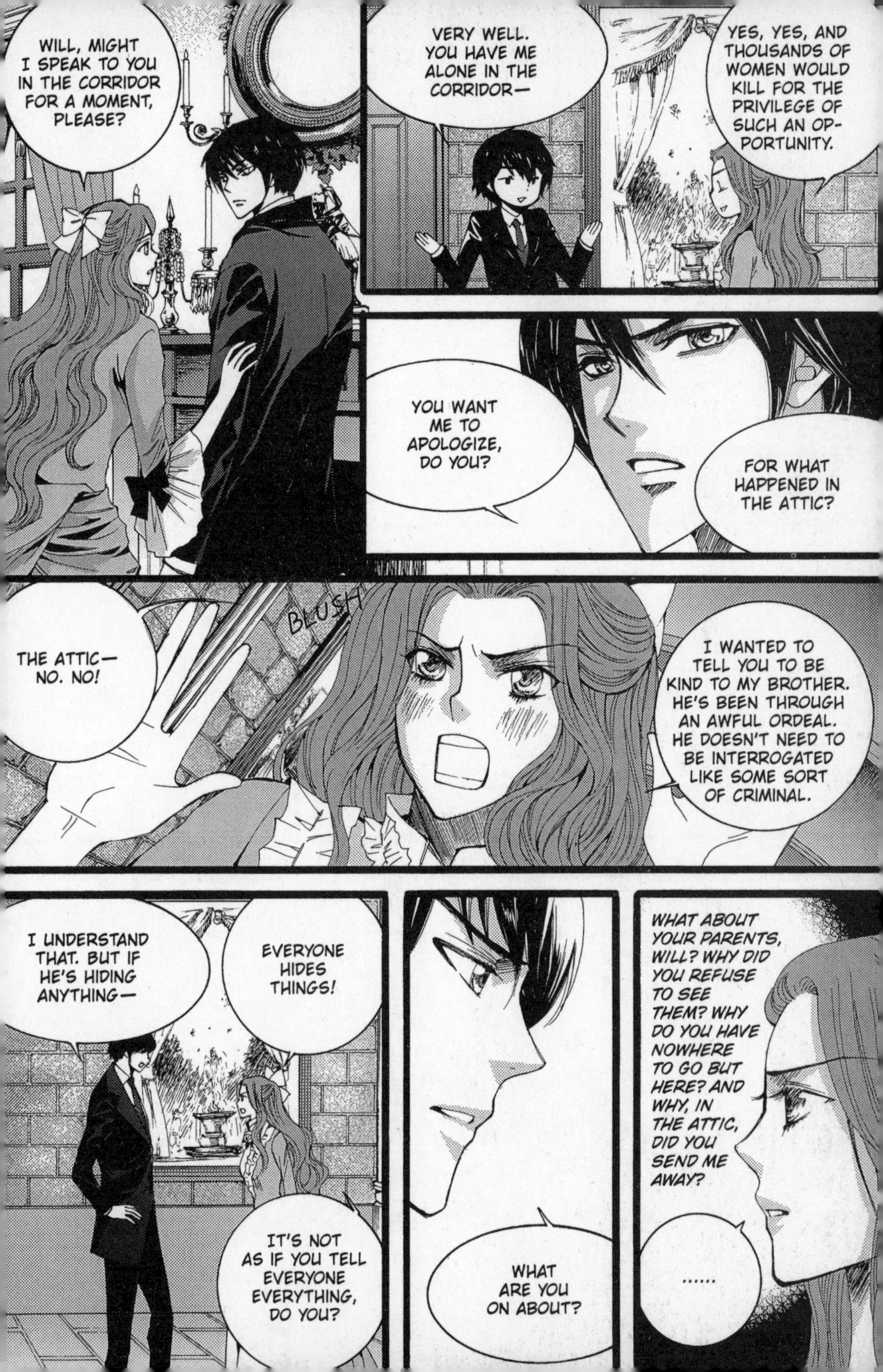
WILL, MIGHT I SPEAK TO YOU IN THE CORRIDOR FOR A MOMENT, PLEASE?
VERY WELL. YOU HAVE ME ALONE IN THE CORRIDOR—
YES, YES, AND THOUSANDS OF WOMEN WOULD KILL FOR THE PRIVILEGE OF SUCH AN OP-PORTUNITY.
YOU WANT ME TO APOLOGIZE, DO YOU?
FOR WHAT HAPPENED IN THE ATTIC?
THE ATTIC— NO. NO!
BLUSH
I WANTED TO TELL YOU TO BE KIND TO MY BROTHER. HE'S BEEN THROUGH AN AWFUL ORDEAL. HE DOESN'T NEED TO BE INTERROGATED LIKE SOME SORT OF CRIMINAL.
I UNDERSTAND THAT. BUT IF HE'S HIDING ANYTHING—
EVERYONE HIDES THINGS!
IT'S NOT AS IF YOU TELL EVERYONE EVERYTHING, DO YOU?
WHAT ARE YOU ON ABOUT?
WHAT ABOUT YOUR PARENTS, WILL? WHY DID YOU REFUSE TO SEE THEM? WHY DO YOU HAVE NOWHERE TO GO BUT HERE? AND WHY, IN THE ATTIC, DID YOU SEND ME AWAY?
......

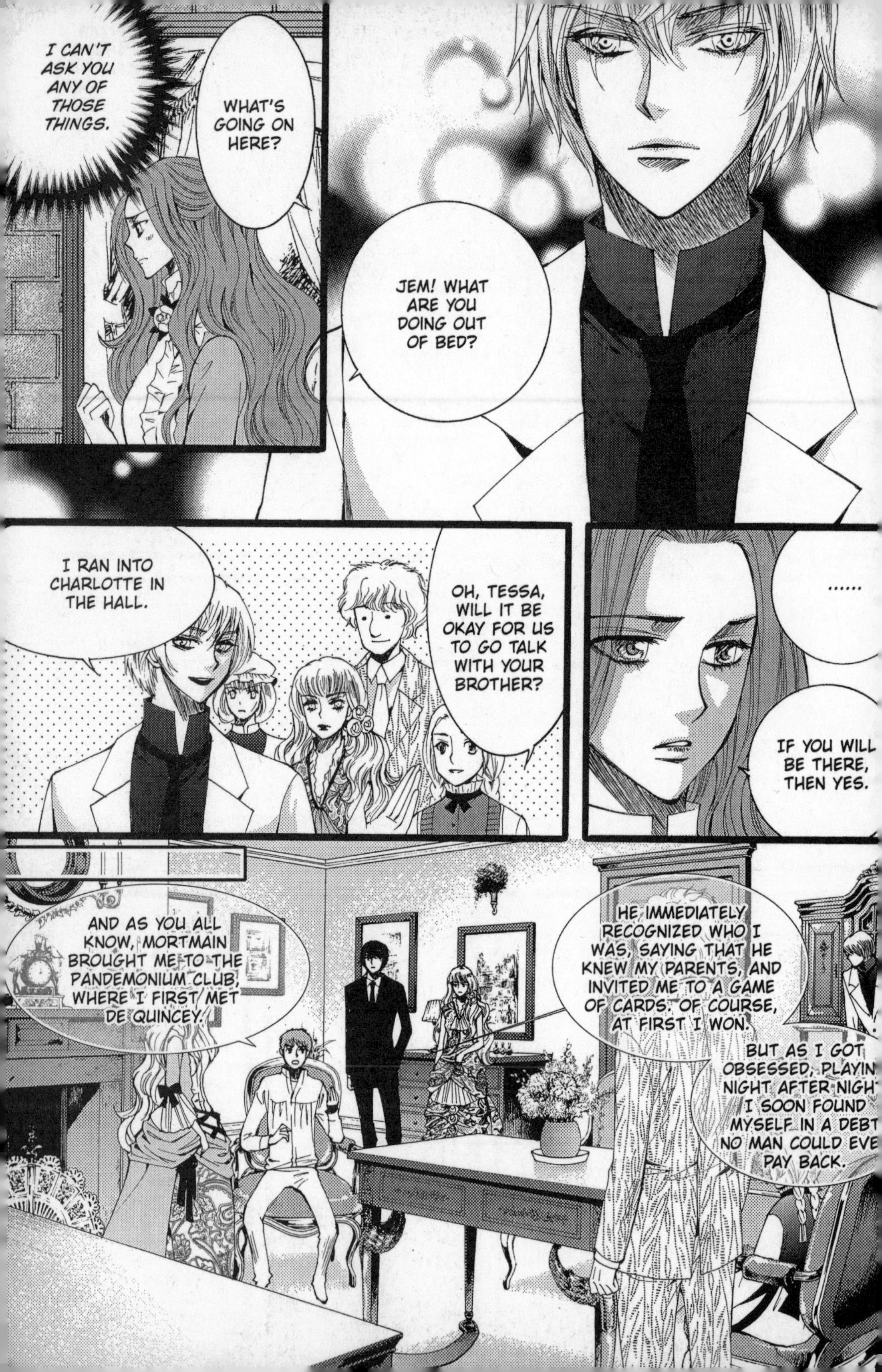
I CAN'T ASK YOU ANY OF THOSE THINGS.
WHAT'S GOING ON HERE?
JEM! WHAT ARE YOU DOING OUT OF BED?
I RAN INTO CHARLOTTE IN THE HALL.
OH, TESSA, WILL IT BE OKAY FOR US TO GO TALK WITH YOUR BROTHER?
......
IF YOU WILL BE THERE, THEN YES.
AND AS YOU ALL KNOW, MORTMAIN BROUGHT ME TO THE PANDEMONIUM CLUB, WHERE I FIRST MET DE QUINCEY.
HE IMMEDIATELY RECOGNIZED WHO I WAS, SAYING THAT HE KNEW MY PARENTS, AND INVITED ME TO A GAME OF CARDS. OF COURSE, AT FIRST I WON.
BUT AS I GOT OBSESSED, PLAYIN NIGHT AFTER NIGH I SOON FOUND MYSELF IN A DEBT NO MAN COULD EVE PAY BACK.

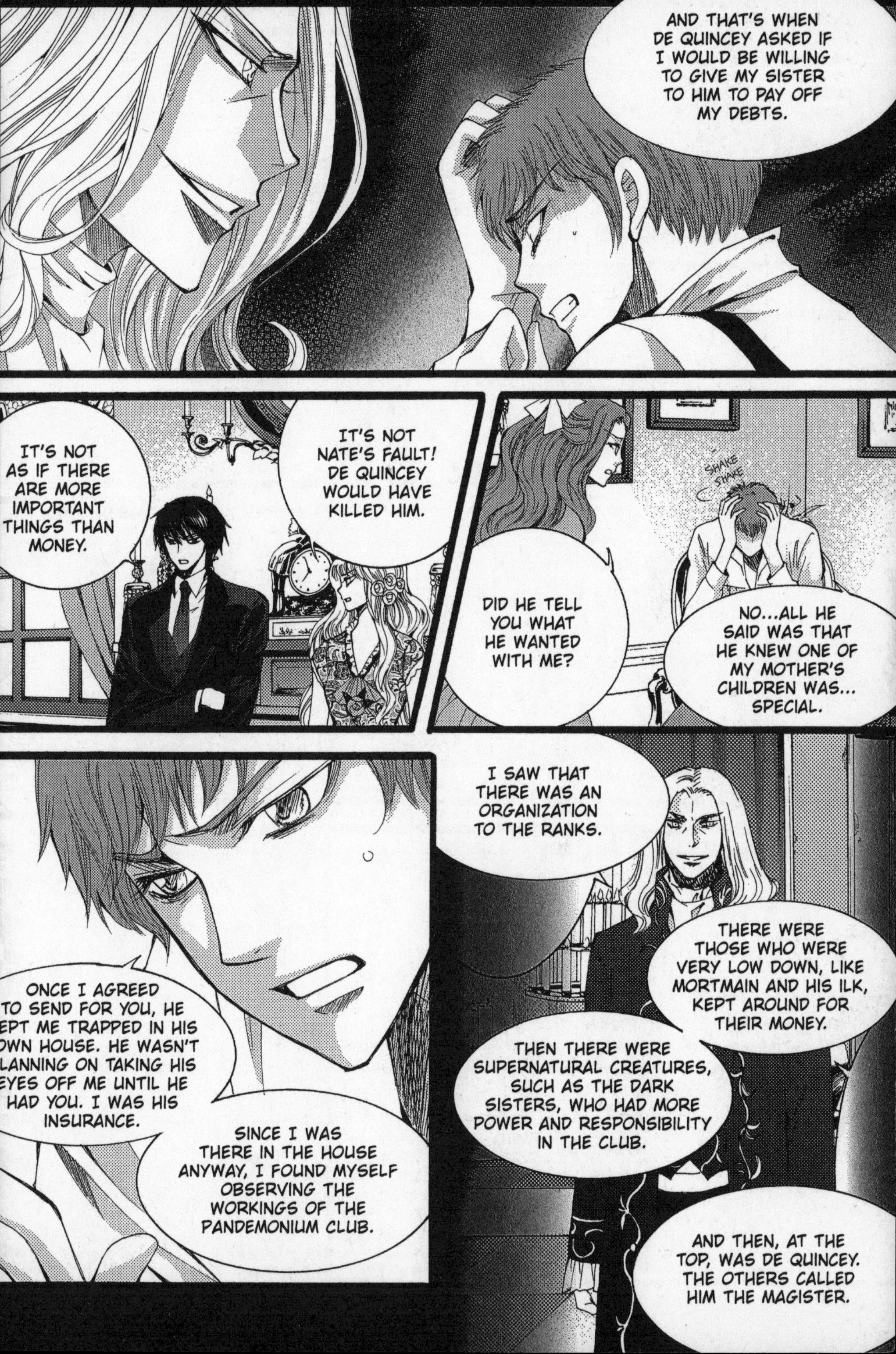
AND THAT'S WHEN DE QUINCEY ASKED IF I WOULD BE WILLING TO GIVE MY SISTER TO HIM TO PAY OFF MY DEBTS.
IT'S NOT AS IF THERE ARE MORE IMPORTANT THINGS THAN MONEY.
IT'S NOT NATE'S FAULT! DE QUINCEY WOULD HAVE KILLED HIM.
SHAKE SHAKE
DID HE TELL YOU WHAT HE WANTED WITH ME?
NO...ALL HE SAID WAS THAT HE KNEW ONE OF MY MOTHER'S CHILDREN WAS... SPECIAL.
ONCE I AGREED TO SEND FOR YOU, HE EPT ME TRAPPED IN HIS WN HOUSE. HE WASN'T LANNING ON TAKING HIS EYES OFF ME UNTIL HE HAD YOU. I WAS HIS INSURANCE.
SINCE I WAS THERE IN THE HOUSE ANYWAY, I FOUND MYSELF OBSERVING THE WORKINGS OF THE PANDEMONIUM CLUB.
I SAW THAT THERE WAS AN ORGANIZATION TO THE RANKS.
THERE WERE THOSE WHO WERE VERY LOW DOWN, LIKE MORTMAIN AND HIS ILK, KEPT AROUND FOR THEIR MONEY.
THEN THERE WERE SUPERNATURAL CREATURES, SUCH AS THE DARK SISTERS, WHO HAD MORE POWER AND RESPONSIBILITY IN THE CLUB.
AND THEN, AT THE TOP, WAS DE QUINCEY. THE OTHERS CALLED HIM THE MAGISTER.

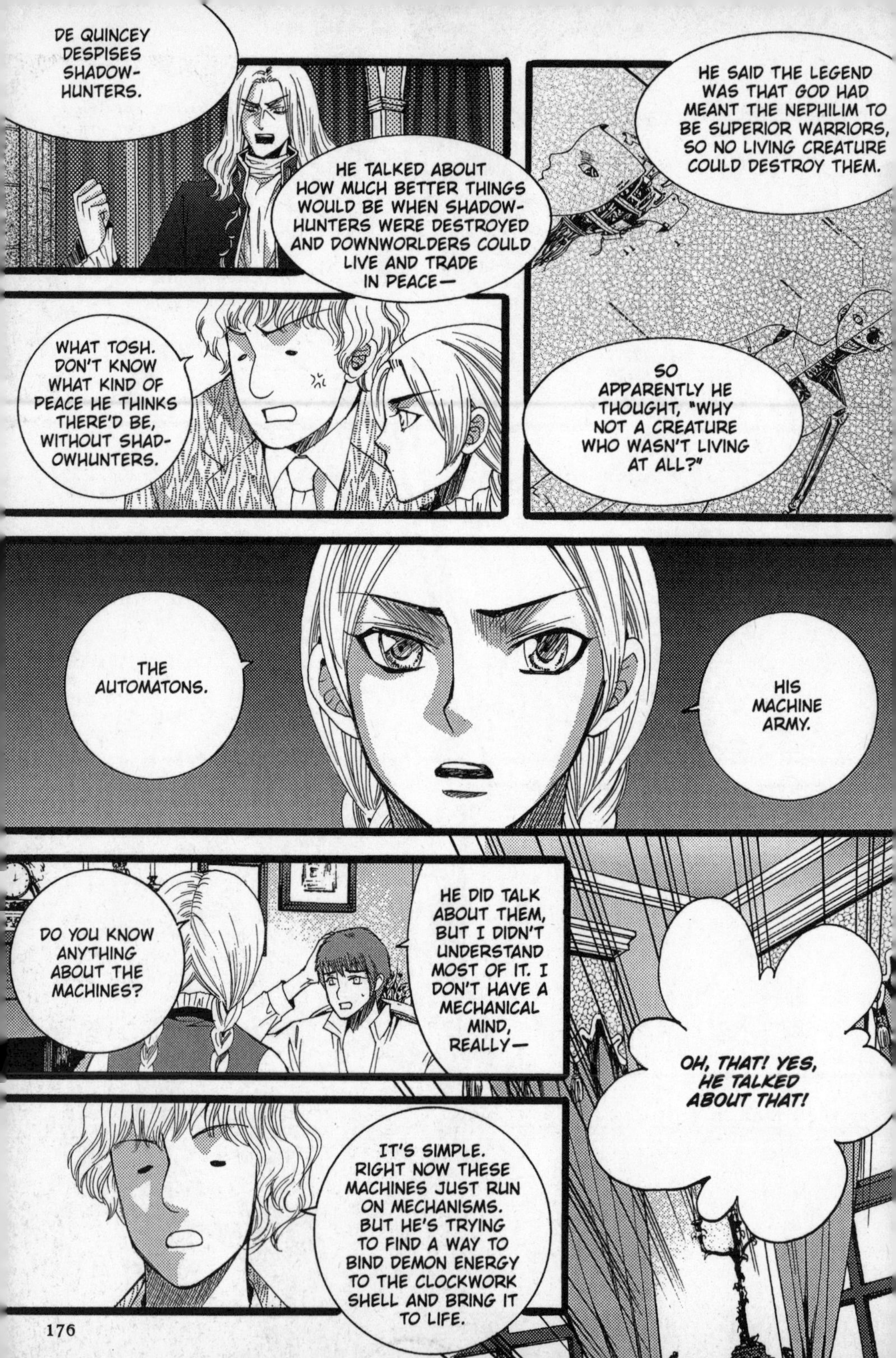
DE QUINCEY DESPISES SHADOW-HUNTERS.
HE TALKED ABOUT HOW MUCH BETTER THINGS WOULD BE WHEN SHADOW-HUNTERS WERE DESTROYED AND DOWNWORLDERS COULD LIVE AND TRADE IN PEACE—
HE SAID THE LEGEND WAS THAT GOD HAD MEANT THE NEPHILIM TO BE SUPERIOR WARRIORS, SO NO LIVING CREATURE COULD DESTROY THEM.
WHAT TOSH. DON'T KNOW WHAT KIND OF PEACE HE THINKS THERE'D BE, WITHOUT SHAD-OWHUNTERS.
SO APPARENTLY HE THOUGHT, "WHY NOT A CREATURE WHO WASN'T LIVING AT ALL?"
THE AUTOMATONS.
HIS MACHINE ARMY.
DO YOU KNOW ANYTHING ABOUT THE MACHINES?
HE DID TALK ABOUT THEM, BUT I DIDN'T UNDERSTAND MOST OF IT. I DON'T HAVE A MECHANICAL MIND, REALLY—
OH, THAT! YES, HE TALKED ABOUT THAT!
IT'S SIMPLE. RIGHT NOW THESE MACHINES JUST RUN ON MECHANISMS. BUT HE'S TRYING TO FIND A WAY TO BIND DEMON ENERGY TO THE CLOCKWORK SHELL AND BRING IT TO LIFE.

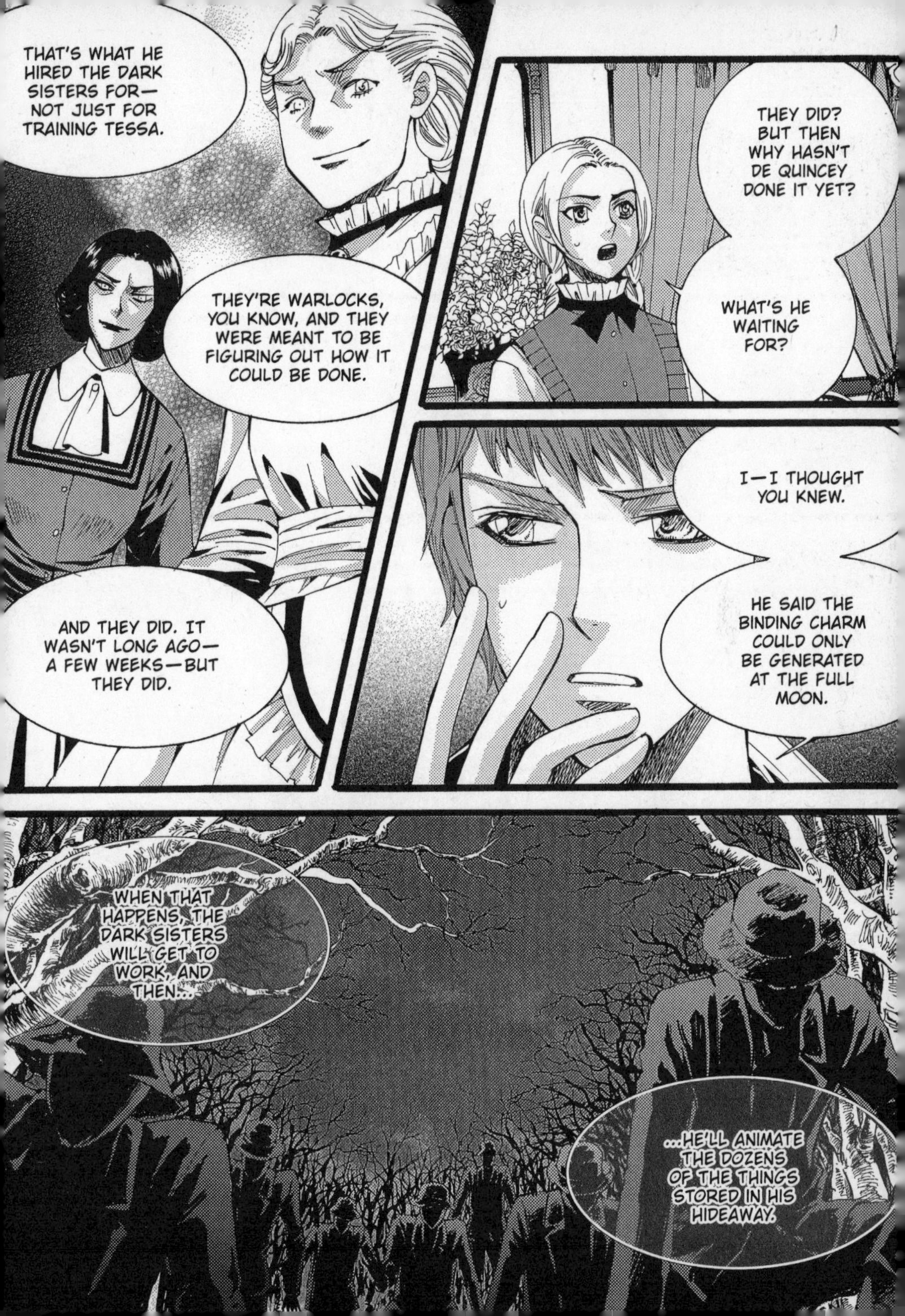
THAT'S WHAT HE HIRED THE DARK SISTERS FOR—NOT JUST FOR TRAINING TESSA.
THEY'RE WARLOCKS, YOU KNOW, AND THEY WERE MEANT TO BE FIGURING OUT HOW IT COULD BE DONE.
THEY DID? BUT THEN WHY HASN'T DE QUINCEY DONE IT YET?
WHAT'S HE WAITING FOR?
AND THEY DID. IT WASN'T LONG AGO—A FEW WEEKS—BUT THEY DID.
I—I THOUGHT YOU KNEW.
HE SAID THE BINDING CHARM COULD ONLY BE GENERATED AT THE FULL MOON.
WHEN THAT HAPPENS, THE DARK SISTERS WILL GET TO WORK, AND THEN...
...HE'LL ANIMATE THE DOZENS OF THE THINGS STORED IN HIS HIDEAWAY.

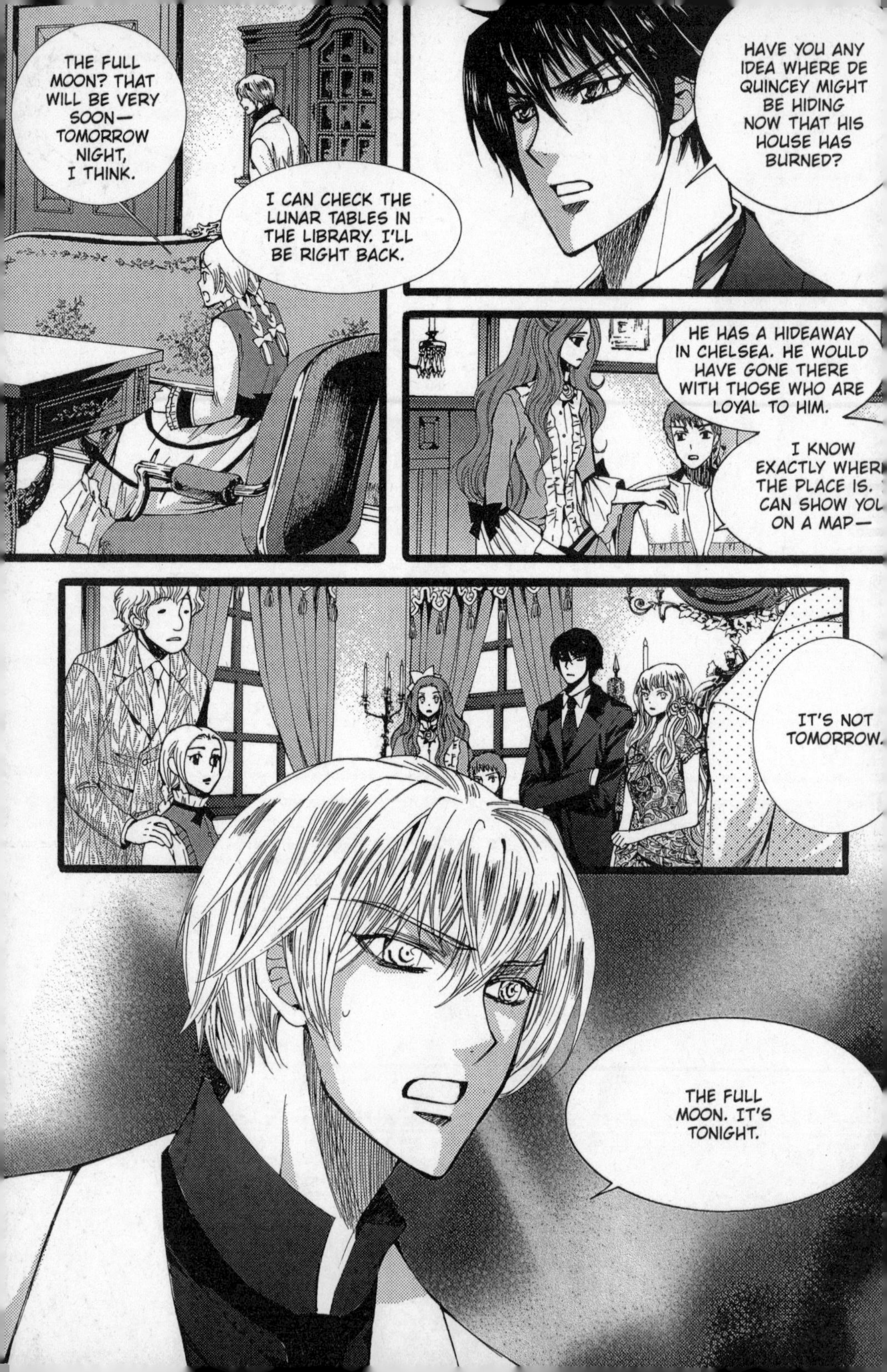
THE FULL MOON? THAT WILL BE VERY SOON—TOMORROW NIGHT, I THINK.
I CAN CHECK THE LUNAR TABLES IN THE LIBRARY. I'LL BE RIGHT BACK.
HAVE YOU ANY IDEA WHERE DE QUINCEY MIGHT BE HIDING NOW THAT HIS HOUSE HAS BURNED?
HE HAS A HIDEAWAY IN CHELSEA. HE WOULD HAVE GONE THERE WITH THOSE WHO ARE LOYAL TO HIM.
I KNOW EXACTLY WHER THE PLACE IS. CAN SHOW YO ON A MAP—
IT'S NOT TOMORROW.
THE FULL MOON. IT'S TONIGHT.

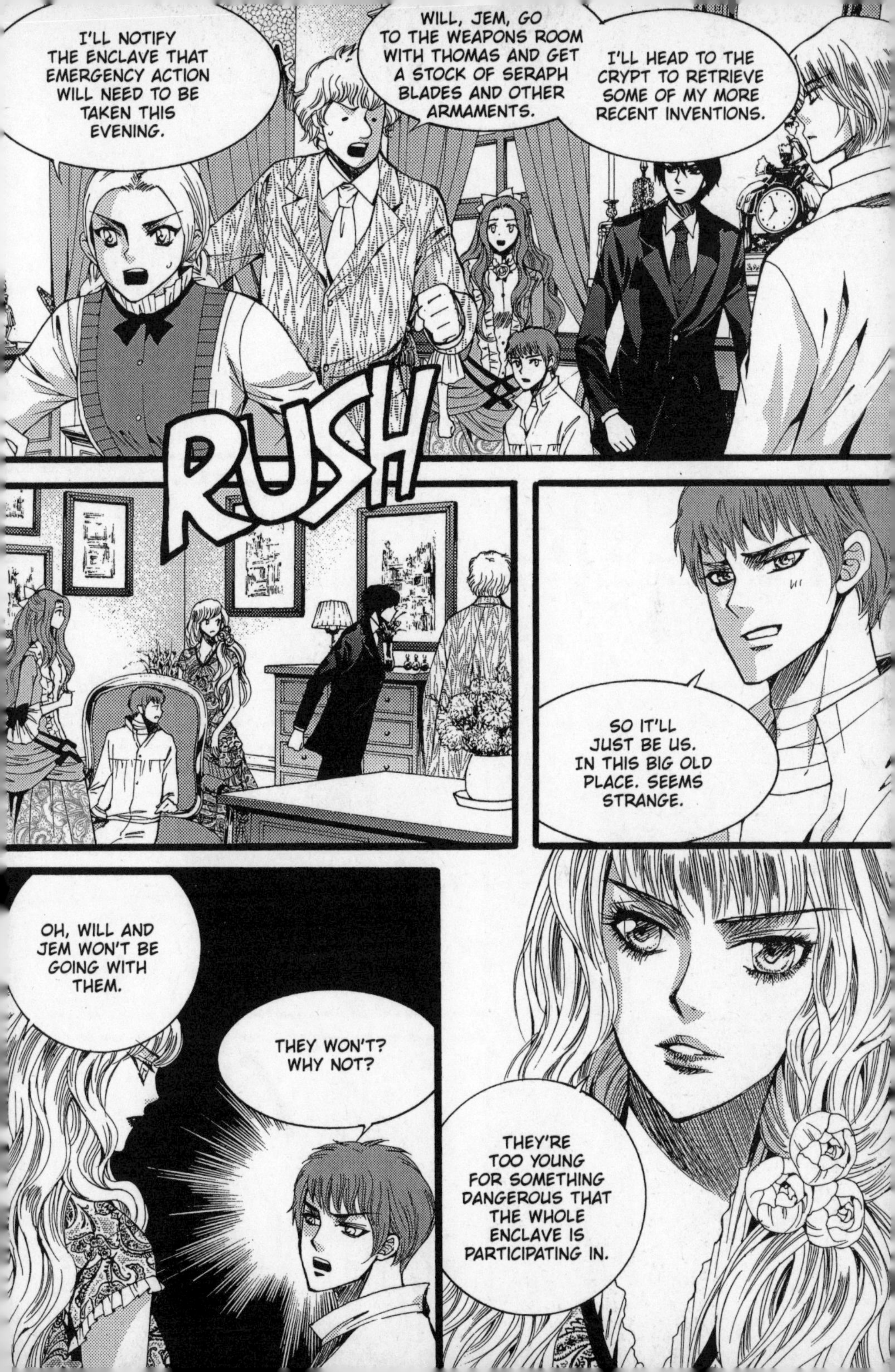
I'LL NOTIFY THE ENCLAVE THAT EMERGENCY ACTION WILL NEED TO BE TAKEN THIS EVENING.
WILL, JEM, GO TO THE WEAPONS ROOM WITH THOMAS AND GET A STOCK OF SERAPH BLADES AND OTHER ARMAMENTS.
I'LL HEAD TO THE CRYPT TO RETRIEVE SOME OF MY MORE RECENT INVENTIONS.
RUSH
SO IT'LL JUST BE US. IN THIS BIG OLD PLACE. SEEMS STRANGE.
OH, WILL AND JEM WON'T BE GOING WITH THEM.
THEY WON'T? WHY NOT?
THEY'RE TOO YOUNG FOR SOMETHING DANGEROUS THAT THE WHOLE ENCLAVE IS PARTICIPATING IN.

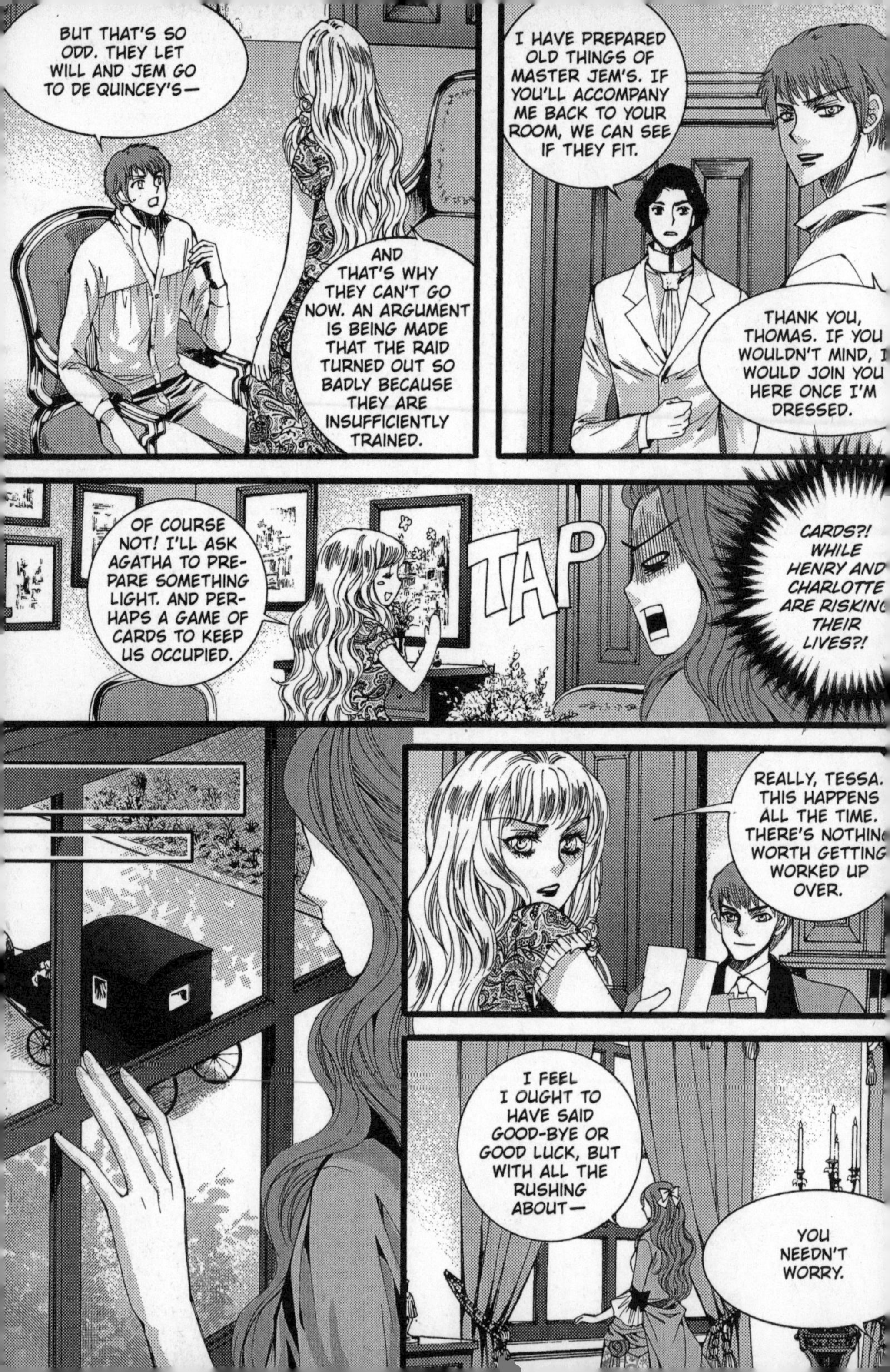

BUT THAT'S SO ODD. THEY LET WILL AND JEM GO TO DE QUINCEY'S—
AND THAT'S WHY THEY CAN'T GO NOW. AN ARGUMENT IS BEING MADE THAT THE RAID TURNED OUT SO BADLY BECAUSE THEY ARE INSUFFICIENTLY TRAINED.
I HAVE PREPARED OLD THINGS OF MASTER JEM'S. IF YOU'LL ACCOMPANY ME BACK TO YOUR ROOM, WE CAN SEE IF THEY FIT.
THANK YOU, THOMAS. IF YOU WOULDN'T MIND, I WOULD JOIN YOU HERE ONCE I'M DRESSED.
OF COURSE NOT! I'LL ASK AGATHA TO PREPARE SOMETHING LIGHT. AND PERHAPS A GAME OF CARDS TO KEEP US OCCUPIED.
TAP
CARDS?! WHILE HENRY AND CHARLOTTE ARE RISKING THEIR LIVES?!
REALLY, TESSA. THIS HAPPENS ALL THE TIME. THERE'S NOTHING WORTH GETTING WORKED UP OVER.
I FEEL I OUGHT TO HAVE SAID GOOD-BYE OR GOOD LUCK, BUT WITH ALL THE RUSHING ABOUT—
YOU NEEDN'T WORRY.

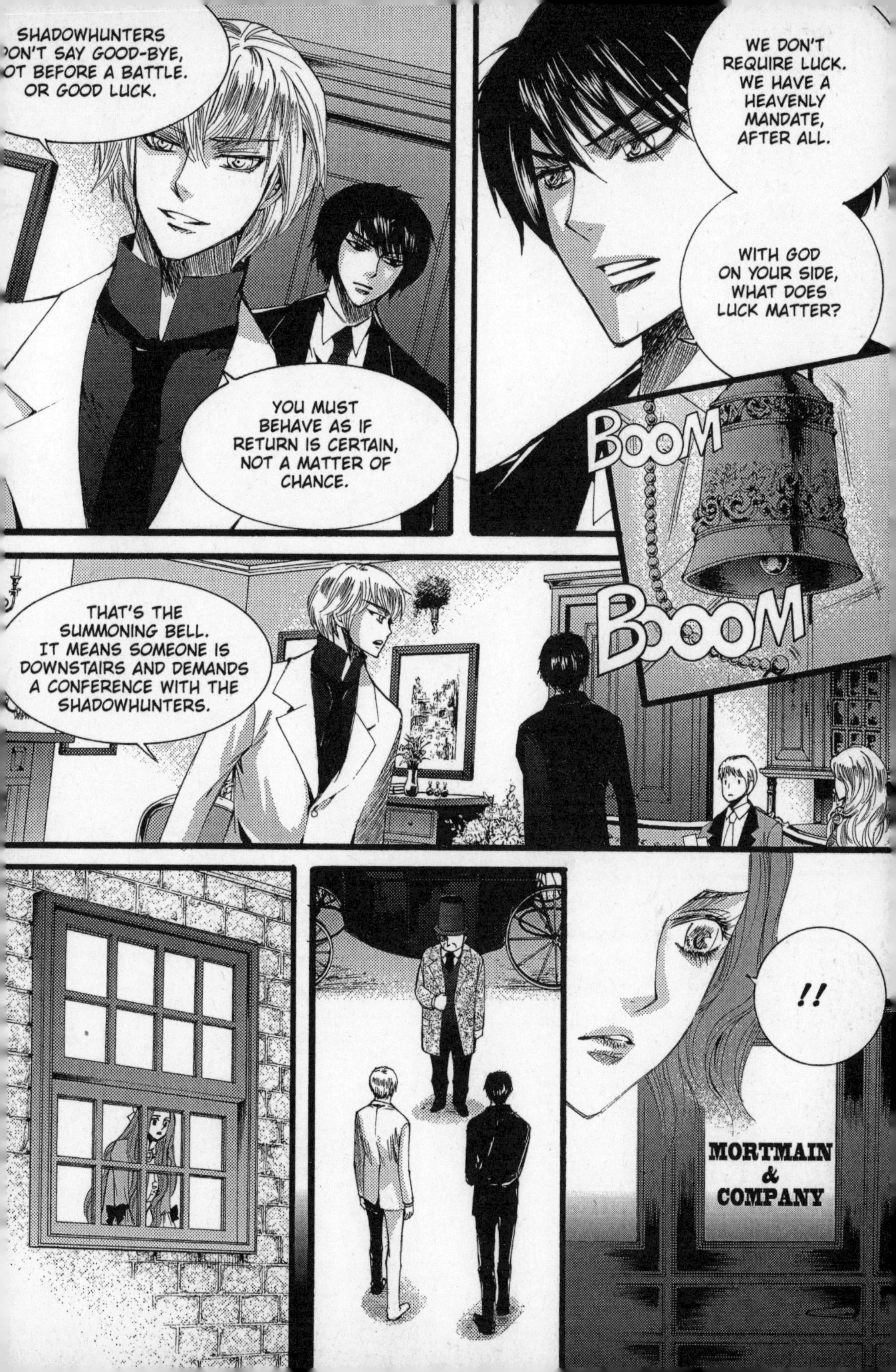
SHADOWHUNTERS DON'T SAY GOOD-BYE, NOT BEFORE A BATTLE. OR GOOD LUCK.
YOU MUST BEHAVE AS IF RETURN IS CERTAIN, NOT A MATTER OF CHANCE.
WE DON'T REQUIRE LUCK. WE HAVE A HEAVENLY MANDATE, AFTER ALL.
WITH GOD ON YOUR SIDE, WHAT DOES LUCK MATTER?
BOOM
BOOOM
THAT'S THE SUMMONING BELL. IT MEANS SOMEONE IS DOWNSTAIRS AND DEMANDS A CONFERENCE WITH THE SHADOWHUNTERS.
!!
MORTMAIN & COMPANY

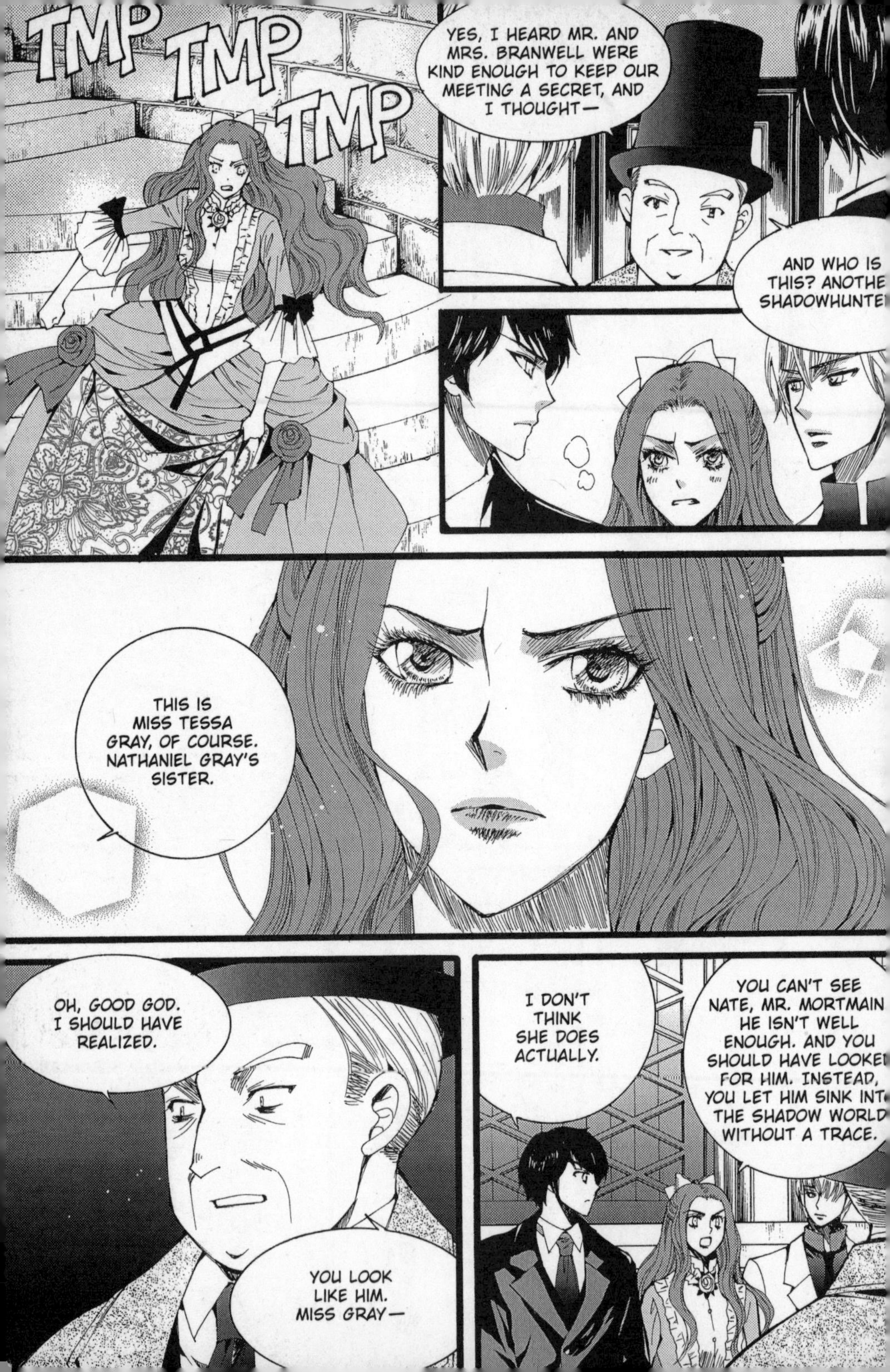
TMP TMP TMP
YES, I HEARD MR. AND MRS. BRANWELL WERE KIND ENOUGH TO KEEP OUR MEETING A SECRET, AND I THOUGHT—
AND WHO IS THIS? ANOTHE SHADOWHUNTE
THIS IS MISS TESSA GRAY, OF COURSE. NATHANIEL GRAY'S SISTER.
OH, GOOD GOD. I SHOULD HAVE REALIZED.
YOU LOOK LIKE HIM. MISS GRAY—
I DON'T THINK SHE DOES ACTUALLY.
YOU CAN'T SEE NATE, MR. MORTMAIN HE ISN'T WELL ENOUGH. AND YOU SHOULD HAVE LOOKE FOR HIM. INSTEAD, YOU LET HIM SINK INT THE SHADOW WORLD WITHOUT A TRACE.

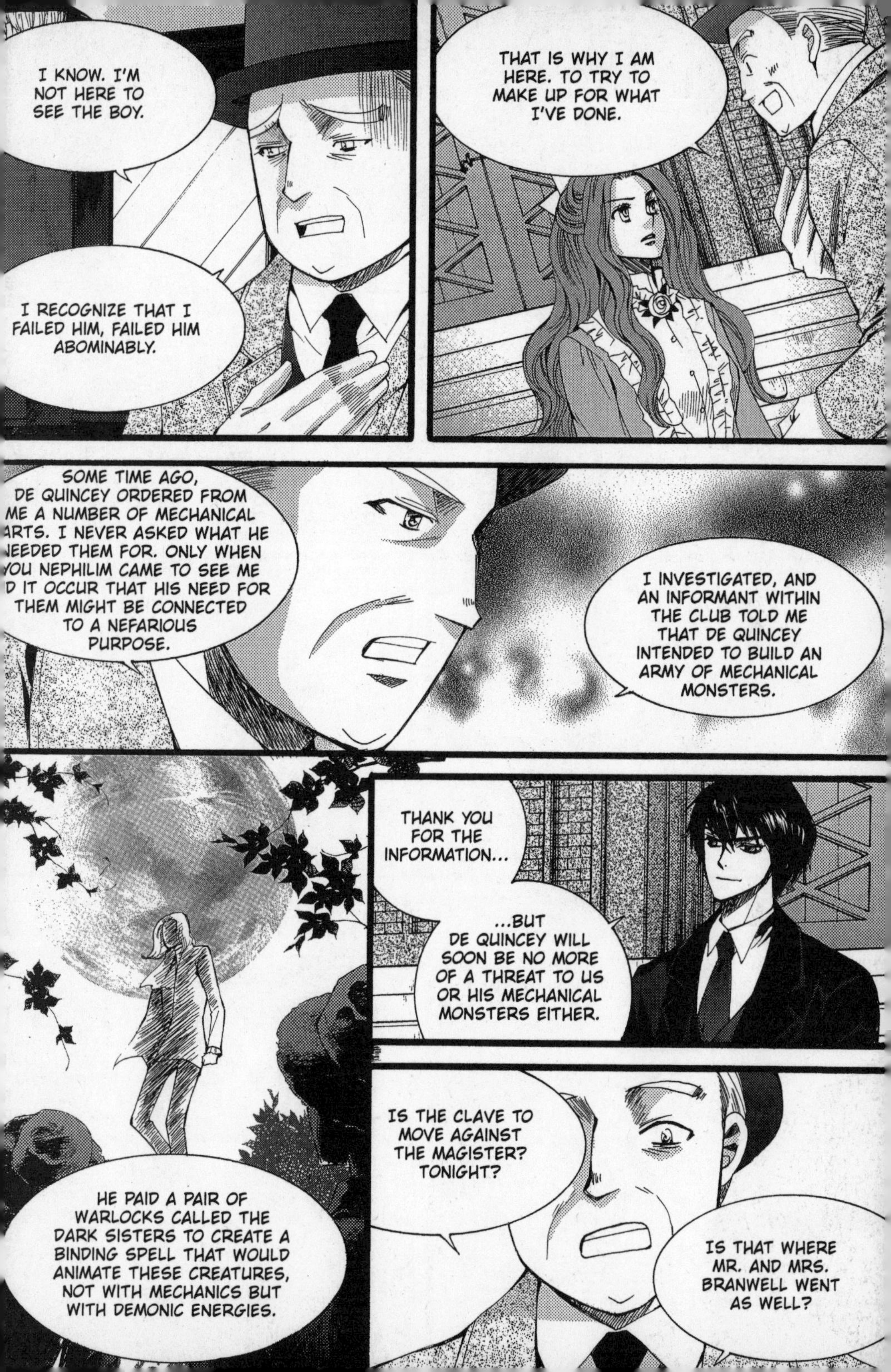
I KNOW. I'M NOT HERE TO SEE THE BOY.
I RECOGNIZE THAT I FAILED HIM, FAILED HIM ABOMINABLY.
THAT IS WHY I AM HERE. TO TRY TO MAKE UP FOR WHAT I'VE DONE.
SOME TIME AGO, DE QUINCEY ORDERED FROM ME A NUMBER OF MECHANICAL ARTS. I NEVER ASKED WHAT HE IEEDED THEM FOR. ONLY WHEN YOU NEPHILIM CAME TO SEE ME D IT OCCUR THAT HIS NEED FOR THEM MIGHT BE CONNECTED TO A NEFARIOUS PURPOSE.
I INVESTIGATED, AND AN INFORMANT WITHIN THE CLUB TOLD ME THAT DE QUINCEY INTENDED TO BUILD AN ARMY OF MECHANICAL MONSTERS.
HE PAID A PAIR OF WARLOCKS CALLED THE DARK SISTERS TO CREATE A BINDING SPELL THAT WOULD ANIMATE THESE CREATURES, NOT WITH MECHANICS BUT WITH DEMONIC ENERGIES.
THANK YOU FOR THE INFORMATION...
...BUT DE QUINCEY WILL SOON BE NO MORE OF A THREAT TO US OR HIS MECHANICAL MONSTERS EITHER.
IS THE CLAVE TO MOVE AGAINST THE MAGISTER? TONIGHT?
IS THAT WHERE MR. AND MRS. BRANWELL WENT AS WELL?

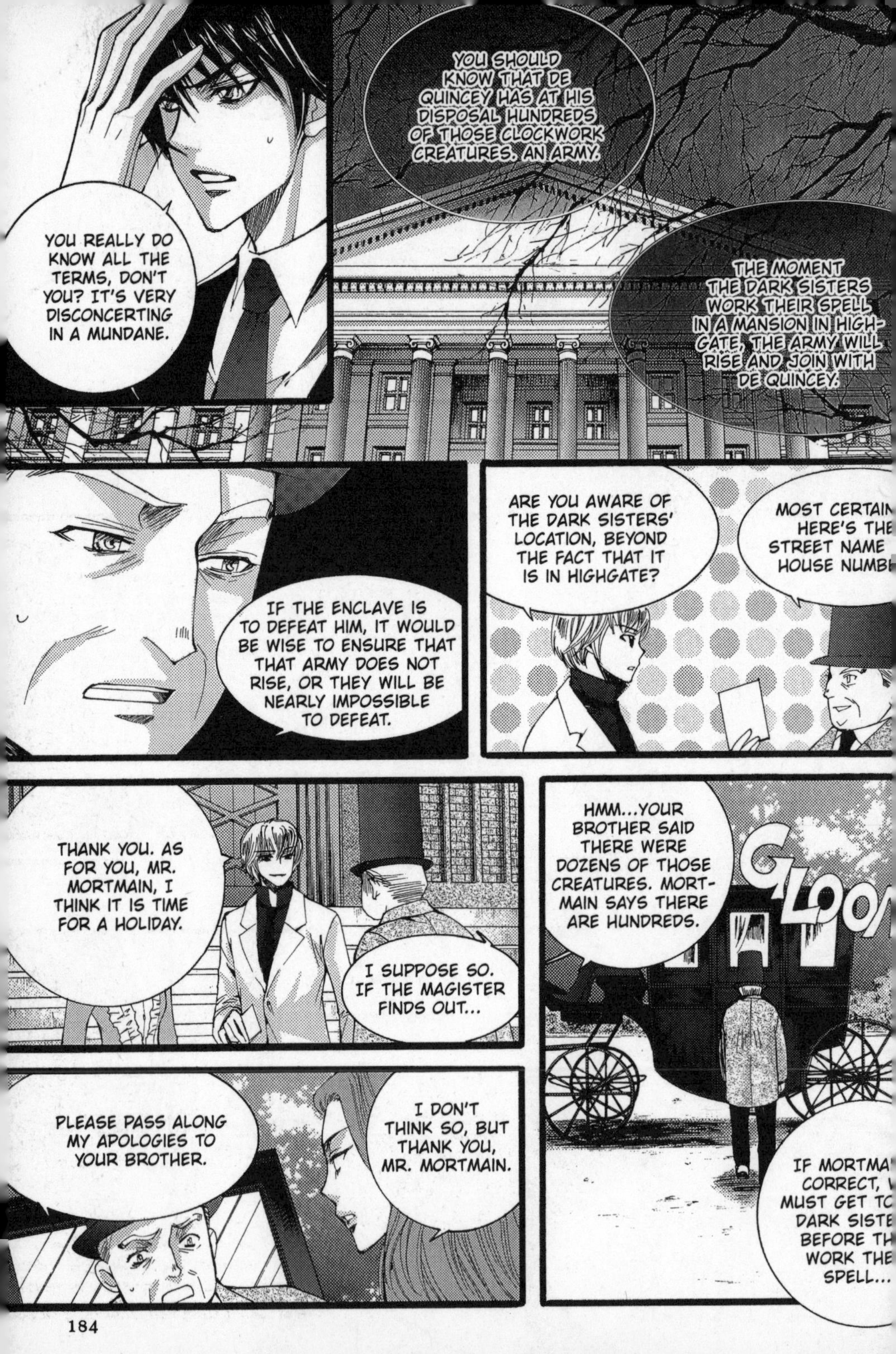
YOU REALLY DO KNOW ALL THE TERMS, DON'T YOU? IT'S VERY DISCONCERTING IN A MUNDANE.
YOU SHOULD KNOW THAT DE QUINCEY HAS AT HIS DISPOSAL HUNDREDS OF THOSE CLOCKWORK CREATURES. AN ARMY.
THE MOMENT THE DARK SISTERS WORK THEIR SPELL IN A MANSION IN HIGH-GATE, THE ARMY WILL RISE AND JOIN WITH DE QUINCEY.
IF THE ENCLAVE IS TO DEFEAT HIM, IT WOULD BE WISE TO ENSURE THAT THAT ARMY DOES NOT RISE, OR THEY WILL BE NEARLY IMPOSSIBLE TO DEFEAT.
ARE YOU AWARE OF THE DARK SISTERS' LOCATION, BEYOND THE FACT THAT IT IS IN HIGHGATE?
MOST CERTAIN HERE'S THE STREET NAME HOUSE NUMB
THANK YOU. AS FOR YOU, MR. MORTMAIN, I THINK IT IS TIME FOR A HOLIDAY.
I SUPPOSE SO. IF THE MAGISTER FINDS OUT...
PLEASE PASS ALONG MY APOLOGIES TO YOUR BROTHER.
I DON'T THINK SO, BUT THANK YOU, MR. MORTMAIN.
HMM...YOUR BROTHER SAID THERE WERE DOZENS OF THOSE CREATURES. MORT-MAIN SAYS THERE ARE HUNDREDS.
GLOO
IF MORTMA CORRECT, MUST GET TO DARK SISTE BEFORE TH WORK THE SPELL...

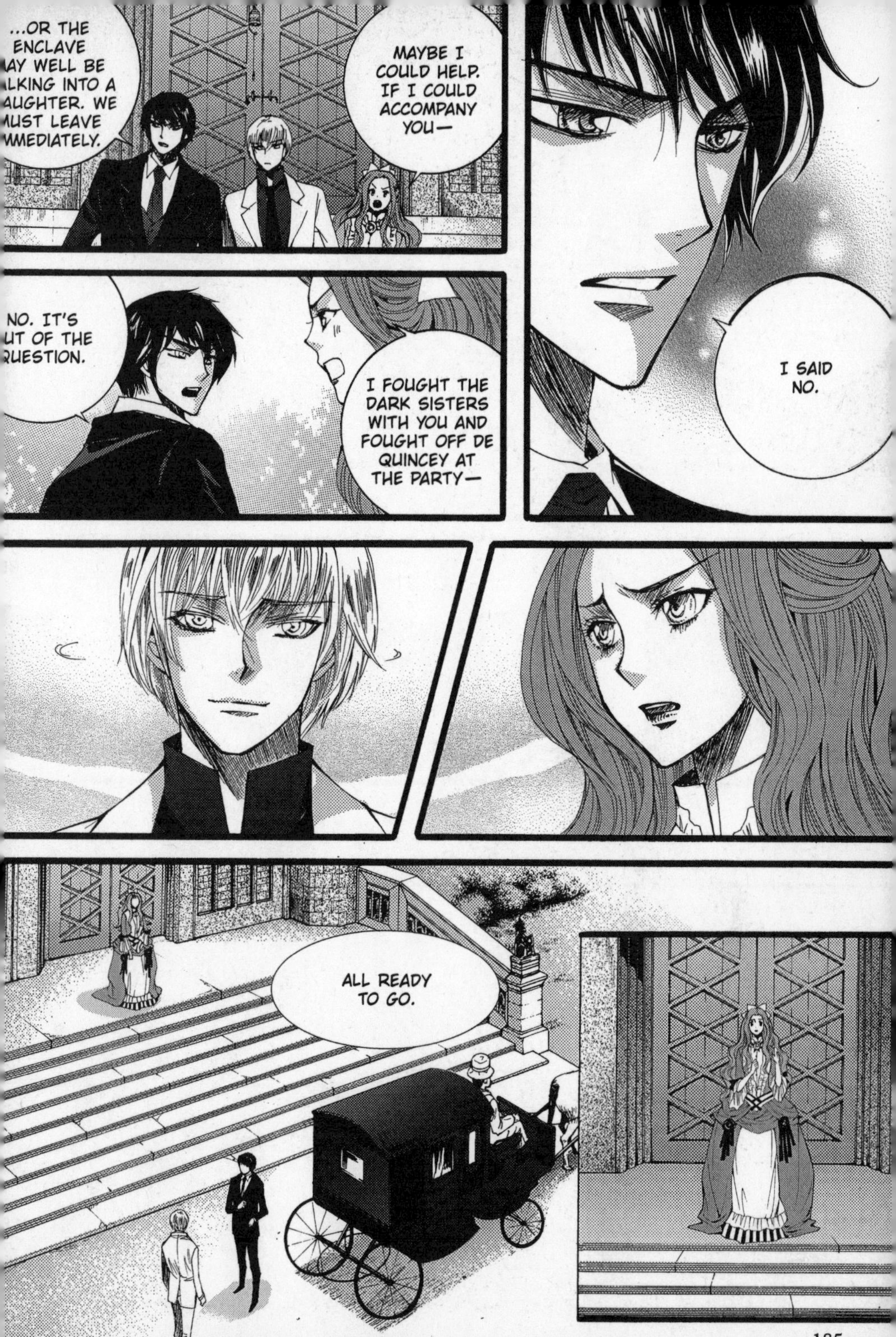
...OR THE ENCLAVE AY WELL BE ALKING INTO A AUGHTER. WE MUST LEAVE MMEDIATELY.
MAYBE I COULD HELP. IF I COULD ACCOMPANY YOU—
NO. IT'S UT OF THE UESTION.
I FOUGHT THE DARK SISTERS WITH YOU AND FOUGHT OFF DE QUINCEY AT THE PARTY—
I SAID NO.
ALL READY TO GO.

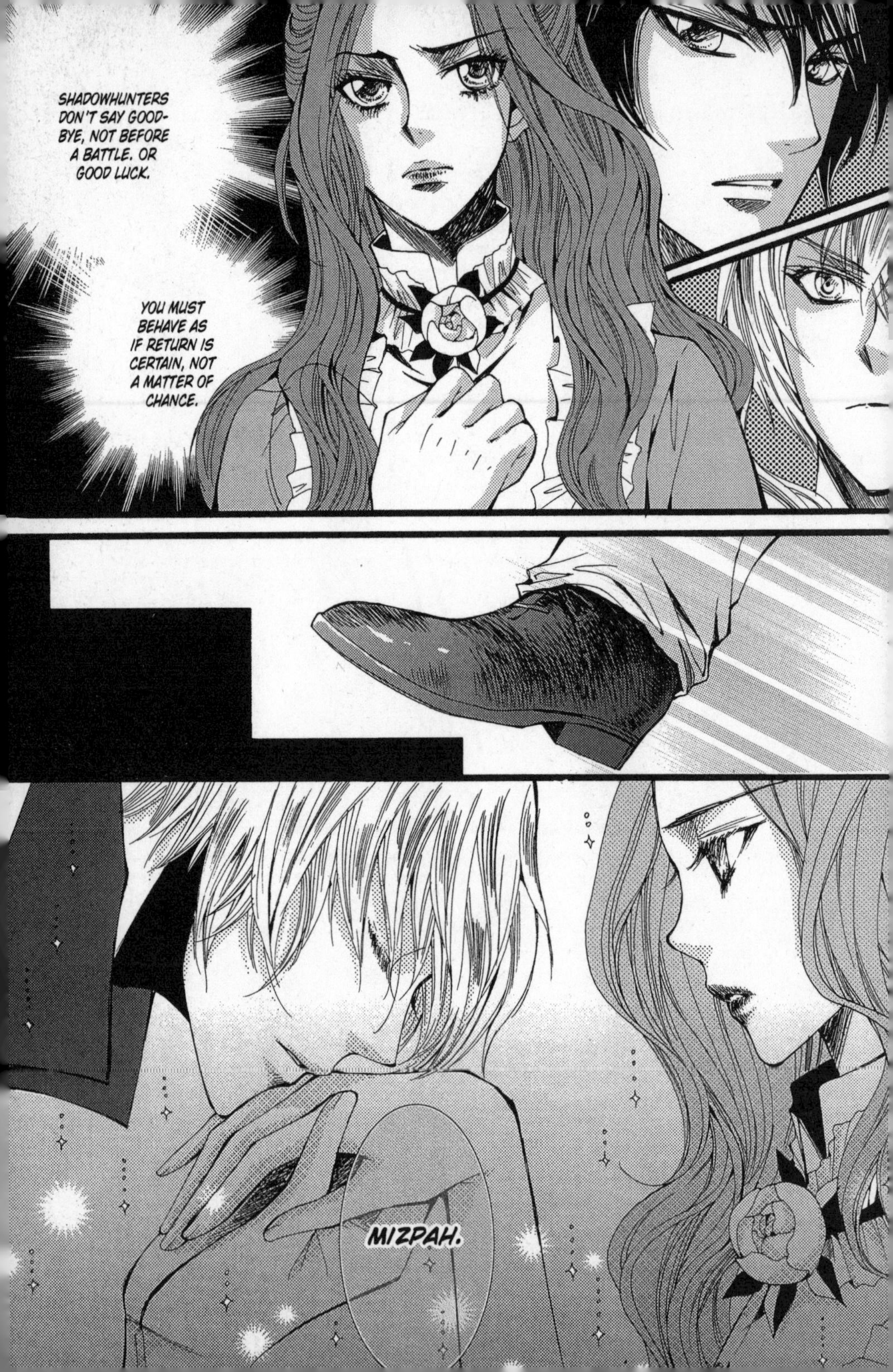
SHADOWHUNTERS DON'T SAY GOOD-BYE, NOT BEFORE A BATTLE. OR GOOD LUCK.
YOU MUST BEHAVE AS IF RETURN IS CERTAIN, NOT A MATTER OF CHANCE.
MIZPAH.

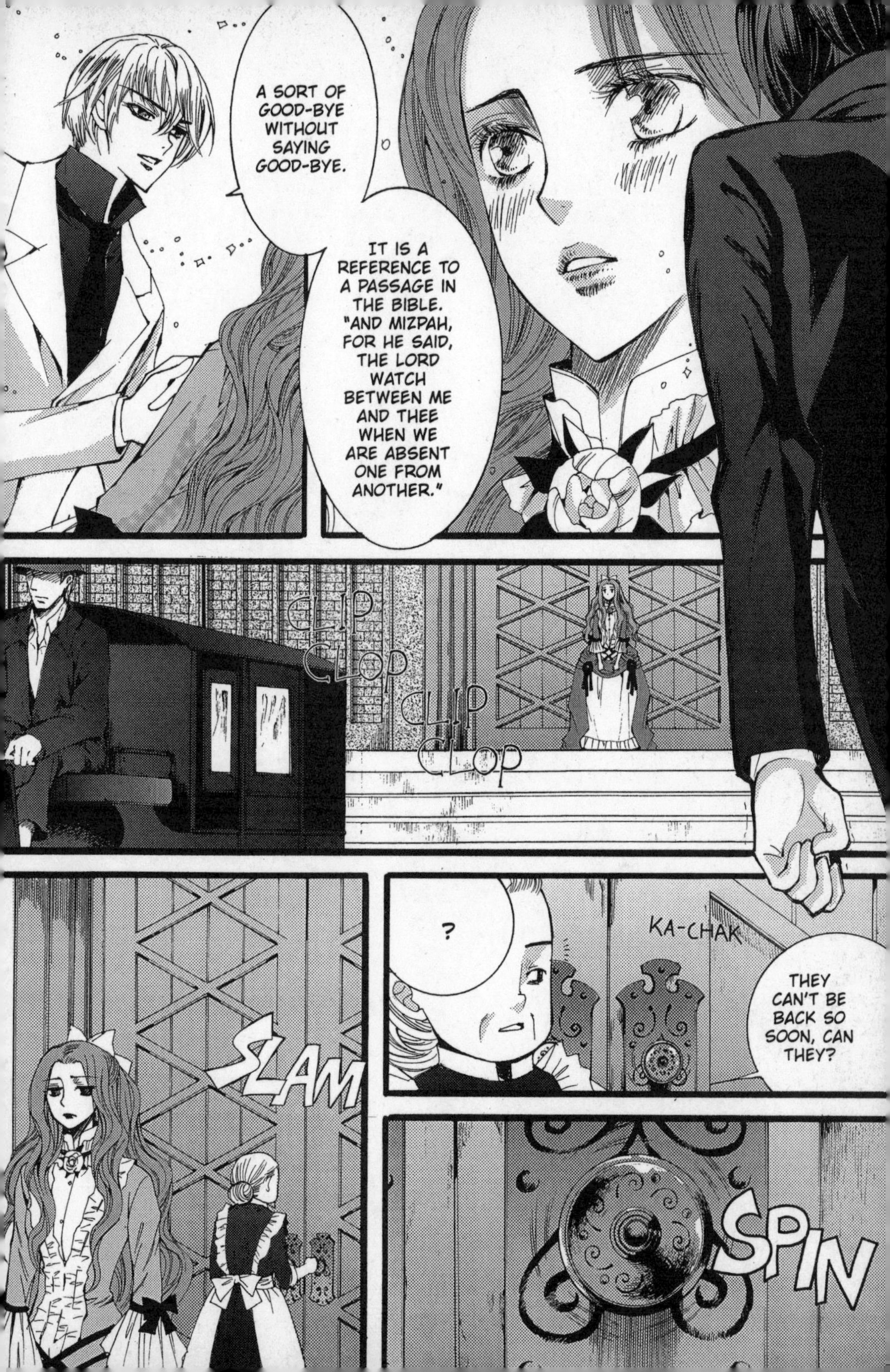

A SORT OF GOOD-BYE WITHOUT SAYING GOOD-BYE.
IT IS A REFERENCE TO A PASSAGE IN THE BIBLE. "AND MIZPAH, FOR HE SAID, THE LORD WATCH BETWEEN ME AND THEE WHEN WE ARE ABSENT ONE FROM ANOTHER."
CLIP CLOP
CLIP CLOP
SLAM
?
KA-CHAK
THEY CAN'T BE BACK SO SOON, CAN THEY?
SPIN

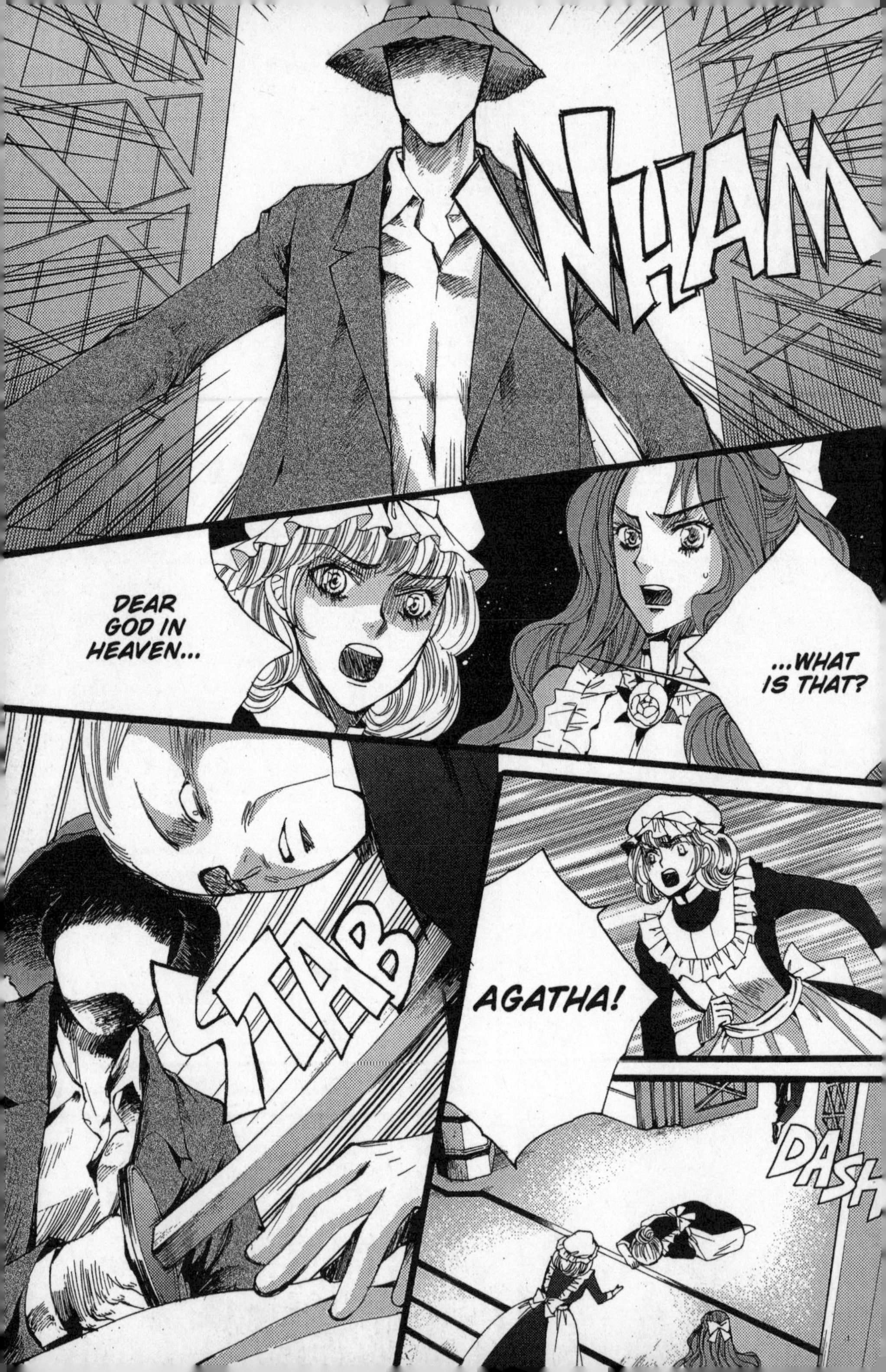
WHAM
DEAR GOD IN HEAVEN...
...WHAT IS THAT?
STAB
AGATHA!
DASH

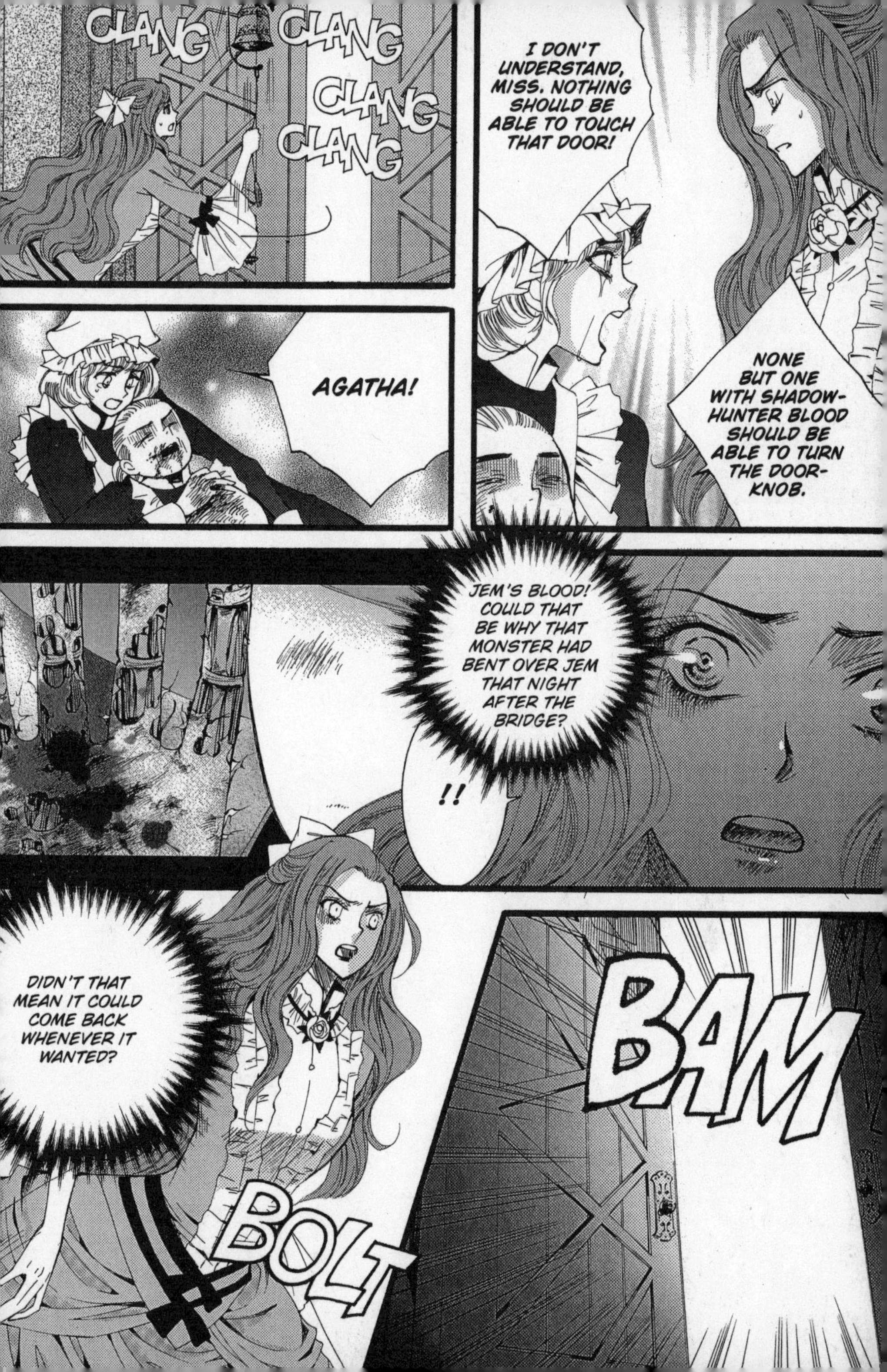
CLANG CLANG
CLANG
CLANG
I DON'T UNDERSTAND, MISS. NOTHING SHOULD BE ABLE TO TOUCH THAT DOOR!
AGATHA!
NONE BUT ONE WITH SHADOW-HUNTER BLOOD SHOULD BE ABLE TO TURN THE DOOR-KNOB.
JEM'S BLOOD! COULD THAT BE WHY THAT MONSTER HAD BENT OVER JEM THAT NIGHT AFTER THE BRIDGE?
!!
DIDN'T THAT MEAN IT COULD COME BACK WHENEVER IT WANTED?
BAM
BOLT

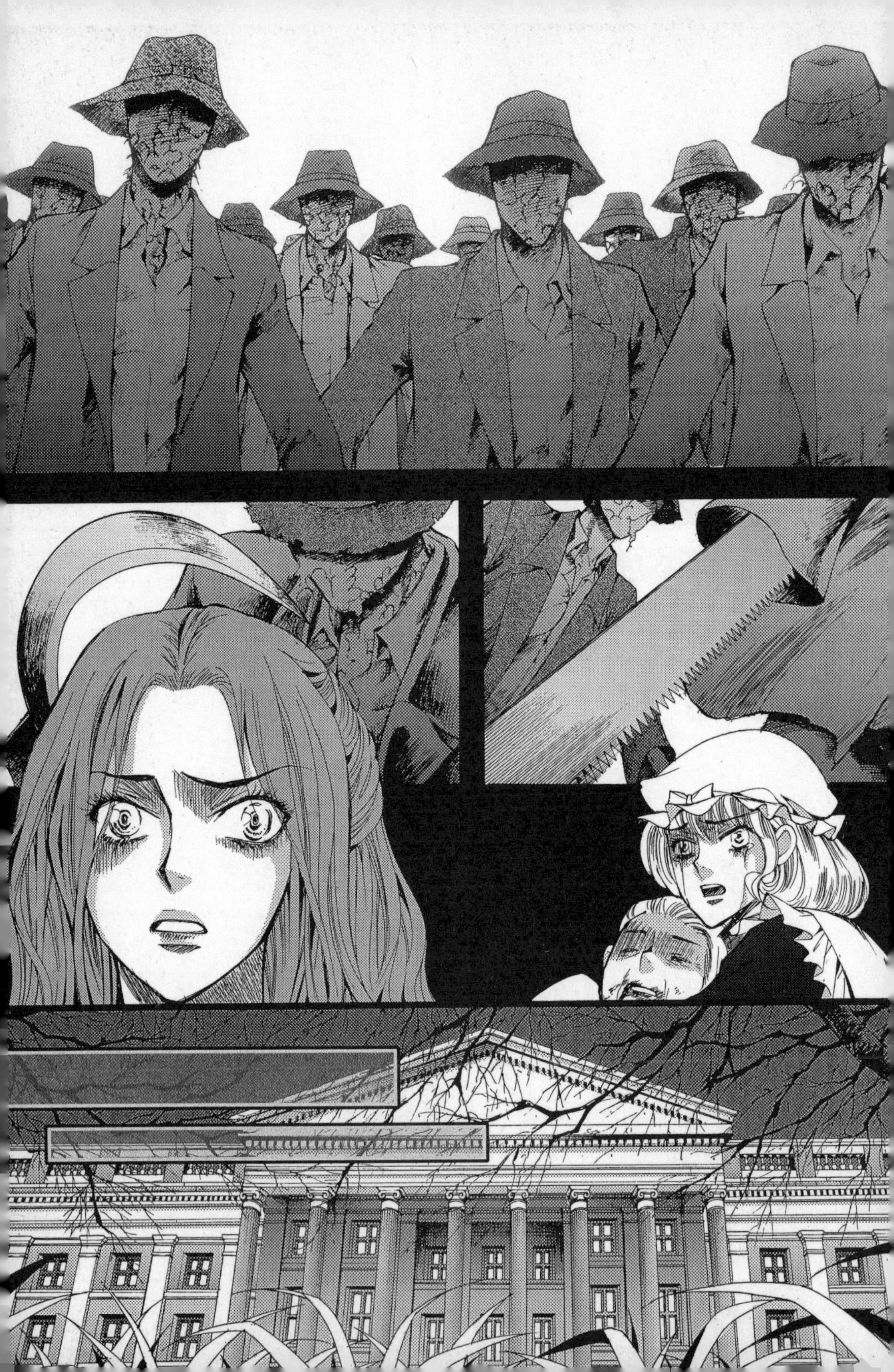

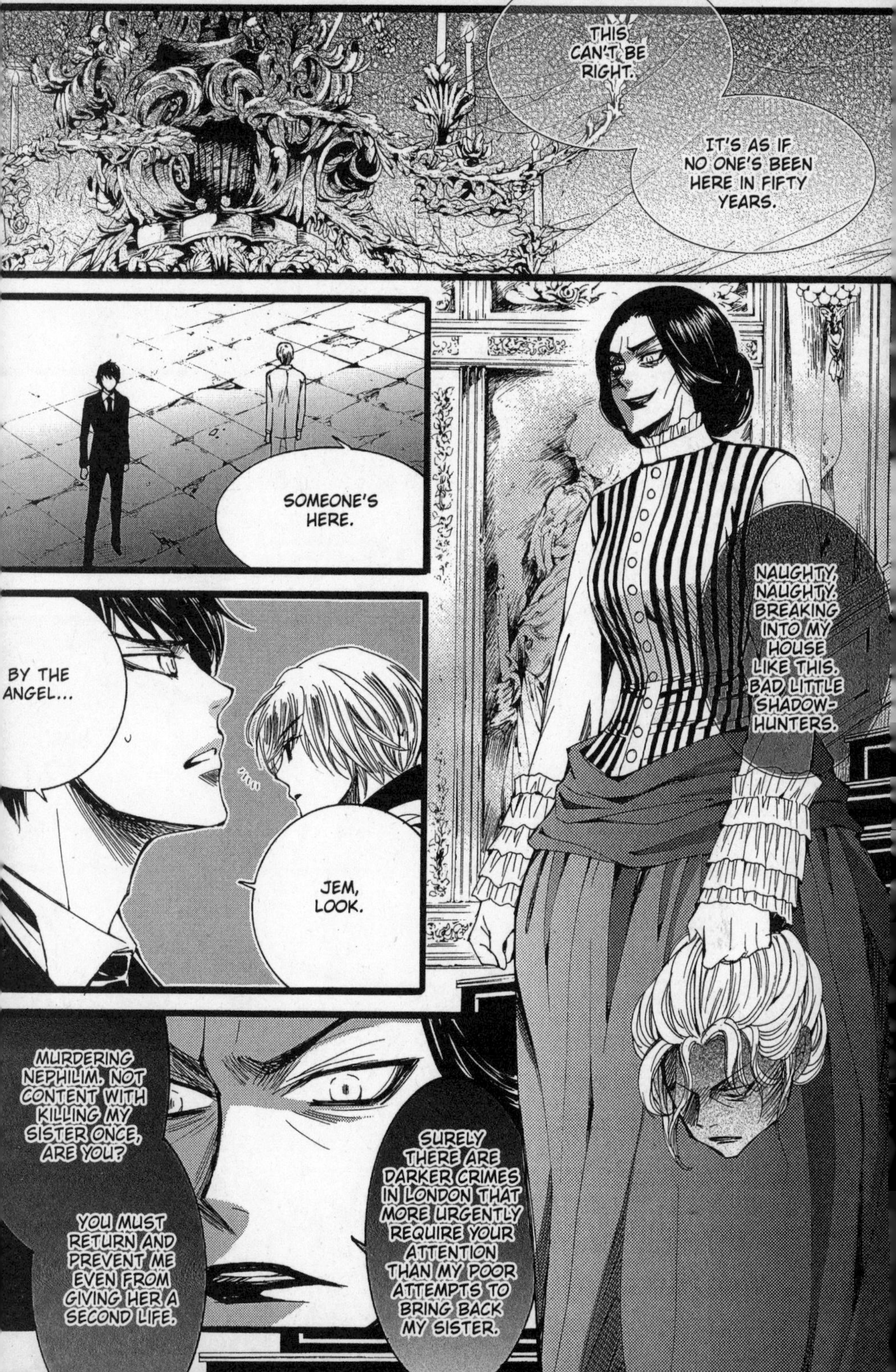
THIS CAN'T BE RIGHT.
IT'S AS IF NO ONE'S BEEN HERE IN FIFTY YEARS.
SOMEONE'S HERE.
BY THE ANGEL...
...
JEM, LOOK.
NAUGHTY, NAUGHTY. BREAKING INTO MY HOUSE LIKE THIS. BAD LITTLE SHADOW-HUNTERS.
MURDERING NEPHILIM. NOT CONTENT WITH KILLING MY SISTER ONCE, ARE YOU?
YOU MUST RETURN AND PREVENT ME EVEN FROM GIVING HER A SECOND LIFE.
SURELY THERE ARE DARKER CRIMES IN LONDON THAT MORE URGENTLY REQUIRE YOUR ATTENTION THAN MY POOR ATTEMPTS TO BRING BACK MY SISTER.

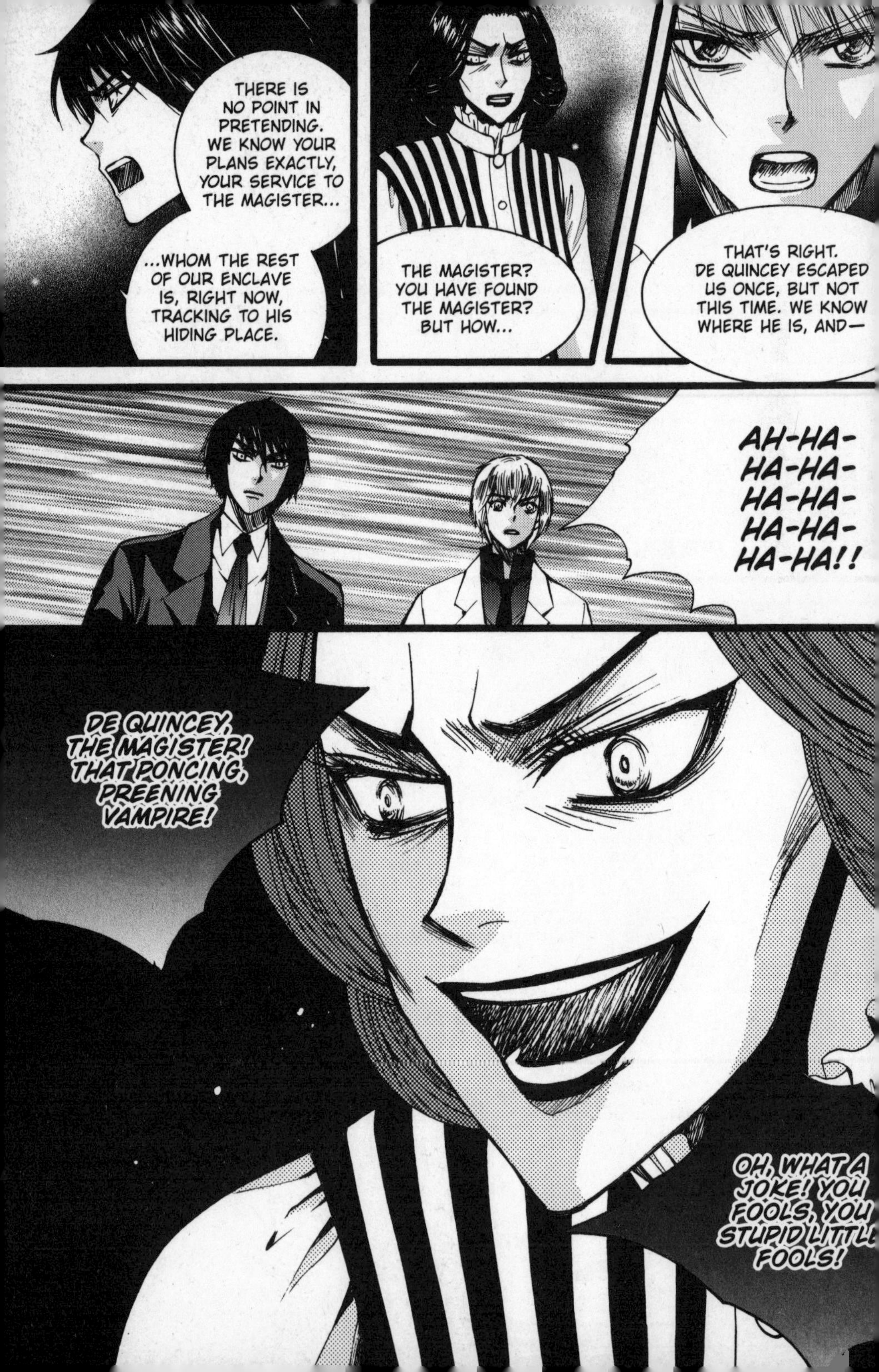
THERE IS NO POINT IN PRETENDING. WE KNOW YOUR PLANS EXACTLY, YOUR SERVICE TO THE MAGISTER...
...WHOM THE REST OF OUR ENCLAVE IS, RIGHT NOW, TRACKING TO HIS HIDING PLACE.
THE MAGISTER? YOU HAVE FOUND THE MAGISTER? BUT HOW...
THAT'S RIGHT. DE QUINCEY ESCAPED US ONCE, BUT NOT THIS TIME. WE KNOW WHERE HE IS, AND—
AH-HA-HA-HA-HA-HA-HA-HA-HA-HA!!
DE QUINCEY, THE MAGISTER! THAT PONCING, PREENING VAMPIRE!
OH, WHAT A JOKE! YOU FOOLS, YOU STUPID LITTL FOOLS!

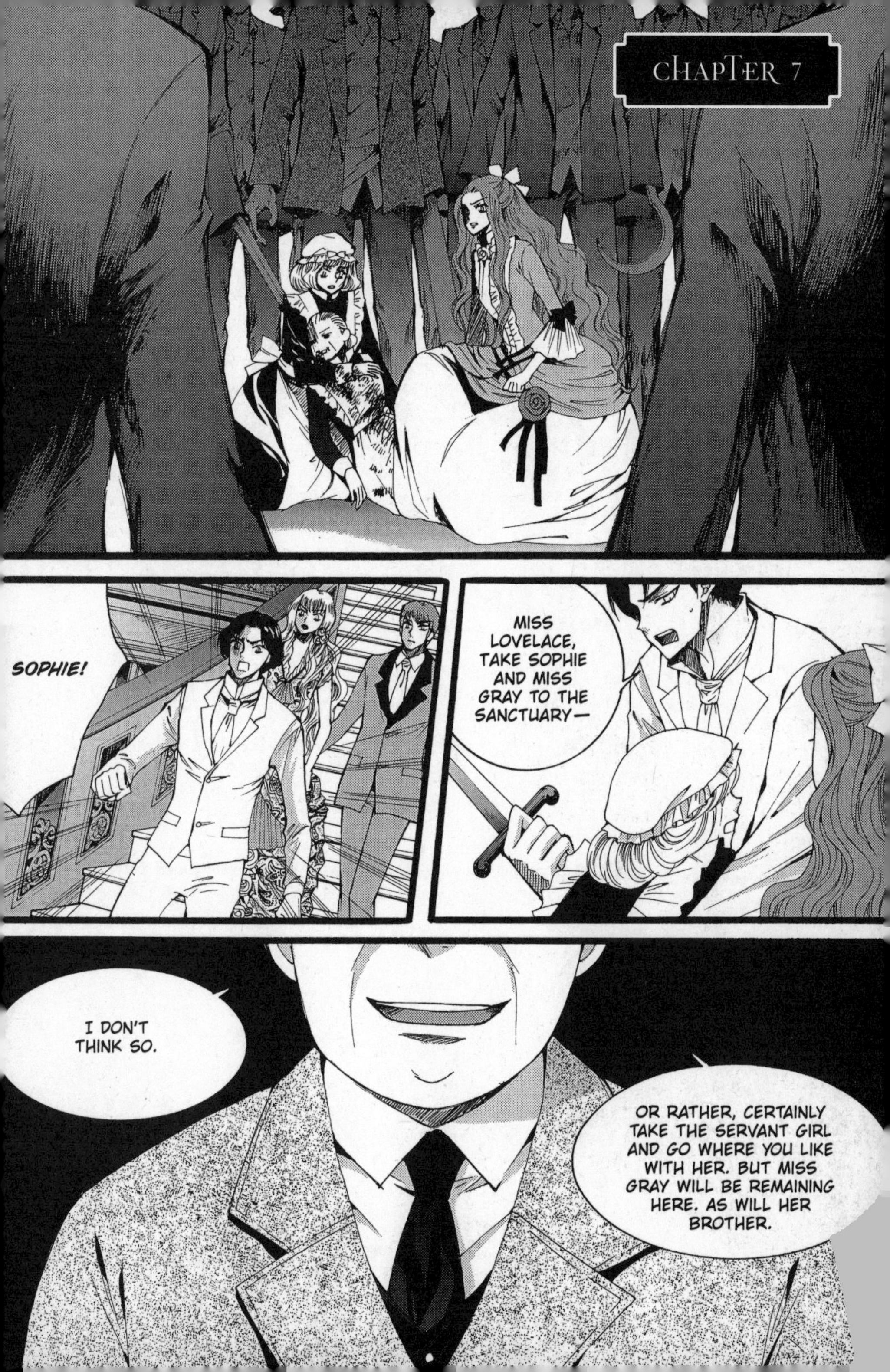
CHAPTER 7
SOPHIE!
MISS LOVELACE, TAKE SOPHIE AND MISS GRAY TO THE SANCTUARY—
I DON'T THINK SO.
OR RATHER, CERTAINLY TAKE THE SERVANT GIRL AND GO WHERE YOU LIKE WITH HER. BUT MISS GRAY WILL BE REMAINING HERE. AS WILL HER BROTHER.

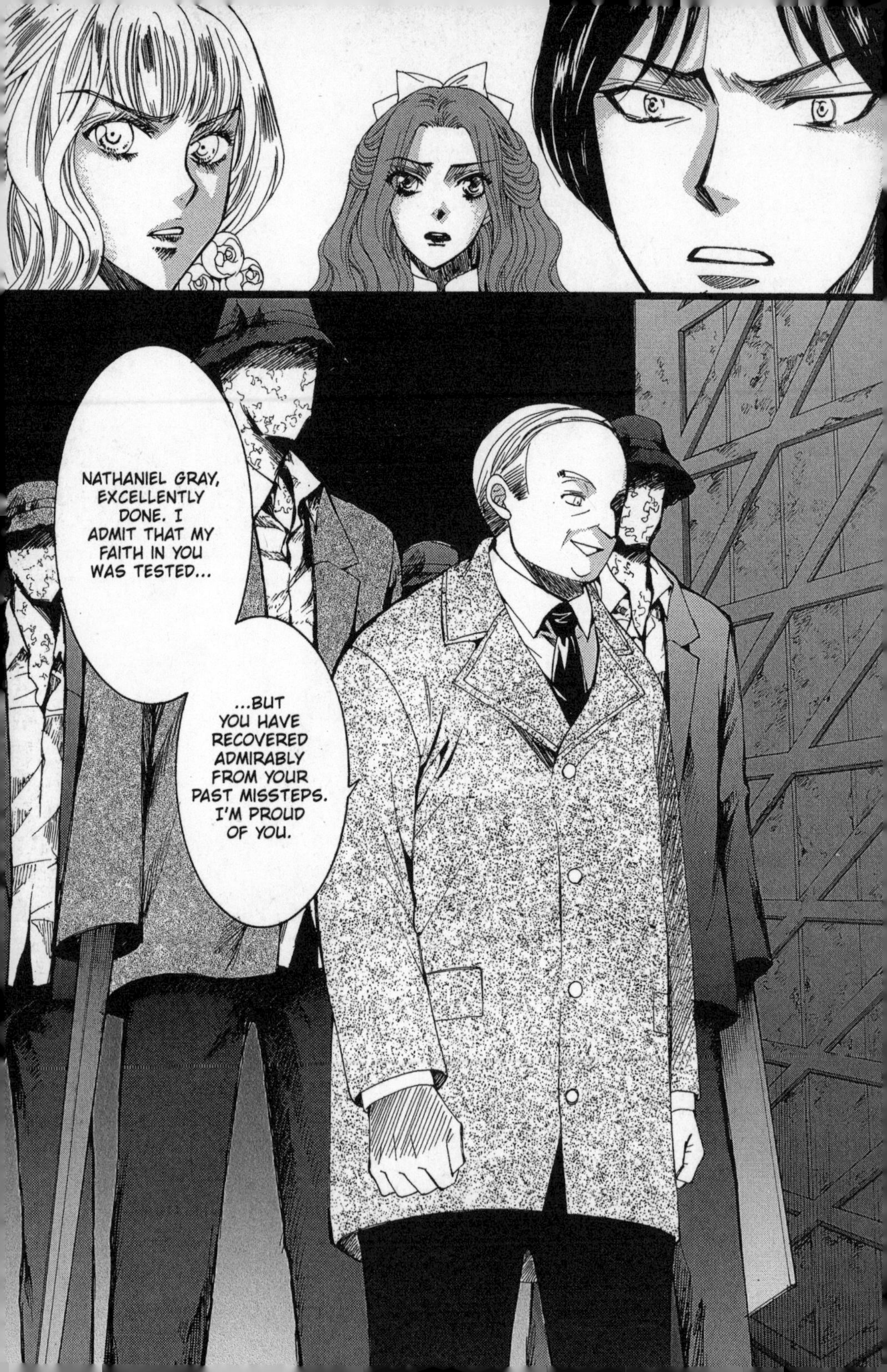
NATHANIEL GRAY, EXCELLENTLY DONE. I ADMIT THAT MY FAITH IN YOU WAS TESTED...
...BUT YOU HAVE RECOVERED ADMIRABLY FROM YOUR PAST MISSTEPS. I'M PROUD OF YOU.

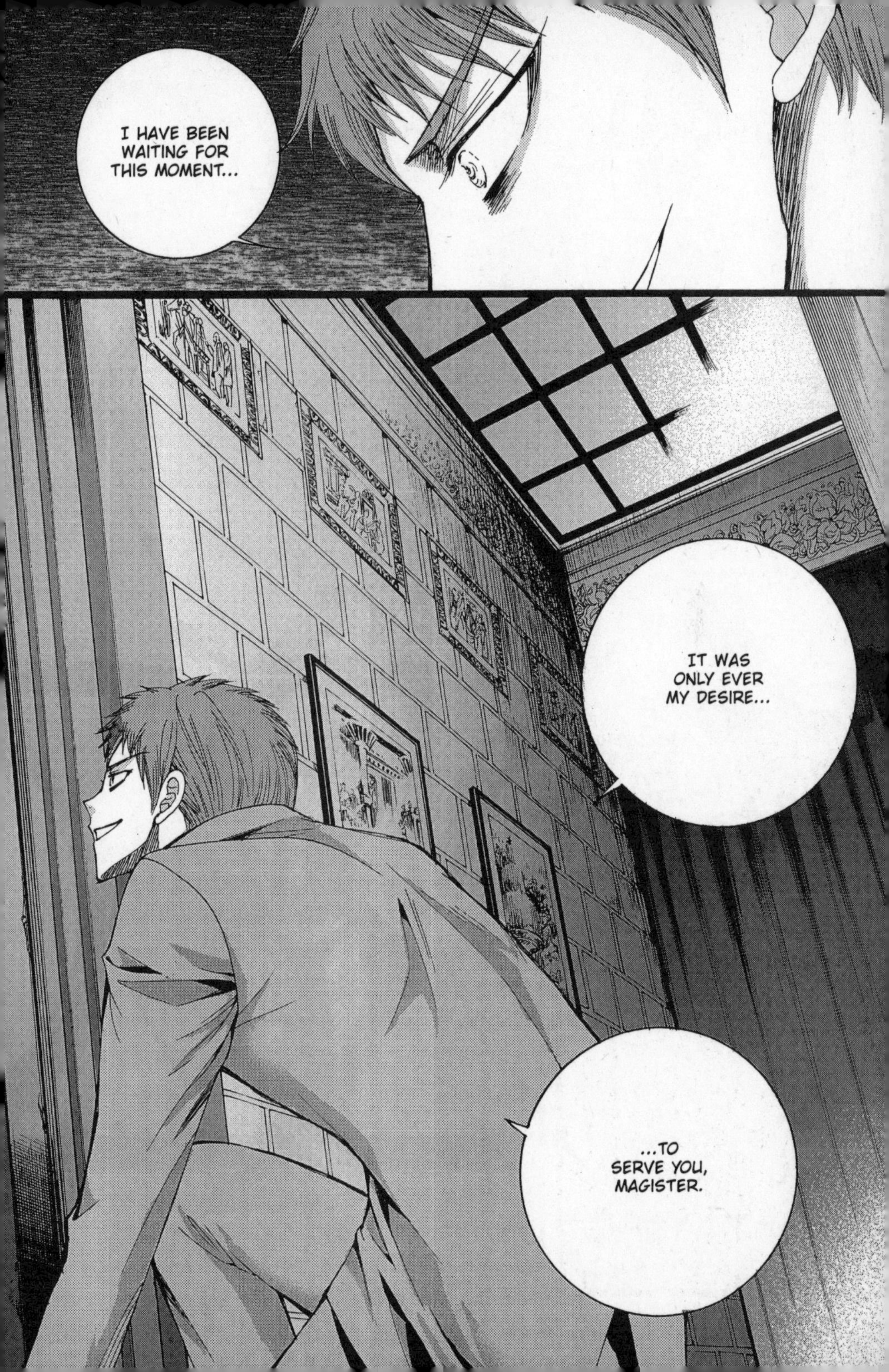
I HAVE BEEN WAITING FOR THIS MOMENT...
IT WAS ONLY EVER MY DESIRE...
...TO SERVE YOU, MAGISTER.

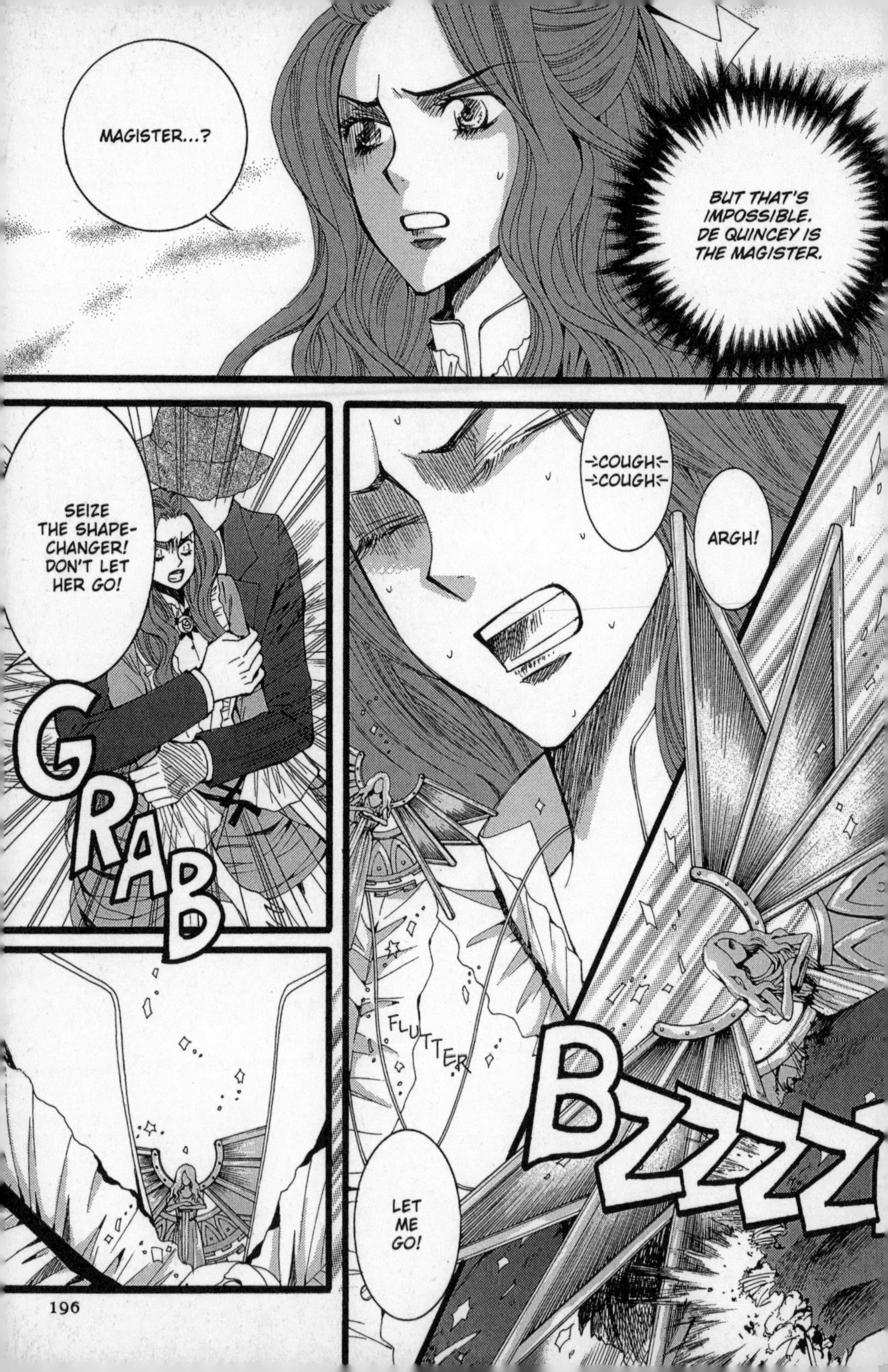
MAGISTER...?
BUT THAT'S IMPOSSIBLE. DE QUINCEY IS THE MAGISTER.
SEIZE THE SHAPE-CHANGER! DON'T LET HER GO!
GRAB
COUGH COUGH
ARGH!
FLUTTER
BZZZZ
LET ME GO!

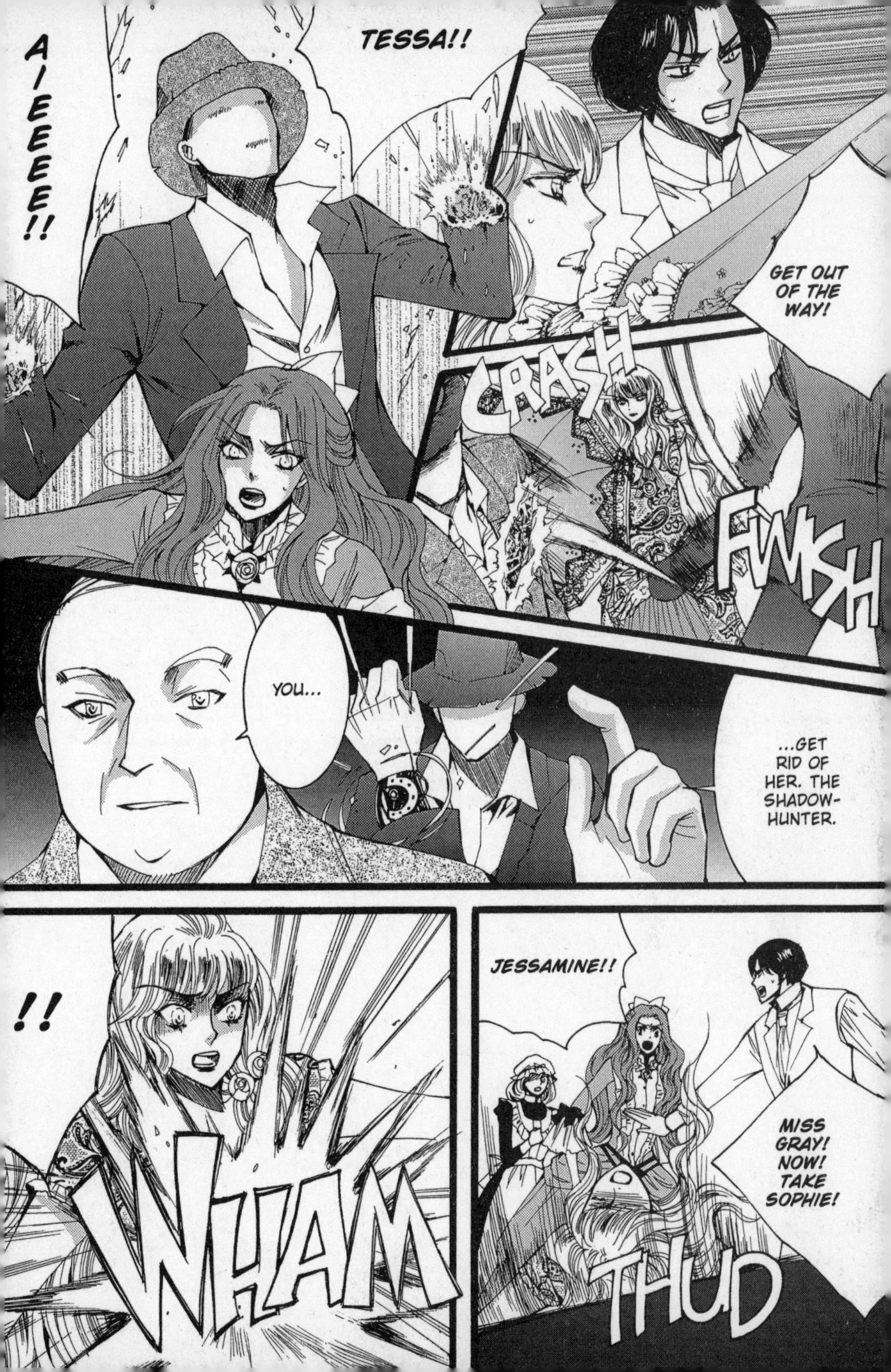
AIEEEEE!!
TESSA!!
GET OUT OF THE WAY!
CRASH
FWISH
YOU...
...GET RID OF HER. THE SHADOW-HUNTER.
!!
WHAM
JESSAMINE!!
MISS GRAY! NOW! TAKE SOPHIE!
THUD

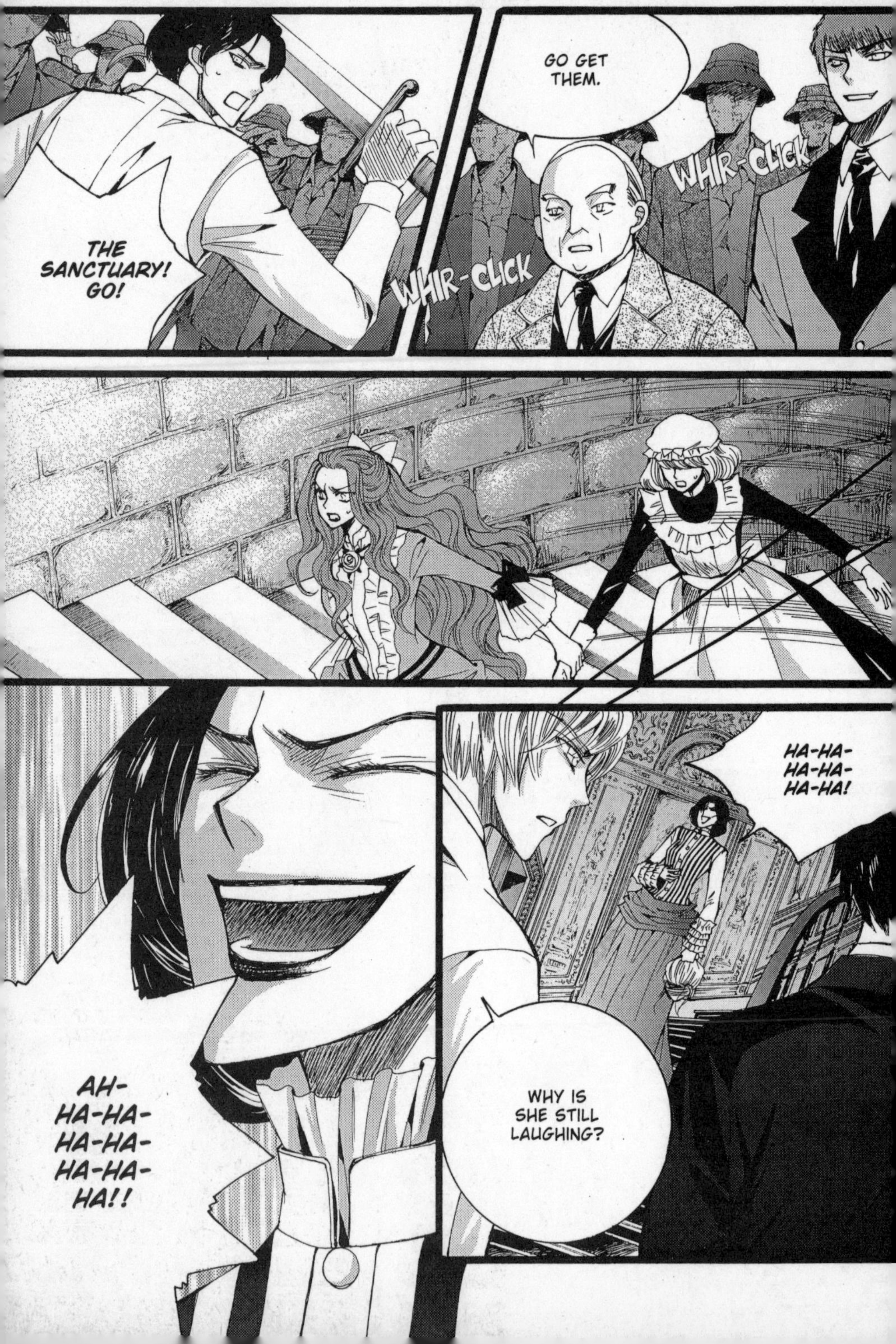
THE SANCTUARY! GO!
GO GET THEM.
WHIR-CLICK
WHIR-CLICK
AH-HA-HA-HA-HA-HA-HA-HA!!
HA-HA-HA-HA-HA-HA!
WHY IS SHE STILL LAUGHING?

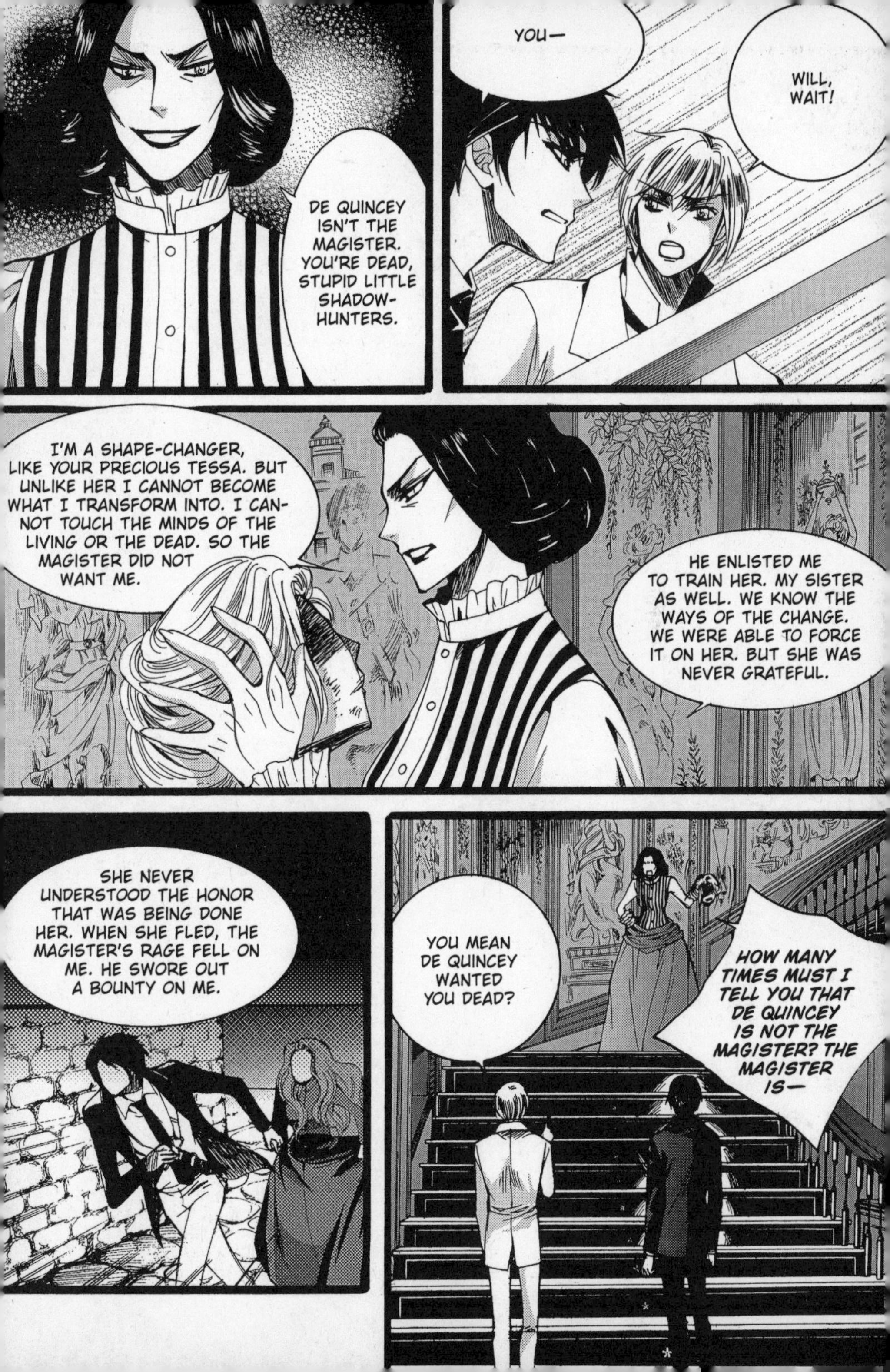
DE QUINCEY ISN'T THE MAGISTER. YOU'RE DEAD, STUPID LITTLE SHADOW-HUNTERS.
YOU—
WILL, WAIT!
I'M A SHAPE-CHANGER, LIKE YOUR PRECIOUS TESSA. BUT UNLIKE HER I CANNOT BECOME WHAT I TRANSFORM INTO. I CANNOT TOUCH THE MINDS OF THE LIVING OR THE DEAD. SO THE MAGISTER DID NOT WANT ME.
HE ENLISTED ME TO TRAIN HER. MY SISTER AS WELL. WE KNOW THE WAYS OF THE CHANGE. WE WERE ABLE TO FORCE IT ON HER. BUT SHE WAS NEVER GRATEFUL.
SHE NEVER UNDERSTOOD THE HONOR THAT WAS BEING DONE HER. WHEN SHE FLED, THE MAGISTER'S RAGE FELL ON ME. HE SWORE OUT A BOUNTY ON ME.
YOU MEAN DE QUINCEY WANTED YOU DEAD?
HOW MANY TIMES MUST I TELL YOU THAT DE QUINCEY IS NOT THE MAGISTER? THE MAGISTER IS—

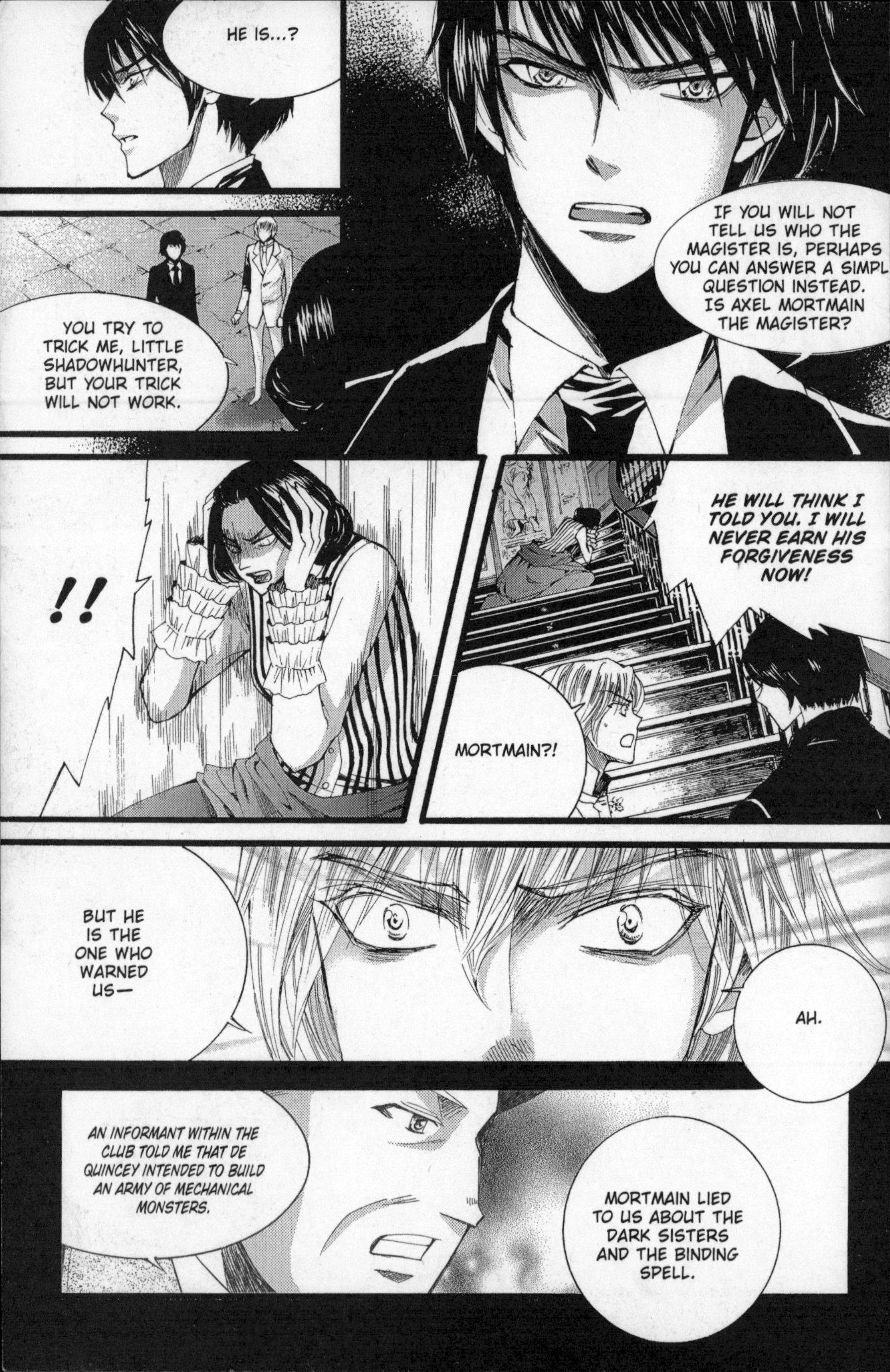
HE IS...?
YOU TRY TO TRICK ME, LITTLE SHADOWHUNTER, BUT YOUR TRICK WILL NOT WORK.
IF YOU WILL NOT TELL US WHO THE MAGISTER IS, PERHAPS YOU CAN ANSWER A SIMPL QUESTION INSTEAD. IS AXEL MORTMAIN THE MAGISTER?
!!
HE WILL THINK I TOLD YOU. I WILL NEVER EARN HIS FORGIVENESS NOW!
MORTMAIN?!
BUT HE IS THE ONE WHO WARNED US—
AH.
AN INFORMANT WITHIN THE CLUB TOLD ME THAT DE QUINCEY INTENDED TO BUILD AN ARMY OF MECHANICAL MONSTERS.
MORTMAIN LIED TO US ABOUT THE DARK SISTERS AND THE BINDING SPELL.

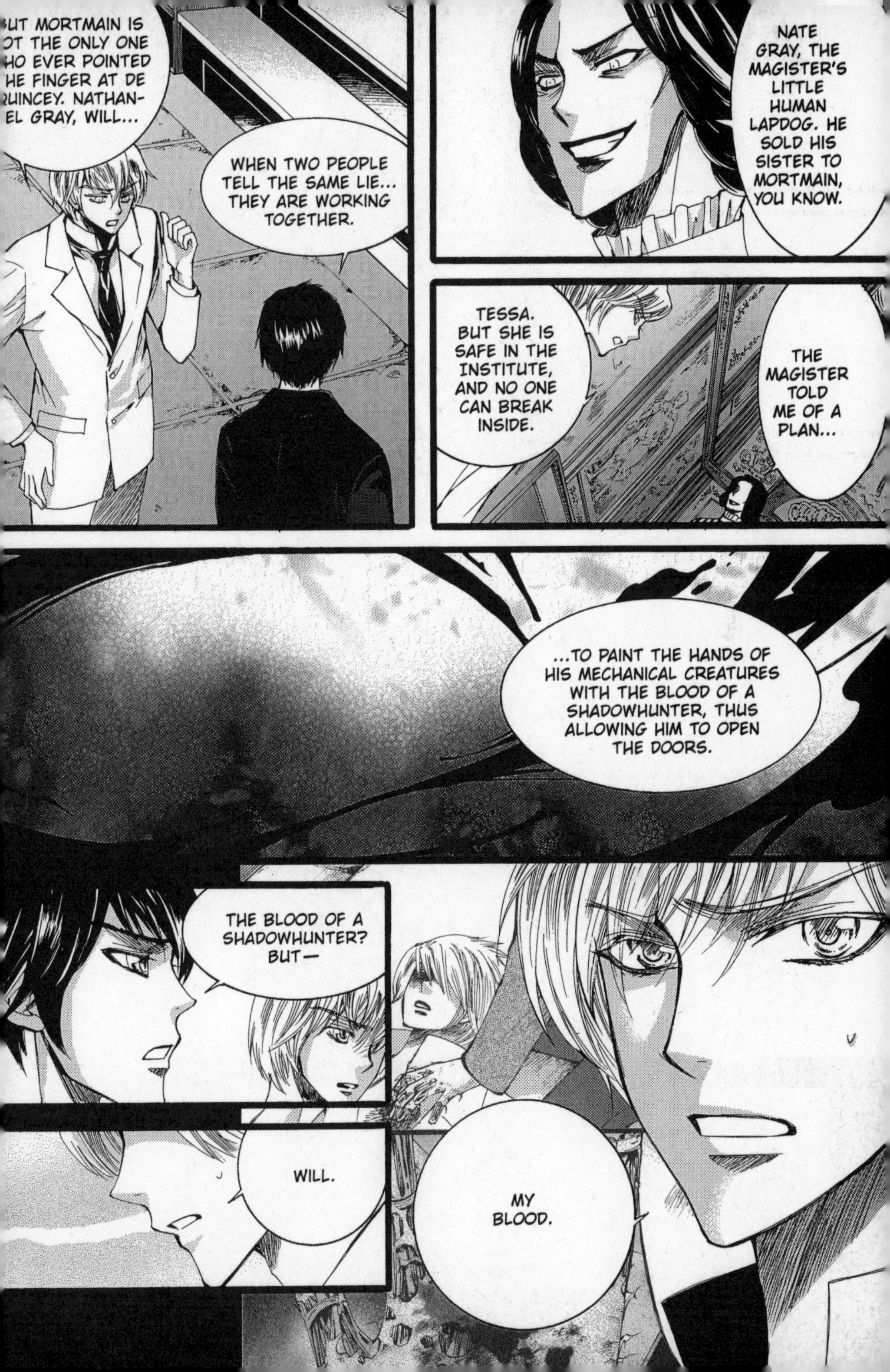
BUT MORTMAIN IS NOT THE ONLY ONE WHO EVER POINTED THE FINGER AT DE QUINCEY. NATHANIEL GRAY, WILL...
WHEN TWO PEOPLE TELL THE SAME LIE... THEY ARE WORKING TOGETHER.
NATE GRAY, THE MAGISTER'S LITTLE HUMAN LAPDOG. HE SOLD HIS SISTER TO MORTMAIN, YOU KNOW.
TESSA. BUT SHE IS SAFE IN THE INSTITUTE, AND NO ONE CAN BREAK INSIDE.
THE MAGISTER TOLD ME OF A PLAN...
...TO PAINT THE HANDS OF HIS MECHANICAL CREATURES WITH THE BLOOD OF A SHADOWHUNTER, THUS ALLOWING HIM TO OPEN THE DOORS.
THE BLOOD OF A SHADOWHUNTER? BUT—
WILL.
MY BLOOD.

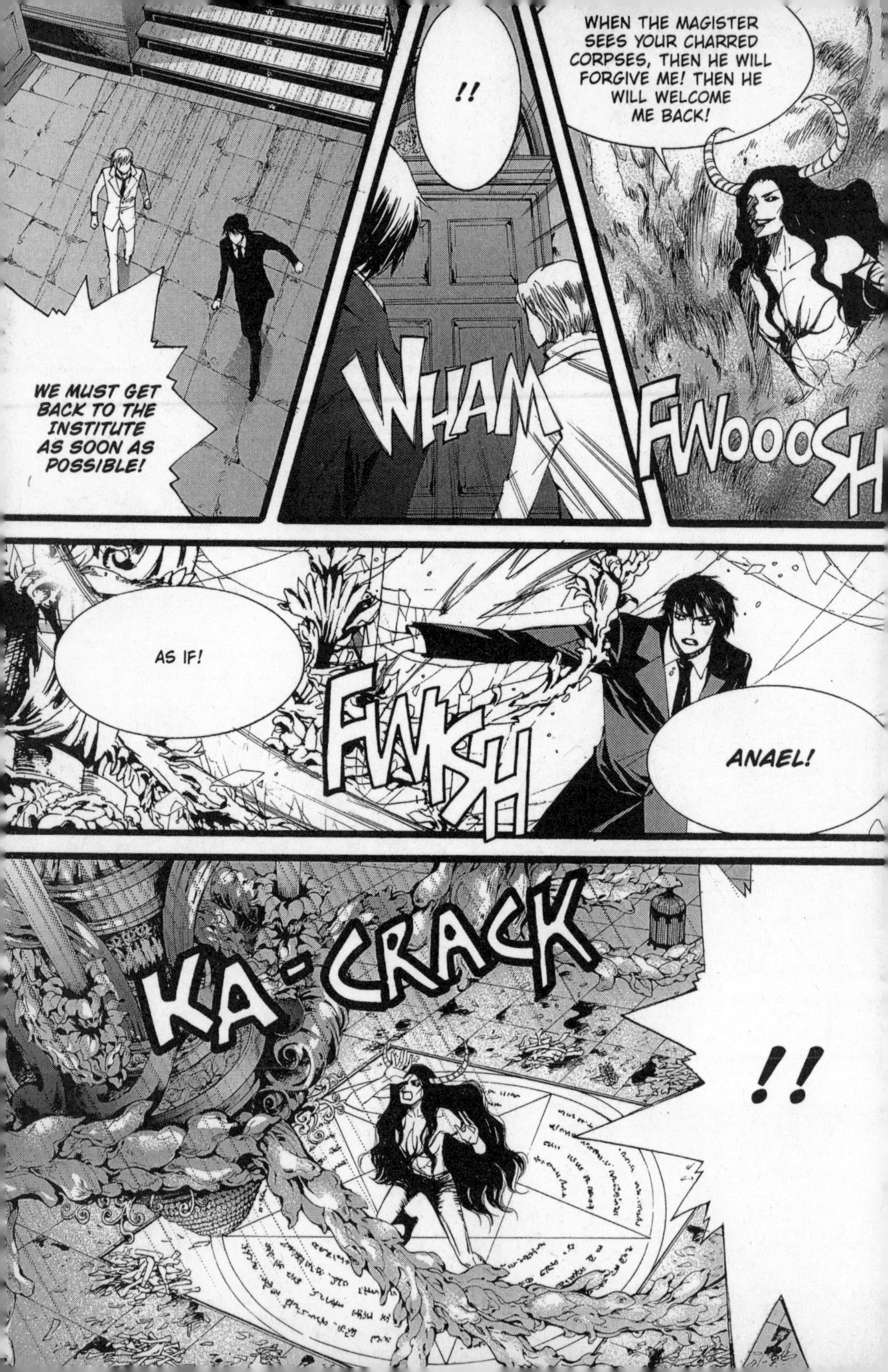
WE MUST GET BACK TO THE INSTITUTE AS SOON AS POSSIBLE!
!!
WHAM
WHEN THE MAGISTER SEES YOUR CHARRED CORPSES, THEN HE WILL FORGIVE ME! THEN HE WILL WELCOME ME BACK!
FWOOOSH
AS IF!
FWISH
ANAEL!
KA-CRACK
!!

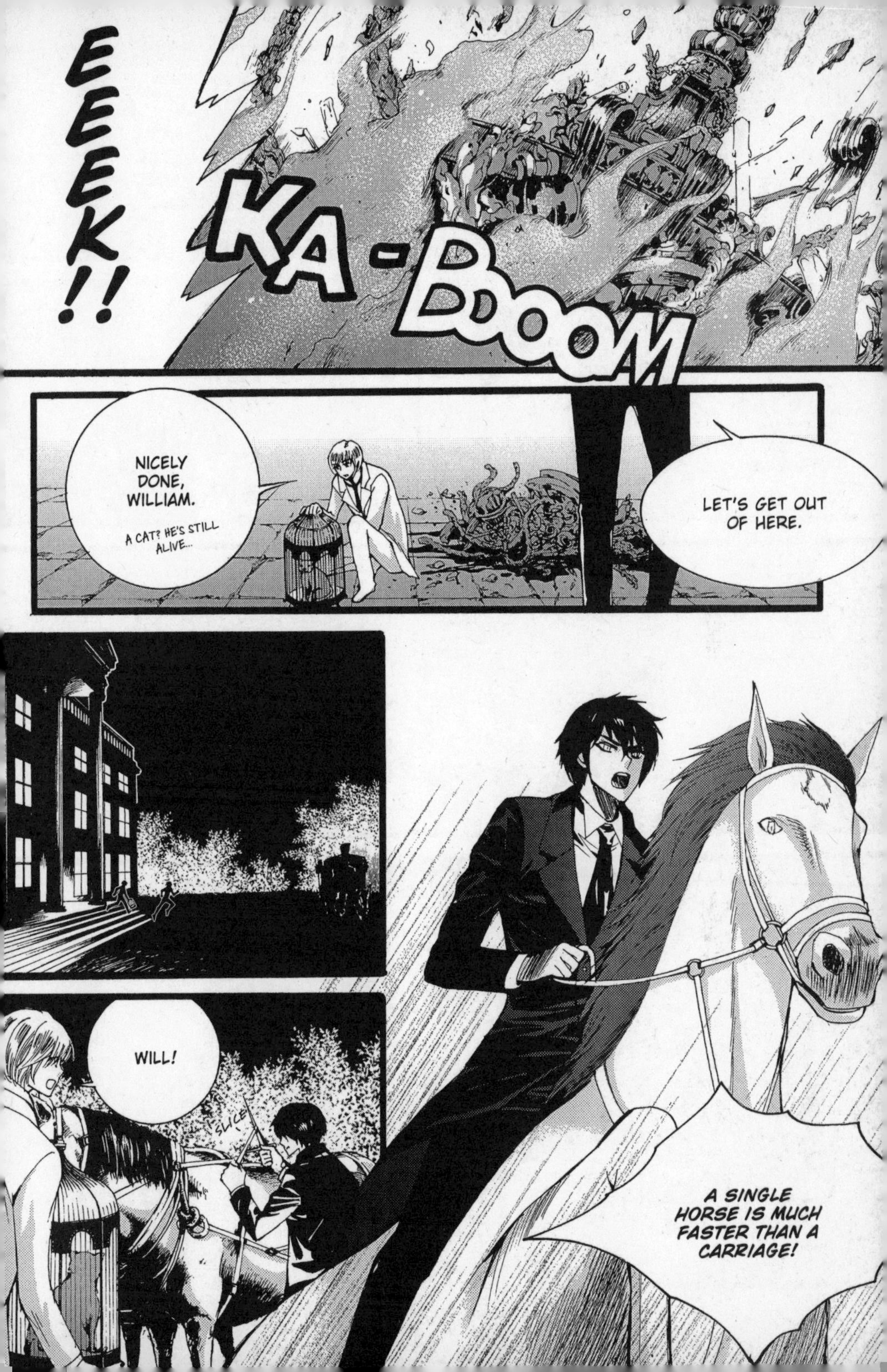
EEEEK!!
KA-BOOOM
NICELY DONE, WILLIAM.
A CAT? HE'S STILL ALIVE...
LET'S GET OUT OF HERE.
WILL!
SLICE
A SINGLE HORSE IS MUCH FASTER THAN A CARRIAGE!

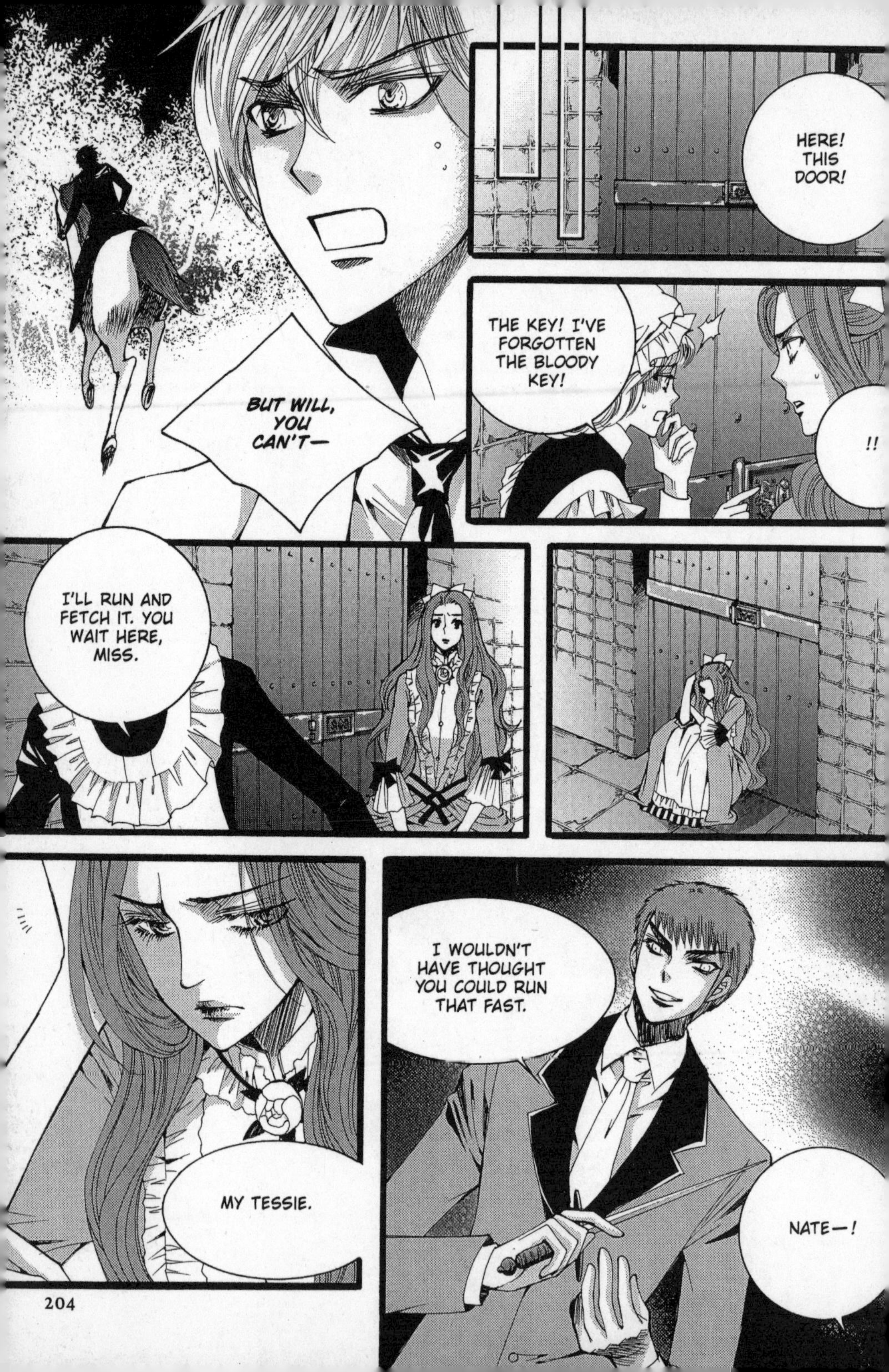

BUT WILL, YOU CAN'T—
HERE! THIS DOOR!
THE KEY! I'VE FORGOTTEN THE BLOODY KEY!
!!
I'LL RUN AND FETCH IT. YOU WAIT HERE, MISS.
MY TESSIE.
I WOULDN'T HAVE THOUGHT YOU COULD RUN THAT FAST.
NATE—!

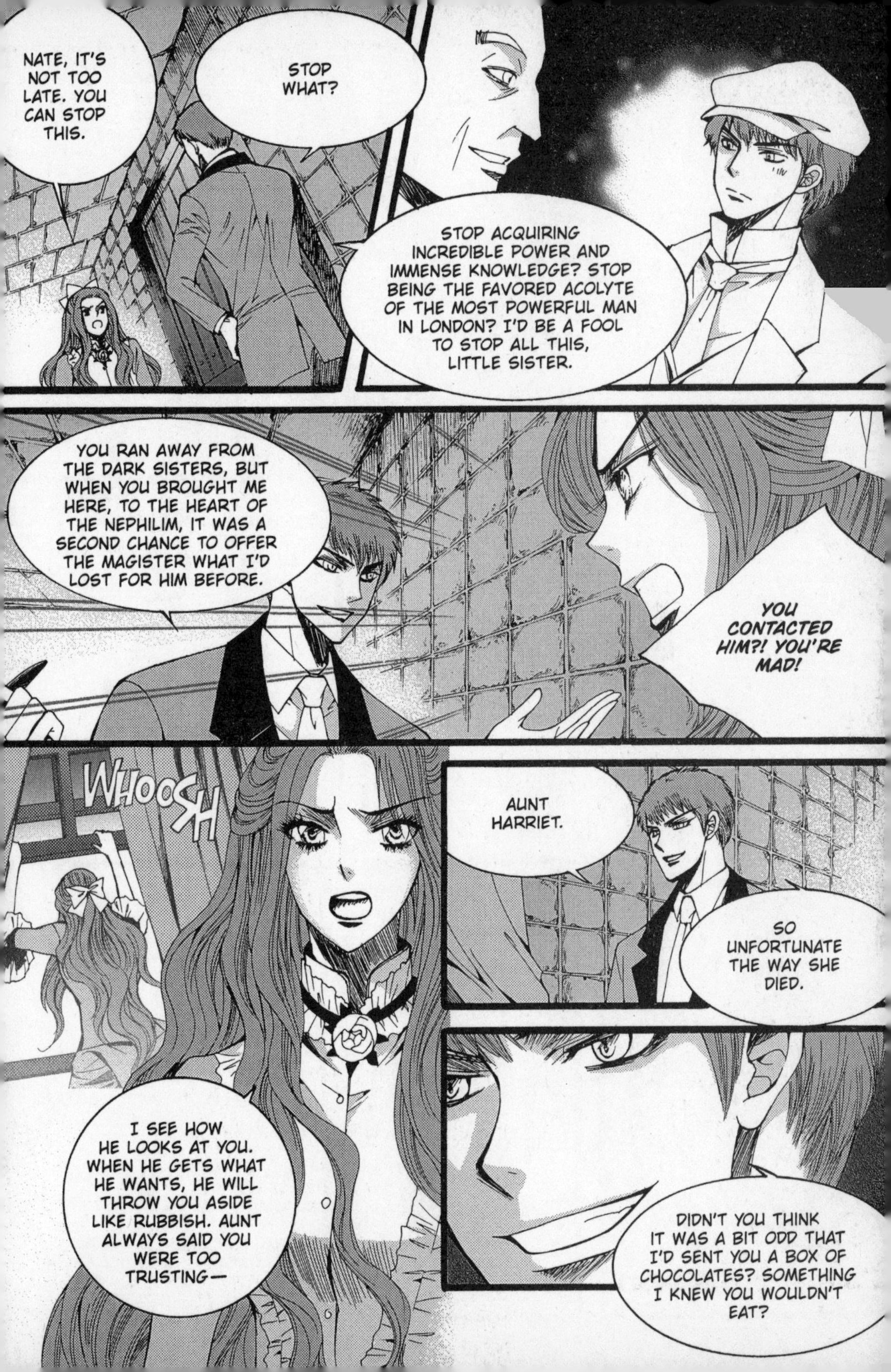
NATE, IT'S NOT TOO LATE. YOU CAN STOP THIS.
STOP WHAT?
STOP ACQUIRING INCREDIBLE POWER AND IMMENSE KNOWLEDGE? STOP BEING THE FAVORED ACOLYTE OF THE MOST POWERFUL MAN IN LONDON? I'D BE A FOOL TO STOP ALL THIS, LITTLE SISTER.
YOU RAN AWAY FROM THE DARK SISTERS, BUT WHEN YOU BROUGHT ME HERE, TO THE HEART OF THE NEPHILIM, IT WAS A SECOND CHANCE TO OFFER THE MAGISTER WHAT I'D LOST FOR HIM BEFORE.
YOU CONTACTED HIM?! YOU'RE MAD!
WHOOSH
I SEE HOW HE LOOKS AT YOU. WHEN HE GETS WHAT HE WANTS, HE WILL THROW YOU ASIDE LIKE RUBBISH. AUNT ALWAYS SAID YOU WERE TOO TRUSTING—
AUNT HARRIET.
SO UNFORTUNATE THE WAY SHE DIED.
DIDN'T YOU THINK IT WAS A BIT ODD THAT I'D SENT YOU A BOX OF CHOCOLATES? SOMETHING I KNEW YOU WOULDN'T EAT?

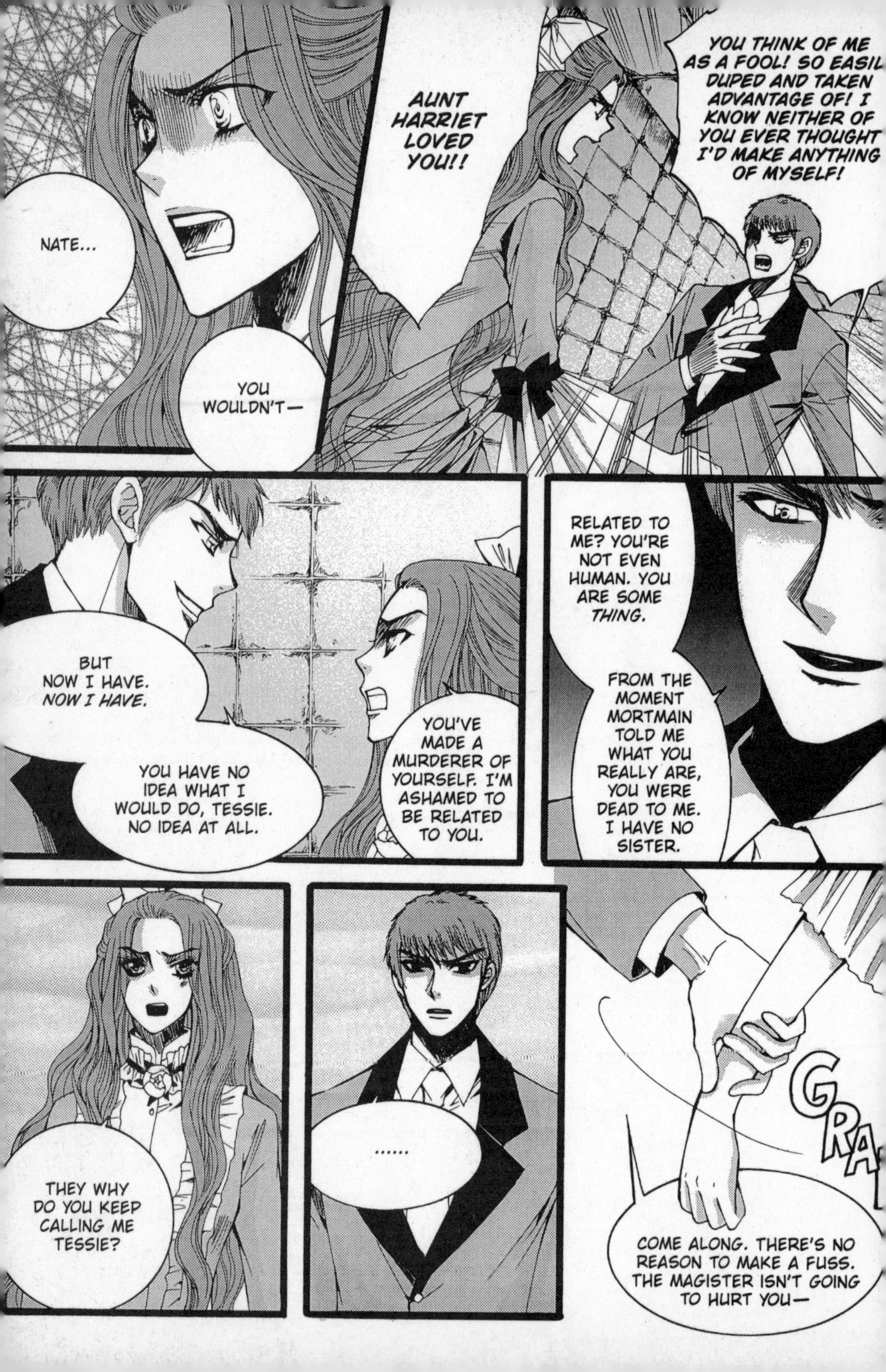
NATE...
YOU WOULDN'T—
AUNT HARRIET LOVED YOU!!
YOU THINK OF ME AS A FOOL! SO EASIL DUPED AND TAKEN ADVANTAGE OF! I KNOW NEITHER OF YOU EVER THOUGHT I'D MAKE ANYTHING OF MYSELF!
BUT NOW I HAVE. *NOW I HAVE.*
YOU HAVE NO IDEA WHAT I WOULD DO, TESSIE. NO IDEA AT ALL.
YOU'VE MADE A MURDERER OF YOURSELF. I'M ASHAMED TO BE RELATED TO YOU.
RELATED TO ME? YOU'RE NOT EVEN HUMAN. YOU ARE SOME *THING*.
FROM THE MOMENT MORTMAIN TOLD ME WHAT YOU REALLY ARE, YOU WERE DEAD TO ME. I HAVE NO SISTER.
THEY WHY DO YOU KEEP CALLING ME TESSIE?
......
GRA
COME ALONG. THERE'S NO REASON TO MAKE A FUSS. THE MAGISTER ISN'T GOING TO HURT YOU—

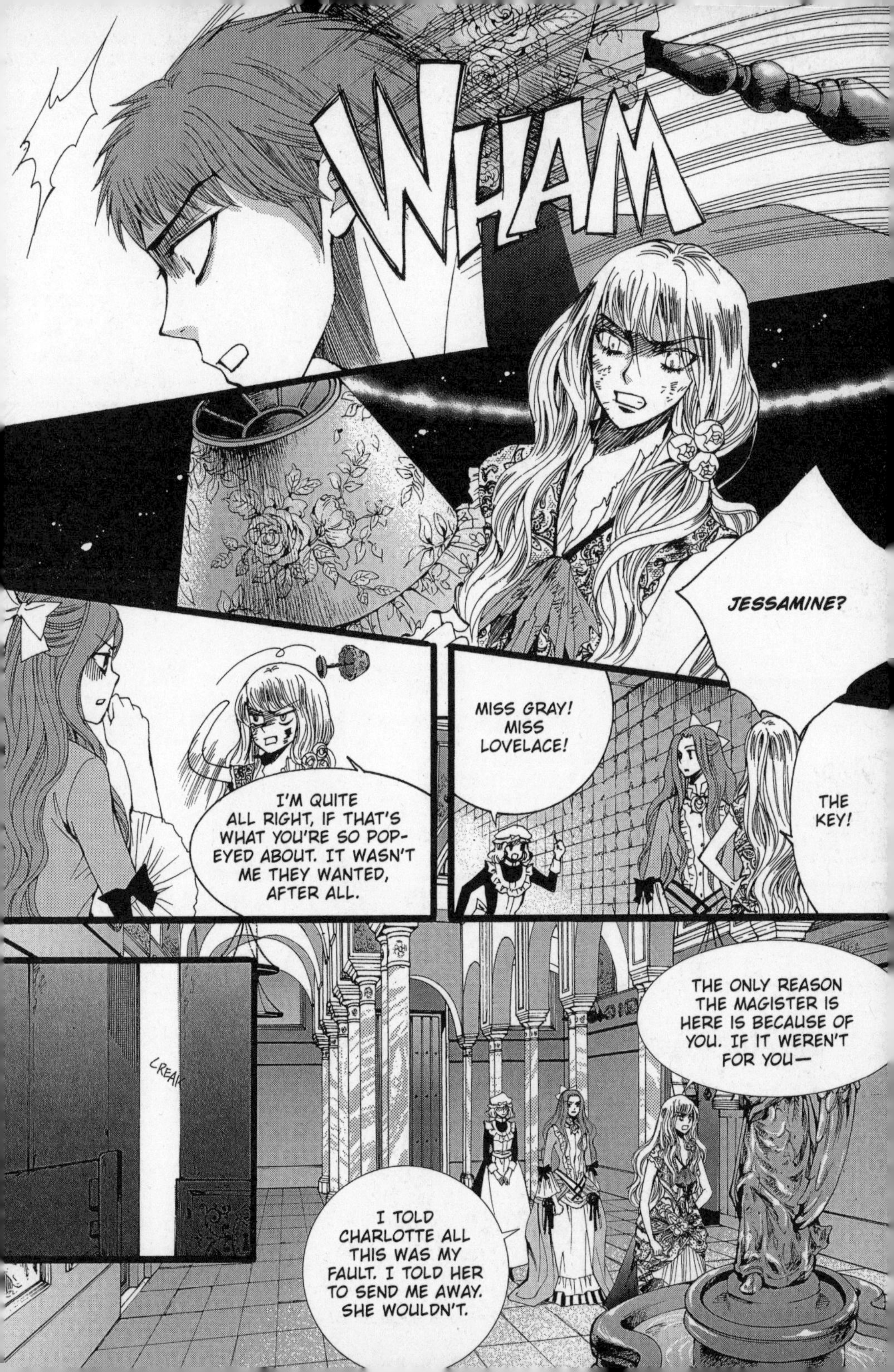
WHAM
JESSAMINE?
I'M QUITE ALL RIGHT, IF THAT'S WHAT YOU'RE SO POP-EYED ABOUT. IT WASN'T ME THEY WANTED, AFTER ALL.
MISS GRAY! MISS LOVELACE!
THE KEY!
CREAK
THE ONLY REASON THE MAGISTER IS HERE IS BECAUSE OF YOU. IF IT WEREN'T FOR YOU—
I TOLD CHARLOTTE ALL THIS WAS MY FAULT. I TOLD HER TO SEND ME AWAY. SHE WOULDN'T.

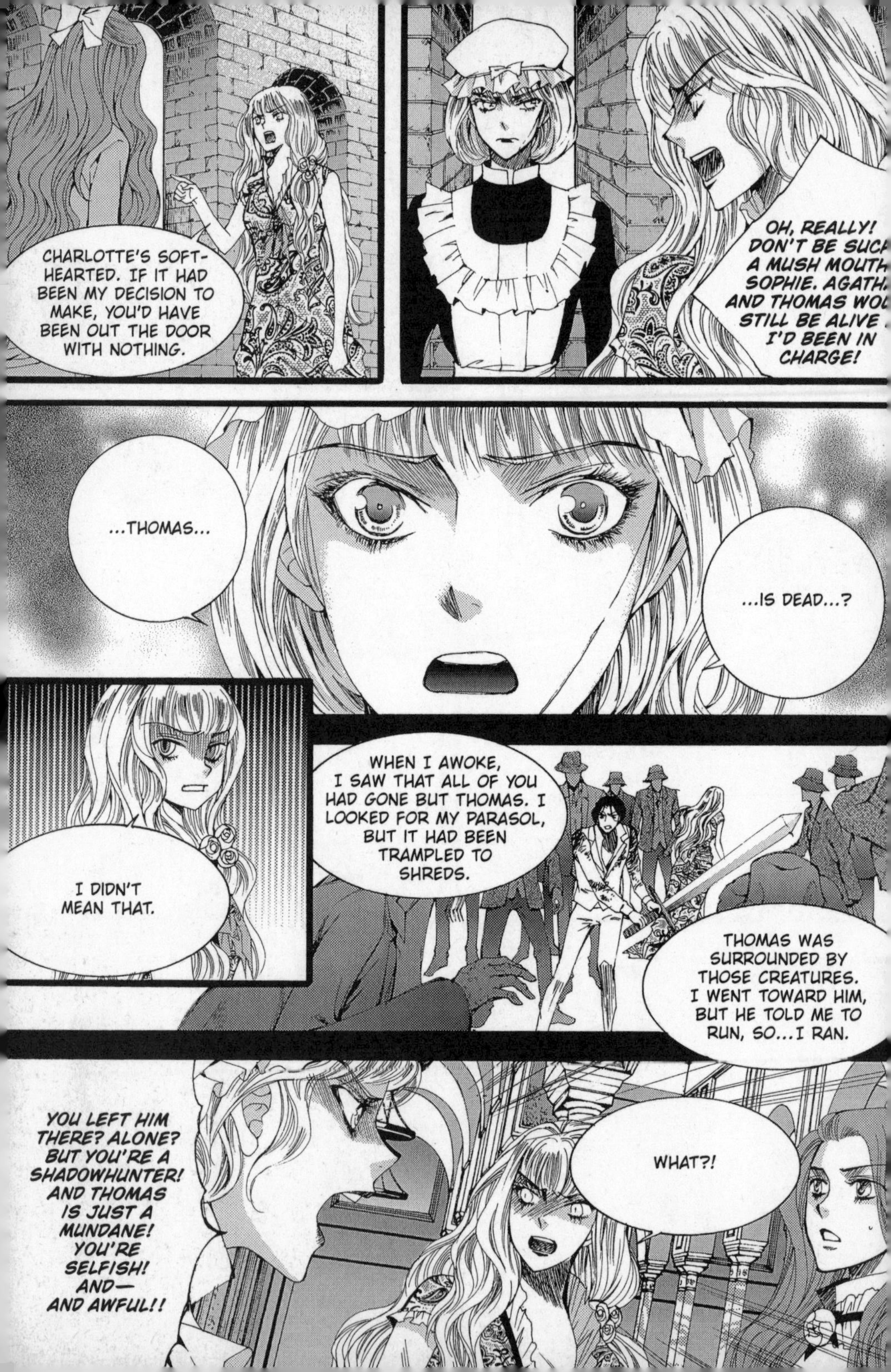
CHARLOTTE'S SOFT-HEARTED. IF IT HAD BEEN MY DECISION TO MAKE, YOU'D HAVE BEEN OUT THE DOOR WITH NOTHING.
OH, REALLY! DON'T BE SUCH A MUSH MOUTH SOPHIE. AGATH AND THOMAS WOU STILL BE ALIVE I'D BEEN IN CHARGE!
...THOMAS...
...IS DEAD...?
I DIDN'T MEAN THAT.
WHEN I AWOKE, I SAW THAT ALL OF YOU HAD GONE BUT THOMAS. I LOOKED FOR MY PARASOL, BUT IT HAD BEEN TRAMPLED TO SHREDS.
THOMAS WAS SURROUNDED BY THOSE CREATURES. I WENT TOWARD HIM, BUT HE TOLD ME TO RUN, SO...I RAN.
YOU LEFT HIM THERE? ALONE? BUT YOU'RE A SHADOWHUNTER! AND THOMAS IS JUST A MUNDANE! YOU'RE SELFISH! AND— AND AWFUL!!
WHAT?!

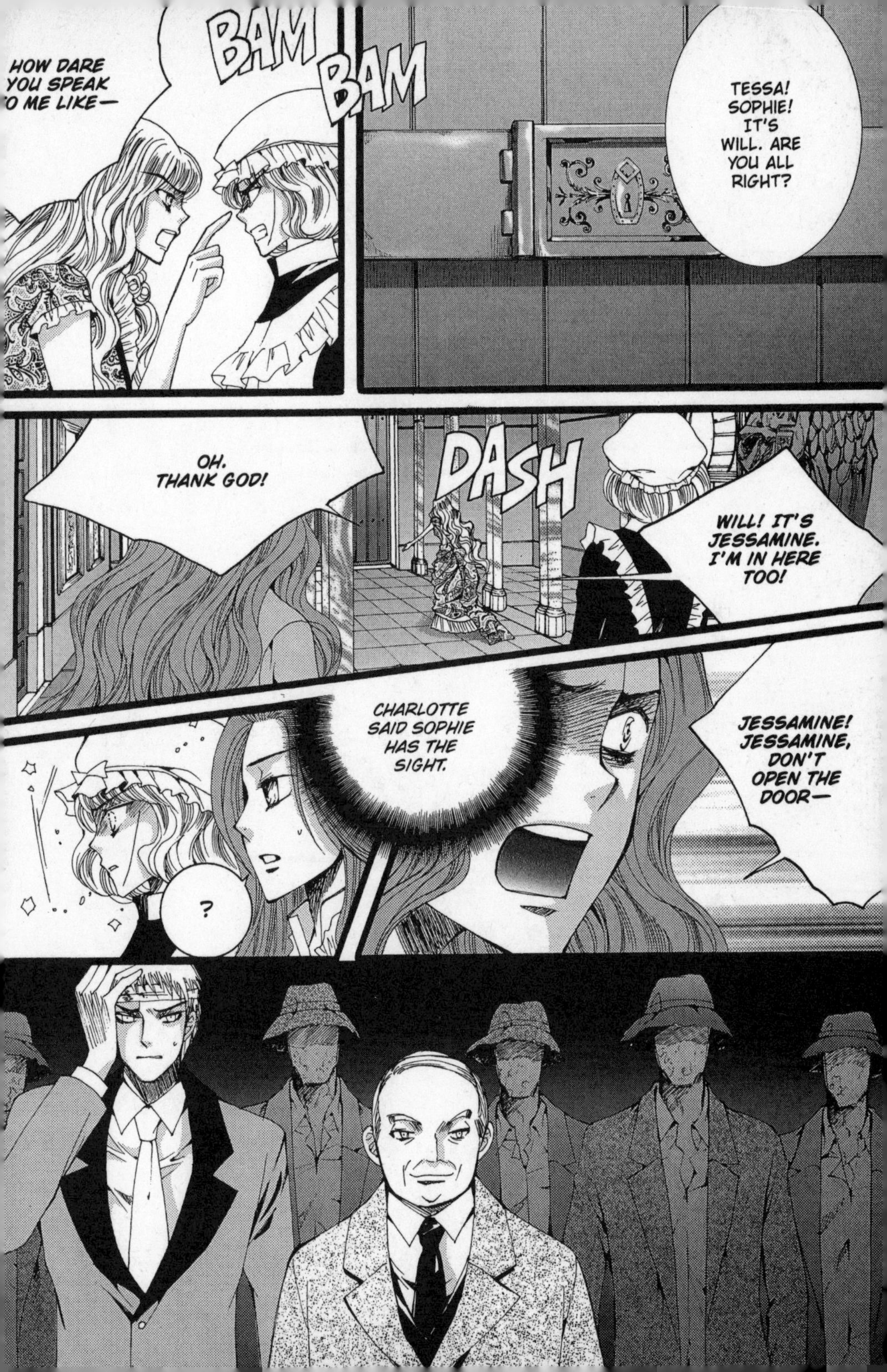
HOW DARE YOU SPEAK TO ME LIKE—
BAM BAM
TESSA! SOPHIE! IT'S WILL. ARE YOU ALL RIGHT?
OH. THANK GOD!
DASH
WILL! IT'S JESSAMINE. I'M IN HERE TOO!
CHARLOTTE SAID SOPHIE HAS THE SIGHT.
?
JESSAMINE! JESSAMINE, DON'T OPEN THE DOOR—

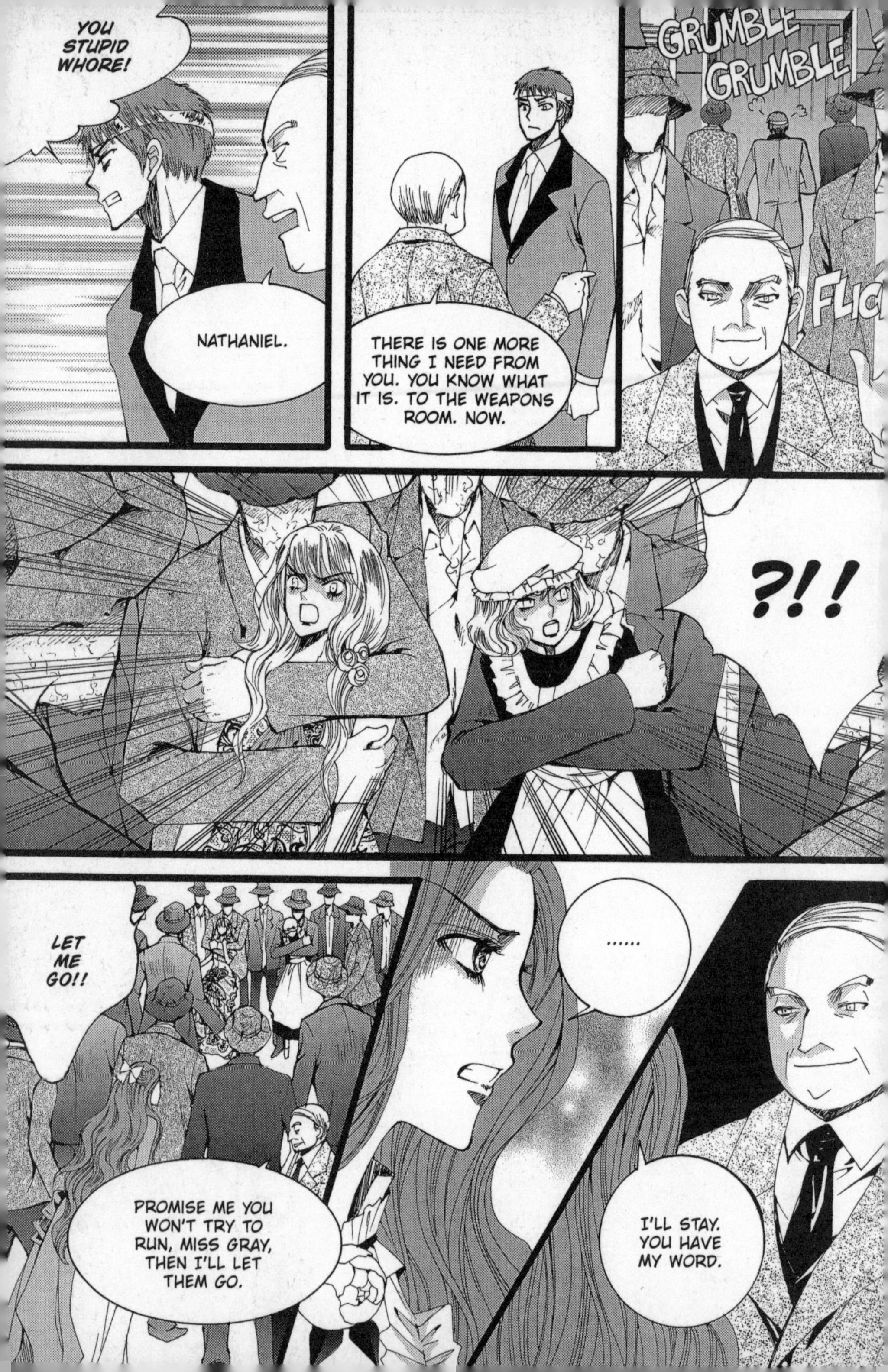
YOU STUPID WHORE!
NATHANIEL.
THERE IS ONE MORE THING I NEED FROM YOU. YOU KNOW WHAT IT IS. TO THE WEAPONS ROOM. NOW.
GRUMBLE GRUMBLE
FLICK
?!!
LET ME GO!!
PROMISE ME YOU WON'T TRY TO RUN, MISS GRAY, THEN I'LL LET THEM GO.
......
I'LL STAY. YOU HAVE MY WORD.

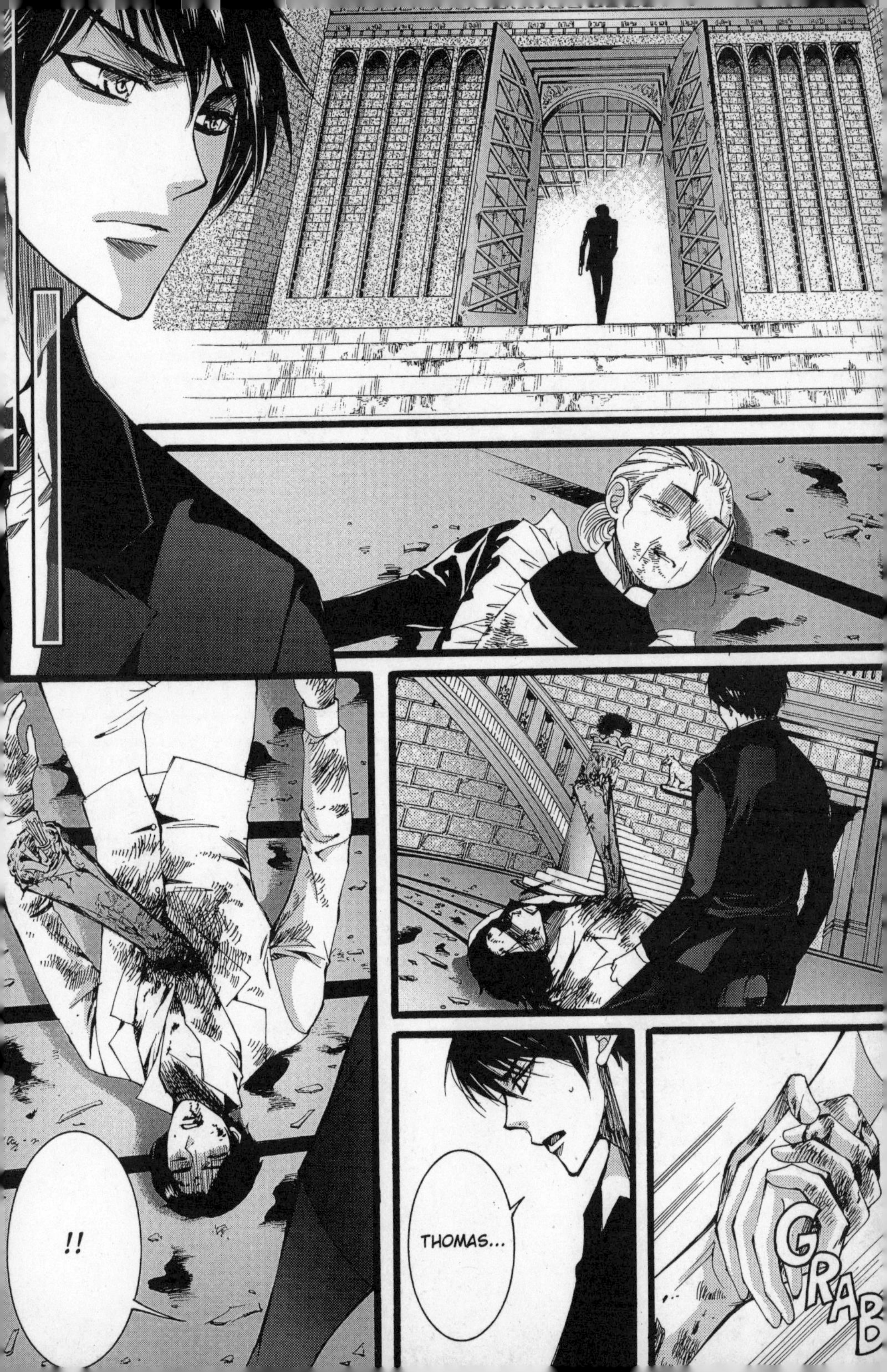
!!
THOMAS...
...
GRAB

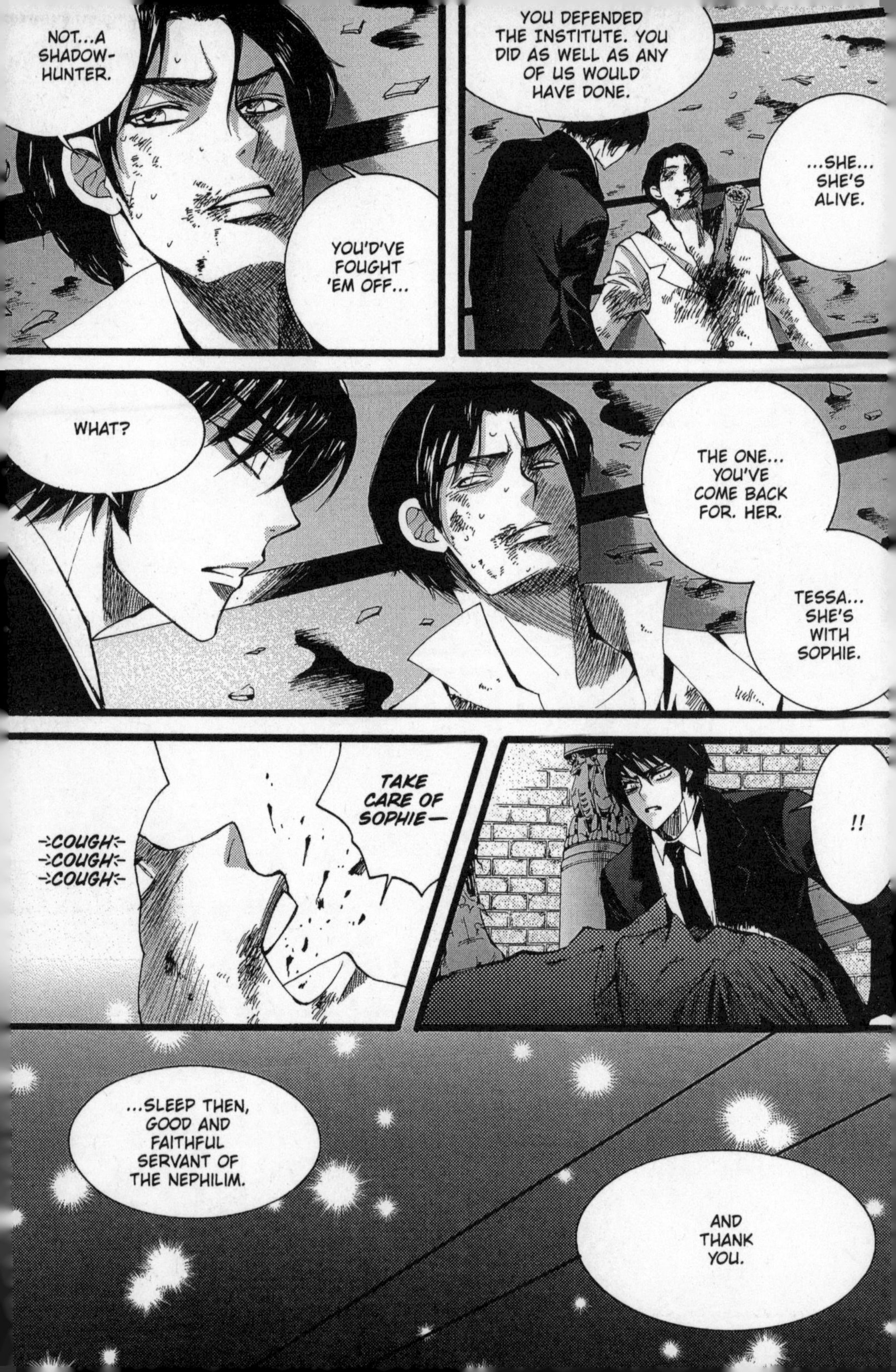
NOT...A SHADOW-HUNTER.
YOU'D'VE FOUGHT 'EM OFF...
YOU DEFENDED THE INSTITUTE. YOU DID AS WELL AS ANY OF US WOULD HAVE DONE.
...SHE... SHE'S ALIVE.
WHAT?
THE ONE... YOU'VE COME BACK FOR. HER.
TESSA... SHE'S WITH SOPHIE.
TAKE CARE OF SOPHIE—
-COUGH- -COUGH- -COUGH-
!!
...SLEEP THEN, GOOD AND FAITHFUL SERVANT OF THE NEPHILIM.
AND THANK YOU.

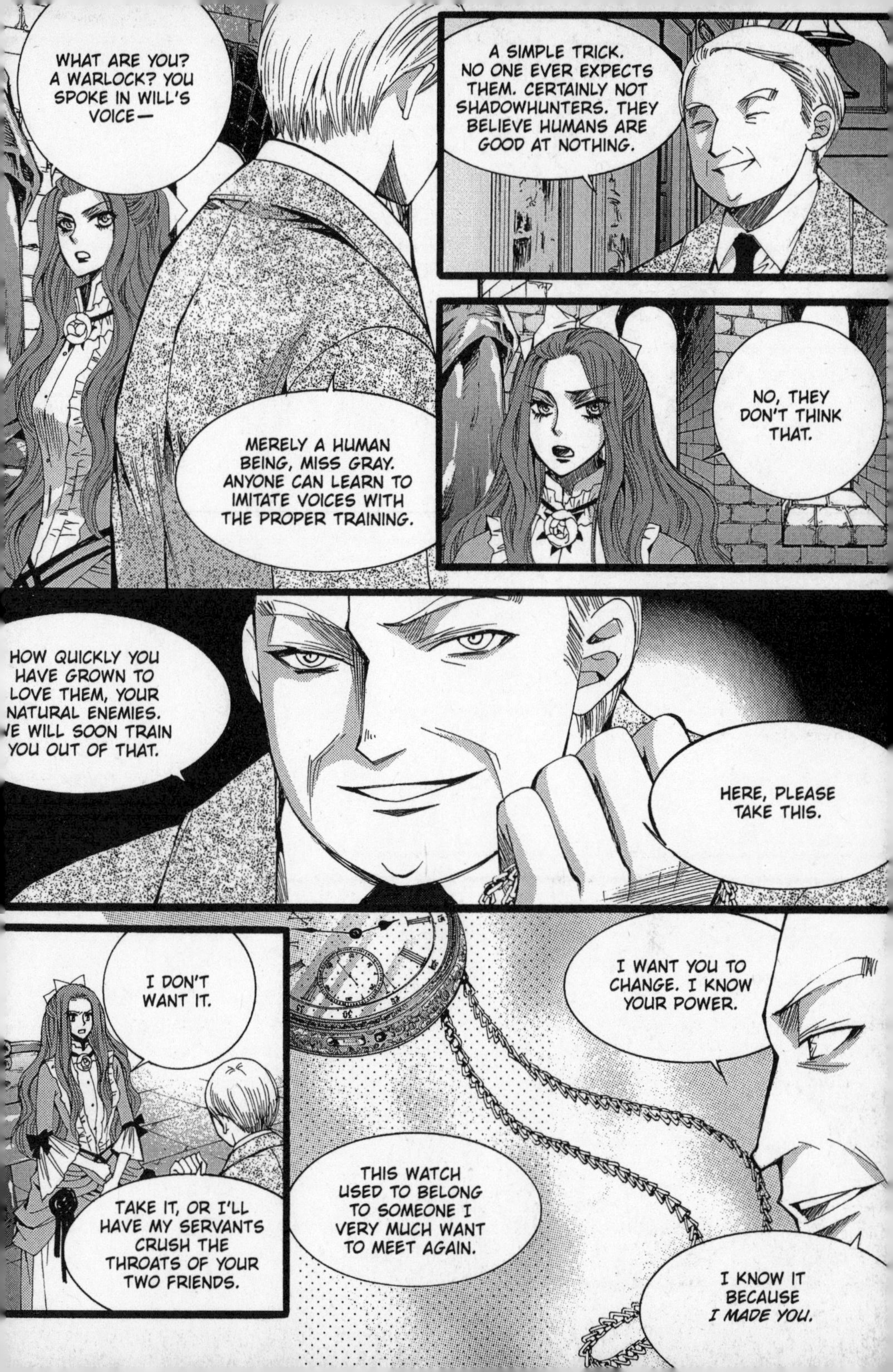
WHAT ARE YOU? A WARLOCK? YOU SPOKE IN WILL'S VOICE—
MERELY A HUMAN BEING, MISS GRAY. ANYONE CAN LEARN TO IMITATE VOICES WITH THE PROPER TRAINING.
A SIMPLE TRICK. NO ONE EVER EXPECTS THEM. CERTAINLY NOT SHADOWHUNTERS. THEY BELIEVE HUMANS ARE GOOD AT NOTHING.
NO, THEY DON'T THINK THAT.
HOW QUICKLY YOU HAVE GROWN TO LOVE THEM, YOUR NATURAL ENEMIES. E WILL SOON TRAIN YOU OUT OF THAT.
HERE, PLEASE TAKE THIS.
I DON'T WANT IT.
TAKE IT, OR I'LL HAVE MY SERVANTS CRUSH THE THROATS OF YOUR TWO FRIENDS.
I WANT YOU TO CHANGE. I KNOW YOUR POWER.
THIS WATCH USED TO BELONG TO SOMEONE I VERY MUCH WANT TO MEET AGAIN.
I KNOW IT BECAUSE *I MADE YOU.*

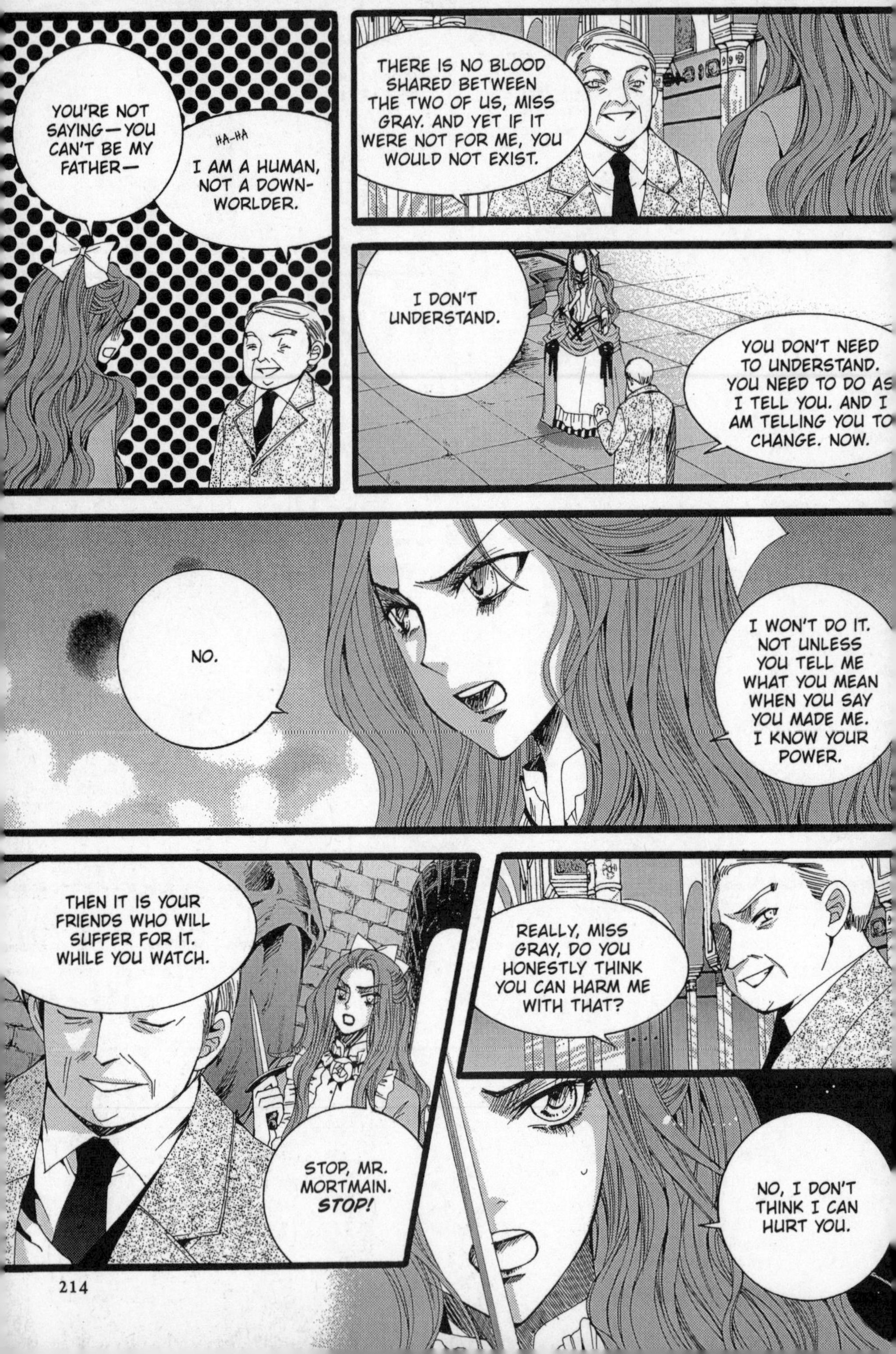
YOU'RE NOT SAYING—YOU CAN'T BE MY FATHER—
HA-HA
I AM A HUMAN, NOT A DOWN-WORLDER.
THERE IS NO BLOOD SHARED BETWEEN THE TWO OF US, MISS GRAY. AND YET IF IT WERE NOT FOR ME, YOU WOULD NOT EXIST.
I DON'T UNDERSTAND.
YOU DON'T NEED TO UNDERSTAND. YOU NEED TO DO AS I TELL YOU. AND I AM TELLING YOU TO CHANGE. NOW.
NO.
I WON'T DO IT. NOT UNLESS YOU TELL ME WHAT YOU MEAN WHEN YOU SAY YOU MADE ME. I KNOW YOUR POWER.
THEN IT IS YOUR FRIENDS WHO WILL SUFFER FOR IT. WHILE YOU WATCH.
STOP, MR. MORTMAIN. *STOP!*
REALLY, MISS GRAY, DO YOU HONESTLY THINK YOU CAN HARM ME WITH THAT?
NO, I DON'T THINK I CAN HURT YOU.

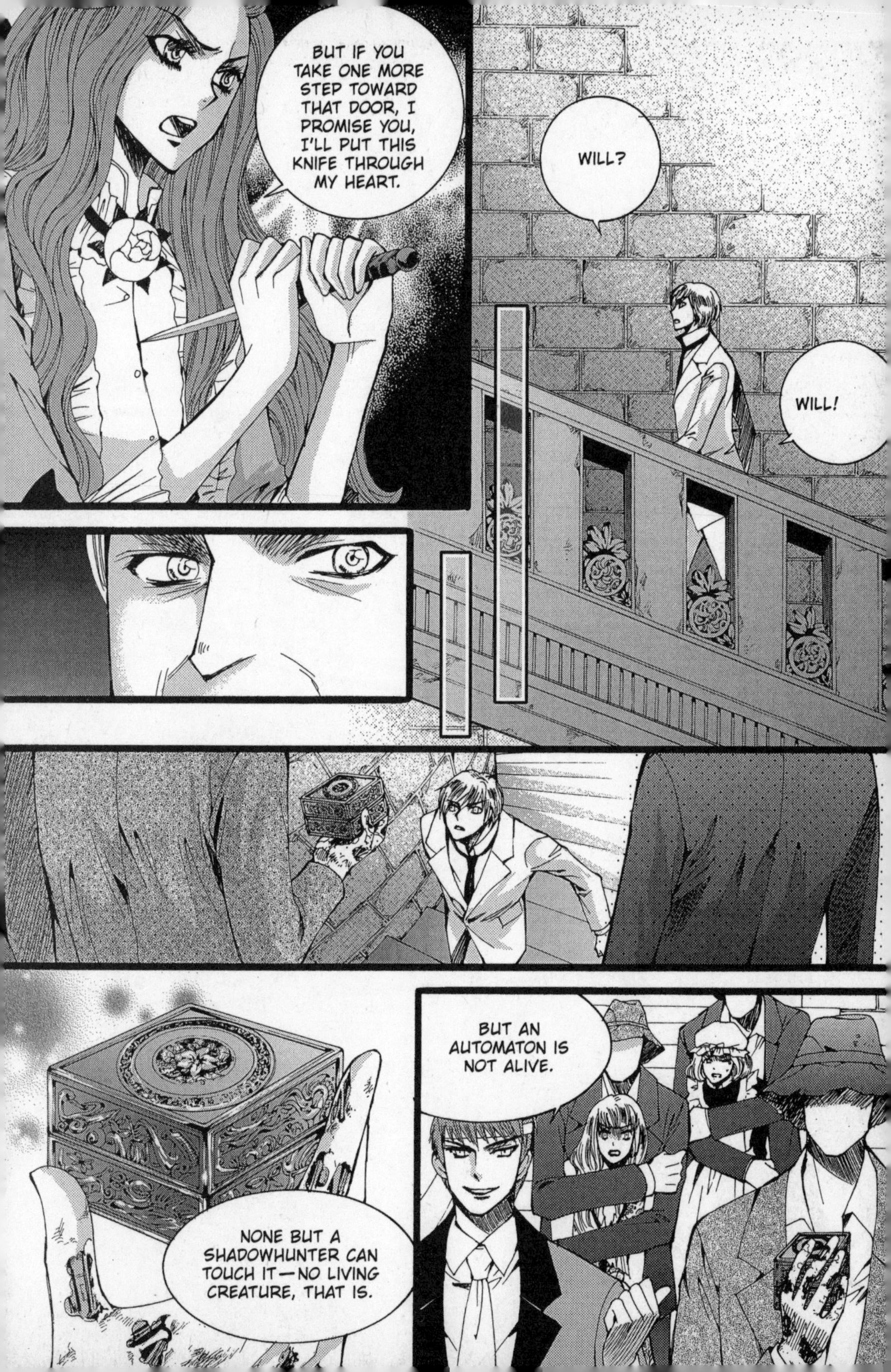
BUT IF YOU TAKE ONE MORE STEP TOWARD THAT DOOR, I PROMISE YOU, I'LL PUT THIS KNIFE THROUGH MY HEART.
WILL?
WILL!
NONE BUT A SHADOWHUNTER CAN TOUCH IT—NO LIVING CREATURE, THAT IS.
BUT AN AUTOMATON IS NOT ALIVE.

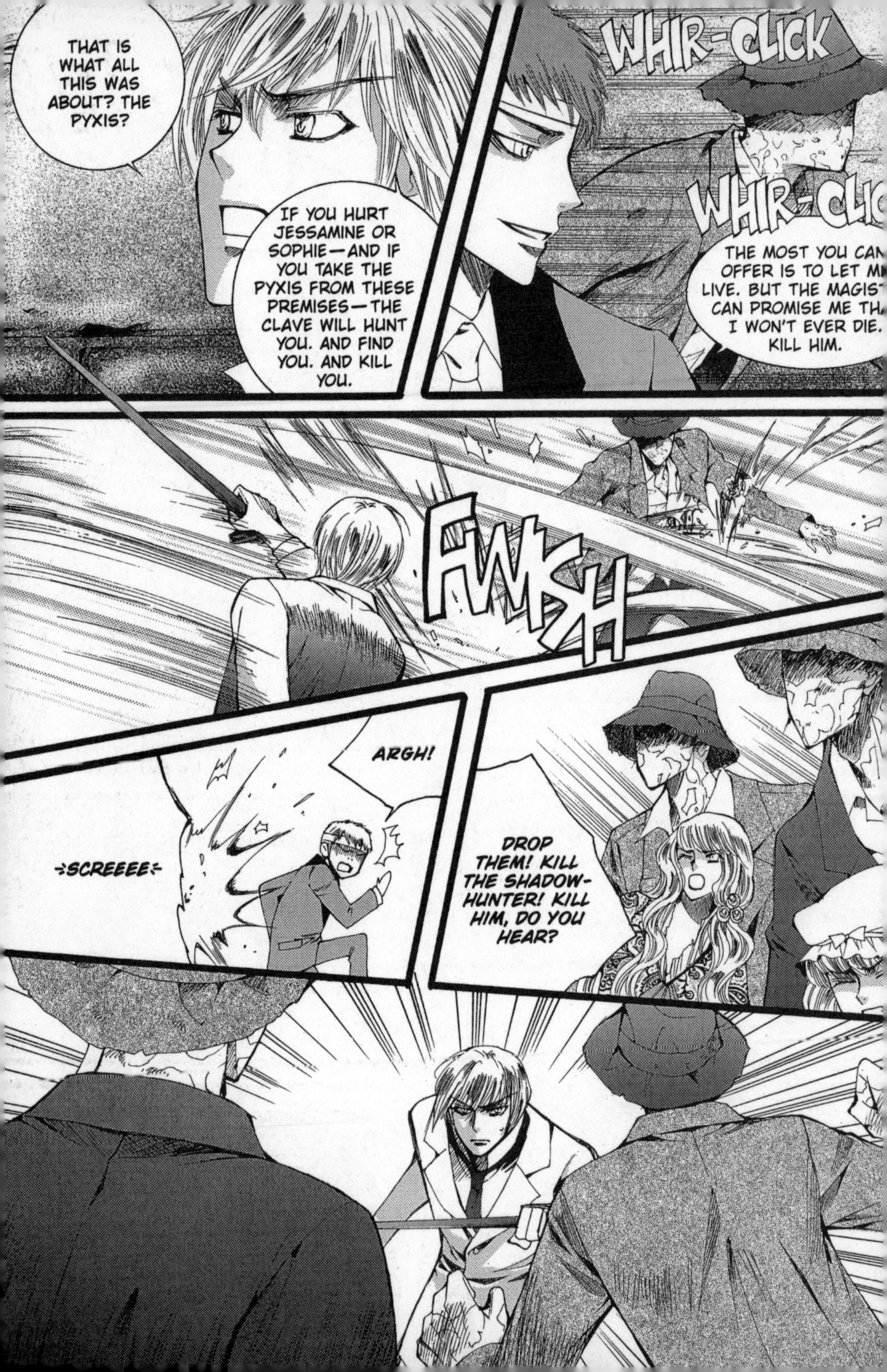
THAT IS WHAT ALL THIS WAS ABOUT? THE PYXIS?
IF YOU HURT JESSAMINE OR SOPHIE—AND IF YOU TAKE THE PYXIS FROM THESE PREMISES—THE CLAVE WILL HUNT YOU. AND FIND YOU. AND KILL YOU.
WHIR-CLICK
WHIR-CLIC
THE MOST YOU CAN OFFER IS TO LET M LIVE. BUT THE MAGIST CAN PROMISE ME TH I WON'T EVER DIE. KILL HIM.
FWISH
ARGH!
SCREEEE
DROP THEM! KILL THE SHADOW-HUNTER! KILL HIM, DO YOU HEAR?

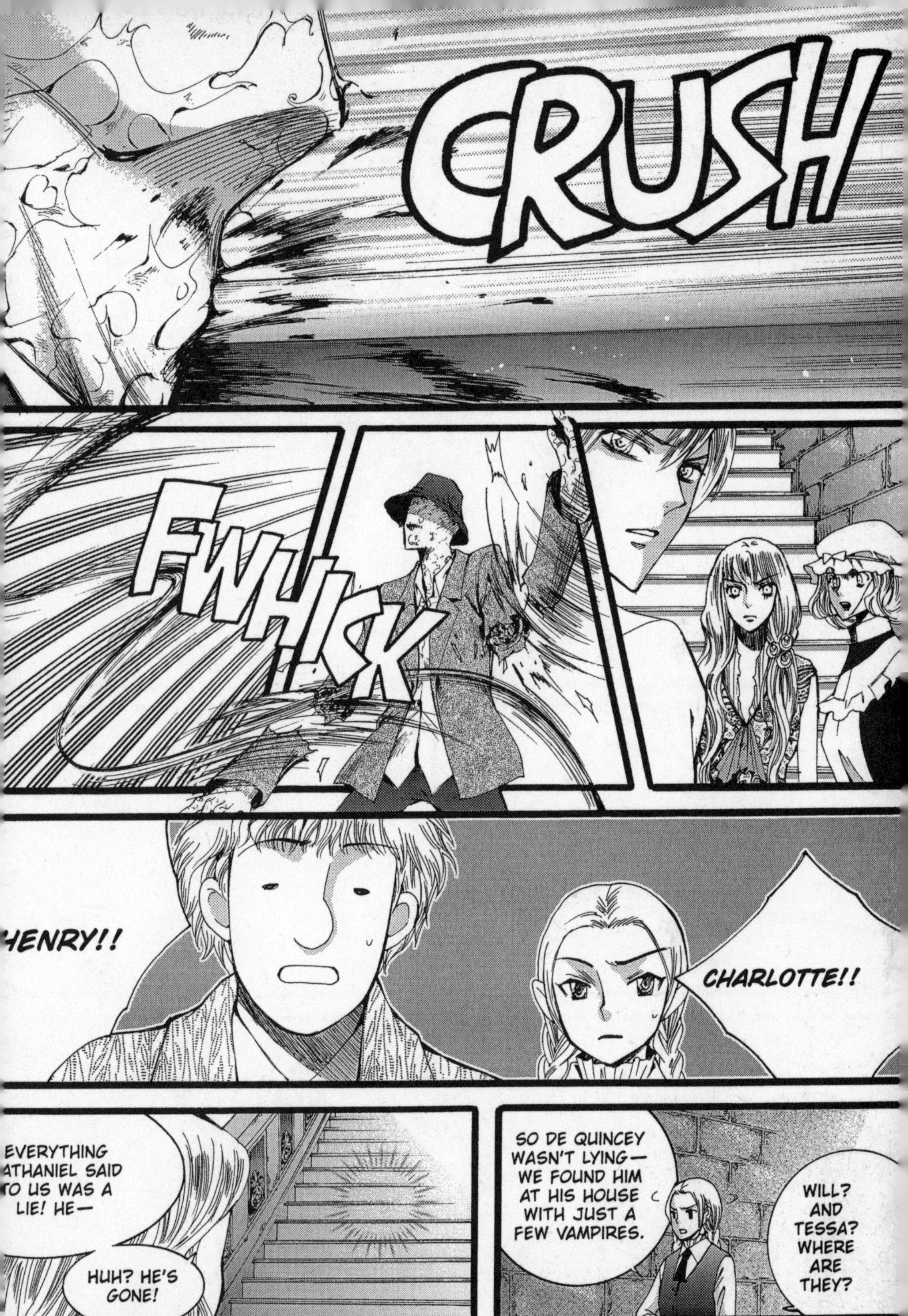
CRUSH
FWHISK
HENRY!!
CHARLOTTE!!
EVERYTHING
ATHANIEL SAID
TO US WAS A
LIE! HE—
HUH? HE'S
GONE!
SO DE QUINCEY
WASN'T LYING—
WE FOUND HIM
AT HIS HOUSE
WITH JUST A
FEW VAMPIRES.
WILL?
AND
TESSA?
WHERE
ARE
THEY?

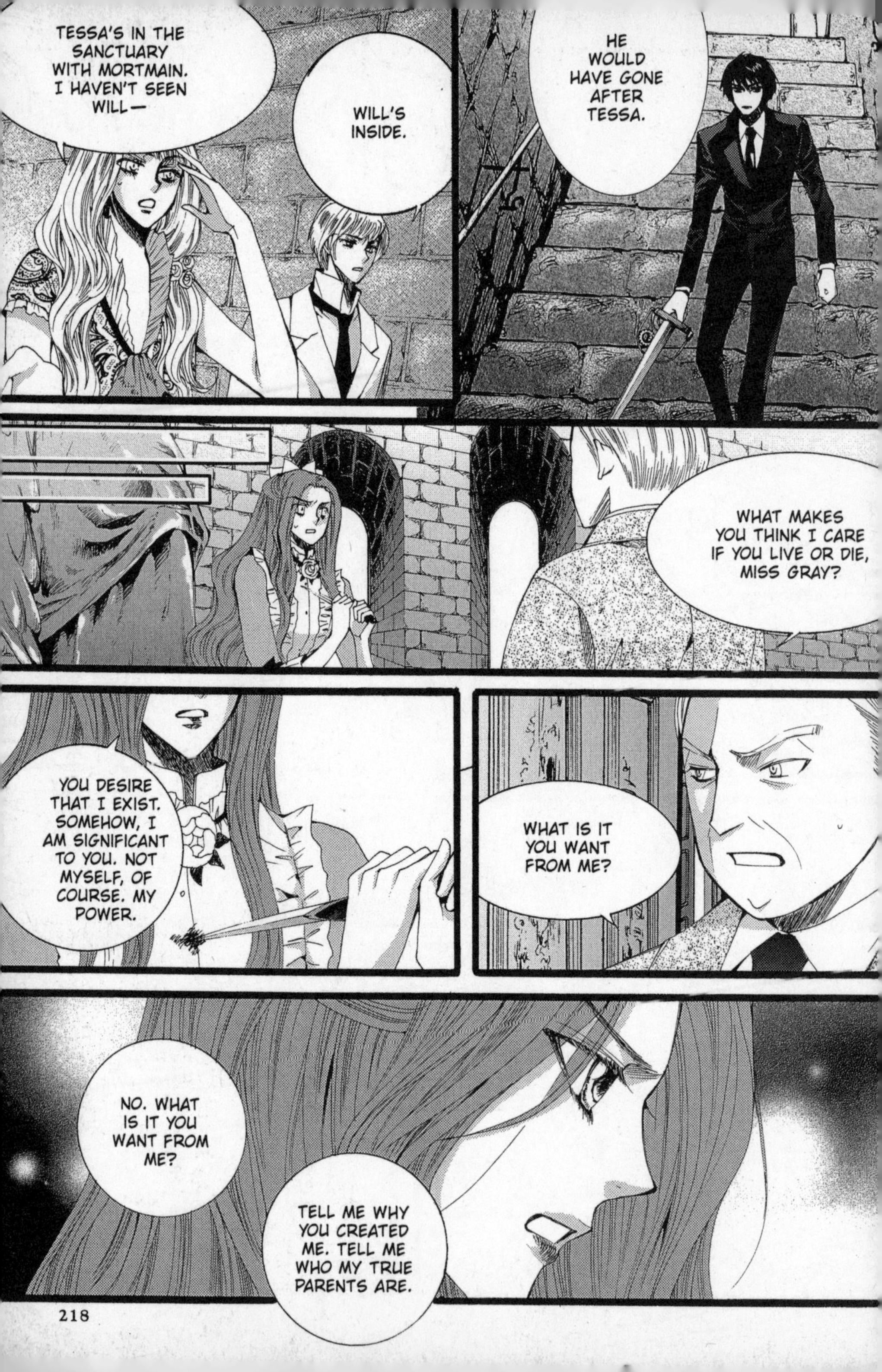
TESSA'S IN THE SANCTUARY WITH MORTMAIN. I HAVEN'T SEEN WILL—
WILL'S INSIDE.
HE WOULD HAVE GONE AFTER TESSA.
WHAT MAKES YOU THINK I CARE IF YOU LIVE OR DIE, MISS GRAY?
YOU DESIRE THAT I EXIST. SOMEHOW, I AM SIGNIFICANT TO YOU. NOT MYSELF, OF COURSE. MY POWER.
WHAT IS IT YOU WANT FROM ME?
NO. WHAT IS IT YOU WANT FROM ME?
TELL ME WHY YOU CREATED ME. TELL ME WHO MY TRUE PARENTS ARE.

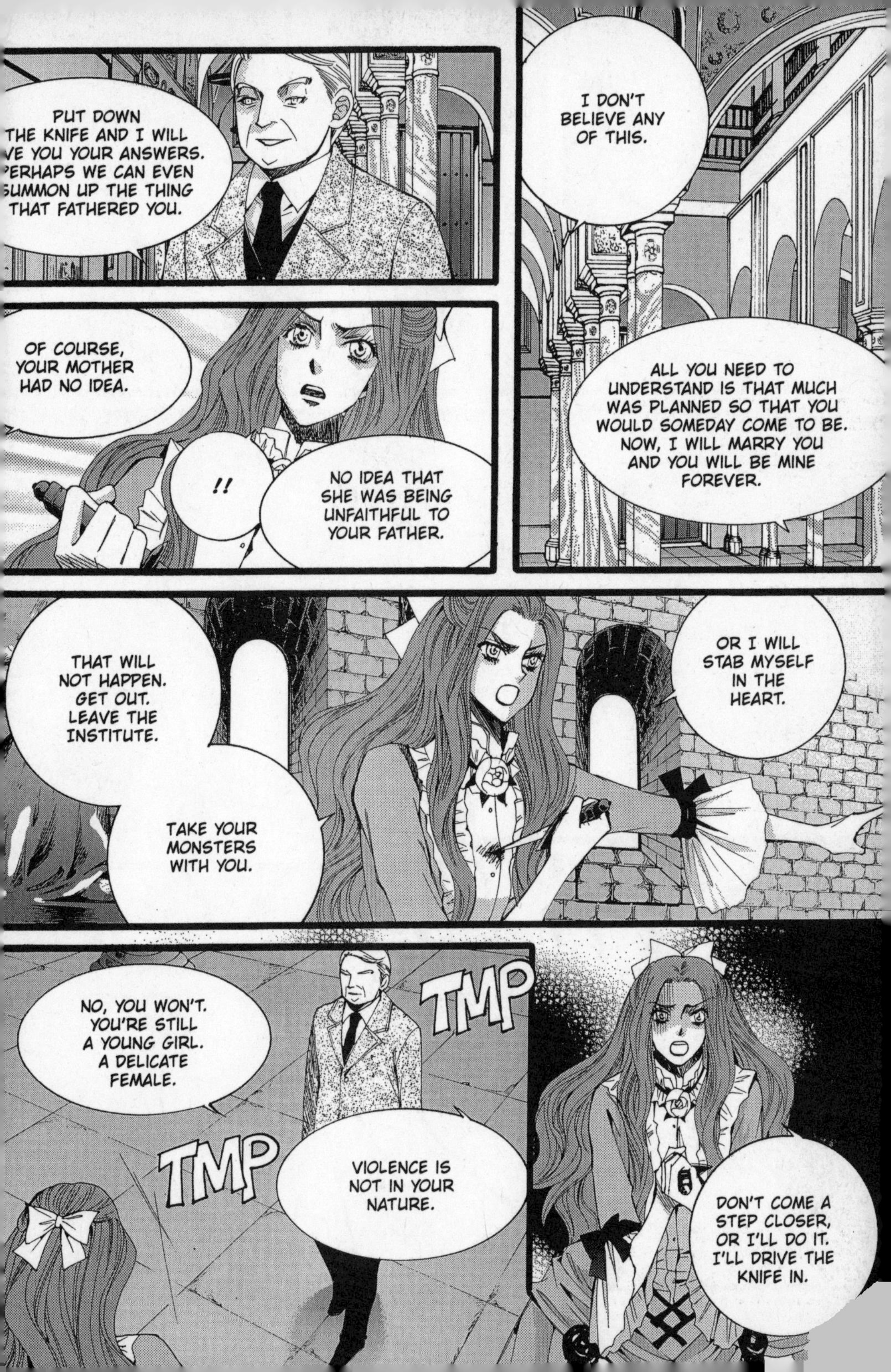
PUT DOWN THE KNIFE AND I WILL VE YOU YOUR ANSWERS. ERHAPS WE CAN EVEN SUMMON UP THE THING THAT FATHERED YOU.
OF COURSE, YOUR MOTHER HAD NO IDEA.
!!
NO IDEA THAT SHE WAS BEING UNFAITHFUL TO YOUR FATHER.
I DON'T BELIEVE ANY OF THIS.
ALL YOU NEED TO UNDERSTAND IS THAT MUCH WAS PLANNED SO THAT YOU WOULD SOMEDAY COME TO BE. NOW, I WILL MARRY YOU AND YOU WILL BE MINE FOREVER.
THAT WILL NOT HAPPEN. GET OUT. LEAVE THE INSTITUTE.
TAKE YOUR MONSTERS WITH YOU.
OR I WILL STAB MYSELF IN THE HEART.
NO, YOU WON'T. YOU'RE STILL A YOUNG GIRL. A DELICATE FEMALE.
TMP
TMP
VIOLENCE IS NOT IN YOUR NATURE.
DON'T COME A STEP CLOSER, OR I'LL DO IT. I'LL DRIVE THE KNIFE IN.

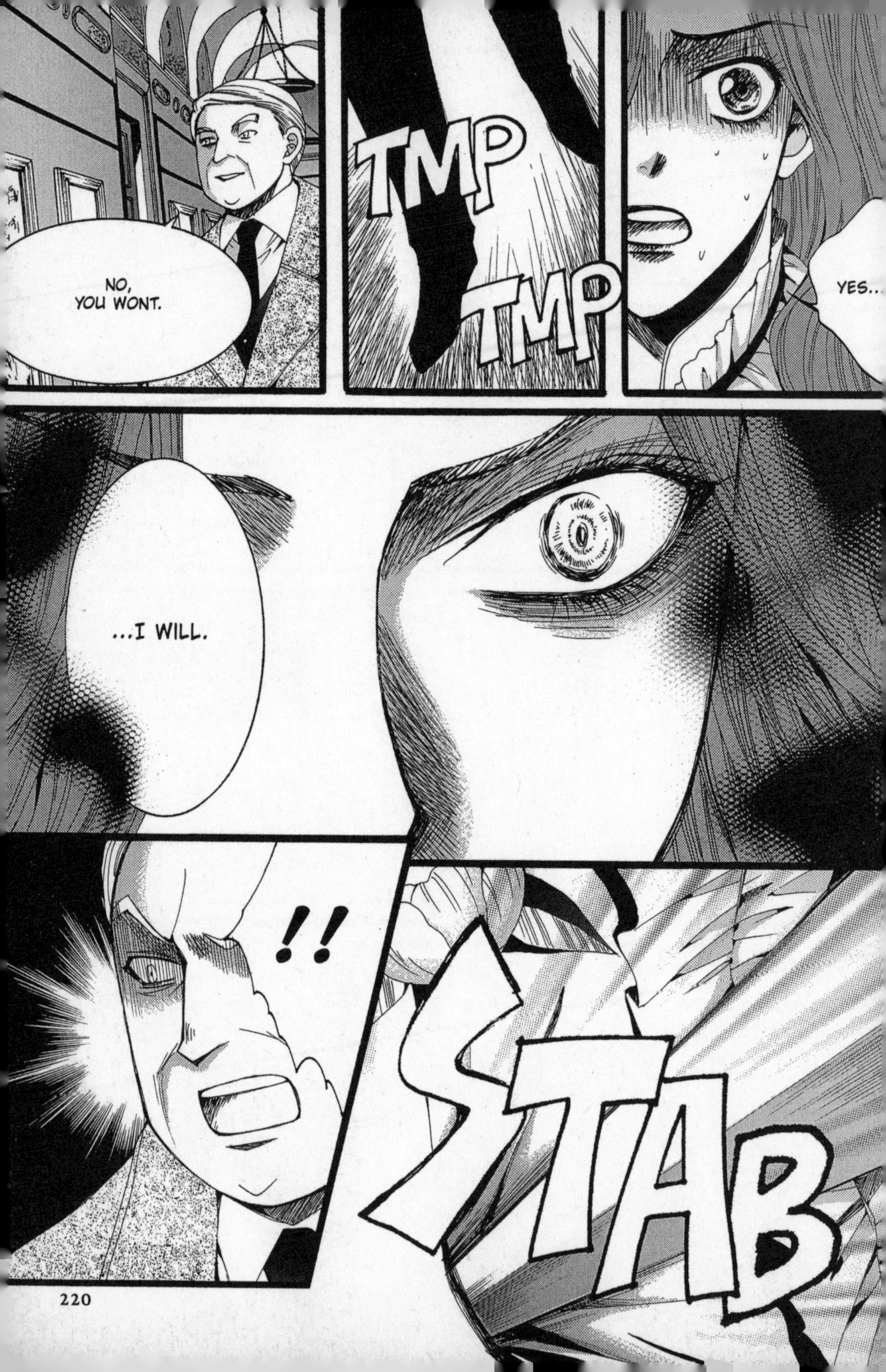
NO, YOU WONT.
TMP
TMP
YES...
...I WILL.
!!
STAB

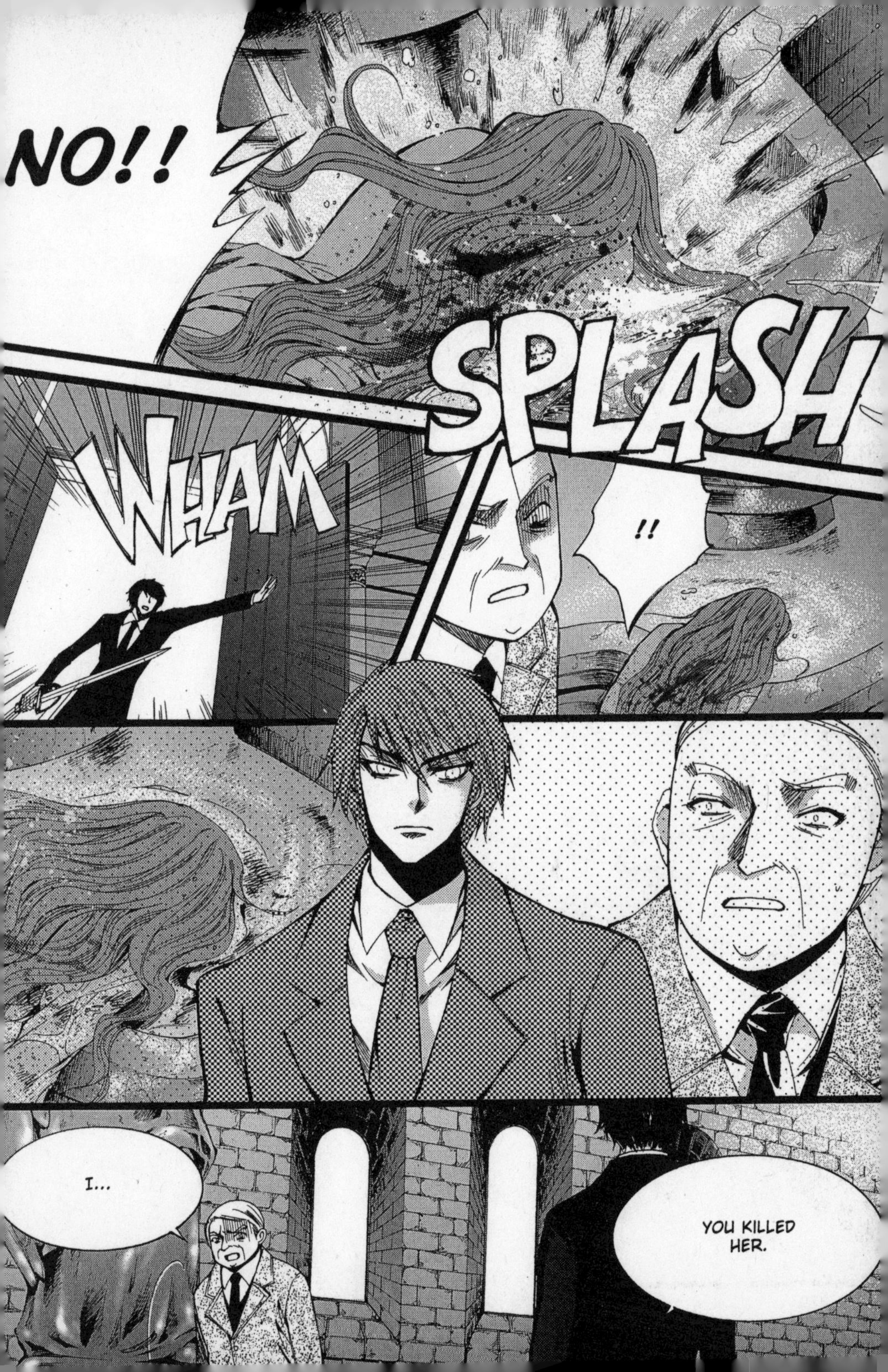
NO!!
SPLASH
WHAM
!!
I...
YOU KILLED HER.

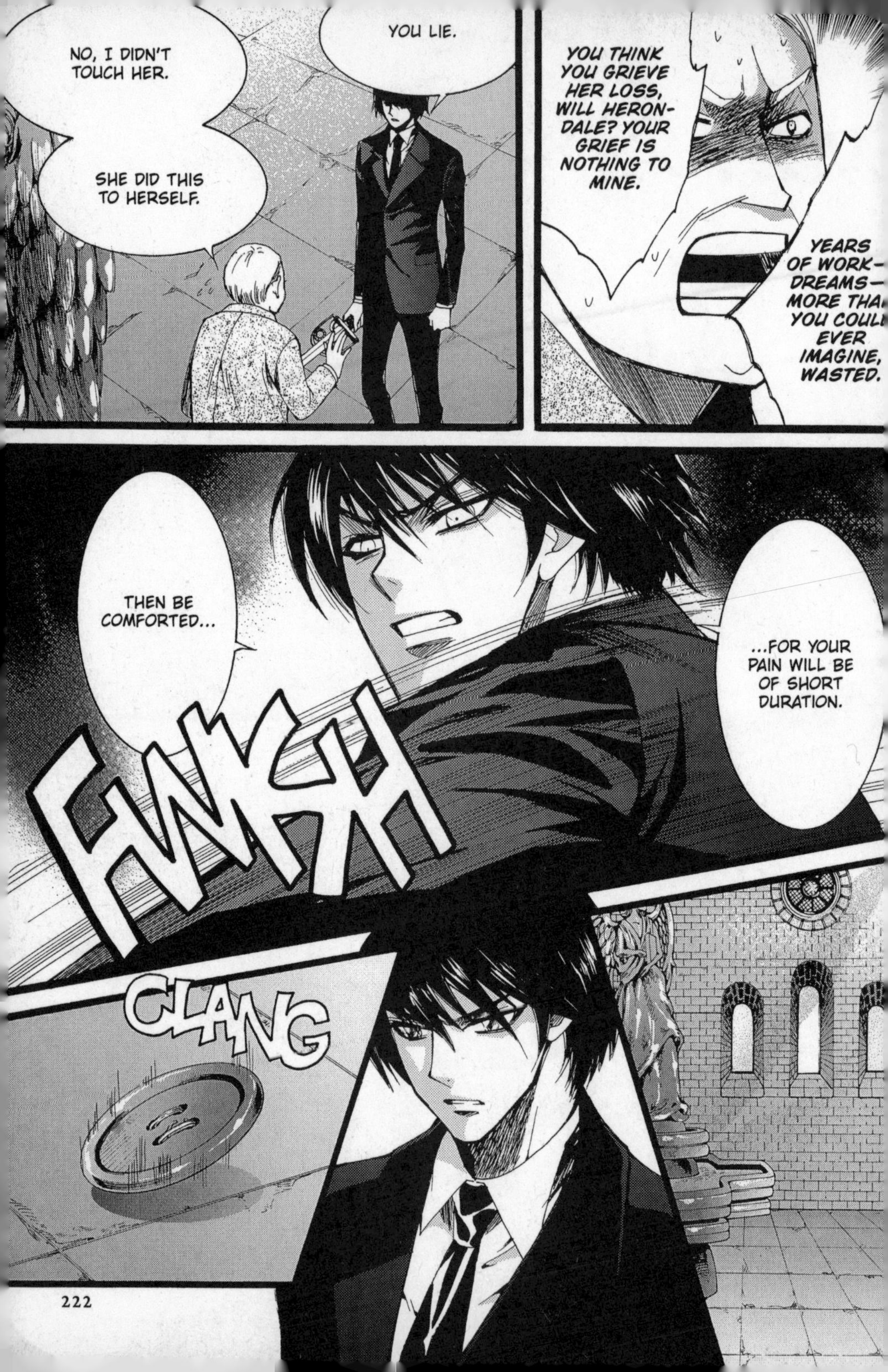
NO, I DIDN'T TOUCH HER.
SHE DID THIS TO HERSELF.
YOU LIE.
YOU THINK YOU GRIEVE HER LOSS, WILL HERON-DALE? YOUR GRIEF IS NOTHING TO MINE.
YEARS OF WORK— DREAMS— MORE THA YOU COUL EVER IMAGINE, WASTED.
THEN BE COMFORTED...
...FOR YOUR PAIN WILL BE OF SHORT DURATION.
FWWSH
CLANG

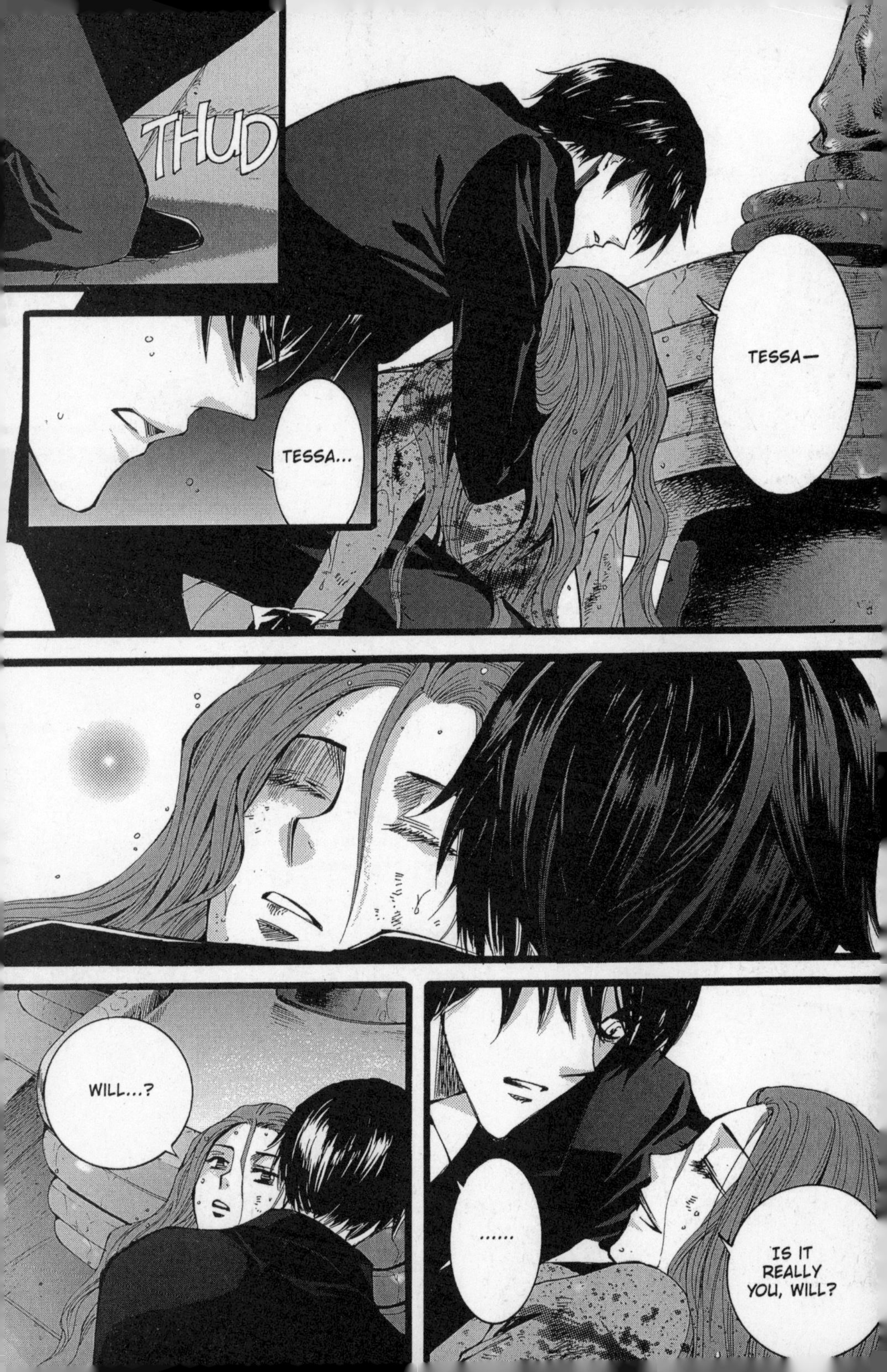
THUD
TESSA...
TESSA—
WILL...?
......
IS IT REALLY YOU, WILL?

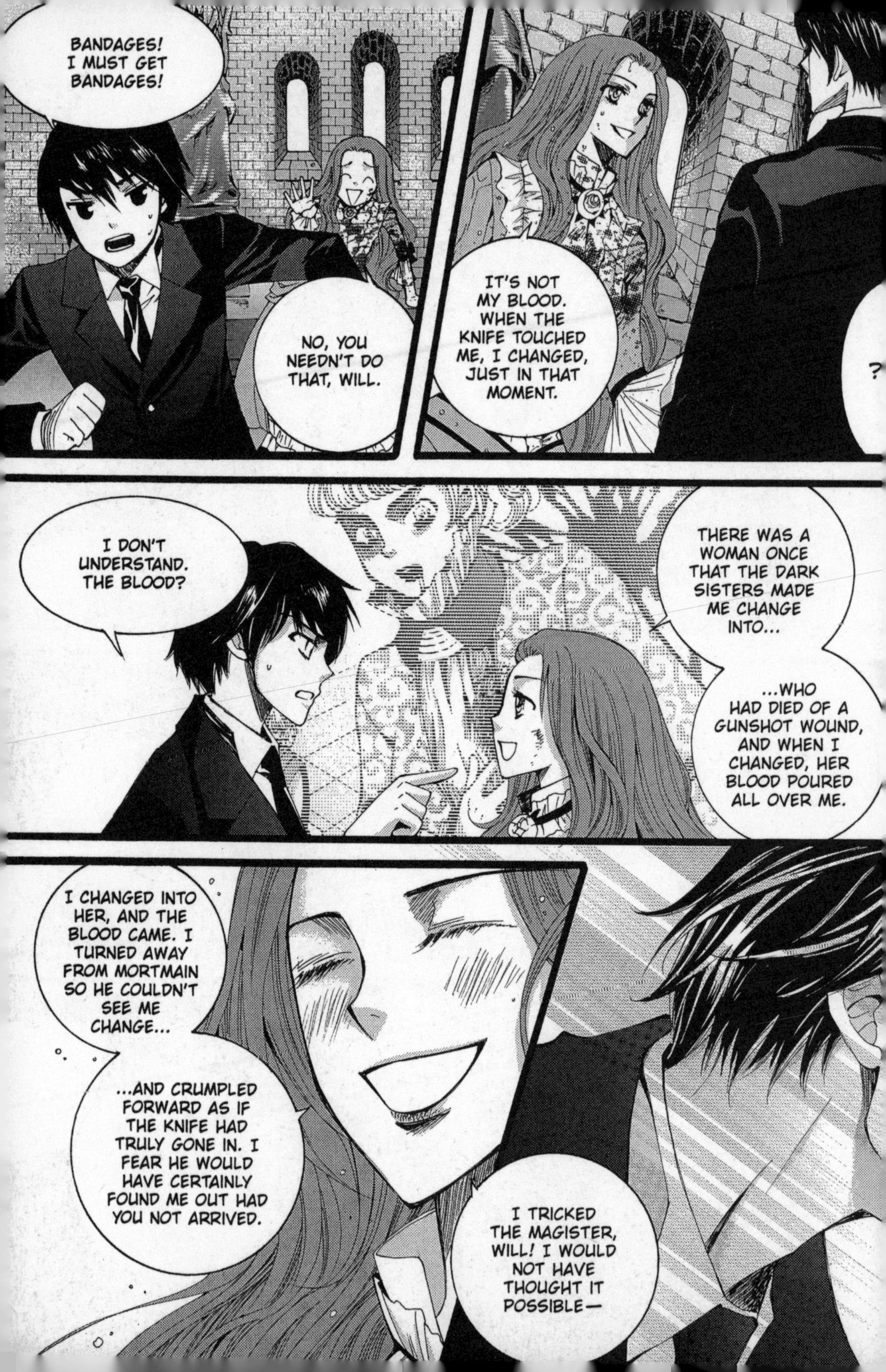
BANDAGES! I MUST GET BANDAGES!
NO, YOU NEEDN'T DO THAT, WILL.
IT'S NOT MY BLOOD. WHEN THE KNIFE TOUCHED ME, I CHANGED, JUST IN THAT MOMENT.
?
I DON'T UNDERSTAND. THE BLOOD?
THERE WAS A WOMAN ONCE THAT THE DARK SISTERS MADE ME CHANGE INTO...
...WHO HAD DIED OF A GUNSHOT WOUND, AND WHEN I CHANGED, HER BLOOD POURED ALL OVER ME.
I CHANGED INTO HER, AND THE BLOOD CAME. I TURNED AWAY FROM MORTMAIN SO HE COULDN'T SEE ME CHANGE...
...AND CRUMPLED FORWARD AS IF THE KNIFE HAD TRULY GONE IN. I FEAR HE WOULD HAVE CERTAINLY FOUND ME OUT HAD YOU NOT ARRIVED.
I TRICKED THE MAGISTER, WILL! I WOULD NOT HAVE THOUGHT IT POSSIBLE—

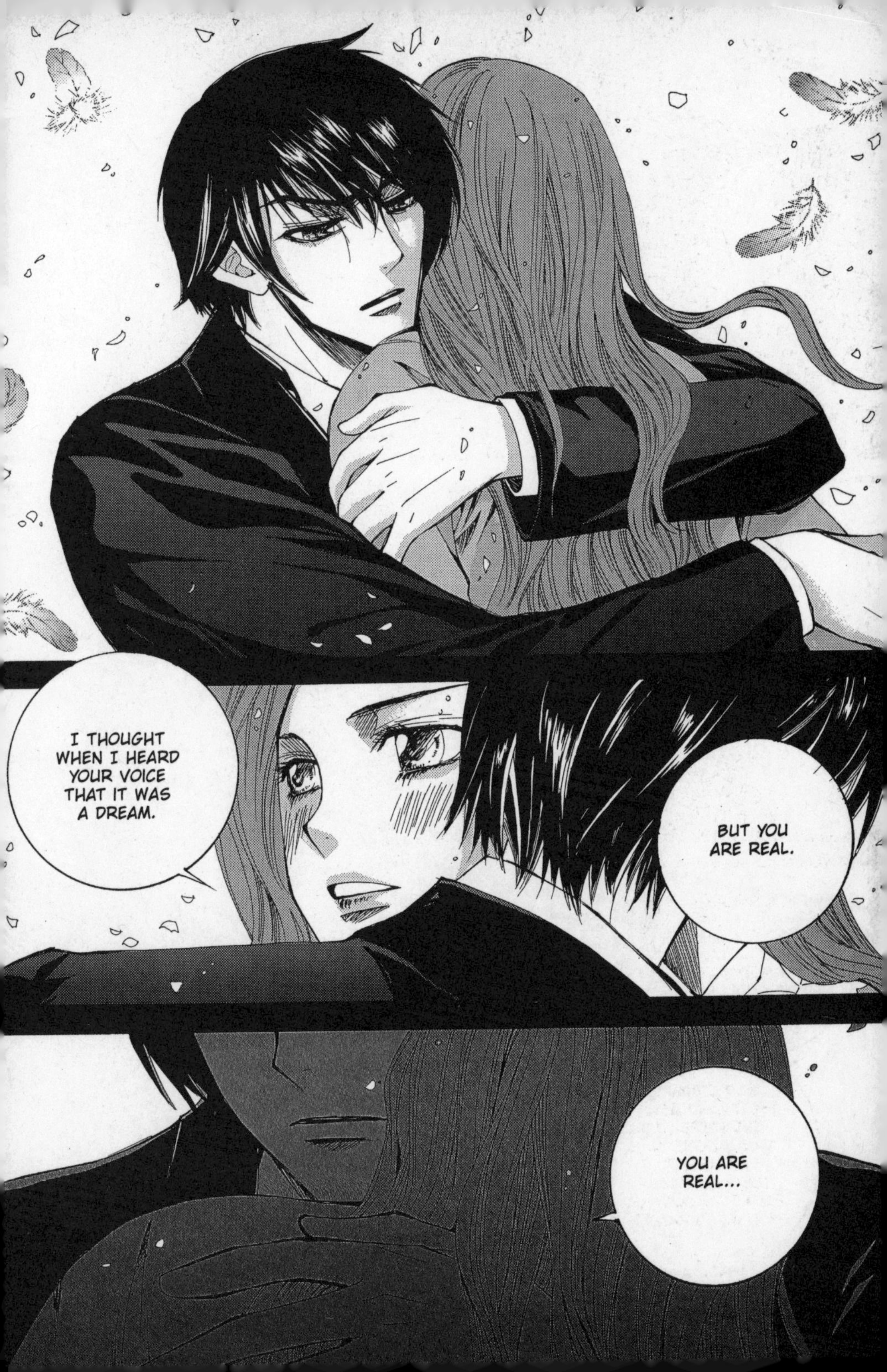
I THOUGHT WHEN I HEARD YOUR VOICE THAT IT WAS A DREAM.
BUT YOU ARE REAL.
YOU ARE REAL...

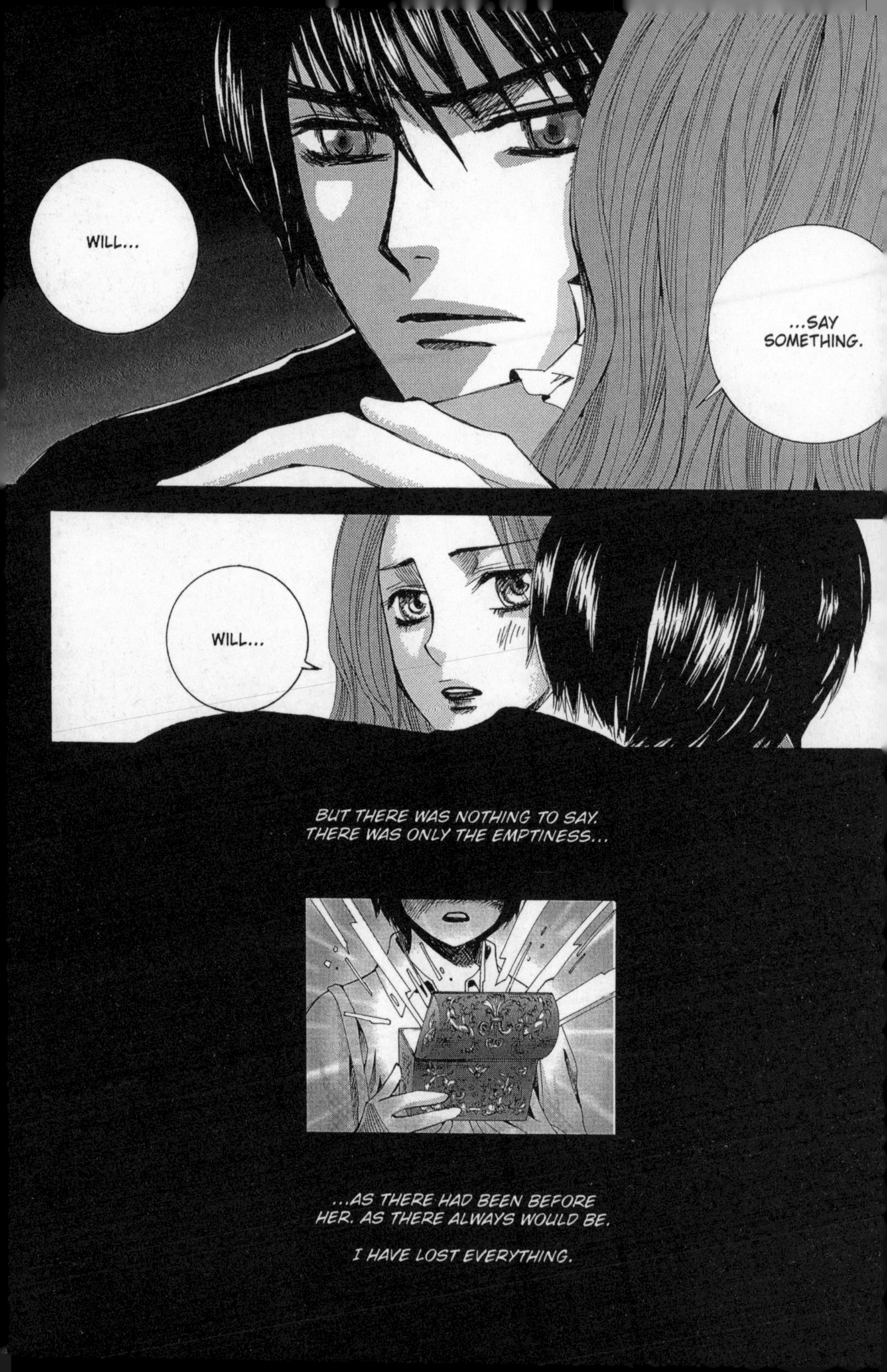
WILL...
...SAY SOMETHING.
WILL...
BUT THERE WAS NOTHING TO SAY. THERE WAS ONLY THE EMPTINESS...
...AS THERE HAD BEEN BEFORE HER. AS THERE ALWAYS WOULD BE.
I HAVE LOST EVERYTHING.

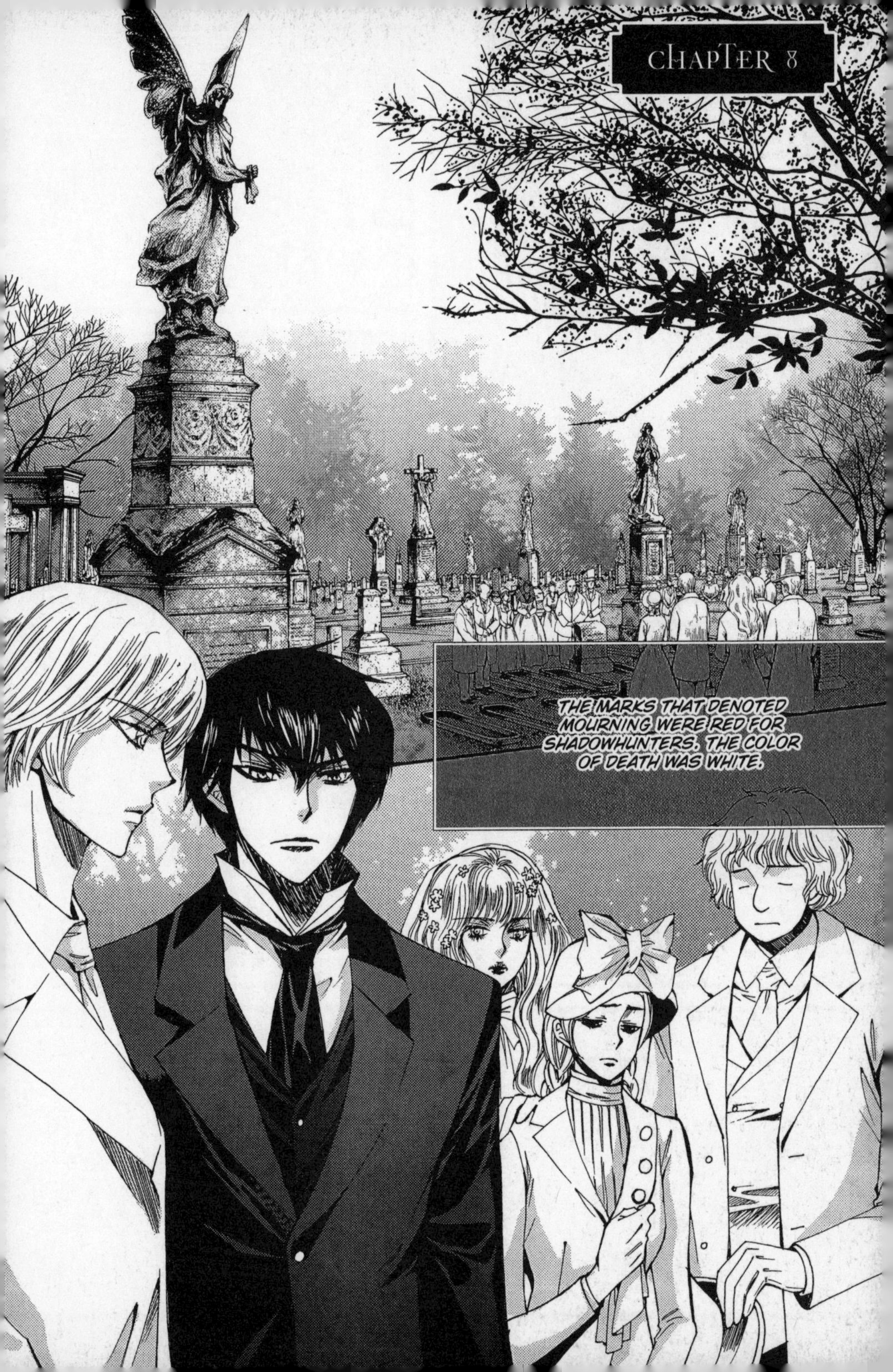
CHAPTER 8
THE MARKS THAT DENOTED MOURNING WERE RED FOR SHADOWHUNTERS. THE COLOR OF DEATH WAS WHITE.

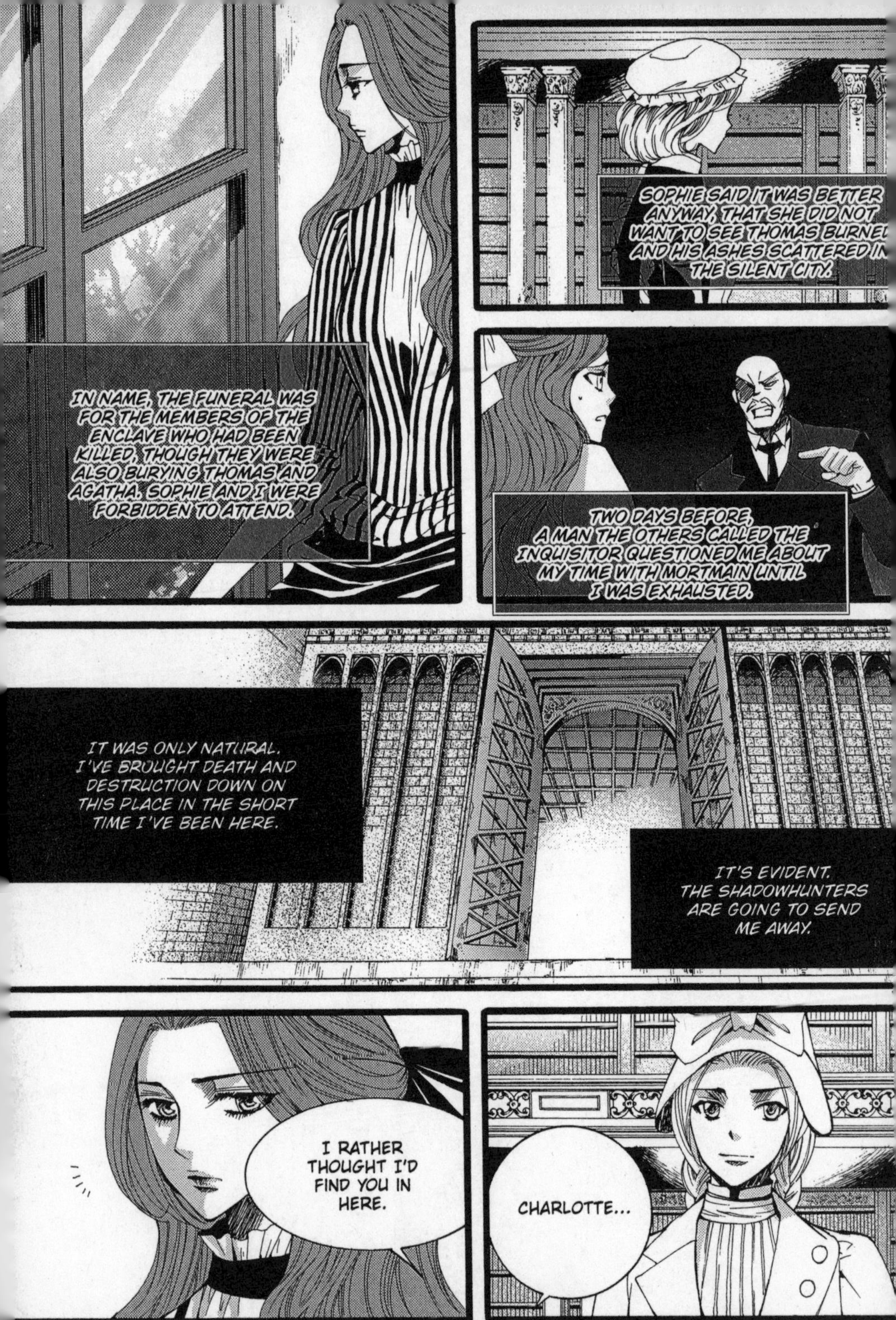
IN NAME, THE FUNERAL WAS FOR THE MEMBERS OF THE ENCLAVE WHO HAD BEEN KILLED, THOUGH THEY WERE ALSO BURYING THOMAS AND AGATHA. SOPHIE AND I WERE FORBIDDEN TO ATTEND.
SOPHIE SAID IT WAS BETTER ANYWAY, THAT SHE DID NOT WANT TO SEE THOMAS BURNED AND HIS ASHES SCATTERED IN THE SILENT CITY.
TWO DAYS BEFORE, A MAN THE OTHERS CALLED THE INQUISITOR QUESTIONED ME ABOUT MY TIME WITH MORTMAIN UNTIL I WAS EXHAUSTED.
IT WAS ONLY NATURAL. I'VE BROUGHT DEATH AND DESTRUCTION DOWN ON THIS PLACE IN THE SHORT TIME I'VE BEEN HERE.
IT'S EVIDENT. THE SHADOWHUNTERS ARE GOING TO SEND ME AWAY.
I RATHER THOUGHT I'D FIND YOU IN HERE.
CHARLOTTE...

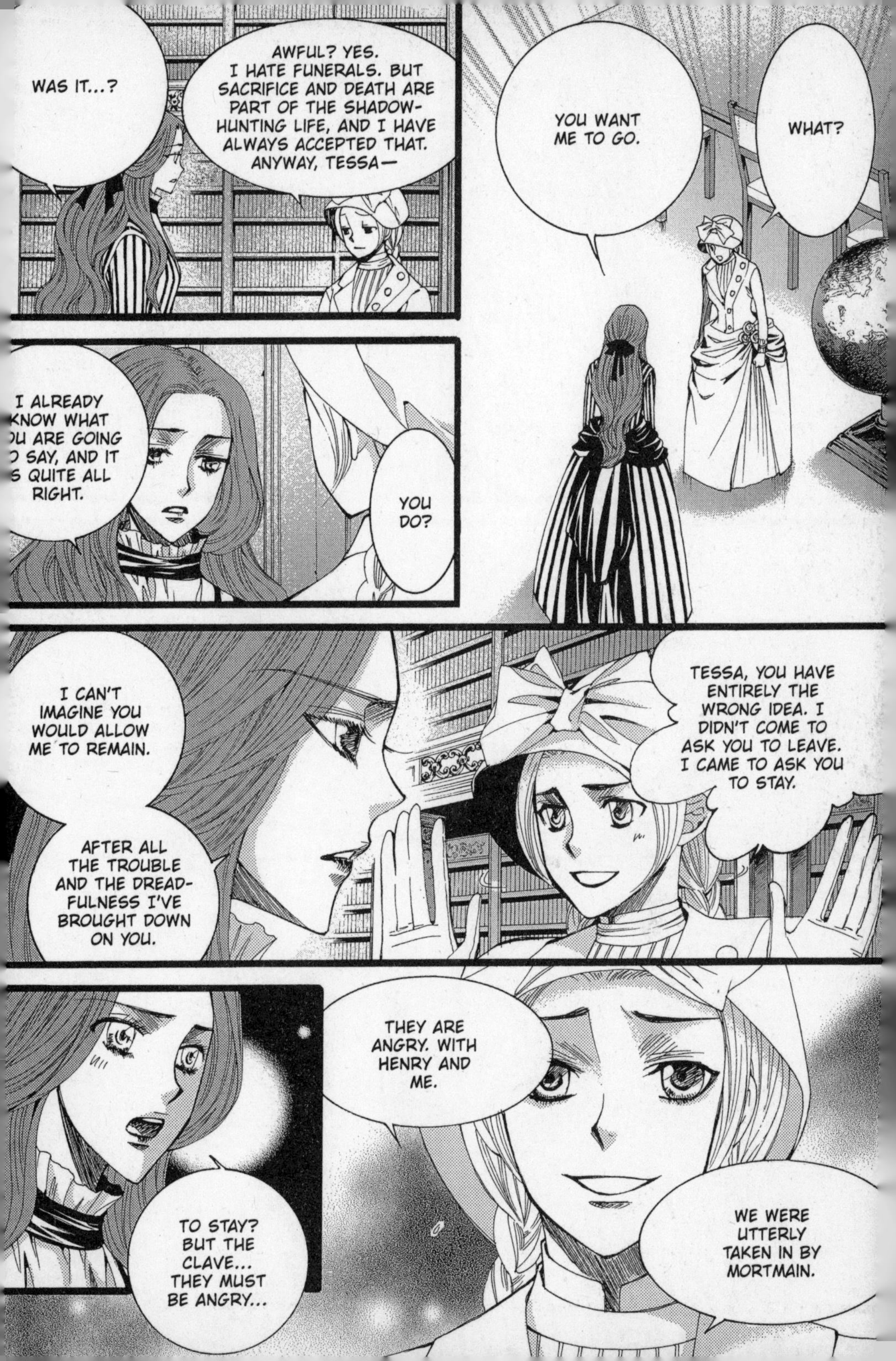
WAS IT...?
AWFUL? YES. I HATE FUNERALS. BUT SACRIFICE AND DEATH ARE PART OF THE SHADOW-HUNTING LIFE, AND I HAVE ALWAYS ACCEPTED THAT. ANYWAY, TESSA—
I ALREADY KNOW WHAT OU ARE GOING O SAY, AND IT S QUITE ALL RIGHT.
YOU DO?
YOU WANT ME TO GO.
WHAT?
I CAN'T IMAGINE YOU WOULD ALLOW ME TO REMAIN.
AFTER ALL THE TROUBLE AND THE DREAD-FULNESS I'VE BROUGHT DOWN ON YOU.
TESSA, YOU HAVE ENTIRELY THE WRONG IDEA. I DIDN'T COME TO ASK YOU TO LEAVE. I CAME TO ASK YOU TO STAY.
TO STAY? BUT THE CLAVE... THEY MUST BE ANGRY...
THEY ARE ANGRY. WITH HENRY AND ME.
WE WERE UTTERLY TAKEN IN BY MORTMAIN.

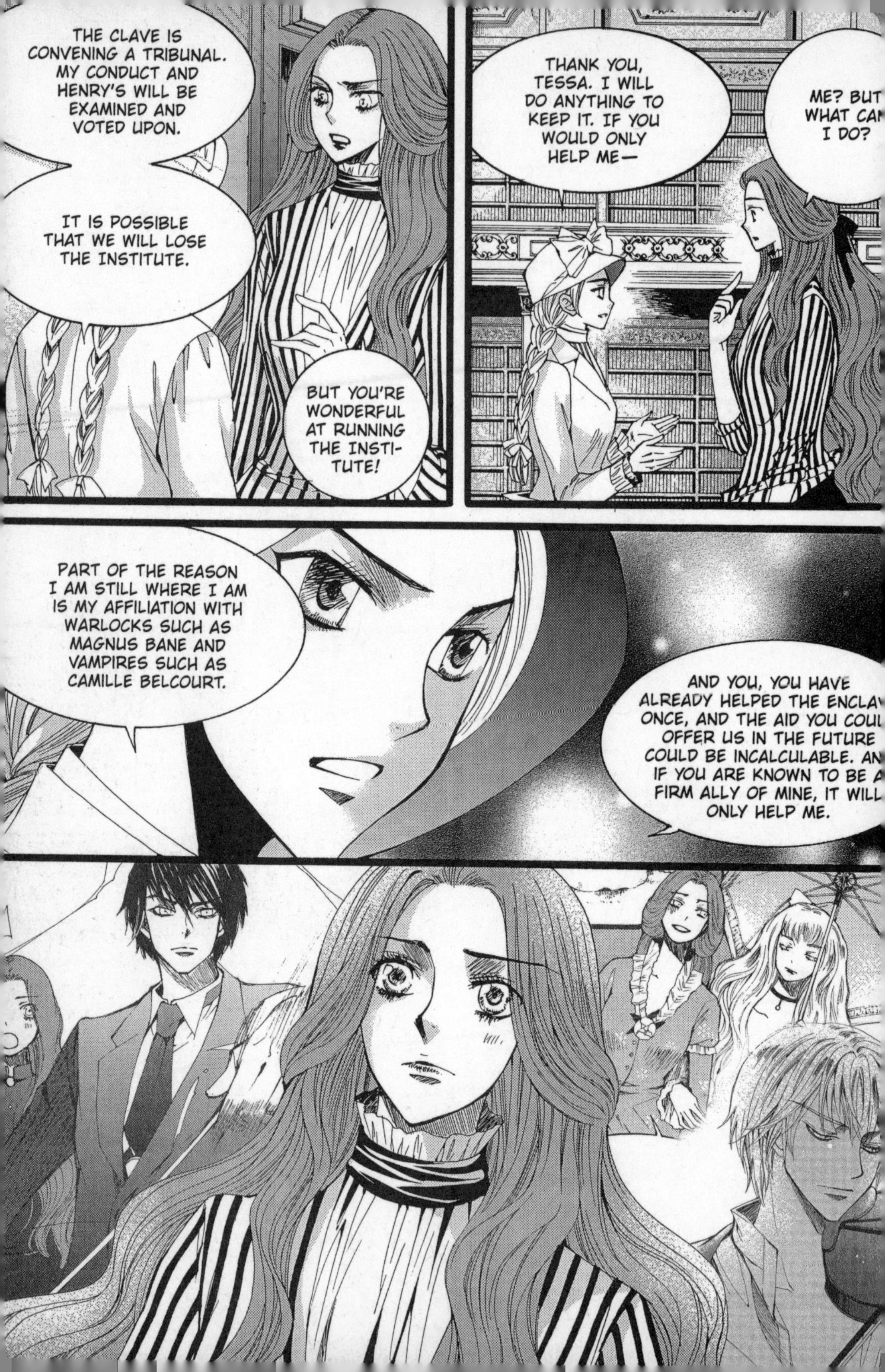
THE CLAVE IS CONVENING A TRIBUNAL. MY CONDUCT AND HENRY'S WILL BE EXAMINED AND VOTED UPON.
IT IS POSSIBLE THAT WE WILL LOSE THE INSTITUTE.
BUT YOU'RE WONDERFUL AT RUNNING THE INSTI-TUTE!
THANK YOU, TESSA. I WILL DO ANYTHING TO KEEP IT. IF YOU WOULD ONLY HELP ME—
ME? BUT WHAT CA I DO?
PART OF THE REASON I AM STILL WHERE I AM IS MY AFFILIATION WITH WARLOCKS SUCH AS MAGNUS BANE AND VAMPIRES SUCH AS CAMILLE BELCOURT.
AND YOU, YOU HAVE ALREADY HELPED THE ENCLAV ONCE, AND THE AID YOU COUL OFFER US IN THE FUTURE COULD BE INCALCULABLE. AN IF YOU ARE KNOWN TO BE A FIRM ALLY OF MINE, IT WILL ONLY HELP ME.

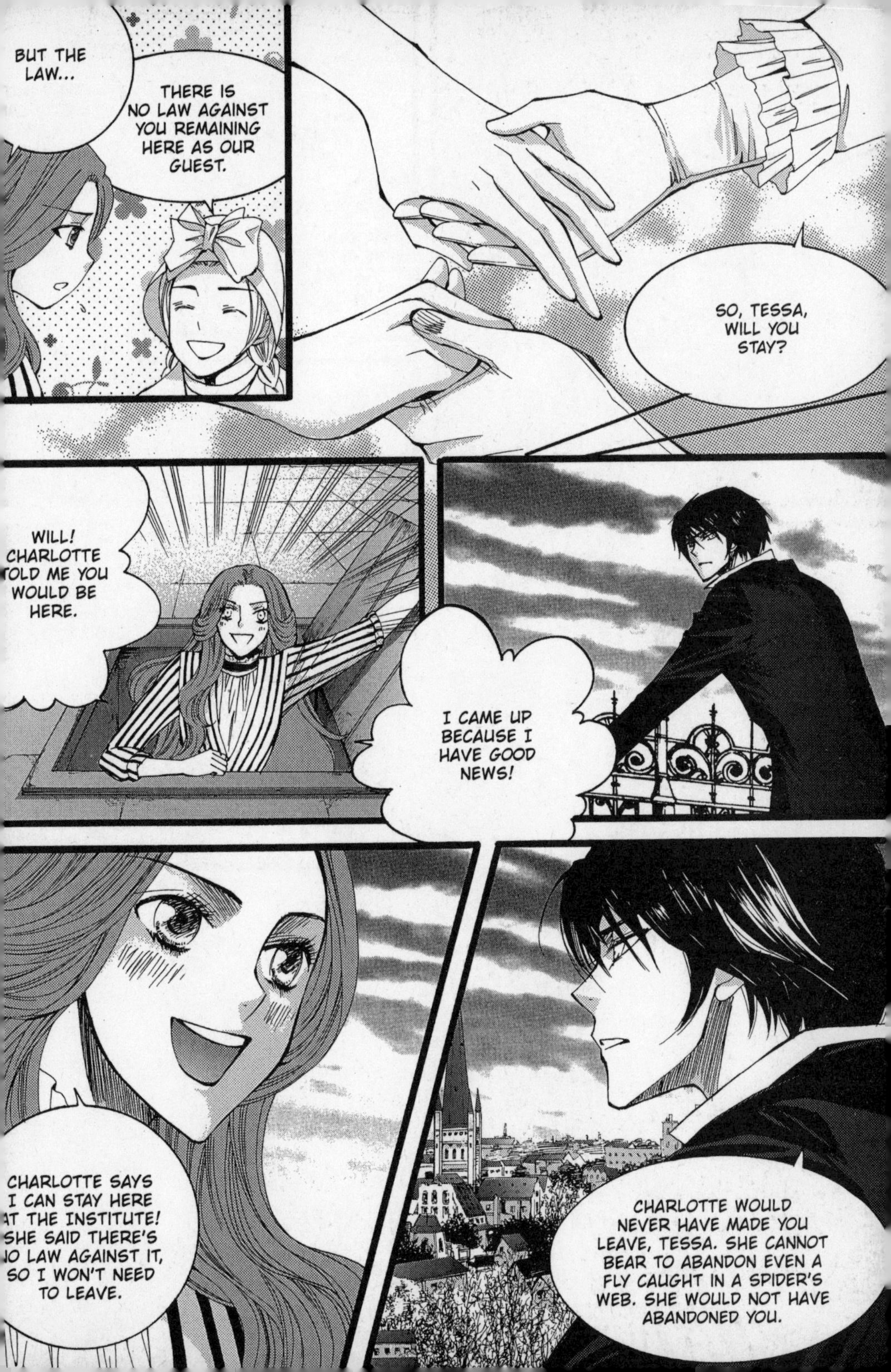

BUT THE LAW...
THERE IS NO LAW AGAINST YOU REMAINING HERE AS OUR GUEST.
SO, TESSA, WILL YOU STAY?
WILL! CHARLOTTE TOLD ME YOU WOULD BE HERE.
I CAME UP BECAUSE I HAVE GOOD NEWS!
CHARLOTTE SAYS I CAN STAY HERE AT THE INSTITUTE! SHE SAID THERE'S NO LAW AGAINST IT, SO I WON'T NEED TO LEAVE.
CHARLOTTE WOULD NEVER HAVE MADE YOU LEAVE, TESSA. SHE CANNOT BEAR TO ABANDON EVEN A FLY CAUGHT IN A SPIDER'S WEB. SHE WOULD NOT HAVE ABANDONED YOU.

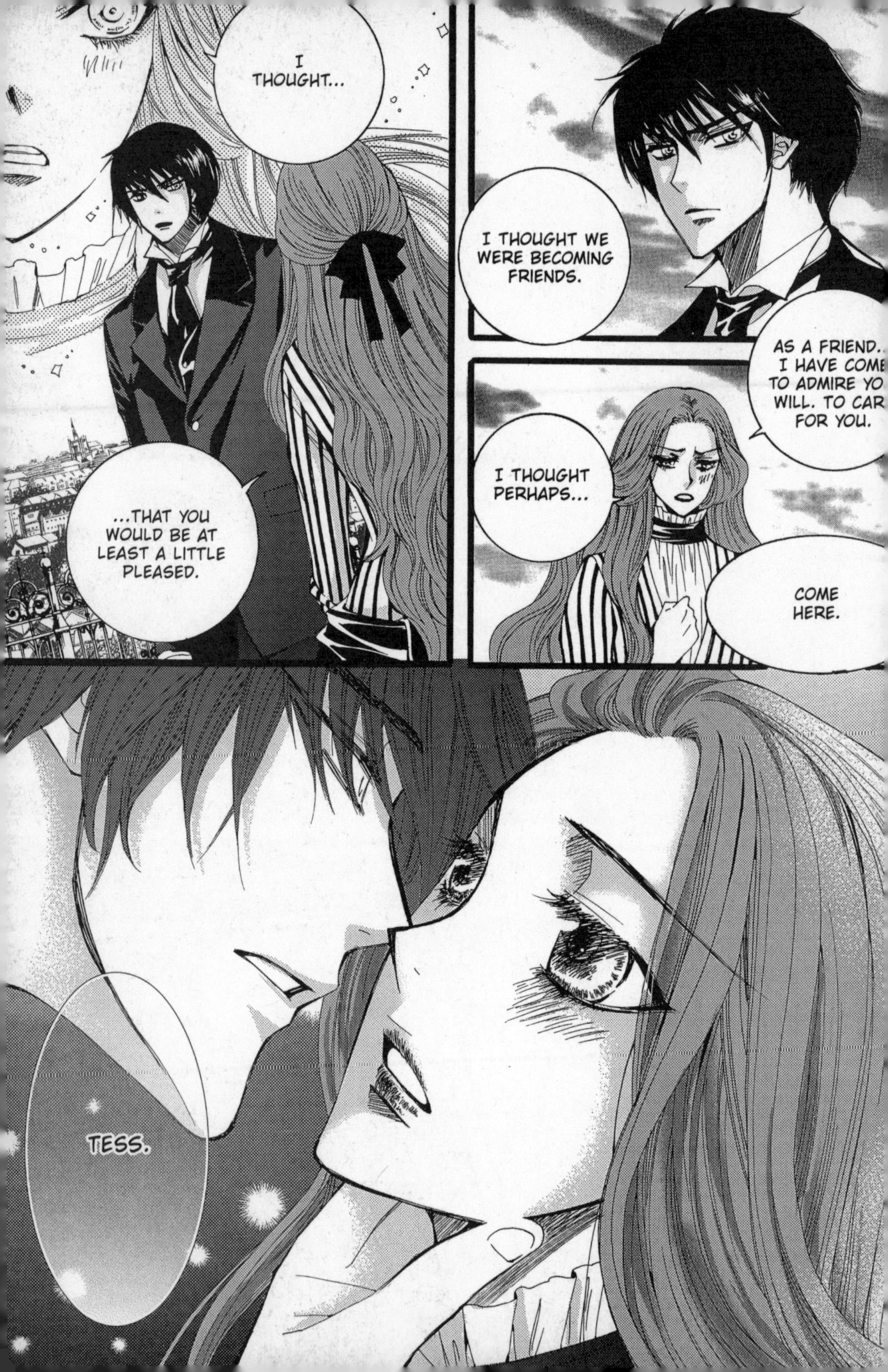
I THOUGHT...
...THAT YOU WOULD BE AT LEAST A LITTLE PLEASED.
I THOUGHT WE WERE BECOMING FRIENDS.
AS A FRIEND... I HAVE COME TO ADMIRE YO WILL. TO CAR FOR YOU.
I THOUGHT PERHAPS...
COME HERE.
TESS.

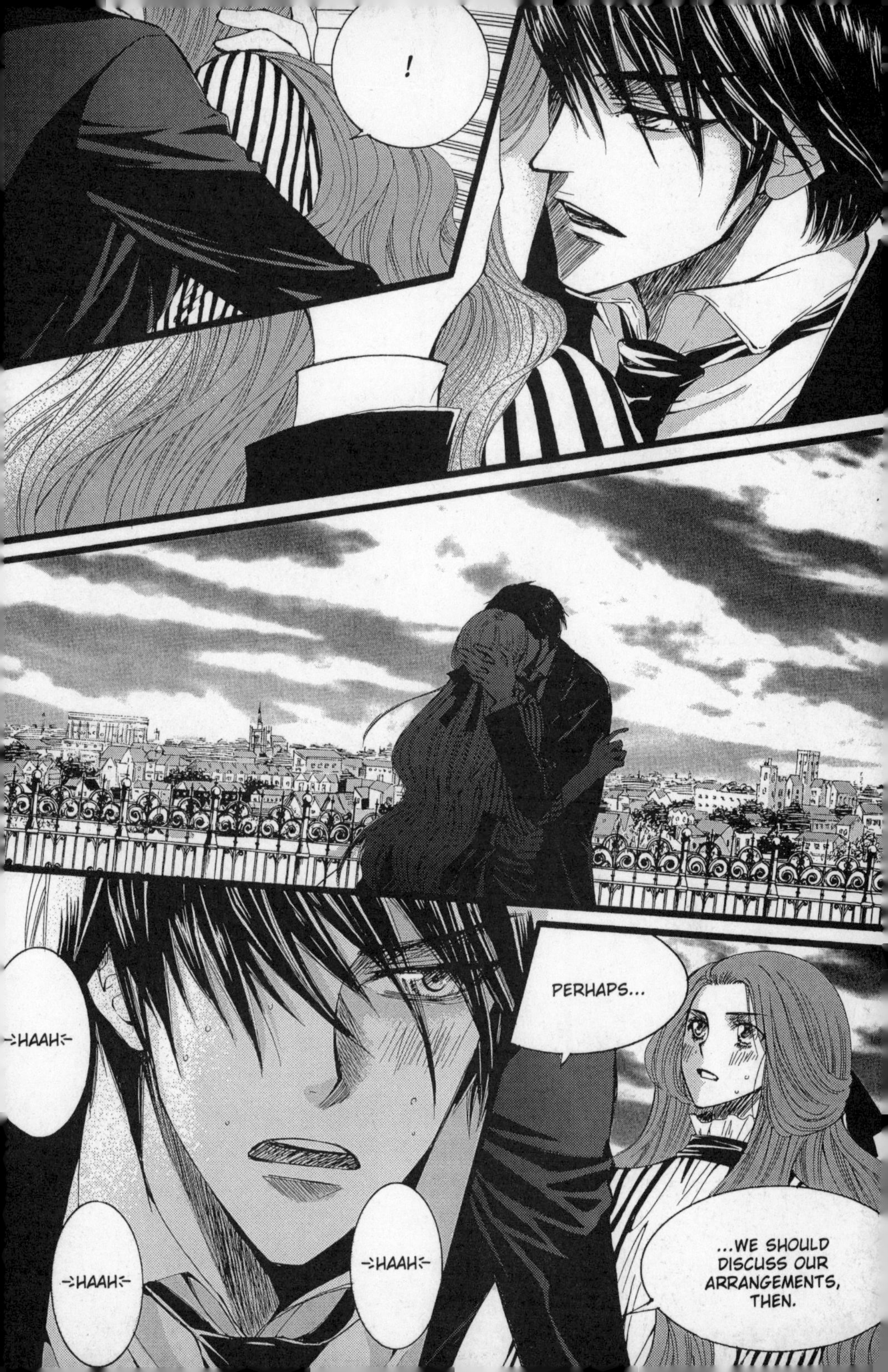
!
~HAAH~
PERHAPS...
~HAAH~
~HAAH~
...WE SHOULD DISCUSS OUR ARRANGEMENTS, THEN.

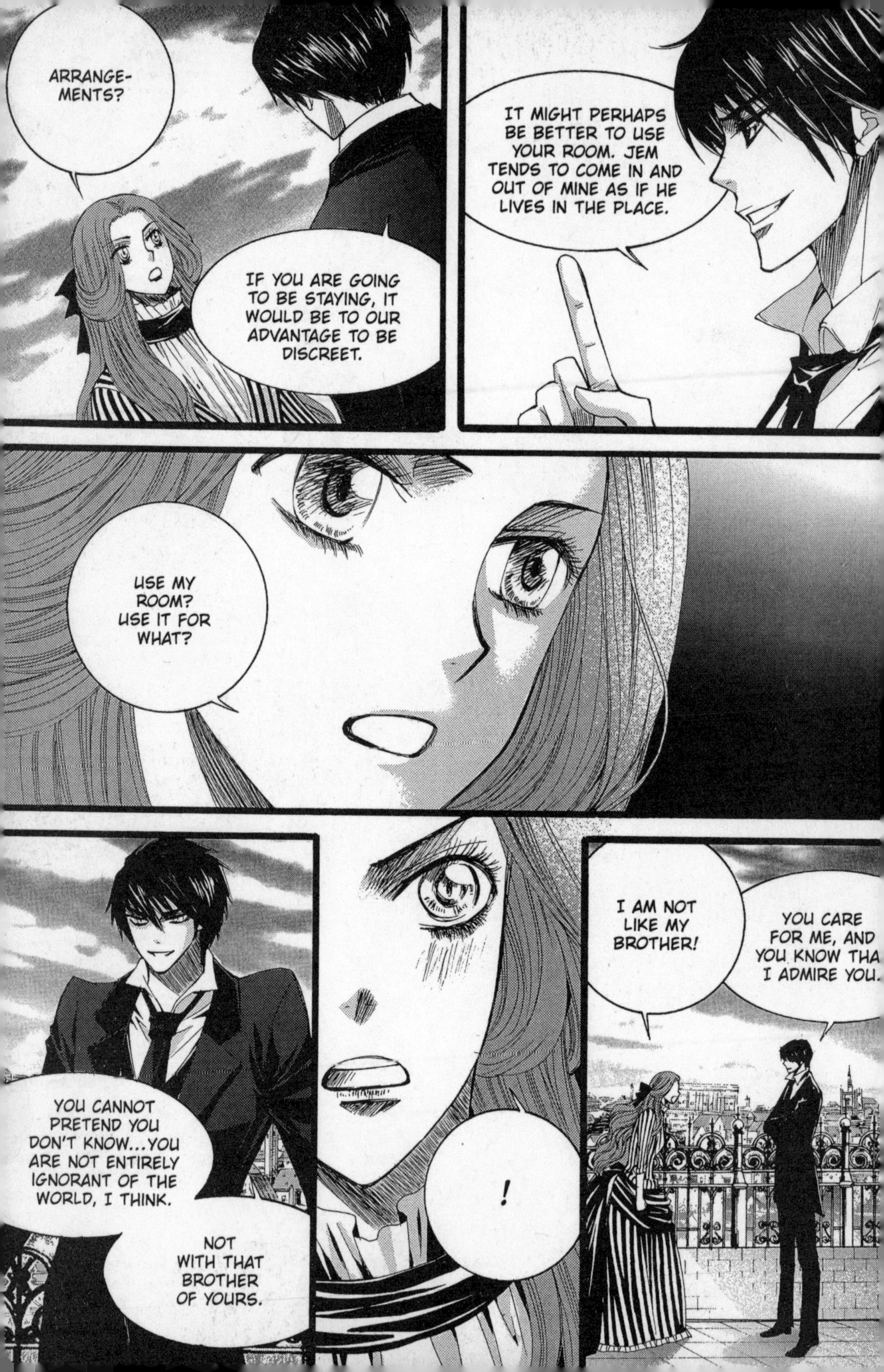
ARRANGE-MENTS?
IF YOU ARE GOING TO BE STAYING, IT WOULD BE TO OUR ADVANTAGE TO BE DISCREET.
IT MIGHT PERHAPS BE BETTER TO USE YOUR ROOM. JEM TENDS TO COME IN AND OUT OF MINE AS IF HE LIVES IN THE PLACE.
USE MY ROOM? USE IT FOR WHAT?
YOU CANNOT PRETEND YOU DON'T KNOW...YOU ARE NOT ENTIRELY IGNORANT OF THE WORLD, I THINK.
NOT WITH THAT BROTHER OF YOURS.
!
I AM NOT LIKE MY BROTHER!
YOU CARE FOR ME, AND YOU KNOW THA I ADMIRE YOU.

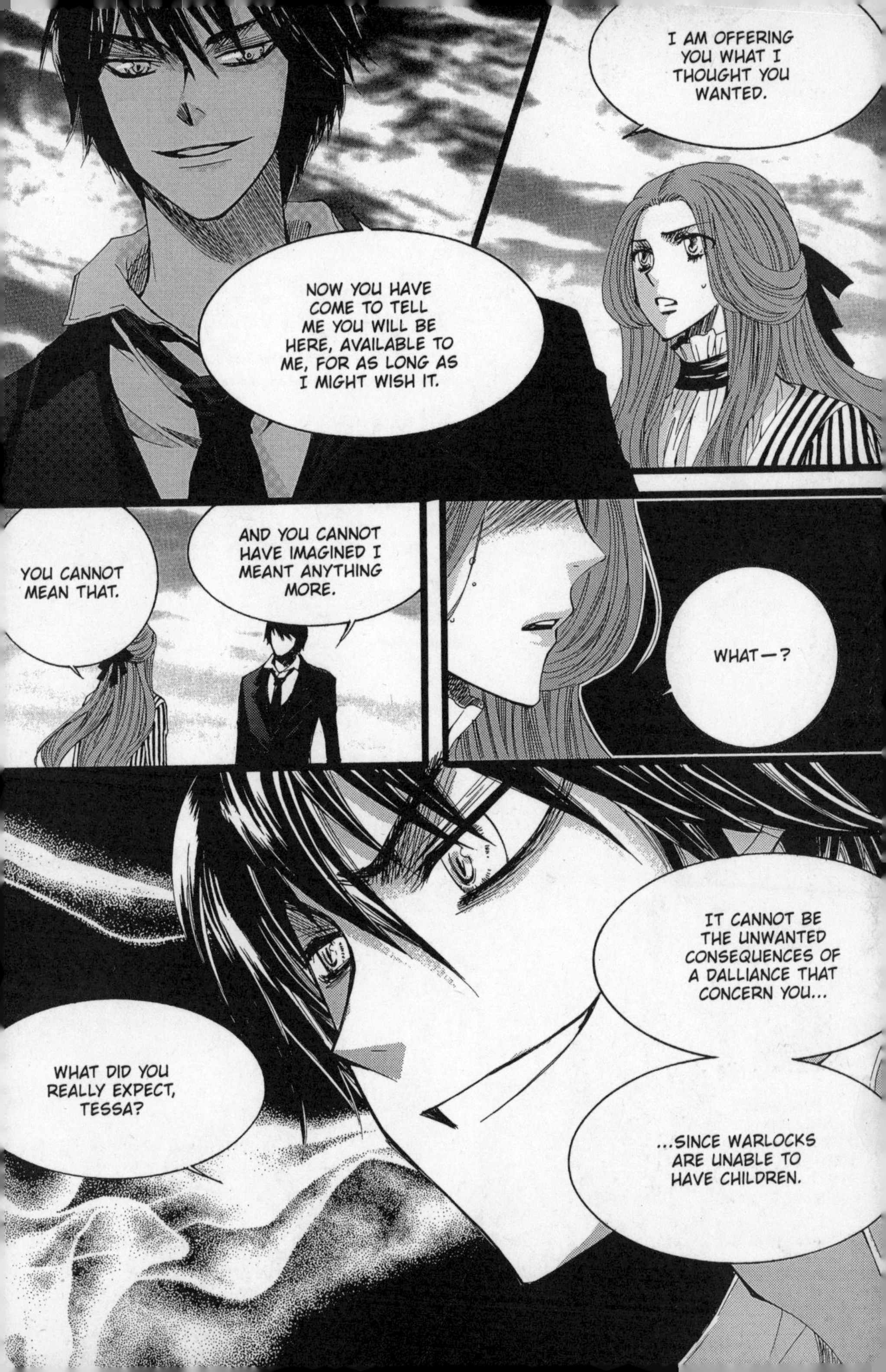
NOW YOU HAVE COME TO TELL ME YOU WILL BE HERE, AVAILABLE TO ME, FOR AS LONG AS I MIGHT WISH IT.
I AM OFFERING YOU WHAT I THOUGHT YOU WANTED.
YOU CANNOT MEAN THAT.
AND YOU CANNOT HAVE IMAGINED I MEANT ANYTHING MORE.
WHAT—?
IT CANNOT BE THE UNWANTED CONSEQUENCES OF A DALLIANCE THAT CONCERN YOU...
WHAT DID YOU REALLY EXPECT, TESSA?
...SINCE WARLOCKS ARE UNABLE TO HAVE CHILDREN.

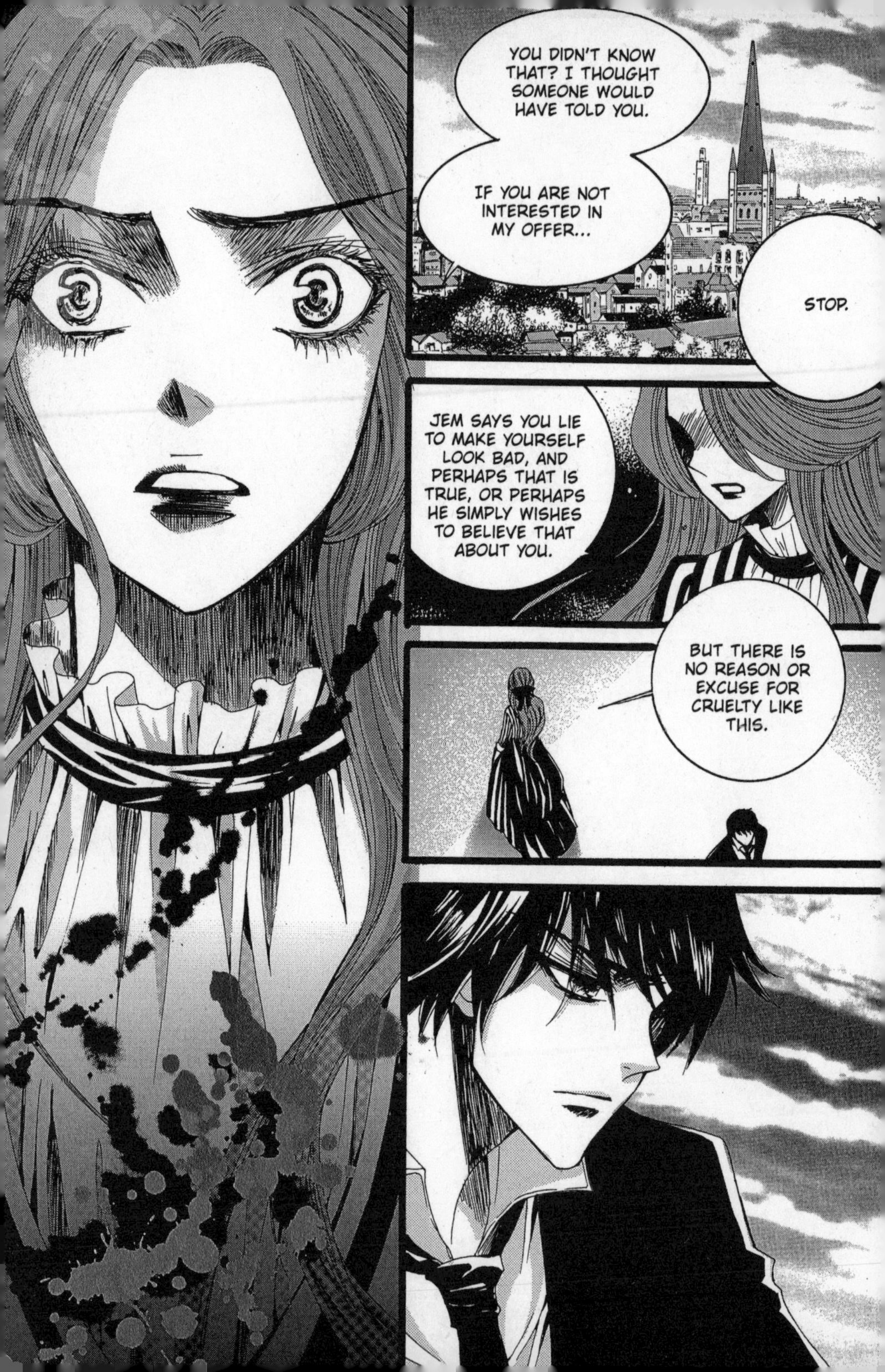
YOU DIDN'T KNOW THAT? I THOUGHT SOMEONE WOULD HAVE TOLD YOU.
IF YOU ARE NOT INTERESTED IN MY OFFER...
STOP.
JEM SAYS YOU LIE TO MAKE YOURSELF LOOK BAD, AND PERHAPS THAT IS TRUE, OR PERHAPS HE SIMPLY WISHES TO BELIEVE THAT ABOUT YOU.
BUT THERE IS NO REASON OR EXCUSE FOR CRUELTY LIKE THIS.

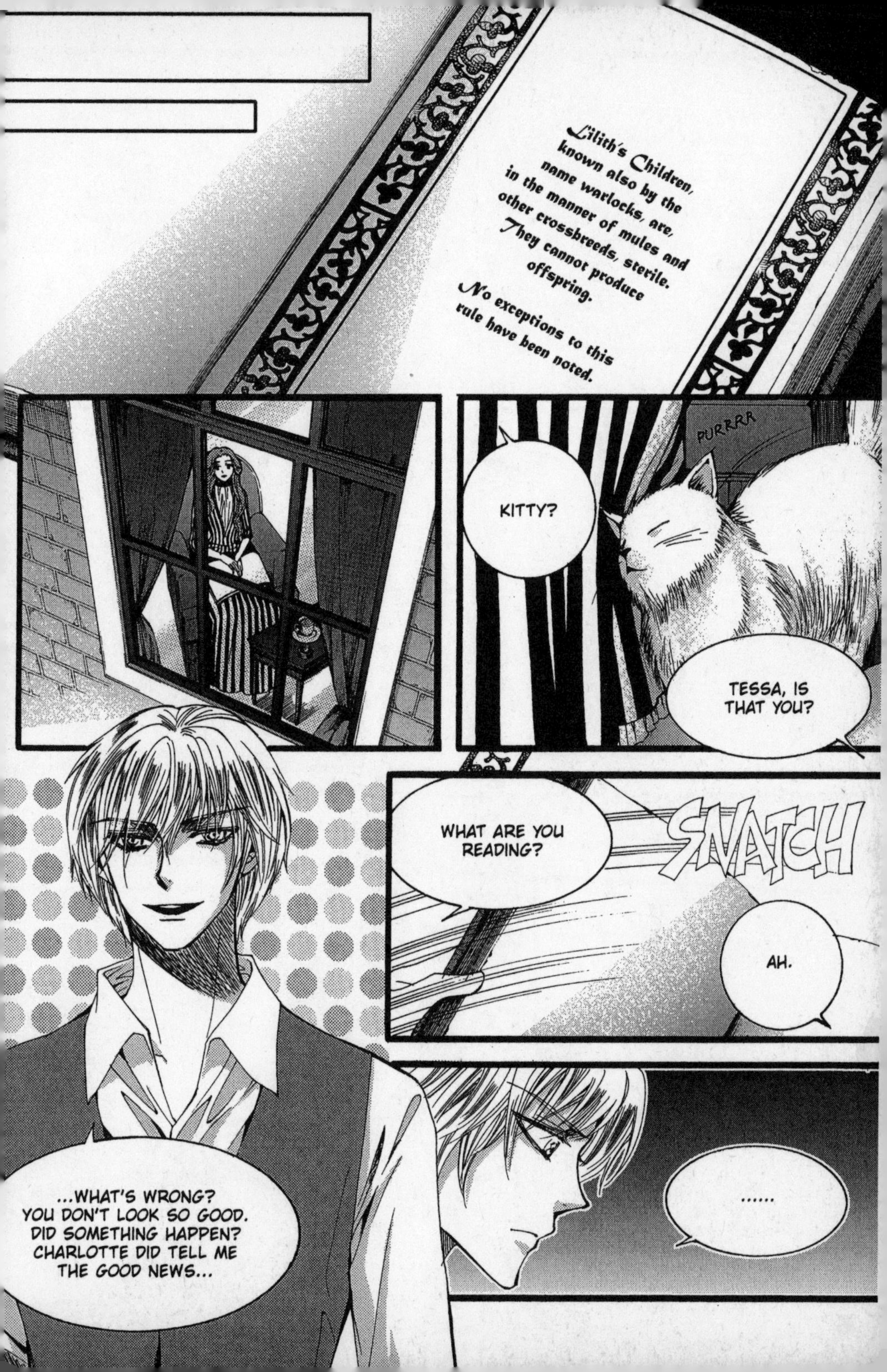
Lilith's Children, known also by the name warlocks, are, in the manner of mules and other crossbreeds, sterile. They cannot produce offspring.
No exceptions to this rule have been noted.
KITTY?
PURRRR
TESSA, IS THAT YOU?
WHAT ARE YOU READING?
SNATCH
AH.
...WHAT'S WRONG? YOU DON'T LOOK SO GOOD. DID SOMETHING HAPPEN? CHARLOTTE DID TELL ME THE GOOD NEWS...
......

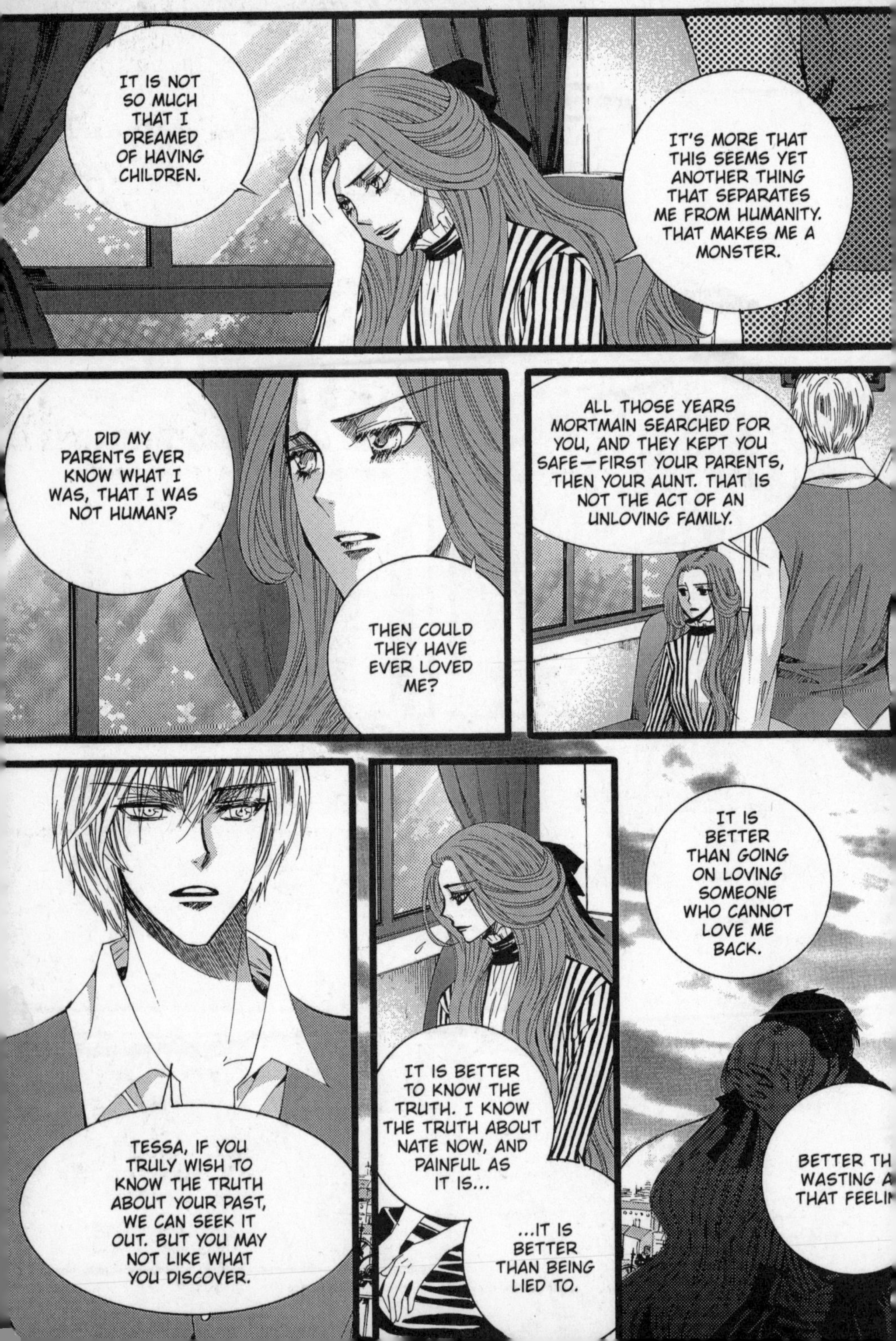
IT IS NOT SO MUCH THAT I DREAMED OF HAVING CHILDREN.
IT'S MORE THAT THIS SEEMS YET ANOTHER THING THAT SEPARATES ME FROM HUMANITY. THAT MAKES ME A MONSTER.
DID MY PARENTS EVER KNOW WHAT I WAS, THAT I WAS NOT HUMAN?
THEN COULD THEY HAVE EVER LOVED ME?
ALL THOSE YEARS MORTMAIN SEARCHED FOR YOU, AND THEY KEPT YOU SAFE—FIRST YOUR PARENTS, THEN YOUR AUNT. THAT IS NOT THE ACT OF AN UNLOVING FAMILY.
TESSA, IF YOU TRULY WISH TO KNOW THE TRUTH ABOUT YOUR PAST, WE CAN SEEK IT OUT. BUT YOU MAY NOT LIKE WHAT YOU DISCOVER.
IT IS BETTER TO KNOW THE TRUTH. I KNOW THE TRUTH ABOUT NATE NOW, AND PAINFUL AS IT IS...
...IT IS BETTER THAN BEING LIED TO.
IT IS BETTER THAN GOING ON LOVING SOMEONE WHO CANNOT LOVE ME BACK.
BETTER TH
WASTING A
THAT FEELI

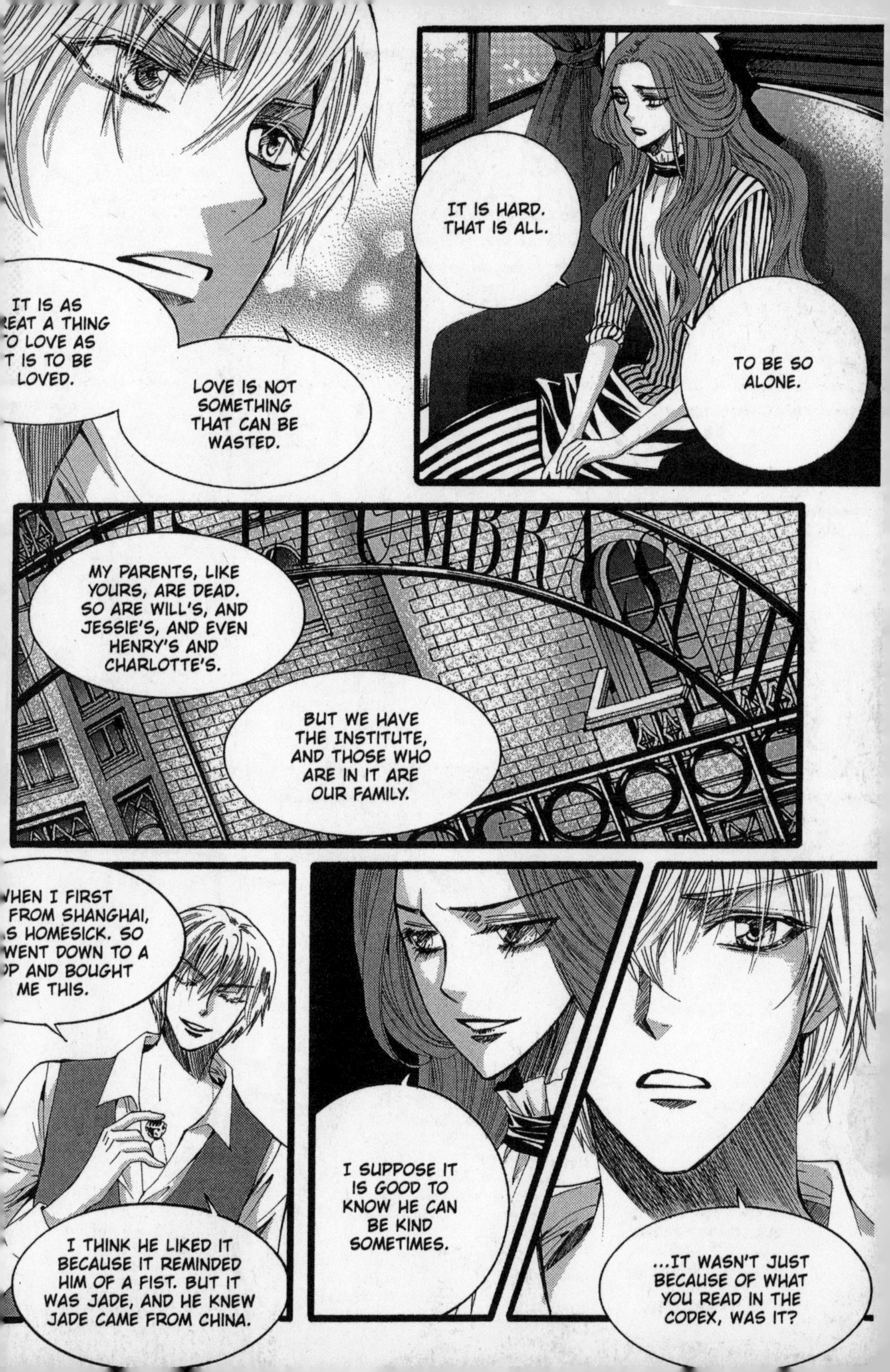
IT IS AS EAT A THING O LOVE AS T IS TO BE LOVED.
LOVE IS NOT SOMETHING THAT CAN BE WASTED.
IT IS HARD. THAT IS ALL.
TO BE SO ALONE.
MY PARENTS, LIKE YOURS, ARE DEAD. SO ARE WILL'S, AND JESSIE'S, AND EVEN HENRY'S AND CHARLOTTE'S.
BUT WE HAVE THE INSTITUTE, AND THOSE WHO ARE IN IT ARE OUR FAMILY.
HEN I FIRST FROM SHANGHAI, S HOMESICK. SO WENT DOWN TO A P AND BOUGHT ME THIS.
I THINK HE LIKED IT BECAUSE IT REMINDED HIM OF A FIST. BUT IT WAS JADE, AND HE KNEW JADE CAME FROM CHINA.
I SUPPOSE IT IS GOOD TO KNOW HE CAN BE KIND SOMETIMES.
...IT WASN'T JUST BECAUSE OF WHAT YOU READ IN THE CODEX, WAS IT?

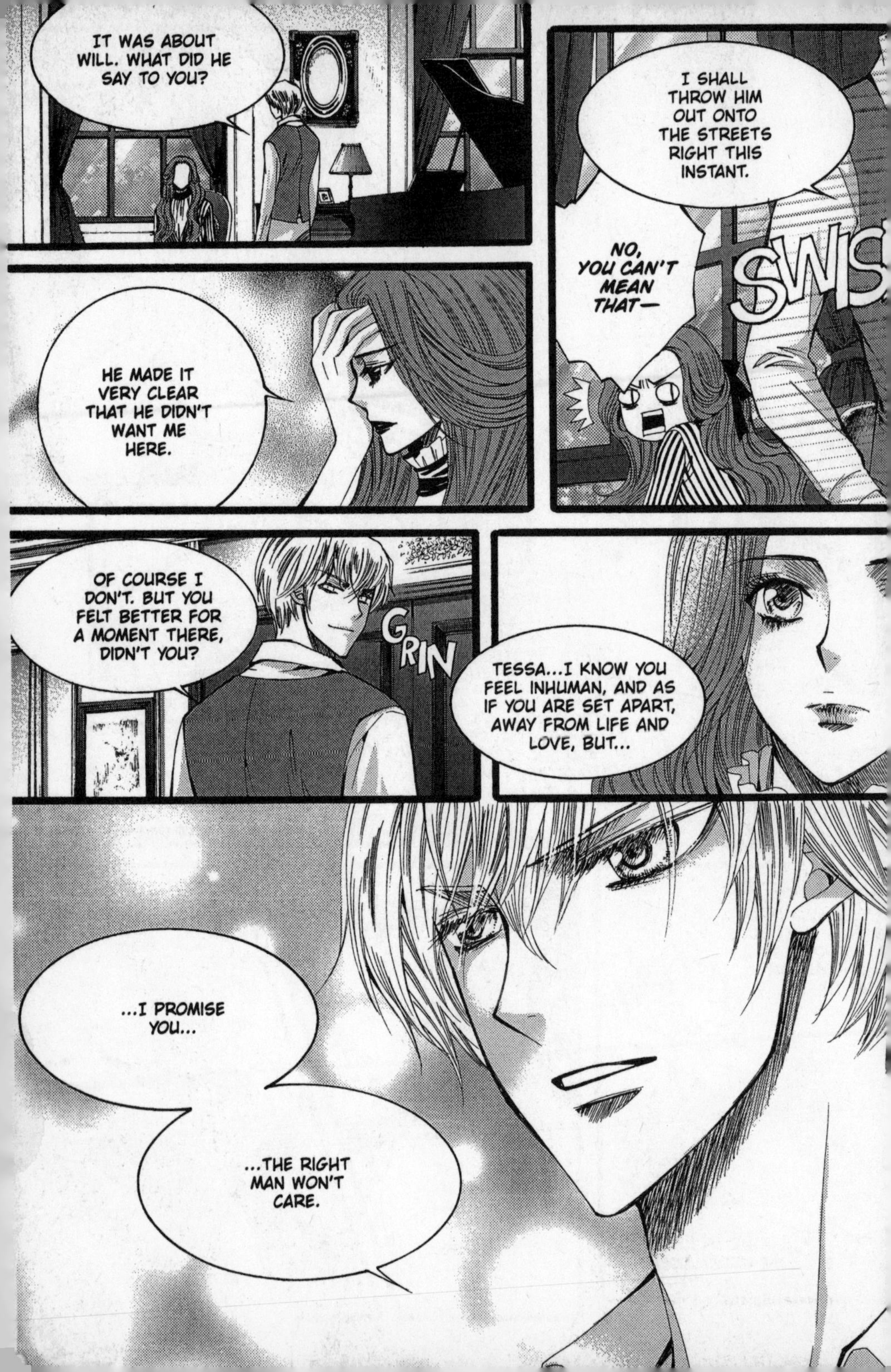
IT WAS ABOUT WILL. WHAT DID HE SAY TO YOU?
I SHALL THROW HIM OUT ONTO THE STREETS RIGHT THIS INSTANT.
NO, YOU CAN'T MEAN THAT—
SWISH
HE MADE IT VERY CLEAR THAT HE DIDN'T WANT ME HERE.
OF COURSE I DON'T. BUT YOU FELT BETTER FOR A MOMENT THERE, DIDN'T YOU?
GRIN
TESSA...I KNOW YOU FEEL INHUMAN, AND AS IF YOU ARE SET APART, AWAY FROM LIFE AND LOVE, BUT...
...I PROMISE YOU...
...THE RIGHT MAN WON'T CARE.

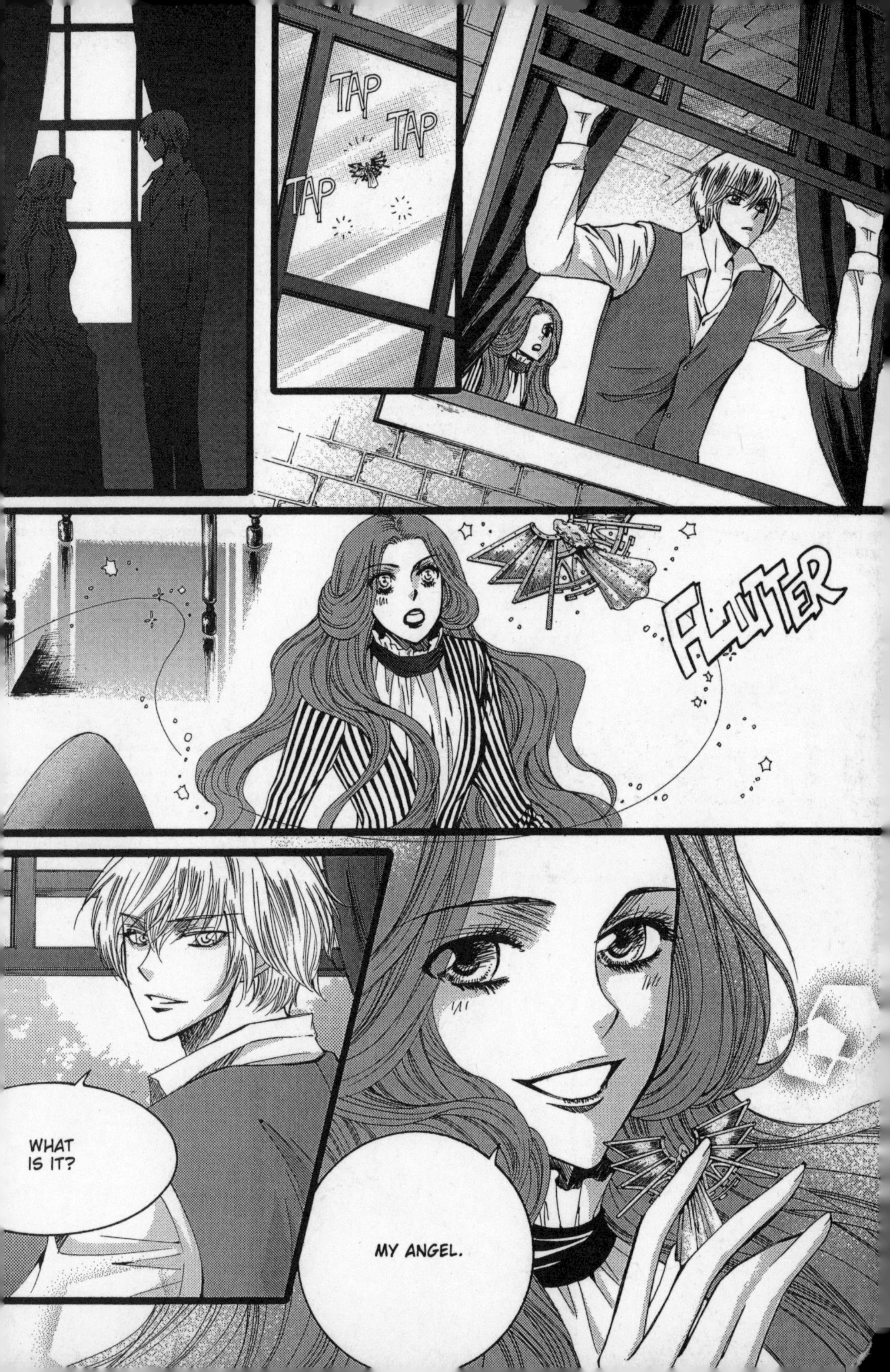
TAP
TAP
TAP
FLUTTER
WHAT IS IT?
MY ANGEL.

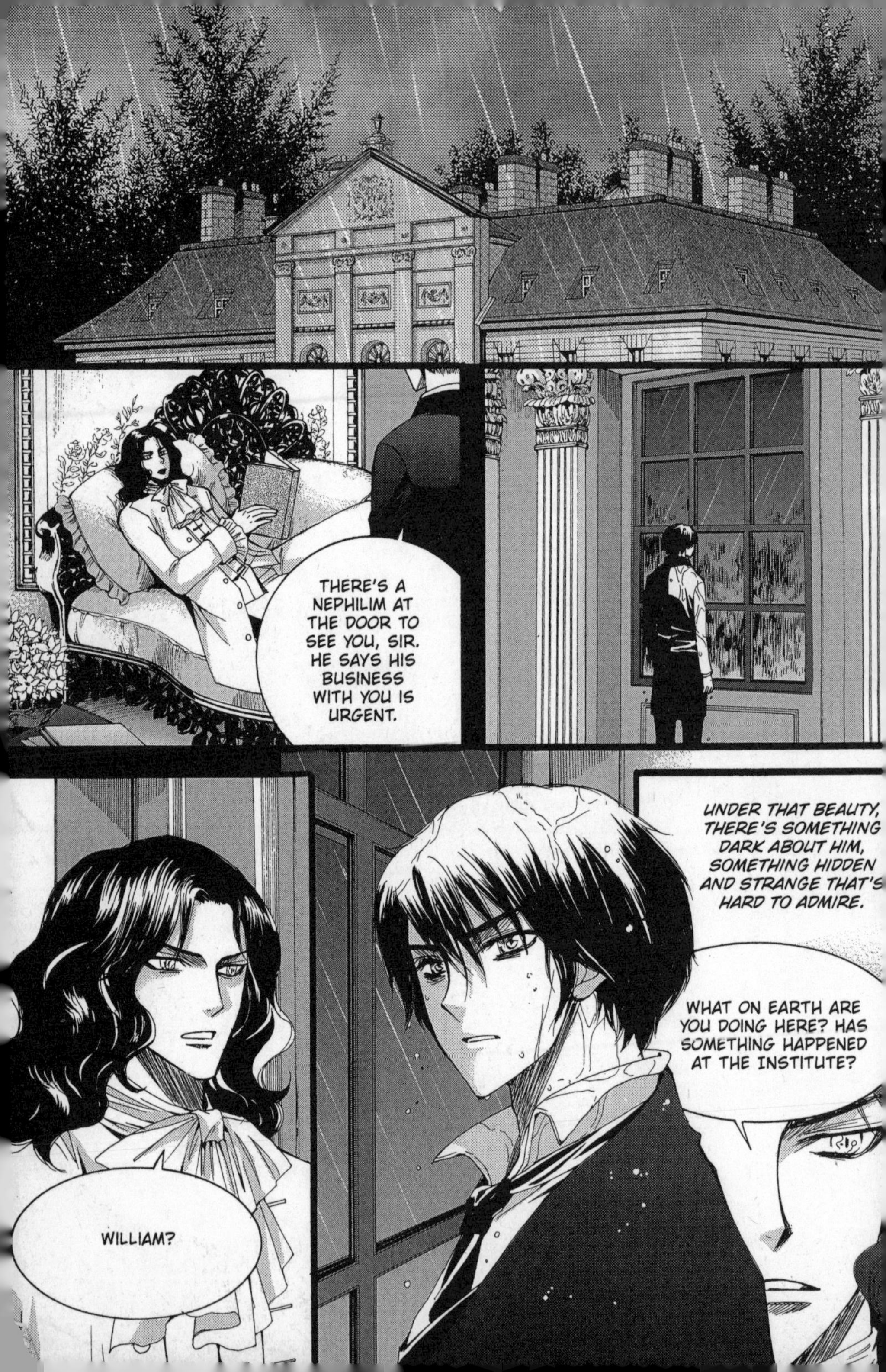
THERE'S A NEPHILIM AT THE DOOR TO SEE YOU, SIR. HE SAYS HIS BUSINESS WITH YOU IS URGENT.
WILLIAM?
UNDER THAT BEAUTY, THERE'S SOMETHING DARK ABOUT HIM, SOMETHING HIDDEN AND STRANGE THAT'S HARD TO ADMIRE.
WHAT ON EARTH ARE YOU DOING HERE? HAS SOMETHING HAPPENED AT THE INSTITUTE?

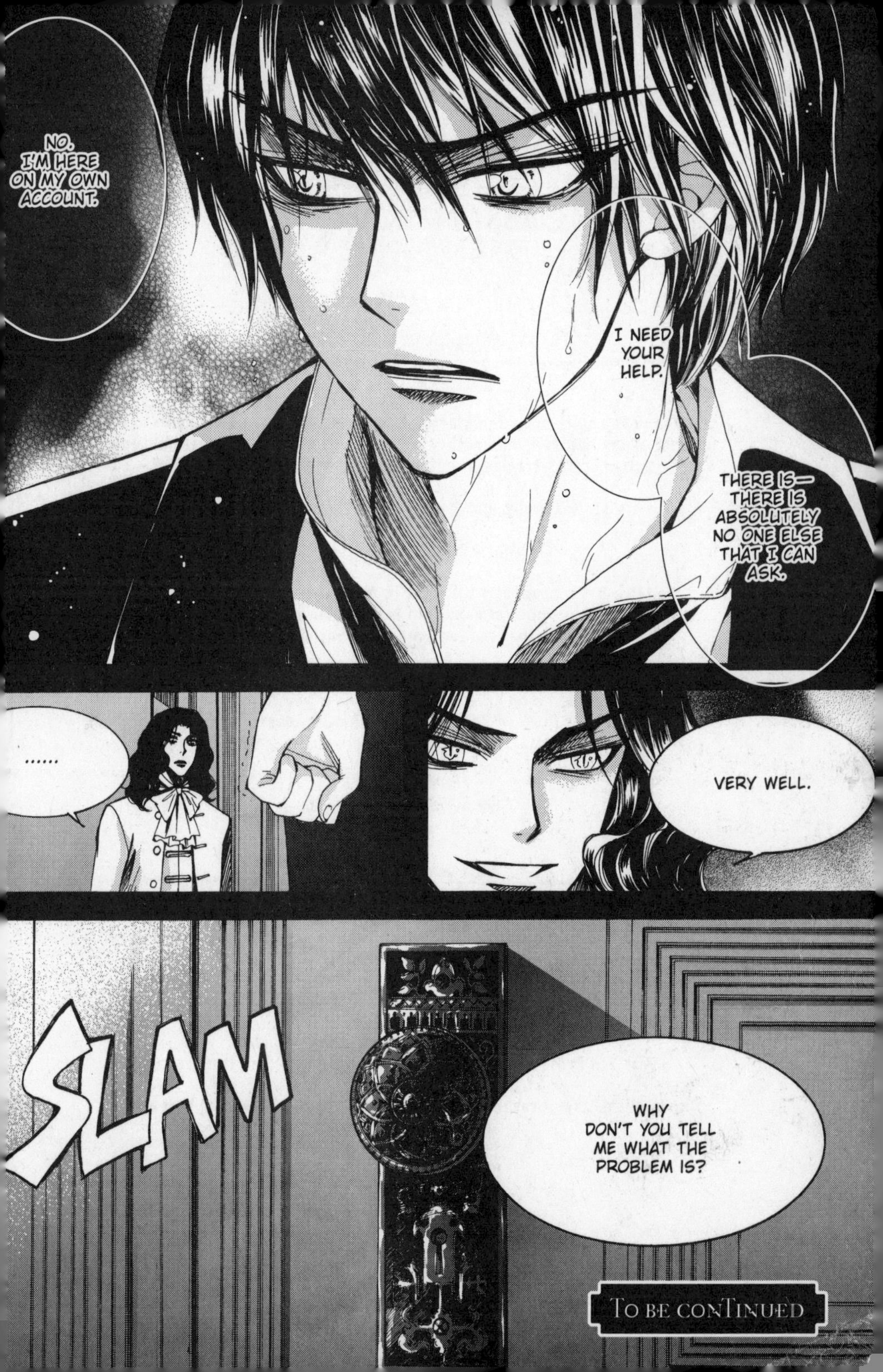
NO. I'M HERE ON MY OWN ACCOUNT.
I NEED YOUR HELP.
THERE IS— THERE IS ABSOLUTELY NO ONE ELSE THAT I CAN ASK.
......
VERY WELL.
SLAM
WHY DON'T YOU TELL ME WHAT THE PROBLEM IS?
TO BE CONTINUED

THE INFERNAL DEVICES: CLOCKWORK ANGEL

CASSANDRA CLARE
HYEKYUNG BAEK

Art and Adaptation: HyeKyung Baek

Lettering: JuYoun Lee

Yen Press
1290 Avenue of the Americas
New York, NY 10104

Visit us at yenpress.com
facebook.com/yenpress
twitter.com/yenpress
yenpress.tumblr.com
instagram.com/yenpress

First Yen Press Edition: October 2012

Yen Press is an imprint of Yen Press, LLC.
The Yen Press name and logo are trademarks of Yen Press, LLC.

The publisher is not responsible for websites (or their content) that are not owned by the publisher.

ISBN: 978-0-316-20098-1

10 9

BVG

Printed in the United States of America